INTRODUCTION TO PALI

INTRODUCTION TO PALI

Second Edition
(With corrections and additions)

A. K. WARDER, B.A., Ph.D.
Professor in the Department of East Asian Studies,
University of Toronto

yogād rūḍhir balīyasī

— Prabhākara

Published by
THE PALI TEXT SOCIETY, LONDON
Distributed by
ROUTLEDGE & KEGAN PAUL
LONDON, BOSTON, MELBOURNE AND HENLEY
1984

First published 1963
Second Edition 1974
Reprinted as a paperback 1984

ISBN 0-7102-0356-X

PRINTED IN GREAT BRITAIN BY
REDWOOD BURN LIMITED, TROWBRIDGE, WILTSHIRE

To

I. B. HORNER

dhammakathikā vinayadharā mahāpaññā

who illustrates, organizes and encourages the study of Pali

dhīrāya mahāpaññāya khippabhiññāya dhammakathikāya
mettāvihāriyā vinayadharāya bahussutāya muditāya
anukampikāya bhagavatiyā tassā sāvako ahaṃ asmi

PREFACE

The purpose of this book is to introduce the student, by the most direct path, to the language of the Pali Canon. Existing primers and readers for the study of Pali teach the later language of the Commentaries and other medieval writings, and indeed of the present day—for this very copious and flexible language is still in use. In Ceylon and other countries where Pali is taught at school the method is to begin with the later language—in fact the language as the Buddhist monks still use it—and the ancient canonical language is taught only to advanced pupils. To the beginner who knows no Indo-Aryan language (except, perhaps, Sanskrit), however, the ancient Pali is somewhat easier than the medieval. It is also far more interesting. Our interpretation admittedly rests largely on the exegesis of the Commentaries and the scholarly works of medieval monks, but the beginner need not at first study the exegetical literature himself—he can be given the results of its study, without the distractions and confusions of later usages, through the medium of a language he knows already. Studying only the ancient texts he will soon become familiar with the idioms and with the precise meanings of expressions in those texts, instead of with broader and vaguer meanings based on texts ranging over more than two millennia of usages changing against a changing social background. Our grammatical analysis is based on the admirable science of the medieval monks. Their terminology is given, to aid reference, but may of course be ignored by the beginner. The intention here is to cover Pali grammar and syntax in a comprehensive manner: in other words to provide a grammar of Pali in its ancient phase within the framework of graded lessons and exercises. This grammar differs from earlier grammars in being a description of the Canonical language as a relatively homogeneous and consistent form of speech, ignoring later usages (which would confuse the description and sometimes confound the interpretation). It is also " descriptive " in being an analysis of Canonical usage as far as possible without historical " squinting " at other languages. The historical philologist is already well provided with comparative grammars of Pali ; the point here, however, is not simply to avoid burdening the description with distractions but to apply a different method : the internal study of the usage of a particular language at a particular time from the meaning of its texts and sentences, falling back on the conjectures of etymology and comparative philology only when all else fails. It is hoped that this method will lead to greater precision and clarity in interpretation and a better understanding of Pali.

The sentences and passages for reading are taken, with only the unavoidable minimum of editing in the first exercises, from prose texts in the *Dīgha Nikāya* of the Canon. There are three reasons for using prose texts and avoiding verse. Firstly the pedagogical ; secondly that they are more interesting to read ; thirdly that—in the belief of the present writer—they are more authentic in their preservation of the utterances and dialogues of the Buddha.

Prose sentences provide the student with straightforward examples of the language, unconstrained by metrical considerations (which in verse distort the word order, influence the choice of words, lead to the insertion of superfluous words to fill the lines, produce irregular spellings through poetic licence, and induce the poet to use archaic words and inflections). The student needs to know first the normal word order, the natural choice and collocation of words, which words are essential as opposed to mere flourishes into which he should not attempt to read deep meanings, the regular spellings, and the current usage and grammar of one period ; this knowledge will help his appreciation of the poetry when he reads it later. Prose sentences can provide also authentic models for composition in the language studied—a useful exercise, in small quantities, to consolidate the ground covered even when, as in the majority of cases, the student does not expect to use his knowledge of the language except for reading. All the examples given are taken verbatim from the *Dīgha Nikāya*, except that in the early lessons some simplification was inevitable. The object is to give only such collocations of words as occur in the texts in order to ensure that the sentences and meanings are fully idiomatic. The sentences for translation into Pali have likewise been chosen with idiomatic Pali versions—often to be found in the *Dīgha Nikāya*—in view, especially the earlier exercises (at a later stage the student may try translating idiomatic English into Pali). By taking a single book (the *Dīgha Nikāya*), though a sufficiently extensive one (900 pages in the PTS edition), it was intended to produce a description of a single phase of Pali, as homogeneous as possible, without raising the question whether all the Canonical texts are contemporary and homogeneous. In fact the *Dīgha* language presented here appears to be sufficiently representative of Canonical Pali as a whole to provide an adequate introduction to any text, except possibly the very latest additions to the Canon. The *Dīgha* usage collected here should provide a standard with which future students can check how far the language of other books may diverge from it, an investigation of considerable interest.

The texts from which extracts are given expound the philosophy of Buddhism fairly systematically, but in narrative and dialogue style against a historical background of the Buddha's wanderings and meetings with a variety of characters.

The poetical sections of the Canon appear to be in the main later additions to the original corpus of *Dhamma-Vinaya* discourses collected by the followers of the Buddha. They are very heterogeneous, the work of many poets over several centuries. No doubt the prose collections also were expanded and rearranged during the same period, but their homogeneous style seems to preserve that of the original collection.

The arrangement of the book is based on the experience that extensive reading is the easiest way to learn a language. The vocabulary and grammar are made familiar and meanings are made explicit by sufficient numbers of encounters with the various forms in the course of reading—not in monotonous and sleep inducing repetition as forms to learn by heart but in constantly varying contexts where the reader is stimulated and entertained by the content of a dialogue or narrative. Since language learning is desirable for the majority of people, it is highly objectionable if text books are written only from the viewpoint of the tiny minority of specialists interested in linguistics for its own sake and able to pick up grammar from bare paradigms.

The reader is recommended at first to hurry through the early lessons and exercises, noting the main features (such as 3rd person singular of a given tense, form of active and passive sentences, uses of cases, forms of pronouns, the common indeclinables, use of participles and other infinite verb forms), in order to reach the more extensive reading passages which follow. The grammar set out in the earlier lessons can of course be consolidated as desired later. Though the lessons and exercises are numbered, and the lessons are of roughly comparable size (giving an idea of the total extent of grammar to be studied), it is not intended that the work should be spread evenly over a similar number of equal intervals of time, such as weeks. On the contrary, progress should agree rather with the number of pages to be covered, and the main objective should be seen as the reading of the long passages in Pali in the later exercises. Thus about half the lessons (by number) should be read in the first few weeks in order to enter into the reading passages as soon as possible. During the reading in the months that follow the grammar and vocabulary may then be consolidated at leisure. (If the work is to be distributed over a three-term university course, for which it has in fact been planned, it is desirable to reach Exercise 16 by the end of the first term. The remaining terms might divide the rest of the lessons and exercises evenly at about seven each.) The reading passages are of course graded according to the exposition of grammar in the preceding lessons, with a very few anticipations explained in footnotes. The most essential grammar has been covered by Lesson 16 (cases, tenses, participles, commonest declension and common conjugations, basic syntax including use of pronouns and adjectives, and an introduction to compounds) and will form a solid basis for reading. Lessons 17–23 add the other declensions as they are met with in the passages, and other less common forms, and carry the study of the use of compounds through the more difficult *bahubbīhi* (completed in Lesson 24). Lessons 24–30 cover the rarest forms, besides treating the advanced branches of grammar which give greater precision in interpretation (and which are important for composition in Pali if this is required): auxiliary verbs, derivation, survey of sentence construction.

The study of early Buddhism will always be the objective of the majority of those who take up Pali, though in addition to the interest of the language itself we must stress the importance of the texts for the study of the history of Indian literature, especially secular literature (literature as literature, "fine" literature, Pali *kāveyyaṃ* : Sanskrit *kāvya*—the latter embracing the prose novel and the drama as well as poetry). Buddhism has been the subject of the most varied fantasies in the West. The few reliable guides are overlooked in the mass of claptrap, humbug, and pure fiction. Inevitably serious work is less readable than journalistic antithesis and exoticism. Moreover in the field of early Buddhism and Pali studies, at least, even the most serious scholars have remained obstinately various in their interpretations. It must still be said that the Pali texts themselves are the only reliable authority as to their meaning. The further advance of these studies depends on the deeper analysis of these texts. Rather than add another volume to the bewildering mass of books on "Buddhism", it seems more constructive to open a door directly on the Pali. The meanings of the key terms cannot be guessed at, nor determined by etymology (which in the study of philosophy especially is utterly irrelevant and misleading); they must be elucidated by a delicate judging of the contexts in which they occur, working if possible from concrete everyday language (as in the stories in our earlier reading passages) to the less obvious dialogues of philosophers. This has been attempted here, and may show the way for future studies of a more ambitious kind. It is not to be expected that all or even most of the meanings suggested in our vocabularies will prove final, particularly as the present study is a general survey of the language and not a deep penetration at particular points. The aim here is rather a demonstration of method, in which the student may see much of the evidence used as well as the conclusions offered, and afterwards go his own way. *attadīpā viharatha attasaraṇā anaññasaraṇā*. The object is to lay open before the reader the actual texts of ancient Buddhism, if possible without adding explanations and interpretations, and to let them speak for themselves in their own language.

It remains to acknowledge the help of all those (in addition to the authorities given in the Bibliography) who have contributed to this project. In the first place the patient labours of the late Dr. W. Stede to give a difficult student a grounding in Pali must be remembered, though it is to be feared he might not approve the result. He himself long meditated writing a Pali grammar, but unhappily was prevented by chronic illness from bringing his later projects to fruition. Through the favour of his widow, Mrs. Helen Stede, a quantity of notes for this projected grammar are now in the hands of the writer, reinforcing the notes from his teaching. As in his contribution to the *Pali-English Dictionary*, Stede was primarily concerned with the comparative study of Pali, Sanskrit, and the other Indo-European languages—in the great tradition of German *Indogermanische Sprachwissenschaft* to which he belonged. He projected a Pali grammar (all phases of Pali) illuminated by comparative grammar and especially comparative syntax. The present *Introduction* has, as explained above, no such historical aim, but these notes from a different viewpoint were valuable even when the methods of the Indian tradition followed here obliged the student to go a different way.

In the severe, precise, and complex discipline of Buddhist studies the only authorities are the ancient texts in Pali and Sanskrit, but the best guide in a modern language has been Th. Stcherbatsky (F. I. Shcherbatskoy), a true *bodhisatta* who has shown us the way to understand these authorities. Though he worked on the Sanskrit texts (according to the Tibetan and Mongolian schools of interpretation) his methods and basic conclusions are equally valid for the Pali texts (and the Ceylonese and Burmese schools), with allowance for the exigencies of extending the survey to another *vāda*, to an earlier phase of Buddhism than the Sabbatthivāda *Abhidharma*, and above all to literary (*suttanta*) texts instead of abstract treatises. Here we seek the link between philosophical terminology and the living language.

In the study of Pali itself and of early Buddhism the writer owes much to the brilliant pioneering work of T. W. Rhys Davids, whose appreciative insight into the texts and their social background made light of every difficulty and yet is confirmed much more often than criticized by the more specialized studies of other investigators. The merit of specializing to establish detail is undeniable, but the significance of the details appears only in the broad context grasped only by such a wide-ranging mind as Rhys Davids'. Rhys Davids' translation of the *Dīgha*, including his extensive comments and introductions to its component dialogues, gave the original impulse to the study of this text in preference to all others, with its promise of varied interest and excellent style spiced with humour.

Since 1959 these lessons and exercises have been used in typescript as the textbook for the first year's Pali Course in Edinburgh, and those who have taken part in the discussions (K. H. Albrow, B. Annan, B. B. Kachru, and T. Hill) must be thanked for contributing greatly by their criticisms to the elimination of errors and inconsistencies and the clarification of explanations. Mr. Hill, of the Linguistic Survey of Scotland, helped especially with the phonetic descriptions and made many other useful suggestions. Mr. Albrow and the Ven. Saddhātissa Mahāthera have read the whole book in proof and made a number of corrections, helping to keep the misprints as few as is humanly possible.

Miss I. B. Horner, President of the Pali Text Society, has encouraged the work from an early stage—already a major factor in the completion of a project of daunting proportions and doubtful prospects—and has had the great kindness to read all the lessons and vocabularies and to make many important suggestions in the light of her unparalleled experience and learning in this field. May the merit thus transferred to this volume outweigh the original errors which have escaped detection. Finally, my wife has endured far more for this book than anyone else by typing out the whole illegible and exceptionally tangled manuscript, and retyping many revised pages, with a willing and cheerful heart. *ā airyə̄mā išyō rafəδrāi jantū . . . vaŋhə̄us rafəδrāi manaŋhō yā daēnā vairīm hanāṯ mīzdəm . . .*

A. K. Warder.

and altered studies of [illegible] investigation. The merit of [illegible] detail [illegible] but the significance of detail appears only in the broad context granted only to such a wide ranging mind as [illegible]. The translation of the [illegible] introductions to its component chapters; even the original impulse to the study of this text in [illegible] with [illegible] and [illegible] spent with him.

[illegible] have been [illegible] in preparing [illegible] the textbook for the [illegible] to Edinburgh, and those who have taken part in the discussions ([illegible]) must be thanked for contributing greatly by their criticism to the elimination of errors and obscurities and the clarification of explanations. [illegible] of Scotland, helped especially with the [illegible] and made many [illegible] suggestions. [illegible] have read the whole book in proof and made a number of [illegible] helping to [illegible] as [illegible].

Miss I. B. Horner, President of the Pali Text Society, has encouraged this work from an early stage [illegible] the completion of the project [illegible] and doubtful passages [illegible] and the great kindness [illegible] all the [illegible] to make [illegible] suggestions on the [illegible] in this field. [illegible] translated in this volume [illegible]. Finally [illegible] for [illegible] this book than anyone else [illegible] and [illegible] many [illegible] with [illegible] and [illegible] of [illegible].

A. K. WARDER

CONTENTS

INTRODUCTION

The Alphabet

Pali (*pāḷi*) is written in a number of scripts derived from the ancient Indian Brāhmī character, and in the romanized script used in this book (sometimes with slight variations). The Indian script was a phonetic one based on an approximately phonemic analysis of the language, one letter (*akkhara*) being assigned to each significantly distinct sound (*vaṇṇa*).[1] The derivative scripts preserve this characteristic, and the roman alphabet likewise has been adapted and enlarged so that one roman letter is assigned to each Indian letter (counting the aspirates *kh*, etc., written as digraphs, as single letters). The ancient Indian grammarians classified the letters, or rather the sounds they represent, as shown in the table (p. 2).

Pronunciation : roughly as in English except :—

the aspirate consonants are accompanied by a strong breath-pulse from the chest, as when uttering English consonants very emphatically (e.g. " tush ! " = *th-*, " pish ! " = *ph-*, etc.),

the non-aspirate consonants are accompanied by a much weaker breath-pulse than any English consonants,

c is like ch in " choose " (so is *ch*, but with strong breath-pulse), except that the middle of the tongue (*jivhāmajjha*) only, not the tip, touches the palate (position as in English g),

the cerebrals are pronounced with the tip of the tongue rather further behind the teeth than in the English t and d, giving a somewhat hollow sound (this is the most characteristic sound of Indian languages),

the dentals are pronounced with the tip of the tongue (*jivhagga*) touching the very tips of the teeth (position as in

[1] Since Pali probably represents a language spoken between the 5th and 3rd centuries B.C. the precision of the script can now be checked only by inference from historical linguistics, including comparison with the statements of contemporary Indian phoneticians about Sanskrit, and partly by metrical considerations (see Lesson 30). Purists might suggest that in analysing the language of a text of the 5th–3rd centuries B.C. we should (despite the tradition of spoken Pali and of reciting the ancient texts) take the precaution of speaking only of " graphetics " and of substituting " graph " for " sound " or " phon- " throughout—we are after all analysing the language of a written text. In fact such caution seems unnecessary, since we can assert that the pronunciation is approximately known.

Place of articulation (*ṭhāna*)	Manner of articulation (*payatana*)										
	Consonants (*vyañjana*)							Vowels (*sara*)			Pure Nasal (*niggahīta*)
	Stops (*phuṭṭha* [1] or *vagga*)					Semi-vowel [2] (*īsaka phuṭṭha*)[3] (voiced)	Sibilant (*sakāra*) (voiceless)	Short (*rassa*)	Long (*dīgha*)	Compound (*asamāna*)	(nasal only, i.e. no release in the mouth, *avivaṭena mukhena*)
	voiceless (*aghosa*) non-aspirate (*sithila*)	voiceless aspirate (*dhanita*)	voiced (*ghosavant*) non-aspirate	voiced aspirate	voiced nasal (*nāsika*)						
Gutturals [4] (*kaṇṭhaja*)	*k*	*kh*	*g*	*gh*	*ṅ* [ŋ]	*h* [5] [ɦ]		*a*	*ā*	*e* [7]	
Palatals (*tāluja*)	*c*	*ch*	*j*	*jh*	*ñ*	*y*		*i*	*ī*		
Cerebrals [4] (*muddhaja*)	*ṭ* [ʈ]	*ṭh*	*ḍ*	*ḍh*	*ṇ*	*r*, *ḷ*, *ḷh* [ɭ]					*ṃ* [m̃]
Dentals (*dantaja*)	*t*	*th*	*d*	*dh*	*n*	*l*	*s*				
Labials (*oṭṭhaja*)	*p*	*ph*	*b*	*bh*	*m*	*v* [6]		*u*	*ū*	*o* [8]	

(long vowels are sometimes written *â*, *î*, *û*, the pure nasal sometimes *ṁ* or ŋ.)
Footnotes on opposite page.

English th, but of course with plosive, not fricative, manner of articulation),

of the three cerebral semivowels *r* is everywhere a clear consonant r as in " ram ", " burrow " ; *ḷ* and *ḷh* (historically, phonetic substitutes for *ḍ* and *ḍh* when isolated between vowels) are laterals like *l* but in cerebral instead of dental position, respectively unaspirate and aspirate,

v may be somewhat similar to English v when standing alone (as initial or between vowels), but (despite Aggavaṃsa's description) like English w when combined with another consonant ; many speakers of Pali pronounce *v* always as English w (i.e. as a pure labial),

s is never voiced (there are no z sounds in Pali),

a is like English u in " hut ", " utter ",

ā is like English a in " barn ", " aunt ",

i is like English i in " bit ", " it ",

ī is like English ee in " beet ", " tree ",

u is like English u in " put " and oo in " foot ",

ū is like English u in " brute " and oo in " boot ",

e is like English a in " bake ", " ache " (but sometimes when followed by a double consonant and therefore short it tends towards English e in " bed ", " eddy "),

NOTES TO PAGE 2.

[1] As Aggavaṃsa points out, the Brahmanical tradition of linguistics (*Śabdaśāstra*) uses this term for all the stops, but the Buddhist tradition uses it as a synonym for "aspirate" only and *aphuṭṭha* as a synonym for "non-aspirate".

[2] " Semi-vowel " is used here in a wider sense than is usual.

[3] " Imperfectly occluded " (in *Śabdaśāstra* terminology).

[4] Modern phoneticians prefer the terms " velar " for " guttural " and " retroflex " for " cerebral ", whereas the terms used here are more literal equivalents of the Pali terms. " Velar " is certainly more precise than " in the throat ", but " retroflex " upsets the Indian system of classification by the places of articulation. " Cerebral " or " in the head " is vague, referring loosely to the top of the mouth cavity between the teeth and the palate, but as an arbitrary term for the back of the ridge behind the teeth it is quite convenient. The terms used here are current in the comparative grammars of Pali. As to retroflection of the tongue, this is described in the Pali tradition (e.g. Aggavaṃsa p. 609, line 8) under the topic of the instruments (*karaṇa*) of articulation (i.e. the parts of the tongue in the case of palatals, cerebrals, and dentals, otherwise the places themselves) as *jivhopagga*, the " sub-tip of the tongue ".

[5] " Pulmonic " (*urasija*), not guttural, when conjoined with another semi-vowel, i.e. simple aspiration.

[6] Labio-dental according to Aggavaṃsa, but perhaps originally or sometimes bilabial [w].

[7] Gutturo-palatal (*kaṇṭhatāluja*).

[8] Gutturo-labial (*kaṇṭhoṭṭhaja*).

o is like English o in " note ", " ode " (or, before a double consonant, more like o in " not ", " odd "),

unlike the English vowels, all Pali vowels are free from diphthongalization (English " sago " tends towards what might in Pali be written *seigou*),

the pure nasal is the humming sound produced when the mouth is closed but air escapes through the nose with voicing (vibration of the vocal chords), it is *m* without release (consequently without place of articulation except the nose).[1]

The distinction of quantity (short and long vowels or syllables) is very important in Pali, but distinctions of stress are insignificant. A syllable is long if its vowel is long or if the vowel, though short, is followed by the pure nasal or by two or more consonants. A long syllable is exactly equal to two short syllables. (The total length of a long syllable being constant, a double consonant tends to compress and shorten a long vowel preceding it, and itself to be shortened by the long vowel.) Double consonants are very frequent in Pali and must be strictly pronounced as long consonants, thus *nn* is like English nn in " unnecessary ".[2]

The dictionary order of letters is *a, ā, i, ī, u, ū, e, o, ṃ* (this may also stand in the place of one of the other nasals, according to the consonant which follows), stops: guttural (*k, kh,* etc.), palatal . . . labial, *y, r, l, ḷ, ḷh, v, s, h.*

The Sentence

The analysis and the learning of any language should be based on the study of sentences, that is of the language as it is actually found in use. It is useful to study words in order to understand the sentences, but, like roots and stems, isolated words are in fact mere abstractions devised by grammarians for the analysis of language. (In the Indian tradition of writing " words " are not separated and each sentence appears as a continuous piece, as in speech. Only by grammatical analysis

[1] Consequently we might well follow the practice of some manuscripts, and also of many ancient inscriptions in dialects close to Pali, of writing only *ṃ*, and not the *vagga* nasals, as the first member of any conjunct, including *ṃm* instead of *mm* (but this is not the practice of modern editors).

[2] In English these double consonants are rare and the orthographies tt, pp, etc., represent something quite different. Only when the English consonants belong to separate words are they generally pronounced double; thus the Pali word *passa* is similar not to English " pusser " but to " pus, sir ! "

can words be abstracted: marked by certain " inflections ".) It is the sentences which are the natural units of discourse and which are the minimum units having precise, fully articulated meaning. For purposes of study we have to assign approximate meanings to words and list these in vocabularies, but these generalized meanings of words are extremely vague, whereas sentences have exact meanings. In translation one may find close equivalents for sentences, whilst it is often impossible to give close equivalents for words.

Ideally one should learn a language as children pick up their mother tongue, by learning a sufficiently large number of its sentences, but this would take too long for most students. Hence the study of words and inflections offers a short cut to proficiency, though at the risk of lack of precision and of idiomatic fluency.

The uninflected form of a Pali word, without an ending, is called the stem. In dictionaries and vocabularies nouns (*nāma*) are usually listed in their stem forms, less often in the form of the nominative singular. Verbs (*ākhyāta*), however, are usually given under the form of the third person singular of the present tense (indicative active), sometimes under the " root ". In this book verbs are given in the root form (but with their prefixes where these are used, hence in the alphabetical position of the prefixes in these cases), nouns in the stem form except in the case of stems in *-a*, where it is more convenient to learn them in the form of the nominative singular since thereby one learns the gender at the same time (*-o* = masculine, *-aṃ* = neuter).

The prefixes (*upasagga*), of which there are about twenty, are regarded as a separate part of speech in Pali (whose characteristic is that it cannot stand alone, but only be prefixed to another word). The various verbs, consisting of prefix + root, have all to be learned separately as regards meanings. Although the separate prefixes and roots can be assigned meanings—usually rather broad and vague ones—the meaning of a prefix + root cannot usually be accounted for adequately as simply the product of the two separate meanings. A good many roots are used also without prefixes, but prefixed forms are very much more frequent in Pali. A number of verbs have two or three prefixes to their roots.

In theory (elaborated by the ancient Indian grammarians and their Sinhalese and Burmese pupils) all words in Pali are " derived "[1] from a limited number of " roots ". In other words all words are analysable into roots plus suffixes (= any modification). A root (*dhātu*) is an element, not further analysable at the grammatical or lexical levels, having a very vague and general meaning. It is rarely, if ever, found in its pure state (without suffix or prefix) except in grammar books and dictionaries. An indefinite number of stems (i.e. words in their " stem forms ") may be derived from any root by the addition of suffixes and by certain changes to the root itself, such as lengthening the vowel, substituting a compound vowel, inserting a nasal, reduplicating the root or contracting a semivowel + *a* into the vowel corresponding in place to the semivowel. For the beginner it saves time in the case of nouns to neglect the processes of derivation and learn the derived words and their precise meanings as they are used in the language. In the case of verbs the derivation has to be noticed since each verb has a variety of stems for its different parts (tenses, participles, etc.), all bearing the same meaning except for the grammatical[2] distinctions of tense, etc. (a glance at the table of Roots and Principal Parts will show the patterns of " derivation ", or rather it will show in most cases the linguistic material on the basis of which a root has been set up as a common denominator).

After this derivation of word stems (*liṅga*) by the addition of suffixes (*paccaya*) to roots (and sometimes of secondary suffixes to these suffixes), inflectional endings (*vibhatti*) are added to form actual words (*pada*) as they occur in sentences in different grammatical relations (the inflections corresponding to grammatical relations : the grammatical distinctions we

[1] " Derived " here must not be taken to imply a historical process of derivation (such as is given, e.g., in the Pali Text Society's *Pali-English Dictionary*, which gives reconstructed Proto-Indo-European roots for Pali verbs), but a synchronic grammatical system (strictly Pali roots).

[2] Thus the derivation of nouns may be regarded as non-grammatical (not belonging to a finite system) and as lexical, and their forms may simply be listed in a dictionary with their various meanings, whereas the derivation of verb forms is purely grammatical (the forms belong to finite systems) and non-lexical (the meanings of verb forms derived from one verb differ only according to the grammatical system of tenses, persons, etc.). The definitions of " lexical " and " grammatical " are due to Dr. M. A. K. Halliday.

make are so many descriptions of formal distinctions occurring in Pali).

Thus far the analysis of sentences into words, roots, suffixes and inflections. We have noticed also that words may be classified as verbs (these are defined as taking the tense-inflections *-ti*, etc.), nouns (defined as taking the case inflections *si*,[1] etc.) and prefixes (defined as prefixed to other words). There is one other class, that of indeclinables (*nipāta*), defined as not taking any inflections. Examples of indeclinables are *evaṃ*, meaning " thus ", " so," *ti*, meaning " end quote " and *yena*, meaning " towards ".

In Pali these four " parts of speech " (*padajāti* : " classes of words ") were recognized by the ancient Indian grammarians, according to the types of inflection or lack of inflection or to their dependence as prefixes (as always in the Indian grammatical tradition, description proceeds by way of accounting for the formal distinctions found in analysing a language in the simplest way possible, and not by setting up conceptual categories and attempting to fit the forms into them).

In Pali we find two numbers (" singular " and " plural ") in both nouns and verbs, three persons in the verb and in pronouns (" third " = " he ", etc., " second " = " you ", " first " = " I " : pronouns are not regarded as a separate class of words but as a kind of noun, although their inflections do not entirely coincide with those of nouns), eight cases in the noun and three genders (" masculine ", " neuter ", and " feminine ") in nouns. As a rule " substantive " nouns have only one gender each, whilst " adjectives " (and pronouns) have all three genders according to the nouns with which they " agree " as attribute-words : the inflections of adjectives are the same as those of

[1] Here " *si* " is a symbol for any inflection to be described as " nominative singular ", it is not itself one of these inflections (which are very varied, so that no common denominator is apparent). It is as if one were to call it " *x* ", explaining : " where ' *x* ' = any inflection described as ' nominative singular '." In the case of *-ti* this is the actual inflection of the third person singular present tense of all verbs. Thus in one sense there is only one " conjugation " of the present tense of Pali verbs, since all take the same set of inflections ; the seven or eight conjugations distinguished by the grammarians are based on the differences of present stem formation from the roots. On the other hand there are several " declensions " of nouns, since their inflections vary considerably according to their stems (in *-a*, *-an*, *-ant*, *-i*, *-u*, *-ar*, etc.).

nouns of the corresponding genders, hence they are not regarded as a separate class of words.

In sentences (*vākya*) there is usually one verb, which generally expresses an action (*kiriyā*), and a noun, ordinarily[1] in the nominative case, expressing the agent (*kattar*) who does the action. (Often there is another noun, ordinarily[1] in the "accusative" case, expressing the patient (*kamma*) who or which undergoes the action.) The agent and the verb agree in number. Thus in the sentence: *loko vivaṭṭati*, meaning "the world evolves", the verb is *vivaṭṭati*, derived from the root *vaṭṭ* (meaning "turn", "roll", "circle") via the present stem *vaṭṭa* (suffix -*a*) with the inflection of the present tense active, third person singular, *ti*, and the prefix *vi* (meaning "apart", "asunder").[2] The noun *loko* is derived from the root *lok* (meaning "see") via the noun stem *loka* (suffix -*a*), in which the ending of the nominative singular of the masculine -*a* declension, which is *o*, is substituted for the stem vowel.[3] In Pali there is usually nothing to express "indefinite" and "definite", corresponding to the "articles" in some languages.

Verb stems and noun stems may coincide in form, and in Pali both verbs and nouns with stems in *a* are much commoner than any others. The inflections of verbs and nouns, however, are nearly all quite distinct. Those of verbs are described according to tense (*lakāra*),[4] person (*purisa*) and number (*saṃkhā*), those of nouns according to number, gender (*liṅga*), and case (*kāraka*). The various cases express relations between the noun and a verb, or between the noun and another noun.

[1] The alternative but much rarer form of sentence called "passive" has the agent in the "instrumental" case and the patient in the nominative, with a different form of the verb (see Lessons 7 and 9).

[2] The meanings of *vi* and *vaṭṭ* are vague whereas the meaning of *vi-vaṭṭ* is most precise: it does not mean any kind of "rolling apart" but only the evolution of the universe.

[3] The stem vowel *a* is seen in most of the other cases, e.g. *lokaṃ* (+ *ṃ*, "accusative"), *lokassa* (+ *ssa*, "genitive"). Some grammarians say the nominative singular inflection here is *u* and that -*a* + *u* > -*o*, which is another, but more complicated, way of analysing the same thing.

[4] There are six tenses and two voices in Pali, "moods" being counted as tenses (i.e. tenses, *lakāras*, are not described according to the concept of time, but simply as alternative sets of forms according to inflection. The six are called "present", "imperative," "aorist" (or "past"), "optative," "future," and "conditional". There is also a "causative" conjugation (having a distinctive stem) of many verbs, and various participles, etc.

Pali sentences do not all contain verbs. When it is asserted simply that a thing is something (as epithet or attribute or " predicate ") two nouns (one of them usually an adjective or pronoun) may merely be juxtaposed. Usually the " subject " stands first. In translating into English the verb " to be " must be used. e.g. : *eso samaṇo,* " this (is) the philosopher " (*eso* is a pronoun, nominative singular masculine, meaning " he ", " this ", *samaṇo,* meaning " philosopher ", is a noun like *loko*). This type of sentence is especially common in philosophical discourse, e.g. : *idaṃ dukkhaṃ,* " this is unhappiness " (*idaṃ* is a pronoun, nominative singular neuter, meaning " it ", " this ", *dukkhaṃ,* meaning " unhappiness ", is a neuter noun in *-a*, nominative singular).

LESSON 1

First Conjugation

The inflection of the present tense (indicative active) of a verb of the *bhū* or first conjugation (*bhuvādi gaṇa*) is as follows :—

	Singular	Plural
3rd person (*paṭhamapurisa*) [1] "he", "it", "she", "they"	*bhavati* "he is"	*bhavanti*
2nd person (*majjhimapurisa*) "you"	*bhavasi*	*bhavatha*
1st person (*uttamapurisa*) "I", "we"	*bhavāmi*	*bhavāma*

(In the old Indian systems of grammar the order of persons is the reverse of the European : this is followed here as the third person is the most frequent in use and is the form given in most dictionaries. The European names of the persons are used. It is worth noting also that in the Indian tradition students learn person by person—and in nouns case by case—and not number by number, thus we would read across the page : *bhavati bhavanti, bhavasi bhavatha, bhavāmi bhavāma.* This practice is recommended.)

The root of this verb is *bhū*, and the meaning "to be". The root appears more clearly in other forms derived from it, such as the past participle *bhūta*, "been." The theory of derivation of the present tense stems of verbs of the first conjugation is that within certain limits the vowel in the root is "strengthened" by alteration into the compound vowel nearest in place of articulation (see next section : "Vowel Gradation"). Where the vowel is *a, ā, e,* or *o* no change is made ; where it is followed by a double consonant no change is made ; the long vowels *ī* and *ū* are not changed when followed in the root by any consonant. Thus the changes are : *i* becomes *e* and *u* becomes *o* unless two consonants follow ; *ī* becomes *e* and

[1] The literal meanings would be *paṭhama* = "first", *majjhima* = "middle", *uttama* = "last". Indian grammarians follow the reverse order to that traditional in Europe, for very sound reasons. We of course translate not literally but into the actual English equivalents.

ū becomes *o* unless any consonant follows. The stem vowel *a* is then added, before which *e* becomes *ay* and *o* becomes *av*.

Verbs of the first conjugation ; root and 3rd person singular :

kam [1] (to walk) (with the prefixes *upa*, meaning " up to ", " towards ", and *saṃ*, meaning " together ")	*upasaṃkamati*	he goes to, he approaches
kam [1] (with the prefix *(p)pa*,[2] meaning " out ", " away ")	*pakkamati*	he goes away
cu	*cavati*	he falls (from a form of existence), he dies
jīv	*jīvati*	he lives (is alive, makes a living)
pass	*passati*	he sees
pucch	*pucchati*	he asks
bandh	*bandhati*	he binds
bhās	*bhāsati*	he says, he speaks
bhū	*bhavati*	he is, there exists
vad	*vadati*	he says
sīd (to sit) (with the prefix *ni*, meaning " down ")	*nisīdati*	he sits (down)
har	*harati*	he takes
har (with the prefix *ā*, meaning " to ")	*āharati*	he brings
hū	*hoti*	he is, there is

[1] In this root and some others the initial consonant is usually doubled when compounded with a prefix. This may be explained as a historical survival from an older phase of the language, but the roots could more conveniently be regarded as *kkam*, etc., the doubling being retained only under certain conditions (close combination with a preceding vowel). The solution adopted in this book is to show consonants liable to doubling in close junction with a bracketed twin : *(k)kam*, etc.

[2] The initial consonant of this prefix also is liable to doubling (e.g. when another prefix ending in a vowel is prefixed to it), cf. preceding footnote.

(*hū* is in fact a weaker form of *bhū* and *o* here a " contraction " of *ava*. In the present tense *hoti* is far commoner than *bhavati*, which is probably used only for special effect : elevated or poetic speech. On the other hand in certain tenses only the forms from *bhū* are used.)

Vowel Gradation

The Indian grammarians described the commonest (in the old Indo-Aryan languages) processes of strengthening of roots, or of syllables generally in morphology (derivation), as a prefixing of *a* to the letter actually strengthened. There are then three grades : zero or weak (*avuddhika* : no *a*-), strong (*guṇa* : *a*- prefixed), lengthened (*vuddhi* = " increase " : a second *a*- prefixed). In the case of vowels (which is the most important) the three grades are seen for example in : *bhūta* (zero), *bhavati* and *hoti* (strong), *bhāveti* (lengthened). The system of vowel gradation may be set out as follows :—

Zero	Strong	Lengthened
— [1]	*a*	*ā*
i or *ī*	*e* or *ay*	*e* [2] or *āy*
u or *ū*	*o* or *av*	*o* [2] or *āv*

Present Tense

The present (*vattamānā*) tense (*lakāra*) is used to express present (*paccuppanna*) time (*kāla*), the limits of which are somewhat vague, or indefinite time (timeless statements such as " eternal truths "), sometimes the immediate future (which may include a shade of " imperative " sense ; cf. English " I'm going ") and sometimes the past (" historic present "). It is used to express the duration of an action " until ", a fixed

[1] Roots such as (*k*)*kam* and *vad* could be given as (*k*)*km* and *vd* (" zero grade of *m* and *d* "), but these forms are never found. The convention is to give them already in the strong grade form, then, as they are already strong they are not further strengthened in the derivation of the first conjugation present tense stem.

[2] The theoretical prefixed *a*- is merged in *e* or *o*.

future time (a vivid future visualized as present) " when ", and in certain other constructions.

It is not necessary to express the person by a pronoun, as this may be understood from the inflection alone. (Pronouns in Pali usually refer back to words in previous sentences or merely emphasize the person.) The inflected forms express " she " and " it " as well as " he ".

Masculine Nouns in -a

Nouns (masculine) inflected like *loka* > *loko*, nominative case singular :—

upāsako	lay disciple, the lay disciple, a lay disciple
kāyo	body, substance
khattiyo	warrior, noble (member of the military-aristocratic class)
gāmo	village
tathāgato	thus-gone (from worldliness to a state of calm : epithet of the Buddha—usually—or of others like him)
devo	god (usual meaning), king (as term of respectful address)
putto	son
puriso	man, person
brāhmaṇo	priest, brahman (member of the hereditary priesthood)
maggo	road, way
manusso	human being, person
amanusso	non-human being (i.e. a god, etc.) (negative prefix *a*)
mahāmatto	minister
loko	world, people, universe
samaṇo	ascetic, wanderer, philosopher [1]
samayo	a time, occasion (any time, time of an event)

Nominative Case

(In Pali eight case-categories are needed in order to describe the colligations in which nouns are used. In the singular of

[1] Other than a hereditary priest : one like the Buddha who has left ordinary life and social ties.

the masculine *-a* declension all are formally distinct ; elsewhere some are formally alike, but the colligations must still be distinguished.)

The nominative (*paṭhamā, paccatta*) case is used for the agent (or " subject ") of an active sentence (or " subject " of an active verb).[1] E.g. *brāhmaṇo passati,* " the priest sees ".

The nominative case is used for any attribute of an agent in the nominative, including one " predicated " [2] of it by means of a verb meaning " to be " (sometimes there is no verb in Pali in this type of sentence : see above, last paragraph of the Introduction). The attribute usually follows the agent [3]. E.g. (with verb) : *brāhmaṇo mahāmatto hoti,* " the priest is a minister ". Without verb : *eso samaṇo,* " this is the philosopher." This curious feature of verbs meaning " to be " (the " copula "), distinguishing them from all other verbs, must be firmly fixed in mind. When there is a verb expressing an action as well, such an attribute may still be applied to the agent (without any verb meaning " to be ") : *brāhmaṇo mahāmatto passati,* " the priest (who is) the minister sees ". As far as possible in Pali words referring to the same thing agree in case, number, gender, and person (exception : cases of relative pronouns).

The nominative is used with (" governed by " in traditional European terminology) certain indeclinables relating it to the action, in place of another case related directly to the verb. E.g. *yena gāmo . . . upasaṃkamati* = " he approaches . . . towards the village ".

The nominative form is used when a word is quoted or cited (to refer simply to itself). E.g. *kāyo ti* = " ' body ' ". (It is in accordance with this convention that Indian dictionaries and grammars cite words in the nominative, not in the stem form.)

[1] See Lesson 7 for the nominative as patient of passive sentences.

[2] Logical terms such as " subject " and " predicate " are as a rule to be eschewed in linguistic analysis. Their use in traditional European grammar is unscientific and misleading, what is needed being terms suited to the description of a natural language, not of a few artificial propositions in traditional European logic. Sometimes we can make a rough use of these words in our descriptions, though not of their traditional definitions. It may be noted as a general rule that in Pali a " predicate ", like an attribute or epithet, goes in the same case as its " subject ". In grammar we may distinguish " nexus " (cf. " predicate ") and " junction " (adjective and noun).

[3] It thus contrasts in position with adjectives, which usually precede the nouns they qualify (except when several adjectives qualify a single noun, cf. Lesson 11).

Word Order

The normal prose order of a sentence is : agent—attribute—patient (Lesson 2)—action, thus the verb is usually at the end. The order is very rarely of grammatical value (the agent will still be the agent even if it follows the patient or the verb), but it is stylistically important.

EXERCISE 1

Translate into English :—

tathāgato bhāsati	mahāmatto nisīdati
upāsako pucchati	samaṇo tathāgato hoti
puriso evaṃ vadati	putto upāsako passati
devo amanusso hoti	brāhmaṇo upasaṃkamati
evaṃ vadāmi	manusso jīvati
khattiyo pakkamati	evaṃ vadanti

Translate into Pali :—

The man speaks	The minister is a priest
The ascetic is " thus-gone "	The noble approaches
The priest goes away	The god dies
The god says so	You say so (Sing.)
There is a time	You say so (Plur.)
The son sits down	We say so

LESSON 2

Nominative Plural

The nominative plural of masculine nouns in *a* has the inflection *ā*. E.g. *gāmā*, " villages."

First Conjugation Verbs with Irregular Stems

Many verbs included in the first conjugation have irregularly formed present stems. Some show the root unchanged where strengthening would be expected, others have the root enlarged or altered in various ways. When a suffix beginning with a consonant is added to a root ending in a consonant the preceding consonant is often " assimilated " to the following one. E.g. : *s* + *ch* > *cch*. (In a consonant cluster only the last consonant can be aspirated unless this is a semivowel, when the preceding consonant can retain its aspiration.) Once the stem is given, the inflection is perfectly regular :—

*vis** [1] (to enter) (with the prefix (*p*)*pa*)	*pavisati*	he enters (no *guṇa* strengthening)
*phus**	*phusati*	he touches, he reaches, he attains
is	*icchati*	he wishes, he desires (*ch* added to root)
gam	*gacchati*	he goes
gam (with the prefix *ā*)	*āgacchati*	he comes
(*t*)*ṭhā*	*tiṭṭhati*	he stands, he remains, he stays (root " reduplicated ")
dā	(*dadāti* or) *deti*	he gives (reduplicated, and a contracted form, the latter being used more commonly : 2 sg. *desi*, 1 sg. *demi*, etc.)
hā (to abandon) (with the prefix (*p*)*pa*)	*pajahati*	he gives up, he renounces (root reduplicated)
(*v*)*vaj* (to go) (with the prefix (*p*)*pa*)	*pabbajati* [2]	he goes forth (he gives up ordinary life and becomes a wandering ascetic or philosopher)
(*j*)*jhe*	*jhāyati*	he meditates (root lengthened, *e* > *āy*,—*vuddhi*)
i	*eti*	he goes (stem vowel *a* not added to the root)

(The verb *i* is synonymous with *gam* but " poetic " or " elevated " and hence rarely used ; in the imperative tense,[3]

[1] In this book first conjugation verbs whose root vowels are not strengthened are marked by an asterisk (following the Roman numeral indicating the conjugation, thus : I*). Some grammarians give these verbs as a separate conjugation.

[2] A double *v* is never written in Pali. Where it would occur in junction the articulation becomes " stop " instead of semivowel : *bb*.

[3] Lesson 6.

however, *i* is normal, not *gam*—which illustrates the meaning of our rather vague term " elevated ".)

i (with the prefix *upa*)	*upeti* (also " elevated ")	he goes to (in the junction of prefix and root vowels the vowels coalesce ; in this case -*a* + *i*- > *e* just as in " strengthening ")

Accusative Case

The " patient " (*kamma*) which undergoes the action of an active verb (the " direct object ") is expressed by the " accusative " (*dutiyā, upayoga*) case ending. Masculines in *a* have the accusative singular inflection *aṃ*. E.g. :—

purisaṃ bandhati, " he binds the man "
samaṇaṃ vadati, " he says to the ascetic "

The accusative case is also used to express the goal of motion :

gāmaṃ pavisati, " he enters the village "

The accusative case may likewise express the (extent [1] of) space traversed :

maggaṃ paṭipajjati, " he follows the road " (*paṭipajjati* is a third conjugation verb—Lesson 11)

The accusative is used for an attribute of another accusative :

khattiyo brāhmaṇaṃ mahāmattaṃ passati, " the warrior sees the priest who is the minister "

This type of construction includes such sentences as " he declares (that) time (is) the cause ", where *kālo* (" time ") and *paccayo* (" condition ", " cause ") will both be in the accusative (*kālaṃ paccayaṃ* . . .).

Alternatively cases like this might be regarded as examples of what the old commentators call the " accusative of specification of state " (*itthambhūtākkhyānatthe upayogavacanaṃ*), usually translatable : " with reference to ". E.g. *Gotamaṃ evaṃ* . . .

[1] This type of construction usually includes a numeral specifying the extent, as in " the smell carries 100 leagues "—*yojanasataṃ* acc. Sing. (*yojana* = " league ", *sata* = " hundred " : both neuter -*a* stems). Similarly in " he goes half-way " " half-way " is accusative in Pali—*upaḍḍhapathaṃ*.

saddo = " the report (*saddo*) . . . thus (which follows in the next sentence) with reference to Gotamo (proper name) ". This idiom is not common, " with reference to " generally being expressed by the locative case (Lesson 16). The accusative is also used to specify the person in greetings and imprecations, with an indeclinable (example in Exercise 6).

Some verbs take two patients (*dvikammaka*). These include verbs meaning to call, tell, or ask (someone something), and to take or bring (something somewhere) :—

> *samaṇaṃ atthaṃ pucchāmi,* " I ask the philosopher the meaning (*attho*) "

The accusative is used to express the pure duration of time or casual point of time. This usage is not of common occurrence (when the time is that through which or necessarily at which something is accomplished the instrumental case is used—Lesson 8) :—

> *aḍḍhamāsaṃ āgacchati,* " he comes after a fortnight "
> *ekaṃ samayaṃ* . . . ", one time . . . ", " once . . . " (beginning a narrative)

The accusative singular neuter form of some adjectives is used as an " adverb " (Lesson 17) :—

> *rassa* (" short "—adjective in *-a*) > *rassaṃ passasāmi,* " I breathe out shortly ", i.e. expel a short breath ((*p*)*pa*-(*s*)*sas*)

The accusative plural inflection of masculines in *a* is *e*. E.g. *upāsake passati,* " he sees the lay disciples ".

Transitive and Intransitive Verbs

Verbs which can take a patient are called " transitive " (*sakammaka*). Verbs which cannot take a patient are called " intransitive " (*akammaka*). (Verbs which can take two patients are called bitransitive, *dvikammaka,* cf. above.) Verbs which are transitive in one language are not necessarily translated by verbs which are transitive in another, hence these properties must be noticed as they occur in Pali verbs. Transitivity is of course a property of verbs, not of their roots, thus the verbs *bhū* and *hū* are intransitive but the verbs *pari-bhū*

(" despise ") and *anu-bhū* (" experience ") are transitive, whilst *pātu(r)-bhū* (" appear ") and *(p)pa-hū* (" be able ") are intransitive. The roots *bhū* and *hū* are neither.

Vocabulary

Nouns inflected like *loko* :—

aggo	top
attho	prosperity, wealth, welfare, purpose, meaning, subject-matter
dhammo	(true, natural) doctrine, natural element, natural substance, natural phenomenon [1]
patto	bowl
pamādo	negligence, pastime
piṇḍo	alms
bhavo	existence, good fortune
vādo	debate, argument, statement
satto	being, creature
saddo	noise, report
sugato	well-gone (title of the Buddha)

EXERCISE 2

Translate into English :—

sugato dhammaṃ bhāsati
upāsako pattaṃ āharati
manussā bhavaṃ icchanti
gāmaṃ gacchāma
samaṇo āgacchati
tathāgato sugato hoti
brāhmaṇo purise pucchati
devā cavanti
vādaṃ vadanti
puttā pabbajanti
satto tiṭṭhati
samaṇe atthaṃ pucchanti

Translate into Pali :—

They go to the minister
The men see the ministers
The god, who is not a human being, approaches the " thus-gone "

[1] This word has several meanings, for some of which it is hard to find English equivalents. The central idea is that of " nature ", " a nature ", " a naturally occurring phenomenon ", hence a (true) doctrine conforming to nature, to reality. The universe, including imponderable and mental phenomena as well as ponderable matter, is regarded as consisting of a finite number (less than 100) of these substances and phenomena.

You ask the philosopher (about) the doctrine
We ask the philosopher who is " well-gone "
The " thus-gone " gives up negligence
The lay disciples enter the village
The ascetics meditate
The substance remains
He reaches the top
We ask the philosopher the meaning
He gives alms

LESSON 3

Declension of bhagavant, brahman, *and* rājan

A few masculine nouns in stems other than *a* are of common occurrence. The usual title for the Buddha in Pali texts has the stem form *bhagavant*, meaning " the fortunate ", " the bountiful ", " the Master " (translations vary: " the blessed one ", " the exalted one ", etc.). The inflections in the nominative and accusative are as follows :—

	Singular	Plural
Nom.	*bhagavā*	*bhagavanto* [1]
Acc.	*bhagavantaṃ*	

[1] *N.B.*—Except in the masculine declension in *a* and in the present participle the accusative plural is always the same as the nominative.

The noun *brahman*, meaning " God " (the supreme being and creator in the Brahmanical religion of the hereditary priesthood of India), is inflected in the nominative and accusative singular as follows :—

	Singular
Nom.	*brahmā*
Acc.	*brahmānaṃ*

The noun *rājan*, " king ", is similarly inflected in these cases.

Seventh Conjugation

Verbs of the *cur* or seventh conjugation (*curādi gaṇa*)[1] form present stems with the vowel *e* (or, much less often, with the fuller suffix *aya*, of which *e* is a contraction). The root vowel is strengthened and sometimes lengthened. As in the first conjugation *i* and *u* become *e* and *o*, but *a* is often lengthened (*vuddhi*) to *ā*. The personal endings are similar to those of the first conjugation. From the root *dis*, " to teach " :—

	Singular	Plural
3rd person	*deseti*	*desenti*
2nd person	*desesi*	*desetha*
1st person	*desemi*	*desema*

Similarly conjugated are :—

kath	*katheti*	he relates, he tells
kam	*kāmeti*	he loves
chaḍḍ	*chaḍḍeti*	he throws away, he abandons
(ñ)ñap (with the prefix *(p)pa*)	*paññāpeti*	he prepares, he declares (he regulates) (*ñ* is always doubled when between two vowels: or we can say initial *ñ* is always in fact *(ñ)ñ*)
dhar	*dhāreti*	he holds, he wears, he has, he accepts (with two patients/accusatives : x as y), he remembers
mant	*manteti*	he takes counsel, he discusses (confidentially)

[1] Some grammars reckon this as the eighth conjugation. There are in practice six conjugations in Pali, the so-called fourth (*svādi gaṇa*) containing only one verb actually used in the Canon, which, moreover, is itself usually conjugated according to the fifth conjugation. Most of the old Pali grammarians reckon seven conjugations, some by splitting the fifth make eight. Each conjugation (*gaṇa*) is named after one of the roots belonging to it.

mant (with the prefix *ā*)	*āmanteti*	he addresses
vañc	*vañceti*	he deceives
vad (to speak) (with the prefix *abhi*, meaning "towards," "about")	*abhivādeti*	he salutes, he greets, he takes leave
vās (to dress) (with the prefix *ni*)	*nivāseti*	he dresses
vid (to feel) (with the prefixes (*p*)*paṭi*, meaning "towards", "back", and *saṃ*)	*paṭisaṃvedeti*	he feels, he experiences (something to be something)
veṭh (to twist, to wrap) (with the prefix *ni*(*r*),[1] meaning "out)"	*nibbeṭheti*	he untwists, he unravels, he explains, he rebuts

Vocabulary

Masculine nouns in *a* :—

kālo	time, opportunity, proper time (appropriate time)
paccayo	condition, cause
bhāro	burden, load
lābho	gain
vipāko	result
vihāro	life, way of life, dwelling (also used figuratively of a mental state, e.g., of happiness)
hattho	hand

EXERCISE 3

Translate into English :—

bhagavā dhammaṃ deseti
rājānaṃ vañcesi

[1] This prefix is often given as *ni*, coinciding in form with *ni*, "down". The form *nir* is seen when a vowel follows. When any consonant follows, the *r* is assimilated to that consonant, which thus appears doubled as here.

upāsakaṃ brāhmaṇaṃ dhāreti
rājā purise āmanteti
brāhmaṇo brahmānaṃ passati
rājā khattiyo mahāmattaṃ pucchati
brāhmaṇā rājānaṃ vadanti
puriso bhāraṃ chaḍḍeti
evaṃ kathenti
kālaṃ paccayaṃ paññāpenti

Translate into Pali :—

The lay disciples salute the fortunate one
He binds the hands
I experience the result
The king addresses the priest
The priest who is minister speaks thus to the fortunate one
Existence (is) the condition
He remembers the meaning
The fortunate one dresses
The gods discuss the matter
The fortunate one asks the king
He enters the dwelling
You rebut the argument
The king takes counsel
He renounces gain

LESSON 4

Past (Aorist) Tense

The usual past tense, which is called the " aorist " (*ajjatanī*) tense, is generally formed directly from the root (more rarely from the present stem) by adding special inflections. Sometimes the vowel *a* is prefixed to the root as an indication of past time, though the difference of inflections avoids ambiguity in most cases. This *a* goes between the prefix (*upasagga*), if any, and the root. It is called the " augment ". The root is sometimes changed to form a special aorist stem. There are three main forms of aorist according to the stem used, having some differences in inflection also (they correspond only partially to the conjugations of the present tense).

The first form of the aorist, followed by the majority of verbs, simply adds a set of inflections beginning with the vowel *i* to the root (sometimes to the present stem). It may be illustrated from the root (*k*)*kam* with the prefixes *upa* and *saṃ*. The augment is not used with this root.

	Singular	Plural
3rd person	*upasaṃkami*, " he approached "	*upasaṃkamiṃsu*
2nd person	*upasaṃkami*	*upasaṃkamittha*
1st person	*upasaṃkamiṃ*	*upasaṃkamimhā* (or *-imha* [1])

[1] The 1st person plural aorist is of infrequent occurrence in the texts and the manuscript tradition is not consistent about the quantity of the final *a*.

The following verbs are inflected in the same way :—

as (to be)	*āsi*	he was, it was (note presence of augment : $a + a > \bar{a}$) (but 3rd pl. is *āsuṃ*)
(*p*)*pa*-(*k*)*kam*	*pakkāmi*	he went away, pl. *pakkamiṃsu* (the singular has irregular lengthening of the root vowel in all three persons, the plural is regular)
(*j*)*jhe*	*jhāyi*	he meditated (using the present stem)
pucch	*pucchi*	he asked
bandh	*bandhi*	he bound
bhās	*abhāsi*	he said, he spoke (this root takes the augment)
(*p*)*pa*-(*v*)*vaj*	*pabbaji*	he went forth
(*p*)*pa-vis*	*pāvisi*	he entered, he went in (note presence of augment between prefix and root, forming a long vowel : *pa* + *a* > *pā*)
ni-sīd	*nisīdi*	he sat down

A second form of aorist is taken by verbs of the seventh conjugation. Here an aorist stem is formed by adding *s* to the present stem in *e*. The singular inflections are as in the first form of aorist. The 3rd person plural inflection is *uṃ*; the other plural persons are not used (> first form on strong root).

	Singular	Plural
3rd person	*desesi*, " he taught "	*desesuṃ*
2nd person	*desesi*	*desittha*
1st person	*desesiṃ*	*desimha*

(*desesi* coincides in form with the 2nd person singular present and has to be distinguished by the context.)

Similarly inflected are :—

kath	*kathesi*	he related, he told
dev (to lament) (with the prefix *pari*, meaning " round ", " around ")	*paridevesi*	he lamented, he grieved
ā-mant	*āmantesi*	he addressed

A third form of aorist is taken by a small but important group of verbs, mostly with roots ending in *ā*. Like the second form it has a stem in *s* and the usual singular inflections, but the plural inflections begin with the vowel *a*. The root *kar*, " to make," " to do," " to work," takes this form of aorist after changing irregularly to *kā*. Several verbs of this group take the augment.

	Singular	Plural
3rd person	*akāsi*, " he made "	*akaṃsu*
2nd person	*akāsi*	*akattha*
1st person	*akāsiṃ*	*akamhă*

Similarly inflected are :—

(ṭ)ṭhā	*aṭṭhāsi*	he stood, he remained
dā	*adāsi*	he gave
(p)pa-hā	*pahāsi*	he renounced

The root *hū* is very irregular in the aorist. The singular takes strengthening (*guṇa*) and *s*, the 3rd plural substitutes *e* for the root vowel :—

	Singular	Plural
3rd person	*ahosi*, " he was, " " there was "	*ahesuṃ*
2nd person	*ahosi*	*ahuvattha*
1st person	*ahosiṃ*	*ahumha*

(The root *bhū* is seen in the aorist only with prefixes, when it usually follows the above inflections : *-bhosi*, etc.)

The aorist is used for all kinds of past actions, including besides the " historical " or " narrative " past particularly the (present-) perfect : *desesiṃ* = " I have taught ". (When more precise demarcations of time relations are needed, participles are used in conjunction with the main verb, as will be illustrated below—Lesson 24.) The second and first persons plural are not often found in the Pali texts. The third person is extremely common, both singular and plural.

Agreement of Verb and Agent

When a verb has two or more agents it usually agrees with the sum of the agents and is plural ; more rarely it may agree with the nearest agent only or with the agents taken as a collective, being singular. If the persons conflict, the second takes precedence over the third and the first over both.

Vocabulary

Some indeclinables (*nipāta*) :—

atha	then (*atha kho* combined mean " then ", " moreover ", " rather ")
ettha	here

kho	indeed (slight emphasis)
ca	and (always follows the word it connects, or the first word of a phrase it connects: called therefore an "enclitic" or "postpositive". Very often repeated after each connected word)
tadā	then
nāma	by name (used after the name) (sometimes merely emphatic, "indeed")
bhūtapubbaṃ	formerly, once upon a time
sace	if

Masculine nouns in *a* :—

kumāro	boy, prince
purohito	high priest, (approx.) prime minister (the priest who is chief adviser to the king, "instructing": *anu-sās*, him in both secular matters and religious duties)
māṇavo	boy, young priest
rājaputto	prince
sahāyo	friend

EXERCISE 4

Translate into English :—

upāsakā nisīdiṃsu

bhūtapubbaṃ rājā Disampati nāma ahosi. Reṇu nāma kumāro putto ahosi. Govindo nāma brāhmaṇo purohito ahosi. Jotipālo nāma māṇavo putto ahosi. Reṇu ca rājaputto Jotipālo ca māṇavo sahāyā ahesuṃ. atha kho Govindo brāhmaṇo kālam akāsi.[1] rājā Disampati paridevesi.

evaṃ tadā āsi

Translate into Pali :—

The priest went away

The fortunate one entered the village

The son was called Uttara

The fortunate one addressed Ānanda [2]

[1] This idiom "made his time" means "he died".

[2] A famous disciple of the Buddha, his personal attendant and "dragon" (for keeping time-wasters at bay).

I have taught the doctrine
The nobles approached the prince
I spoke thus
The prince went forth

LESSON 5

Pronouns: Personal and Demonstrative

The personal pronouns are inflected as follows :—

FIRST PERSON (stem *ma(d)*) [1]

	Singular	Plural
Nom.	*ahaṃ*, " I "	*mayaṃ*, " we "
Acc.	*maṃ*, " me "	*amhe*, " us "

SECOND PERSON (stem *ta(d)*)

	Singular	Plural
Nom.	*tvaṃ*, " thou ", " you "	*tumhe*, " you "
Acc.	*taṃ* (or *tvaṃ*) " thee ", " you "	

THIRD PERSON (stem *ta(d)*)

	Singular		Plural	
	Masculine	Feminine	Masculine	Feminine
Nom.	*so*, " he " (sometimes *sa*)	*sā*, " she "	*te*	*tā*
Acc.	*taṃ*, " him "	*taṃ*, " her "		

[1] The declension of pronouns is very irregular. The forms given as " stems " are those which appear in compounds (Lesson 13). (In practice the 1st and 2nd person pronouns are hardly used in compounds.)

Although the person is expressed by the inflection of the verb, the pronouns of the first and second persons are frequently used, giving a slight emphasis to the subject. The third person pronoun is less often used in this way. The third personal pronoun is used also as a demonstrative, meaning " that ", " it ", in three genders. It is generally used as what is known as an " anaphoric " pronoun, that is to say it refers back to someone or something previously mentioned in a narrative. As opposed to the use in conversation and other direct speech of " pronouns of presence " referring to someone or something present (" this man says ", " in that jar "), *ta*(*d*) is thus called a " pronoun of absence " because it is most often used to speak of someone or something in a story and therefore not present to the listeners. It may serve to connect the sentences of a narrative into a continuous paragraph or longer section. It is used also as an emphatic pronoun (in combination with another pronoun or occasionally with 1st person verb in sense of emphatic 1st person), for example in the expression *so 'haṃ* " I " (literally " that I "). In combination with a noun it is again emphatic and may sometimes be translated " the ". The masculine and feminine demonstrative (anaphoric) pronouns are as above, the neuter inflections are :—

	Singular	Plural
Nom. and Acc.[1]	*taṃ* or *tad*	*tāni*

[1] Neuter words in Pali have always the same form for the nominative and accusative cases.

Another form of the demonstrative pronoun is used to denote a present object or person, corresponding roughly to the English " he ", " she ", " it ", and " this " (also to " that " when the object is pointed at, i.e. present). It may be called a " deictic " pronoun, pointing to someone or something present to the hearers in direct speech. The inflections are the same, with the prefix *e* :—

(stem *eta(d)*)

	Singular			Plural		
	Masculine	Feminine	Neuter	Masculine	Feminine	Neuter
Nom.	*eso* (sometimes *esa*)	*esā*	*etaṃ* or *etad*	*ete*	*etā*	*etāni*
Acc.	*etaṃ*	*etaṃ*	*etaṃ* or *etad*	*ete*	*etā*	*etāni*

Another demonstrative pronoun, also "deictic" or "present" and translatable "he", "she", "it", or "this" and so hardly[1] distinguishable in meaning from *eta(d)*, is inflected as follows :—

(stem *idaṃ-*)

	Singular			Plural		
	Masculine	Feminine	Neuter	Masculine	Feminine	Neuter
Nom.	*ayaṃ*	*ayaṃ*	*idaṃ*	*ime*	*imā*	*imāni*
Acc.	*imaṃ*	*imaṃ*	*idaṃ*	*ime*	*imā*	*imāni*

There being no "definite article" in Pali the demonstrative pronouns are sometimes used where English would use the definite article, and may sometimes be translated "the" rather than "he", "that", "this", etc.

Demonstrative pronouns must agree in number and gender with the nouns to which they refer.

The Verb as

The verb *as*, "to be", asserts with emphasis the existence of something or somebody. (On the other hand *hoti* is not emphatic and is used also to state attributes : the minister is a priest, etc., and of something which happens or "becomes" : a man

[1] Where there is any distinction *idaṃ-* indicates a nearer object or emphasizes the nearness : *this* one, whilst *eta(d)* is simply indefinite.

is/becomes pleased, etc. The usual and more emphatic verb for " becomes ", " comes into existence ", however, is *uppajjati*—third conjugation: see Lesson 10). The verb *as* is very irregular; the present tense is as follows :—

	Singular	Plural
3rd person	*atthi*	*santi*
2nd person	*asi*	*attha*
1st person	*asmi* or *amhi*	*amha* (sometimes *amhā*)

Frequently *as* is used, unlike other verbs, at the beginning of a statement: " There is . . ." The meaning is emphatic assertion of what is stated.

Negation

There are two main negative indeclinables, *na* and *mā*. The first is the usual negative " not ", placed in front of the word or phrase negated, or at the beginning of a negative sentence :—

tvaṃ na passasi, " you do not see "

The vowel of *na* is often elided when the word following it begins with a vowel :—

n' atthi, " it is not ", " it doesn't exist "

The second negative is used for prohibitions or negative injunctions or wishes, usually with the second person of the aorist tense, which loses its time reference and applies to the present or future (sometimes a verb otherwise augmented appears without the augment in this construction) :—

mā paridevesi, " don't grieve "

More rarely *mā* appears, sometimes with the particle *eva*, or *h' eva*,[1] with the third person of the verb :—

mā h' eva rājā kālam akāsi, " may the king not die " (*mā h' eva* means " don't " or simply " not ").

[1] *h'* is the emphatic particle *ha*, " indeed," with elision of its vowel before another vowel.

mā with the third person appears regularly in polite address (see next Lesson).

A double negation is equivalent to a strong affirmation :—

mā h' eva kho kumāro na rajjaṃ kāresi, " don't let the prince not rule (*kāresi* : aor. 3 sg.) the kingdom (*rajjaṃ*) ", i.e. let him rule, he *must* rule.

Aorist of vac

The aorist of the verb *vac*, to say, is very irregular :—

	Singular	Plural
3rd person	*avoca*, " he said "	*avocuṃ*
2nd person	*avoca* (also *avaca*)	*avocuttha* (also *avacuttha*)
1st person	*avocaṃ*	*avocumha* (or *-umhā*)

Vocative Case

The vocative case, or " nominative of address ", of masculine nouns in *a* has in the singular merely the uninflected stem : *deva*, " O king." The plural is the same as the nominative plural. The vocative is used " enclitically ", i.e. it does not stand at the beginning of a sentence.

Vocabulary

Verb of the first conjugation :—

apa-i	*apeti*	he goes from, he goes away (poetic)

Indeclinables :—

tuṇhī	silent, silently
tena	this way, that way
pi	also, too (like *ca* this follows the word, or the first word of the phrase, connected by it)
ha	indeed

Masculine nouns in *a* :—

issaro	lord, god
nirodho	cessation (of unhappiness and of perception, sensation and mental states), peace of mind, calm
paribbājako	wanderer
mahārājā	great king, king (nom. sg. as *rājan-*, but rest follows *a* declension on stem *-rāja-*, e.g.: acc. *mahārājaṃ*. The nom. pl. may be written either *~ā* or *~āno*)[1]

EXERCISE 5

Translate into English :—

Reṇu rājaputto rājānaṃ Disampatiṃ etad avoca. mā kho tvaṃ deva paridevesi. atthi deva Jotipālo nāma māṇavo putto ti.
atha kho rājā Disampati purisaṃ āmantesi.
ahaṃ ime dhamme desesiṃ
rājā khattiyo taṃ purisaṃ etad avoca
mā samaṇaṃ upasaṃkami
ahaṃ purohito brāhmaṇo ahosiṃ
ahaṃ asmi brahmā issaro
idaṃ avoca bhagavā [2]
te rājaputtaṃ avocuṃ
mā saddam akattha
so nirodhaṃ phusati
samaṇā amha
na taṃ deva vañcemi
eso mahārāja bhagavā
mayaṃ bhagavantaṃ upasaṃkamimhā
atthi kāyo
upeti pi apeti pi
evam [3] etaṃ brāhmaṇa

[1] In compounds words sometimes lose their characteristic stems, the new compound-words being assimilated to the *a* declension.
[2] Rhetorical and emotive inversion of agent and verb, for emphasis. In their context these words follow the utterance of an important statement.
[3] *ṃ* may change to *m* when a vowel follows in close junction.

Translate into Pali :—

The wanderer said this to the fortunate one
Those wanderers were silent
I teach the doctrine
I am a priest
This king is a human being, I too am a human being
I love her
Don't go in (sing., use two words only)
We said to that fortunate one
Don't grieve (plur.)
He goes forth (use pronoun)
Then (add *kho*) Mahāgovinda the priest towards those nobles approached that way
He said this to those nobles
They ask me the meaning
He said this to us
She said this to me
I teach this doctrine
This (is) cessation (use *idaṃ*-)
You are (emphatically) priests, O Vāseṭṭhas (word order: pronoun, *kho*, verb, vocative . . .)

LESSON 6

Imperative Tense

The imperative (*pañcamī*) tense is formed from the present stem with some special inflections :—

	Singular	Plural
3rd person	*bhavatu*	*bhavantu*
2nd person	*bhava*	*bhavatha*
1st person	*bhavāmi*	*bhavāma*

—the first persons and the second person plural coincide with the present indicative. The second person singular has usually no inflection but sometimes the inflection *hi* is added, in which case the stem vowel *a* is lengthened. The following verbs, and all verbs of the seventh conjugation, regularly have the *hi* inflection :—

jīv	*jīvāhi*	live !, make your living !
i	*ehi*	go !, you must go
vad	*vadehi*	say !, speak ! (the stem vowel is irregularly changed to *e*)
hū	*hohi*	be !

The third person singular imperative of *hū* is *hotu.* From *as* the 3rd person singular is occasionally used :—

atthu, it may be, may it be, it shall be (always impersonal).

(*as* rarely appears as imperative in other persons, an example is *attha* = " you be ! ")

The imperative expresses commands and prohibitions, but also invitations and wishes. In the second person the sense is usually that of a command, whereas the 3rd person imperative used in a similar situation with the title or name of the person addressed, or the polite pronoun, expresses a polite invitation.

The imperative verb often stands at the beginning of a sentence.

The imperative of (*t*)*ṭhā* is used (besides the sense " wait ", " remain " : *ettha tiṭṭha,* " wait here ") in the meaning : " let it be," " never mind," " let him not," " don't trouble." Eg. *tiṭṭhatha tumhe,* " don't you bother."

Respectful Address

The stem *bhavant-* (of the present participle of *bhū*) is used as a pronoun of polite or respectful reference or address (*tvaṃ* being restricted to familiar address) but with a verb of the 3rd person (except in the vocative case : see Lesson 8) :—

	Singular
Nom.	*bhavaṃ,* " you ", " sir ", " his honour "
Acc.	*bhavantaṃ*

Quotation

The indeclinable *ti* means " end quote " and stands at the

end of any passage in direct speech. It is used also to mark something thought. Anything quoted, whether a line of verse or a single word (e.g. in giving a definition or in mentioning a word or concept : *kāyo ti* = " 'body' ", *kusalan ti*[1] = " the word 'good' ", " the good ", " the concept of the good "), is marked in the same way. Indirect speech is exceedingly rare in Pali, so that instead of such English constructions as " he said (or thought) that so and so " or " when he asked so and so " we find direct speech with *ti* : " so and so *ti* he said."

Any short vowel immediately preceding *ti* is lengthened. The pure nasal *ṃ* is changed to the dental nasal *n*.

evaṃ devā ti, " (it is) so, O king " (end quote)

n' eso n' atthī ti vadāmi, " I don't say 'This doesn't exist'." (Here the first *na* goes with *vadāmi* and the second with *atthi* ; the quotation starts after the first *na*, with " *eso* . . .")

This indeclinable sometimes appears in a fuller form : *iti*, which is emphatic and may generally be translated " this ", " that ", " thus ". It may refer to a statement (or a philosophical view or conception) from a distance instead of marking the end of the actual words. The two forms may be used together for emphasis.

Sixth Conjugation

Verbs of the *tan* or sixth conjugation (*tanādi gaṇa*)[2] form present stems with the suffix *o*. The personal endings are the same as for the first conjugation. From the root *kar*, " to do," " to make," " to work," the present tense is :—

	Singular	Plural
3rd person	*karoti*	*karonti*
2nd person	*karosi*	*karotha*
1st person	*karomi*	*karoma*

The imperative tense is *karotu* (3rd sing.), *karontu* (3rd plur.), *karohi* (2nd sing.), etc. (rest as present).

[1] *kusalaṃ* is a neuter word (nom. sing. in *-aṃ*). Before *ti*, *ṃ* > *n*.
[2] Some grammars reckon this as the seventh conjugation.

Similarly conjugated are :—

(p)pa-ap(p)	*pappoti*	he attains, he arrives (a rare, "poetic" verb ; cf. in ordinary speech *phusati* and *upasaṃkamati*)
vi-ā-kar	*vyākaroti*	he explains
tan	*tanoti*	it expands, it stretches
sak(k)	*sakkoti*	he can, he is able to (used with the infinitive—Lesson 19)

(In the aorist this verb follows the third form, with *s*, but $k + s > kh$, hence : *asakkhi*, he could)

kar is the only verb of this conjugation which is frequently used. It is found in many idioms, such as : take in the hand, assume an appearance or expression, perform a feat, make a reply ; also to do an action which is specified by a patient-noun, as *sajjhāyaṃ karoti*, "he does studying," i.e. "he studies".

Vocabulary

Verbs of the first conjugation :—

anu-sās (to rule) (the prefix *anu* means "after", "following")	*anusāsati*	he advises, he instructs (used especially of ministers of a king, also figuratively of a teacher)
abhi-(k)kam	*abhikkamati*	he goes forward, he advances
ā-i	*eti*	he comes (the vowels coalesce : only the context can decide whether the meaning is "goes" or "comes")
khād	*khādati*	he eats, he bites, he chews
pā	*pivati*	he drinks (irregular stem)
(p)pa-hū	*pahoti*	he can (more emphatic than *sak(k)*)

Masculine nouns in *a* :—

okāso	opportunity
thūpo	monument, pagoda
pariyāyo	course (lit. and fig., including discourse and manner of doing something)
vaṇṇo	colour, beauty, praise, class

saṅkho conch (trumpet)
sajjhāyo learning, studying, study

Indeclinable :—

bhavaṃ good fortune !, best wishes ! (in greetings, with imperative of *as*)

EXERCISE 6

Translate into English :—

ehi tvaṃ purisa. yena Jotipālo māṇavo ten' [1] upasaṃkama. Jotipālaṃ māṇavaṃ evaṃ vadehi . . . evaṃ [2] devā ti . . . so puriso Jotipālaṃ māṇavaṃ etad avoca : bhavam [3] atthu bhavantaṃ Jotipālaṃ [4] māṇavaṃ. rājā Disampati bhavantaṃ Jotipālaṃ māṇavaṃ āmanteti . . . Jotipālo māṇavo yena rājā Disampati ten' upasaṃkami. Jotipālaṃ māṇavaṃ rājā Disampati etad avoca. anusāsatu bhavaṃ Jotipālo māṇavo . . . te atthe anusāsati.

gaccha tvaṃ Ānanda
idaṃ hara
etu bhagavā
ayaṃ samaṇo Gotamo [5] āgacchati
nibbeṭhehi sace pahosi
desetu sugato dhammaṃ
pivatha khādathā ti
abhikkama mahārāja
thūpaṃ karonti
etha tumhe

Translate into Pali :—

Let the fortunate one sit down
Bring that !
That man must come
Let the priest not trouble

[1] Elision of final *a* before another vowel.

[2] *evaṃ* with a vocative as here signifies assent. It may be translated " so (be it) " or simply " yes ".

[3] *ṃ* > *m* before a vowel.

[4] This greeting is idiomatic, using the accusative of the person greeted with an indeclinable and the imperative of the verb *as* ; cf. the " accusative of specification of state ", Lesson 2.

[5] Name of the clan (*gotta*) to which the Buddha belonged. Used like a surname.

He makes an opportunity
The king said this : " We must go "
I do not say this world doesn't exist
Give that up !
Let not the honourable Govinda go forth
Study ! (plur.)
Ask the fortunate one (about) this subject-matter
This conch makes a noise

LESSON 7

Past Participle

The past participle is usually formed from the root with the suffix *ta* or *ita*. Thus :—

(p)pa-(k)kam	*pakkanta*	gone away, left (assimilation *m* + *t* > *nt*)
kar	*kata*	done (final *r* elided)
kilam	*kilanta*	tired
kup (to be angry)	*kupita*	angered
gam	*gata*	gone (final *m* elided)
adhi-gam (the prefix *adhi* means " over ")	*adhigata*	understood
ā-gam	*āgata*	come
saṃ-anu-ā-gam	*samannāgata*	endowed, acquired (*anu-ā* > *anvā* > *annā* by assimilation)
ni-(g)gah (to seize, to grasp)	*niggahīta*	refuted
chaḍḍ	*chaḍḍita*	thrown away, abandoned
(p)pa-(ñ)ñap	*paññatta*	declared, prepared (*p* assimilated to *t*)
(ṭ)ṭhā	*ṭhita*	stood, stayed (final vowel elided)
saṃ-tus (to be pleased)	*santuṭṭha*	contented, satisfied
dis	*desita*	taught (present stem is used)

(d)dis	*diṭṭha*	seen (irregular assimilation)
pucch	*puṭṭha*	asked (assimilation *cch* + *ta* > *ṭṭh*)
bandh	*baddha*	bound (nasal elided, *t* assimilated to *dh*)
bhās	*bhāsita*	spoken
bhū	*bhūta*	been
ni(r)-mā (to measure)	*nimmita*	created
vi-muc (to become free)	*vimutta*	freed
ni-rudh (to obstruct)	*niruddha*	stopped, ceased, ended
vac	*vutta*	said (irregular formation : a form of weakening of the root)
(p)pa-(v)vaj	*pabbajita*	gone forth
sam	*santa*	calmed
(s)su (to hear)	*suta*	heard

The past participle is normally passive (*kammapada*) in meaning, but past participles of intransitive verbs (and even of some transitive verbs used intransitively), especially of those meaning " go ", " move ", " go forth ", are sometimes constructed as active. The past participle may be equivalent to a (normally passive) finite verb in the past tense. It then appears in the nominative case and agrees in number and gender with the agent (if active) or the patient (if passive). Usually it indicates the " present-perfect ", as in conversation, e.g. :—

> *mayaṃ . . . upasaṃkantā*, " we have approached . . .", " we have come . . ." (announcing their arrival to see someone).

Instead of standing alone as equivalent to a finite verb the past participle may be accompanied (usually followed) by the present tense of verbs meaning " to be ", stressing the " present-perfect " sense.[1]

[1] These constructions, which are called " periphrastic ", will be discussed further in Lesson 24.

Some past participles are used as nouns (e.g. *bhāsitaṃ* may mean " what was spoken ", " speech ", " saying "), and all of them may be used as " adjectives " (e.g. *kupita* = " angry ") qualifying and agreeing with nouns in gender, case, and number. Some have acquired special meanings as nouns. They are inflected like nouns in *a*, in the three genders.

Neuter Nouns in -a

Neuter nouns in *a* have their nominative singular in *aṃ* (as well as their accusative) and their nominative and accusative plural in *āni*. The rest of their declension is the same as for masculines in *a*. Thus from the stem *yāna*, " carriage," we have :—

	Singular	Plural
Nom. and Acc.	*yānaṃ*	*yānāni*

Instrumental Case

The third or instrumental (*tatiyā, karaṇa*) case is used to express the instrument by means of which an action is done. Masculine and neuter nouns in *a* have the singular instrumental inflection *ena* and the plural *ehi*. The first personal pronoun has in the singular the forms *mayā* and *me*, " by me," the latter form being enclitic (it need not follow the word with which it is most closely connected, but cannot stand at the beginning of a sentence). The instrumental plural is *amhehi*. Eg. : *kāyena phusati*, " he touches with (his) body." Likewise " he acquiesced by his silence " is . . . *tuṇhībhāvena* ; bringing water " in a bowl " is *pattena*. The instrumental embraces a wide range of idioms, including " covered with dust ", " . . . with clothes (dressing) ", " pleased with " or " by " a saying or by seeing, and a series of special uses which will be considered in the next Lesson.

Passive Sentences

When the action of a sentence is expressed by a passive (*kammapada*) verb, the agent is expressed by the instrumental case. A common construction is the past participle used as an impersonal (*bhāva*) passive verb and inflected in the nominative singular neuter as sentence-verb :—

evaṃ me sutaṃ, " thus it was heard by me," or " thus I have heard " (" present-perfect ").

If there is a patient, and the action is expressed by a past participle, the patient will be in the nominative case and the participle will agree with it in gender, case, and number, as if it were an adjective :—

mayā ime sattā nimmitā, " by me these beings were (/have been) created," " I (have) created these beings."

N.B.—The agent (*kattar*) may be expressed either by the nominative or by the instrumental, and the patient (*kamma*) either by the accusative or by the nominative, according to the active or passive construction of the sentence.

The stems in consonants form instrumentals with the inflection *ā* :—

Stem	Instrumental
bhagavant	*bhagavatā*
brahman	*brahmunā*
rājan	*raññā* (*j* + *n* assimilated to *ññ*)

The other pronouns form instrumentals as follows :—

Nominative	Instrumental Singular	Instrumental Plural
tvaṃ	*tayā, te*	*tumhehi*
so and *taṃ*	*tena*	*tehi*
sā	*tāya*	*tāhi*
ayaṃ	*iminā* (M. and N.) *imāya* (F.)	*imehi* (M. and N.) *imāhi* (F.)

Neuter nouns in *a*, nominative singular :—

āsanaṃ seat
kammaṃ work

kiccham	difficulty
geham	house, building
gottam	clan
cīvaram	robe
dānam	gift, donation, alms
dukkham	unhappiness, misery, suffering
dvāram	door, gate
dhanam	money, wealth
puññam	merit, good, goodness, meritorious action
maranam	death
yojanam	league (actually about 4·5 miles)
sahassam	thousand
sīlam	virtue, good conduct
sukham	happiness

Vocabulary

Indeclinable :—

āma yes

EXERCISE 7

Translate into English :—

iminā mayaṃ nimmitā
mayaṃ brahmunā nimmitā
desito Ānanda mayā dhammo [1]
iminā tvaṃ purisa dhanena jīvāhi
vimutto tathāgato
te ca me evaṃ puṭṭhā āmā ti vadanti
idam [2] āsanaṃ paññattaṃ
ete manussā gehaṃ pavisanti
niggahīto 'si [3]
kilanto 'smi
dānaṃ detha

Translate into Pali :—

They experience happiness
The doctrine has been declared by me

[1] *desito* placed at the beginning for emphasis. As a rule departures from the usual word order in prose indicates emphasis, strong emotion.
[2] *ṃ* may change to *m* when a vowel follows.
[3] *asi* with elision of the first vowel.

The wanderer is (*hoti*) contented
Death (is) misery
I have heard this
I did the work
He gives a donation
The body (is) tired

LESSON 8

Further Uses of the Instrumental Case

The other more or less distinct uses of the instrumental case may be noted here for reference.

Accompaniment: *brāhmaṇena saddhiṃ,* "with the priest," "accompanied by the priest."

The indeclinable *saddhiṃ,* "with," is generally used in these expressions, following the noun, and we may equally say that *saddhiṃ* requires the instrumental. "Talking", "discussing" (*mant*) with a person need not take *saddhiṃ.*

Possession (endowment): a past participle meaning "endowed with", or the instrumental of the reflexive pronoun *attan* (see Lesson 22), is used with the word indicating the virtue or vice in question in the instrumental: *sīlehi samannāgato,* "endowed with virtues."

Filled "with water"; filled "with happiness"; filled "with noise" (*saddena*).

Cause (but in scientific/philosophical discourse the ablative case is used to express causal connections: Lesson 14): *bhagavatā vādena kupito,* "angry at (with) the fortunate one's statement"; *cīvarena santuṭṭho,* "satisfied with the robe"; *atthena,* "because of that business/matter"; *karaṇīyena,* "(engaged in some) business"; *iminā p' aṅgena,* "(you shouldn't go) for this reason" (*aṅgaṃ* = "limb", "characteristic", "factor", and so is used in expressions such as "because of this": related to "endowment").

Equality: *samasamo vaṇṇena,* "quite equal in beauty." In making a comparison the instrumental may be used only if the act of comparison is first described generally and indefinitely: *purisena purisaṃ,* "(comparing) a man with a man" (for a specific, conclusive comparison, " this is better than that," the ablative case is used : see Lesson 14).

Price : *sahassena,* " for a thousand " (i.e. sell for 1,000 *kahāpaṇas,* the standard silver coin).

Way (which way, direction) : " by one way " ; " by another way " ; *dvārena,* " by the gate " (entering, leaving).

Direction, orientation : " from West to East " (both in instrumental) and each followed by the indeclinable *ca* ; " from North to South ".

Manner : *iminā,* " in this way " ; *iminā pariyāyena,* " through this course (procedure) ", " in this manner " ; *kāyena paṭisaṃvedeti,* " he experiences through his body " ; *santena,* " calmly " (thus instrumentals may be used like " adverbs of manner ") ; " on his right side " (manner of lying) ; *kicchena adhigataṃ,* " understood with difficulty " ; " he sat practising a certain kind of meditation " (instrumental, as if " manner " of sitting). This sense is in fact adjacent to the ordinary " instrument " sense, as we see in expressions such as : serving with actions (*kammena*), whether physical or mental, or with speech ; honouring, entertaining, etc., with music, dancing, garlands, etc.

Means of livelihood, means of explanation or description (cf. instrument), means of acquiring goodness, *puññaṃ,* such as *dānena,* " by giving," or of expiating past deeds (*kammaṃ*).

Vehicle : *yānena gacchati,* " he goes in (by) a carriage," *nāgena,* " by elephant."

Motive : *gāravena,* " through respect " (he did not speak).

Time by means of which (at the end of which) or particular time at which : *aparena samayena,* " after some time," " in due course " ; *tena samayena,* " at that time " ; *accayena,* " through (after) the passage/passing away " (of time or of a person : specified in the genitive case).

Age at which.

Measure (cf. the ablative case, Lesson 14) : *dvādasayojanāni ahosi āyāmena,* " it (a city) was twelve leagues in length " ; *sattayojanāni vitthārena,* " seven leagues in breadth." Compounds ending in the word *matta-,* meaning " measure ", are also used in the instrumental case : *jannumattena,* " knee deep."

Classification: birth, clan, family, kind, and similar relations: *Gotamo gottena*, "a Gotama by clan"; *jātivādena*, "in respect of class (station by birth)."

Dissociation (cf. accompaniment: we find in a number of words and expressions a tendency to associate opposite and contradictory ideas; in the present case there is fortunately no ambiguity): *adaṇḍena*, "without force" (negative prefix *a-*); also instrumental used with the indeclinable *aññatra*, "except for," "apart from": *aññatra brāhmaṇena*, "except for the priest."

Other idioms with the instrumental:—

āsanena nimanteti, "he invites to sit down," "he offers a seat";

kālena kālaṃ, "from time to time," "regularly";

lābhena lābhaṃ, "from gain to gain" (wishing always for more gain, with one gain on to another);

aññena aññaṃ ("one with another", literally "other with other"), "irrelevantly";

sabbena sabbaṃ ("all with all", i.e.) "completely", "absolutely thoroughly" (as in knowing some doctrine).

Present Participle

Present participles (*missakiriyā*), active in meaning, are formed from the present stem of verbs by adding the suffixes *nt* or *māna* and declining like nouns. They indicate an action which takes place simultaneously with (*missa*) the main action of the sentence. From *bhū* are formed the stems *bhavant* and *bhavamāna*, both meaning "being". The *nt* stem, which is much more commonly used for almost all verbs, is inflected as follows, for example from *gam*:—

	Singular	Plural
Nom.	*gacchaṃ* or *gacchanto*, "going"	*gacchantā*
Acc.	*gacchantaṃ*	*gacchante*
Instru.	*gacchatā*	*gacchantehi*

Note the weak form of stem (without nasal) in the ins. sg.

From other conjugations, masculine nominative singular: *karonto,* "doing"; *paññāpento,* "declaring."

The forms in *māna* are inflected in exactly the same way as other nouns in *a*. From *as* we have as stem *samāna,* "being," masculine nominative singular *samāno,* which is used quite frequently—more frequently than *sant,* though the latter is also current. Since the words *bhavant* (and *bhava*) and *sant* have certain special meanings [1] as well as that of "being", *samāna,* which has not, avoids ambiguity.

Present participles are used like "adjectives" (as past participles may be) "qualifying" nouns, with which they agree in gender, case, and number.

The Pronoun bhavant

Bhavant is inflected like *gacchant* when it means "being". From the same stem is formed the honorific pronoun *bhavant,* "you," "sir," "your honour," "his honour," which has largely divergent inflections :—

	Masculine	
	Singular	Plural
Nom.	*bhavaṃ*	*bhavanto* or *bhonto* (by contraction of *ava* > *o*)
Acc.	*bhavantaṃ*	*bhavante*
Instru.	*bhotā*	*bhavantehi*

Vocative singular : *bho* (plural as nominative : *bhonto*).

The nominative case of this pronoun is used for the 3rd person, the vocative for the 2nd person : *ayaṃ bhavaṃ,* "this honourable"; *tvaṃ bho,* "you, sir."

[1] For *bhavant,* see below, though with special inflections. *Bhavo* means "existence", "good fortune"; *sant* means "existing", hence "true", more rarely "good".

Gerund

The gerund (*pubbakiriyā*), an indeclinable participle, is used to express an action preceding (*pubba*) the action of the main verb of a sentence. It may thus conclude a subordinate clause. The agent of the gerund is the same as that of the main action. Complex sentences are constructed with clauses concluded by participles or gerunds preceding the main clause with the main verb. In this way the agent is described as performing a group or series of actions. Each clause may have its own patient (i.e. gerunds may take patients in the accusative, like other verb forms). The gerund is usually (but far from always) formed from the same stem as the past participle by adding the suffixes *tvā*, *itvā*, or *ya* :—

upa-saṃ-(k)kam	*upasaṃkamitvā*	having approached
kar	*katvā*	having done ; *karitvā* is also used
gam	*gantvā*	having gone
(g)gah	*gahetvā*	having taken
chid	*chinditvā*	having cut
u(d)-(ṭ)ṭhā (the prefix *u(d)* means " up " [1])	*uṭṭhāya*	having stood up
ā-dā	*ādāya*	having taken (often equivalent to simply " taking " in English)
(d)dis	*disvā*	having seen
vac	*vatvā*	having said
abhi-vad	*abhivādetvā*	having greeted
ni-vās	*nivāsetvā*	having dressed
vi-vic (to separate)	*vivicca*	having become separated from, having become isolated (*vic* + *ya* > *vicca*)
(p)pa-vis	*pavisitvā*	having entered
(s)su	*sutvā*	having heard

[1] It is sometimes given as simply *u*, since the *d* rarely appears in practice, but after this *u* any consonant is doubled (= assimilation of the *d* to it).

(p)paṭi-(s)su	*paṭissutvā*	having agreed, having assented
(p)pa-hā	*pahāya*	having renounced
hū	*hutvā*	having been

Vocabulary

Verbs of the first conjugation :—

ji	*jayati*	he conquers, he wins, he defeats
labh	*labhati*	he obtains, he gets
(p)pa-su (to crush, to extract (liquids), to produce)	*pasavati*	he generates

Nouns :—

āyāmo	length
gāravo	respect
daṇḍo	stick, force, punishment
nāgo	elephant
pañho	question
bhūto	living being (p.p. of *bhū* used as a noun)
vitthāro	breadth
agāraṃ	house, home
annaṃ	food
cittaṃ	thought, mind, heart (figuratively)
jīvitaṃ	life
jhānaṃ	meditation
ṭhānaṃ	place
nagaraṃ	city
nibbānaṃ, *parinibbānaṃ*	extinction (of existence), liberation (from existence), Nirvāṇa [1]
pānaṃ	drink
bhāsitaṃ	speaking, saying (p.p. of *bhās* used as a noun)
bhojanaṃ	meal, food
vatthaṃ	garment (plural : clothes, dress)

[1] The prefix *pari* is generally used when referring not to Nirvāṇa itself as a state, or non-state, but to the event of an individual's (final) attainment of it at the end of his worldly life, and especially to the Parinibbāna of the Buddha himself.

viññāṇaṃ	consciousness
veraṃ	hatred
saraṇaṃ	protection, refuge
senāsanaṃ	abode, resting place

Indeclinables :—

diṭṭhā	excellent, splendid !, it's lucky, it's wonderful
vata (enclitic)	surely, indeed ! (strong emphasis or mild expletive, expressing a wish, regret, reproach or surprise : cf. " alas ! ", " I say ! ")
handa	well !

EXERCISE 8

Translate into English :—

ahaṃ tena samayena rājā Mahāsudassano ahosiṃ
dānena n' atthi puññaṃ
te 'haṃ [1] upasaṃkamitvā evaṃ vadāmi
maṃ abhivādetvā pakkāmi
disvā evaṃ avocumha
diṭṭhā bho satta jīvasi
jayaṃ veraṃ pasavati
brāhmaṇo brahmunā manteti
evaṃ bho ti
handa vata bho gacchāma
kālaṃ karonto avoca
rājā samāno idaṃ labhati
jhānaṃ jhāyati
mayaṃ bhagavantaṃ saraṇaṃ gacchāma, dhammañ ca [2]
jīvitaṃ demi

Translate into Pali :—

They enter by this gate
The king, having greeted the fortunate one, sat down
Having approached (and) greeted the fortunate one, they sat down
Having approached them I ask these questions
Having dressed, taking a bowl I entered the village

[1] *ahaṃ* with elision of initial *a* after another vowel.
[2] Assimilation *ṃ* + *c* > *ñc* in junction.

Gentlemen ! do not say thus
The honourable Jotipāla went forth
(As he is) going he sees
I do not take counsel with God
He entered the house
He gives a drink
I do not get food
He sees the garment
He is (*hoti*) satisfied with the resting place
Living beings experience unhappiness
The lay disciples come to the place

LESSON 9

Passive Conjugation

Verbs form passive stems with the suffix *ya* or *īya* added to the root. The root is usually unchanged, but some roots show a weaker form. Normally the root has the same form as in the past participle. Roots ending in a vowel often lose the vowel. The inflections are the same as in the active. It is the stem which shows whether a verb is active or passive.

Root (*p*)*pa-hā*, present indicative passive (*kammapada*) :—

(Root vowel elided)

	Singular	Plural
3rd person	*pahīyati* " it is given up "	*pahīyanti*
2nd person	*pahīyasi*	*pahīyatha*
1st person	*pahīyāmi*	*pahīyāma*

The simple verb *hā* (" to abandon ", " to diminish ") may have the unweakened stem *hāya*.

Frequently the *ya* suffix is assimilated to the final consonant of a root, and sometimes its presence is inferred merely from the apparent doubling of this consonant.

Other passives are :—

kar (to do)	*karīyati*	it is done (the *i* may be long or short ; another spelling is *kayirati*)
(*ñ*)*ñā* (to know) (with the prefix (*p*)*pa*)	*paññāyati*	it is understood
dā (to give)	*dīyati*	it is given
(*d*)*dis* (to see)	*dissati*	he is seen
vac (to say)	*vuccati*	it is said, it is called (cf. the past participle : *vutta*)
han (to kill)	*haññati*	he is killed

Passive verbs are not very common in Pali, which has a strong preference for the active except in certain favoured expressions with past participles.

An aorist passive is sometimes formed by adding the aorist inflections to the passive stem : *haññiṃsu*, " they were killed."

A present participle passive is formed by adding the suffix *māna* to the passive stem and inflecting as a participle : *kayiramāna*, " being done."

Feminine Nouns in -ā

Feminine nouns in *ā* have the following inflections in the first three cases :—

	Singular	Plural
Nom.	*kathā*, " talk," " story "	(*kathā* or) *kathāyo*
Acc.	*kathaṃ*	
Ins.	*kathāya*	*kathāhi*

(cf. the inflection of the pronoun *sā*, " she.")

Feminine nouns in *ā* :—

avijjā	ignorance
upāsikā	female lay disciple
taṇhā	desire, " thirst "

devatā	deity, divine being, spirit
paññā	understanding, wisdom
parisā	assembly
mālā	garland
vācā	speech
vijjā	science, knowledge
vedanā	sensation
saññā	perception
sālā	hall

Vocabulary

Verb of the first conjugation :—

apa-(k)kam (the prefix *apa* means " off ", " away ")	*apakkamati*	he goes off, he withdraws

Noun :—

ajo goat

Indeclinables :—

bhante sir ! (polite address to a Buddhist monk)
vā or, either (enclitic, used like *ca*—Vocab. 4)
saccaṃ it is true that, is it true that ? (whether this is interrogative can appear only from the context—and no doubt from the intonation in speaking)

EXERCISE 9

Translate into English :—

kāyā hāyanti
ayaṃ kho sā brāhmaṇa paññā
esā taṇhā pahīyati
bhojanaṃ dīyati
saccaṃ Nigrodha bhāsitā te esā vācā (interrogative)
saccaṃ bhante bhāsitā me esā vācā (affirmative reply to the preceding sentence)
idaṃ vuccati cittan ti vā viññāṇan ti vā
tā devatā maṃ etad avocuṃ

atthi kho bho Maṇikā [1] nāma vijjā
saññā ca vedanā ca niruddhā honti [2]
Sujātā nāma bhante upāsikā kālakatā [3]
evam pi kho Sunakkhatto mayā vuccamāno apakkami
samaṇo Gotamo imaṃ parisaṃ āgacchati

Translate into Pali, using the present passive in the present time sentences :—

These phenomena are abandoned
Goats are killed
The priest is seen
Ignorance is given up
He is called an ascetic
This is called misery
Taking a garland they went to the hall

LESSON 10

Future Tense

The future (*bhavissantī*) tense has the same inflections as the present, added usually to a stem having a strong form of the root and the suffix *iss*, or in the seventh conjugation usually *ess* :—

gam	*gamissati*	he will go
dis	*desessati*	he will teach
bhū	*bhavissati*	he will be, there will be

(*as* and other verbs meaning " to be " rarely form their own futures, *bhavissati* is used for all of them)

labh	*labhissati*	he will get
saṃ-vi-bhaj (to resort to)	*saṃvibhajissati*	he will share

[1] A magic science for thought-reading.

[2] As here, *hū* is sometimes used as an " auxiliary " verb with a past particle : " are stopped," " have ceased." This construction is described as " periphrastic ", cf. Lesson 24, and is equivalent to a single passive verb. It is much more commonly used than the latter.

[3] Cf. *kālam akāsi* in Exercise 4 ; here *kāla-* is compounded with the participle, the whole functioning grammatically as a past participle.

The meanings include the expression of the probable (*bhavissati* in particular often has this sense) and of the hypothetical future as well as of certainty or (in the 1st person) determination or decision. *sace ahaṃ . . . labhissāmi, saṃvibhajissāmi . . .*, " if I get . . . I will share . . ." Obedience to a law of nature and also habit (innate or acquired) may also be expressed by the future : all living beings (must/will) die = . . . *nikkhipissanti*, literally " will throw down, put down " (the body). This is more emphatic than the use of the present tense to express an " eternal truth " : they *will* do this ; it may also express the emotional colour of regret or disapproval. Indignation (or disapproval) may be expressed by the future tense, usually in a phrase beginning *kathaṃ hi nāma . . .*, " for how could (' will ') he . . ." The future also expresses perplexity, surprise, and wonder, for example in : *kim ev' idaṃ bhavissati*, " what can this be ? ", " what is this (stuff) ? ".

Future passive verbs are formed by adding the same suffix and inflections to passive stems :—

(*p*)*pa-hā* *pahīyissati* it will be given up

Genitive Case

The sixth or genitive (*chaṭṭhī, sāmin*) case expresses normally a relation (*sambandha*) between two nouns. All the other cases except the vocative are grouped together as *kāraka* (" acting ") cases, since they normally connect directly with the verb (action). The genitive may often be translated by " of ", and serves as a " possessive " case. Two main and characteristic uses are distinguished : denoting the " possessor " (*sāmin*), or the whole of which the related word denotes a part (*avayava*). Of these the possessive genitive is much the more frequent and has many shades of meaning.

The inflections of the genitive are as follows :—

Nominative.	Genitive.
loko	*lokassa*
lokā	*lokānaṃ*
cittaṃ	*cittassa*
cittāni	*cittānaṃ*

Nominative	Genitive
kathā	*kathāya* (sing. : same as instrumental), *kathānaṃ* (plur.)
bhagavā	*bhagavato*
rājā	*rañño*
brahmā	*brahmuno*
ahaṃ	*mama*,[1] *me* (enclitic form)
mayaṃ	*amhākaṃ*
tvaṃ	*tava*, *te* (enclitic form)
tumhe	*tumhākaṃ*
(*e*)*so* and *tad*	(*e*)*tassa*
sā	*tassā*
te and *tāni*	*tesaṃ*
tā	*tāsaṃ*
ayaṃ	*assa* or *imassa* (masc.), *assā* or *imassā* (fem.)
ime	*imesaṃ*
imā	*imāsaṃ*
bhavaṃ	*bhoto*

Usually the genitive word immediately precedes the word to which it relates : *rañño thūpo*, " a king's monument."

A construction with a possessive genitive is very often equivalent to an English construction with the verb " to have ". (In Pali " to have " is hardly ever expressed by a verb but almost always by the genitive case.) The verb " to be " (*hū*) is used if there is no other verb in the sentence : *idaṃ assa hoti*, literally " of him there is this ", " he has this ". A frequent idiom of this type is *tassa evaṃ hoti* . . . (or *ahosi*, etc.) introducing direct speech which is thought by the agent, literally " of him thus it is . . ." (or was, etc.), " he has this thought . . .", " he thinks thus . . .".

As noted in Lesson 8, an idiom consisting of the genitive of the word denoting the period + *accayena* expresses the time after which (or through the passage of which) something is done :—

sattāhassa accayena . . . pabbajissāma, after a week . . . we will go forth

[1] Sometimes *mamaṃ*.

A similar idiom is *mama* + *accayena* = " after me " in the sense of " after I have passed away ", " after my death/ *parinibbāna* ".

The very general and comprehensive nature of mere relationship between nouns, which the genitive basically " means ", allows the genitive case to be used somewhat loosely where precision is unnecessary. Since the nouns include participles,[1] we quite often find a participle in its verbal function (equivalent to a finite verb : Lesson 7) preceded by a noun in the genitive expressing either the agent or the patient of the action of the participle (so-called " subjective genitive " and " objective genitive " respectively). Formally these constructions are of the regular genitive type (*sambandha*) described above, but in interpretation old commentators have often explained them as substitutes for the *kāraka* cases instrumental (agent) or accusative (patient), which are also used with participles. This has led some later writers to institute the " subjective " and " objective " genitives in Pali as if the genitive were used as a *kāraka* case (the medieval Pali grammarians describe the use of the genitive here as merely substitution for another case, or they assume ellipsis of another noun in the required case—to which the genitive would relate ; some modern writers have simply ignored the distinction between *kāraka* and *sambandha*).

Examples of agent-genitive (" subjective genitive ") :—

brāhmaṇassa pūjito (*Soṇadaṇḍo*) = " (Soṇadaṇḍo was) honoured of (= by) the priest "

yesaṃ . . . *devā* . . . *adiṭṭhā* = " those . . . who have not seen . . . the gods (negative participle : *a*-) " (" of (= by) whom the gods are unseen " ; Commentary explains *yesaṃ* by *yehi*)

Example of patient-genitive (" objective genitive ") :—

ahaṃ . . . *tassa yaññassa yājetā* [2] = " I . . . (was) the performer of that sacrifice "

[1] Also other " verbal nouns " : the " agent noun " (Lesson 23) and " action nouns " (Lesson 19), which have much in common with participles.

[2] *yājetā* is an " agent noun " (Lesson 23), nominative singular, meaning " sacrificer " (from the verb *yaj* I, " to sacrifice ").

The genitive is also regarded as a substitute for the instrumental when it is used in connection with "filling" (cf. Lesson 8). Example with the adjective (Lesson 11) *pūra*, "full" (not a participle, but similar in meaning to a participle as the translation suggests) :—

kumbhiṃ[1] . . . *pūraṃ* . . . *suvaṇṇassa* = "pot . . . full . . . of gold"

The genitive is also used with certain indeclinables, such as *piṭṭhito*, "behind"; *purato*, "before," "in front of"; *antarena*, "between": *me purato*, "in front of me"; *kāyānam antarena*, "between the bodies" ("body" here = ultimate body, element, atom, and the context is cutting between atomic particles). Others will be noted as they occur in later exercises. With these three positional relations may be compared the idiom *uttaraṃ nagarassa*, "north of the city."

A construction called the "genitive absolute" consists of a noun (or pronoun) followed by a participle, both inflected in the genitive. This nexus stands apart from the other words of the sentence and means "while (the noun was doing the participle)" . . . The agent in the absolute nexus is different from the agent of the main sentence. Often the genitive absolute has the special sense of disregarding: "despite (the noun doing the participle)", "under their very noses," as when the participle means "seeing", "looking on". E.g. *telassa jhāyamānassa*, "as (while) the oil is burning" ((*j*)*jhe*, "to burn," *jhāyati*, a homonym of (*j*)*jhe*, "meditate"); *mātāpitunnaṃ*[2] . . . *rudantānaṃ* . . . *pabbajito*, "though his parents were weeping, he went forth" (i.e. "despite their weeping"). The genitive absolute is useful for constructing a sentence with two agents, but the similarly constructed locative absolute (Lesson 16) is much more frequently used, not being restricted to special circumstances.

Vocabulary

Verbs of the first conjugation :—

arah	*arahati*	he deserves, he must, he ought
kilam	*kilamati*	he becomes tired

[1] Accusative of *kumbhī*, "pot" (feminine noun in -*ī*).
[2] Genitive plural, see Lesson 23.

*rud**	*rudati*	he weeps
vīj	*vījati*	he fans
subh	*sobhati*	he makes it clear (intransitive)

Verbs of the seventh conjugation :—

pūj	*pūjeti*	he honours
veṭh	*veṭheti*	he wraps

Nouns :—

anto	side, end, extreme
jayo	victory
dāso	slave
bhāgo	share
yañño	sacrifice (ritual)
telaṃ	oil (sesame oil)
bhayaṃ	danger
ratanaṃ	gem, precious thing
sarīraṃ	body (of a man or animal : *kāyo* has this sense but also the wider meanings of " substance ", " particle "), the plural *sarīrāni* is used to mean " (bodily) relics " (of the Buddha after his cremation)
suvaṇṇaṃ	gold

Indeclinables :—

antarena	between (with genitive)
ciraṃ	for a long time, after a long time
pana (enclitic)	but, however
piṭṭhito	behind (with genitive)
purato	before, in front of (with genitive)

Past participle :—

āropita	disproved (from *ropeti* : Lesson 13)

EXERCISE 10

Translate into English :—

na ciraṃ tathāgatassa parinibbānaṃ bhavissati
imassa jayo bhavissati

brāhmaṇā brahmuno puttā
dukkhass' antaṃ karissanti
āropito te vādo
ayaṃ imassa bhāsitassa attho
mā me purato aṭṭhāsi
so maṃ pañhena, ahaṃ veyyākaraṇena sobhissāmi
tena kho pana samayena Ānando bhagavato piṭṭhito ṭhito hoti bhagavantaṃ vījamāno [1]
kammaṃ kho pana me karontassa kāyo kilamissati
tassa ratanāni bhavanti

Translate into Pali :—

These people will have sons
I am his slave
There will be danger
He will teach the doctrine
I will be an ascetic
The priest has a son
They wrap the king's body in a garment (instrumental)
This is the pagoda of that fortunate one
We deserve a share of the relics of the fortunate one

LESSON 11

Adjectives

Adjectives (*guṇanāma*) [2] are inflected in the same way as other nouns, in the three genders according to the nouns they qualify as attribute-words. Most adjectives in *a* form feminines in *ā*. Adjectives also agree in case and number with the nouns they qualify. When an adjective is common to two or more

[1] Notice how the last two words are tacked on after the main verb. An additional clause of this sort is frequently so placed, as if it were an afterthought, when its action (or state) is simultaneous with the main action. This stylistic feature is very characteristic of old Pali prose.

[2] The Pali term *nāma* includes all nouns and adjectives. As adjectives are called *guṇanāma* ("quality noun"), *appadhānaliṅga* ("subordinate stem"), or *vāccaliṅga* ("qualifying stem") so nouns in the narrower sense, that is "substantives", are called *guṇipada* ("word for thing possessing a quality"), *padhānaliṅga* ("main stem"), or *abhidheyyaliṅga* ("name stem"). Adjectives are also called *visesana*, "distinguishing".

nouns it may agree with the sum of these (and be plural) or with the nearest. Thirdly the qualified words may be taken as collective and singular and the adjective be singular. Where the genders conflict, the masculine takes precedence over the feminine, the neuter over both.[1] An adjective usually precedes the noun it qualifies (thus contrasting with attribute-nouns : cf. Lesson 1), but when there are several adjectives with one noun very often only one adjective precedes and the rest follow the noun. A demonstrative pronoun relating to the same noun will precede the whole group. When an adjective, or (all the) adjectives, follows its noun this usually indicates that it is being "predicated" of the noun, or in other words that the attribute in question is being emphasized. One should then translate "... who is/which is ...". If we use the terms "nexus" and "junction" then the word order adjective + noun usually indicates junction and the order noun + adjective (or equally another noun in the same case) indicates nexus. When there is no verb in the sentence, however, we understand a nexus regardless of the order ; then the placing of a nexus-adjective first indicates emphasis of it (as in an argument).[2]

Adjectives in *a* :—

akusala	bad
atīta	past
ananta	infinite
iddha	powerful
kanta (p.p. *kam* (VII))	agreeable, lovely
kalyāṇa	beautiful, good
kusala	good
dakkhiṇa	right (hand), southern
dhuva	fixed
nicca	permanent
pacchima	last, western
pahūta	much, many
piya	dear
phīta	prosperous

[1] Cf. agreement of verb and agent : Lesson 4 (the principles are similar).

[2] In Pali word order is important chiefly for the sake of being able to deviate from it for effect. This may explain why some severe philologists have refused to countenance it.

vāma	left
sassata	eternal
sukara	easy
sukha	happy

Past participles may acquire special meanings when used as adjectives : *diṭṭha,* " visible."

The distinction between " substantives " and " adjectives " is not absolute, a good many words being used in both functions. Thus *kusalaṃ* = " the good ", *kusala* = " good ", " good at " ; *sukhaṃ* = " happiness ", *sukha* = " happy " ; likewise *kalyāṇa* and other words which are usually adjectives may appear in the neuter gender as abstract nouns.

Third Conjugation

Verbs of the *div* or third conjugation (*divādi gaṇa*) form present stems with the suffix *ya.* In form they therefore resemble passives in *ya.* The personal endings are the same as for the first conjugation. From the root *man,* " to think " (stem : *man* + *ya* > *mañña*) :—

	Singular	Plural
3rd person	*maññati*	*maññanti*
2nd person	*maññasi*	*maññatha*
1st person	*maññāmi*	*maññāma*

Similarly conjugated are :—

chid	*chijjati*	he cuts (down)
jan	*jāyati*	he is born (intransitive verb ; stem irregularly formed)
ā-dā	*ādiyati*	he takes (irregular elision of root vowel, cf. passive conjugation ; here *ĭ*)
ā-pad	*āpajjati*	he acquires, he produces, he gets, he has (intransitive in the latter meaning)

pad (to go) (with the prefix *u*(*d*))	*uppajjati*	it happens, it arises, it becomes
upa-pad	*upapajjati*	he transmigrates, he is reborn
upa-saṃ-pad	*upasampajjati*	he enters into
ni-pad	*nipajjati*	he lies down
(*p*)*paṭi-pad*	*paṭipajjati*	he engages in, he follows, he practises, he behaves (habitually)
vi-muc	*vimuccati*	he is freed
ni-rudh	*nirujjhati*	it stops, it ceases
vid	*vijjati*	it is, it occurs, it is found (to be the case)

In an idiom with *ṭhānaṃ*, *vijjati* expresses the possibility of an event or inference : *ṭhānaṃ etaṃ vijjati* = " this/it is possible " (literally " this place is found "), " it is the case " ; *n' etaṃ ṭhānaṃ vijjati* = " this is impossible ", " it is not the case". These two phrases may be placed immediately after the statement quoted (. . . *ti*) as possible or impossible, or this may follow and be introduced by a relative pronoun (Lesson 12).

Imperatives are formed from these stems just as in the first conjugation. Note the aorist form from *u*(*d*)-*pad* : *udapādi*, " it arose." [1] In forming aorists from these verbs the present stem is sometimes used : -*pajji*, etc., likewise in the future : -*pajjissati*, etc.

Passive forms occasionally coincide with the active : the meaning must in such cases be inferred from the context : *rukkhā chijjanti* must mean " trees are cut down ". Many verbs of the third conjugation are intransitive. Sometimes it is difficult to decide whether a word should be regarded as passive or merely as intransitive. The form *hāyati* (Lesson 9) is regarded as intransitive active by some grammarians, taking it to mean " diminishes ", " withers away", as against (*pa*)*hīyati* meaning " is abandoned ".

[1] But cf. Lesson 20, aorist passive.

Past Participles in -na

Certain verbs form their past participles with the suffix *na*, often there is assimilation of a final root consonant to the *n* :—

chid	*chinna*	cut off
dā	*dinna*	given
ā-pad	*āpanna*	possessing, having
u(d)-pad	*uppanna*	happened, arisen
upa-pad	*upapanna*	transmigrated, reborn, arisen, come into existence
(p)paṭi-pad	*paṭipanna*	engaged in, following, practising
sam-pad	*sampanna*	endowed with, having
bhid	*bhinna*	divided, split
ni-sīd	*nisinna*	seated
hā	*hīna*	diminished, eliminated

Aorists of (d)dis *and* gam

The root *(d)dis*, " to see," forms an aorist with inflections in *ā*, changing its root vowel to *a* :—

	Singular	Plural
3rd person	*addasā*	*addasaṃsu*
2nd person	*addasā*	*addasatha*
1st person	*addasaṃ*	*addasāma*

A few verbs may form an aorist with double inflection, taking the *ā* inflection of *addasā* plus *s* and some of the inflections found with *s* aorists. Some of these forms from *gam* are regularly used, mixed with single forms corresponding to those of *(d)dis* :—

	Singular	Plural
3rd person	*agamāsi* " he went "	*agamaṃsu* (with the double inflection)
2nd person	*agamā* (without the double inflection)	(*agamittha* : following the first aorist form)
1st person	*agamāsiṃ*	*agamamhā*

From (*d*)*dis* itself the double form *addasāsuṃ* (3rd plural) is used alongside *addasaṃsu*.

Vocabulary

Verb of the first conjugation :—

abhi-u(*d*)-*kir** (to scatter)	*abbhukkirati*	he sprinkles (when a dissimilar vowel follows it, *i* sometimes changes to *y* ; in the present case the *y* is further assimilated to the preceding consonant, hence *abhi-u* > *abhyu* > *abbhu*)

Past participles :—

cu	*cuta*	fallen, passed away
vi-pari-ṇam	*vipariṇata*	changed

Nouns :—

ābādho	illness
kārako	doer
bhiṅkāro	vase, ceremonial water vessel
rukkho	tree
saṃvaro	restraint
cakkaṃ	wheel
disā	direction
samaññā	designation, agreed usage

Indeclinables :—

āvuso	sir ! (polite address between equals, also to juniors)
idha	here, in this connection
kuto pana	(whence then ?—rhetorical question) : much less, let alone
tato	thence, then, from there, from that
micchā	wrongly, badly } (these are sometimes written as compounds with verbs or nouns, like the prefixes)
sammā	rightly, perfectly }

EXERCISE 11

Translate into English :—

na kho ahaṃ āvuso addasaṃ
ayaṃ tathāgatassa pacchimā vācā
pāmujjaṃ bhavissati, sukho ca vihāro
addasā [1] kho bhagavā tā devatāyo
iminā kho evaṃ bho pariyāyena Jotipālassa māṇavassa Mahāgovindo ti samaññā udapādi
sassato loko
so gacchati dakkhiṇaṃ disaṃ
kusalan ti pi na bhavissati, kuto pana kusalassa kārako
ahaṃ kho maggaṃ agamāsiṃ
kalyāṇaṃ vuccati brāhmaṇa
atha kho rājā Mahāsudassano vāmena hatthena bhiṅkāraṃ gahetvā dakkhiṇena hatthena cakkaratanaṃ [2] abbhukkiri
idaṃ kusalaṃ
ayaṃ Jambudīpo [3] iddho c' eva bhavissati phīto ca
micchā paṭipanno tvam asi, aham asmi sammā paṭipanno
so tato cuto idhūpapanno [4]
addasā paribbājako bhagavantaṃ āgacchantaṃ
saññā uppajjanti pi nirujjhanti pi
bhagavato ābādho uppajji
saṃvaraṃ āpajjati
ahaṃ kho kammaṃ akāsiṃ. kammaṃ kho pana me karontassa kāyo kilanto, handāhaṃ [5] nipajjāmi
imaṃ mayaṃ addasāma idha upapannaṃ

Translate into Pali :—

The universe is infinite
This is not easy (use the neuter : impersonal statement)
I followed the road
The king saw the boy
The city was prosperous

[1] *addasā* often stands at the beginning of its sentence.
[2] A compound word : " wheel-gem," a symbol of imperial power.
[3] India (as continent : see the first footnote in Exercise 30).
[4] When two vowels meet, sometimes the first is elided and the second is lengthened (*idha* + *upapanno*).
[5] This combination may be regarded as an instance of that described in footnote 4 above, or of *a* + *a* > *ā* by coalescence of similar vowels.

He (is) fixed, permanent, eternal (four words, order as here)
We saw the fortunate one
The speech (is) agreeable
My life (was) given by him (he spared my life), his life (was) given by me (I spared his life)
See ! Ānanda—They (are) past, ended, changed
He has much gold

LESSON 12

Dative Case

The fourth or dative (*catutthī, sampadāna*) case is used to express the purpose for which an action is done and the person to whom something is given (" indirect object "). The dative may express the person for whom something is done or to whom something which happens is advantageous (" dative of advantage "). It is used also with a number of individual verbs (see below). Formally the Pali dative largely coincides with the genitive. Where the form is ambiguous the case may generally be known from its relating either to another noun (genitive) or to the verb (dative). In *all* declensions " genitive " forms are used for the dative also,[1] but a special dative inflection exists alongside this for the singular of masculines and neuters in *a* :—

Nominative	Dative
piṇḍo	*piṇḍāya* or *piṇḍassa*
nibbānaṃ	*nibbānāya* or *nibbānassa*

The inflection in *āya* has the specialized meaning of purpose : *gāmaṃ piṇḍāya pāvisi,* " he entered the village for alms."

Among the verbs which take the dative are the following. We may add here also some other words which take a dative and some miscellaneous dative constructions. The dative is used with the verb (*k*)*kham* meaning " to please " [2] (someone

[1] This of course leads to some difficulties in analysis (i.e. in our grammatical descriptions).
[2] But *ā-rādh* takes the accusative.

= dative) and with the same verb when it means "to forgive" (someone = dative, something = accusative). The verb *(p)paṭi-(s)su* meaning "to assent to (someone)" takes the dative. It is used with the verb *upa-(ṭ)ṭhā*, meaning to serve, attend on/to someone or something (dative), especially in the causative conjugation (see Lesson 13): to cause nurses to attend to the boy (dative); to cause the mind to attend to knowledge. The verb *dhar* in the sense of "hold for/over" takes the dative of the person sheltered, and in the sense of "owe" it takes the dative of the person to whom something is owed. The verb *ā-ruc* ("to inform") takes the dative of the person informed (whereas *ā-mant* takes the accusative). Verbs meaning to be angry at (*kup*, etc.), to curse (*sap*), to long for (*pih*), and to be clear to ((*p*)*pa-*(*k*)*khā*: visible, apparent), to appear to (*pātu*(*r*)*-bhū*: manifest) take the dative.

The adjective (of verbal import) *piya*, "dear", takes the dative of the person to whom.

"For the sake of" (= dative of purpose, above) is expressed by *atthāya* preceded by the genitive of the person or object of the endeavour.

The indeclinable *alaṃ* ("sufficient", "enough", "adequate", "perfected") takes the dative. Besides the ordinary sense of "sufficient" (for any purpose) it has the idiomatic meaning of a refusal or objection ("enough!" = "stop!", "I won't!", etc.) with dative of the person for whom it is sufficient or superfluous ("I won't" = *alaṃ me*; "it is sufficient for you" = *alaṃ vo*).

The negative participle (future passive: see Lesson 16) *abhabba*, which functions as an adjective meaning "unable", "incapable", takes the dative of the action which cannot be done, if the latter is expressed by a noun ("action noun").

When wishes (good wishes) are expressed, the dative is used for the person for whom they are expressed: "may there be (*hotu*) long life for him"; "good luck to you" (*bhaddaṃ bhavato hotu*); "welcome to you" (*svāgataṃ bhavato hotu*). Like *svāgataṃ* ("welcome!") the indeclinables *sotthi* "safety", "safely") and *namo* ("hail!") take the dative.

In a number of expressions there may be doubt whether the case used is dative or genitive. Modern European philologists have disagreed with the classifications of Indian linguistics in several instances, chiefly because they have followed different principles, but the old commentators and grammarians themselves are not unanimous on all points. The genitive meaning " to have " (Lesson 10) has been regarded as dative (this is popular in Europe, especially in France and Germany, reflecting the usages of the philologists' own languages) and the dative with *(p)paṭi-(s)su* as genitive (by some old commentators, who explain the construction as ellipsis of a word meaning " speech "). The noun *vippaṭisāro,* " regret ", may be said to take the dative of the person who regrets—or this may be regarded as a simple relation between two nouns : *rañño . . . vippaṭisāro,* " (there may be) regret . . . to/of the king," = " the king may regret ". There are several similar instances. The chief criterion of the case is : is it " adnominal " (relating to a noun) and genitive or is it " adverbial " (relating to a verb) and dative ? Interpretations of border line instances vary, and the verbal nouns and adjectives introduce further ambiguity. There is no absolute and immutable " dative " or " genitive " in reality : grammarians set up their own principles of description and classify the constructions they find accordingly.

It should be borne in mind that the infinitive of verbs (Lesson 19) overlaps in meaning with the dative of purpose.

A very important idiomatic construction with the dative case refers to the proper time for something, the opportunity for something. Thus *etassa kālo* means " it is the time for this ", " it is the right time for this " ; *akālo . . . yācanāya* means " it is not the right time for asking " ; *yassa* [1] *dāni kālaṃ maññasi* means literally " for which you think it is now (*dāni*) the right time ". The last expression is extremely common in saying (formally) goodbye (spoken by the host, not the guest—who for his part has made the excuse of pressure of work), being roughly equivalent to " well, if you really must go . . ." It is used also by servants reporting to their master that preparations are completed, implying " you can start whenever you wish ", etc.

[1] See the relative pronoun, next page.

Aorist of (s)su

The aorist of the verb (*s*)*su* is inflected as follows :—

	Singular	Plural
3rd person	*assosi*, " he heard "	*assosuṃ*
2nd person	*assosi*	*assuttha*
1st person	*assosiṃ*	*assumha*

(cf. the second form of aorist given in Lesson 4, but note presence of the augment here ; cf. *hū*.)

From (*p*)*paṭi*-(*s*)*su* we have *paccassosi*.[1]

Relative Pronoun

The relative pronoun has the stem *ya*(*d*), " who," " which," which is inflected in the three genders in the same way as the demonstrative *so*, *sā*, *taṃ*, or *tad* :—

	Singular			Plural		
	Masc.	Neut.	Fem.	Masc.	Neut.	Fem.
Nom.	*yo*	*yaṃ* or *yad*	*yā*	*ye*	*yāni*	*yā*
Acc.	*yaṃ*	*yaṃ* or *yad*	*yaṃ*			
Ins.	*yena*		*yāya*	*yehi*		*yāhi*
Dat. Gen.	*yassa*		*yassā*	*yesaṃ*		*yāsaṃ*

Relative pronouns are used mostly in relative clauses, but some of the case-forms are also used as indeclinables.

Relative Clause

The relative clause (*aniyamuddesa*) is the regular form of " subordinate clause " in Pali (clauses with participles and

[1] (*p*)*paṭi* + *a* > *pacca* in junction.

gerunds are also freely used—cf. Lesson 8—but this is not the same kind of " subordination "). Its use is extremely frequent. The clear articulation of the sentence into a subordinate clause introduced by a relative word (a pronoun or an indeclinable such as *yattha,* " where ") and a main clause introduced by a demonstrative word (*niyamato paṭiniddesa*) is an outstanding characteristic of Pali. Complex sentences or " periods " may be built up by combinations of relative clauses and demonstrative clauses, co-ordinate clauses (joined by conjunctive particles such as *ca*), direct speech and so forth. The usages of sentence and period construction will be more extensively surveyed in Lesson 27, when the main elements of construction have been studied and can be reviewed together. A more detailed review of relative clause construction with indeclinables will also be found there.

The relative clause regularly precedes the main clause. The relative word introduces the clause, but may be preceded by indeclinables connecting the whole sentence to the narrative of which it forms a part. E.g. :—

> *atha kho ye icchiṃsu te akaṃsu,* " then (indeed) those who wished, worked " (literally : ". . . who wished, they worked.")

The relative pronoun must be in the same number and gender as the noun or demonstrative pronoun it refers to, but it may be in any case—connecting it with the words in its own relative clause or sentence. E.g. :—

> *yena dvārena nikkhami taṃ Gotamadvāraṃ nāma ahosi,* " the gate by which he left was called Gotama Gate " (" by which (ins.) gate he left, that (nom.) Gotama Gate named was ").

Besides the demonstrative, other pronouns may serve as correlatives, for example the personal pronouns and also the " pronominal adjective " (see below) *sabba,* " all " :—

> *ye . . . ahesuṃ, . . . sabbe . . . bhakkhesi,* " those . . . who were there, . . . he devoured (*bhakkh* (VII)) them all."

Sometimes the main clause has no correlative word (this may of course depend on its having a special form, such as direct speech), but as a rule the correlative demonstrative is used. A proper name (with title) in the main clause is quite often used without a demonstrative.

Repetition of a relative word emphasizes that the clause is universal: *yo yo* = "whoever". The correlative also is repeated. E.g.:—

> *yo yo . . . ādiyissati tassa tassa . . . anuppadassāmi,*[1] "whoever will take . . . to him I will grant . . ."

A demonstrative pronoun immediately following a relative pronoun is emphatic (cf. Lesson 5: *so 'haṃ*): *yo so* = "he who", "that which". Thus we may have a more complex sentence with emphatic and correlative demonstratives. The example which follows has a direct speech clause at the end:—

> *yo so satto paṭhamaṃ*[2] *upapanno, tassa evaṃ hoti: ahaṃ asmi brahmā,* "that being who has come into existence first (in the evolution of the universe) thinks he is God." ("Who that being first is reborn, has this thought: I am God.")

Relative Indeclinables

Besides such indeclinables as *yattha, yathā* ("as"), *yadā* ("when"), *yadi* ("if"), and *yato* ("whence", "because", "since"), certain forms of the relative pronoun have, besides their ordinary uses, uses as indeclinables.

Thus the neuter forms of the nominative-accusative singular (especially *yaṃ*) are used in the impersonal sense of "that", "what", covering a wide range of shades of meaning.

hoti kho so samayo yaṃ . . . ayaṃ loko vivaṭṭati, "there is indeed the (*so*) time that (i.e. when) . . . this world evolves." (Here the relative clause follows the main clause = elevated speech or emphasis of main clause. The main clause has *samayo* as its subject/agent, the subordinate clause *loko*, the subordination of the *loko* clause is indicated by the *yaṃ* with which it begins—the omitted words say "some time, after a long time".)

[1] Future of *dā*.

[2] *paṭhamaṃ* is here an indeclinable meaning "first", "firstly". It is derived from the ordinal numeral *paṭhama*, "first."

yaṃ frequently appears after the expression *ṭhānaṃ etaṃ vijjati*, introducing the statement of what is possible : *ṭhānaṃ etaṃ vijjati yaṃ* . . . = " it is possible that . . ." (here of course the *yaṃ* may be regarded as correlative with the demonstrative *etaṃ*).

yad is used in close combination with another indeclinable word : the forms *tad* and *yad* of the neuter pronouns are junction forms of *taṃ* and *yaṃ* taken when following words are closely associated with them syntactically (and hence in utterance) : *yad idaṃ* (cf. masculine *yo so* with a different demonstrative), " which that ", is used as an indeclinable emphatic demonstrative, " that is," " i.e.," " as for example," " as," " such as," " to wit."

The instrumental *yena* used with a verb of motion means " where ", " towards " (cf. the instrumental of the way by which). It " governs " the nominative case (Lesson 1). When doubled it means " wherever " : *yena yena gacchati*, " wherever he goes." It is often used with the correlative *tena* preceding the verb : *yena gāmo tena upasaṃkami*, " he approached the village."

Interrogative Pronoun

The interrogative pronoun has the stem *kiṃ*, " who ? ", " which ? ", " what ? " :—

	Singular			Plural		
	Masc.	Neut.	Fem.	Masc.	Neut.	Fem.
Nom.	*ko*	*kiṃ*	*kā*	*ke*	*kāni*	*kā*
Acc.	*kaṃ*	*kiṃ*	*kaṃ*			
Ins.	*kena*		*kāya*	*kehi*		*kāhi*
Dat. / Gen.	*kassa* or *kissa*		*kassā*	*kesaṃ*		*kāsaṃ*

There is no equivalent to the question mark in Pali (though modern editors sometimes insert question marks in their texts to assist students). As a general rule if a sentence contains an interrogative word the whole sentence is interrogative, but a few interrogative sentences contain no interrogative word and must be understood from the context (see the example in Exercise 9). Sometimes inversion is used: *khamati te idaṃ*, "does this please you?", "do you approve of this?" (*idaṃ me khamati* = "this pleases me", "I like this"). The neuter singular form *kiṃ* is sometimes used as an indeclinable, simply making the sentence interrogative (= inversion + "?" in English): *kiṃ saddaṃ assosi* = "Did he hear the noise?" As Pali favours direct speech *kiṃ saddaṃ assosī ti* . . . will translate "(. . . he asked) whether he heard the noise". The interrogative usually stands at the beginning of its clause. Cf. also the indeclinables *nu* (in Vocabulary below) and *api* (Vocabulary 14).

" *Pronominal Adjectives* "

Certain pronouns (sometimes called "pronominal adjectives" because they function as both pronouns and adjectives) follow the declension of *ya(d)* and must be carefully distinguished from adjectives on account of the difference of inflection in the nominative and genitive-dative plural masculine. Thus from *sabba*, "all," we have: nominative singular *sabbo* (M.), *sabbaṃ* (N.: only form), *sabbā* (F.); nominative and accusative plural masculine *sabbe*, like *ye* and unlike *kusalā* (masculine nominative plural), *kusale* (masculine accusative plural); genitive and dative plural masculine *sabbesaṃ* (cf. *yesaṃ*, *kusalānaṃ*).

Similar pronouns are:—

añña	other
aññatara	a certain, a
apara	another
para	other, another
sabba	all, entire

Vocabulary

Verbs:—

ā-kaṅkh (I)	*ākaṅkhati*	he wishes
(k)kham (I)	*khamati*	it pleases, it suits, he approves, he likes (dative of person)

ni(r)-(k)kam (I)	*nikkhamati* [1]	he goes out, he leaves
saṃ-ni-pat (I) (to fall)	*sannipatanti*	they assemble
upa-ḷas (VII) (to exercise an art)	*upaḷāseti*	he plays, he sounds

Nouns :—

upasamo	calm
janapado	country
jīvo	life-principle, soul
paccantajo	borderer, foreigner
saṅkhadhamo	conch blower
dassanaṃ	seeing
phalaṃ	fruit

Adjectives :—

kamanīya	lovely
paccantima	bordering, foreign
madanīya	intoxicating
rajanīya	exciting

Indeclinables :—

ajja	to-day
ambho	sir ! (not very respectful)
taṃ	then, so, now (accusative of *ta(d)* used adverbially)[2]
nu	? (enclitic : an interrogative particle reinforcing an interrogative pronoun or combined with another indeclinable to make it interrogative : *nanu*, " (is) not ? " ; or by itself = " does ? ")
yathā	as, how

EXERCISE 12

Passage for reading :—

bhūtapubbaṃ aññataro saṅkhadhamo saṅkhaṃ ādāya paccantimaṃ janapadaṃ agamāsi. so yen' aññataro gāmo

[1] *r + k > kkh.*

[2] The adverbial use of certain cases of the pronouns is confusing ; the contexts must be carefully considered in order to arrive at the meanings : whether adverbial or not.

ten' upasaṃkami. upasaṃkamitvā saṅkhaṃ upaḷāsitvā saṅkhaṃ nikkhipitvā nisīdi. atha kho tesaṃ paccantajānaṃ manussānaṃ etad ahosi : kissa nu kho eso saddo evaṃ rajanīyo evaṃ kamanīyo evaṃ madanīyo ti. sannipatitvā taṃ saṅkhadhamaṃ etad avocuṃ : ambho kissa nu kho eso saddo evaṃ rajanīyo evaṃ kamanīyo evaṃ madanīyo ti. eso kho bho saṅkho nāma yass' eso saddo evaṃ rajanīyo evaṃ kamanīyo evaṃ madanīyo ti.

Translate into English :—

yen' ajja samaṇo Gotamo dvārena nikkhamissati taṃ Gotamadvāraṃ nāma bhavissati
vatthāni pi 'ssa na yathā aññesaṃ
imassa ko attho
mayaṃ yaṃ icchissāma taṃ karissāma
kissa nu kho me idaṃ kammassa phalaṃ, kissa kammassa vipāko
taṃ kiṃ maññanti bhonto devā
n' atthi paro loko
ko 'si tvaṃ āvuso
kiṃ kusalaṃ kiṃ akusalaṃ
ke tumhe
rājā samāno kiṃ labhati
iminā me upasamena Udāyibhaddo kumāro samannāgato hotu
puccha mahārāja yad ākaṅkhasi
karoti te bhagavā okāsaṃ
yaṃ kho 'ssa na kkhamati taṃ pajahati

Translate into Pali :—

He gave to me
Prince Udāyibhadda (is) dear to me
The fortunate one, taking a bowl, entered the village for alms
He teaches the doctrine for " extinction "
He eats what he likes
Then (*atha*) the gate by which the fortunate one left was named Gotama Gate
What do you think, then, great king ?
We have come here to see the honourable Gotama
Did you hear a noise, sir ? I didn't hear a noise, sir !
We do not see his soul leaving

LESSON 13

Compounds

Nouns (including participles, adjectives, and pronouns) are very frequently combined in compounds (*samāsa*).[1] In a compound only the last noun is inflected, those prefixed to it being usually in their stem form.[2] The compound functions grammatically in a sentence as if it were a single word, but the meaning is often simply the combination of the meanings of the words forming it—just as if they were separate words in a sentence. The prefixed uninflected member stands for the plural as well as the singular, according to the context. Sometimes, though not often, compound words have special, restricted meanings. In English the word " blackbird " is a compound, but it means a particular species of bird, not any black bird. The same thing holds for " grasshopper ", though this term may be used more loosely. " Madhouse " on the other hand means any " house for the mad " (or any place resembling one). " Pond-life " includes all animals and vegetables living in ponds. As other types of compound in English may be quoted " fourteen " (= " four and ten "), " whitewashed " (= having a white wash on it, as a building), " alongside " (= " along the side of "), " twelvemonth " (= a collection of twelve months, a year). The six types of compound in Pali corresponding to " grasshopper ", " fourteen ", " blackbird ", " whitewashed ", " alongside ", and " twelvemonth " will be explained in Lessons 13, 15, 16, 19, 25, and 26 respectively.

In order to understand Pali sentences containing compounds, a classification of compounds is made according to the relation between their members and between the compounds and other words of the sentences.

Tappurisa *Compounds*

In the class known as *tappurisa* (no English equivalents have been invented for the names of compounds, so we use the Pali

[1] Indeclinables and prefixes also may be combined with nouns to form compounds. The combination of prefixes with roots is a different matter and is not treated under " compounds ". Finite verbs are not compounded with nouns, but participles and other nouns derived from verbs may be.

[2] Words in *-ant* have the weak stem *-at*, those in *-an* drop the *-n*.

names [1]) the prior member is associated with the posterior by a direct relation. The whole compound functions grammatically as a noun. The English example " madhouse " illustrates this: in Pali the relation " *for* the mad " might be expressed by the dative case (purpose), which would be the case in which the prior word would appear if there were no compounding. In " grasshopper " the relation " in the grass " would be expressed by the locative case (Lesson 16). In Pali any case-relation may occur in a *tappurisa*, that of the genitive being the most frequent as it is the usual case to express a relation between two nouns. The " genitive " relation may be very general or vague; other cases may express very specific relations, including those to an action (when the second noun is more or less verbal). Examples :—

brāhmaṇaparisā, " an assembly of priests (" priest-assembly ")

rājaputto, " son of a king " (" kingson "), " prince " (stems in *an* lose the *n* in compounds)

The last word in a compound, when the compound is a noun, usually retains its original gender.

Participles likewise occur as the final members of *tappurisas*, and it is in these *tappurisas* that the other case relations are most often found, such as the accusative relation when the first member is the patient (" direct object ") of the participle.

Compounds are very freely formed in Pali (much more freely than in English, except perhaps in some modern styles which many English speakers would regard as jargon). They are not restricted to two members, compounds of three or more members, variously related, being quite common. Thus *kūṭāgārasālā* = " hall of the house with a gable (*kūṭo*) ".[2]

Causative Conjugation

A special conjugation of verbs has the meaning to cause someone or something else to do the action of the root, to have something done, and is called the " causative " (*kārita*).

[1] Most of these names are examples of the forms; thus *tappurisa* = *tad* + *purisa* (*d* + *p* > *pp*) = *tassa purisa*, " his man," " his servant."

[2] *kūṭo* = point, peak (of a mountain), ridge (of a roof). This refers to the high ridged, overhanging barrel-vaulted roof characteristic of ancient India.

Formally (in formation and inflection) it frequently coincides with the seventh conjugation, just as the passive coincides with the third conjugation. There is, however, a distinctive causative suffix *(ā)p* which is sometimes added to roots. Roots conjugated in any conjugation for the ordinary present indicative may appear in causative meanings with the stem in *e* or a " fuller " form *aya* (or *pe, āpe, paya, āpaya*). As in the seventh conjugation the root vowel is usually strengthened or lengthened (cf. Lesson 3). The meaning may be the straightforward causative one or a more specialized and idiomatic one. Thus from *vac*, " to speak," we have the causative *vāceti*, (" he makes speak "), " he reads aloud," " he recites," whilst from *vad*, " to say," we have the causative *vādeti* (" he makes say "), " he plays (a musical instrument)." Sometimes it is not easy to decide whether to class a verb as an independent seventh conjugation root or as the causative form of some other verb of perhaps widely divergent meaning. There is a certain amount of disagreement among grammarians over the proper classification (e.g. of *vādeti*).

With *(ā)p* we have from *chid chedāpayati* (" he causes to cut ") ; from *(ṭ)ṭhā ṭhă̄payati*, in which the root vowel is usually shortened (as opposed to most causatives) and which often has the meaning " he leaves aside ", " he excepts ", instead of the more literal meaning " makes stand ", " erects ". Besides the possibility of a " double " formation with *(ā)p* alongside a causative form in *e* (which may have double meaning as well as double form), " triple " forms are sometimes made by adding *(ā)p* twice, thus from *ruh* " grow ", we have a causative form (with elision of *h*) *ropeti*, " he plants " (causes to grow), and another causative form *ropāpeti*, meaning " he causes to cause to grow ", " he has planted ".

As with ordinary verbs, the agent of a causative verb (*hetukattar*) goes in the nominative case. The person or " instrument " through whom the action is performed goes usually in the accusative (the instrumental may be used instead, on account of the sense of " instrument ") ; thus a causative verb may take one patient more than the equivalent ordinary verb : the causative of an intransitive verb may take one patient (the verb may be said to " become transitive "), the causative of a transitive verb may take two patients, the causative of a verb which ordinarily takes two accusatives may take three patients. For example " to be " is intransitive and takes no patient ; " to cause to be " (i.e. to develop, etc., as " to develop 1 the mind ") takes one. " To enter " may take one patient (enter 1 a house) ; " to cause to enter " may take two (cause to enter 1 a man 2 a house). " To take," " to lead," etc., may take two patients (take 1 to a village 2 a goat) ; in theory (in practice the extravagance seems to be avoided) " to cause to take " may take three (cause to take 1 (by) a man 2 to a village 3 a goat : *puriso* (agent) 1 *purisaṃ* 2 *gāmaṃ* 3 *ajaṃ nāyeti*, or *puriso purisena gāmaṃ ajaṃ nāyeti* with instrumental).

The causative conjugation includes the various tenses and participles, formed from causative stems as from seventh conjugation stems.

Present causative of *bhū* :—

	Singular	Plural
3rd person	*bhāveti*	*bhāventi*
2nd person	*bhāvesi*	*bhāvetha*
1st person	*bhāvemi*	*bhāvema*

Causatives :—

kapp ((VII): *kappeti*, he arranges, he puts in order, he organizes)	*kappāpeti*	he causes to be got ready, he has put in order, he has organized
kar	*kāreti*	he causes to work, he causes to make, (of kings) he governs, he rules (causes the kingdom to function)
	kārāpeti	he causes to make, he has built
chid	*chedāpeti*	he causes to cut
jan	*janeti*	he causes to be born, he produces

(j)jhe	*jhāpeti*	he causes to burn, he sets fire to
(ṭ)ṭhā	*ṭhapeti* *ṭhāpayati*	he causes to stand, he erects, he makes stand up, he causes to remain, he excepts
ni-pat	*nipāteti*	he causes to fall down, he drops, he puts down
pā	*pāyeti*	he causes to drink
bhū	*bhāveti*	he causes to be, he develops
ā-mant	*āmantāpeti*	he causes to be addressed, he has invited
muc	*muñcāpeti*	he causes to be free, he sets free
(p)paṭi-yat (to prepare)	*paṭiyādāpeti*	he causes to be prepared (irregular change of *t* > *d*)
yā	*yāpeti*	he causes to go, he keeps going
yuj ((VII) : *yojeti*)	*yojāpeti*	he causes to be yoked (carriage)
ā-ruc	*ārocāpeti*	he causes to be announced
ruh	*ropeti* *ropāpeti*	he causes to grow, he plants he causes to cause to grow, he has planted
ā-ruh (climb, mount)	*āropeti*	he causes to mount, he puts on top of, he shows, he shows up, he disproves
(p)pa-vatt	*pavatteti*	he causes to go, he sets going
ni(r)-vā	*nibbāpeti*	he causes to be extinct, he extinguishes (e.g. fire)
(p)pa-vid (*vid* (I) : " know ", but the primary present system is not used)	*pavedeti*	he makes known
(p)pa-vis	*paveseti*	he causes to enter, he brings in

(p)pa-(v)vaj	*pabbājeti*	he causes to go forth, he banishes (he has banished)
ni-sīd	*nisīdāpeti*	he causes to sit down
(s)su	*sāveti*	he causes to hear
pari-sudh (III) (to become pure/clean)	*parisodheti*	he causes to become pure

Other tenses of the causative :—

Imperative : *kappāpehi*
Aorist : *kārāpesi ; ṭhapesuṃ ; ārocāpesi, ārocāpesuṃ ; ropāpesi ; āropesuṃ*
Future : *jhāpessati ; bhāvessati*

Participles :—

Present : *kārento, kārayato* (genitive) ; *chedāpento, chedāpayato* (genitive) ; *dāpento ; pācento* (*pac* = cook, torment), *pācayato* (genitive) ; *yojāpento*
Past : *kappita ; kārita, kārāpita ; bhāvita ; pavattita ; pavedita* (usually in *ita*, as with the seventh conjugation)
Gerund : *kārāpetvā ; āmantāpetvā ; paṭiyādāpetvā ; yojāpetvā ; āropetvā ; pavesetvā*

Despite the mechanical appearance of the causative in theory, as a kind of tense of the ordinary verb, in practice the meaning and usage of causative verbs is highly idiomatic and each one requires careful attention.

Vocabulary

Verbs :—

ā-kuṭ (VII)	*ākoṭeti*	he strikes
gaves (I)	*gavesati*	he looks for, he searches for
(p)pa-ikkh (I)	*pekkhati*	he looks on, he watches
bhaj (I)	*bhajati*	he resorts to

Nouns :—

kammāro	smith
(k)khandho	group, collection, mass

paccatthiko	enemy
pabbato	mountain
pāsādo	palace
puñjo	heap
bālo	fool
bhedo	division, splitting up
manto	prayer, hymn
migo	beast, deer
samudayo	origin, origination
sīho	lion
araññaṃ	forest
indriyaṃ	faculty
khādaniyaṃ	foods, dishes (collective singular)
palālaṃ	straw
bhattaṃ	meal
mūlaṃ	root, base, capital (money)
samma (voc.)	(my) dear ! (familiar address : only the vocative is used)

Adjectives :—

anuttara	unsurpassed, supreme
abbhokāsa	open, free, out of doors, open air
ariya	excellent, exalted, noble
uttāna	stretched out, lying down
gambhīra	profound
nava	new
niṭṭhita	completed, ready
paṇīta	excellent, delightful, delicious
puratthima	east

Past participle :—

vivitta (*vi-vic*)	separated, isolated

Indeclinables :—

ayoniso	unmethodically, haphazardly, erratically, inconsequentially, unscientifically
uddhaṃ	above, up
kacci	perhaps ?, did ?, I doubt whether ?, I hope ?, aren't you ? (with *na*)

kathaṃ	how ?, why ?
tikkhattuṃ	thrice
dāni	now (enclitic: cannot stand at beginning of sentence)
passena	on its side (instrumental of *passo*, side, used adverbially)
yāva	as far as, up to, as much, to what extent

EXERCISE 13

Passage for reading :—

te taṃ saṅkhaṃ uttānaṃ nipātesuṃ : vadehi bho saṅkha, vadehi bho saṅkhā ti. n' eva so saṅkho saddaṃ akāsi. te taṃ saṅkhaṃ passena nipātesuṃ . . . uddhaṃ ṭhapesuṃ . . . daṇḍena ākoṭesuṃ . . . sandhuniṃsu [1] : vadehi bho saṅkha, vadehi bho saṅkhā ti. n' eva so saṅkho saddaṃ akāsi. atha kho tassa saṅkhadhamassa etad ahosi : yāva bālā ime paccantajā manussā. kathaṃ hi nāma ayoniso saṅkhasaddaṃ gavesissantī ti. tesam pekkhamānānaṃ [2] saṅkhaṃ gahetvā tikkhattuṃ saṅkhaṃ upaḷāsitvā saṅkhaṃ ādāya pakkāmi.

Translate into English :—

brāhmaṇo mante vācesi
so taṃ cittaṃ bhāveti
na taṃ (2nd. person) deva paccatthikānaṃ demi
ayaṃ dukkhasamudayo
rājā kumārassa (dative) pāsāde kārāpesi
so iminā ca ariyena sīlakkhandhena samannāgato iminā ariyena indriyasaṃvarena samannāgato . . . vivittaṃ senāsanaṃ bhajati : araññaṃ, rukkhamūlaṃ, pabbataṃ, . . . abbhokāsaṃ palālapuñjaṃ
idha tathāgatena anuttaraṃ dhammacakkaṃ pavattitaṃ
idaṃ paṇītaṃ
ye mālaṃ āropessanti, tesaṃ taṃ bhavissati sukhāya
tvaṃ pana samma Jīvaka kiṃ tuṇhī
kacci maṃ samma Jīvaka na paccatthikānaṃ desi

[1] Aorist of *saṃ-dhū* (V : Lesson 15), " to shake."
[2] Genitive absolute, cf. Lesson 10.

Translate into Pali, using compounds where indicated by hyphens :—

This is the cessation-of-unhappiness
(It is) now the time-for-extinction of the fortunate one
Cunda the son-of-a-smith, having had delicious dishes prepared, had the time announced to the fortunate one : " (it is) time, sir,[1] the meal (is) ready " [2]
The lion, king-of-the-beasts, went out
There are (*atthi* : the singular verb may be used for the plural also in this sense) other profound, delightful, doctrines which the " thus-gone " makes known
He develops that thought
The king, having had the priests invited, said this : " let the priests see the boy "
The king, having made the boy sit down, instructs (him)
The priest had a new house built to the east (instrumental or accusative) of the city
Recite the prayers ! (plural)
I set free the goats

LESSON 14

Indefinite Pronoun

The indeclinable particle *ci*(*d*) is added to inflected interrogative pronouns to form indefinite pronouns :—

ko ci	anyone, someone
kassa ci	of anyone
kiñ ci	anything, some (*ṃ* of *kiṃ* assimilated to *c*, becoming the palatal nasal)

With relative :—

yaṃ kiñ ci whatever

[1] Use the form of address to a monk.
[2] Invert the order of the last two words (= emphasis or exclamation).

With the negative :—

na kiñ ci nothing, none at all

The junction form *cid* often appears when another word follows closely.

Optative Tense

The optative (or " potential ") (*sattamī*) tense is used for any hypothetical action. It may be translated by " should ", " would ", " may ", etc. It is formed from the present stem of all conjugations with special inflections :—

	Singular	Plural
3rd person	*bhaveyya*, " he should be," " could be," " may be."	*bhaveyyuṃ*
2nd person	*bhaveyyāsi*	*bhaveyyātha*
1st person	*bhaveyyaṃ* (also *bhaveyyāmi*)	*bhaveyyāma*

From other conjugations (all have the *e* stem) :—

man (III) *maññeyya* he should think
kar (VI) *kareyya* he should do
dis (VII) *deseyya* he may teach

The verb *as*, " to be," has two forms of optative tense, though there is little distinction of meaning. The first type is much more frequent, the second more elevated or " poetic ", only the 3rd person singular being used regularly :—

	Singular	Plural
3rd person	*assa*, " there would be "	*assu*
2nd person	*assa*	*assatha*
1st person	*assaṃ*	*assāma*

	Singular	Plural
3rd person	*siyā*, " there may be," " there would be," " it might be "	*siyaṃsu* (*rarely used*) (*siyuṃ*)
2nd person	(*siyā*)	—
1st person	(*siyaṃ*)	—

The second type is usually impersonal, and hardly occurs except in the 3rd person singular. Thus : *siyā . . . kaṅkhā*, " there may be doubt " (with agent in the genitive : " subjective genitive "). The bracketed forms are sometimes found in poetry.

Sometimes *assa* and *siyā* are used together in one sentence, and it is this which makes it convenient to have two different forms. Thus *siyā kho pana bhoto rañño evam assa* = " but it might be (that) of his majesty (*bhoto*) the king there would be thus (thought, idea) ". Here we may see a distinction of meaning between *siyā* and *assa* : in such sentences they always have the same positions and functions, *siyā* (" it might be ") leading and *assa* (" there would be ") following. On the whole *siyā* is used as optative of *atthi*, whilst *assa* is used as optative of *hoti*. Thus *siyā* is used quite frequently in philosophical discourse to assert a possibility, in contrast to the categorical *atthi* and *n' atthi*. Like *atthi*, *siyā* may be used for the plural as well as the singular.

Optatives may be formed also for the passive and causative conjugations.

The range of meaning of the optative includes a mild form of command or a strong injunction, as well as requests, invitations, wishes, possibilities, suppositions, and hypotheses.

The hypothetical meaning is by far the most usual (cf. meanings of future, Lesson 10). When a relative or other subordinate clause expresses a condition on which a main clause depends, its verb may be in the optative, depending on the degree of uncertainty. There is, however, a tendency for both verbs, of the main and subordinate clauses, to be in the same tense (by " attraction " or assimilation). Thus if the effect of the condition is quite hypothetical (as: " if you ask, he may accept," *sace . . . yāceyyāsi . . . atha . . . adhivaseyya*) both verbs are usually in the optative. On the other hand if the result is considered certain and factual (by the speaker or writer, in narrative by the narrator but not necessarily by the speaker he quotes) both verbs may be in the present tense (as: " if a virtuous man approaches an assembly, he approaches without shame "); or both may be in the future if instead of an " eternal truth ", as above, a particular future action is considered (as: " if I have them salute (future of causative) one by one, the fortunate one will be (future) unsaluted by them (all) before daybreak "; likewise " I will not . . . until . . ."—both futures). Different tenses may also be used: " as . . . he explains (present), so . . . you should (must) report (optative) " (command of a king to an emissary) = *yathā . . . vyākaroti taṃ . . . āroceyyāsi*; " I shall teach (future) a course of doctrine with which one may explain (optative) " = *dhammapariyāyaṃ desessāmi yena samannāgato . . . vyākareyya.*

The optative is often used after the idiom *ṭhānaṃ . . . vijjati yaṃ . . .*, " there exists (present) the case that . . . (optative of the possible action or event) ", but the present is sometimes used (when the possibility is considered as definitely attested); when the idiom is negative (" it is not possible ") the future is usual. Without *yaṃ*, and preceding the idiom, the case considered may be given simply as a quotation ending with *ti*. (There is also a conditional tense in Pali, but it is not often used, being restricted to the statement of impossible hypotheses—see Lesson 29.)

With reference to the distinction between the optative and the future, used of future events which are respectively hypothetical and certain, the following example is instructive: " if he should get the kingdom he would share it " (both verbs optative), ". . . if I do (' shall ') get the kingdom I will share it " (both verbs future).

Ablative Case

The fifth or ablative (*pañcamī, nissakka, apādāna*) case is used to express the point from which an action begins. The action may be physical or mental. The ablative also expresses the cause or origin from which something arises. Formally the ablative may coincide with the instrumental except in the singular of the *a* stems and the masculine and neuter demonstrative and relative pronouns and other pronouns or " pronominal adjectives " inflected like them. There is also a special ablative singular suffix, *to,* which may be added to any stem. Moreover the pronominal inflection of the ablative singular, *smā* or *mhā,* is sometimes added to various noun stems.

Nominative.	Ablative.
janapado	*janapadā*
āsanaṃ	*āsanā*
so and *tad*	*tasmā* or *tamhā*
ayaṃ	*imasmā* or *imamhā*
paccatthiko	*paccatthikato* " from an enemy " (suffix *to*)

Examples of the use of the ablative :—

uṭṭhāy' āsanā, " having got up from (his) seat " (in this phrase the usual order of words is always inverted)

gāmā gāmaṃ, " from village to village "

agārasmā pabbajito (noun with pronominal inflection), " gone forth from home "

dasahi ca lokadhātūhi [1] *devatā . . . sannipatitā,* " and the gods . . . assembled from the ten universes "

kiṃ kāraṇā, " from what cause ? ", " for what reason ? ", " why ? "

The ablative of cause is very important, and is always used in philosophical statements :—

vedanāpaccayā taṇhā, " desire (is) from the sensation-cause [2] ", " desire is caused by sensation "

kimpaccayā bhavo, " from what cause [2] (is) existence ? "

kissa nirodhā bhavanirodho, " from the cessation of what (is there) cessation of existence ? "

The ablatives of some pronouns in *-asmā* are used as indeclinables with causal meaning : *kasmā* = " why ? ", *tasmā* = " therefore ".

[1] Instrumental-ablative plural of a stem in *u*, *dasahi* of *dasa*, " ten."
[2] Or " condition ".

Subsidiary uses of the ablative :—

—isolated, separated, secluded from :

vivicca akusalehi dhammehi, " having become separated from bad phenomena " (with *vivicca* as with *uṭṭhāya* inversion is usual)

—fear, danger from :

na kuto ci bhayaṃ . . . yad idaṃ paccatthikato ". . . fear (danger) from nowhere, such as from an enemy " (ablative in *to* and similarly formed indeclinable *kuto* = " whence ? ")

—cleaned or purified from (literal : " from dirt " and figurative) :

padosā cittaṃ parisodheti, " he makes his mind pure from anger," " he purifies his mind from anger "

—freed from (from slavery, etc.) :

cittaṃ āsavehi vimuccati, " the mind is freed from the influxes "

—direction from (with genitive of the origin) :

dakkhiṇato nagarassa, " south of the city "

—distance from (space and time) ; this meaning appears always with the suffix *to* and mostly in the indeclinables with suffix *to* (especially *ito* = from here/now), otherwise the instrumental is usually used (cf. Lesson 8) :

ito . . . ekatiṃso kappo, " the thirty-first aeon from (before) now "

ito tiṇṇaṃ māsānaṃ accayena, " after three months from now " (notice the combination of the three cases : ablative-genitive-instrumental)

dūrato āgacchantaṃ (seen) " coming from the distance "

—abstinence from, revulsion from :

virato methunā gāmadhammā, " has abstained (past participle of *vi-ram*) from sexual vulgar (" village ") custom "

pisuṇāya vācāya paṭivirato, " has abstained from malicious speech "

—recover from (illness) :

tamhā ābādhā mutto, " freed (recovered) from that illness "

—limit up to (within) which (with *yāva*) :

yāva brahmalokā, " as far as the world of God (heaven) "
yāva sattamā, " up to the seventh "

—with the verb *u(d)-(ṭ)ṭhā,* " to rise up (from)," "come out from " (literally and figuratively) :

paṭisallānā vuṭṭhito, " come out from seclusion (privacy, withdrawing ; sometimes spelt *paṭi-*) "

jhānā vuṭṭhahitvā, " having risen up (come out) from a meditation (trance) " (and passing into a higher or lower trance)

—" with reference to ", " from the standpoint of " = *-to* :

tathāgato atīte buddhe . . . gottato pi anussarati, " the thus-gone recollects past enlightened ones (Buddhas) with reference to (their) clan(s) also "

With indeclinables :—

—*aññatra* :

aññatra phassā, " except for contact," " without touch " (*aññatra* often takes the instrumental, cf. Lesson 8, and this *ā* inflection with it is sometimes regarded as a form of instrumental, cf. the instrumentals in *ā* : *bhagavatā, raññā* [1])

—*adho,* " below " :

adho kesamatthakā, " below the top (*matthako*) of the hair "

—*ārakā,* " far from " :

ārakā sāmaññā, " far from asceticism (*sāmaññaṃ*)

ārakā . . . vijjācaraṇasampadāya, " far from success (*sampadā* : feminine) in knowledge and practice (*caraṇaṃ*) "

—*uddhaṃ,* " above," " after," " beyond " :

uddhaṃ pādatalā, " above the soles (*talaṃ,* ' surface ') of the feet "

kāyassa bhedā uddhaṃ, " after the splitting up (death) of the body "

—*paraṃ,* " after " :

param maraṇā, " after death "

—*yāva,* " up to," " as far as " (see above, under " limit ")

[1] We find also *saha parinibbānā* = " (simultaneously) with the extinction ", unless it should be regarded as meaning caused by the extinction, in which case *saha* would seem superfluous.

The ablative is sometimes used in comparison or distinction (when the sense is " most " the genitive is used, see Lesson 18) :

na . . . vijjati añño samaṇo vā brāhmaṇo vā bhagavatā (ablative) *bhiyyo 'bhiññataro*, " there is . . . not any other philosopher or priest more learned than the fortunate one " (*abhiññataro* comparative of *abhiñña*, " learned " ; see Lesson 18 on comparison ; *bhiyyo*, " more," is used also with *kuto* : *kuto bhiyyo* (lit. = " whence more "), meaning idiomatically " let alone more ", " how could it be more ? ")

ito bhiyyo, " more than this "

The instrumental is sometimes used in comparison, just as it overlaps with the ablative in some other uses (cause, measure).

Dependent Words in Tappurisa *Compounds*

A dependent word (*samāsanta*) is a word which can appear only at the end of a compound (it is a " bound form "). It cannot be used independently. In certain *tappurisas*[1] such words are found, generally indicating the action of a root from which they are immediately derived :—

—*karo*, " doing," " working " (*kar*) : *kammakaro* " worker "

—*kāro*, " making " (*kar*, causative) : *kumbhakāro*, " potter " (*kumbho* = " pot ")

—*ggāho*, " seizing " ((*g*)*gah*) : *candaggāho*, " eclipse of the moon (*cando*) "

—*dharo*, " holding," " remembering " (*dhar*) : *dhammadharo*, " memorizer of the doctrine "

—*pāto*, " dropping," " offering," " collecting " (*pat*, " to fall," causative) : *piṇḍapāto*, " alms offering," " alms collecting " (this has the sense of the food collected by a begging monk).

As with the other cases, ablative *tappurisas* may be formed :—

piṇḍapātapaṭikkanto, " (monk) returned from an alms collecting "

[1] Called " *upapada* compounds " after the *first* member, the " adjacent word " (*upapada*), in virtue of which the dependent form may be used.

Vocabulary

Verbs :—

adhi-gam (I)	*adhigacchati*	acquires
anu-(s)sar (I)	*anussarati*	recollects
u(d)-(ṭ)ṭhā (I)	*uṭṭhāti* or *uṭṭhahati* or *vuṭṭhāti* (with *v* as junction consonant—see Lesson 25—between *u* and a preceding vowel)	rises up, gets up, arises, comes out from, emigrates
ni-mant (VII)	*nimanteti*	invites (*āsanena* ~ = ~ to sit down, offers a seat)
pari-pucch (I)	*paripucchati*	asks about, asks advice
ā-yā (I)	*āyāti*	comes, approaches

Nouns :—

āsavo	influx, influence [1]
deso	point (topic)
padoso	anger
phasso	contact, touch
sahāyako	friend
upādānaṃ	attachment
gāmapadaṃ	site of a village
dāsavyaṃ	slavery
bandhanaṃ	bond, fetter
vedayitaṃ	sensation, experience
sāṇaṃ	hemp

Indeclinables :—

api or *app* (stands at beginning of sentence or clause ; *app* is a junction form before a vowel)	(with optative) perhaps, (with indicative) does ?, do ?, did ? (i.e. makes sentence interrogative : polite form of question)

[1] They are, in Buddhist doctrine, passion, existence, opinion, and ignorance ; freedom from these is equivalent to the attainment of *nibbānaṃ*, to absolute peace.

etarahi	now, at present
ettha	here, (also means) in this case
tattha	there, in that/this connection
tena hi	now! (admonitory)
pubbe	before, formerly
yattha	where
yan nūna	what now if?, what if?, now if, supposing?
sabbaso	completely

Adjectives :—

pisuṇa	malicious
purāṇa	old

Numeral :—

ubho (nominative and accusative, all genders)	both

Past participle :—

khīṇa ((*k*)*khī* (III))	exhausted, wasted, perished (irregular *ṇ* for *n*)

EXERCISE 14

Passage for reading :—

bhūtapubbaṃ aññataro janapado vuṭṭhāsi. atha kho sahāyako sahāyakaṃ āmantesi : āyāma samma. yena so janapado ten' upasaṃkamissāma. app eva nām' ettha kiñ ci dhanaṃ adhigaccheyyāmā ti. evaṃ sammā ti kho sahāyako sahāyakassa paccassosi. te yena so janapado yen' aññataraṃ gāmapadaṃ ten' upasaṃkamiṃsu. tatth' addasaṃsu pahūtaṃ sāṇaṃ chaḍḍitaṃ. disvā sahāyako sahāyakaṃ āmantesi : idaṃ kho samma pahūtaṃ sāṇaṃ chaḍḍitaṃ. tena hi samma tvañ [1] ca sāṇabhāraṃ bandha, ahañ ca sāṇabhāraṃ bandhissāmi. ubho sāṇabhāraṃ ādāya gamissāmā ti. evaṃ sammā ti kho sahāyako sahāyakassa paṭissutvā sāṇabhāraṃ bandhi.

[1] *ṃ* palatalized to *ñ* before *c*.

Translate into English :—

puccheyyām' ahaṃ bhante kañ cid eva desaṃ
devā tamhā kāyā cavanti
upādānapaccayā bhavo
yan nūna mayaṃ kusalaṃ kareyyāma
na hi bhagavā evaṃ vadeyya
na dān' ime imamhā ābādhā vuṭṭhahissanti
te kālena kālaṃ upasaṃkamitvā paripuccheyyāsi (= " should " : exhortation)
tassa evam assa : ahaṃ kho pubbe dāso ahosiṃ. so [1] 'mhi etarahi tamhā dāsavyā mutto
yattha pan' āvuso sabbaso vedayitaṃ n' atthi, api nu kho tattha " asmī " ti siyā
khīṇā me āsavā
na maṃ ko ci āsanena pi nimantesi
āyantu bhonto
idha samaṇo vā brāhmaṇo vā kusalaṃ dhammaṃ adhigaccheyya. kusalaṃ dhammaṃ adhigantvā na parassa āroceyya. kiṃ hi paro parassa karissati.[2] seyyathā pi nāma purāṇaṃ bandhanaṃ chinditvā aññaṃ navaṃ bandhanaṃ kareyya.

Translate into Pali :—

I got up from my seat and left
If the philosopher Gotama should come to this assembly we will ask (optative) him this question
What should we do ?
I should do meritorious actions
Sensation is caused by (" from the condition of ") contact
You should explain it as it pleases you (*te* ; both verbs optative)
We would invite him to sit down
There will be an eclipse of the moon
There is nothing here
The priests would banish the priest from the city

[1] *so* used with 1st person verb as emphatic pronoun (1st person), cf. Lesson 5.
[2] *kiṃ . . . karissati* = " what will/can he/it do ? " means much the same as " what's the use of ? "

LESSON 15

Fifth Conjugation

Verbs of the *ki* or fifth conjugation (*kiyādi gaṇa*) form present stems with the suffix *nā*. The personal endings are the same as for the first conjugation. From the root (*ñ*)*ñā*, "to know" (learn, find out), which before the present suffix is changed to *jā*, we have :—

	Singular	Plural
3rd person	*jānāti*	*jānanti*
2nd person	*jānāsi*	*jānātha*
1st person	*jānāmi*	*jānāma*

Similarly conjugated are :—

ji	*jināti*	he wins
abhi-(*ñ*)*ñā*	*abhijānāti*	he knows, he is aware of, he ascertains, he discovers
ā-(*ñ*)*ñā*	*ājānāti*	he learns, he grasps (fig.)
(*p*)*pa-*(*ñ*)*ñā*	*pajānāti*	he understands, he has insight
(*p*)*paṭi-*(*ñ*)*ñā*	*paṭijānāti*	he admits
vi-(*ñ*)*ñā*	*vijānāti*	he is conscious of, he discerns
saṃ-(*ñ*)*ñā*	*saṃjānāti*	he experiences, he perceives

In some verbs the suffix is *ṇā* with cerebral *ṇ* :—

(*k*)*ki*	*kiṇāti*	he buys
(*s*)*su*	*suṇāti*	he hears

The root (*g*)*gah*, "to take," "to seize," inverts the order of the final consonant of the root and the *ṇ* (which is cerebral) of the suffix :—

gaṇhāti he takes

In consequence of this special feature some grammars place it in a separate conjugation of its own, known as the *gah* conjugation (*gahādi gaṇa*), making it the sixth of the eight conjugations they accordingly reckon. They place with it some roots of nouns which show the same inversion.

With prefixes :—

u(d)-(g)gah	*ugganhāti*	he learns, he memorizes
(p)paṭi-(g)gah	*paṭigganhāti*	he accepts

Other tenses are formed as follows :—

Imperative : *jānātu* (3rd sing.), *jānāhi* (2nd sing. : always with -*hi*), etc.

Optative : *jāneyya*, etc. (also a rarer form, *jaññā*, of the 3rd person sing.)

Present participle : *jānaṃ* or *jānanto* (masc. nom. sing.), *jānatā* (ins.), etc.

Aorist : *aññāsi* ((*ñ*)*ñā* and *ā*-(*ñ*)*ñā*),[1] *jāniṃsu* (for aorist of (*s*)*su*, see Lesson 12)

Future : *jānissati*, etc.

Gerund : *aññāya* (from *ā*-(*ñ*)*ñā*, *ā* shortened before the doubled consonant ; *ñatvā* from (*ñ*)*ñā* itself is not often used) ; *abhiññāya* ; *sutvā* ; *gahetvā*

Past participle : *ñāta* (*aññāta* is usually the negative : " unknown ") ; *suta* ; *gahīta* (sometimes *gahita*)

Passive : *paññāyati*

Causative : *sāveti*

Dvanda *Compounds*

Two or more nouns forming a list can be made into a compound instead of being connected by the particle *ca*. (cf. in English " fourteen " = " four and ten "). This type of compound is called *dvanda* (" twin "). It may be used as a collective noun, neuter (regardless of the gender of the members) and inflected in the singular number, or (retaining the gender), inflected in the plural as meaning two or more items. The component words may signify one or more than one item. The more important or leading object, if any, sometimes occupies the second position, which is normally the dominant position in Pali (cf. the *tappurisa* compound). In English the order may then be reversed :—

candimasuriyā (plural), " the sun and the moon "
samaṇabrāhmaṇā (plural), " priests and ascetics "

[1] As a rule, when in close junction a long vowel may not stand before a double consonant : here *ā* is shortened (cf. Introduction, pronunciation of *e* and *o*, and such verbs as *ā*-(*k*)*khā*—Vocabulary 17).

Sāriputtamoggallānaṃ (neuter singular), " Moggallāna and Sāriputta " (the two leading disciples of the Buddha)
pattacīvaraṃ, " robe and bowl "

Negative and other Prefixes to Nouns

Nouns (including adjectives) can be made negative by adding the prefix *a*, which before vowels becomes *an*. Several examples have been met with already : *akusala* (" non-good "), *amanusso* (" non-human "), *avijjā* (" non-knowledge "), *ananta* (" unending " : *an*). Finite verbs are not negatived in this way, but participles may be : *vimutta* = " freed " ; *avimutta* = " not freed " ; *anuppanna* = " not arisen " ; *adinna* = " not-given " ; present participles and gerunds are more rarely negatived : *adisvā* = " not having seen " ; *appahāya* = " not having renounced ". Other prefixes added to nouns, etc., are *su*, meaning " well ", " good ", and *du*(*r*), meaning " ill ", " bad " (and they cover a wide range of similar conceptions : easy/difficult, pleasant/unpleasant, etc.) : *subhāsita* = " well-spoken ", *dullabha* = " rare " (" hard to get " : *labh*).

These words with prefixes are regarded as compounds, see below pp. 108 and 137.

Vocabulary

Past participles :—

abhi-u(*d*)*-gam*	*abbhuggata*	disseminated, spread (report)
saṃ-nah	*sannaddha*	tied up ($h + t > ddh$)
ā-bhar	*ābhata*	brought, carried
jan	*jāta*	born

Nouns :—

āvasatho	room, cell
kāmo	love, passion, liking, pleasure
gandho	scent, perfume
vinayo	discipline
anagāriyaṃ	homelessness
ñāṇaṃ	knowledge
duccaritaṃ	bad conduct
padīpeyyaṃ	lamp

vilepanaṃ	ointment, cosmetic
sucaritaṃ	good conduct
suttaṃ	thread
kaṅkhā	doubt
seyyā	bed

Pronoun :—

ekacca	someone

Indeclinables :—

eva	(enclitic ; in junction sometimes *va* or *yeva*) only, alone, just, surely
khippaṃ	quickly
tathā	thus, true
no	not (emphatic form of *na*)
yadi	whether

EXERCISE 15

Passage for reading :—

te ubho sāṇabhāraṃ ādāya yen' aññataraṃ gāmapadaṃ ten' upasaṃkamiṃsu. tatth' addasaṃsu pahūtaṃ sāṇasuttaṃ chaḍḍitaṃ. disvā sahāyako sahāyakaṃ āmantesi : yassa kho samma atthāya iccheyyāma sāṇaṃ, idaṃ pahūtaṃ sāṇasuttaṃ chaḍḍitaṃ. tena hi samma tvañ ca sāṇabhāraṃ chaḍḍehi, ahañ ca sāṇabhāraṃ chaḍḍessāmi. ubho sāṇasuttabhāraṃ ādāya gamissāmā ti. ayaṃ kho me samma sāṇabhāro durābhato ca susannaddho ca. alam[1] me ; tvaṃ pajānāhī ti. atha kho so sahāyako sāṇabhāraṃ chaḍḍetvā sāṇasuttabhāraṃ ādiyi.

Translate into English :—

tena hi brāhmaṇa suṇāhi

na tvaṃ imaṃ dhammavinayaṃ ājānāsi. ahaṃ imaṃ dhammavinayaṃ ājānāmi

idha tathāgato jāto

[1] A final *ṃ* may be assimilated to a following labial when the words are closely connected grammatically. It may become *m* also when a vowel follows, under the same conditions (in verse under stress of metre too, since *ṃ* makes the preceding syllable long whilst *m* does not).

ko imaṃ dhammaṃ khippam eva ājānissati
ekacco dānaṃ deti samaṇassa vā brāhmaṇassa vā annaṃ pānaṃ vatthaṃ yānaṃ mālāgandhavilepanaṃ seyyāvasathapadīpeyyaṃ
ko nu kho pana bho jānāti.[1] madanīyā kāmā
jānāhi yadi vā taṃ bhavantaṃ Gotamaṃ tathā santaṃ [2] yeva saddo abbhuggato, yadi vā no tathā
tassa evaṃ jānato evaṃ passato kāmāsavā pi cittaṃ vimuccati bhavāsavā pi cittaṃ vimuccati avijjāsavā pi cittaṃ vimuccati
yaṃ kiñ ci samudayadhammaṃ, sabban taṃ nirodhadhammaṃ
n' atthi jātassa amaraṇaṃ

Translate into Pali :—

What I know, you know ; what you know, I know
I learn the saying of the fortunate one
He will grasp what I explain (fut.) quickly
After some time he hears the excellent doctrine
The fortunate one, taking robe-and-bowl, entered Rājagaha [3] for alms
Stop ! Ānanda, don't grieve
He understands that (use direct speech) these beings (are) endowed with bad-conduct-of-the-body
Not-memorizing that speech, I left
Why (is) this unexplained by the philosopher Gotama ?
You (plur.) have gone forth from house to homelessness

LESSON 16

Locative Case

The seventh or locative (*sattamī*, *bhumma*, *adhikaraṇa*, *okāsa*) case expresses the place where, the time when or the situation in which an action takes place. The plural is used to express the society in which the action takes place.

The locative is also used in the senses of " about ", " in the

[1] This is an idiom and may be translated " who knows ? ", " you never know ", " you never can tell ".
[2] Present participle of *as*, cf. Lesson 8.
[3] Capital of Magadha.

case of ", " with reference to " (e.g. : " to agree on some points "), " in the situation of ", and in certain idioms meaning : knowledge " about ", doubt " about ", established " in " office or " in " circumspect behaviour, training " under " a teacher and confidence " in " him, putting " into " a jar, disappearing " in " (from) a place. It is frequently used in an " absolute " construction (equivalent to a subordinate clause).

Masculine and neuter nouns in *a* have the locative inflections *e* in the singular and *esu* in the plural : *loke,* " in the world " ; *devesu,* " among the gods." Feminines in *ā* have either *āyaṃ* or simply *āya* in the singular and *āsu* in the plural : *kathāyaṃ, kathāya, kathāsu.* The demonstrative and relative pronouns have the following locative inflections :—

Singular :

Masculine and neuter, *yasmiṃ* or *yamhi* ; feminine, *yāyaṃ* or *yāya* or *yassaṃ*

Plural :

Masculine and neuter, *yesu* ; feminine, *yāsu*

From *idaṃ-* : Singular :

Masculine and neuter, *asmiṃ* or *imasmiṃ* ; feminine, *imāyaṃ* or *imāya*

From *idaṃ-* : Plural :

Masculine and neuter, *imesu* ; feminine, *imāsu*

Examples of the use of the locative :

Place :

dhammā raññe, " qualities in a king "
Nāḷandāyaṃ [1] *viharanto,* " dwelling in Nāḷandā "
rukkhamūle nisinnaṃ, " seated at the foot of a tree " (literally " at the root ", which is appropriate for a tropical tree)
devatā ākāse, " deities in the sky "

Time :

tasmiṃ samaye vedanaṃ vedeti, " he feels a sensation on that occasion "

[1] A town in Magadha.

vassānaṃ pacchime māse, " in the last month of the rainy season "

Situation :

tasmiṃ yaññe . . . na rukkhā chijjiṃsu, " in that sacrifice . . . no trees were cut down "

āpadāsu na vijahati, " he does not abandon (him) in misfortune "

Society :

Māgadhesu viharati, " he lives in Magadha " (literally " among the Magadhans ")

Reference, etc. :

idam pi 'ssa hoti sīlasmiṃ, " he has this as regards (moral) character "

citte cittānupassī viharati, " with reference to the mind, he lives observing the mind "

dhammesu . . . ñāṇaṃ, " knowledge of (about) phenomena "

kaṅkhā . . . dhamme, " doubt about the doctrine "

jīvite apekhaṃ, " hope for life "

(the locative may also be used after *yad idaṃ*)

Establishment :

pettike ṭhāne ṭhapesi, " appointed (him) in his father's place "

satipaṭṭhānesu supatiṭṭhitacitta, " (whose) mind is well established in the conditions of self-possession " (*sati* is variously translated, usually by " mindfulness ")

Confidence :

pasanno ahaṃ bhagavati, " I have confidence in the fortunate one " (Loc. Sg. of *bhagavant*)

dhamme pasannā, " she has confidence in the doctrine "

bhagavati brahmacariyaṃ caritvā, " having lived the God-like life under the fortunate one "

Disappearing :

brahmaloke antarahito, " vanished from God's world " (and appeared on Earth) (this is by supernatural power—*iddhi*—of a monk or deity : ordinary mortals can move away only gradually as expressed by the ablative case).

The locative absolute consists (like the genitive absolute, cf. Lesson 10) of a nexus of noun (or pronoun) + participle. Both are in the locative case. The noun is agent to the participle, which is often but not necessarily passive, and this agent cannot be the same as the agent of the main sentence within which the absolute construction forms a subordinate clause. Further words inflected in the locative in concord with the locative agent, such as adjectives, pronouns, and predicate nouns, may be included in the absolute construction. If the participle has a patient, instrument, etc., this will be in its proper case (accusative, etc.). There may also be indeclinables included in the absolute phrase. A sentence may contain several locative absolutes, each with its own agent, indicating a number of distinct subordinate actions. E.g. : "Though it is raining, it is pouring down, lightning is flashing, a thunderbolt cracking—that he should not see (anything), nor hear a sound ! " (four locative absolutes in the Pali). The locative absolute is used much more frequently than the genitive, not being restricted to a special type of relation between the subordinate and main actions. The subordinate action may precede the main action or be simultaneous with it. Any kind of subordinate action may be expressed. The absolute phrase usually precedes the main clause of the sentence, but is sometimes inserted parenthetically.

Examples :—

parinibbute bhagavati . . . Sakko . . . imaṃ gāthaṃ abhāsi, " when the fortunate one was " liberated " . . . Sakko [1]. . . spoke this verse "

imasmiṃ ca pana veyyākaraṇasmiṃ bhaññamāne Sakkassa . . . dhammacakkhuṃ [2] udapādi, " and moreover as this explanation was being spoken . . . the ' eye of the doctrine ' arose in (' of ') Sakka "

[1] The king of the gods.
[2] *u* stem, " eye."

upādāne kho sati bhavo hoti, " attachment being, existence is," " when there is attachment there is existence "
Disampatimhi [1] *raññe kālakate . . . rājaputtaṃ rajje abhisiñciṃsu*, " after king Disampati died . . . they consecrated the prince in the kingdom."

Future Passive Participle

A future participle (*kicca*) formed with the suffixes *tabba*, *anīya* [2] or *ya* is normally passive, like the past participle. It is usually called the " future passive participle " (an active participle, formed with the same suffix as the present participle but added to the future instead of the present stem, is also formed, but it is hardly ever used : in the entire Pali Canon only one unambiguous example has so far been pointed out, in a verse ; in Pali the " future passive participle " is used in any construction requiring a future participle). The construction is mostly the same as for the past participle, and the future passive participle may be used as sentence verb or as adjective, a few being used also as nouns. Though all the forms of future passive participle are used all these ways, that in *tabba* is more often used as sentence verb and that in *anīya* as adjective. The inflection is in the three genders on the *a*/*ā* stem just as in the case of the past participle.

The sense of the future passive participle is generally not simply future but rather imperative or optative : " this must be done," " this should be done," " this ought to be done," also " this can be done ".

A strong form of the root is normally used in the future passive participle :—

With suffix *tabba* (or *itabba*) :

(k)kam	*kamitabba*	to be walked
kar	*kātabba*	to be done
gam	*gantabba*	to be gone, must be gone
car	*caritabba*	must be lived, to be practised

[1] Locative of *i* stem.
[2] Rarely *aniya*.

jīv	*jīvitabba*	to be lived
(ñ)ñā	*jānitabba*	to be known
dā	*dātabba*	to be given, must be given, should be given
(d)dis	*daṭṭhabba*	to be seen, must be seen (as), should be viewed, must be envisaged, should be considered (in such and such a way)
pad	*pajjitabba* (on present stem)	(used with various prefixes in the corresponding meanings)
pā	*pātabba*	to be drunk
pucch	*pucchitabba*	to be asked
bhās	*bhāsitabba*	to be spoken, should be spoken
vac	*vattabba*	to be spoken
vid (II)	*veditabba*	to be known, to be found out, to be discovered, to be ascertained
(s)su	*soṭabba*	to be heard
sev	*sevitabba*	to be indulged in, to be pursued
han	*hantabba*	to be killed

Causative :

kar	*kāretabba*	must be caused to be made, should be caused to be made
(ṭ)ṭhā	*ṭhāpetabba*	to be established
bhū	*bhāvetabba*	to be developed

With suffix *anīya* :

kam	*kamanīya*	to be loved, lovely

kar	*karaṇīya* [1]	what must be done; duty, business (neuter)
(*k*)*kham*	*khamanīya*	to be pleased; pleasure, contentment (neuter)
khād	*khādanīya*	to be chewed; (hard) foods (neuter)
(*d*)*dis*	*dassanīya*	what must be seen, beautiful
bhuj	*bhojanīya*	to be eaten; (soft) foods (neuter)
mad (III) ("to become intoxicated")	*madanīya*	intoxicating
rañj (I) ("to become impassioned", "to be excited about")	*rajanīya*	exciting
ram	*ramaṇīya* [1]	to be delighted in, delightful
vac	*vacanīya*	to be said, what ought to be said

With suffix *ya* (or *yya*):

kar	*kicca*	to be done, what should be done; business (neuter)
dā	*deyya*	to be given, gift (neuter)
pā	*peyya*	to be drunk
bhū	*bhabba*	capable
labh	*labbha*	to be obtained, possible

With prefixes the forms are the same. Like the past participle (but rather less often), the future passive participle can be made negative by the prefix *a* (or *an*): *abhabba*, "incapable."

[1] When the suffix follows a root containing the letter *r*, the *n* is often cerebralized to *ṇ*. This cerebralization of *ṇ* is seen in some other suffixes under similar conditions. As a rule it occurs only when no consonant which would move the tongue intervenes (thus it does not occur in *rajanīya*).

Examples of the use of the future passive participle :—

As impersonal (neuter or agreeing with patient, if expressed) passive, with agent in instrumental :—

te vo bhāvetabbā, " they must be developed by you "
thūpo kātabbo, " a pagoda should be built "
iminā . . . pariyāyena veditabbaṃ, " it should be ascertained in this way (' by this course ') "
kathaṃ paṭipajjitabbaṃ, " how should one proceed (behave, conduct oneself) ? "

The active use of future passive participles of intransitive verbs meaning " go ", " move ", " go forth ", etc., is rare. They are much more frequently constructed passively.

Sometimes the future passive participle is accompanied (followed) by the present or future tense of a verb meaning " to be " (" periphrastic construction " : Lesson 24) :—

. . . maggo gantabbo hoti, ". . . the road has to be travelled "
maggo kho me gantabbo bhavissati, " the road will have to be travelled by me," " I shall have to travel along the road "
n' amhi kena ci upasaṃkamitabbo, " I am not to be approached (visited) by anyone."

The future passive participle is used with *man* (III : " think ") to express what one thinks (present), thought (aorist) or might think (optative) of doing or suitable to be done :—

upasaṃkamitabbaṃ maññeyya, " he may think it (an assembly) is to be approached," " he might consider it worth approaching."

As adjective (see also *rajanīyo,* etc., in the passage in Exercise 12) :—

ramaṇīyo pabbato, " the mountain is delightful ."

As noun :—

pure vacanīyaṃ pacchā avaca, " you said last (after) what ought to be said first (before)."

Kammadhāraya *Compounds*

A class of compound somewhat similar to the *tappurisa* (and sometimes included in it as a sub-variety) is the *kammadhāraya.*[1] Like the *tappurisa*, the *kammadhāraya* compound functions as a noun, but in this class the two component words refer to the same locus or object (cf. in English " blackbird "). In place of relation we have identity of locus, the first member being an attribute of the second. If they were not compounded, the members would have to be in the same case, since they would be noun and attribute or two nouns in apposition. If a *tappurisa* were divided, the first member would show the case relation inherent in the compound, the second member the same case as the original compound, determined by its function in the sentence. If a *kammadhāraya* were divided, the second member would again retain the same case as the original compound, but so would the first, since it would have to agree with the second in case.

Examples :—

akālamegho, " an untimely cloud " : *megho* = " cloud " ; *akāla* = " untimely " : i.e. out of the usual season.

rājisi, " king-sage " : *rājan* + *isi* with elision of the *-an* of the stem *rājan*.

adhammakāro, " unlawful acting " ; (for *-kāro* see Lesson 14). *adhamma* = " non-law "—*dhamma* here in the ancient sense of religion-custom-law, not in the restricted sense of the Buddhist doctrine, though the latter represents the two as ultimately one and based on the immutable natural law of the universe, varying only in their degree of nearness and fidelity to the truth.

The word *adhammo* in itself and other similar negative formations are regarded as *kammadhāraya* compounds (*a* + *dhammo*) of a perhaps looser kind. A further, rather rare, group of *kammadhārayas* expresses a comparison between the members, which are nouns in apposition.

cakkaratanaṃ, " wheel jewel ", might be interpreted as a

[1] The name is obscure : " character bearing " ? (taking *kamma* in the ethical sense of the character or habit or tendencies resulting from action, which is held to determine destiny, and hence as character or attribute in general).

simple apposition or as a comparison: a jewel shaped like a wheel. (The wheel-jewel is one of seven symbolic gems supposed to appear when there is a " universal emperor " in the world.)

Abbreviation

Frequently in Pali texts a passage is repeated verbatim or with only one or two words changed. This is often indicated by giving only the opening words of the passage followed by the word *pe*, " and so on," " etc.," itself an abbreviation of the word *peyyāla*, " etcetera."

Vocabulary

Verbs :—

u(d)-(g)ghar (I) (to make wet)	*uggharati*	it oozes
(p)pa-(g)ghar (I)	*paggharati*	it trickles, it drips
car (I)	*carati*	he proceeds, lives, conducts, carries on (it is difficult to give a general equivalent, *car* means following a particular way of life, as animals grazing, monks begging, etc.)
(p)pa-(t)thar (I) (to spread)	*pattharati*	he spreads out
pari-bhū (I)	*paribhavati*	he despises
makkh (VII)	*makkheti*	he smears
ā-rādh (VII)	*ārādheti*	he satisfies
(p)pa-vass (I) (to rain)	*pavassati*	it rains heavily
u(d)-vah (I) (to carry)	*ubbahati*	he carries off
vi-har (I)	*viharati*	he dwells, he lives

Nouns :—

aggo	(also means) tip, the supreme
amacco	minister (privy councillor)
ākāso	sky, space
uttarāsaṅgo	cloak
gūtho	dung
candimā (masculine, stem *candima-*)	moon (used only in nominative singular and in compounds)
nakho	fingernail, toenail
posako	rearer, breeder
megho	cloud
viggaho	quarrel, strife
vippaṭisāro	regret
vivādo	dispute
suriyo	sun
sūkaro	pig
khomaṃ	flax
vassaṃ	rain, rainy season (plural), year
sīsaṃ	lead
sīsaṃ	head
bhaṇḍikā	parcel, bundle
sajjhu(ṃ) (neuter)	silver (stem in *u*, cf. Lesson 19)

Adjectives :—

ummatta	mad
bahuka	much, plenty
veceta	daft
vyatta	intelligent
saka	own (= his own, her own, etc.)
sukkha	dry
mahant (inflected like *bhagavant*)	great

Indeclinables :—

antarā	within, between, meanwhile, whilst
pe	and so on, etc. (as abbreviation)
bhaṇe	I say !
yagghe	hear !
yoniso	methodically, consequently

EXERCISE 16

Passages for reading :—

1. te yen' aññataraṃ gāmapadaṃ ten' upasaṃkamiṃsu. tatth' addasaṃsu pahūtaṃ khomaṃ chaḍḍitaṃ. disvā. pe. pahūtaṃ khomasuttaṃ chaḍḍitaṃ. disvā. pe. [a whole range of commodities of increasing value is enumerated] pe. pahūtaṃ suvaṇṇaṃ chaḍḍitaṃ. disvā sahāyako sahāyakaṃ āmantesi : yassa kho samma atthāya iccheyyāma sāṇaṃ vā sāṇasuttaṃ vā . . . sīsaṃ vā sajjhuṃ vā, idaṃ pahūtaṃ suvaṇṇaṃ chaḍḍitaṃ. tena hi samma tvañ ca sāṇabhāraṃ chaḍḍehi, ahañ ca sajjhubhāraṃ chaḍḍessāmi. ubho suvaṇṇabhāraṃ ādāya gamissāmā ti. ayaṃ kho me samma sāṇabhāro durābhato ca susannaddho ca. alam me ; tvaṃ pajānāhī ti . . .

2. bhūtapubbaṃ aññataro sūkaraposako puriso sakamhā gāmā aññaṃ gāmaṃ agamāsi. tatth' addasā pahūtaṃ sukkhagūthaṃ chaḍḍitaṃ. disvān' [1] assa etad ahosi : ayaṃ me bahuko sukkhagūtho chaḍḍito, mamañ ca sūkarabhattaṃ. yan nūnāhaṃ ito sukkhagūthaṃ hareyyan ti. so uttarāsaṅgaṃ pattharitvā pahūtaṃ sukkhagūthaṃ āharitvā bhaṇḍikaṃ bandhitvā sīse ubbāhetvā [2] agamāsi. tassa antarā magge mahā akālamegho pāvassi. so uggharantaṃ paggharantaṃ yāva agganakhā gūthena makkhito gūthabhāraṃ ādāya agamāsi. tam enaṃ [3] manussā disvā evam āhaṃsu [4] : kacci no tvaṃ

[1] *disvāna* is an archaic form of *disvā* used mostly in verse ; sometimes the form *disvān'* is used in prose, when a vowel follows.

[2] Causative in same meaning as simple verb ; the double form of causative of this verb is used in the meaning " to have someone carry off ".

[3] *enaṃ* = " him "—accusative singular masculine of a pronoun of the 3rd person, used only in accusative as enclitic form.

[4] *āhaṃsu* = " they said "—Lesson 21.

bhaṇe ummatto, kacci veceto. kathaṃ hi nāma uggharantaṃ paggharantaṃ yāva agganakhā gūthena makkhito gūthabhāraṃ harissasī ti. tumhe kho ettha bhaṇe ummattā tumhe vecetā tathā hi pana me sūkarabhattan ti.

Translate into English :—

Bhagavā Rājagahe viharati
ime candimasuriyā parasmiṃ loke na imasmiṃ
kismiṃ vo viggaho, kismiṃ vivādo
evaṃ vutte aññataro rājāmacco rājānaṃ etad avoca
na dāni tena ciraṃ jīvitabbaṃ bhavissati
so bhotā raññā vippaṭisāro na karaṇīyo
na kho pan' etaṃ Poṭṭhapāda evaṃ daṭṭhabbaṃ
kiñ cid eva karaṇīyaṃ uppajji
idaṃ sevitabbaṃ, idaṃ na sevitabbaṃ

Translate into Pali (this is a Pali passage for retranslation, given as literally as possible to show the construction of long sentences with conjunctive particles and direct speeches, as well as the repetitive and ponderous style of debating priests and philosophers in which much of the Pali Canon is written) :—

If (*ce*) now (*va kho pana*) I (put first) were to ask (optative) the philosopher Gotama a question, if (*ce*) in that connection the philosopher Gotama were to ask me thus : " Priest,[1] this question, now (*ca*), should not be asked (future passive participle) thus, but (*nāma*) thus, priest, this question should be asked," this assembly would despise me for that (*tena*—place at beginning of clause) : " The priest Soṇadaṇḍa is a fool (put first), unintelligent, he could (*sak*(*k*), aorist) not ask (*pucchituṃ*—infinitive of *pucch*, Lesson 19 ; place at end of clause) the philosopher Gotama a question consequently (precedes ' question ')."

If now (as before) the philosopher Gotama were to ask me (put first) a question, and I were not to satisfy (optative) (his : omit) mind (accusative) with (my) explanation of his question, if in that connection the philosopher Gotama were to say to me (accusative) thus : " Priest, this question, now, should not be

[1] Word order : " Not now this, priest, question thus should be asked."

explained thus, but thus, priest, this question should be explained," this assembly would despise me for that: "The priest Soṇadaṇḍa is a fool, unintelligent, he couldn't satisfy (*ārādhetuṃ*—infinitive) (his) mind with (his) explanation of the philosopher Gotama's question."

LESSON 17

Declension of Masculine and Neuter Nouns in -a *and Feminine Nouns in* -ā

As all the cases of the nouns in *a* have been given we can now recapitulate the whole declension, adding the various pronominal inflections (such as the ablatives in *asmā* and *amhā*) which are sometimes used with these nouns :—

Masculine stem in *a*, *loka* :

		Singular	Plural
1.	Nom. Voc.	*loko* *loka*	*lokā*
2.	Acc.	*lokaṃ*	*loke*
3.	Instr.	*lokena*	*lokehi*
4.	Dative	*lokāya, lokassa*	*lokānaṃ*
5.	Abl.	*lokā, lokasmā, lokamhā* (*lokato*)	*lokehi*
6.	Gen.	*lokassa*	*lokānaṃ*
7.	Loc.	*loke, lokasmiṃ*	*lokesu*

Neuters in *a* :

—have the special forms nominative singular in *aṃ* and nominative and accusative plural in *āni* : *cittaṃ, cittāni* ; otherwise they are inflected in the same way as the masculines.

Declension of feminine stems in *ā* :

	Singular	Plural
Nom.	*kathā*	(*kathā*) or *kathāyo*
Voc.	*kathe*	(*kathā*) or *kathāyo*
Acc.	*kathaṃ*	(*kathā*) or *kathāyo*
Ins.	*kathāya*	*kathāhi*
Dat.	*kathāya*	*kathānaṃ*
Abl.	*kathāya*	*kathāhi*
Gen.	*kathāya*	*kathānaṃ*
Loc.	*kathāya* or *kathāyaṃ*	*kathāsu*

Declension of Pronouns

Recapitulation of the pronominal declension :—

Stem *ya*(*d*) (relative pronoun) :

	Singular			Plural		
	Masc.	Neut.	Fem.	Masc.	Neut.	Fem.
Nom.	*yo*	*yaṃ* or *yad*	*yā*	*ye*	*yāni*	*yā*
Acc.	*yaṃ*	*yaṃ* or *yad*	*yaṃ*	*ye*	*yāni*	*yā*
Ins.	*yena*		*yāya*	*yehi*		*yāhi*
Dat.	*yassa*		*yassā*	*yesaṃ*		*yāsaṃ*
Abl.	*yasmā* or *yamhā*		*yāya*	*yehi*		*yāhi*
Gen.	*yassa*		*yassā*	*yesaṃ*		*yāsaṃ*
Loc.	*yasmiṃ* or *yamhi*		*yāya*(*ṃ*) *or* *yassaṃ*	*yesu*		*yāsu*

Personal pronouns :

	First—*ma*(*d*) or *mam-*		Second—*ta*(*d*)	
	Singular	Plural	Singular	Plural
Nom.	*ahaṃ*	*mayaṃ*	*tvaṃ*	*tumhe*
Acc.	*maṃ*	*amhe* or *no* [1]	*tvaṃ* or *taṃ*	*tumhe* or *vo* [1]
Ins.	*mayā* or *me* [1]	*amhehi* or *no*	*tayā* or *te* [1]	*tumhehi* or *vo*
Dat.	*mama*(*ṃ*) or *me*, sometimes *mayhaṃ*	*amhākaṃ* [3] or *no*	*tava* or *te*	*tumhākaṃ* [2] or *vo*
Abl.	*mayā*	*amhehi*	*tayā*	*tumhehi*
Gen.	*mama*(*ṃ*) or *me*, sometimes *mayhaṃ*	*amhākaṃ* [3] or *no*	*tava* or *te*	*tumhākaṃ* [2] or *vo*
Loc.	*mayi*	*amhesu*	*tayi*	*tumhesu*

[1] *me*, *no*, *te*, and *vo* are unemphatic forms used as enclitics.
[2] Occasionally *tumhaṃ*.
[3] Occasionally *asmākaṃ*.

Third—*ta*(*d*)

Nominative singular : *so* (sometimes *sa*), *taṃ* or *tad*, *sā* ; rest as *ya*(*d*).

Demonstrative *idaṃ-* : singular masculine and feminine nominative *ayaṃ*, accusative *imaṃ* ; neuter *idaṃ* ; instrumental masculine and neuter *iminā*, feminine *imāya* ; genitive/dative masculine and neuter *assa*, feminine *assā* ; ablative masculine and neuter *imamhā* or *imasmā*, feminine *imāya* ; locative masculine and neuter *asmiṃ* or *imasmiṃ*, feminine *imāya*(*ṃ*).

Plural follows the declension of *ya*(*d*), in all genders, on the stem *ima*.

Interrogative *kiṃ* as *ya*(*d*) (stem *ka*) except : neuter nominative accusative singular *kiṃ* ; masculine and neuter dative and genitive singular either *kassa* or *kissa* ; masculine and neuter locative singular *kismiṃ* or *kimhi*.

A demonstrative pronoun with the stem *na* is inflected in the same way as *ta*(*d*) : accusative singular *naṃ*, genitive plural *nesaṃ*, etc. The nominative does not seem to be used. The meaning is hardly distinguishable from that of *ta*(*d*).

Adverbial Accusative

The accusative singular neuter of a noun or adjective (i.e., a masculine noun is made neuter, etc.) may be used as an " adverb " or indeclinable. This kind of adverb is called *bhāvanapuṃsaka*, " impersonal-neuter " or " neuter of state ", or *kiriyāvisesana*, " action-qualifier." E.g. :—

Adjective.	Adverb.
cira long (time)	*ciraṃ* (for a) long (time)
dīgha long (place or time)	*dīghaṃ* long
rassa short	*rassaṃ* shortly (e.g. in breathing " shortly ")
sādhuka good	*sādhukaṃ* well

Numerals eka, dvi, pañca, sataṃ, sahassaṃ

The numeral stem *eka*, " one," is inflected like the relative pronoun, except in the feminine, where in the dative, genitive, and locative singular, a stem in *i* appears instead of *a*. It is used like an adjective or pronoun, or like the indefinite article in English : " a " (but only to emphasize the indefiniteness when required). In the plural it means " some " :—

	Singular			Plural		
	Masc.	Neut.	Fem.	Masc.	Neut.	Fem.
Nom.	*eko*	*ekaṃ*	*ekā*	*eke*	*ekāni*	*ekā*
Acc.	*ekaṃ*	*ekaṃ*	*ekaṃ*			
Inst.	*ekena*		*ekāya*	*ekehi*		*ekāhi*
Dat.	*ekassa*		*ekissā*	*ekesaṃ*		*ekāsaṃ*
Abl.	*ekasmā* or *ekamhā*		*ekāya*	*ekehi*		*ekāhi*
Gen.	*ekassa*		*ekissā*	*ekesaṃ*		*ekāsaṃ*
Loc.	*ekasmiṃ* or *ekamhi*		*ekissā*	*ekesu*		*ekāsu*

The numerals *dvi,*[1] "two" and *pañca,* "five," which are used like adjectives, are inflected as follows for all genders :—

Nom. Acc.	*dve*	*pañca*
Ins.	*dvīhi*	*pañcahi*
Dat.	*dvinnaṃ*	*pañcannaṃ*
Abl.	*dvīhi*	*pañcahi*
Gen.	*dvinnaṃ*	*pañcannaṃ*
Loc.	*dvīsu*	*pañcasu*

The numerals *sataṃ,* "hundred" and *sahassaṃ,* "thousand" are neuter nouns, inflected like neuters in *a* and used in apposition with other nouns (i.e. *not* agreeing in gender but only in case) or with nouns in the genitive. They are used in both singular and plural : *sataṃ purisaṃ* or *satāni purisā* or *sataṃ purisā* or *satāni purisaṃ* or *sataṃ purisānaṃ,* all meaning "a hundred men". Alternatively a compound may be formed : *purisasataṃ* (genitive *tappurisa*).

Conjunctive Indeclinables

Phrases or sentences may be joined to make a continuous "period" or paragraph by "conjunctive" (also "disjunctive", etc.) indeclinables, several of which have been met already. Here we may recapitulate these in a synopsis of the main indeclinables of this type, grouped according to function (with references to passages for reading in previous exercises in which some of them have occurred).

"Conjunctive" (*samuccaya*) in the literal sense :—

ca (enclitic) "and", "now" (see Exercises 14, 16—second passage and translation into Pali)

pi (enclitic) "also", "too" (see Exercise 15, sentence for translation)

atha (initial) "then" (see Exercise 12).

[1] In derivatives and compounds the stems *dvi, du, dve,* and *dvā* are used.

" Disjunctive " (*vikappana*) :—

vā (enclitic) " or ", " either " (see Exercise 15, sentence for translation)

udāhu (initial) " or ? " (used in interrogative disjunctions) (see Exercises 17, 18, sentences for translation).

" Adversative " (*visesa*) :—

pana (enclitic) " but ", " however " (see Exercises 11, 17).

" Causal " (*kāraṇa*) :—

hi (enclitic) " for ", " because " (see Exercises 13, 14)

tasmā " therefore "

tena " therefore " (see Exercise 16, translation into Pali) (" conclusive ")

tad, taṃ " then ", " so " (" illative ").

" Emphatic " (*ekaṃsa*) :—

kho (enclitic) " indeed " (see Exercises 12, 14)

khalu (enclitic) " indeed "

ha " indeed ", " truly "

(emphasize the whole sentence)

" Hypothetical " (*saṃkā*) :—

ce (enclitic) " if " (see Exercise 16, translation into Pali)

sace (initial) " if " (examples in Lessons 10, 14 illustrating use of future and optative).

" Interrogative " (*pucchana*) :—

nu (enclitic) " ? ", " now ? " (see Exercise 12)

nanu " isn't it ? "

udāhu " or ? " (introduces second member of a disjunction, cf. above).

(Some of these indeclinables have other uses besides the connecting of phrases or sentences : cf. Vocabulary.)

Vocabulary

Verbs :—

anu-pa[1]*-(k)khand* (I) *anupakkhandati* he goes over to, he is converted to, he joins

[1] *pa* here not > *ppa* (cf. *anu-pa-gam* in Vocabulary 28 : here too we might restore *-pi-*).

ā-(k)khā (I)	*akkhāti* [1]	he tells, he reports (especially tradition)
ā-(s)sas (I)	*assasati* [1]	he breathes in
pari-ā-dā (III)	*pariyādiyati*	he uses up, he exhausts
vi-bhaj (I)	*vibhajati*	he divides
apa-vad (I)	*apavadati*	he disparages

→

Nouns :—

bhāgineyyo	nephew (sister's son)
sakaṭo (also neuter)	cart
sattho	caravan
satthavāho	caravan-merchant
udakaṃ	water
kaṭṭhaṃ	firewood
tiṇaṃ	grass
micchā	wrong, misconduct
sabhā	assembly hall

Adjectives :—

uttara	northern
haritaka	green, fresh

Pronoun :—

katama	which ?, which one ?

Indeclinables :—

ekaṃsena	for certain, certainly, definitely
ekato	on one side, together, on either side
dvidhā	twofold, twice, in two
yaṃ (as *nipāta*)	since, if, that . . . (with optative)
saha	along with, according to (usually with instrumental)

[1] Cf. footnote in Lesson 15.

EXERCISE 17

Passage for reading :—

bhūtapubbaṃ mahā sakaṭasattho sakaṭasahassaṃ puratthimā janapadā pacchimaṃ janapadaṃ agamāsi. so yena yena gacchati khippam eva pariyādiyati tiṇakaṭṭhodakaṃ [1] haritakavaṇṇaṃ. tasmiṃ kho pana satthe dve satthavāhā ahesuṃ ; eko pañcannaṃ sakaṭasatānaṃ, eko pañcannaṃ sakaṭasatānaṃ. atha kho tesaṃ satthavāhānaṃ etad ahosi : ayaṃ kho mahā sakaṭasattho sakaṭasahassaṃ. te mayaṃ yena yena gacchāma khippam eva pariyādiyati tiṇakaṭṭhodakaṃ haritakavaṇṇaṃ. yan nūna mayaṃ imaṃ satthaṃ dvidhā vibhajeyyāma ekato pañca sakaṭasatāni.

Translate into English :—

tena hi brāhmaṇa suṇāhi, bhāsissāmi
dīghaṃ assasāmi
mā ekena [2] dve agamittha
disvā va mayaṃ taṃ bhagavantaṃ Gotamaṃ gamissāma (disvā is put first for emphasis)
devā sabhāyaṃ sannisinnā honti
santān' [3] eva nu kho saddāni nāssosi, udāhu asantāni
aham pana agārasmā anagāriyaṃ pabbajissāmi
katame pañca
kāmesu micchā na caritabbā
yaṃ sukho bhavaṃ taṃ sukhā mayaṃ, yaṃ dukkho bhavaṃ taṃ dukkhā mayaṃ

Translate into Pali:—

Priests declare (one) endowed with these five characteristics a priest.

Of these five characteristics let us except class, for what will class effect (*kar*) ?

" Don't you bother, let the priest Soṇadaṇḍa discuss with me." When it had been spoken thus the priest Soṇadaṇḍa said this to the fortunate one : " Let the honourable Gotama not trouble, let the honourable Gotama be silent, I by myself

[1] The vowels *a* + *u* combine as *o*, hence *kaṭṭha* + *udakaṃ* combine as here in a compound.

[2] Instrumental of way by which, here meaning : " one way ", " the same way ".

[3] Elision of final *i* before a following vowel in close junction.

(*eva*) will make a reply to them according to the doctrine." Then (add *kho* for emphasis) the priest Soṇadaṇḍa said this to those priests: "Sirs! Do not speak thus: 'His honour Soṇadaṇḍa surely disparages class, disparages prayers,[1] certainly his honour Soṇadaṇḍa is going over to the argument of the philosopher Gotama himself (*eva*),' I do not, sir, disparage either class or prayers."

At that very (*kho pana*) time a young priest called Aṅgaka, a nephew of the priest Soṇadaṇḍa, was sitting (past participle and *hoti*) in that assembly.

Do you see (3rd person), sirs, this young priest Aṅgaka, our nephew? (make interrogative merely by inversion of agent and verb). Yes (*evaṃ*), sir.

Where (there is) virtue, there (there is) wisdom, where wisdom, virtue.

It is reported (passive) that (omit "that" and put the subject spoken of in the accusative—"specification of state") in the world the supreme is of-virtue-and-wisdom.

LESSON 18

Declension of Masculine and Neuter Nouns in -i *and* -in

A few nouns in all genders have stems in *i*. The masculines and neuters are inflected as follows:—

	MASCULINE—*pāṇi*, "hand"		NEUTER—*akkhi*, "eye"	
	Singular	Plural	Singular	Plural
Nom.	*pāṇi* }	*pāṇayo* or *pāṇī*	*akkhi* or *akkhiṃ*	*akkhīni* or *akkhī*
Acc.	*pāṇiṃ* }	for both cases	for both cases	for both cases
Inst.	*pāṇinā*	*pāṇīhi*		
Dat.	*pāṇino*	*pāṇīnaṃ*	Rest as masculine.	
Abl.	{ *pāṇinā* / *pāṇito*	*pāṇīhi*		
Gen.	{ *pāṇino* / *pāṇissa*	*pāṇīnaṃ*		
Loc.	*pāṇismiṃ*	*pāṇīsu*		

[1] Here the phrases are not joined by a conjunctive particle but simply juxtaposed, the verb being repeated, as in the English. Cf. the imperatives above. Note the emboxing of direct speeches here as an element in period construction.

(the vocative is the same as the nominative) (the stem vowel may be long or short in the instrumental to locative plural).

The extremely rare adjectives in *i* follow the same declension.

The suffix *in* added to noun stems in place of the stem vowel forms possessive adjectives or (more rarely) nouns specialized from them. Thus from *saññā*, perception, is formed a stem *saññin* "having perception", "sentient", inflected as follows :—

	MASCULINE.		
	Singular.	Plural.	
Nominative	*saññī*	*saññino* (nominative and accusative)	
Accusative	*saññinaṃ*		
Instrumental	*saññinā*	*saññīhi*	note that these cases coincide with the *i* declension except for the locative singular form.
Dative	*saññino*	*saññīnaṃ*	
Ablative	*saññinā*	*saññīhi*	
Genitive	*saññino*	*saññīnaṃ*	
Locative	*saññini*	*saññīsu*	

(vocative : *saññi*).

Neuter : (extremely rare : inflections as *akkhi* above).

The feminine stem is formed by adding *ī* (as *saññinī*), it is inflected in the same way as other feminines in *ī* (see below, Lesson 20).

These possessives appear frequently as final members of compounds.

The above declensions have also forms borrowed from the pronominal declension for the ablative and locative singular :—

Ablative : *pāṇismā, pāṇimhā ; saññismā, saññimhā*
Locative : *pāṇismiṃ, pāṇimhi ; saññismiṃ, saññimhi*
(the only forms used)

Second Conjugation

Verbs of the second conjugation (*rudhādi gaṇa*) form present stems by strengthening the root with a nasal and adding the stem vowel *a*. The nasal is inserted between the root vowel and the following consonant, and is articulated in the same place as that consonant or is the pure nasal if the consonant is *s*. The personal endings are the same as for the first conjugation. From the root *bhuj*, " to eat " :—

	Singular	Plural
3rd person	*bhuñjati*	*bhuñjanti*
2nd person	*bhuñjasi*	*bhuñjatha*
1st person	*bhuñjāmi*	*bhuñjāma*

Similarly conjugated are :—

chid	*chindati*	he cuts
muc	*muñcati*	he frees
sic	*siñcati*	he sprinkles
his	*hiṃsati*	he injures

Other tenses :—

Optative : *bhuñjeyya*
Present participle : *chindanto* (nom.), *chindato* (gen.) ; *bhuñjamāna* ; —of causative : *chedāpento*
Gerund : *chinditvā, bhuñjitvā*
Past participle : *chinna, bhutta*
Aorist : *chindi*
Future : *chindissati*
Passive : *chijjati*
Causative : *muñcāpeti*

Comparison

Comparison is effected by the use of certain suffixes added to the stems of adjectives (and occasionally of indeclinables). The usual suffix is *tara*, and its meaning includes both the " comparative " and the " superlative " according to the context. The suffix can be added direct to any stem ending in a vowel. Consonant stems may be used by first adding *a*. Comparative adjectives in *tara* are inflected like other adjectives in *a* (fem. *ā*).

Examples :—

garu " heavy "	*garutara* " heavier "
dassanīya " beautiful "	*dassanīyatara* " more beautiful ", " most beautiful "
paṇīta " delightful "	*paṇītatara* " more delightful ", " most delightful "
vaṇṇavant " handsome ", " beautiful " (consonant stem)	*vaṇṇavantatara* " more handsome "

Comparatives are constructed with the ablative of the word denoting that with which comparison is made : *imamhā* . . . *phalaṃ* . . . *paṇītataraṃ*, " a fruit more delightful than this." The indeclinable *ito*, " from this," " than this," is sometimes used in comparisons. When the meaning is superlative, the ablative (= " from ", " than ") is replaced by the genitive (= partitive genitive, the meaning being " best of ", " best among ") : *nesaṃ* . . . *dassanīyataro*, " the most beautiful among them."

Some comparatives use other suffixes. Whereas *tara* is added to any stem, two special suffixes, one usually comparative and the other usually superlative, are used when the derivation is made directly from a root (" primary derivation " : cf. Lesson 25). They are (*ĭ*)(*y*)*ya* (comparative) and *iṭṭha* (superlative), inflected as adjectives in *a* (fem. *ā*). Only a few of these are commonly used :—

kaṇ (" decrease ")	(*khudda* " small ", " minor ")	—	*kaṇiṭṭha* " younger ", " youngest "
ja (" increase ")	(*vuḍḍha* " old ", " elder ")	—	*jeṭṭha* " elder ", " eldest ", " (most) senior "
pāp	*pāpa* " bad "	*pāpīya* " worse "	—[1]
bhū	(*bahu* " much ")	*bhiyya* " more "	—

[1] The rare *pāpiṭṭha*, " worst," is not found in the *Dīgha* (it has a remarkable form with superlative and comparative suffixes : *pāpiṭṭhatara*).

(*sirī*)	(*kalyāṇa* "good")	*seyya* "better"	*seṭṭha* "best"

Some of these are used in certain forms as indeclinables (adverbs): *bhiyyo*, "more"; *seyyo*, "better."

A superlative suffix *tama* is rarely seen except in the pronoun *katama*, "which one?" (used in plural also). The sense is "which of these things?", or "which of all possible things (indefinite)?"

Ordinal Numerals

The first six ordinal numerals are as follows:—

paṭhama	first
dutiya	second
tatiya	third
catuttha	fourth
pañcama	fifth
chaṭṭha	sixth

They are declined like adjectives in *a*, the feminine being usually in *ā* except in the case of *pañcamī* (*catutthī* and *chaṭṭhī* are occasionally used also).

Vocabulary

Verbs:—

anu-(p)pa-dā (I)	*anuppadeti*	grant
anu-yuj (II)	*anuyuñjati*	submit (p.p. *anuyutta*)
antara-dhā (III) (the prefix *antara* means "within")	*antaradhāyati*	disappear (p.p. *antarahita* with *dhā* > *hi* as weak form of the root)
abhi-ni-vajj (VII)	*abhinivajjeti*	avoid
ā-(c)chad (VII)	*acchādeti*	dress
o-sakk (I) (to go) (the prefix *o* means "down", "off")	*osakkati*	draw back, retire
o-har (I)	causative: *ohāreti* =	shave off
gil (I*)	*gilati*	swallow

div (III)	*dibbati*	play, gamble
(*p*)*paṭi*[1]-(*t*)*ṭhā* (I)	*patiṭṭhahati*	set up, station itself
(*p*)*paṭi-vi-ram* (I)	*paṭiviramati*	abstain (p.p. *paṭivirata*)
(*p*)*pa-dā* (I)	*padeti*	give to, hand over (aorist *pādāsi*)
pari-kujj (I) (to bend, to fold)	*palikujjati* (in a few words *pari* is changed to *pali*)	squat down (gerund *palikujjitvā*)
pari-bhū (I)	*paribhavati*	despise (causative *paribhāveti* treat with, penetrate with, fill with)
(*p*)*pa-vatt* (I)	*pavattati*	go on, continue, proceed, set going, start
pātu(*r*)-*bhū* (I) (the prefix *pātu*(*r*) means " manifest ")	*pātubhavati* (*r* dropped in the present tense)	become manifest, appear
budh (III)	*bujjhati*	know, be aware of
mān (VII)	*māneti*	honour, respect
lip (II)	*limpati*	smear (p.p. *litta*)
vatt (I)	*vattati*	proceed, conduct oneself, go on (doing) (imp. 2nd sing. *vattāhi*)
vi-ati-sār (VII) (the prefix *ati* means " over ", " very ", " exceedingly ")	*vītisāreti*[2]	converse, make (conversation : *kathā*)
saṃ-anu-sās (I)	*samanusāsati*	install, appoint (as ruler)

[1] Before a root beginning with (*t*)*th*, and occasionally elsewhere, (*p*)*paṭi* is changed to *pati*.

[2] Sometimes when two vowels meet the second is elided and the first lengthened.

saṃ-ā-dā (III)	*samādiyati*	conform (to a rule or way of life) (p.p. *samādiṇṇa*)
saṃ-mud (I)	*sammodati*	greet, exchange greetings with (*saddhiṃ* and instrumental) (aorist *sammodi*)

Nouns :—

akkhadhutto	gambler
akkho	die (in dice : but played by drawing several dice of different values)
acelo	naked ascetic
abhisamparāyo	future state
ākappo	deportment, style
odano	boiled rice
kukkuravatiko	canine (ascetic) (dog-vower)
kukkuro	dog
kummāso	barley bread
keso	hair (of the head)
govatiko	bovine (ascetic)
jānapado	country dweller
negamo	town dweller
padeso	place, locality, region
pāṇo	life (breath, animal life), living being
mado	drink (intoxicating), excess
(v)vataṃ [1]	vow
vāso	dwelling place, camp
ahitaṃ	disadvantage, hardship
āvaraṇaṃ	shelter
kaṭukaṃ	bitterness
dāyajjaṃ	inheritance
dukkaraṃ	hard task
→ *majjaṃ*	intoxicant, liquor, drink
rajjaṃ	kingdom
vattaṃ	conduct, duty, government

[1] The initial is doubled in some compounds but not in others : *sīlabbataṃ* but *kukkuravataṃ*, although an occasional variant would substitute *kukkuravattaṃ* for the latter.

vijitaṃ	realm, kingdom
visaṃ	poison
satthaṃ	sword
hitaṃ	benefit, welfare
anattamanatā	worry, disquiet, anxiety
chamā	earth, ground
disā	direction, region
musā	falsehood
rakkhā	safety
sahavyatā	association, condition, union (with genitive)
paṭirājan-	hostile king (declined like *rājan-*)

→ Masculine nouns declined like *pāṇi* :—

isi	sage, seer
kali	unlucky die, bad luck, the iron age (the present decadent period of civilization, which began c. 1000 B.C. with the discovery of iron and consequent increased horrors of warfare)
gahapati	householder
cakkavatti	emperor
muṭṭhi	fist
samādhi	concentration
sārathi	charioteer

Adjectives declined like *saññin* :—

ātāpin	energetic (with ascetic energy)
-kārin	doing
-cārin	living, behaving, carrying on, going on
brahmacārin	celibate (living like God)
-vihārin	living, dwelling, being
Noun : *pakkhin*	bird (" winged ")

Adjectives :—

adhana	poor
anattamana	disturbed, worried
abhiñña	learned
kāsāya	brown, orange, saffron (colour of the robes of Buddhist monks and of some

other ascetics: original shade uncertain, now saffron)

dibba	divine, heavenly
dhammika	just
parama	most, highest
pāpa	evil
pettika	paternal
mānusaka	human
sammodanīya	agreeable, pleasant
sārāṇīya	polite
hīna	inferior

Indeclinables :—

addhā	certainly
anvad	after (behind) (this word is always followed by *eva*)
api ca	nevertheless
apubbaṃ acarimaṃ	simultaneously
āgatāgataṃ	each time it came
iṅgha	here !
ekantikena	finally, conclusively
tāta	my son ! (affectionate address)
dīgharattaṃ	long (time)
pacchā	afterwards, back, behind, west
re	damn you !, hey ! (contemptuous address)
va (enclitic)	like
(*s*)*sudaṃ*	even

Gerund :—

nissāya	depending on, leaning on (*ni*-(*s*)*sī* (I))

EXERCISE 18

Passages for reading :—

1. bhūtapubbaṃ dve akkhadhuttā akkhehi dibbiṃsu. eko akkhadhutto āgatāgataṃ kaliṃ gilati. addasā kho dutiyo akkhadhutto taṃ akkhadhuttaṃ āgatāgataṃ kaliṃ gilantaṃ. disvā akkhadhuttaṃ etad avoca : tvaṃ kho samma ekantikena

jināsi, dehi samma akkhe, pajohissāmī [1] ti. evaṃ sammā ti kho so akkhadhutto tassa akkhadhuttassa akkhe pādāsi. atha kho so akkhadhutto akkhe visena paribhāvetvā taṃ akkhadhuttaṃ etad avoca: ehi kho samma akkhehi dibbissāmā ti. evaṃ sammā ti kho so akkhadhutto tassa akkhadhuttassa paccassosi. dutiyam pi kho te akkhadhuttā akkhehi dibbiṃsu, dutiyam pi kho so akkhadhutto āgatāgataṃ kaliṃ gilati. addasā kho dutiyo akkhadhutto taṃ akkhadhuttaṃ dutiyam pi āgatāgataṃ kaliṃ gilantaṃ. disvā taṃ akkhadhuttaṃ etad avoca:—

littaṃ paramena tejasā [2]
gilam akkhaṃ puriso na bujjhati
gila re gila pāpadhuttaka
pacchā te kaṭukaṃ bhavissatī ti.

2. bhūtapubbaṃ rājā Daḷhanemi nāma ahosi cakkavatti dhammiko dhammarājā [3] . . . atha kho rājā Daḷhanemi vassasahassānaṃ accayena aññataraṃ purisaṃ āmantesi. yadā tvaṃ ambho purisa passeyyāsi dibbaṃ cakkaratanaṃ [4] osakkitaṃ ṭhānā cutaṃ, atha me āroceyyāsī ti. evaṃ devā ti kho so puriso rañño Daḷhanemissa paccassosi. addasā kho so puriso vassasahassānaṃ accayena dibbaṃ cakkaratanaṃ osakkitaṃ ṭhānā cutaṃ. disvā yena rājā Daḷhanemi ten' upasaṃkami, upasaṃkamitvā rājānaṃ Daḷhanemiṃ etad avoca. yagghe deva jāneyyāsi dibbaṃ te cakkaratanaṃ osakkitaṃ ṭhānā cutan ti. atha kho rājā Daḷhanemi jeṭṭhaputtaṃ kumāraṃ āmantāpetvā etad avoca. dibbaṃ kira me tāta kumāra cakkaratanaṃ osakkitaṃ ṭhānā cutaṃ. sutaṃ kho pana m' etaṃ, yassa rañño cakkavattissa dibbaṃ cakkaratanaṃ osakkati ṭhānā cavati, na dāni tena raññā ciraṃ jīvitabbaṃ hotī ti. bhuttā kho pana me mānusakā kāmā, samayo dibbe kāme pariyesituṃ.[5] ehi tvaṃ tāta kumāra imaṃ paṭhaviṃ [6] paṭipajja. ahaṃ pana kesamassuṃ [7] ohāretvā,

[1] " I shall make a votive offering ".
[2] Instrumental of *tejo*, " heat," " energy," " potency."
[3] *dhammo* here is the way or custom of good behaviour and good government, justice, supposed to have been followed by ancient emperors in a less degenerate period of civilization than ours.
[4] The *dibbaṃ cakkaratanaṃ* in this narrative suggests a comet, fancied to remain in the sky throughout the reign of a just emperor.
[5] " to seek ", infinitive, see next Lesson.
[6] Accusative of *paṭhavī* (fem.), " earth."
[7] *massu(ṃ)*, " beard."

kāsāyāni vatthāni acchādetvā, agārasmā anagāriyaṃ pabbajissāmī ti. atha kho rājā Daḷhanemi jeṭṭhaputtaṃ kumāraṃ sādhukaṃ rajje samanusāsitvā, kesamassuṃ ohāretvā kāsāyāni vatthāni acchādetvā, agārasmā anagāriyaṃ pabbaji. sattāhapabbajite kho pana rājisimhi dibbaṃ cakkaratanaṃ antaradhāyi. atha kho aññataro puriso yena rājā khattiyo ten' upasaṃkami, upasaṃkamitvā rājānaṃ khattiyaṃ etad avoca : yagghe deva jāneyyāsi dibbaṃ cakkaratanaṃ antarahitan ti.

atha kho rājā khattiyo dibbe cakkaratane antarahite anattamano ahosi. so yena rājisi ten' upasaṃkami, upasaṃkamitvā rājisiṃ etad avoca : yagghe deva jāneyyāsi dibbaṃ cakkaratanaṃ antarahitan ti. evaṃ vutte rājisi rājānaṃ khattiyaṃ etad avoca : mā kho tvaṃ tāta dibbe cakkaratane antarahite anattamano ahosi. na hi te tāta dibbaṃ cakkaratanaṃ pettikaṃ dāyajjaṃ. iṅgha tvaṃ tāta ariye cakkavattivatte vattāhi. ṭhānaṃ kho pan' etaṃ vijjati yan te dibbaṃ cakkaratanaṃ pātubhavissatī ti. katamaṃ pan' etaṃ deva ariyaṃ cakkavattivattan ti. tena hi tvaṃ tāta dhammaṃ yeva nissāya dhammaṃ mānento dhammaṃ pūjento dhammikaṃ rakkhāvaraṇaguttiṃ [1] saṃvidahassu [2] khattiyesu anuyuttesu brāhmaṇagahapatikesu negamajānapadesu samaṇabrāhmaṇesu migapakkhīsu. mā ca te tāta vijite adhammakāro pavattittha.[3] ye ca te tāta vijite adhanā assu, tesañ ca dhanam anuppadeyyāsi. ye ca te tāta vijite samaṇabrāhmaṇā madappamādā paṭiviratā, te kālena kālaṃ upasaṃkamitvā paripuccheyyāsi : kiṃ bhante kusalaṃ kiṃ akusalaṃ, kiṃ me kayiramānaṃ dīgharattaṃ ahitāya dukkhāya assa, kiṃ vā pana me kayiramānaṃ dīgharattaṃ hitāya sukhāya assā ti. tesaṃ sutvā yaṃ akusalaṃ taṃ abhinivajjeyyāsi, yaṃ kusalaṃ taṃ samādāya vatteyyāsi. idaṃ kho tāta taṃ ariyaṃ cakkavattivattan ti. evaṃ devā ti kho rājā khattiyo rājisissa paṭissutvā ariye cakkavattivatte vatti. tassa ariye cakkavattivatte vattamānassa dibbaṃ cakkaratanaṃ pāturahosi. disvā rañño khattiyassa etad ahosi : sutaṃ kho pana m' etaṃ : yassa rañño khattiyassa dibbaṃ

[1] *gutti* (fem.), " protection."
[2] " provide," " arrange," " organize " : *saṃ-vi-dhā*, 2nd singular imperative " middle " (Lesson 28).
[3] *(p)pa-vatt*, 3rd singular aorist " middle " (Lesson 28). The meaning is the same as the ordinary aorist, but probably poetic and emotive.

cakkaratanaṃ pātubhavati, so hoti cakkavattī ti. assaṃ nu kho ahaṃ rājā cakkavattī ti.

atha kho taṃ cakkaratanaṃ puratthimaṃ disaṃ pavatti, anvad eva rājā cakkavatti saddhiṃ caturaṅginiyā [1] senāya. yasmiṃ kho pana padese cakkaratanaṃ patiṭṭhāsi, tattha rājā cakkavatti vāsaṃ upagacchi saddhiṃ caturaṅginiyā senāya. ye kho pana puratthimāya disāya paṭirājāno, te rājānaṃ cakkavattiṃ upasaṃkamitvā evam āhaṃsu [2] : ehi kho mahārāja, svāgataṃ te mahārāja, sakan te mahārāja, anusāsa mahārājā ti. rājā cakkavatti evam āha [2] : pāṇo na hantabbo. adinnaṃ n' ādātabbaṃ. kāmesu micchā na caritabbā. musā na bhāsitabbā. majjaṃ na pātabbaṃ. yathābhuttañ [3] ca bhuñjathā ti. ye kho pana puratthimāya disāya paṭirājāno, te rañño cakkavattissa anuyuttā ahesuṃ . . . dakkhiṇaṃ disaṃ pavatti. pe. pacchimaṃ. pe. uttaraṃ. pe. ye kho pana uttarāya disāya paṭirājāno, te rañño cakkavattissa anuyuttā ahesuṃ.

Translate into English :—

brāhmaṇo va seṭṭho vaṇṇo

purisena purisaṃ karitvā khattiyā va seṭṭhā hīnā brāhmaṇā

na c' etarahi vijjati añño samaṇo vā brāhmaṇo vā bhagavatā bhiyyo 'bhiññataro

tiṇhena satthena sīsaṃ chindati

na odanakummāsaṃ bhuñjeyyaṃ

aggo 'ham asmi lokassa, jeṭṭho 'ham asmi lokassa, seṭṭho 'ham asmi lokassa

na mayaṃ ito bhiyyo pajānāma

idaṃ hīnaṃ, idaṃ paṇītaṃ

saññā nu kho bhante pathamaṃ uppajjati pacchā ñāṇaṃ, udāhu paṭhamaṃ ñāṇaṃ uppajjati pacchā saññā, udāhu saññā ca ñāṇaṃ ca apubbaṃ acarimaṃ uppajjanti.

Translate into Pali :—

Once, the fortunate one was dwelling (use present tense, which in contexts like this expresses a continuing state in the

[1] Instrumental singular of the feminine (*caturaṅginī*) of the adjective *caturaṅgin*, "having four arms (infantry, cavalry, chariotry, elephantry : cf. chess)."

[2] *āhaṃsu*, "they said" ; *āha*, "he said" (Lesson 21).

[3] "according to what is eaten," "in moderation," adverb.

past) among the Koḷiyas. Then (*atha kho*) Puṇṇa, a Koḷiyan (*Koḷiyaputto*), a bovine, and a naked ascetic Seniya, a canine, approached (aorist : past event at a point of time) this way towards the fortunate one. Having approached, Puṇṇa (the) Koḷiyan (who was) a bovine, having saluted the fortunate one, sat down to one side (*ekam-antaṃ* : used as an indeclinable-compound). The naked ascetic Seniya, however, (the) canine, exchanged greetings with the fortunate one ; having made agreeable polite conversation (word order : agreeable conversation polite), squatting (gerund) like a dog, he sat down to one side. Puṇṇa the Koḷiyan bovine, seated to one side (put this clause first) said this to the fortunate one : " Sir, this naked ascetic Seniya (is) a canine, a doer-of-hard-tasks. He eats (what is) thrown-on-the-ground. He (use genitive and past participle) has long (*dīgharattaṃ*) conformed (to) that dog-vow. What (will be) his future state ? " " Enough, Puṇṇa, don't bother with this. Don't ask me this." [Puṇṇa asks a second and a third time : the convention being that, however reluctant, one must satisfy an inquirer who persists in asking up to three times. In the Pali of this story the question is repeated with abbreviation (*pe*) in place of the second statement. The fortunate one reluctantly answers.] ". . . Nevertheless I will explain to you (*te*). In this connection, Puṇṇa, someone develops the dog-vow perfectly (*paripuṇṇaṃ* : accusative used as adverb) . . . Having developed the dog-vow perfectly, having developed the-virtue-of-a-dog perfectly, having developed the-mind-of-a-dog perfectly, having developed the-style-of-a-dog perfectly, after death he is reborn in the condition (acc.) of dogs. But if (*sace*) he has the opinion (*diṭṭhi*, fem. : Lesson 20) : ' By this virtue or vow I shall be a god,' that (fem.) is his wrong-opinion." (Wrong-opinion produces as future state either purgatory or birth as an animal.)

LESSON 19

Declension of Masculine and Neuter Nouns in -u

Nouns and adjectives in *u* follow a declension parallel to that in *i*, substituting *ŭ* for *ĭ* and *v* for *y* in the stem.

	MASCULINE—*bhikkhu*, " monk "		NEUTER—*vatthu*, " thing," " (building) site," " position "	
	Singular	Plural	Singular	Plural
Nom.	*bhikkhu*	*bhikkhavo* or *bhikkhū* for both cases	*vatthu* or *vatthuṃ*	*vatthūni*
Acc.	*bhikkhuṃ*			
Ins.	*bhikkhunā*	*bhikkhūhi*		
Dat.	*bhikkhuno*	*bhikkhūnaṃ*		
Abl.	*bhikkhunā*	*bhikkhūhi*	Rest as masculine.	
Gen.	*bhikkhuno* or *bhikkhussa*	*bhikkhūnaṃ* or *bhikkhunnaṃ*		
Loc.	*bhikkhusmiṃ*	*bhikkhūsu*		

Vocative as nominative except for the special additional form in the plural : *bhikkhave,* " monks ! "—only in this word.

Adjectives in *u* are similarly declined.

Infinitive

The infinitive is formed by adding the suffixes *tuṃ*, *ituṃ* to a strong form of the root or to the present stem. Stems in consonants take *ituṃ* ; some roots in vowels take *tuṃ*. Verbs of the 7th conjugation and causatives have *tuṃ* following the stem vowel *e*. The infinitive is used as an indeclinable. Usually it expresses purpose, and is interchangeable with a dative of purpose :—

rādh (VII)	*ārādhetuṃ*	to please, to satisfy
(*k*)*kam*	*upasaṃkamituṃ*	to approach
kar	*kātuṃ*	to do

gam	*gantuṃ*	to go
jīv	*jīvituṃ*	to live
(j)jhe	*jhāyituṃ*	to meditate
(ñ)ñā	*ñātuṃ*	to know
tar	*tarituṃ*	to cross
dā	*dātuṃ*	to give
dis (VII)	*desetuṃ*	to teach
(ñ)ñap	*paññāpetuṃ*	to declare
is (I) [1]	*pariyesituṃ* [2]	to seek
vis	*pavisituṃ*	to enter
pucch	*pucchituṃ*	to ask
bhū	*bhavituṃ*	to be
bhās	*bhāsituṃ*	to speak
bhuj (II)	*bhuñjituṃ*	to eat
muc (II)	*muñcituṃ*	to free
(ṭ)ṭhā	*vuṭṭhātuṃ*	to rise, to get up
(ñ)ñā	*saññāpetuṃ* (caus.)	to make perceive
(s)su	*sotuṃ*	to hear

The infinitive is neutral as regards active and passive and hence is used in passive as well as active sentences. Thus in a passive sentence with the agent in the instrumental: *kula-puttena upasaṃkamituṃ*, literally "to be approached by a respectable person". In an active sentence: *na sakkoti āsanā pi vuṭṭhātuṃ*, "he can't even get up from his seat."

The infinitive may be made negative by compounding with the prefix *a-*: *adātuṃ*, "not to give."

Among the more or less idiomatic constructions with the infinitive we may note the following:—

evaṃ arahati bhavituṃ = "it should be so" ("deserves to be"), "it must be so" (expressing probability, not certainty, concerning facts)

iccheyyāma mayaṃ . . . sotuṃ = "we would like to hear . . ."

[1] There are two roots *is* of the first conjugation, the (regular) one, traditionally called *is(a)*, present tense *esati*, past participle *iṭṭha*, and the one traditionally called *is(u)* which takes the suffix *cha*: present tense *icchati*, past participle *icchita*. In this book we have omitted the exponents (*anubandha*) such as (*a*), (*u*), with which almost all roots are traditionally given.

[2] Before a root beginning with a vowel the prefix *pari* becomes *pariy*.

arahati . . . samaṇaṃ dassanāya upasaṃkamituṃ = " he ought . . . to go and see the philosopher " (dative and infinitive in conjunction)

iccheyyātha no tumhe . . . sotuṃ = " would you not like to hear ? . . ."

sakkā nu kho . . . paññāpetuṃ = " is it possible to define . . . ? " (*sak(k)* is frequently used with the infinitive ; *sakkā* is an impersonal indeclinable derivative from this root meaning " it is possible " or " is it possible ? " according to the context)

sakkā pan' etaṃ bhante mayā ñātuṃ = " but is it possible, sir, for me to know (lit. : " to be known by me ") this ? "

devā yesaṃ na sakkā . . . āyuṃ saṃkhātuṃ = " gods whose age cannot be . . . reckoned "

nāhaṃ sakkomi . . . pañca vassāni āgametuṃ = " I cannot . . . wait for five years " (causative of *ā-gam* means " wait ")

(any tense of *sak(k)* may be used with the infinitive) (cf. also Exercise 16, Translation into English : ***nāsakkhi***, " he could not," with infinitives).

na labhanti gāmaṃ . . . pavisituṃ = " they did not obtain entry into a village . . .", " they were not allowed to enter a village . . ." (idiomatic use of *labh*, i.e. " to be permitted ", " to qualify for ")

atha agārāni upakkamiṃsu kātuṃ tass' eva asaddhammassa paṭicchādanatthaṃ = " then they went into houses in order to do the purpose of concealment of just that evil ", i.e. in order to accomplish the evil in secret (*a-sad-dhamma* = " non-good-custom " ; *paṭicchādanā* = " covering ", " concealment ". It is also possible to regard the genitive in constructions like this as objective to the infinitive and *-atthaṃ* as an adverb)

abhabbo . . . bhikkhu . . . gantuṃ = " a monk . . . is unable to go . . ."

(cf. use of dative in a parallel construction).

bhikkhū . . . alaṃ . . . dhammaṃ desetuṃ = " monks . . . able (*alaṃ* = ' fit ', ' adequate for ') . . . to teach the doctrine."

Bahubbīhi *Compounds* (1)

The *bahubbīhi* [1] class of compounds consists of those whose meanings are subordinate to the meanings of words other than the members of the compounds themselves (cf. in English " whitewashed "). Unlike *tappurisas*, *dvandas*, and *kammadhārayas* they thus function as adjectives. In explaining a *bahubbīhi* it is necessary to ascertain to whom or to what the compound pertains. *Bahubbīhis* are inflected in the three genders like adjectives, according to the gender of the dominating noun. A *bahubbīhi* compound is always equivalent to a relative (subordinate) clause : " who has/was . . .", " which has/was . . .".

From *pahūta* and *jivhā* (" tongue ") we may form a compound *pahūtajivha-* as an epithet of, say, *kumāra-* (hence with masculine inflections), meaning " a boy who has a large tongue ". From *lohita* (" red ") and *akkhi*, *lohitakkhi* (*puriso*) = " (a man) having red eyes ". From *kaddamo* (" mud ") and *makkhita*, *kaddamamakkhitaṃ* (*cakkaṃ*) = " (a wheel) smeared with mud ". From *sa-* (" with ", " possessing ") and *dhaññaṃ* (" grain ", " crops ") we have the *bahubbīhi sadhañña*, " grain-bearing," as the epithet of a place. Frequently other classes of compound are enclosed within *bahubbīhis*, thus *satiṇakaṭṭhodaka* means " possessing grass, firewood, and water " (*dvanda* within a *bahubbīhi*). It may be noted that *sa* in these compounds is not used as an independent word (the equivalent independent word is *saha*) : a number of such substitute or secondary words are used in compounds in place of independent forms. The form *sa-* is used also for *saka*, " own."

Bahubbīhis may be subdivided into several distinct groups, of which the ordinary two-member compounds and those beginning with *sa-* (= *saha*) form two. Those beginning with the negative *a-*/*an-* (= *na*), such as *asama* (*bhagavant*), " unequalled (fortunate one) " form another group, some of which have occurred in earlier exercises.[2] Compounds which formally resemble *tappurisas*, *kammadhārayas*, or *dvandas* may be used

[1] *bahubbīhi* = *bahu* + (*v*)*vīhi* (" rice ")—*vv* > *bb*—an example of the class : *bahubbīhi* (*deso*) = " (a country) having much rice " (i.e. a fertile, prosperous country).

[2] With *sa-* and *a-* contrasting pairs are formed : *sadhana*/*adhana*.

as *bahubbīhis*. Thus most of the ordinary two-member *bahubbīhis* have a case relation between the members, whilst the negative *bahubbīhis* resemble negative *kammadhārayas*. In a two-member *bahubbīhi* the order of the members may be reversed (as compared with the strict order of the *tappurisa*) :—

katapuñña (*purisa*) = " (a man) who has done good "
chinnapapañca (*Buddha*) = " (a Buddha) who has cut through obstacles "
vajirapāṇi (*yakkha*) = " (a god) who has a thunderbolt in his hand ".

Very often the sense of compounds is spontaneously evident, but at times it is obscure, hence the need to consider their usage. Other groups of *bahubbīhis* will be indicated in subsequent lessons.

Action Nouns

Nouns expressing an action, such as those ending in *-ana* (e.g. *dassana*, " seeing ") sometimes take a patient (" direct object " of the action) in the accusative or genitive (" objective genitive ") case. These " action nouns " may also take a " subjective " (agent) in the genitive or in the instrumental. In these constructions the action noun often (though not always) appears in the dative case, expressing purpose, and may be compared with the infinitive. It may also appear in the accusative as representing the objective of the main action (with its own objective in the genitive).

Examples of action nouns with patients in the accusative :—

mayaṃ bhavantaṃ Gotamaṃ dassanāya idh' upasaṃkantā, " we have come here to see (for seeing) the honourable Gotama."
dūrā vat' amhā āgatā tathāgataṃ dassanāya, " we have indeed come from far to see the thus-gone."
kathaṃ savanāya, " to hear (some) talk."

Vocabulary

Verbs :—

adhi-ā-vas (I)	*ajjhāvasati*	live on, exploit
anu-bhū (I)	*anubhavati*	experience, enjoy, observe

abhi-(p)pa-vass (I)	*abhippavassati*	rain down on, pour down (heavy rain, cloudburst) (p.p. *abhippavaṭṭa*)
abhi-vaḍḍh (I)	*abhivaḍḍhati*	increase
abhi-vi-ji (V)	*abhivijināti*	conquer (ger. *abhivijiya*)
ā-gam (I)	causative : *āgameti*	= wait
ā-sic (II)	*āsiñcati*	shower over, pour over (pp. *āsitta*)
u(d)-tar (I)	*uttarati*	cross
u(d)-sah (I)	*ussahati*	try, undertake, take up
u(d)-sīd	causative : *ussādeti*	= lift on to
u(d)-har (I)	*uddharati*	collect, raise
upa-gam (I)	*upagacchati*	go to
garu-kar (VI) [1]	*garukaroti*	give respect to
nat (III)	*naccati*	dance
ni(r)-tar (I)	*nittharati*	cross over
(p)pa-kapp (VII)	*pakappeti*	dispense, pay (wages)
(p)paṭi-vas (I)	*paṭivasati*	dwell
(p)paṭi-vid (I)	only causative : *paṭivedeti*	= inform, announce
(p)pa-yā (I)	*payāti*	set out
bhakkh (VII)	*bhakkheti*	eat, devour
mud (I)	*modati*	rejoice
vi-heṭh (VII)	*viheṭheti*	harass
sat-kar (VI) [1]	*sakkaroti*	entertain
saṃ-u(d)-han (I)	*samūhanati*	suppress, abolish (pp. of caus. *samugghāta*)
saṃ-kaḍḍh (I)	*saṃkaḍḍhati*	collect (ger. *saṃkaḍḍhitvā*)
saṃ-tapp (VII)	*saṃtappeti*	gratify, please
sis (VII)	*seseti*	leave

Nouns :—

akiccaṃ	what should not be done
aṭṭhikaṃ	bone
aṇṇavo	flood

[1] Adjective compounded with verb : see Lesson 20.

atithi masc.	guest
adhammo	false doctrine, bad nature, bad custom, injustice, bad mental object, bad idea
anayo	misfortune, misery
apāraṃ	hither, this world
arahant- masc. (declined like *bhagavant-* or like a present participle)	worthy one, perfected one
avasesako	one who remains, survivor
āsaṅkā	apprehension, doubt, fear
upakaraṇaṃ	resources
upapīḷā	oppression, trouble
upamā	simile
ussado	abundance
kaṇṭakaṃ	(" thorn "), subversive element, rebel, bandit
kaddamo	mud
kantāro	wilderness, semi-desert
kalāpo	bundle, quiver
kiccaṃ	what should be done
kumudaṃ	white water-lily
kulo	tribe
kullo	raft
koṭṭhāgāraṃ	granary, storehouse
koso	treasury
khattar- masc. (irregular noun : nom. sing. *khattā*, acc. sing. *khattaṃ*, voc. sing. *khatte*)	steward
khīlo	stake (boundary)
khettaṃ	field, territory, land
gaṇo	group, aggregate
gadrabho	donkey
gamanaṃ	going
garahā	blame, reproof, threat
gahaṇaṃ	seizing, keeping
gahapatiko	householder
guṇaṃ (sometimes masc.)	string, strand, quality

gorakkhā	cattle breeding
gharaṃ	house
ghāto	attacking, destruction
cārikā	travel, journey, mission
jātarūpaṃ	gold
ñāti masc.	relative, kinsman
tīraṃ	shore, bank
thalaṃ	land, dry land
dāyo	gift
divāseyyā	day-bed, siesta bed
duhano	robbery
dhaññaṃ	grain
dhammo	good mental object, good mental phenomenon, good idea (when opposed to *adhammo* as bad ~, otherwise *dhammo* as natural phenomenon includes bad phenomena as well as good)
nāvā	boat, ship
nigamo	town
nittharaṇaṃ	crossing over
nemitto	diviner, prognosticator, astrologer
(p)paṭibhayaṃ	danger, terror
paṇiyaṃ	commodity
pantho	road
pabbājanā	banishment
pariṇāyako	leader
parivitakko	reflection, idea
palāso	foliage
pābhataṃ	present, gratuity, capital
pāraṃ	thither, across, beyond
porisaṃ	service
→ *bali* masc.	tithe, religious tax or contribution
bījaṃ	seed
brahmadeyyaṃ	(" gift to God " : i.e. grant of land/villages to a priest of the Brahman religion) grant, fief, benefice
bhaṇḍaṃ	goods, stores, supplies
bhogo	property

bhoggaṃ	property, proprietary rights
maṇḍalaṃ	circle, disc
mitto	friend
yakkho	spirit, god, demon
yoggaṃ	draught animal, ox
rajataṃ	silver
ratho	chariot, cart
rājadāyo	gift by the king, royal endowment
rājabhoggaṃ	crown property (crown land, as opposed to land owned by peasant/village communities)
rāsiko	accumulation
vaṭumaṃ	road
vaṇijjā	commerce
vadho	execution
vetanaṃ	wages, pay
vyasanaṃ	disaster
saṃvidhānaṃ	arrangement, policy
saṃgho	community, group
satthiko	caravan merchant
saddhā	confidence, trust, conviction
sampadā	success
sākhā	branch
sāro	value
sālohito	blood relation

Past Participles :—

anuppatta (*anu-(p)pa-ap(p)*)	arrived at
apanaddha (*apa-nah*)	tied back, untied
tiṇṇa (*tar* (I))	crossed
paripuṇṇa (*pūr*)	full, perfect
sambuddha (*budh*)	enlightened
hata (*han*)	killed

Future Passive Participle :—

pahātabba (*(p)pa-hā*)	to be given up, to be renounced

Adjectives :—

aḍḍha	rich
attamana	assured

aneka	many
apāruta	open
appa	little
amuka	such and such
alla	wet
ahata	new
ura	bosom, own (child)
orima	nearer, this side
kāḷa	black
khema	secure, safe
gaṇībhūta	crowded together
gimhika	summer
tividha	threefold
paṇḍita	wise
paṭisallīna	retired, secluded
pasuta	intent on
pārima	further, other side
bahukāra	very useful
bāla	foolish
bhadda	good (repeated = very good)
mahesakkha	superior
muda	glad, joyful
yathākata	usual, customary
rahogata	alone, in privacy
lohita	red
vassika	rainy (for the rainy season)
vipula	large, abundant
saṃghāsaṃghin	in groups
saṃghāsaṃghīgaṇībhūta	clustered in groups
hemantika	winter

Masculine Nouns in *u* :—

aṇu	atom
dassu [1]	brigand, thief (~ *khīlo*, " brigand-stake " marking territory under rebel control)
pasu	animal

[1] Originally the name of the non-Āryan people of (N.W.) India conquered by the Āryan invaders *c*. 1600 B.C.

bhikkhu	monk
setu	causeway, dam, bridge
hetu	cause

Neuter Nouns in *u* :—

āyu	life, age
utu	season (the gender of the word fluctuates)
cakkhu	eye
massu	beard
vatthu	thing, (building) site, position, mode (of argument)
sajjhu	silver

Adjectives in *u* :—

aṇu	minute, atomic
uju	straight, erect
garu	heavy
phāsu	comfortable
bahu	much, many
maṅku	shamefaced
lahu	light (weight)
sādhu	good (as adverb = well)

Gerund :—

āgamma (*ā-gam* I)	depending on, as a result of (acc.) (*āgantvā* on the other hand means having come, having returned)

Ordinal Numeral :—

sattama	seventh

Indeclinables :—

upari	on top (of) (precedes the word it relates to, which is usually in the locative)
evam eva	just so, likewise
kira	really, now, they say
kuto	whence ?

kuhiṃ	where (to) ?
tatra	there
tāva	so much, so long, first, now
tv eva (enclitic)	but (emphatic)
divā	by day
pag eva	how much more so, let alone, still more, still less
paṭipathaṃ	the opposite way, in the opposite direction
maññe	I think, no doubt
yatra	where
yadā	when
sīghaṃ	fast (repeated = very fast)
seyyathā	as, just like (introducing a simile)
sotthinā	safely

EXERCISE 19

Passages for reading :—

1. te taṃ satthaṃ dvidhā vibhajiṃsu ekato pañca sakaṭasatāni ekato pañca sakaṭasatāni. eko tāva satthavāho bahuṃ tiṇañ ca kaṭṭhañ ca udakañ ca āropetvā satthaṃ pāyāpesi. dvīhatīhapāyāto [1] kho pana so sattho addasā purisaṃ kāḷaṃ lohitakkhiṃ apanaddhakalāpaṃ [2] kumudamālaṃ allavatthaṃ allakesaṃ kaddamamakkhitehi cakkehi gadrabharathena paṭipathaṃ āgacchantaṃ. disvā etad avoca : kuto bho āgacchasī ti. amukamhā janapadā ti. kuhiṃ gamissasī ti. amukaṃ nāma janapadan ti. kacci bho purato kantāre mahāmegho abhippavaṭṭo ti. evaṃ kho bho purato kantāre mahāmegho abhippavaṭṭo, āsittodakāni vaṭumāni, bahuṃ tiṇañ ca kaṭṭhañ ca udakañ ca, chaḍḍetha bho purāṇāni tiṇāni kaṭṭhāni udakāni, lahubhārehi sakaṭehi sīghaṃ sīghaṃ gacchatha, mā yoggāṇi kilamethā ti.

atha kho so satthavāho satthike āmantesi : ayaṃ bho puriso evam āha : purato kantāre mahāmegho abhippavaṭṭo, āsittodakāni vaṭumāni, bahuṃ tiṇañ ca kaṭṭhañ ca udakañ ca, chaḍḍetha bho purāṇāni tiṇāni kaṭṭhāni udakāni, lahubhārehi

[1] " when it was two or three days since it had set out " (*bahubbīhi*).
[2] *bahubbīhi* : " with quiver tied behind " (Commentary), " with hair untied " (meaning suggested by *Critical Pali Dictionary*).

sakaṭehi sīghaṃ sīghaṃ gacchatha, mā yoggāni kilamethā ti chaḍḍetha bho purāṇāni tiṇāni kaṭṭhāni udakāni, lahubhārehi sakaṭehi satthaṃ pāyāpethā ti. evam bho ti kho te satthikā tassa satthavāhassa paṭissutvā, chaḍḍetvā purāṇāni tiṇāni kaṭṭhāni udakāni lahubhārehi sakaṭehi satthaṃ pāyāpesuṃ. te paṭhame pi satthavāse na addasaṃsu tiṇaṃ vā kaṭṭhaṃ vā udakaṃ vā, dutiye pi satthavāse . . . tatiye pi satthavāse . . . catutthe pi satthavāse . . . pañcame pi satthavāse . . . chaṭṭhe pi satthavāse . . . sattame pi satthavāse na addasaṃsu tiṇaṃ vā kaṭṭhaṃ vā udakaṃ vā, sabbe va anayavyasanaṃ āpajjiṃsu. ye ca tasmiṃ satthe ahesuṃ manussā vā pasū vā sabbe so yakkho amanusso bhakkhesi, aṭṭhikān' eva sesesi.

yadā aññāsi dutiyo satthavāho : bahunikkhanto kho dāni so sattho ti, bahuṃ tiṇañ ca kaṭṭhañ ca udakañ ca āropetvā satthaṃ pāyāpesi. dvīhatīhapāyāto kho pan' eso sattho addasā purisaṃ kāḷaṃ lohitakkhiṃ apanaddhakalāpaṃ kumudamālaṃ allavatthaṃ allakesaṃ kaddamamakkhitehi cakkehi gadrabharathena paṭipathaṃ āgacchantaṃ. disvā etad avoca : kuto bho āgacchasī ti. amukamhā janapadā ti. kuhiṃ gamissasī ti. amukaṃ nāma janapadan ti. kacci kho purato kantāre mahāmegho abhippavaṭṭo ti. evaṃ bho purato kantāre mahāmegho abhippavaṭṭo, āsittodakāni vaṭumāni, bahuṃ tiṇañ ca kaṭṭhañ ca udakañ ca, chaḍḍetha bho purāṇāni tiṇāni kaṭṭhāni udakāni, lahubhārehi sakaṭehi sīghaṃ sīghaṃ gacchatha, mā yoggāni kilamethā ti.

atha kho so satthavāho satthike āmantesi : ayaṃ bho puriso evam āha : purato kantāre mahāmegho abhippavaṭṭo, āsittodakāni vaṭumāni bahuṃ tiṇañ ca kaṭṭhañ ca udakañ ca, chaḍḍetha bho purāṇāni tiṇāni kaṭṭhāni udakāni, lahubhārehi sakaṭehi sīghaṃ sīghaṃ gacchatha, mā yoggāni kilamethā ti. ayaṃ kho bho puriso n' ev' amhākaṃ mitto na pi ñātisālohito, kathaṃ mayaṃ imassa saddhāya gamissāma. na kho chaḍḍetabbāni purāṇāni tiṇāni kaṭṭhāni udakāni, yathākatena bhaṇḍena satthaṃ pāyāpetha, na vo purāṇaṃ chaḍḍessāmā ti. evaṃ bho ti kho te satthikā tassa satthavāhassa paṭissutvā yathākatena bhaṇḍena satthaṃ pāyāpesuṃ. te paṭhame pi satthavāse na addasaṃsu tiṇaṃ vā kaṭṭhaṃ vā udakaṃ vā, dutiye pi satthavāse . . . tatiye pi satthavāse . . . catutthe pi satthavāse . . . pañcame pi satthavāse . . . chaṭṭhe pi satthavāse . . . sattame pi satthavāse na addasaṃsu tiṇaṃ vā kaṭṭhaṃ vā udakaṃ vā, tañ ca satthaṃ addasaṃsu anayavyasanaṃ āpannaṃ. ye va tasmiṃ satthe ahesuṃ manussā vā pasū vā, tesañ ca aṭṭhikān' eva addasaṃsu tena yakkhena amanussena bhakkhitānaṃ.

atha kho so satthavāho satthike āmantesi : ayaṃ kho bho so sattho anayavyasanaṃ āpanno yathā taṃ tena bālena satthavāhena pariṇāyakena. tena hi bho yān' asmākaṃ satthe appasārāni paṇiyāni, tāni chaḍḍetvā, yāni imasmiṃ satthe mahāsārāni paṇiyāni tāni ādiyathā ti. evaṃ bho ti kho te satthikā tassa satthavāhassa paṭissutvā yāni sakasmiṃ satthe appasārāni paṇiyāni tāni chaḍḍetvā, yāni tasmiṃ satthe mahāsārāni paṇiyāni tāni ādiyitvā, sotthinā taṃ kantāraṃ nittharimsu yathā taṃ paṇḍitena satthavāhena pariṇāyakena.

2. evam me sutaṃ. ekaṃ samayaṃ bhagavā Māgadhesu cārikaṃ caramāno mahatā bhikkhusaṃghena saddhiṃ yena Khānumataṃ nāma Māgadhānaṃ brāhmaṇagāmo tad avasari. tatra sudaṃ bhagavā Khānumate viharati Ambalaṭṭhikāyaṃ. tena kho pana samayena Kūṭadanto brāhmaṇo Khānumataṃ ajjhāvasati sattussadaṃ satiṇakaṭṭhodakaṃ sadhaññaṃ rājabhoggaṃ raññā Māgadhena Seniyena Bimbisārena [1] dinnaṃ rājadāyaṃ brahmadeyyaṃ.

tena kho pana samayena Kūṭadanto brāhmaṇo upari pāsāde divāseyyaṃ upagato hoti. addasā kho Kūṭadanto brāhmaṇo Khānumatake brāhmaṇagahapatike Khānumatā nikkhamitvā saṃghāsaṃghīgaṇībhūte yena Ambalaṭṭhikā ten' upasaṃkamante. disvā khattaṃ āmantesi : kin nu kho bho khatte Khānumatakā brāhmaṇagahapatikā Khānumatā nikkhamitvā saṃghāsaṃghīgaṇībhūtā yena Ambalaṭṭhikā ten' upasaṃkamantī ti. atthi kho bho samaṇo Gotamo Sakyaputto Sakyakulā pabbajito. Māgadhesu cārikaṃ caramāno mahatā bhikkhusaṃghena saddhiṃ Khānumataṃ anuppatto Khānumate viharati Ambalaṭṭhikāyaṃ. tam ete bhagavantaṃ Gotamaṃ dassanāya upasaṃkamantī ti. atha kho Kūṭadantassa brāhmaṇassa etad ahosi : sutaṃ kho pana m' etaṃ : samaṇo Gotamo tividhayaññasampadaṃ jānātī ti. na kho panāhaṃ [2] jānāmi

[1] Reigned B.C. 546 (?)–494.
[2] Junction *a* + *a* = *ā*.

tividhayaññasampadaṃ, icchāmi cāhaṃ[1] mahāyaññaṃ yajituṃ. yan nūnāhaṃ[1] samaṇaṃ Gotamaṃ upasaṃkamitvā tividhayaññasampadaṃ puccheyyan ti.

atha kho Kūṭadanto brāhmaṇo taṃ khattaṃ āmantesi : tena hi bho khatte yena Khānumatakā brāhmaṇagahapatikā ten' upasaṃkama, upasaṃkamitvā Khānumatake brāhmaṇagahapatike evaṃ vadehi : Kūṭadanto bho brāhmaṇo evam āha : āgamentu kira bhavanto, Kūṭadanto pi brāhmaṇo samaṇaṃ Gotamaṃ dassanāya upasaṃkamissatī ti. evaṃ bho ti kho so khattā Kūṭadantassa brāhmaṇassa paṭissutvā yena Khānumatakā brāhmaṇagahapatikā ten' upasaṃkami, upasaṃkamitvā Khānumatake brāhmaṇagahapatike etad avoca : Kūṭadanto bho brāhmaṇo evam āha : āgamentu kira bhavanto, Kūṭadanto pi brāhmaṇo samaṇaṃ Gotamaṃ dassanāya upasaṃkamissatī ti. tena kho pana samayena anekāni brāhmaṇasatāni Khānumate paṭivasanti : Kūṭadantassa brāhmaṇassa mahāyaññaṃ anubhavissāmā ti. assosuṃ kho te brāhmaṇā : Kūṭadanto kira brāhmaṇo samaṇaṃ Gotamaṃ dassanāya upasaṃkamissatī ti. atha kho te brāhmaṇā yena Kūṭadanto brāhmaṇo ten' upasaṃkamiṃsu, upasaṃkamitvā Kūṭadantaṃ brāhmaṇaṃ etad avocuṃ : saccaṃ kira bhavaṃ Kūṭadanto samaṇaṃ Gotamaṃ dassanāya upasaṃkamissatī ti. evaṃ kho me bho hoti aham pi samaṇaṃ Gotamaṃ dassanāya upasaṃkamissāmī ti. mā bhavaṃ Kūṭadanto samaṇaṃ Gotamaṃ dassanāya upasaṃkami, na arahati bhavaṃ Kūṭadanto samaṇaṃ Gotamaṃ dassanāya upasaṃkamituṃ. sace bhavaṃ Kūṭadanto samaṇaṃ Gotamaṃ dassanāya upasaṃkamissati, bhoto Kūṭadantassa yaso[2] hāyissati, samaṇassa Gotamassa yaso abhivaḍḍhissati. yam pi bhoto Kūṭadantassa yaso hāyissati, samaṇassa Gotamassa yaso abhivaḍḍhissati, iminā p' aṅgena na arahati bhavaṃ Kūṭadanto samaṇaṃ Gotamaṃ dassanāya upasaṃkamituṃ. samaṇo tv eva Gotamo arahati bhavantaṃ Kūṭadantaṃ dassanāya upasaṃkamitun ti. evaṃ vutte Kūṭadanto brāhmaṇo te brāhmaṇe etad avoca : tena hi bho mama pi suṇātha yathā mayam eva arahāma taṃ bhavantaṃ Gotamaṃ dassanāya upasaṃkamituṃ, na tv eva arahati so bhavaṃ Gotamo

[1] Junction $a + a = \bar{a}$.
[2] *yaso* = " reputation ", see next Lesson.

amhākaṃ dassanāya upasaṃkamituṃ. samaṇo khalu bho Gotamo Khānumataṃ anuppatto Khānumate viharati Ambalaṭṭhikāyaṃ. ye kho pana ke ci samaṇā vā brāhmaṇā vā amhākaṃ gāmakkhettaṃ āgacchanti atithī no te honti. atithī kho pan' amhehi sakkātabbā garukātabbā mānetabbā pūjetabbā. yam pi bho samaṇo Gotamo Khānumataṃ anuppatto Khānumate viharati Ambalaṭṭhikāyaṃ atith' amhākaṃ samaṇo Gotamo. atithi kho pan' amhehi sakkātabbo garukātabbo mānetabbo pūjetabbo. iminā p' aṅgena na arahati so bhavaṃ Gotamo amhākaṃ dassanāya upasaṃkamituṃ, atha kho mayam eva arahāma tam bhavantaṃ Gotamaṃ dassanāya upasaṃkamitun ti.

atha kho Kūṭadanto brāhmaṇo mahatā brāhmaṇagaṇena saddhiṃ yena Ambalaṭṭhikā yena bhagavā ten' upasaṃkami, upasaṃkamitvā bhagavatā saddhiṃ sammodi sammodanīyaṃ kathaṃ sārāṇīyaṃ vītisāretvā ekamantaṃ nisīdi. ekamantaṃ nisinno kho Kūṭadanto brāhmaṇo bhagavantaṃ etad avoca : sutaṃ m' etaṃ bho Gotama : samaṇo Gotamo tividhayaññasampadaṃ jānātī ti. na kho panāhaṃ jānāmi tividhayaññasampadaṃ, icchāmi cāhaṃ mahāyaññaṃ yajituṃ. sādhu me bhavaṃ Gotamo tividhayaññasampadaṃ desetū ti. tena hi brāhmaṇa suṇohi,[1] bhāsissāmī ti. evaṃ bho ti kho Kūṭadanto brāhmaṇo bhagavato paccassosi. bhagavā etad avoca : bhūtapubbaṃ brāhmaṇa rājā Mahāvijito nāma ahosi aḍḍho mahaddhano mahābhogo pahūtajātarūparajato pahūtavittūpakaraṇo[2] pahūtadhanadhañño paripuṇṇakosakoṭṭhāgāro. atha kho brāhmaṇa rañño Mahāvijitassa rahogatassa patisallīnassa evaṃ cetaso[3] parivitakko udapādi : adhigatā kho me vipulā mānusakā bhogā, mahantaṃ paṭhavimaṇḍalaṃ abhivijiya ajjhāvasāmi. yan nūnāhaṃ mahāyaññaṃ yajeyyaṃ yaṃ mama assa dīgharattaṃ hitāya sukhāyā ti. atha kho brāhmaṇa rājā Mahāvijito purohitaṃ brāhmaṇaṃ āmantāpetvā etad avoca : idha mayhaṃ brāhmaṇa rahogatassa patisallīnassa evaṃ cetaso parivitakko udapādi : adhigato me vipulā mānusakā bhogā, mahantaṃ paṭhavimaṇḍalaṃ abhivijiya ajjhāvasāmi.

[1] Imperative second person singular ; *(s)su* here follows the fourth conjugation, see Lesson 28.

[2] *vitti*, feminine, " pleasure." In the vowel junction here the first vowel is elided and the second lengthened.

[3] Genitive of *ceto*, " mind," see next Lesson.

yan nūnāhaṃ mahāyaññaṃ yajeyyaṃ, yaṃ mama assa dīgharattaṃ hitāya sukhāyā ti. icchām' ahaṃ brāhmaṇa mahāyaññaṃ yajituṃ. anusāsatu maṃ bhavaṃ yaṃ mama assa dīgharattaṃ hitāya sukhāyā ti.

evaṃ vutte brāhmaṇa purohito brāhmaṇo rājānaṃ Mahāvijitaṃ etad avoca: bhoto kho rañño janapado sakaṇṭako saupapīḷo, gāmaghātā pi dissanti nigamaghātā pi dissanti nagaraghātā pi dissanti panthaduhanā pi dissanti. bhavañ ce kho pana rājā evaṃ sakaṇṭake janapade saupapīḷe balim uddhareyya, akiccakārī assa tena bhavaṃ rājā. siyā kho pana bhoto rañño evam assa: aham etaṃ dassukhīlaṃ vadhena vā bandhena vā jāniyā [1] vā garahāya vā pabbājanāya vā samūhanissāmī ti, na kho pan' etassa dassukhīlassa evaṃ sammā samugghāto hoti. ye te hatāvasesakā bhavissanti, te pacchā rañño janapadaṃ viheṭhessanti. api ca kho idaṃ saṃvidhānaṃ āgamma evam etassa dassukhīlassa sammā samugghāto hoti. tena hi bhavaṃ rājā ye bhoto rañño janapade ussahanti kasigorakkhe [2] tesam bhavaṃ rājā bījabhattaṃ anuppadetu, ye bhoto rañño janapade ussahanti vaṇijjāya tesam bhavaṃ rājā pābhataṃ anuppadetu, ye bhoto rañño janapade ussahanti rājaporise tesam bhavaṃ rājā bhattavetanaṃ pakappetu, te ca manussā sakammapasutā rañño janapadaṃ na viheṭhessanti, mahā ca rañño rāsiko bhavissati, khemaṭṭhitā janapadā akaṇṭakā anupapīḷā manussā ca mudā modamānā ure putte naccentā apārutagharā maññe viharissantī ti.

3. jāte kho pana bhikkhave Vipassimhi [3] kumāre, Bandhumato [4] rañño paṭivedesuṃ: putto te deva jāto, taṃ devo passatū ti. addasā kho bhikkhave Bandhumā rājā Vipassīkumāraṃ, disvā nemitte brāhmaṇe āmantāpetvā etad avoca: passantu bhonto nemittā brāhmaṇā kumāran ti. addasāsuṃ kho bhikkhave nemittā brāhmaṇā Vipassīkumāraṃ, disvā Bandhumantaṃ rājānaṃ etad avocuṃ: attamano deva hohi, mahesakkho te deva putto uppanno. sace agāraṃ ajjhāvasati,

[1] *jāni* (fem.), inst., "confiscation."
[2] *kasi* (fem.), "cultivation," "agriculture."
[3] *Vipassin*: a prince who lived millions of years ago (when human life was immensely long) and became a Buddha, one of the predecessors of "our" Buddha.
[4] *Bandhumant*: father of *Vipassin*.

rājā hoti cakkavatti dhammiko dhammarājā. sace kho pana agārasmā anagāriyaṃ pabbajati, arahaṃ hoti sammā sambuddho ti. atha kho bhikkhave Bandhumā rājā nemitte brāhmaṇe ahatehi vatthehi acchādāpetvā sabbakāmehi santappesi. atha kho bhikkhave Bandhumā rājā Vipassissa kumārassa tayo [1] pāsāde kārāpesi, ekaṃ vassikaṃ ekaṃ hemantikaṃ ekaṃ gimhikaṃ, pañca kāmaguṇāni upaṭṭhāpesi.

Translate into Pali :—

" O monks, I will teach you the doctrine having-a-raft-as-simile (*bahubbīhi* : raft-simile ; this word stands first, for emphasis), for-the-purpose-of-crossing-over [2], not (emphatic : *no*) for-the-purpose-of-keeping. Just like a man who-had-followed-a-road : he might see a great flood-of-water, the nearer shore with-fear, with-danger, the further shore secure, without-danger (*a*-), and there might not be a boat or a causeway for going from hither across,—he would have (the thought) thus : " Indeed this flood of water (is) great, and the nearer shore (is) with-fear, with-danger, the further shore secure, without-danger, and there isn't a boat or a causeway for going from hither across. What now if I, having collected grass-firewood-branches-and-foliage, having bound a raft, depending on that raft, should cross thither safely ? " Then, indeed (*kho*), that man, having collected grass-firewood-branches-and-foliage, having bound a raft, depending on that raft would cross thither safely. Crossed, gone thither (past participles), he might have (the thought) thus : " Indeed this raft (is) very useful. What now if, having put (" mounted ") this raft on my head, I should go away ? " What do you think (of) that, monks ? Perhaps (*api*) that man thus-doing (*-kārin, bahubbīhi*) (with reference) to that raft (loc.) would be doing-what-should-be-done ? (*nu*) ". " Indeed not (*no h'*) this, sir ! (*bhante*) ". . ." In this connection, monks, that man, crossed, gone thither, might have (the thought) thus : ". . . What now (if), having lifted this raft on to (dry) land, I should go away (?) " Thus-doing, indeed, that man would be doing-what-should-be-done with (loc.) that raft.

[1] " three " (cf. Lesson 26).
[2] *a* + *a* > *ā* > *ă* before a double consonant in close junction.

Likewise, indeed, monks, the doctrine is taught by me having-a-raft-as-simile, for-the-purpose-of-crossing-over, not for-the-purpose-of-keeping. By your (*vo*) learning (present participle, instrumental plural) the raft-simile, monks, even good mental phenomena (are) to be given up by you (*vo*), how much more so bad mental phenomena."

LESSON 20

Declension of Feminine Nouns in -i *and* -ī

Feminines in *i* and *ī* (nouns and adjectives) are declined as follows :—

jāti, " birth "

	Singular	Plural
Nom.	*jāti*	*jātiyo*
Voc.	*jāti*	*jātiyo*
Acc.	*jātiṃ*	*jātiyo*
Ins.	*jātiyā*	*jātīhi*
Dat.	*jātiyā*	*jātīnaṃ*
Abl.	*jātiyā*	*jātīhi*
Gen.	*jātiyā*	*jātīnaṃ*
Loc.	*jātiyā* (loc. also *jātiyaṃ*)	*jātīsu*

devī, " queen "

	Singular	Plural
Nom.	*devī*	*deviyo*
Voc.	*devi*	*deviyo*
Acc.	*deviṃ*	*deviyo*
	rest as *jāti* . . .	

(Within a compound the stem vowel is often shortened.)

A few words, among them *itthī*, " woman," may have either the long or the short vowel in the nominative singular.

Occasionally some of these words are written with assimilation. For example from *nadī*, " river," genitive singular *najjā*.

Numeral catu(r)

The numeral stem *catu(r)*, " four," is inflected in three genders as follows. It is used like an adjective.

	Masc.	Neut.	Fem.
Nom. and Acc.	*cattāro*	*cattāri*	*catasso*
Ins. and Abl.		*catŭ̄hi*	
Dat. and Gen.		*catunnaṃ*	
Loc.		*catŭ̄su*	

Declension of bhagavant *and Adjectives in* -ant, rājan, addhan, muddhan *and* puman

Among the nouns having stems ending in consonants, *bhagavant*, " the fortunate," and *rājan*, " king ", are inflected as follows (both are masculine) :—

	Singular	Plural	Singular	Plural
Nom.	*bhagavā*	*bhagavanto* (Nom. and Acc.)	*rājā*	*rājāno* (Nom. and Acc.)
Acc.	*bhagavantaṃ*		*rājānaṃ*	
Inst.	*bhagavatā*	*bhagavantehi*	*raññā* [1]	*rājūhi*
Dat.	*bhagavato*	*bhagavantānaṃ*	*rañño*	*raññaṃ*
Abl.	*bhagavatā*	*bhagavantehi*	*raññā*	*rājūhi*
Gen.	*bhagavato*	*bhagavantānaṃ*	*rañño*	*raññaṃ* or *rājūnaṃ*
Loc.	*bhagavati*	*bhagavantesu*	*rājini* or *raññe*	*rājūsu*

[1] Assimilation of *rāj* + *n* > *rañň* : note that the vowel is shortened before the double consonant.

The vocatives of these words are not used : the *bhagavant* is addressed as *bhante*, etc., according to the speaker, and a king as *mahārāja* or *deva*. Stem in compounds : *bhagavat-*, *rāja-*.

A number of adjectives in *ant* are inflected in the same way as *bhagavant* (vocative same as nominative or with *-ă* in singular).

addhan, " road " (figuratively : " time ") (masc.) has the following inflections :—

	Singular	Plural
Nom.	*addhā*	*addhā*
Acc.	*addhānaṃ* (often used adverbially for time elapsed)	
Inst.	*addhunā*	
Gen.	*addhuno*	

Rest not used. Two stems, *addhāna-* as well as *addha-*, are used in compounds.

From *muddhan*, " head," we have nominative singular *muddhā* but accusative *muddhaṃ* (the locative singular *muddhani* occurs in a verse in the *Dīgha*). The word may be regarded as poetic or elevated.

Forms from a stem *puman*, " man," following the declension of *addhan*, are exceedingly rare, and the word may be regarded as poetic (it is also inflected according to the *a* declension on the stem *puma-*).

Declension of Nouns in -as

Stems in *as* are inflected as follows :—

manas, " mind " (masc., rarely neut.)

	Singular	
Nom. / Acc.	*mano*	In the plural these nouns follow the masculine (or neuter) *a* declension, on the stem without *s* : *mana-*.
Ins.	*manasā*	
Dat.	*manaso*	
Abl.	*manasā*	
Gen.	*manaso*	
Loc.	*manasi*	

(Stem in compounds : *mano-*.)

Declension of Masculine Nouns in -ū

A few masculine nouns have stems in *ū*. They are immediate derivatives from roots or compounds ending in such derivatives.

Except in the nominative singular and nominative and accusative plural they are inflected like masculines in *ŭ*. From *viññū* (< *vi-(ñ)ñā*, " discern "), " discerning person," we have :—

	Singular	Plural
Nom.	*viññū*	*viññū* (or *viññŭno*)
Acc.	*viññuṃ*	*viññū* (or *viññŭno*)

Bahubbīhi *Compounds* (2)

In a *bahubbīhi* compound the members may refer to the same thing (as in *lohitakkhi puriso*) or to different things (as in *vajirapāṇi yakkho*). All kinds of relations are possible : cf. other kinds of compounds used as *bahubbīhis* or within *bahubbīhis*, as mentioned in the preceding Lesson. As examples of more complex *bahubbīhis*, with three members, we have :—

bhagavā onītapattapāṇi (*onīta* from *o-nī* = " withdrawn ", " removed " ; explained as . . . *onīto pattato pāṇi yena*), "the fortunate one who had removed (his) hand from the bowl " (". . . by whom the hand was removed from the bowl ") (compound equivalent to a passive subordinate clause)

mahāpuriso sīhapubbaddhakāyo (*pubbaddhaṃ* = " front half ", " fore-part ", from *addho*, " half," and could itself be regarded as a compound ; explained as . . . *sīhassa pubbaddhaṃ viya kāyo assa,—viya* = "like "), " a great man whose body (is like) the front half of a lion."

In the latter example we have a comparison (metaphor) expressed in a *bahubbīhi*, other examples of which are :—

bhagavā suvaṇṇavaṇṇo, " the fortunate one whose colour is like gold "

bhagavā brahmassaro, ((*s*)*saro* = " voice "), "the fortunate one whose voice is like God's " (?—or " having the best voice ", " having the supreme voice ").

Aorist Passive Formed Directly from a Root

An aorist passive, having a 3rd person singular only, may be formed directly from a root. The root has the *vuddhi* (> *ā*) lengthening, the augment is prefixed, and the inflection is *-i*. The meaning is the same as that of the ordinary aorist passive (Lesson 9). The form is exceedingly rare and may be regarded as poetic. Since it differs from the ordinary aorist (active) only in having the lengthening of the root vowel it may sometimes be difficult to distinguish between the two forms (a few verbs, e.g. (*k*)*kam*, have this lengthening in the aorist active).

From *tan* (VI), " stretch," we have :—

(3rd sing.) *atāni*, " it was stretched "

From *u*(*d*)-*pad* (III), " arise," " happen," we have, if in fact it belongs here :—

(3rd sing.) *udapādi*, " it was arisen," " it arose "

(Cf. Lesson 11 : in this case the meaning does not tell us whether the form should be regarded as active or passive, and it is often taken as an ordinary active aorist, a merely formal alternative to *uppajji*. Moreover we find from the same root, without augment, *upapādi*, " he transmigrated," " he was reborn " (passive ??) and 1st person *upapādiṃ*, " I was reborn.")

Nouns and Adjectives Compounded with Verbs

A number of nouns and adjectives are sometimes combined with verbs in the same way as prefixes, and take an indeclinable form when so combined. The verbs usually concerned are *kar* and *bhū*, and the meaning is that of the noun/adjective transformed into a verb with more or less idiomatic divergence. We have already met *garu-kar* = " give respect to " (" make heavy ") and *sat-kar* = " entertain " (" make well ", from the weak stem of *sant-*). The adverbial form is often derived by substituting *ī* for a final *a* : *udakī-bhū* = " consist of water ". Besides the past participle *bhūta*, which may be used as a noun, the noun derivative (from *bhū*) *bhāvo*, " nature ", " state of," may be used in the same combination, thus *ekī-bhāvo* = " one-nature ", " unity " (lit. : " only-nature," " oneish-nature.")

Feminine nouns in *i*, inflected like *jāti* :—

aṅguli	finger, toe
anugati	following, imitation
iddhi	power (marvellous)

kasi	cultivation, agriculture
gutti	protection
jāni	confiscation
(ṭ)ṭhiti	duration, persistence
nirutti	language
paññatti	concept
pīti	joy
bhūmi	earth, ground, place
yoni	womb, origin, source
ratti	night
vitti	pleasure
vimutti	release, liberation
sati	self-possession, mindfulness
samāpatti	attainment
sambodhi	enlightenment
sāli	rice

Feminine nouns in *ī*, inflected like *devī* :—

kalyāṇī	a beautiful girl
kumārī	girl, princess (girl of the military-aristocratic class)
gopānasī	(roof) bracket
dāsī	slave-woman, slave-girl
dhātī	nurse
nadī	river
paṭhavī	earth
brāhmaṇī	(priestess) woman of the hereditary priest-class
bhikkhunī	nun
vacī	speech
—*itthī̆*	woman (has both forms)

Feminines of the present participle and of adjectives, inflected like *devī* :—

gacchantī	going
gabbhinī	pregnant
dhammī	doctrinal
mahatī	great
saññinī	sentient (similarly other feminines of possessive adjectives and nouns in *-in*).

Nouns (stems) inflected like *manas* :—

āpas	water
cetas	mind
tejas	heat, energy, potency
divas	day
payas	milk
yasas	reputation
rajas	dust
vayas	age
vāyas	air
siras	head

Adjectives inflected like *bhagavant* :—

cakkhumant	having eyes, having insight, intelligent
mahant	great
vaṇṇavant	beautiful, handsome
vusitavant	having lived (properly), having (truly) lived (as a monk)
satimant	self-possessed, mindful

The feminines are formed by adding *ī* to the weak stem, as *mahatī*, etc., inflected like *devī*.

A masculine noun, nominative singular *candimā* (in compounds *candima-* ; no other cases are used), " moon," is also assigned to this declension by some grammarians.

Vocabulary

Verbs :—

adhi-upa-gam (I)	*ajjhūpagacchati*	join, adhere to
anu-(ñ)ñā (V)	*anujānāti*	allow
abhi-ā-cikkh (I)	*abbhācikkhati*	slander, calumniate
abhi-ruh (I*)	*abhirūhati*	mount, get into, board
ā-(k)kus (I) (to cry out)	*akkosati*	abuse, scold
āṇa	only causative : *āṇāpeti*	order, command
upa-(k)kam (I)	*upakkamati*	attack, fall upon, go into
upa-subh (I)	*upasobhati*	appear beautiful, shine
o-(k)kam (I)	*okkamati*	descend into, arise within

o-dhā (I)	*odahati*	put down (p.p. *ohita*)
o-ruh (I)	*orohati*	descend
(k)khī (III)	*khīyati*	exhaust, waste, perish (p.p. *khīṇa*)
garah (I)	*garahati*	blame (p.p. *garahita*)
chad (VII)	*chādeti*	be pleased
jīr (I)	*jīrati*	become old, age (p.p. *jiṇṇa*)
ni(r)-yā (I)	*niyyāti*	go out to
ni(r)-vā (III)	*nibbāyati*	become cool
(p)pa-(j)jhe (I)	*pajjhāyati*	be consumed with regret
(p)pa-(ñ)ñā	in passive, *paññāyati* = be discerned	
(p)paṭi-ā-gam (I)	*paccāgacchati*	return
(p)paṭi-ā-ni(r)-yā (I)	*paccāniyyāti*	go back, return
pari-(k)khī (III)	*parikkhīyati*	exhaust, eliminate (p.p. *parikkhīṇa*)
pari-bhās (I)	*paribhāsati*	defame, slander
pari-bhuj (II)	*paribhuñjati*	eat, enjoy
pari-vas (I)	*parivasati*	live among
pari-hā	in passive, *parihāyati* = be eliminated, come to an end	
(p)pa-vedh (I)	*pavedhati*	tremble
(p)pa-saṃs (I)	*pasaṃsati*	praise (p.p. *pasattha*)
vi-jan (III)	*vijāyati*	give birth (aorist : *vijāyi*)
saṃ-vaṭṭ (I)	*saṃvaṭṭati*	involve, dissolve
saṃ-tan (VI)	*saṃtanoti*	stretch out, spread out
(s)sar (I)	*sarati*	remember
sā (III)	*sāyati*	taste
sudh (III)	*sujjhati*	become pure

Nouns :—

aññā	knowledge, insight
atipāto	slaying, killing
antalikkhaṃ	sky
antepuraṃ	citadel, palace
andhakāro	darkness, obscurity
apacco	offspring
apuññaṃ	demerit, evil

assādo	tasting, enjoyment
ācāro	conduct
ādānaṃ	taking
ālumpaṃ	bit, piece
itthattaṃ	this world
uyyānaṃ	park
khuddaṃ	honey (of small wild bees)
gaṇikā	courtesan, geisha
gandho	odour
gītaṃ	singing
jano	person, people (collective singular)
jarā	old age
tārakā	star
timisā	darkness
dāyādo	inheritor, heir
dovāriko	porter, doorkeeper
nakkhattaṃ	constellation, esp. lunar mansion
naccaṃ	dancing
navanītaṃ	butter
pacchāyā	shade
paññāsā	fifty
paṭisallānaṃ	retirement, seclusion
pabhā	radiance
paribhāsā	slander
palāpo	nonsense
pādo	foot
pokkharatā	complexion
porāṇaṃ	antiquity, ancient tradition
bandhu masc.	Kinsman, —a name of *brahmā* (= God as father or grandfather of all creatures)
bhāvo	nature, state, status
mattā	measure
māso	month
mukhaṃ	mouth
yobbanaṃ	youth (state of)
raso	taste, piquancy, enjoyment (aesthetic experience, source of aesthetic experience)
rūpaṃ	form, matter

vāditaṃ	instrumental music
vesso	husbandman, farmer, merchant, bourgeois (member of the hereditary agricultural-mercantile class [1])
saṃyojanaṃ	connection, union
saṃvaccharaṃ	year
saṃkhyā (also spelt *saṃkhā*)	enumeration, calculation, denomination, classification

(The idiom *saṅkh(y)aṃ gacchati* means " counts as ", " is conceived of as ", " is considered as ".)

sakkāro	entertainment
sadattho	the true (good) purpose, the true (good) objective (cf. *attho*)
santānakaṃ	film, skin
sappi n.	ghee
samphaṃ	frivolity, chatter
savanaṃ	hearing
sāyaṇho	evening
suddo	helot (member of the servile or working class [1])
subhaṃ	lustre, glory

Adjectives :—

atipātin	slaying, killing
attarūpa	personal (following the Commentary ; *contra CPD* : full, complete)
atthika	aspiring, wishful, desirous
anatīta	not-passing, not escaping
aneḷaka	pure
abhijjhālu (fem. *-unī* ; sometimes masc. *-ū* and plur. *-uno*)	covetous
amanāpa	displeasing

[1] The *vessas* were originally the third, most numerous, and only productive class among the three classes of Āryan society. After their conquests of the 2nd millennium B.C. the Āryans, adopting the ways of civilization (presumably from the Indus people they had conquered), instituted the fourth class, the *suddas*, as a servile and sometimes enslaved class of subjected people serving, working for, the Āryan classes, for example as labourers and artisans. The *vessa* in the *Dīgha Nikāya* may thus be a farmer using *sudda* labourers or a merchant using *sudda* craftsmen.

ātura	afflicted
ādāyin	taking
iddha	powerful
ibbha	domestic
orasa	own (cf. *ura*)
kaṇha	black, dark
-kulīna	by tribe
khudda	small, minor
gilāna	ill
-jacca	by birth
-jātika	of the genus/kind/class/nature
-(ṭ)ṭhāyin	staying, remaining
diṭṭhin	seeing
dukkhin	unhappy
dummana	depressed
padakkhiṇa	dexterous, skilful in, good at (loc.)
parāyana	depending on
palāpin	nonsensical, talking nonsense
pāsādika	lovely
pharusa	harsh, rough
bhogga	bent
madhu	sweet (as neut. noun = " honey ")
manomaya	mental, spiritual (consisting of mind)
muṇḍaka	shaven-headed
Rājagahaka	of Rājagaha
lola	restless, fickle, wanton
vaṅka	crooked
vādin	speaking
vyāpanna	malevolent, violent
saṃvaṭṭanika	involved in, dissolved in
sukka	white, light coloured

Past Participles :—

abhisaṭa (*abhi-sar*)	visited, met
ekodakībhūta (*ekodakī-bhū*)	consisting entirely of water ; as neuter noun = nature/universe consisting only of water
tatta(*tap* I)	hot
vokiṇṇa (*vi-o-kir*)	mixed (with)

Pronoun :—

ubhaya	both

Dependent words :—

-cara (*car*)	living
-ja· (*jan* : cf. Lesson 25)	born (of)
-bhakkha (*bhakkh*)	eating, feeding on

Gerund :—

hitvā (*hā*)	having abandoned

Indeclinables :—

ayye (voc.)	lady !
ettāvatā	so far, to that extent
kadā	when ?
kadā ci	at any time, at some time, ever
karaha ci	at some time
taggha	certainly, assuredly
tv eva (or *t' eva*)	(also = *ti* + *eva* with exceptional junction *i* + *e* > *ve* :) end quote + emphasis (usually marking and stressing a single word or expression, which may be repeated), *that* is its designation ; or simply = " indeed ", " definitely " (i.e. the preceding word is correct, as after *atthi* = " it *is* " : somewhat similar to the use of italics)
dhi(*r*)	fie !, confound (him/it) !
na cirass' eva	soon
puna(*d*)	again
bhiyyoso	still more (so), still greater
bhiyyoso mattāya	to a still greater extent/degree (abl.)
yato	whence, because, since
yatra hi nāma	in as much as (may express wonder, etc.)
yathā kathaṃ	in what way ?
yebhuyyena	mostly, the majority of

santikā (directly) from (at first hand) (with gen.) (abl. of *santikaṃ*, " presence ")
sayaṃ oneself, self

EXERCISE 20

Passages for reading :—

1. atha kho bhikkhave Vipassī kumāro bahunnaṃ vassānaṃ bahunnaṃ vassasatānaṃ bahunnaṃ vassasahassānaṃ accayena sārathiṃ āmantesi : yojehi samma sārathi bhaddāni bhaddāni yānāni, uyyānabhūmiṃ gacchāma bhūmiṃ dassanāyā ti. evaṃ devā ti kho bhikkhave sārathi Vipassissa kumārassa paṭissutvā bhaddāni bhaddāni yānāni yojāpetvā Vipassissa kumārassa paṭivedesi : yuttāni kho te deva bhaddāni bhaddāni yānāni, yassa dāni kālaṃ maññasī ti. atha kho bhikkhave Vipassī kumāro bhaddaṃ yānaṃ abhiruhitvā bhaddehi bhaddehi yānehi uyyānabhūmiṃ niyyāsi. addasā kho bhikkhave Vipassī kumāro uyyānabhūmiṃ niyyanto purisaṃ jiṇṇaṃ gopānasivaṅkaṃ bhoggaṃ daṇḍaparāyanaṃ pavedhamānaṃ gacchantaṃ āturaṃ gatayobbanaṃ. disvā sārathiṃ āmantesi : ayam pana samma sārathi puriso kiṃ kato, kesā pi 'ssa na yathā aññesaṃ, kāyo pi 'ssa na yathā aññesan ti. eso kho deva jiṇṇo nāmā ti. kim pan' eso samma sārathi jiṇṇo nāmā ti. eso kho deva jiṇṇo nāma : na dāni tena ciraṃ jīvitabbaṃ bhavissatī ti. kim pana samma sārathi aham pi jarādhammo jaraṃ anatīto ti. tvañ ca deva mayañ c' amhā sabbe jarādhammā jaraṃ anatītā ti. tena hi samma sārathi alan dān' ajja uyyānabhūmiyā, ito va antepuraṃ paccāniyyāhī ti. evaṃ devā ti kho bhikkhave sārathi Vipassissa kumārassa paṭissutvā tato va antepuraṃ paccāniyyāsi. tatra sudaṃ bhikkhave Vipassī kumāro antepuragato dukkhī dummano pajjhāyati : dhir atthu kira bho jāti nāma, yatra hi nāma jātassa jarā paññāyissatī ti.

2. evam me sutaṃ. ekaṃ samayaṃ bhagavā Sāvatthiyaṃ [1] viharati Pubbārāme. tena kho pana samayena Vāseṭṭha-Bhāradvājā bhikkhūsu parivasanti bhikkhubhāvaṃ ākaṅkhamānā. atha kho bhagavā sāyaṇhasamayaṃ patisallānā vuṭṭhito pāsādā orohitvā pāsādapacchāyāyaṃ abbhokāse

[1] Capital of the kingdom of Kosala.

caṅkamati.[1] addasā kho Vāseṭṭho bhagavantaṃ sāyaṇhasamayaṃ patisallānā vuṭṭhitaṃ pāsādā orohitvā pāsādapacchāyāyaṃ abbhokāse caṅkamantaṃ. disvā Bhāradvājaṃ āmantesi: ayaṃ āvuso Bhāradvāja bhagavā sāyaṇhasamayaṃ patisallānā vuṭṭhito pāsādā orohitvā pāsādapacchāyāyaṃ abbhokāse caṅkamati. āyām' āvuso Bhāradvāja yena bhagavā ten' upasaṃkamissāma. app eva nāma labheyyāma bhagavato santikā dhammiṃ kathaṃ savanāyā ti. evam āvuso ti kho Bhāradvājo Vāseṭṭhassa paccassosi. atha kho Vāseṭṭha-Bhāradvājā yena bhagavā ten' upasaṃkamiṃsu, upasaṃkamitvā bhagavantaṃ abhivādetvā bhagavantaṃ caṅkamantaṃ anucaṅkamiṃsu.[2]

atha kho bhagavā Vāseṭṭhaṃ āmantesi: tumhe khv [3] attha Vāseṭṭhā [4] brāhmaṇajaccā brāhmaṇakulīnā brāhmaṇakulā agārasmā anagāriyaṃ pabbajitā. kacci vo Vāseṭṭhā brāhmaṇā na akkosanti na paribhāsantī ti. taggha no bhante brāhmaṇā akkosanti paribhāsanti attarūpāya paribhāsāya paripuṇṇāya no aparipuṇṇāyā ti. yathākathaṃ pana vo Vāseṭṭhā brāhmaṇā akkosanti paribhāsanti attarūpāya paribhāsāya paripuṇṇāya no aparipuṇṇāyā ti. brāhmaṇā bhante evam āhaṃsu: brāhmaṇo va seṭṭho vaṇṇo, hīno añño vaṇṇo; brāhmaṇo va sukko vaṇṇo kaṇho añño vaṇṇo; brāhmaṇā va sujjhanti no abrāhmaṇā; brāhmaṇā va brahmuno puttā orasā mukhato jātā brahmajā brahmanimmitā brahmadāyādā. te tumhe seṭṭhaṃ vaṇṇaṃ hitvā hīnam attha vaṇṇaṃ ajjhūpagatā, yadidaṃ muṇḍake samaṇake ibbhe kaṇhe bandhupādāpacce ti. evaṃ kho no bhante brāhmaṇā akkosanti . . . ti. taggha vo Vāseṭṭhā brāhmaṇā porāṇaṃ assarantā evam āhaṃsu. dissanti kho pana Vāseṭṭhā brāhmaṇānaṃ brāhmaṇiyo gabbhiniyo pi vijāyamānā pi, te ca brāhmaṇā yonijā va samānā evam āhaṃsu. te brahmānañ c' eva abbhācikkhanti musā ca bhāsanti bahuñ ca apuññaṃ pasavanti. cattāro 'me Vāseṭṭhā vaṇṇā, khattiyā brāhmaṇā vessā suddā. khattiyo pi kho Vāseṭṭhā idh' ekacco pāṇātipātī hoti, adinnādāyī hoti, kāmesu micchācārī hoti, musāvādī hoti, pisuṇāvāco hoti,

[1] " He walks up and down " (see Lesson 29 on this verb), the inflections are the same as those of *kamati* with *caṅ* prefixed.
[2] " they walked up and down with."
[3] *kho* > *khv* before a vowel.
[4] Vocative plural, the second name being understood as included in the first.

pharusāvāco hoti, samphappalāpī hoti, abhijjhālū hoti, vyāpannacitto hoti, micchādiṭṭhī hoti. brāhmaṇo pi kho Vāseṭṭhā. pe. vesso pi. pe. suddo pi. pe. micchādiṭṭhī hoti. khattiyo pi kho Vāseṭṭhā idh' ekacco pāṇātipātā paṭivirato hoti, adinnādānā paṭivirato hoti. pe. suddo pi. pe. sammādiṭṭhī hoti. imesu kho Vāseṭṭhā catūsu vaṇṇesu evam ubhayavokiṇṇesu vattamānesu kaṇhasukkesu dhammesu viññūgarahitesu c' eva viññūpasatthesu ca yad ettha brāhmaṇā evam āhaṃsu : brāhmaṇo va seṭṭho vaṇṇo. pe. brahmadāyādā ti, taṃ tesaṃ viññū nānujānanti.[1] taṃ kissa hetu. imesaṃ hi Vāseṭṭhā catunnaṃ vaṇṇānaṃ yo hoti bhikkhu arahaṃ khīṇāsavo vusitavā katakaraṇīyo ohitabhāro anuppattasadattho parikkhīṇabhavasaṃyojano sammadaññāvimutto,[2] so tesaṃ aggam akkhāyati dhammen' eva no adhammena. dhammo hi Vāseṭṭhā seṭṭho jan' [3] etasmiṃ diṭṭhe c' eva dhamme abhisamparāyañ ca.

hoti kho so Vāseṭṭhā samayo yaṃ kadā ci karaha ci dīghassa addhuno accayena ayaṃ loko saṃvaṭṭati. saṃvaṭṭamāne loke yebhuyyena sattā ābhassarasaṃvaṭṭanikā [4] honti. te tattha honti manomayā pītibhakkhā sayampabhā antalikkhacarā subhaṭṭhāyino ciraṃ dīgham addhānaṃ tiṭṭhanti. hoti kho so Vāseṭṭhā samayo yaṃ kadā ci karaha ci dīghassa addhuno accayena ayaṃ loko vivaṭṭati. vivaṭṭamāne loke yebhuyyena sattā ābhassarakāyā cavitvā itthattaṃ āgacchanti. te ca honti manomayā pītibhakkhā sayampabhā antalikkhacarā subhaṭṭhāyino, ciraṃ dīgham addhānaṃ tiṭṭhanti. ekodakībhūtaṃ kho pana Vāseṭṭhā tena samayena hoti andhakāro andhakāratimisā. na candimasuriyā paññāyanti, na nakkhattāni tārakarūpāni paññāyanti, na rattindivā [5] paññāyanti, na māsaḍḍhamāsā paññāyanti, na utusaṃvaccharā paññāyanti, na itthipumā paññāyanti. sattā sattā tv eva saṅkhyaṃ gacchanti. atha kho tesaṃ Vāseṭṭhā sattānaṃ kadā ci karaha ci dīghassa addhuno accayena rasapaṭhavī udakasmiṃ samatāni. seyyathā pi nāma payaso tattassa nibbāyamānassa upari santānakaṃ hoti, evam eva pāturahosi. sā ahosi vaṇṇasampannā gandhasampannā

[1] *na* + *anu*-.
[2] *sammad* is junction form of *sammā* when a vowel follows.
[3] < *jane* with elision.
[4] *ābhassara*, " the world of radiance."
[5] Irregular nasal in junction of compound.

rasasampannā, seyyathā pi nāma sampannaṃ vā sappi, sampannaṃ vā navanītaṃ evaṃvaṇṇā [1] ahosi ; seyyathā pi nāma khuddaṃ madhu aneḷakaṃ evamassādā ahosi.

atha kho Vāseṭṭhā aññataro satto lolajātiko, ambho kim ev' idaṃ bhavissatī ti, rasapaṭhaviṃ aṅguliyā sāyi. tassa rasapaṭhaviṃ aṅguliyā sāyato acchādesi, taṇhā c' assa okkami. aññatare pi kho Vāseṭṭhā sattā tassa sattassa diṭṭhānugatiṃ āpajjamānā rasapaṭhaviṃ aṅguliyā sāyiṃsu. tesaṃ rasapaṭhaviṃ aṅguliyā sāyataṃ acchādesi, taṇhā ca tesaṃ okkami. atha kho te Vāseṭṭhā sattā rasapaṭhaviṃ hatthehi ālumpakārakaṃ [2] upakkamiṃsu paribhuñjituṃ. yato kho Vāseṭṭhā sattā rasapaṭhaviṃ hatthehi ālumpakārakaṃ upakkamiṃsu paribhuñjituṃ atha tesaṃ sattānaṃ sayampabhā antaradhāyi. sayampabhāya antarahitāya candimasuriyā pāturahesuṃ. candimasuriyesu pātubhūtesu, nakkhattāni tārakarūpāni pāturahesuṃ. nakkhattesu tārakarūpesu pātubhūtesu, rattindivā paññāyiṃsu. rattindivesu paññāyamānesu, māsaḍḍhamāsā paññāyiṃsu. māsaḍḍhamāsesu paññāyamānesu, utusaṃvaccharā paññāyiṃsu. ettāvatā kho Vāseṭṭhā ayaṃ loko puna vivaṭṭo hoti.

Translate into Pali :—

At that time Vesālī [3] (was) powerful and prosperous. The geisha Ambapālī was (*hoti*) beautiful, lovely, endowed with the highest beauty-of-complexion. (She was) skilled in dancing and singing and instrumental music. Visited by (use genitive) aspiring men (she) went (present time) for a night for fifty (*kahāpaṇas*) ; and through her Vesālī appeared (present tense) beautiful in still greater measure (ablative). Then (add *kho*) a burgher of Rājagaha went (aorist) to Vesālī on (ins.) some business. He saw Vesālī powerful and prosperous, and the geisha Ambapālī, and through her Vesālī appearing beautiful in still greater measure. Then (+ *kho*) the burgher returned to Rājagaha. He approached the king, Māgadha Seṇiya Bimbisāra, and having approached he said this to the king : " Vesālī, O king, (is) powerful and prosperous, etc., and through her

[1] *bahubbīhi*, " of such a colour."
[2] Compound used as adverb.
[3] Capital of the Vajjī Republic, which was north of the kingdom of Magadha (the Ganges forming the boundary).

Vesālī appears beautiful in still greater measure. (It would be) good, O king, (if) we too were to establish (optative of causative of *ụ*(*d*)-(*ṭ*)*ṭhā* : *vuṭṭhāpeyy-*) a geisha." "Then (*tena hi*), I say,[1] find out a girl whom you would establish (as) geisha!" Just at that time in Rājagaha there was (*hoti*) a girl named Sālavatī, beautiful, lovely, endowed with the highest beauty-of-complexion. Then the burgher established the girl Sālavatī as geisha. Then Sālavatī soon became skilled in dancing, singing, and instrumental music. Visited by aspiring men she went (present tense) for a night for a hundred. Then Sālavatī soon became pregnant. Then Sālavatī thought: "A pregnant woman (is) displeasing to men. If anyone knows (future) I am pregnant (use direct speech: "Sālavatī (is) pregnant") all my entertainment will be eliminated. What now (if) I were to announce that I am ill (direct speech)?" Then Sālavatī ordered the porter: "Porter, I say, don't let any man enter (*mā* with aorist 3rd person), (he) who asks (about) me you must inform that I am ill." "Yes, lady," assented the porter to Sālavatī the geisha.

LESSON 21

Declension of Feminine Nouns in -u *and* -ū

Feminine nouns and adjectives in *u* and *ū* are declined as follows:—

dhātu, "element"

	Singular	Plural
Nom.	*dhātu*	*dhātuyo*
Voc.	*dhātu*	*dhātuyo*
Acc.	*dhātuṃ*	*dhātuyo*
Ins.	*dhātuyā*	*dhātūhi*
Dat.	*dhātuyā*	*dhātūnaṃ*
Abl.	*dhātuyā*	*dhātūhi*
Gen.	*dhātuyā*	*dhātūnaṃ*
Loc.	*dhātuyā*	*dhātusu*

[1] *bhaṇe* is often used by high personages in speaking to inferiors.

vadhū, " bride "

	Singular	Plural
Nom.	*vadhū*	*vadhuyo*
Voc.	*vadhu*	
Acc.	*vadhuṃ*	
	rest as *dhātu* . . .	

Declension of Present Participles in -ant

The inflection of present participles in *ant* is as follows :—

	Masculine		Feminine
	Singular	Plural	(inflected like *devī*)
Nom.	*gacchaṃ* or *gacchanto*	*gacchantā*	*gacchantī*
Acc.	*gacchantaṃ*	*gacchante*	*gacchantiṃ*
Ins.	*gacchatā* (or *gacchantena*)	*gacchantehi*	*gacchantiyā*
Dat.	*gacchato*	*gacchataṃ*	etc.
Abl.	*gacchatā*	*gacchantehi*	
Gen.	*gacchato* (or *gacchantassa*)	*gacchataṃ*	
Loc.	*gacchati* (rarely *-ante*)	*gacchantesu*	

This differs from the adjectives in *ant* in having the nominative singular in *aṃ*, also in using the strong stem instead of the weak in the feminine.

The present participle may be made negative by the prefix *a-*.

The present participle (*sant*) of *as*, " be," " exist," the inflection of which is regular,[1] has the meanings " real ", " true ", " good ", as an adjective, as well as the simple participial meaning " being ", " existing ". The weak stem *sat* is used in forming compounds, e.g., *sadattho*,[2] " the true (good) purpose " ; *sat-kar* (here used adverbially as prefix), " entertain " (" make well ").

[1] But *sati* is used as fem. loc. sing. as well as masc.
[2] In close junction a final consonant may be voiced when followed by a vowel.

Declension of the Pronoun bhavant

The full declension of the pronoun *bhavant,* " you," " sir," " his honour," is as follows :—

	Masculine		Feminine
	Singular	Plural	
Nom.	*bhavaṃ*	*bhavanto* (or *bhonto*)	*bhotī* (inflected like *devī*)
Acc.	*bhavantaṃ*	*bhavante*	
Ins.	*bhotā*	*bhavantehi*	
Dat.	*bhoto*	*bhavataṃ*	
Abl.	*bhotā*	*bhavantehi*	
Gen.	*bhoto*	*bhavataṃ*	
Loc.	*bhoti*	*bhavantesu*	
Voc.	*bho*	*bhonto*	

The form *bhante* is an indeclinable particle which is used alone as a polite vocative or in association with another vocative or with a word in any other case. Its use is generally restricted to addressing Buddhist monks.

" *Perfect* " *Tense of* ah

Another form of past tense, the so-called perfect (*parokkha*) is extremely rare except for the 3rd persons of the " defective " verb *ah,* " to say," which are favoured in narrative. The meaning is indefinite time—often present (cf. Lesson 24).

	Singular	Plural
3rd person	*āha,* " he said," " he says "	*āhaṃsu* (sometimes *āhu* in verse)

No other forms or tenses from the root *ah* are used.

The perfect tense is distinguished in form by reduplication of the initial part of the root (here *a — ah* > *āh*) and the inflections, particularly the 3rd singular in *a.* Perfect forms from various verbs are occasionally affected in later Pali poetry.

Repetition

In Pali repetition (*āmeṇḍita*) of a word or expression is quite frequent. The meaning may be emphasis (= " very "), as *bhaddāni bhaddāni* (*yānāni*), " very fine (carriages)." Often, particularly with pronouns and indeclinables, the meaning is " distributive " : *yo yo*, " whoever," *yathā yathā*, " in whatever way," " just as," " however " (with answering *tathā tathā*, " so "). Repetition also expresses strong emotion of any kind, in which case a whole phrase may be repeated.

Further examples :—

sīghaṃ sīghaṃ, " very fast "
saṇḍasaṇḍā sāliyo, " rice plants in thick clusters " (compound)
abhikkantaṃ bhante abhikkantaṃ bhante, " very fine indeed, sir ! ", expressing great praise or admiration
aho rasaṃ aho rasaṃ, " ah ! what piquancy ! ", expressing wonder
diṭṭhā bho satta jīvasi diṭṭhā bho satta jīvasi, ". . . it's wonderful to see you alive ! ", expressing happiness
āyāmi āvuso āyāmi āvuso, " I'm coming, sir ! ", expressing assurance
abhikkamatha Vāseṭṭhā abhikkamatha Vāseṭṭhā, " hurry forward, O Vāseṭṭhas ! ", enjoins haste
mā bhavaṃ Soṇadaṇḍo evaṃ avaca mā bhavaṃ Soṇadaṇḍo evaṃ avaca, " let not the honourable Soṇadaṇḍa speak thus ! ", expresses anger or blame
nassa asuci nassa asuci, " perish, vile one ! ", expresses anger, contempt, and disgust
tuvaṃ tuvaṃ, " you, you ! " (in a quarrel), expresses disrespect and contempt (*tuvaṃ* is a form of *tvaṃ*, here presumably emphatic).

Vocabulary

Verbs :—

ā-(g)gah (V)	*aggaṇhāti*	seize
ati-pat causative :	*atipāteti*	slay, kill
ati-man (III)	*atimaññati*	despise

anu-(t)thu (V)	*anutthunāti*	lament, complain
anu-pat (I)	*anupatati*	follow, chase after
abhi-ni(r)-vatt (I)	*abhinibbattati*	be produced
ā-har (I)	*āharati*	bring, fetch (aorist : 3rd sing. *āhāsi*, but 1st plur. *āharāma* ; cf. *addasāma* ; p.p. *āhata*)
ā-hiṇḍ (I) (to wander)	*āhiṇḍati*	wander
upa-jīv (I)	*upajīvati*	live by, live upon
upa-ni-(j)jhe (I)	*upanijjhāyati*	observe, think about
upa-ni(r)-vatt (I)	*upanibbattati*	derive (p.p. *upanibbatta*)
(k)khip (I*)	*khipati*	throw (gerund *khipitvā*)
(k)khī (III)	*khīyati*	means also "become indignant"
nas (III)	*nassati*	perish
ni(r)-vah (I)	*nibbahati*	lead out (passive : *nibbuyhati*)
ni(r)-har (I)	*nīharati*	take out, take away (*irh* > *īh*)
(p)pa-āp (V) (this root is sometimes given as *ăp*)	(cf. *(p)pa-ap(p)* (VI) in Lesson 6) used in the figurative sense of "attain": *pāpuṇāti* (this use is very restricted in Canonical Pali. aorist *pāpuṇi* ; p.p. *patta*)	
(p)pa-(k)khip (I*)	*pakkhipati*	put into
pac (I)	*pacati*	cook, torture, torment
(p)paṭi-vi-ruh (I*)	*paṭivirūhati*	grow again (p.p. *paṭivirūḷha*)
(p)paṭi-sev (I)	*paṭisevati*	indulge in
pari(y)-o-nah (II)	*pariyonandhati*	cover over, envelop
pari-rakkh (I)	*parirakkhati*	guard
(p)pa-har (I)	*paharati*	hit, beat
pus (VII)	*poseti*	rear, look after (p.p. of caus. : *posāpita*)
phand (I)	*phandati*	throb, quiver
bhaṇ (I)	*bhaṇati*	say
rañj (I)	*rañjati*	be excited, be glad, be delighted

vi-han (I)	*vihanati*	distress, trouble
saṃ-ā-pad (III)	*samāpajjati*	attain
saṃ-man (VI) (to consider)	*sammannati* (*mano/manva/manna* by substitution of *va* for *o*)	agree on, elect (p.p. *sammata*)
sikkh (I)	*sikkhati*	train, study, learn (p.p. *sikkhita*)
suc (I)	*socati*	grieve, sorrow
han (I)	*hanati*	kill (caus.: *ghāteti*)

Feminine nouns in *u* :—

dhātu	element
natthu	nose
rajju	rope
hanu	jaw(s)

Feminine noun in *ū* :—

vadhū	bride

Nouns :—

akiriyaṃ	inaction
akkharaṃ	expression
aṭṭhāhaṃ	eight days
atimāno	arrogance, contempt
apadānaṃ	reaping, harvest
abhinibbatti (fem.)	production, origin
ahi (masc.)	snake
ahicchattako	mushroom, toadstool
āgamo	coming
ācariyo	teacher
āhāro	food (in the most general sense, sometimes figurative), gathering
upaṭṭhānaṃ	serving, attending on, audience
ekāgāriko	burglar, burglary
kaṇo	the fine red powder between the grain and husk of rice (Childers)

kattarasuppo	old winnowing-basket
kalambukā	a creeper : (*Convolvulus repens* ?)
kāko	crow
kharattaṃ	roughness
khalaṃ	threshing (floor)
khuraṃ	razor
gabbho	embryo
gomayaṃ	cow dung
catuhaṃ	four days
chatta(ka)ṃ	sunshade
jīvikā	livelihood
taṇḍulaṃ	rice grain, husked rice
tīhaṃ	three days
thuso	husk, chaff
damo	taming, restraint
dārako	boy
dāro (sometimes -*ā*)	wife
dvīhaṃ	two days
nāmaṃ	name
nidānaṃ	cause, source, origin
nillopo	plunder
paṃsu (masc.)	dust, mud
pati (masc.)	lord
pappaṭako	fungus
paripantho	ambush
paripāko	ripening
pariḷāho	burning, lust
pātarāso	breakfast, morning meal
pātavyatā	indulgence
badālatā	creeper
bhesajjaṃ	medicine, drug
maṃsaṃ	flesh, meat
mariyādā	boundary
mahājano	the people
mahābhūto	element
māno	pride, conceit
rājakulaṃ	royal court
liṅgaṃ	characteristic

leḍḍu (masc.)	clod
viññutā	discernment, discretion
vejjo	doctor, physician
vevaṇṇatā	discoloration
saṃyamo	self-control, abstinence
saṃkārakūṭo	rubbish heap
saccavajjaṃ	speaking the truth, truthfulness
saṇḍo	cluster
sandhi (masc.)	junction, joint, breach
sannidhi (masc.)	store
sāmaññaṃ	state of being a wanderer/ascetic/philosopher, profession of asceticism, etc. (cf. *samaṇo*)
sāyamāso	evening meal
sārāgo	passion
sippaṃ	craft, trade, profession
seṭṭhi (fem. ?)	ash

Adjectives :—

akaṭṭha	uncultivated, unploughed
akaṇa	without the red coating which lies underneath the husk
aggañña	knowing the beginning, primeval, original
ativela	excessive
athusa	without husk
aparisesa	without remainder, complete, absolute
abhirūpa	handsome
alasa	lazy
asuci	impure, dirty, vile
dubbaṇṇa	discoloured, ugly
pakka	ripe
pariyanta	bordered, encircled
pāka	ripe, ripened
pāmokkha	foremost
methuna	sexual
-yāniya	leading to
sadisa	like, of such sort
sandiṭṭhika	visible

Past Participles :—

lūna (*lū* (V))	reaped, mown
samāhita (*saṃ-ā-dhā*)	concentrated
samparikiṇṇa (*saṃ-pari-kir*)	surrounded by, covered with

Gerunds :—

anvāya (*anu-i*)	following, in consequence of (acc.)
netvā (*nī*)	having led

Indeclinables :—

agge	since (*tad agge* = since then)
ativelaṃ	too long, excessively
anupubbena	in due course, in succession
aho	ah ! : expresses surprise (approving) and delight
itthaṃ	thus, in this way
kattha	where ?
je (enclitic)	you ! (form of address by a master/mistress to a slave woman ; preceded by *handa, kiñ*, etc., or by *gaccha*)
ñeva	= *eva* (junction form sometimes used after *ṃ*)
pāto	in the morning
saki(*d*) (*eva*) (or *sakiṃ*)	once
samantā	on all sides, all round
sāyaṃ	in the evening
(*s*)*su*	even, isn't it ? (or merely emphatic)
seyyathīdaṃ	as, to wit
handa je	you there ! (cf. *je* above)

EXERCISE 21

Passages for reading :—

1. evaṃ vutte bhante Pūraṇo Kassapo [1] maṃ etad avoca :

[1] Died *c.* 503 B.C. A *samaṇo*, one of the leaders of the Ājīvaka movement, which was amalgamated in 489 B.C. and was for a time probably the most important non-orthodox sect. Their fundamental doctrine was that of fatalism (*niyati*) as propounded by their supreme leader Makkhali Gosālo. It will be seen that the doctrine expounded here can be harmonized with this. For Gosāla's doctrine see Exercise 28 (English into Pali).

karato kho mahārāja kārayato chindato chedāpayato pacato pācayato socayato kilamayato phandato phandāpayato pāṇaṃ atipātāpayato adinnaṃ ādiyato sandhiṃ chindato nillopaṃ harato ekāgārikaṃ karoto paripanthe tiṭṭhato paradāraṃ gacchato musā bhaṇato, karoto na karīyati pāpaṃ. khurapariyantena ce pi cakkena yo imissā paṭhaviyā pāṇe ekamaṃsakhalaṃ ekamaṃsapuñjaṃ kareyya, n'atthi tatonidānaṃ pāpaṃ, n'atthi pāpassa āgamo. dakkhiṇañ ce pi Gaṅgātīraṃ[1] āgaccheyya hananto ghātento chindanto chedāpento pacanto pācento, n' atthi tatonidānaṃ pāpaṃ, n' atthi pāpassa āgamo. uttarañ ce pi Gaṅgātīraṃ gaccheyya dadanto dāpento yajanto yajāpento, n' atthi tatonidānaṃ puññaṃ, n' atthi puññassa āgamo. dānena damena saṃyamena saccavajjena n' atthi puññaṃ, n' atthi puññassa āgamo ti. itthaṃ kho me bhante Pūraṇo Kassapo sandiṭṭhikaṃ sāmaññaphalaṃ puṭṭho samāno akiriyaṃ vyākāsi.

2. atha kho te Vāseṭṭhā sattā rasapaṭhaviṃ paribhuñjantā tambhakkhā tadāhārā ciraṃ dīgham addhānaṃ aṭṭhaṃsu. yathā yathā kho te Vāseṭṭhā sattā rasapaṭhaviṃ paribhuñjantā tambhakkhā tadāhārā ciraṃ dīgham addhānaṃ aṭṭhaṃsu, tathā tathā tesaṃ sattānaṃ kharattañ c' eva kāyasmiṃ okkami, vaṇṇavevaṇṇatā ca paññāyittha.[2] ek' idaṃ sattā vaṇṇavanto honti, ek' idaṃ dubbaṇṇā. tattha ye te sattā vaṇṇavanto, te dubbaṇṇe satte atimaññanti. mayam etehi vaṇṇavantatarā, amheh' ete dubbaṇṇatarā ti. tesaṃ vaṇṇātimānapaccayā mānātimānajātikānaṃ rasapaṭhavī antaradhāyi. rasāya paṭhaviyā antarahitāya sannipatiṃsu, sannipatitvā anutthuniṃsu, aho rasaṃ, aho rasan ti. tad etarahi pi manussā kiñ cid eva sādhu rasaṃ labhitvā evam āhaṃsu, aho rasaṃ, aho rasan ti. tad eva porāṇaṃ aggaññaṃ akkharaṃ anupatanti, na tv ev' assa atthaṃ ājānanti.

atha kho tesaṃ Vāseṭṭhā sattānaṃ rasāya paṭhaviyā antarahitāya bhūmipappaṭako pāturahosi. seyyathā pi nāma ahicchattako, evam evaṃ pāturahosi. so ahosi vaṇṇasampanno gandhasampanno rasasampanno. seyyathā pi nāma sampannaṃ

[1] *Gaṅgā*, the River Ganges.
[2] Aorist passive with " middle " inflection (cf. Lesson 28), " it was discerned."

vā sappi sampannaṃ vā navanītaṃ, evaṃvaṇṇo ahosi. seyyathā pi nāma khuddaṃ madhu aneḷakaṃ, evamassādo ahosi. atha kho te Vāseṭṭhā sattā bhūmipappaṭakaṃ upakkamiṃsu paribhuñjituṃ. te taṃ paribhuñjantā tambhakkhā tadāhārā ciraṃ dīgham addhānaṃ aṭṭhaṃsu. yathā yathā kho te Vāseṭṭhā sattā bhūmipappaṭakaṃ paribhuñjantā tambhakkhā tadāhārā ciraṃ dīgham addhānaṃ aṭṭhaṃsu, tathā tathā tesaṃ sattānaṃ bhiyyoso mattāya kharattañ c'eva kāyasmiṃ okkami, vaṇṇavevaṇṇatā ca paññāyittha. ek' idaṃ sattā vaṇṇavanto honti, ek' idaṃ sattā dubbaṇṇā. tattha ye te sattā vaṇṇavanto, te dubbaṇṇe satte atimaññanti. mayam etehi vaṇṇavantatarā, amheh' ete dubbaṇṇatarā ti. tesaṃ vaṇṇātimānapaccayā mānātimānajātikānaṃ bhūmipappaṭako antaradhāyi. bhūmipappaṭake antarahite badālatā pāturahosi. seyyathā pi nāma kalambukā, evam evaṃ pāturahosi. sā ahosi vaṇṇasampannā gandhasampannā rasasampannā. seyyathā pi nāma sampannaṃ vā sappi sampannaṃ vā navanītaṃ, evaṃvaṇṇā ahosi. seyyathā pi nāma khuddaṃ madhu aneḷakaṃ, evamassādā ahosi.

atha kho te Vāseṭṭhā sattā badālataṃ upakkamiṃsu paribhuñjituṃ. te tam paribhuñjantā tambhakkhā tadāhārā ciraṃ dīgham addhānaṃ aṭṭhaṃsu. yathā yathā kho te Vāseṭṭhā sattā badālataṃ paribhuñjantā tambhakkhā tadāhārā. pe. badālatāya antarahitāya sannipatiṃsu, sannipatitvā anutthuniṃsu, ahu [1] vata no, ahāyi vata no badālatā ti. tad etarahi pi manussā kena cid eva dukkhadhammena phuṭṭhā evam āhaṃsu : ahu vata no, ahāyi vata no ti. tad eva porāṇaṃ aggaññaṃ akkharaṃ anupatanti, na tv ev' assa atthaṃ ājānanti.

atha kho tesaṃ Vāseṭṭhā sattānaṃ badālatāya antarahitāya akaṭṭhapāko sāli pāturahosi, akaṇo athuso sugandho taṇḍulapphalo. yan taṃ sāyaṃ sāyamāsāya āharanti, pāto taṃ hoti pakkaṃ paṭivirūḷhaṃ. yan taṃ pāto pātarāsāya āharanti sāyaṃ taṃ hoti pakkaṃ paṭivirūḷhaṃ, nāpadānaṃ paññāyati. atha kho te Vāseṭṭhā sattā akaṭṭhapākaṃ sāliṃ paribhuñjantā tambhakkhā tadāhārā. pe. vaṇṇavevaṇṇatā ca paññāyittha. itthiyā ca itthiliṅgaṃ pāturahosi, purisassa purisaliṅgaṃ. itthī ca sudaṃ ativelaṃ purisaṃ upanijjhāyati,

[1] " it was " : " root aorist " (cf. Lesson 30).

puriso ca itthiṃ. tesaṃ ativelaṃ aññam aññaṃ upanijjhāyataṃ sārāgo udapādi, pariḷāho kāyasmiṃ okkami. te pariḷāhapaccayā methunaṃ dhammaṃ paṭisevimsu. ye kho pana te Vāseṭṭhā tena samayena sattā passanti methunaṃ dhammaṃ paṭisevante, aññe paṃsuṃ khipanti, aññe seṭṭhiṃ khipanti, aññe gomayaṃ khipanti. nassa asuci, nassa asucī ti. kathaṃ hi nāma satto sattassa evarūpaṃ karissatī ti. tad etarahi pi manussā ekaccesu janapadesu vadhuyā nibbuyhamānāya aññe paṃsuṃ khipanti, aññe seṭṭhiṃ khipanti, aññe gomayaṃ khipanti. tad eva porāṇaṃ aggaññaṃ akkharaṃ anupatanti, na tv ev' assa atthaṃ ājānanti.

adhammasammataṃ kho pana Vāseṭṭhā tena samayena hoti, tad etarahi dhammasammataṃ. ye kho pana Vāseṭṭhā tena samayena sattā methunaṃ dhammaṃ paṭisevanti, te māsam pi dvemāsam pi na labhanti gāmaṃ vā nigamaṃ vā pavisituṃ. yato kho Vāseṭṭhā te sattā tasmiṃ samaye asaddhamme ativelaṃ pātavyataṃ āpajjiṃsu, atha agārāni upakkamiṃsu kātuṃ tass' eva asaddhammassa paṭicchādanatthaṃ.

atha kho Vāseṭṭhā aññatarassa sattassa alasajātikassa etad ahosi : ambho kim evāhaṃ vihaññāmi sāliṃ āharanto sāyaṃ sāyamāsāya pāto pātarāsāya. yan nūnāhaṃ sāliṃ āhareyyaṃ sakid eva sāyapātarāsāyā ti. atha kho so Vāseṭṭhā satto sāliṃ āhāsi sakid eva sāyapātarāsāya. atha kho Vāseṭṭhā aññataro satto yena so satto ten' upasaṃkami, upasaṃkamitvā taṃ sattaṃ etad avoca : ehi bho satta sālāhāraṃ gamissāmā ti. alaṃ bho satta āhato me sāli sakid eva sāyapātarāsāyā ti. atha kho so Vāseṭṭhā satto tassa sattassa diṭṭhānugatiṃ āpajjamāno sāliṃ āhāsi sakid eva dvīhāya, evam pi kira bho sādhū ti. atha kho Vāseṭṭhā aññataro satto yena so satto ten' upasaṃkami, upasaṃkamitvā taṃ sattaṃ etad avoca : ehi bho satta sālāhāraṃ gamissāmā ti. alaṃ bho satta āhato me sāli sakid eva dvīhāyā ti. atha kho so Vāseṭṭhā satto tassa sattassa diṭṭhānugatiṃ āpajjamāno sāliṃ āhāsi sakid eva catuhāya, evam pi kira bho sādhū ti. atha kho Vāseṭṭhā aññataro satto yena so satto ten' upasaṃkami, upasaṃkamitvā taṃ sattaṃ etad avoca : ehi bho satta sālāhāraṃ gamissāmā ti. alaṃ bho satta āhato me sāli sakid eva catuhāyā ti. atha kho so Vāseṭṭhā satto tassa sattassa diṭṭhānugatiṃ āpajjamāno sāliṃ āhāsi sakid eva aṭṭhāhāya, evam pi kira bho sādhū ti. yato kho te

Vāseṭṭhā sattā sannidhikārakaṃ sāliṃ upakkamiṃsu paribhuñjituṃ atha kaṇo pi taṇḍulaṃ pariyonandhi, thuso pi taṇḍulaṃ pariyonandhi, lūnam pi na ppaṭivirūḷhaṃ apadānaṃ paññāyittha, saṇḍasaṇḍā sāliyo aṭṭhaṃsu.

atha kho te Vāseṭṭhā sattā sannipatiṃsu sannipatitvā anutthuniṃsu pāpakā vata bho dhammā sattesu pātubhūtā, mayaṃ hi pubbe manomayā ahumhā pītibhakkhā sayampabhā antalikkhacarā subhaṭṭhāyino, ciraṃ dīgham addhānaṃ aṭṭhamhā. tesaṃ no amhākaṃ kadāci karahaci dīghassa addhuno accayena rasapaṭhavī udakasmiṃ samatāni. sā ahosi vaṇṇasampannā gandhasampannā rasasampannā. te mayaṃ rasapaṭhaviṃ hatthehi ālumpakārakaṃ upakkamimhā paribhuñjituṃ, tesaṃ no rasapaṭhaviṃ hatthehi ālumpakārakaṃ upakkamataṃ paribhuñjituṃ sayampabhā antaradhāyi. sayampabhāya antarahitāya, candimasuriyā pāturahesum. candimasuriyesu pātubhūtesu nakkhattāni tārakarūpāni pāturahesuṃ. nakkhattesu tārakarūpesu pātubhūtesu rattiṃdivā paññāyiṃsu. rattiṃdivesu paññāyamānesu māsaḍḍhamāsā paññāyiṃsu. māsaḍḍhamāsesu paññāyamānesu utusaṃvaccharā paññāyiṃsu. te mayaṃ rasapaṭhaviṃ paribhuñjantā tambhakkhā tadāhārā ciraṃ dīgham addhānaṃ aṭṭhamhā, tesaṃ no pāpakānaṃ ñeva akusalānaṃ dhammānaṃ pātubhāvā rasapaṭhavī antaradhāyi. rasapaṭhaviyā antarahitāya bhūmipappaṭako pāturahosi. so ahosi vaṇṇasampanno gandhasampanno rasasampanno. te mayaṃ bhūmipappaṭakaṃ upakkamimhā paribhuñjituṃ. te mayaṃ taṃ paribhuñjantā tambhakkhā tadāhārā ciraṃ dīgham addhānaṃ aṭṭhamhā. tesaṃ no pāpakānaṃ ñeva akusalānaṃ dhammānaṃ pātubhāvā bhūmipappaṭako antaradhāyi. bhūmipappaṭake antarahite badālatā pāturahosi. sā ahosi vaṇṇasampannā gandhasampannā rasasampannā. te mayaṃ badālataṃ upakkamimhā paribhuñjituṃ. te mayaṃ taṃ paribhuñjantā tambhakkhā tadāhārā ciraṃ dīgham addhānaṃ aṭṭhamhā. tesaṃ no pāpakānaṃ ñeva akusalānaṃ dhammānaṃ pātubhāvā badālatā antaradhāyi. badālatāya antarahitāya akaṭṭhapāko sāli pāturahosi, akaṇo athuso suddho sugandho taṇḍulapphalo. yan taṃ sāyaṃ sāyamāsāya āharāma pāto taṃ hoti pakkaṃ paṭivirūḷhaṃ. yan taṃ pāto pātarāsāya āharāma, sāyan taṃ hoti pakkaṃ paṭivirūḷhaṃ nāpadānaṃ paññāyittha. te mayaṃ akaṭṭhapākaṃ sāliṃ paribhuñjantā tambhakkhā tadāhārā ciraṃ dīgham addhānaṃ aṭṭhamhā. tesaṃ no pāpakānaṃ ñeva akusalānaṃ dhammānaṃ pātubhāvā kaṇo pi taṇḍulam pariyonandhi, thuso pi taṇḍulam pariyonandhi, lūnam pi na paṭivirūḷhaṃ, apadānaṃ paññāyittha, saṇḍasaṇḍā sāliyo ṭhitā. yan nūna mayaṃ sāliṃ vibhajeyyāma, mariyādaṃ ṭhapeyyāmā ti. atha kho te Vāseṭṭhā sattā sāliṃ vibhajiṃsu, mariyādaṃ ṭhapesuṃ. atha kho Vāseṭṭhā aññataro satto lolajātiko sakaṃ bhāgaṃ parirakkhanto aññataraṃ bhāgaṃ adinnaṃ ādiyitvā paribhuñji. tam enaṃ aggahesuṃ, gahetvā etad avocuṃ : pāpakaṃ vata bho satta karosi, yatra hi nāma sakaṃ bhāgaṃ parirakkhanto aññataraṃ bhāgaṃ adinnaṃ ādiyitvā paribhuñjasi. mā ssu bho satta puna pi evarūpam akāsī ti. evaṃ bho ti kho Vāseṭṭhā so satto tesaṃ sattānaṃ paccassosi. dutiyam pi kho Vāseṭṭhā so satto . . . pe . . . tatiyam pi kho Vāseṭṭhā so satto sakaṃ bhāgaṃ parirakkhanto aññataraṃ bhāgaṃ adinnaṃ ādiyitvā paribhuñji. tam enaṃ aggahesuṃ, aggahetvā etad avocuṃ : pāpakaṃ vata bho satta karosi, yatra hi nāma sakaṃ bhāgaṃ parirakkhanto aññataraṃ bhāgaṃ adinnaṃ ādiyitvā paribhuñjasi. mā ssu bho satta puna pi evarūpam akāsī ti. aññe pāṇinā pahariṃsu, aññe leḍḍunā pahariṃsu, aññe daṇḍena pahariṃsu. tad agge kho pana Vāseṭṭhā adinnādānaṃ paññāyati, garahā paññāyati, musāvādo paññāyati, daṇḍādānaṃ paññāyati.

atha kho te Vāseṭṭhā sattā sannipatiṃsu, sannipatitvā anutthuniṃsu, pāpakā vata bho dhammā sattesu pātubhūtā, yatra hi nāma adinnādānaṃ paññāyissati, garahā paññāyissati, musāvādo paññāyissati, daṇḍādānaṃ paññāyissati, yan nūna mayaṃ ekaṃ sattaṃ sammanneyyāma. so no sammākhīyitabbaṃ khīyeyya, sammāgarahitabbaṃ garaheyya, sammāpabbājetabbaṃ pabbājeyya. mayaṃ pan' assa sālīnaṃ bhāgaṃ anuppadassāmā [1] ti. atha kho te Vāseṭṭhā sattā yo nesaṃ satto abhirūpataro ca dassanīyataro ca pāsādikataro ca mahesakkhataro ca, taṃ sattaṃ upasaṃkamitvā etad avocuṃ : ehi bho satta, sammākhīyitabbaṃ khīya, sammāgarahitabbaṃ garaha, sammāpabbājetabbaṃ pabbājehi. mayaṃ pana te sālīnaṃ bhāgaṃ anuppadassāmā ti. evaṃ bho ti kho Vāseṭṭhā so satto tesaṃ sattānaṃ paṭissutvā, sammākhīyitabbaṃ khīyi, sammā-

[1] Future of *-dā*.

garahitabbaṃ garahi, sammāpabbājetabbaṃ pabbājesi. te pan' assa sālīnaṃ bhāgaṃ anuppadaṃsu.

mahājanasammato ti kho Vāseṭṭhā mahāsammato, mahāsammato tv eva paṭhamaṃ akkharaṃ upanibbattaṃ. khettānaṃ patī ti kho Vāseṭṭhā khattiyo, khattiyo tv eva dutiyaṃ akkharaṃ upanibbattaṃ. dhammena pare rañjetī ti kho Vāseṭṭhā rājā, rājā tv eva tatiyaṃ akkharaṃ upanibbattaṃ. iti kho Vāseṭṭhā evam etassa khattiyamaṇḍalassa porāṇena aggaññena akkharena abhinibbatti ahosi. tesaṃ ñeva sattānaṃ anaññesaṃ sadisānaṃ ñeva no asadisānaṃ dhammen' eva no adhammena. dhammo hi Vāseṭṭhā seṭṭho jan' etasmiṃ diṭṭhe c' eva dhamme abhisamparāyañ ca.

3. bhūtapubbaṃ imasmiṃ yeva bhikkhusaṃghe aññatarassa bhikkhuno evaṃ cetaso parivitakko udapādi : kattha nu kho ime cattāro mahābhūtā aparisesā nirujjhanti, seyyathīdaṃ paṭhavīdhātu āpodhātu tejodhātu vāyodhātū ti. atha kho so bhikkhu tathārūpaṃ samādhiṃ samāpajji yathā samāhite citte devayāniyo maggo pāturahosi.

atha kho so bhikkhu yena Cātummahārājikā devā ten' upasaṃkami, upasaṃkamitvā Cātummahārājike deve etad avoca : kattha nu kho āvuso ime cattāro mahābhūtā aparisesā nirujjhanti, seyyathīdaṃ paṭhavīdhātu āpodhātu tejodhātu vāyodhātū ti. evaṃ vutte Cātummahārājikā devā taṃ bhikkhuṃ etad avocuṃ : mayam pi kho bhikkhu na jānāma yatth' ime cattāro mahābhūtā aparisesā nirujjhanti, seyyathīdaṃ paṭhavīdhātu āpodhātu, tejodhātu, vāyodhātu. atthi kho bhikkhu cattāro Mahārājā amhehi abhikkantatarā ca paṇītatarā ca. te kho evaṃ jāneyyuṃ yatth' ime cattāro mahābhūtā aparisesā nirujjhanti, seyyathīdaṃ paṭhavīdhātu āpodhātu tejodhātu vāyodhātū ti.

atha kho so bhikkhu yena cattāro Mahārājā ten' upasaṃkami, upasaṃkamitvā cattāro Mahārāje etad avoca : kattha nu kho āvuso ime cattāro mahābhūtā aparisesā nirujjhanti, seyyathīdaṃ paṭhavīdhātu āpodhātu tejodhātu vāyodhatū ti. evaṃ vutte cattāro Mahārājā taṃ bhikkhuṃ etad avocuṃ : mayam pi kho bhikkhu na jānāma yatth' ime cattāro mahābhūtā aparisesā nirujjhanti, seyyathīdaṃ paṭhavīdhātu āpodhātu tejodhātu vāyodhātu. atthi kho bhikkhu Tāvatiṃsā nāma devā amhehi abhikkantatarā ca paṇītatarā ca. te kho evaṃ jāneyyuṃ yatth' ime cattāro mahābhūtā aparisesā nirujjhantī ti.

Translate into Pali :—

Then, following the ripening of that embryo, the geisha Sālavatī gave birth to a son (acc.). Then Sālavatī ordered a slave girl : " You there ! After (express this simply by using gerunds) putting this boy into an old winnowing-basket (loc.) (and) taking him out throw (him) away on a rubbish heap." . . . At that time a son of the king (*rājakumāro*) named Abhaya, going to the king's-audience just at the (right) time (dat.), saw that boy surrounded by crows. Having seen he asked people : " What (is) that, I say !, surrounded by crows ? " " A boy, O king (title *devo* used in addressing a prince of the blood)." " (Does he) live, I say !(?) " " (He) lives, O king." " Now ! I say ! having led that boy to our citadel give (him) to nurses to rear." . . . They made the name " Jīvaka " for him (thinking) : " (he) lives " ; they made the name " Komārabhacca " (thinking) : " (He) was caused to be reared by the prince." Then Jīvaka Komārabhacca soon attained (see Vocabulary above, (*p*)*pa-āp*) discretion . . . Then he thought this : " These royal courts (are) not easy to live upon without-a-profession (ins. : 'with-a-non-profession'). Supposing I were to learn (opt.) a profession ? " Now at that time there dwelt (present tense) in Takkasilā [1] a doctor who-was-the-foremost-of-(all)-regions. Then Jīvaka Komārabhacca went away to Takkasilā, in due course approached Takkasilā (and) that doctor, (and) having approached said this to that doctor : " O teacher, I wish to learn the profession " . . . Then Jīvaka grasped (present tense) much, grasped lightly . . . When seven (*satta*, inflect as *pañca*) years had passed Jīvaka thought this : " I indeed grasp much . . . the end of this profession is not discerned, when will the end of this profession be discerned ? " Then Jīvaka approached that doctor . . . " Now ! I say, Jīvaka,

[1] The capital of Gandhāra, in North-West India, which in ancient times had a famous university attracting students from all parts of India. The earliest known school of philosophers had flourished here in pre-Buddhist times (*c.* 800 B.C. : Uddālaka, the founder of the school, lived probably in the 9th century B.C.), and the great school of linguistics which culminated with Pāṇini (*c.* 350 B.C.) was also situated here.

taking a gardener's-trowel (*khaṇittī*), wandering for a league on all sides of Takkasilā, whatever non-medicine you may see, bring that." " Yes, teacher "... wandering (he) saw no non-medicine at all . . . ". . . I saw no non-medicine at all." " You have learned (p.p. + *asi*), I say, O Jīvaka, sufficient for your livelihood ! "

LESSON 22

Declension of attan, brahman, san, yuvan, *and* kamman

The noun (masc.) and pronoun *attan*, " self," " soul," is inflected as follows :—

	Singular	Plural
Nom. }	*attā* }	*attāno*
Voc. }		
Acc.	*attānaṃ* }	
Ins.	*attanā*	*attehi* } (following the *a* declension)
Dat.	*attano*	*attānaṃ* }
Abl.	*attanā*	*attehi* }
Gen.	*attano*	*attānaṃ* }
Loc.	*attani*	(does not seem to be used ; according to the grammarians it would be *attanesu*)

The declension of the masculine noun *brahman*, " God," is as follows :—

	Singular	Plural
Nom.	*brahmā*	
Voc.	*brahme*	
Acc.	*brahmānaṃ*	(if used, the plural will be inflected like *attan*)
Ins.	*brahmunā*	
Dat.	*brahmuno*	
Abl.	*brahmunā*	
Gen.	*brahmuno*	
Loc.	*brahmani*	

Two other masculine nouns in *an*, *san*, " dog " and *yuvan*, " youth," have the nominative singular forms *sā* and *yuvā*. No other forms of this declension occur. In place of *san* a stem *suṇa-* is used, inflected according to the *a* declension.

Some neuter nouns have (rarely) inflections using the *an* stem alongside those of the *a* declension. From the stem *kamman*, " action," we have :—

	Singular	Plural
Nom. / Acc.	*kamma*	*kammāni*
Ins.	*kammunā* and *kammanā*	(in the plural only the *a* forms occur)
Dat.	*kammuno*	
Abl.	*kammunā* and *kammanā*	
Gen.	*kammuno*	
Loc.	*kammani*	

The Pronoun attan

The word *attan* has two main uses. As a reflexive (or, in the genitive, possessive) pronoun it means " himself ", " oneself," " myself ", " yourself " (also " his own ", " her own ", " my own ", etc., as " possessive adjective "), etc., in various contexts (it may refer to the body or the mind). As a noun it means the " soul " as usually conceived in the Brahmanical religion (i.e. the essential self, supposed to underlie the individual consciousness, or the animating principle called also *jīva*), a conception which the Buddhists rejected as not corresponding to any reality.

Examples of the use of *attan* as pronoun :—

attānaṃ sukheti[1] *pīṇeti*, " he enjoys and pleases (*pīṇ* (I) caus.) himself "

sā attānañ c' eva jīvitaṃ . . ., " she . . . (will destroy) her own life and . . . " (here *attānañ* is used in apposition to *jīvitaṃ*)

attanā ca jīvāhi . . ., " you must make a living yourself and . . . "

[1] Denominative verb : Lesson 28.

sucibhūtena attanā, "being pure himself" (the instrumental has usually a simple reflexive-intransitive sense : the agent acts, or is, himself, by himself)

attanā attānaṃ vyākareyya, "he would explain himself (ins.) to himself (acc.)" (i.e. know himself)

jānāsi . . . attano gatiṃ, " do you know . . . your own destiny ? "

jānāmi . . . attano gatiṃ, " I do know . . . my own destiny " (the genitive *attano* may usually be translated " own ", " his own ", and is more emphatic than *tassa* or *assa* = simply " his " in similar contexts)

attano samasamaṃ, " equal to myself," " my equal "

ime . . . nīvaraṇe pahīne attani, " (he sees) . . . these . . . obstacles eliminated in himself "

attahitāya, " for his own advantage " (*tappurisa*)

attā pi 'ssa agutto arakkhito hoti . . ., " he himself is unprotected, unsafe (and his wife, etc.) " (nominative with *assa* = " his self ")

The singular may be used for the plural, sometimes with *eka* = " one " in close combination :—

ye . . . samaṇabrāhmaṇā . . . ekam attānaṃ damenti, " priests and philosophers who . . . restrain the self " (" oneself ")

The plural is rarely used.

Reflexive or Possessive Pronouns

With *attan* we may compare the other reflexive or possessive pronouns or adjectives, *sayaṃ*, *sāmaṃ*, *saka*, and *sa*.

We have met *saka*, " own," already ; it is used in all genders like an adjective (agreeing with the word expressing the thing possessed, not with the possessor) :—

yena sako ārāmo tena pāyāsi, " he set out for his own park "

vihaññati . . . sakena cittena, " he is distressed . . . by his own thought/mind "

sake nivesane, " in his own house "

sakasmiṃ satthe, " in their own caravan "

Idiom : *sakan te mahārāja* (in offering submission) = " (let all be) yours, great king ! ", " (let it be) your own . . . "

sa is inflected according to the pronominal declension (Lesson 17) in all genders, but is very rarely used except in verse. The meaning is the same as *saka*. It is found in some compounds in prose: *samata* = " his own opinion ", *sahattha* = " one's own hand ".

sayaṃ and *sāmaṃ* are indeclinables meaning " oneself ", " self ", " myself ", etc. They are synonymous, except that *sāmaṃ* is more usual and *sayaṃ* more poetic and used only in elevated speech :—

sāmaṃ diṭṭhaṃ, " seen by oneself," " seen by myself "
sayaṃ abhiññā, " having ascertained himself " (*abhiññā* = *abhiññāya* with elision of the final syllable)
sayaṃ is used in compounds: *sayaṃpabha* = " self-luminous " ; *sayaṃkata* = " self-made ", " self-evolved," " spontaneous " (e.g. the universe or the soul may be so conceived ; the opposite is *paraṃkata* = " made by another ")

Bahubbīhi *Compounds* (3) (*including Negative Prefixes*)

In the formation of *bahubbīhi* compounds a suffix *-ka* or *-ika* (cf. Lesson 25) is sometimes added to the final member. It may be regarded in these cases as converting a noun into an adjective. It is added more frequently to stems in *i* and *u* than to those in *a*, and there is in fact a tendency for compounds used as adjectives to appear in the *a* declension, nevertheless *-ika* is substituted for *-a* also in a number of *bahubbīhis*. Stems in *-an* and *-ar* (see next Lesson) usually appear as simply *-a* in compounds (in any position) or are replaced by *-ika*, but those in *-ar* occasionally change to *-u* (+ *-ka*) ; those in *-as* generally appear as *-o* within a compound but as *-a* at the end of a compound. Feminine stems in *-ā* are often changed to *-a*.

Examples :—

akālika (*dhamma*) (a doctrine) " which is timeless "
evaṃgatika (*diṭṭhiṭṭhāna*) (from *gati*, " destiny ") (a case/class of opinion) " which has such and such a destiny " (i.e. the holding of which leads one to a certain destiny)
attasaraṇa (*bhikkhu*) (a monk) " having himself as refuge ", " independent "

atītasatthuka (*pāvacana*) (from *satthar*, " teacher ") (the teaching is) " having lost its teacher "

The formation of *bahubbīhi* compounds may be very free, depending only on there being a familiar collocation of a pair (or group) of words :—

antānantika (*samaṇabrāhmaṇa*) " finite or infinite-er " (who maintains that the universe is finite or infinite)
ehipassika (*dhamma*) (from the finite verbs *ehi* and *passa*) (a doctrine) " which is verifiable ", " which is demonstrable " (" come-and-see ! ")
aññadatthudasa (*brahman*) (*aññadatthu*, regarded as an indeclinable, is *añña* + *atthu*, with *d* as junction consonant between two vowels, and means " absolutely ") (God) " seeing absolutely ", " seeing everything "
nevasaññināsaññivāda (*samaṇabrāhmaṇa*) " arguing that it is neither sentient nor insentient " ; " belonging to the school of neither-sentient-nor-insentient " (with reference to the state of the " soul " after death)

The possessive suffix *-in* also is sometimes added to *bahubbīhis*. Some examples will be found in the second reading passage in Exercise 20.

Words formed with the prefixes *su-* and *du*(*r*)- (Lesson 15) may be regarded as compounds. If they function as nouns they will be *kammadhārayas*, if as adjectives, *bahubbīhis*. Thus *sucaritaṃ*, " good conduct," and *duccaritaṃ*, " bad conduct," are *kammadhārayas* ; the following are *bahubbīhis* :—

duddasa (*dhamma*), (a doctrine) " hard to see "
duranubodha (*dhamma*), (a doctrine) " hard to understand "
sukata (*kamma*), (an action) "well done ", " proper to do " (written also *sukaṭa*)
susannaddha (*bhāra*), (a load) " well tied up "

Indeclinables may be used as the first members of *bahubbīhi* compounds :—

itthannāma (*samaṇa*), " thus named "
evaṃvimutta (*bhagavant*), (a fortunate one) " freed in such and such a way "
evaṃgotta (*samaṇa*), " of such and such a clan "

tathārūpa (*cetosamādhi*), (a concentration of the mind) " of such a kind " (fem. : *tathārūpī*)
sayaṃpabha (*satta*), (a being) " self-luminous "

It may be noted here that certain prefixes or prefixed words may serve in place of *a*- to form a negative compound : *ni*(*r*)-, *vi*-, *apagata*- (*apa-gam*, " go away "), *vigata*- (*vi-gam*, " be expended "), *vīta*- (*vi-i*, " vanish "). These may express departure, loss, etc., but sometimes they express mere negation or absence, " without," and are synonymous with *a*- :—

nippītika (*sukha*), (happiness) " free from joy " (i.e. calm)
viraja (*dhammacakkhu*), (the eye of doctrine) " free from dust "
apagatakāḷaka (*vattha*), (a garment) " free from stains " (*kāḷa* = " black ")
vigatakathaṃkatha (*putta*), " free from doubt "
vītamala (*dhammacakkhu*), " without dust ", " clear " (*malaṃ* = " dirt ")

With *a*- prefixed these compounds express strong affirmation (by double negation) : *ahīnindriya* (*attan*) = (a soul) " having every faculty " (" not lacking any faculty ").

Various complex *bahubbīhis* :—

susukkadāṭha (*kumāra*), (a boy) "having very white teeth " (*bahubbīhi* : *susukka* within another *bahubbīhi*)
anaññasaraṇa (*bhikkhu*), (a monk) " not depending on another for refuge "
ākāsānañcāyatanūpaga (*attan*), (a soul) " which attains the sphere of infinite space "
sabbapāṇabhūtahitānukampin (*bhikkhu*), (a monk) " compassionate for the welfare of all living beings " (*pāṇabhūta* is a *kammadhāraya*, *sabba*- is another ; *sabba . . . hita* is a *tappurisa*)

Comparison (simile) may be expressed in a *bahubbīhi* by its ending with a word meaning " type ", " kind ", " form "—several of which may be used as synonyms for " like ".[1] The

[1] Without such a word we have a metaphorical compound as illustrated in Lesson 20.

commonest of these is *-rūpa*, " form " (cf. the compounds with indeclinables above). E.g. :—

vālavedhirūpa (*samaṇabrāhmaṇa*), " like a shooter (*vedhin*) of wild beasts (*vālo*) (i.e. his opponents in debate) "

Vocabulary

Verbs :—

anu-car (I)	*anucarati*	follow, practice
abhi-vad (I)	*abhivadati*	proclaim
ā-cikkh (I)	*ācikkhati*	call, describe
u(d)-chid (III)	*ucchijjati*	Passive : be annihilated
parā-mas (I) (the prefix *parā* means " on ", " on to ")	*parāmasati*	hold on to, be attached to (p.p. *parāmaṭṭha*)
pari-car (I)	caus : *paricāreti* =	enjoy oneself
vi-o-bhid (II)	*vobhindati*	shoot
vi-nas (III)	*vinassati*	perish utterly
saṃ-sar (I)	*saṃsarati*	transmigrate (circulate indefinitely)
sacchi-kar (VI)	*sacchikaroti*	perceive, observe, experience, examine
saṃ-dhāv (I)	*sandhāvati*	transmigrate (pass on)
samaṅgī-bhū (I)	*samaṅgībhavati*	supply with, provide with
saṃ-ati-(k)kam (I)	*samatikkamati*	pass beyond, transcend
saṃ-anu-(g)gah (V)	caus : *samanuggāheti* =	ask for reasons, cross-examine
saṃ-anu-bhās (I)	*samanubhāsati*	criticize, refute
saṃ-anu-yuj (II)	*samanuyuñjati*	take up, cross-question
saṃ-pāy (I) (to succeed)	*sampāyati*	maintain one's position, defend one's thesis

Nouns :—

atthagamo	setting, extinction
adhivutti (fem.)	expression, description

anabhirati (fem.)	discontent, loneliness
anubodho	understanding
anuyogo	practice, examination
antarāyo	obstacle, danger, plague
aparanto	the future, the end, a future or final state
appamādo	diligence, care
abhibhū (masc.)	overlord, conqueror
amarā	perpetuity
avacaro	scope
ākāro	feature, peculiarity
ākiñcaññaṃ	nothingness
āghatanaṃ	death
ātappo	energy (purifying ascetic energy)
ādīnavo	disadvantage
ānañcaṃ	infinity
ābhogo	enjoyment
āyatanaṃ	sphere
ucchedo	annihilation
uddeso	synopsis, summary, summarized description
upāyāso	misery, despair
upekkhā	equanimity, detachment (also spelt *upekhā*)
uppādo	occurrence, arising, production
ubbilāvitattaṃ	elation, exultation
ekattaṃ	unity
ekodibhāvo	singleness, concentration
esikaṃ	pillar
kappo	arrangement, order, rule, aeon
kabaḷiṅkāro	solid matter, solid food
(k)khayo	exhaustion
gati (fem.)	future career, destiny, future course
cavanaṃ	passing away
chandas	will
takko	deduction
diṭṭhi (fem.)	opinion, theory
domanassaṃ	depression, melancholy
doso	aversion, anger
nānattaṃ	diversity

nibbuti (fem.) extinguishing, calming, liberating (from *ni*(*r*)-*vā* (I))
nibbusitattā unsettlement, uneasiness
nivāso life, existence
nissaraṇaṃ liberation
paccaṅgaṃ part
pajānanā understanding
paṭigho repulsion, reacting
paṭibhānaṃ intuition, inspiration
paṇidhi (masc.) aspiration, determination
paṇḍito wise man
padaṃ word
padhānaṃ exertion
parijeguccho disgust
paritassanā longing
paridevo lamentation, grief
pavādo debate
pahānaṃ abandoning
pārisuddhi (fem.) purity
pubbanto origin
bhayaṃ (means also) fear
bhavyo being, future being
manasikāro attention
mandattaṃ dullness, ineptitude
momūhattaṃ extreme stupidity
rāgo passion, desire
rogo illness
vasin master, authority
vālo wild animal
vikkhepo confusion, equivocation
vighāto remorse
vicāro cogitation, pondering
vitakko reasoning
vināso destruction
vibhavo non-existence
vimāno palace, mansion (only of divine beings, in the sky)
virāgo dispassion
vivaṭṭaṃ evolution

viveko	separation, seclusion, discrimination
vūpasamo	calming
vedhin	shooter, archer
saṃvaṭṭaṃ	dissolution, involution
sattattaṃ	existence
samatikkamo	passing beyond, transcending
sampasādanaṃ	serenity
sambhavo	origin, production
sassati (fem.)	eternal thing, eternity
soko	grief, sorrow
somanassaṃ	joy, elation

Adjectives :—

ajjhatta	inner
adhicca	spontaneous, causeless
anudiṭṭhin	contemplating, theorizing
anta	finite
antavant	finite
apariyanta	unlimited
appamāṇa	immeasurable
appesakkha	inferior
arūpin	formless, immaterial
asañña	insentient
-upaga	going to
upe(k)khaka	detached
ekaka	alone
ekanta	extreme
esikaṭṭhāyin	firm as a pillar
opapātika	transmigrating
oḷārika	coarse, gross, material
kūṭaṭṭha (or *kūta-*)	immovable as a peak
gambhīra	profound
takkin	deducing (as masc. noun = deducer, logician)
-dasa	seeing
nipuṇa	subtle
paccatta	individual, personal, independent
paṭisaṃvedin	feeling, experiencing
paritta	small, restricted

pariyāhata	deduced
parivaṭuma	limited, circumscribed
manda	slow, dull, inept
momūha	extremely stupid
yathābhucca	real, proper
rūpin	formed, material
vañjha	barren, sterile
vasavattin	wielding power
vīmaṃsin	investigating (as masc. noun = investigator, exegete, metaphysician)
sata	self-possessed, mindful
sant	existing, true, good
sama	even, equal to, up to, like
sampajāna	conscious
sukhin	happy
suñña	empty

Past participles :—

anabhibhūta (*abhi-bhū*)	unconquered
patta ((*p*)*pa-āp* (V))	attained (fig.)
pariṇata (*pari-nam* (I))	changed, developed
vicārita (*vi-car* (I) caus.)	excogitated, pondered
vitakkita (*vi-takk*)	reasoned
vidita (*vid* (II))	found, known
vihita (*vi-dhā*)	arranged
samappita (*saṃ-app* (VII), to fix in, to apply to)	presented with
samucchinna (*saṃ-u*(*d*)*-chid* (III))	utterly annihilated
samuppanna (*saṃ-u*(*d*)*-pad* (III))	originated

Pronoun :—

ekacca	(means also) some thing(s)

Numerals :—

aṭṭha	eight (inflected like *pañca*)
aṭṭhādasa	eighteen (inflected like *pañca*)

catucattārīsā	forty-four (feminine noun inflected like *kathā* in the singular)
cattārīsā	forty (feminine noun inflected like *kathā*)
dasa	ten (inflected like *pañca*)
satta	seven (inflected like *pañca*)
soḷasa	sixteen (inflected like *pañca*)

Indeclinables :—

aññathā	otherwise
aññadatthu	absolutely, universally
anupādā	without attachment, through non-attachment
amutra	there, yonder
uttari	beyond, further, more
tayidaṃ	with reference to this
tiriyaṃ	horizontally
bahiddhā	outside, apart
yathābhūtaṃ	as it really is, in its true nature
samaṃ	equally, like
sassatisamaṃ	eternally

Gerunds :—

ārabbha (*ā-rabh* (I) begin, start)	with reference to, about (acc.)
viditvā (*vid* (II))	having found, having known
vivicca (*vi-vic* (VII))	having become separated from (cf. Lesson 14 on inverted construction of this gerund with the ablative)

EXERCISE 22

Passage for reading :—

atthi bhikkhave aññ' eva dhammā gambhīrā duddasā duranubodhā santā paṇītā atakkāvacarā nipuṇā paṇḍitavedanīyā, ye tathāgato sayaṃ abhiññā [1] sacchikatvā pavedeti, yehi tathāgatassa yathābhuccaṃ vaṇṇaṃ sammā vadamānā vadeyyuṃ.

[1] *abhiññā* = *abhiññāya*, usually taken as gerund (formally it could also be the instrumental of a feminine noun *abhiññā*, "insight"). [Cf. Wackernagel: *Altindische Grammatik* I, §241 (*b*).]

katame ca pana te bhikkhave dhammā gambhīrā duddasā duranubodhā santā paṇītā atakkāvacarā nipuṇā paṇḍitavedanīyā, ye tathāgato sayaṃ abhiññā sacchikatvā pavedeti, yehi tathāgatassa yathābhuccaṃ vaṇṇaṃ sammā vadamānā vadeyyuṃ.

santi bhikkhave eke samaṇabrāhmaṇā pubbantakappikā pubbantānudiṭṭhino, pubbantaṃ ārabbha anekavihitāni adhivuttipadāni abhivadanti aṭṭhādasahi vatthūhi. te ca bhonto samaṇabrāhmaṇā kim āgamma kim ārabbha pubbantakappikā pubbantānudiṭṭhino pubbantaṃ ārabbha anekavihitāni adhivuttipadāni abhivadanti aṭṭhādasahi vatthūhi.

santi bhikkhave eke samaṇabrāhmaṇā sassatavādā, sassataṃ attānañ ca lokañ ca paññāpenti catuhi vatthūhi. te ca bhonto samaṇabrāhmaṇā kim āgamma kim ārabbha sassatavādā sassataṃ attānañ ca lokañ ca paññāpenti catuhi vatthūhi.

idha bhikkhave ekacco samaṇo vā brāhmaṇo vā ātappam anvāya padhānam anvāya anuyogam anvāya appamādam anvāya sammāmanasikāram anvāya tathārūpaṃ cetosamādhiṃ phusati yathā samāhite citte anekavihitaṃ pubbe nivāsaṃ anussarati — seyyathīdaṃ ekam pi jātiṃ dve pi jātiyo . . . pañca pi jātiyo . . . jātisatam pi jātisahassam pi jātisatasahassam pi anekāni pi jātisatāni anekāni pi jātisahassāni anekāni pi jātisatasahassāni. amutr' āsiṃ evaṃnāmo evaṃgotto evaṃvaṇṇo evamāhāro evaṃsukhadukkhapaṭisaṃvedī evamāyupariyanto. so tato cuto amutra upapādiṃ. tatrā[1] p' āsiṃ evaṃnāmo evaṃgotto evaṃvaṇṇo evamāhāro evaṃsukhadukkhapaṭisaṃvedī evamāyupariyanto. so tato cuto idhūpapanno ti iti sākāraṃ sauddesaṃ anekavihitaṃ pubbe nivāsaṃ anussarati. so evam āha : sassato attā ca loko ca vañjho kūṭaṭṭho esikaṭṭhāyiṭṭhito, te ca sattā sandhāvanti saṃsaranti cavanti upapajjanti, atthi tv eva sassatisamaṃ. taṃ kissa hetu. ahaṃ hi ātappam anvāya . . . pubbe nivāsaṃ anussarāmi. iminā p' āhaṃ etaṃ jānāmi : yathā sassato attā ca loko ca vañjho kūṭaṭṭho esikaṭṭhāyiṭṭhito, te ca sattā sandhāvanti saṃsaranti cavanti upapajjanti, atthi tv eva sassatisaman ti.

idaṃ bhikkhave paṭhamaṃ ṭhānaṃ yam āgamma yam ārabbha ekacce samaṇabrāhmaṇā sassatavādā sassataṃ attānañ ca lokañ ca paññāpenti.

[1] *a* is often lengthened before *pi*.

dutiye ca bhonto samaṇabrāhmaṇā kim ārabbha kim āgamma sassatavādā sassataṃ attānañ ca lokañ ca paññāpenti.

idha bhikkhave ekacco samaṇo vā brāhmaṇo vā ātappam anvāya . . . pubbe nivāsaṃ anussarati — seyyathīdaṃ ekam pi saṃvaṭṭavivaṭṭaṃ dve pi saṃvaṭṭavivaṭṭāni . . . cattāri pi saṃvaṭṭavivaṭṭāni pañca pi saṃvaṭṭavivaṭṭāni dasa pi saṃvaṭṭavivaṭṭāni. amutrāsiṃ evaṃ nāmo . . . anussarāmi. iminā p' āhaṃ etaṃ jānāmi : yathā sassato attā ca loko ca vañjho kūṭaṭṭho esikaṭṭhāyiṭṭhito, te ca sattā sandhāvanti saṃsaranti cavanti upapajjanti, atthi tv eva sassatisaman ti.

idaṃ bhikkhave dutiyaṃ ṭhānaṃ yam āgamma yam ārabbha eke samaṇabrāhmaṇā sassatavādā sassataṃ attānañ ca lokañ ca paññāpenti.

tatiye ca . . . cattārīsam pi saṃvaṭṭavivaṭṭāni . . . paññāpenti.

catutthe ca bhonto samaṇabrāhmaṇā kim āgamma kim ārabbha sassatavādā sassataṃ attānañ ca lokañ ca paññāpenti.

idha bhikkhave ekacco samaṇo vā brāhmaṇo vā takkī hoti vīmaṃsī. so takkapariyāhataṃ vīmaṃsānucaritaṃ sayaṃpaṭibhānaṃ evam āha : sassato attā ca loko ca vañjho kūṭaṭṭho esikaṭṭhāyiṭṭhito, te ca sattā sandhāvanti saṃsaranti cavanti upapajjanti, atthi tv eva sassatisaman ti.

idaṃ bhikkhave catutthaṃ ṭhānaṃ yam āgamma yam ārabbha eke samaṇabrāhmaṇā sassatavādā sassataṃ attānañ ca lokañ ca paññāpenti.

ime kho te bhikkhave samaṇabrāhmaṇā sassatavādā sassataṃ attānañ ca lokañ ca paññāpenti catuhi vatthūhi. ye hi ke ci, bhikkhave, samaṇā vā brāhmaṇā vā sassatavādā sassataṃ attānañ ca lokañ ca paññāpenti, sabbe te imeh' eva catuhi vatthūhi etesaṃ vā aññatarena, n' atthi ito bahiddhā.

tayidaṃ bhikkhave tathāgato pajānāti : ime diṭṭhiṭṭhānā evaṃgahitā evaṃparāmaṭṭhā evaṃgatikā bhavissanti evamabhisamparāyā ti. tañ ca tathāgato pajānāti, tato ca uttaritaraṃ pajānāti, tañ ca pajānanaṃ na parāmasati, aparāmasato c' assa paccattaṃ yeva nibbuti viditā, vedanānaṃ samudayañ ca atthagamañ ca assādañ ca ādīnavañ ca nissaraṇañ ca yathābhūtaṃ viditvā anupādā vimutto, bhikkhave, tathāgato.

ime kho te bhikkhave dhammā gambhīrā duddasā duranubodhā santā paṇītā atakkāvacarā nipuṇā paṇḍitavedanīyā ye tathāgato sayaṃ abhiññā sacchikatvā pavedeti, yehi tathāgatassa yathābhuccaṃ vaṇṇaṃ sammā vadamānā vadeyyuṃ.

santi bhikkhave, eke samaṇabrāhmaṇā ekaccasassatikā ekaccaasassatikā, ekaccaṃ sassataṃ ekaccaṃ asassataṃ attānañ ca lokañ ca paññāpenti catuhi vatthūhi. te ca bhonto samaṇabrāhmaṇā kim āgamma kim ārabbha ekaccasassatikā ekaccaasassatikā ekaccaṃ sassataṃ ekaccaṃ asassataṃ attānañ ca lokañ ca paññāpenti catuhi vatthūhi.

hoti kho so, bhikkhave, samayo yaṃ kadā ci karaha ci dīghassa addhuno accayena ayaṃ loko saṃvaṭṭati. saṃvaṭṭamāne loke yebhuyyena sattā ābhassarasaṃvaṭṭanikā honti. te tattha honti manomayā pītibhakkhā sayaṃpabhā antalikkhacarā subhaṭṭhāyino, ciraṃ dīghaṃ addhānaṃ tiṭṭhanti.

hoti kho so, bhikkhave, samayo yaṃ kadā ci karaha ci dīghassa addhuno accayena ayaṃ loko vivaṭṭati. vivaṭṭamāne loke suññaṃ brahmavimānaṃ pātubhavati. ath' aññataro satto āyukkhayā vā puññakkhayā vā ābhassarakāyā cavitvā suññaṃ brahmavimānaṃ upapajjati. so tattha hoti manomayo pītibhakkho sayaṃpabho antalikkhacaro subhaṭṭhāyī, ciraṃ dīghaṃ addhānaṃ tiṭṭhati.

tassa tattha ekakassa dīgharattaṃ nibbusitattā anabhirati paritassanā uppajjati: aho vata aññe pi sattā itthattaṃ āgaccheyyun ti. atha aññatare pi sattā āyukkhayā vā puññakkhayā vā ābhassarakāyā cavitvā brahmavimānaṃ upapajjanti tassa sattassa sahavyataṃ. te pi tattha honti manomayā pītibhakkhā sayaṃpabhā antalikkhacarā subhaṭṭhāyino, ciraṃ dīghaṃ addhānaṃ tiṭṭhanti.

tatra, bhikkhave, yo so satto paṭhamaṃ upapanno tassa evaṃ hoti: aham asmi brahmā mahābrahmā abhibhū anabhibhūto aññadatthudaso vasavattī issaro kattā [1] nimmātā [1] seṭṭho sañjitā [1] vasī pitā [1] bhūtabhavyānaṃ. mayā ime sattā nimmitā. taṃ kissa hetu. mamaṃ hi pubbe etad ahosi: aho vata aññe pi sattā itthattaṃ āgaccheyyun ti. iti mamañ ca manopaṇidhi, ime ca sattā itthattaṃ āgatā ti. ye pi te sattā pacchā upapannā tesam pi evaṃ hoti: ayaṃ kho bhavaṃ brahmā mahābrahmā abhibhū anabhibhūto aññadatthudaso vasavattī issaro kattā

[1] These four words are nominative singular masculines of stems in *ar*, see next Lesson; *kattā* = "maker", *nimmātā* = "creator", *sañjitā* = "ordainer", *pitā* = "father".

nimmātā seṭṭho sañjitā vasī pitā bhūtabhavyānaṃ. iminā mayaṃ bhotā brahmunā nimmitā. taṃ kissa hetu. imaṃ mayaṃ hi addasāma idha paṭhamaṃ upapannaṃ, mayaṃ pana amhā pacchā upapannā ti.

tatra, bhikkhave, yo so satto paṭhamaṃ upapanno so dīghāyukataro ca hoti vaṇṇavantataro ca mahesakkhataro ca. ye pana te sattā pacchā upapannā te appāyukatarā ca honti dubbaṇṇatarā ca appesakkhatarā ca. ṭhānaṃ kho pan' etaṃ, bhikkhave, vijjati yaṃ aññataro satto tamhā kāyā cavitvā itthattaṃ āgacchati. itthattaṃ āgato samāno agārasmā anagāriyaṃ pabbajati. agārasmā anagāriyaṃ pabbajito samāno ātappam anvāya padhānam anvāya anuyogam anvāya appamādam anvāya sammāmanasikāram anvāya tathārūpaṃ cetosamādhiṃ phusati yathā samāhite citte taṃ pubbe nivāsaṃ anussarati, tato paraṃ nānussarati. so evam āha : yo kho so bhavaṃ brahmā mahābrahmā abhibhū anabhibhūto aññadatthudaso vasavattī issaro kattā nimmātā seṭṭho sañjitā vasī pitā bhūtabhavyānaṃ yena mayaṃ bhotā brahmunā nimmitā, so nicco dhuvo sassato avipariṇāmadhammo sassatisamaṃ tath' eva ṭhassati.[1] ye pana mayaṃ ahumha tena brahmunā nimmitā te mayaṃ aniccā addhuvā appāyukā cavanadhammā itthattaṃ āgatā ti.

idaṃ, bhikkhave, paṭhamaṃ ṭhānaṃ yam āgamma yam ārabbha eke samaṇabrāhmaṇā ekaccasassatikā ekaccaasassatikā ekaccaṃ sassataṃ ekaccaṃ asassataṃ attānañ ca lokañ ca paññāpenti . . .

santi, bhikkhave, eke samaṇabrāhmaṇā antānantikā, antānantaṃ lokassa paññāpenti catuhi vatthūhi. te ca bhonto samaṇabrāhmaṇā kim āgamma kim ārabbha antānantikā antānantaṃ lokaṃ paññāpenti catuhi vatthūhi.

idha, bhikkhave, ekacco samaṇo vā brāhmaṇo vā ātappam anvāya padhānam anvāya anuyogam anvāya appamādam anvāya sammāmanasikāram anvāya tathārupaṃ cetosamādhiṃ phusati yathā samāhite citte antasaññī lokasmiṃ viharati. so evam āha : antavā ayaṃ loko parivaṭumo. taṃ kissa hetu. ahaṃ hi ātappam anvāya . . . pe . . . tathārūpaṃ cetosamādhiṃ phusāmi yathā samāhite citte antasaññī lokasmiṃ viharāmi.

[1] Future of (*ṭ*)*ṭhā* (Lesson 24).

imināpāhaṃ etaṃ jānāmi: yathā antavā ayaṃ loko parivaṭumo ti.

idaṃ, bhikkhave, paṭhamaṃ ṭhānaṃ yam āgamma yam ārabbha eke samaṇabrāhmaṇā antānantikā antānantaṃ lokassa paññāpenti.

dutiye ca bhonto samaṇabrāhmaṇā kim āgamma kim ārabbha antānantikā antānantaṃ lokassa paññāpenti.

idha, bhikkhave, ekacco samaṇo vā brāhmaṇo vā ātappam anvāya padhānam anvāya anuyogam anvaya appamādam anvāya sammāmanasikāram anvāya tathārūpaṃ cetosamādhiṃ phusati yathā samāhite citte anantasaññī lokasmiṃ viharati. so evam āha: ananto ayaṃ loko apariyanto. ye te samaṇabrāhmaṇā evam āhaṃsu: antavā ayaṃ loko parivaṭumo ti tesaṃ musā. ananto ayaṃ loko apariyanto. taṃ kissa hetu. ahaṃ hi ātappam anvāya . . . pe . . . tathārūpaṃ cetosamādhiṃ phusāmi yathā samāhite citte anantasaññī lokasmiṃ viharāmi. imināpāhaṃ etaṃ jānāmi: yathā ananto ayaṃ loko apariyanto ti.

idaṃ, bhikkhave, dutiyaṃ ṭhānaṃ yam āgamma yam ārabbha eke samaṇabrāhmaṇā antānantikā antānantaṃ lokassa paññāpenti.

tatiye ca bhonto samaṇabrāhmaṇā kim āgamma kim ārabbha antānantikā antānantaṃ lokassa paññāpenti.

idha, bhikkhave, ekacco samaṇo vā brāhmaṇo vā ātappam anvāya padhānam anvāya anuyogam anvāya appamādam anvāya sammāmanasikāram anvāya tathārūpaṃ cetosamādhiṃ phusati yathā samāhite citte uddhamadho antasaññī lokasmiṃ viharati, tiriyaṃ anantasaññī. so evam āha: antavā ca ayaṃ loko ananto ca. ye te samaṇabrāhmaṇā evam āhaṃsu: antavā ayaṃ loko parivaṭumo ti tesaṃ musā. ye pi te samaṇabrāhmaṇā evam āhaṃsu: ananto ayaṃ loko apariyanto ti tesam pi musā. antavā ca ayaṃ loko ananto ca. taṃ kissa hetu. ahaṃ hi ātappam anvāya . . . pe . . . tathā rūpaṃ cetosamādhiṃ phusāmi yathā samāhite citte uddhamadho antasaññī lokasmiṃ viharāmi, tiriyaṃ anantasaññī. imināpāhaṃ etaṃ jānāmi: yathā antavā ca ayaṃ loko ananto cā ti.

idaṃ bhikkhave, tatiyaṃ ṭhānaṃ yam āgamma yam ārabbha eke samaṇabrāhmaṇā antānantikā antānantaṃ lokassa paññāpenti.

catutthe ca bhonto samaṇabrāhmaṇā kim āgamma kim ārabbha antānantikā antānantaṃ lokassa paññāpenti.

idha, bhikkhave, ekacco samaṇo vā brāhmaṇo vā takkī hoti vīmaṃsī. so takkapariyāhataṃ vīmaṃsānucaritaṃ sayaṃpaṭibhānaṃ evam āha : n' evāyaṃ loko antavā na panānanto. ye te samaṇabrāhmaṇā evam āhaṃsu : antavā ayaṃ loko parivaṭumo ti tesaṃ musā. ye pi te samaṇabrāhmaṇā evam āhaṃsu : ananto ayaṃ loko apariyanto ti tesam pi musā. ye pi te samaṇabrāhmaṇā evam āhaṃsu : antavā ca ayaṃ loko ananto cā ti tesam pi musā. n' evāyaṃ loko antavā na panānanto ti.

idaṃ, bhikkhave, catutthaṃ ṭhānaṃ yam āgamma yam ārabbha eke samaṇabrāhmaṇā antānantikā antānantaṃ lokassa paññāpenti . . .

santi, bhikkhave, eke samaṇabrāhmaṇā amarāvikkhepikā, tattha tattha pañhaṃ puṭṭhā samānā vācāvikkhepaṃ āpajjanti amarāvikkhepaṃ catuhi vatthūhi. te ca bhonto samaṇabrāhmaṇā kim āgamma kim ārabbha amarāvikkhepikā tattha tattha pañhaṃ puṭṭhā samānā vācāvikkhepaṃ āpajjanti amarāvikkhepaṃ catuhi vatthūhi.

idha, bhikkhave, ekacco samaṇo vā brāhmaṇo vā idaṃ kusalan ti yathābhūtaṃ na ppajānāti, idaṃ akusalan ti yathābhūtaṃ na ppajānāti. tassa evaṃ hoti : ahaṃ kho idaṃ kusalan ti yathābhūtaṃ na ppajānāmi, idaṃ akusalan ti yathābhūtaṃ na ppajānāmi. ahañ c' eva kho pana idaṃ kusalan ti yathābhūtaṃ appajānanto, idaṃ akusalan ti yathābhūtaṃ appajānanto, idaṃ kusalan ti vā vyākareyyaṃ idaṃ akusalan ti vā vyākareyyaṃ, tattha me assa chando vā rāgo vā doso vā paṭigho vā. yattha me assa chando vā rāgo vā doso vā paṭigho vā taṃ mam' assa musā. yaṃ mam' assa musā so mam' assa vighāto. yo mam' assa vighāto so mam' assa antarāyo ti. iti so musāvādabhayā musāvādaparijegucchā n' ev' idaṃ kusalan ti vyākaroti, na pana idaṃ akusalan ti vyākaroti, tattha tattha pañhaṃ puṭṭho samāno vācāvikkhepaṃ āpajjati amarāvikkhepaṃ : evam pi me no. tathā ti pi me no. aññathā ti pi me no. no ti pi me no. no no ti pi me no ti.

idaṃ, bhikkhave, paṭhamaṃ ṭhānaṃ yam āgamma yam ārabbha eke samaṇabrāhmaṇā amarāvikkhepikā tattha tattha pañhaṃ puṭṭhā samānā vācāvikkhepaṃ āpajjanti amarāvikkhepaṃ.

dutiye ca . . . upādānabhayā . . .

tatiye ca . . . ahañ c' eva kho pana idaṃ kusalan ti yathābhūtaṃ appajānanto, idaṃ akusalan ti yathābhūtaṃ appajānanto, idaṃ kusalan ti vā vyākareyyaṃ idaṃ akusalan ti vā vyākareyyaṃ — santi hi kho pana samaṇabrāhmaṇā paṇḍitā nipuṇā kataparappavādā vālavedhirūpā vobhindantā maññe caranti paññāgatena diṭṭhigatāni — te maṃ tattha samanuyuñjeyyuṃ samanuggāheyyuṃ samanubhāseyyuṃ. ye maṃ tattha samanuyuñjeyyuṃ samanuggāheyyuṃ samanubhāseyyuṃ tesāhaṃ na sampāyeyyaṃ. yesāhaṃ na sampāyeyyaṃ so mam' assa vighāto. yo mam' assa vighāto so mam' assa antarāyo ti. iti so anuyogabhayā anuyogaparijegucchā n' ev' idaṃ kusalan ti vyākaroti, na pan' idaṃ akusalan ti vyākaroti, tattha tattha pañhaṃ puṭṭho samāno vācāvikkhepaṃ āpajjati amarāvikkhepaṃ : evam pi me no. tathā ti pi me no. aññathā ti pi me no. no ti pi me no. no no ti pi me no ti.

idaṃ, bhikkhave, tatiyaṃ ṭhānaṃ yaṃ āgamma yam ārabbha eke samaṇabrāhmaṇā amarāvikkhepikā tattha tattha pañhaṃ puṭṭhā samānā vācāvikkhepaṃ āpajjanti amarāvikkhepaṃ.

catutthe ca bhonto samaṇabrāhmaṇā kim āgamma kim ārabbha amarāvikkhepikā tattha tattha pañhaṃ puṭṭhā samānā vācāvikkhepaṃ āpajjanti amarāvikkhepaṃ.

idha, bhikkhave, ekacco samaṇo vā brāhmaṇo vā mando hoti momūho. so mandattā momūhattā tattha tattha pañhaṃ puṭṭho samāno vācāvikkhepaṃ āpajjati amarāvikkhepaṃ : atthi paro loko ti iti ce maṃ pucchasi, atthi paro loko ti iti ce me assa, atthi paro loko ti iti te naṃ vyākareyyaṃ. evam pi me no. tathā ti pi me no. aññathā ti pi me no. no ti pi me no. no no ti pi me no. n' atthi paro loko ti . . . pe . . . atthi ca n' atthi ca paro loko. n' ev' atthi na n' atthi paro loko — atthi sattā opapātikā. n' atthi sattā opapātikā. atthi ca n' atthi ca sattā opapātikā. n' ev' atthi na n' atthi sattā opapātikā — atthi sukatadukkatānaṃ kammānaṃ phalaṃ vipāko. n' atthi sukatadukkatānaṃ kammānaṃ phalaṃ vipāko. atthi ca n' atthi ca sukatadukkatānaṃ kammānaṃ phalaṃ vipāko. n' ev' atthi na n' atthi sukatadukkatānaṃ kammānaṃ phalaṃ vipāko — hoti tathāgato param maraṇā. na hoti tathāgato param maraṇā. hoti ca na hoti ca tathāgato param maraṇā. n' eva hoti na na hoti tathāgato param maraṇā ti iti ce maṃ pucchasi, n' eva hoti na na hoti tathāgato param maraṇā ti iti ce me assa, n' eva hoti na na hoti tathāgato param maraṇā ti iti te naṃ vyākareyyaṃ. evam pi me no. tathā ti pi me no. aññathā ti pi me no. no ti pi me no. no no ti pi me no ti.

idaṃ, bhikkhave, catutthaṃ ṭhānaṃ yam āgamma yam ārabbha eke samaṇabrāhmaṇā amarāvikkhepikā tattha tattha pañhaṃ puṭṭhā samānā vācāvikkhepaṃ āpajjanti amarāvikkhepaṃ. . . .

santi, bhikkhave, eke samaṇabrāhmaṇā adhiccasamuppannikā, adhiccasamuppannaṃ attānañ ca lokañ ca paññāpenti dvīhi vatthūhi. te ca bhonto samaṇabrāhmaṇā kim āgamma kim ārabbha adhiccasamuppannikā adhiccasamuppannaṃ attānañ ca lokañ ca paññāpenti.

santi, bhikkhave, asaññasattā nāma devā, saññuppādā ca pana te devā tamhā kāyā cavanti. ṭhānaṃ kho pan' etaṃ, bhikkhave, vijjati yaṃ aññataro satto tamhā kāyā cavitvā itthattaṃ āgacchati, itthattaṃ āgato samāno agārasmā anagāriyaṃ pabbajati. agārasmā anagāriyaṃ pabbajito samāno ātappam anvāya padhānam anvāya anuyogam anvāya appamādam anvāya sammāmanasikāram anvāya tathārūpaṃ cetosamādhiṃ phusati yathā samāhite citte saññuppādam anussarati, tato paraṃ nānussarati. so evam āha : adhiccasamuppanno attā ca loko ca. taṃ kissa hetu. ahaṃ hi pubbe nāhosiṃ, so 'mhi etarahi ahutvā sattattāya pariṇato ti.

idaṃ, bhikkhave, paṭhamaṃ ṭhānaṃ yam āgamma yam ārabbha eke samaṇabrāhmaṇā adhiccasamuppannikā adhiccasamuppannaṃ attānañ ca lokañ ca paññāpenti.

dutiye ca bhonto samaṇabrāhmaṇā kim āgamma kim ārabbha adhiccasamuppannikā adhiccasamuppannam attānañ ca lokañ ca paññāpenti.

idha, bhikkhave, ekacco samaṇo vā brāhmaṇo vā takkī hoti vīmaṃsī. so takkapariyāhataṃ vīmaṃsānucaritaṃ sayaṃpaṭibhānaṃ evam āha : adhiccasamuppanno attā ca loko cā ti . . .

ime kho te, bhikkhave, samaṇabrāhmaṇā pubbantakappikā pubbantānudiṭṭhino pubbantaṃ ārabbha anekavihitāni adhivuttipadāni abhivadanti aṭṭhādasahi vatthūhi. ye hi keci, bhikkhave, samaṇā vā brāhmaṇā vā pubbantakappikā pubbantānudiṭṭhino pubbantaṃ ārabbha anekavihitāni adhivuttipadāni abhivadanti, sabbe te imeh' eva aṭṭhādasahi vatthūhi etesaṃ vā aññatarena, n' atthi ito bahiddhā.

tayidaṃ, . . . yathābhūtaṃ viditvā anupādā vimutto, bhikkhave, tathāgato.

ime kho te, bhikkhave, dhammā gambhīrā . . . vaṇṇaṃ sammā vadamānā vadeyyuṃ.

santi, bhikkhave, eke samaṇabrāhmaṇā aparantakappikā aparantānudiṭṭhino, aparantaṃ ārabbha anekavihitāni adhivuttipadāni abhivadanti catucattārīsāya vatthūhi. te ca bhonto samaṇabrāhmaṇā kim āgamma kim ārabbha aparantakappikā aparantānudiṭṭhino aparantaṃ ārabbha anekavihitāni adhivuttipadāni abhivadanti catucattārīsāya vatthūhi.

santi, bhikkhave, eke samaṇabrāhmaṇā uddhamāghatanikā saññivādā, uddham āghatanā saññim attānaṃ paññāpenti soḷasahi vatthūhi. te ca bhonto samaṇabrāhmaṇā kim āgamma kim ārabbha uddhamāghatanikā saññivādā uddham āghatanā saññim attānaṃ paññāpenti soḷasahi vatthūhi.

rūpī attā hoti arogo param maraṇā saññī ti naṃ paññāpenti. arūpī attā hoti arogo param maraṇā saññī ti naṃ paññāpenti. rūpī ca arūpī ca attā hoti . . . pe . . . n' eva rūpī nārūpī . . . antavā attā hoti . . . anantavā . . . antavā ca anantavā ca . . . n' ev' antavā nānantavā . . . ekattasaññī attā hoti . . . nānattasaññī . . . parittasaññī . . . appamāṇasaññī . . . ekantasukhī attā hoti . . . ekantadukkhī . . . sukhadukkhī . . . adukkhamasukhī attā hoti arogo param maraṇā saññī ti naṃ paññāpenti.

ime kho te, bhikkhave, samaṇabrāhmaṇā uddhamāghatanikā saññivādā uddham āghatanā saññiṃ attānaṃ paññāpenti soḷasahi vatthūhi . . .

santi, bhikkhave, eke samaṇabrāhmaṇā uddhamāghatanikā asaññivādā, uddham āghatanā asaññiṃ attānaṃ paññāpenti aṭṭhahi vatthūhi. te ca bhonto samaṇabrāhmaṇā kim āgamma kim ārabbha uddhamāghatanikā asaññivādā uddham āghatanā asaññim attānaṃ paññāpenti aṭṭhahi vatthūhi.

rūpī attā hoti arogo param maraṇā asaññī ti naṃ paññāpenti. arūpī . . . pe . . . rūpī ca arūpī ca . . . n' eva rūpī nārūpī . . . antavā ca . . . anantavā . . . antavā ca anantavā ca . . . n' ev' antavā nānantavā attā hoti arogo param maraṇā asaññī ti naṃ paññāpenti.

ime kho te, bhikkhave, samaṇabrāhmaṇā uddhamāghatanikā asaññivādā uddham āghatanā asaññiṃ attānaṃ paññāpenti aṭṭhahi vatthūhi . . .

santi, bhikkhave, eke samaṇabrāhmaṇā uddhamāghatanikā nevasaññināsaññivādā, uddham āghatanā n' eva saññiṃ nāsaññiṃ attānaṃ paññāpenti aṭṭhahi vatthūhi. te ca bhonto samaṇabrāhmaṇā kim āgamma kim ārabbha uddhamāghatanikā nevasaññināsaññivādā uddham āghatanā n' eva saññiṃ nāsaññiṃ attānaṃ paññāpenti aṭṭhahi vatthūhi.

rūpī attā hoti arogo param maraṇā n' eva saññī nāsaññī ti naṃ paññāpenti. arūpī . . . rūpī ca arūpī ca . . . n' eva rūpī nārūpī . . . antavā . . . anantavā . . . antavā ca anantavā ca . . . n' ev' antavā nānantavā attā hoti arogo param maraṇā n' eva saññī nāsaññī ti naṃ paññāpenti.

ime kho te, bhikkhave, samaṇabrāhmaṇā uddhamāghatanikā nevasaññināsaññivādā uddham āghatanā n' eva saññiṃ nāsaññiṃ attānaṃ paññāpenti aṭṭhahi vatthūhi . . .

santi, bhikkhave, eke samaṇabrāhmaṇā ucchedavādā, sato sattassa ucchedaṃ vināsaṃ vibhavaṃ paññāpenti sattahi vatthūhi. te ca bhonto samaṇabrāhmaṇā kim āgamma kim ārabbha ucchedavādā sattassa ucchedaṃ vināsaṃ vibhavaṃ paññāpenti sattahi vatthūhi.

idha, bhikkhave, ekacco samaṇo vā brāhmaṇo vā evaṃvādī hoti evaṃdiṭṭhī: yato kho bho ayaṃ attā rūpī cātummahābhūtiko mātāpettikasambhavo,[1] kāyassa bhedā ucchijjati vinassati, na hoti param maraṇā, ettāvatā kho bho ayaṃ attā sammā samucchinno hotī ti. itth'[2] eke sato sattassa ucchedaṃ vināsaṃ vibhavaṃ paññāpenti.

taṃ añño evam āha: atthi kho bho eso attā yaṃ tvaṃ vadesi. n' eso n' atthī ti vadāmi. no ca kho bho ayaṃ attā ettāvatā sammā samucchinno hoti. atthi kho bho añño attā dibbo rūpī kāmāvacaro kabaliṅkārāhārabhakkho. taṃ tvaṃ na jānāsi na passasi. tam ahaṃ jānāmi passāmi. so kho bho attā yato kāyassa bhedā ucchijjati vinassati na hoti param maraṇā, ettāvatā kho bho ayaṃ attā sammā samucchinno hotī

[1] *mātar-* = " mother ", see next Lesson.
[2] Elision of *-aṃ* before a vowel.

ti. itth' eke sato sattassa ucchedaṃ vināsaṃ vibhavaṃ paññāpenti.

taṃ añño evam āha: atthi kho bho eso attā yaṃ tvaṃ vadesi. n' eso n' atthī ti vadāmi. no ca kho bho ayaṃ attā ettāvatā sammā samucchinno hoti. atthi kho bho añño attā dibbo rūpī manomayo sabbaṅgapaccaṅgī ahīnindriyo. taṃ tvaṃ na jānāsi na passasi. taṃ ahaṃ jānāmi passāmi. so kho bho attā yato kāyassa bhedā ucchijjati vinassati na hoti param maraṇā, ettāvatā kho bho ayam attā sammā samucchinno hotī ti. itth' eke sato sattassa ucchedaṃ vināsaṃ vibhavaṃ paññāpenti.

taṃ añño evam āha: atthi kho bho eso attā yaṃ tvaṃ vadesi. n' eso n' atthī ti vadāmi. no ca kho bho ayaṃ attā ettāvatā sammā samucchinno hoti. atthi kho bho añño attā sabbaso rūpasaññānaṃ samatikkamā paṭighasaññānaṃ atthagamā nānattasaññānaṃ amanasikārā ananto ākāso ti ākāsānañcāyatanūpago. taṃ tvaṃ na jānāsi na passasi. taṃ ahaṃ jānāmi passāmi. so kho bho attā yato kāyassa bhedā ucchijjati vinassati na hoti param maraṇā, ettāvatā kho bho ayaṃ attā sammā samucchinno hotī ti. itth' eke sato sattassa ucchedaṃ vināsaṃ vibhavaṃ paññāpenti.

taṃ añño evam āha: atthi kho bho eso attā yaṃ tvaṃ vadesi. n' eso n' atthī ti vadāmi. no ca kho bho ayaṃ attā ettāvatā sammā samucchinno hoti. atthi kho bho añño attā sabbaso ākāsānañcāyatanaṃ samatikkamma anantaṃ viññāṇan ti viññāṇānañcāyatanūpago. taṃ tvaṃ na jānāsi na passasi. taṃ ahaṃ jānāmi passāmi. so kho bho attā yato kāyassa bhedā ucchijjati vinassati na hoti param maraṇā, ettāvatā kho bho ayaṃ attā sammā samucchinno hotī ti. itth' eke sato sattassa ucchedaṃ vināsaṃ vibhavaṃ paññāpenti.

taṃ añño evam āha: atthi kho bho eso attā yaṃ tvaṃ vadesi. n' eso n' atthī ti vadāmi. no ca kho bho ayaṃ attā ettāvatā sammā samucchinno hoti. atthi kho bho añño attā sabbaso viññāṇañcāyatanaṃ [1] samatikkamma n' atthi kiñ cī ti ākiñcaññāyatanūpago. taṃ tvaṃ na jānāsi na passasi. taṃ ahaṃ jānāmi passāmi. so kho bho attā yato kāyassa bhedā ucchijjati vinassati na hoti param maraṇā, ettāvatā kho bho

[1] This word is usually written with haplology of *-ān-* as here. The meaning is unchanged.

ayaṃ attā sammā samucchinno hotī ti. itth' eke sato sattassa ucchedaṃ vināsaṃ vibhavaṃ paññāpenti.

taṃ añño evam āha : atthi kho bho eso attā yaṃ tvaṃ vadesi. n' eso n' atthī ti vadāmi. no ca kho bho ayaṃ attā ettāvatā sammā samucchinno hoti. atthi kho bho añño attā sabbaso ākiñcaññāyatanaṃ samatikkamma santaṃ etaṃ paṇītam etan ti nevasaññānāsaññāyatanūpago. taṃ tvaṃ na jānāsi na passasi. taṃ ahaṃ jānāmi passāmi. so kho bho attā yato kāyassa bhedā ucchijjati vinassati na hoti param maraṇā, ettāvatā kho bho ayaṃ attā sammā samucchinno hotī ti. itth' eke sato sattassa ucchedaṃ vināsaṃ vibhavaṃ paññāpenti.

ime kho te, bhikkhave, samaṇabrāhmaṇā ucchedavādā sato sattassa ucchedaṃ vināsaṃ vibhavaṃ paññāpenti sattahi vatthūhi . . .

santi, bhikkhave, eke samaṇabrāhmaṇā diṭṭhadhammanibbānavādā, sato sattassa paramadiṭṭhadhammanibbānaṃ paññāpenti pañcahi vatthūhi. te ca bhonto samaṇabrāhmaṇā kim āgamma kiṃ ārabbha diṭṭhadhammanibbānavādā sato sattassa diṭṭhadhammanibbānaṃ paññāpenti pañcahi vatthūhi.

idha, bhikkhave, ekacco samaṇo vā brāhmaṇo vā evaṃvādī hoti evaṃdiṭṭhī : yato kho bho ayaṃ attā pañcahi kāmaguṇehi samappito samaṅgībhūto paricāreti, ettāvatā kho bho ayaṃ attā paramadiṭṭhadhammanibbānaṃ patto hotī ti. itth' eke sato sattassa paramadiṭṭhadhammanibbānaṃ paññāpenti.

taṃ añño evam āha : atthi kho bho eso attā yaṃ tvaṃ vadesi. n' eso n' atthī ti vadāmi. no ca kho bho ayaṃ attā ettāvatā paramadiṭṭhadhammanibbānappatto hoti. taṃ kissa hetu. kāmā hi bho aniccā dukkhā vipariṇāmadhammā, tesaṃ vipariṇāmaññathābhāvā uppajjanti sokaparidevadukkhadomanassupāyāsā. yato kho bho ayaṃ attā vivicc' eva kāmehi vivicca akusaladhammehi savitakkaṃ savicāraṃ vivekajaṃ pītisukhaṃ paṭhamajjhānaṃ upasampajja viharati, ettāvatā kho bho ayaṃ attā paramadiṭṭhadhammanibbānaṃ patto hotī ti. itth' eke sato sattassa paramadiṭṭhadhammanibbānaṃ paññāpenti.

taṃ añño evam āha : atthi kho bho eso attā yaṃ tvaṃ vadesi. n' eso n' atthī ti vadāmi. no ca kho bho ayaṃ attā ettāvatā paramadiṭṭhadhammanibbānappatto hoti. taṃ kissa hetu. yad eva tattha vitakkitaṃ vicāritaṃ etena etaṃ oḷārikaṃ akkhāyati. yato kho bho ayaṃ attā vitakkavicārānaṃ vūpasamā ajjhattaṃ sampasādanaṃ cetaso ekodibhāvaṃ avitakkaṃ avicāraṃ samādhijaṃ pītisukhaṃ dutiyajjhānaṃ upasampajja viharati, ettāvatā kho bho ayaṃ attā paramadiṭṭhadhammanibbānaṃ patto hotī ti. itth' eke sato sattassa paramadiṭṭhadhammanibbānaṃ paññāpenti.

taṃ añño evam āha : atthi kho bho eso attā yaṃ tvaṃ vadesi. n' eso n' atthī ti vadāmi. no ca kho bho ayaṃ attā ettāvatā paramadiṭṭhadhammanibbānappatto hoti. taṃ kissa hetu. yad eva tattha pītigataṃ cetaso ubbilāvitattaṃ etena etaṃ oḷārikaṃ akkhāyati. yato kho bho ayaṃ attā pītiyā ca virāgā upekkhako ca viharati sato ca sampajāno sukhañ ca kāyena paṭisaṃvedeti yan taṃ ariyā ācikkhanti upekhako satimā sukhavihārī ti tatiyajjhānaṃ upasampajja viharati, ettāvatā kho bho ayaṃ attā paramadiṭṭhadhammanibbānaṃ patto hotī ti. itth' eke sato sattassa paramadiṭṭhadhammanibbānaṃ paññāpenti.

taṃ añño evam āha : atthi kho bho eso attā yaṃ tvaṃ vadesi. n' eso n' atthī ti vadāmi. no ca kho bho ayaṃ attā ettāvatā paramadiṭṭhadhammanibbānappatto hoti. taṃ kissa hetu. yad eva tattha sukham iti cetaso ābhogo etena etaṃ oḷārikaṃ akkhāyati. yato kho bho ayaṃ attā sukhassa ca pahānā dukkhassa ca pahānā pubb' eva somanassadomanassānaṃ atthagamā adukkhaṃ asukhaṃ upekhāsatipārisuddhiṃ catutthajjhānaṃ upasampajja viharati, ettāvatā kho bho ayaṃ attā paramadiṭṭhadhammanibbānaṃ patto hotī ti. itth' eke sato sattassa paramadiṭṭhadhammanibbānaṃ paññāpenti.

ime kho te, bhikkhave, samaṇabrāhmaṇā diṭṭhadhammanibbānavādā sato sattassa paramadiṭṭhadhammanibbānaṃ paññāpenti pañcahi vatthūhi . . .

tayidaṃ, bhikkhave, tathāgato pajānāti : ime diṭṭhiṭṭhānā evaṃgahitā evaṃparāmaṭṭhā evaṃgatikā bhavissanti evamabhisamparāyā ti. tañ ca tathāgato pajānāti, tato ca uttaritaraṃ pajānāti ; tañ ca pajānanaṃ na parāmasati, aparāmasato c' assa paccattaṃ yeva nibbuti viditā, vedanānaṃ samudayañ ca atthagamañ ca assādañ ca ādīnavañ ca nissaraṇañ ca yathābhūtaṃ viditvā anupādā vimutto, bhikkhave, tathāgato.

ime kho te, bhikkhave, dhammā gambhīrā duddasā duranubodhā santā paṇītā atakkāvacarā nipuṇā paṇḍitavedanīyā ye tathāgato sayaṃ abhiññā sacchikatvā pavedeti, yehi tathāgatassa yathābhuccaṃ vaṇṇaṃ sammā vadamānā vadeyyuṃ.

Compose a few connected sentences in Pali describing a visit by a monk or priest to the Buddha. The narrative can open by describing the occasion of the meeting, as in a *Dīgha* dialogue, and continue with the exchange of greetings. The visitor may then ask a question and so open a dialogue, or the Buddha may ask a leading question himself in order to introduce a brief discourse on a point of doctrine.

Similar compositions or " essays " on various topics are recommended for practice as a sufficient vocabulary is acquired. The aim should be to follow the idiom and style of the *Dīgha* closely by appropriate selection of subject matter. Attempts to cover a wider range are (even apart from the question of acquiring the vocabulary) best left until the basic idiom and structure can be reproduced with some fluency within a restricted subject matter.

LESSON 23

Declension of Nouns in -ar, *Agent Noun*

Two kinds of noun have a stem in *ar*. From a root, by adding the suffix *tar* (usually to a strong form of the root) a noun is formed which signifies the agent who carries out the action implied by the root (or by the root with prefixes). Sometimes the vowel *i* is inserted between the root and the suffix. Thus from *bhās*, " to speak," we have *bhāsitar*, " a speaker," from *saṃ-dhā*, " to make peace," we have *sandhātar*, " peacemaker," and from *sās*, " to teach," we have *satthar*, " teacher " (here *s* + *t* becomes *tth*). Such nouns may also be formed from causative stems with causative meaning ; *sāvetar*, from (*s*)*su*, " causer of hearing ", " reciter " ; *viññāpetar*, from *vi*-(*ñ*)*ñā*, " causer of discernment." These nouns are called " agent nouns " : sometimes they can be used like participles, taking a patient (" object "). A group of nouns signifying family relationships, such as *pitar*, " father," and *mātar*, " mother," has the same stem. The "agent nouns" are inflected as follows :—

	Singular	Plural
Nom.	*satthā*	*satthāro*
Acc.	*satthāraṃ*	
Inst.	*satthārā*	(*satthūhi*)
Dat.	*satthu*	(*satthūnaṃ*)
Abl.	*satthārā*	(*satthūhi*)
Gen.	*satthu* (or *satthuno*)	(*satthūnaṃ*)
Loc.	*satthari*	(*satthūsu*)
Voc.	*satthe*	(*satthāro*)

(Only the nominatives singular and plural are at all frequently used—see the syntax below—together with the singular of *satthar*, which is used as an epithet of the Buddha and hence is not restricted syntactically as agent nouns ordinarily are.)

The inflection of relationship nouns differs from that of agent nouns chiefly in that the final *ar* of the stem, where it appears, has only the *guṇa* grade (*ar*) in all cases, whereas the agent nouns have *vuddhi* (*ār*) except in the locative singular (like *i* (*y*) and *u* (*v*), *r* may be considered as having three grades of strengthening by prefixed *a*: zero—*guṇa*—*vuddhi* ; so may *n* and other consonants if desired in grammatical description). The genitive plural usually has the ending *unnaṃ*, sometimes *ūnaṃ* (the agent nouns are supposed to have *ūnaṃ* here, following the *u* declension, or else *ārānaṃ*, but the case occurs so rarely—never in the *Dīgha Nikāya*—that the usage hesitates).

Inflection of the relationship noun *pitar* masculine, "father":—

	Singular	Plural
Nom.	*pitā*	*pitaro*
Acc.	*pitaraṃ*	
Ins.	*pitarā*	*pitūhi*
Dat.	*pitu*	*pitunnaṃ*
Abl.	*pitarā*	*pitūhi*
Gen.	*pitu*	*pitunnaṃ* (sometimes -*ūnaṃ*)
Loc.	*pitari*	*pitūsu*
Voc.	(not used : a son addressing his father uses either a formal title, such as *deva*, or the affectionate *tāta* used also, and more frequently, by a father addressing his son)	

The agent noun may be used in the nominative case as attribute of the nominative agent, agreeing with it in number, and its patient (" object ") may be in either the accusative or the genitive case (" objective genitive "). It may express the main action of a sentence, with the verb " to be " either understood or expressed (*hoti*), it may express the action of a subordinate clause, or it may express merely an attribute of the agent.

Examples :—

tathāgato . . . vācaṃ bhāsitā ahosi = " the thus-gone . . . was the speaker of the speech (acc.) "

ahaṃ assa mante vācetā = " I am his teacher (' causer to speak ') (of) sacred texts [1] (acc.) "

ahaṃ . . . mantānaṃ dātā, tvaṃ mantānaṃ paṭiggahetā, " I am . . . the giver (imparter) of sacred texts, you are the receiver (recipient) of sacred texts (gen.) "

iti bhinnānaṃ va sandhātā = " thus (he is) a peacemaker to (gen.) those who are divided "

tattha n' atthi hantā vā ghātetā vā sotā vā sāvetā vā = " there there is no killer nor causer of killing nor hearer nor reciter "

bhavissanti vattāro = " there will be speakers "

ito sutvā na amutra akkhātā imesaṃ bhedāya, amutra vā sutvā na imesaṃ akkhātā amūsaṃ bhedāya = " hearing (something) from here he doesn't report it there in order to divide these (people), or, hearing from there he doesn't report it to (gen.) these in order to divide those (people) " (*amūsaṃ* is genitive plural of the pronoun (deictic) *amu-* " he ", " that ", " yon " (more remote), which stands to *idaṃ* as *amutra* stands to *idha* or *ettha* ; see next Lesson)

ahan tena samayena purohito brāhmaṇo ahosiṃ tassa yañ-ñassa yājetā = " at that time I was the high priest who performed that sacrifice (gen.) "

tatr' assa dovāriko paṇḍito viyatto [2] *medhāvī aññātānaṃ*

[1] Especially of the Vedic tradition of hymns, prayers, descriptions of divine beings, etc.

[2] *viyatta* is an alternative spelling of *vyatta* : in certain words the orthography hesitates between taking *vya-*, *tva-*, etc., as one syllable or as two (the pronunciation is always *viya-*, but *t(u)va-* is variable).

nivāretā ñātānaṃ pavesetā = " there there might be an astute, intelligent, wise porter (who) kept away strangers (and) showed in friends (' known ') "

siyā kho pana bhoto rañño mahāyaññaṃ yajamānassa ko cid eva vattā =" but someone may say of his majesty the king sacrificing a great sacrifice . . . "

abhijānām' ahaṃ bhante imaṃ pañhaṃ aññe samaṇabrāhmaṇe pucchitā = " I am aware of having asked this question of other priests and philosophers "

Bahubbīhi *Compounds* (4)

A *bahubbīhi* containing two numerals (or numeral expressions) is usually disjunctive. We have met an example in Exercise 19, where the expressions (themselves compounds) *dvīhaṃ*, " two days," and *tīhaṃ*, " three days," are compounded in *dvīhatīhapāyāta* (*sattha*), meaning " (when it was) two or three days (since it) had set out (caravan) ", i.e. *dvīhaṃ vā tīhaṃ vā* . . . Some grammarians very artificially would regard even *dvīhatīhaṃ* by itself as a *bahubbīhi*, in which the word to which the compound is subordinate (being other than a member of the compound itself, hence implying a *bahubbīhi*) is *vā*, " or."

[When two cardinal directions (*disā*) are combined in a *bahubbīhi* the meaning is the intermediate direction (*vidisā* or *anudisā*) : *pubbadakkhiṇā* (*vidisā*) = " the south-east direction " ; *pacchimuttarā* . . . =" north-west . . ." These expressions do not seem to have been used in the Pali Canon, but they are found in later Pali literature.]

A word may be repeated to form a *bahubbīhi*, the stem final of the first member being lengthened and the suffix *-in* being added (cf. Lesson 21 for repetition, and Lesson 22 for *-in* added to *bahubbīhis*). The meaning may be distributive, or intensifying or emphasizing that of the single word, the whole being used as an adjective or, usually, as an adverb.[1] We have already met *saṃghāsaṃghin* (Exercise 19), used adverbially in a compound with the past participle *gaṇībhūta* (*gaṇī-bhū* =" to cluster "),

[1] Like adjectives, compounds otherwise used as *bahubbīhis* may be used in the accusative singular neuter as adverbs or in the neuter as nouns (hence as *tappurisas* or *kammadhārayas*).

meaning " in groups " (*saṃgho* =" group ", " community ")—here distributive and probably intensive as well (= many groups jostling one another) :—

> *saṃghāsaṃghīgaṇībhūta* (*brāhmaṇagahapatika*)—which might be freely rendered : " crowds of householders and priests jostling one another."

The " lengthened " *-ā-* in the seam of these compounds should perhaps be regarded as the prefix *ā*, " to," since other prefixes are sometimes found in a similar position. Thus *dhammānudhammapaṭipanna* (*bhikkhu*) =" (a monk) following the entire doctrine " or (if we take *anudhammo* as a separate word meaning " minor doctrine ") simply " . . . following the (main) doctrine and subsidiary doctrines ". As *dvanda* we find *vādānuvādo*, disjunctive according to the Commentary " *vādo vā anuvādo vā* " =" argument or subsidiary argument ".

Junction

The usages in junction (*sandhi*) may be summarized here for reference. They have mostly been noted above as examples of them occurred.

The alphabets used in writing Pali being phonetic tended to show the pronunciation of complete utterances (of which the minimum is the sentence) rather than of such smaller linguistic units as " words " and " morphemes ". Hence a " word " may show different forms (especially in its final syllable, sometimes in its initial) according to the sounds which precede and follow it and to which it may be assimilated, especially when the junction is close (i.e. when the utterance is rapid through the close syntactic grouping of two or more words). Assimilation is the rule between closely joined words, especially a word and a following " enclitic " (postpositive) such is *ca* or *ti*. Elsewhere it may be quite absent, leaving a " hiatus " for example between two vowels. In most manuscripts and printed books enclitics, and sometimes other closely joined words, are written without word spacing. This has not been done here, except in cases of coalescence of vowels (even there apostrophes have sometimes been used to show elision), for the sake of clarity. Thus for *ko ci, tañ ca, atthī ti, tena hi, ten' upasaṃkami, idam avoca, evam me, atha kho* and the like it is more usual to write *koci, tañca, atthīti, tenahi, tenupasaṃkami, idamavoca, evamme, athakho.*

As a general rule in junction it is the sound which follows which determines the nature of the sound which precedes, not the reverse.

In the junction of vowels most frequently the preceding vowel is elided :—

ha + eva > heva
na + atthi > natthi
eva + idaṃ > evidaṃ
dukkhassa + antaṃ > dukkhassantaṃ
saññā + uppādo > saññuppādo
dāni + ime > dānime
aṭṭhikāni + eva > aṭṭhikāneva
yāni + asmākaṃ > yānasmākaṃ
tiṭṭhatu + eva > tiṭṭhateva
me + etaṃ > metaṃ
vi + o > vo
pi + āsiṃ > pāsiṃ.

When the preceding vowel is elided the following vowel may be lengthened, provided it is not followed by a conjunct consonant or *ṃ* :—

idha + upapanno > idhūpapanno
handa + ahaṃ > handāhaṃ (this can of course equally be regarded as *a + a > ā*)
vitti + upakaraṇo > vittūpakaraṇo
upahato + ayaṃ > upahatāyaṃ
sace + ayaṃ > sacāyaṃ.

In rare cases *ā* is written even before a conjunct, as a result of junction :—

na + assa > nāssa
sa + atthaṃ > sātthaṃ (also written *satthaṃ*)
su + akkhāto > svākkhāto (on *sv* see below)

When a preceding *ă* is elided a following *ĭ* may rarely produce the strong vowel *e* and a following *ŭ*, *o* (i.e. *ă + ĭ > e* and *ă + ŭ > o : guṇa*) :—

kaṭṭha + udakaṃ > kaṭṭhodakaṃ.

Sometimes *ĭ* or *ŭ* followed by a dissimilar vowel is changed to *y* or *v* :—

vi + *ā* > *vyā*
anu + *āya* (*i*, gerund) > *anvāya*.

This *y* or *v* may then be assimilated to the preceding consonant :—

anu + *ā* > *anvā* > *annā*.

Both *tu* + *eva* and *ti* + *eva* produce *tveva* (this exceptional change of *i* > *v* happens only before *eva* ; *t' eva* also is written for *ti* + *eva*).

Sometimes a consonant is inserted between the two vowels. Consonants which regularly appear after certain words are shown bracketed in the vocabularies in this book. *y* is quite often inserted after *i* :—

pari + *ā* > *pariyā*
na + *idaṃ* > *nayidaṃ*
yathā + *idaṃ* > *yathayidaṃ* (or *yathāyidaṃ*)
sammā + *aññā* > *sammădaññā*
añña + *atthu* > *aññadatthu*
tasmā + *iha* > *tasmātiha*
yathā + *iva* > *yathariva*.

(These junction consonants will be reviewed in Lesson 25.)

After final *o* or *e* and sometimes other dissimilar vowels initial *a* is very often elided :—

ko + *asi* > *kosi*
kilanto + *asmi* > *kilantosmi*
niggahīto + *asi* > *niggahītosi*
te + *ahaṃ* > *tehaṃ*
pi + *assa* > *pissa*.

In rare cases a vowel preceding elided *a* is lengthened :—

vi + *ati* > *vīti*.

Occasionally final *i*, *e* and *u*, *o* (especially after a *k*, *kh*, *t*, or *s*) followed by *a* are changed to *y* and *v*, and the *a* is lengthened :—

te + *ahaṃ* > *tyāhaṃ* (or *tehaṃ*)

me + *ayaṃ* > *myāyaṃ*
yesu + *ahaṃ* > *yesvāhaṃ* (or *yesāhaṃ*)
yāvatako + *assa* > *yāvatakvassa*
yato + *adhikaraṇaṃ* > *yatvādhikaraṇaṃ*
so + *ahaṃ* > *svāhaṃ* (besides this form of junction *sohaṃ* also is found, or without junction *so ahaṃ*).

The same change when other vowels follow :—

su + *ākāre* > *svākāre*
kho + *ettha* > *khvettha*
so + *eva* > *sveva*.

Very rarely we find hiatus between two vowels, even in close junction :—

anu + *esi* > *anuesi*
sa + *upapīḷā* > *saupapīḷo* (*bahubbīhi* compound).

A vowel followed by a consonant usually remains unchanged, but before *ti* any short vowel is lengthened and before *pi* short vowels are sometimes lengthened :—

deva + *ti* > *devāti*
atthi + *ti* > *atthīti*
tatra + *pi* > *tatrāpi*.

Before a conjunct consonant a long vowel may be shortened [1] (this is usual in close combination) :—

ā + (*k*)*khā* > *akkhā*-.

A consonant preceded by a vowel may be doubled in all cases where this possibility has been indicated in this book by means of a bracketed initial consonant :—

na + (*k*)*khamati* > *nakkhamati*
na + (*p*)*pajānāti* > *nappajānāti*.

[1] There is a strong tendency in Pali for the length/quantity of the syllable (which for this purpose may be regarded as beginning with the vowel and including all following consonants) to be restricted to two units (*mattā*), where the unit is one short vowel. A consonant may be reckoned as half a unit and *niggahīta* as one unit, hence short vowel plus two consonants = two units and short vowel + *ṃ* = two units.

A consonant is usually doubled after the prefixes *u*(*d*) and *du*(*r*), similarly the *r* of *ni*(*r*) is assimilated :—

u(*d*) + *pajjati* > *uppajjati*
ni(*r*) + *pītika* > *nippītika*
ni(*r*) + *yā* > *niyyā-*
du(*r*) + *caritaṃ* > *duccaritaṃ*.

But *r* + *k* > *kkh*, *r* + *t* > *tth* and *d* + *h* > *ddh* :—

ni(*r*) + (*k*)*kam* > *nikkham-*
ni(*r*) + *tar* > *nitthar-*
u(*d*) + *har* > *uddhar-* (but *u*(*d*) + *han* > *ūhan-* and *ni*(*r*) + *har* > *nīhar-*).

The finals *-ti* and *-ṭi*, *-dhi*, may be changed to *cc*, *jjh*, and *-bhi* may be changed to *bbh*, when followed by vowels :—

iti + *alaṃ* > *iccalaṃ* (also written *iccālaṃ*)
(*p*)*paṭi* + *assosi* > *paccassosi*
adhi + *ā* > *ajjhā*
abhi + *u*(*d*) + *kir* > *abbhukkir-*.

Final *niggahīta* may be written as assimilated to the same place of articulation as a following consonant, becoming *ṅ*, *ñ*, *ṇ*, *n*, or *m* :—

saṃ + (*k*)*kam* > *saṅkam-* (*saṃkam-* is probably more usual)
dhammaṃ + *ca* > *dhammañca*
alaṃ + *dāni* > *alandāni*
saṃ + *ni* > *sanni*
alaṃ + *me* > *alamme*.

ṃ is always assimilated to *ti* :—

kusalaṃ + *ti* > *kusalanti*.

Final *niggahīta* followed by a vowel may become *m* :—

bhavaṃ + *atthu* > *bhavamatthu*
idaṃ + *āsanaṃ* > *idamāsanaṃ*.

Very rarely a final *niggahīta* may be elided :—

idaṃ + *ahaṃ* > *idāhaṃ*.

When *niggahīta* is followed by *eva*, *y* may be inserted :—

santaṃ + *eva* > *santaṃ yeva*
ekaṃ + *eva* > *ekaṃ yeva.*

Final *niggahīta* followed by *y* may combine with it to form *ṃñ* :—

tesaṃ + *eva* > *tesaṃ* + *yeva* > *tesaṃñeva.*

A double *v* is never written in Pali. Where it might occur *bb* is substituted :—

ni(r)-veṭh > *nibbeṭh-*
(p)pa-(v)vaj > *pabbaj-.*

A consonant followed by a vowel may be voiced :—

sat + *attho* > *sadattho.*

All these rules concern the junction of two words (including prefixes). In the derivation of stems and words from roots and stems by the addition of suffixes further changes are seen (e.g. consonant + consonant as *k* + *s* > *kh* : p. 37 above, " cerebralization " of *n* : footnote p. 106), but these are best learnt in connection with the actual derivations. This " internal (to the word) junction " does not always coincide with the " external junction " between words.

Two rules may be noted here : (1) Usually only one cerebral or cerebral cluster is tolerated in a word, except that there may always be a *r* also (cf. next rule), thus in reduplicating *(ṭ)ṭhā* we have *tiṭṭhati*, and the prefix *(p)paṭi* sometimes becomes *(p)pati* (especially before *(ṭ)ṭhā*) ; (2) *n* is usually cerebralized when a *r* occurs before it in the same word, provided no consonant intervenes which would cause the tongue to move. (These phenomena are of the type called " prosodies " by some phoneticians. Some other apparent irregularities difficult to explain by the simple junction of segments—phonemes or syllables—may also be explicable by " prosody " of words.)

Vocabulary

Verbs :—

adhi-o-gāh (I)	*ajjhogāhati*	put out to (sea), cross over (ocean)
adhi-gam (I)	*adhigacchati*	get

anu-ge (I)	*anugāyati*	sing after
anu-bhās (I)	*anubhāsati*	say after
anu-vac (I)	caus. : *anuvāceti* =	recite after
upa-rudh (III)	*uparujjhati*	stop, cease, end
gādh (I)	*gādhati*	be firm, stand fast, hold tight (p.p. *gāḷha*)
tacch (I)	*tacchati*	chop, carve
(*d*)*dis*	caus. : *dasseti* =	show
ni(*r*)-*vatt* (VII)	*nibbatteti*	produce
ni(*r*)-*vā* (III)		go out ; aorist : *nibbāyi*
ni-sidh (I) (*nisedhati*)	caus. : *nisedheti* =	prevent, prohibit
pabb (I)	*pabbati*	thrive, flourish
(*p*)*pa-yuj* (VII)	*payojeti*	undertake
pari-is(*a*) (I)	*pariyesati*	seek, look for, search
pari-car (I)	*paricarati*	tend
(*p*)*pa-vaḍḍh* (I)	*pavaḍḍhati*	increase
(*p*)*pa-sar* (I)	(*pasarati* = stretch out, intransitive) caus. = stretch out, transitive	
(*p*)*pa-sās* (I)	*pasāsati*	govern
saṃ-vid (III)	*saṃvijjati*	be, occur, be found
saṃ-vis (I*)	*saṃvisati*	go home ; caus. = take home
saṃ-jan (III)	*saṃjāyati*	be produced
saṃ-iñj (I)	*sammiñjati* (usual spelling, also written *samiñjati*)	draw in, bend
si (I)	*seti*	lie down

Nouns :—

aggi (masc.)	fire
aññāto	stranger (" unknown ")
anīkaṭṭho	soldier
anudisā	intermediate direction
araṇi (fem.)	kindling stick
assamo	hermitage
āloko	light

obhāso	radiance
kammanto	work, undertaking, business
karīsaṃ	excrement
kāraṇaṃ	cause
khiḍḍā	play
gaṇako	mathematician, treasurer
gatako	goer
ghaccā	destruction
ñāto	friend (" known ")
theyyaṃ	theft
dakkhiṇā	gift, donation
daliddiyaṃ	poverty
nimitto	sign, omen, portent
nisedho	prohibition, prevention
paṇavo	drum
pariyeṭṭhi (fem.)	seeking, looking for, search
pavuttaṃ	recitation
pātubhāvo	appearance, manifestation
pārisajjo	councillor, member of an assembly
bāhā	arm
mataṃ	opinion
muttaṃ	urine
rathiyā	street
vāṇijo	merchant
vāsī	hatchet
vepullaṃ	prevalence
vyādhi (masc.)	disease
sakuṇo	bird
saggo	heaven
samihitaṃ	collection
samuddo	ocean
(*s*)*saro*	sound, voice
sahitaṃ	kindling block
sāsanaṃ	instruction, doctrine
siṅghāṭako	crossroads, square

Agent Nouns (masc.) :—

akkhātar	reporter
aññātar	learner, grasper

kattar	maker
ghātetar	instigator to kill
dātar	giver
nimmātar	creator
nivāretar	keeper away
paṭiggahetar	receiver
pavattar	proclaimer
pavesetar	shower in, usher
pucchitar	asker
bhāsitar	speaker
yājetar	sacrificer
vattar	speaker
vācetar	causer to speak
sañjitar	ordainer
satthar	teacher
sandhātar	peacemaker
sāvetar	causer to hear, reciter
sotar	hearer
hantar	killer

Relationship Nouns :—

pitar (masc.)	father
bhātar (masc.)	brother
mātar (fem.)	mother

Adjectives :—

anidassana	indefinable, invisib
aparaddha	failed, offended
asubha	foul
asesa	without remainder, complete, absolute
ājīvin	living by
ābādhika	ill
uddhaggika	uplifting
khara	rough, harsh
tiṇha	sharp
tīradassi	shore-sighting, land-sighting
tevijja	having the triple knowledge (= the verses, music, and prayers of the Three Vedas)
thūla	gross, large

dakkhin	seeing (fem. *dakkhiṇī*)
daḷha	strong, firm
dahara	young, baby
dukkhita	afflicted
paṭirūpa	proper
pubbaka	former, old
balavant	strong
bāḷha	strong, excessive, violent
brahmakāyika	having a God-like body, of the substance of God (the gods who are the companions, retinue, or courtiers of God)
manāpa	pleasing
muṇḍa	shaven
-vassuddesika	about the age of (numeral-)
vyādhita	diseased, ill
saṃvattanika	leading to
-saṃkhāta	known as, called (p.p. of *saṃ-(k)khā* (I))
sāmuddika	oceanic, ocean going
subha	lustrous, fair
sovaggika	heavenly, leading to heaven

Numeral :—

asīti (fem.)	eighty (inflected like *jāti*)

Past Participle :—

palipanna (*pari-pad* (III))	fallen into

Gerunds :—

atisitvā (*ati-sar*)	having passed over, having ignored
apanetvā (*apa-nī*)	having led away
parinetvā (*pari-nī*)	having led round

Indeclinables :—

iha	here, in this case
kahaṃ	whereabouts ?
yahiṃ	whereabouts

yena	(also means) which way
santike	into the presence of (gen. or acc.)
sabbato	all round
samantā	anywhere, in any direction
sammukhā	in the presence of (gen.)

EXERCISE 23

Passages for reading :—

1. evaṃ vutte brahmakāyikā devā taṃ bhikkhuṃ etad avocuṃ : mayam pi kho bhikkhu na jānāma yatth' ime cattāro mahābhūtā aparisesā nirujjhanti, seyyathīdaṃ paṭhavīdhātu ... pe ... vāyodhātu. atthi kho bhikkhu brahmā mahābrahmā abhibhū anabhibhūto aññadatthudaso vasavattī issaro kattā nimmātā seṭṭho sañjitā vasī pitā bhūtabhavyānaṃ amhehi abhikkantataro ca paṇītataro ca. so kho etaṃ jāneyya yatth' ime cattāro mahābhūtā aparisesā nirujjhanti, seyyathīdaṃ paṭhavīdhātu ... pe ... vāyodhātū ti.

kahaṃ pan' āvuso etarahi so mahābrahmā ti.

mayam pi kho bhikkhu na jānāma yattha vā brahmā yena vā brahmā yahiṃ vā brahmā. api ca bhikkhu yathā nimittā dissanti āloko sañjāyati obhāso pātubhavati brahmā pātubhavissati. brahmuṇo [1] etaṃ pubbenimittaṃ pātubhāvāya yad idaṃ āloko sañjāyati obhāso pātubhavatī ti.

atha kho so mahābrahmā na cirass' eva pāturahosi. atha kho so bhikkhu yena so mahābrahmā ten' upasaṃkami, upasaṃkamitvā brahmāṇaṃ etad avoca : kattha nu kho āvuso ime cattāro mahābhūtā aparisesā nirujjhanti, seyyathīdaṃ paṭhavīdhātu ... pe ... vāyodhātū ti.

evaṃ vutte so mahābrahmā taṃ bhikkhuṃ etad avoca : aham asmi bhikkhu brahmā mahābrahmā abhibhū anabhibhūto aññadatthudaso vasavattī issaro kattā nimmātā seṭṭho sañjitā vasī pitā bhūtabhavyānan ti.

dutiyam pi kho so bhikkhu taṃ brahmāṇaṃ etad avoca : na kho ahan taṃ āvuso evaṃ pucchāmi : tvaṃ 'si [2] brahmā mahābrahmā abhibhū anabhibhūto aññadatthudaso vasavattī

[1] *ṇ* is sometimes written in the inflections of *brahman*, but not usually (cf. *brāhmaṇa*, which always has *ṇ*).

[2] Unusual elision of vowel after *ṃ*, or *si* as variant for *asi*.

issaro kattā nimmātā seṭṭho sañjitā vasī pitā bhūtabhavyānan ti. evañ ca kho ahan taṃ āvuso pucchāmi : kattha nu kho āvuso ime cattāro mahābhūtā aparisesā nirujjhanti, seyyathīdaṃ paṭhavīdhātu . . . pe . . . vāyodhātū ti.

dutiyam pi kho so mahābrahmā taṃ bhikkhuṃ etad avoca : aham asmi bhikkhu brahmā . . . pe . . .

tatiyam pi . . . pe . . . vāyodhātū ti.

atha kho so mahābrahmā taṃ bhikkhuṃ bāhāyaṃ gahetvā ekamantaṃ apanetvā taṃ bhikkhuṃ etad avoca : idha bhikkhu brahmakāyikā devā evaṃ jānanti : n' atthi kiñci brahmuṇo adiṭṭhaṃ, n' atthi kiñci brahmuṇo aviditaṃ, n' atthi kiñci brahmuṇo asacchikatan ti. tasmā ahaṃ tesaṃ sammukhā na vyākāsiṃ. aham pi kho bhikkhu na jānāmi yatth' ime cattāro mahābhūtā aparisesā nirujjhanti, seyyathīdaṃ paṭhavīdhātu . . . pe . . . vāyodhātu. tasmāt [1] iha bhikkhu tumh' ev' etaṃ dukkataṃ, tumh' ev' etaṃ aparaddhaṃ, yaṃ tvaṃ taṃ bhagavantaṃ atisitvā bahiddhā pariyeṭṭhiṃ āpajjasi imassa pañhassa veyyākaraṇāya. gaccha tvaṃ bhikkhu tam eva bhagavantaṃ upasaṃkamitvā imaṃ pañhaṃ puccha, yathā ca te bhagavā vyākaroti tathā naṃ dhāreyyāsī ti.

atha kho so bhikkhu seyyathā pi nāma balavā puriso sammiñjitaṃ vā bāhaṃ pasāreyya, pasāritaṃ vā bāhaṃ sammiñjeyya, evam eva brahmaloke antarahito mama purato pāturahosi. atha kho bhikkhu maṃ abhivādetvā ekamantaṃ nisīdi. ekamantaṃ nisinno kho so bhikkhu maṃ etad avoca : kattha nu kho bhante ime cattāro mahābhūtā aparisesā nirujjhanti, seyyathīdaṃ paṭhavīdhātu āpodhātu tejodhātu vāyodhātū ti.

evaṃ vutte ahaṃ taṃ bhikkhuṃ etad avoca : bhūtapubbaṃ bhikkhu sāmuddikā vāṇijā tīradassiṃ sakuṇaṃ gahetvā nāvāya samuddaṃ ajjhogāhanti. te atīradakkhiṇiyā nāvāya tīradassiṃ sakuṇaṃ muñcanti. so gacchat' eva puratthimaṃ disaṃ, gacchati dakkhiṇaṃ disaṃ, gacchati pacchimaṃ disaṃ, gacchati uttaraṃ disaṃ, gacchati uddhaṃ, gacchati anudisaṃ. sace so samantā tīraṃ passati, tathā gatako va hoti. sace pana so samantā tīraṃ na passati, tam eva nāvaṃ paccāgacchati. evam eva kho tvaṃ bhikkhu yāva yato yāva brahmalokā

[1] The final *t* here is a "junction consonant" between two vowels; cf. Lesson 25.

pariyesamāno imassa pañhassa veyyākaraṇaṃ nājjhagā,[1] atha maṃ yeva santike paccāgato. na kho eso bhikkhu pañho evaṃ pucchitabbo : kattha nu kho bhante ime cattāro mahābhūtā aparisesā nirujjhanti, seyyathīdaṃ paṭhavīdhātu āpodhātu tejodhātu vāyodhātū ti. evañ ca kho eso bhikkhu pañho pucchitabbo :—

kattha āpo ca paṭhavī tejo vāyo na gādhati,
kattha dīghañ ca rassañ ca aṇuṃ thūlaṃ subhāsubhaṃ,
kattha nāmañ ca rūpañ ca asesaṃ uparujjhatī ti.

tatra veyyākaraṇaṃ bhavati :—

viññāṇaṃ anidassanaṃ anantaṃ sabbatopabhaṃ,[2]
ettha āpo ca paṭhavī tejo vāyo na gādhati,
ettha dīghañ ca rassañ ca aṇuṃ thūlaṃ subhāsubhaṃ,
ettha nāmañ ca rūpañ ca asesaṃ uparujjhati,
viññāṇassa nirodhena etth' etaṃ uparujjhatī ti.

2. atha kho bhikkhave Bandhumā rājā sārathiṃ āmantāpetvā etad avoca :—

kacci samma sārathi kumāro uyyānabhūmiyā abhiramittha,[3] kacci samma sārathi kumāro uyyānabhūmiyā attamano ahosī ti.

na kho deva kumāro uyyānabhūmiyā abhiramittha, na kho deva kumāro uyyānabhūmiyā attamano ahosī ti.

kim pana samma sārathi addasā kumāro uyyānabhūmiṃ niyyanto ti.

addasā kho deva kumāro uyyānabhūmiṃ niyyanto purisaṃ jiṇṇaṃ . . . so kho deva kumāro antepuragato dukkhī dummano pajjhāyati : dhir atthu kira bho jāti nāma, yatra hi nāma jātassa jarā paññāyissatī ti.

atha kho bhikkhave Bandhumassa rañño etad ahosi : mā h'

[1] " Root " aorist (see Lesson 30) of *adhi-gam*, 2nd singular.
[2] Several meanings are suggested in the Commentaries for this difficult word : *pabhā* = " ford ", " crossing place " (over the ocean of existence to *nibbānaṃ*) ; *pa(b)ha(va)ṃ* = " able ", " prevailing " (present participle of *pa-(b)hū*) ; *pabhā* = " brilliance ". The *Dīgha* Commentary (*Sumaṅgalavilāsinī*) here prefers the first.
[3] *abhi-ram*, " enjoy," " take pleasure in " ; 3rd singular aorist " middle " (Lesson 28).

eva kho Vipassī kumāro na rajjaṃ kāresi, mā h' eva Vipassī kumāro agārasmā anagāriyaṃ pabbaji, mā h' eva nemittānaṃ brāhmaṇānaṃ saccaṃ assa vacanan ti.

atha kho bhikkhave Bandhumā rājā Vipassissa kumārassa bhiyyoso mattāya pañca kāmaguṇāni upaṭṭhāpesi yathā Vipassī kumāro rajjaṃ kāreyya, yathā Vipassī kumāro na agārasmā anagāriyaṃ pabbajeyya, yathā nemittānaṃ brāhmaṇānaṃ micchā assa vacanaṃ. tatra sudaṃ bhikkhave Vipassī kumāro pañcahi kāmaguṇehi samappito samaṅgībhūto paricāreti.

atha kho bhikkhave Vipassī kumāro bahunnaṃ vassānaṃ . . . pe . . .

addasā kho bhikkhave Vipassī kumāro uyyānabhūmiṃ niyyanto purisaṃ ābādhikaṃ dukkhitaṃ bāḷhagilānaṃ muttakarīse palipannaṃ semānaṃ aññehi vuṭṭhāpiyamānaṃ aññehi saṃvesiyamānaṃ. disvā sārathiṃ āmantesi: ayam pana samma sārathi puriso kiṃ kato, akkhīni pi 'ssa na yathā aññesaṃ, saro pi 'ssa na yathā aññesan ti.

eso kho devá vyādhito nāmā ti.

kim pana eso samma sārathi vyādhito nāmā ti.

eso kho deva vyādhito nāma: app eva nāma tamhā ābādhā vuṭṭhaheyyā ti.

kim pana samma sārathi aham pi vyādhidhammo vyādhiṃ anatīto ti.

tvañ ca deva mayañ c' amhā sabbe vyādhidhammā vyādhiṃ anatītā ti.

tena hi samma sārathi alan dān' ajja uyyānabhūmiyā, ito va antepuraṃ paccāniyyāhī ti.

3. atha kho bhikkhave aññataro puriso yena rājā khattiyo muddhāvasitto ten' upasaṃkami, upasaṃkamitvā rājānaṃ khattiyaṃ muddhāvasittaṃ etad avoca:—

yagghe deva jāneyyāsi dibbaṃ cakkaratanaṃ antarahitan ti.

atha kho bhikkhave rājā khattiyo muddhāvasitto dibbe cakkaratane antarahite anattamano ahosi, anattamanatañ ca paṭisaṃvedesi, no ca kho rājisiṃ upasaṃkamitvā ariyaṃ cakkavattivattaṃ pucchi. so samaten' eva sudaṃ janapadaṃ pasāsati, tassa samatena janapadaṃ pasāsato na pubbe nāparaṃ janapadā pabbanti yathā taṃ pubbakānaṃ rājūnaṃ ariye cakkavattivatte vattamānānaṃ.

atha kho bhikkhave amaccā pārisajjā gaṇakamahāmattā anīkaṭṭhā dovārikā mantass' ājīvino sannipatitvā rājānaṃ khattiyaṃ muddhāvasittaṃ upasaṃkamitvā etad avocuṃ :— na kho te deva samatena janapadaṃ pasāsato pubbe nāparaṃ janapadā pabbanti yathā taṃ pubbakānaṃ rājūnaṃ ariye cakkavattivatte vattamānānaṃ. saṃvijjanti kho te deva vijite amaccā pārisajjā gaṇakamahāmattā anīkaṭṭhā dovārikā mantass' ājīvino, mayañ c' eva aññe ca ye mayaṃ ariyaṃ cakkavattivattaṃ dhārema, iṅgha tvaṃ deva amhe ariyaṃ cakkavattivattaṃ puccha, tassa te mayaṃ ariyaṃ cakkavattivattaṃ puṭṭhā vyākarissāmā ti.

atha kho bhikkhave rājā khattiyo muddhāvasitto amacce pārisajje gaṇakamahāmatte anīkaṭṭhe dovārike mantass' ājīvino sannipātāpetvā ariyaṃ cakkavattivattaṃ pucchi. tassa te ariyaṃ cakkavattivattaṃ puṭṭhā vyākariṃsu. tesaṃ sutvā dhammikaṃ hi kho rakkhāvaraṇaguttiṃ saṃvidahi, no ca kho adhanānaṃ dhanam anuppadāsi, adhanānaṃ dhane ananuppadiyamāne daliddiyaṃ vepullaṃ agamāsi. daliddiye vepullagate aññataro puriso paresaṃ adinnaṃ theyyasaṃkhātaṃ ādiyi. tam etaṃ aggahesuṃ gahetvā rañño khattiyassa muddhāvasittassa dassesuṃ — ayaṃ deva puriso paresaṃ adinnaṃ theyyasaṃkhātaṃ ādiyī ti.

evaṃ vutte bhikkhave rājā khattiyo muddhāvasitto taṃ purisaṃ etad avoca : saccaṃ kira tvaṃ ambho purisa paresaṃ adinnaṃ theyyasaṃkhātaṃ ādiyī ti. saccaṃ devā ti. kiṃ kāraṇā ti. na hi deva jīvāmī ti. atha kho bhikkhave rājā khattiyo muddhāvasitto tassa purisassa dhanam anuppadāsi — iminā tvaṃ ambho purisa dhanena attanā ca jīvāhi, mātāpitaro ca posehi, puttadārañ ca posehi, kammante ca payojehi, samaṇesu brāhmaṇesu uddhaggikaṃ dakkhiṇaṃ patiṭṭhāpehi sovaggikaṃ sukhavipākaṃ saggasaṃvattanikan ti.

evaṃ devā ti kho bhikkhave so puriso rañño khattiyassa muddhāvasittassa paccassosi.

aññataro pi kho bhikkhave puriso paresaṃ adinnaṃ theyyasaṃkhātam ādiyi. tam enaṃ aggahesuṃ gahetvā rañño khattiyassa muddhāvasittassa dassesuṃ — ayaṃ deva puriso paresaṃ adinnaṃ theyyasaṃkhātaṃ ādiyī ti.

evaṃ vutte bhikkhave rājā khattiyo muddhāvasitto purisaṃ etad avoca :—

saccaṃ kira tvaṃ ambho purisa paresaṃ adinnaṃ theyyasaṃkhātaṃ ādiyī ti. saccaṃ devā ti. kiṃ kāraṇā ti. na hi deva jīvāmī ti.

atha kho bhikkhave rājā khattiyo muddhāvasitto tassa purisassa dhanam anuppadāsi — iminā tvaṃ ambho purisa dhanena attanā ca upajīvāhi, mātāpitaro ca posehi, puttadārañ ca posehi, kammante ca payojehi, samaṇesu brāhmaṇesu uddhaggikaṃ dakkhiṇaṃ patiṭṭhāpehi, sovaggikaṃ sukhavipākaṃ saggasaṃvattanikan ti.

evaṃ devā ti kho so bhikkhave puriso rañño khattiyassa muddhāvasittassa paccassosi.

assosuṃ kho bhikkhave manussā : ye kira bho paresaṃ adinnaṃ theyyasaṃkhātaṃ ādiyanti, tesaṃ rājā dhanam anuppadetī ti. sutvāna tesaṃ etad ahosi — yan nūna mayam pi paresaṃ adinnaṃ theyyasaṃkhātaṃ ādiyeyyāmā ti.

atha kho bhikkhave aññataro puriso paresaṃ adinnaṃ theyyasaṃkhātaṃ ādiyi. tam enaṃ aggahesuṃ, gahetvā rañño khattiyassa muddhāvasittassa dassesuṃ — ayaṃ deva puriso paresaṃ adinnaṃ theyyasaṃkhātaṃ ādiyī ti.

evaṃ vutte bhikkhave rājā khattiyo muddhāvasitto taṃ purisaṃ etad avoca : saccaṃ kira tvaṃ ambho purisa paresaṃ adinnaṃ theyyasaṃkhātaṃ ādiyī ti. saccaṃ devā ti. kiṃ kāraṇā ti. na hi deva jīvāmī ti.

atha kho bhikkhave rañño khattiyassa muddhāvasittassa etad ahosi : sace kho ahaṃ yo yo paresaṃ adinnaṃ theyyasaṃkhātaṃ ādiyissati, tassa tassa dhanam anuppadassāmi, evam idaṃ adinnādānaṃ pavaḍḍhissati. yan nūnāhaṃ imaṃ purisaṃ sunisedhaṃ nisedheyyaṃ, mūlaghaccaṃ kareyyaṃ, sīsaṃ chindeyyan ti.

atha kho bhikkhave rājā khattiyo muddhāvasitto purise āṇāpesi : tena hi bhaṇe imaṃ purisaṃ daḷhāya rajjuyā pacchābāhaṃ [1] gāḷhabandhanaṃ bandhitvā, khuramuṇḍaṃ karitvā, kharassarena paṇavena rathiyāya rathiyaṃ siṅghāṭakena siṅghāṭakaṃ parinetvā dakkhiṇena dvārena nikkhamitvā, dakkhiṇato nagarassa sunisedhaṃ nisedhetha, mūlaghaccaṃ karotha, sīsam assa chindathā ti.

[1] Adverbial compound : " with his arms behind his back."

evaṃ devā ti kho bhikkhave te purisā rañño khattiyassa muddhāvasittassa paṭissutvā taṃ purisaṃ daḷhāya rajjuyā pacchābāhaṃ gāḷhabandhanaṃ bandhitvā, khuramuṇḍaṃ karitvā, kharassarena paṇavena rathiyāya rathiyaṃ siṅghāṭakena siṅghāṭakaṃ parinetvā, dakkhiṇena dvārena nikkhamitvā, dakkhiṇato nagarassa sunisedhaṃ nisedhesuṃ, mūlaghaccaṃ akaṃsu, sīsam assa chindiṃsu.

assosuṃ kho bhikkhave manussā, — ye kira bho paresaṃ adinnaṃ theyyasaṃkhātaṃ ādiyanti, te rājā sunisedhaṃ nisedheti, mūlaghaccaṃ karoti, sīsāni tesaṃ chindatī ti. sutvāna tesaṃ etad ahosi : yan nūna mayam pi tiṇhāni satthāni kārāpeyyāma, tiṇhāni satthāni kārāpetvā yesaṃ adinnaṃ theyyasaṃkhātaṃ ādiyissāma, te sunisedhaṃ nisedhessāma, mūlaghaccaṃ karissāma, sīsāni tesaṃ chindissāmā ti.

te tiṇhāni satthāni kārāpesuṃ, tiṇhāni satthāni kārāpetvā gāmaghātam pi upakkamiṃsu kātuṃ, nigamaghātam pi upakkamiṃsu kātuṃ, nagaraghātam pi upakkamiṃsu kātuṃ, panthaduhanam pi upakkamiṃsu kātuṃ. te yesaṃ adinnaṃ theyyasaṃkhātaṃ ādiyanti, te sunisedhaṃ nisedhenti, mūlaghaccaṃ karonti, sīsāni tesaṃ chindanti.

iti kho bhikkhave adhanānaṃ dhane ananuppadiyamāne daliddiyaṃ vepullam agamāsi, daliddiye vepullagate adinnādānaṃ vepullam agamāsi, adinnādāne vepullagate satthaṃ vepullam agamāsi, satthe vepullagate pāṇātipāto vepullam agamāsi, pāṇātipāte vepullagate musāvādo vepullam agamāsi, musāvāde vepullagate tesaṃ sattānaṃ āyu pi parihāyi, vaṇṇo pi parihāyi ; tesaṃ āyunā pi parihāyamānānaṃ vaṇṇena pi parihāyamānānaṃ asītivassasahassāyukānaṃ manussānaṃ cattārīsaṃ vassasahassāyukā puttā ahesuṃ.

cattārīsaṃ vassasahassāyukesu bhikkhave manussesu aññataro puriso paresaṃ adinnaṃ theyyasaṃkhātaṃ ādiyi. tam enaṃ aggahesuṃ, gahetvā rañño khattiyassa muddhāvasittassa dassesuṃ — ayaṃ deva puriso paresaṃ adinnaṃ theyyasaṃkhātaṃ ādiyī ti.

evaṃ vutte bhikkhave rājā khattiyo muddhāvasitto taṃ purisaṃ etad avoca : saccaṃ kira tvaṃ ambho purisa paresaṃ adinnaṃ theyyasaṃkhātaṃ ādiyī ti. na hi devā ti avaca, sampajānamusā 'bhāsi.

Translate into English :—

kim pana Vāseṭṭha ye pi tevijjānaṃ brāhmaṇānaṃ pubbakā isayo, mantānaṃ kattāro mantānaṃ pavattāro, yesam idaṃ etarahi tevijjā brāhmaṇā porāṇaṃ mantapadaṃ gītaṃ pavuttaṃ samihitaṃ tad anugāyanti tad anubhāsanti, bhāsitam anubhāsanti vācitam anuvācenti : seyyathīdaṃ Aṭṭhako,[1] Vāmako, Vāmadevo, Vessāmitto, Yamataggi, Aṅgiraso, Bhāradvājo, Vāseṭṭho, Kassapo, Bhagu — te pi evam āhaṃsu : mayam etaṃ jānāma, mayam etaṃ passāma, yattha vā Brahmā yena vā Brahmā yahiṃ vā Brahmā.

bhavissanti dhammassa aññātāro

tena hi bhavaṃ Govindo sattāhaṃ āgametu yāva mayaṃ sake puttabhātaro rajje anusāsāma

idaṃ satthu sāsanaṃ

ap' āvuso amhākaṃ satthāraṃ jānāsī ti. āma āvuso jānāmi

seyyathā pi Ānanda pitā puttānaṃ piyo hoti manāpo, evam eva kho Ānanda rājā Mahāsudassano brāhmaṇagahapatikānaṃ piyo ahosi manāpo

Translate into Pali :—

Then the ascetic, having got up at (the proper) time, approached the caravan-camp. Having approached, he saw in that caravan-camp a baby-boy abandoned. Having seen he thought : " It is not proper that a human-living-being should die whilst I am looking on. Suppose I led this boy to the hermitage and looked after him." Then the ascetic led that boy to the hermitage and looked after him. When that boy was (present tense) about ten years old, then the ascetic had some business crop up in the country. Then that ascetic said this to that boy : " I wish, my son, to go to the country. You should tend the fire ; now (*ca*) don't let your fire go out. If your fire should go out, this (is the) hatchet, these (are the) sticks (' firewood '—plural), this (is the) kindling-stick-and-block. Having produced fire you should tend the fire." Then that ascetic having thus instructed that boy went to the country.

[1] Names—mostly clan names—of some of the ancient poet-seers who composed the hymns of the *Veda*. The Vāseṭṭha who is being questioned here is of course a later descendant of the same clan as the *isi* Vāseṭṭha. (The Vedic forms (stems) of these names are : Aṣṭaka, Vamraka, Vāmadeva, Viśvāmitra, Jamadagni, Aṅgirasas, Bharadvāja, Vasiṣṭha, Kaśyapa, Bhṛgu.)

Whilst he was intent-on-play (genitive absolute) the fire went out. Then that boy thought this : " Father spoke thus to me : You should tend the fire, my son . . . you should tend the fire. Suppose I were to produce fire and tend the fire." Then he chopped the kindling-stick-and-block with the hatchet, thinking : " Perhaps I shall get fire."

LESSON 24

The Pronoun amu

The demonstrative pronoun *amu*, " he," " she," " it," " that," " yon, " is a deictic like *idaṃ*, but it refers to a more remote object. It is used when it is necessary to distinguish a further object from a nearer, or to contrast two persons or groups. It corresponds to the indeclinable *amutra*, " there," " yonder," as *idaṃ* corresponds to *idha* and *ettha*, " here." The full declension cannot be cited from the *Dīghanikāya*, the bracketed forms below being taken from other Canonical prose texts :—

	Singular			Plural	
	Masc.	Fem.	Neut.	Masc. Fem.	Neut.
Nom.	*asu*		*aduṃ*	(*amū*)	(*amūni*)
Acc.	*amuṃ*				
Ins.	(*amunā*)	—[1]	(rest as masc.)	(*amūhi*)	
Dat.	(*amussa*)	(*amussā*)		(*amūsaṃ*)	
Abl.	(*amumhā*)	—[1]		(*amūhi*)	
Gen.	(*amussa*)	(*amussā*)		*amūsaṃ*	
Loc.	(*amusmiṃ*)	(*amussaṃ*)		—[1]	

[1] Not found : according to the grammarians the form *amuyā* may be used for the instrumental, dative, ablative, genitive and locative singular feminine, and *amūsu* for the locative plural, all genders.

Bahubbīhi *Compounds* (5)

A *bahubbīhi* compound may be made of an infinitive (which drops its final *ṃ*) or an action noun with the noun *kāmo*,

" desire." The compound is used as an adjective expressing the desire to do the action of the infinitive :—

upasaṃkamitukāmo (*ahaṃ*) = " (I) desiring to approach "
taritukāma (*purisa*) = " (a man) wishing to cross over "
gantukāma (*manussa*) = " (a person) wishing to go "

With action noun :—

dassanakāmo (*so*) = " (he) wishing to see "

These compounds, like other *bahubbīhis*, may be used in nominal sentences :—

cirapaṭikā 'haṃ bhante bhagavantaṃ dassanāya upasaṃkamitukāmo = " sir, I have long wished to go and see the fortunate one " (*cira-paṭi-kā* is a feminine noun meaning " since long ", " a long time back " ; here it may perhaps be explained as a *bahubbīhi* with elision of final *o* in junction : *cirapaṭiko* > *cirapaṭik' āhaṃ*, as is done by the Commentary on the *Udāna*, p. 115)

so tumhākaṃ dassanakāmo = " he is desirous of seeing you," " he wishes to see you."

Futures without -i-, *etc.*

In forming their future stems some verbs add the suffix *ss* directly to the root, instead of using the vowel *i* as a link (cf. Lesson 10). In the case of roots ending in consonants the junction with *ss*, not always regular, may make the forms hard to recognize. Among the verbs forming futures in this way are :—

chid	*checchati*	(*d* + *ss* > *cch* ; *chindissati* is more usual)
(*ñ*)*ñā*	*ñassati*	(root vowel shortened before double consonant)
(*ṭ*)*ṭhā*	*ṭhassati*	
dā	*dassati*	
labh	*lacchati*	(*bh* + *ss* > *ch* ; *labhissati* also is used and probably more frequently)
(*s*)*su*	*sossati*	
han	*hañchati*	(in the *Dīgha* only the irregular 1st person singular *āhañchaṃ* is found)
hū	*hessati*	(in verse ; change of stem : cf. aorist 3rd plural *ahesuṃ*).

Very rarely a suffix *h* (or *ih*) appears in place of *ss* (or *iss*). The inflections then begin with *i* instead of *a*: *hohisi* 2nd singular: "you will be" (in prose but perhaps poetic-portentous speech; *bhavissati* is the usual form).

(d)dis has the very irregular *dakkhiti* (*s* + *ss* > *kkh*), and more rarely the double form *dakkhissati* (for irregularity of root vowel cf. the aorist).

Auxiliary Verbs

Sometimes a verb meaning "to be" or a verb implying duration is used more or less as an auxiliary with a form (usually a participle) of another verb. A construction in which two verb forms are thus used as equivalent to a single verb is called "periphrastic". The usual definition of "periphrastic", according to European philologists, is that two verb forms "express a single verbal idea".[1] This seems imprecise, if only because it is hard to define a "single verbal idea" (which varies from language to language): Pali has a "desiderative" conjugation and can express the "idea" wish-to-do-the-action-of-the-verb in a single verb form and apparently as one "idea", hence the alternative constructions *is* + infinitive or *bahubbīhi* in *-kāmo* + *hoti*, etc., would be "periphrastic". If, again, some periphrastic constructions are supposed to have a meaning such as "continuous action" which would not belong to the alternative single verb, then we seem to have two "verbal ideas" after all. It is this latter possibility of expressing nuances of meaning not given by a single verb which is of most interest here, however we define "periphrastic". It may suffice to speak of the use of certain verbs as "auxiliaries". The verbs concerned include, besides *as* and *hū* (*bhū*), *car*, *(ṭ)ṭhā*, *vatt*, and *vi-har*. We may compare with them also *ni-sīd* and *ni-pad*.

as with a past participle emphasizes the meaning of "present perfect" of the latter. The 3rd person of the present tense, however, is not used in this way, except for the emphatic *atthi* or *santi* at the beginning of a sentence, being omitted as

[1] Alternatively it is said that one verb is a mere auxiliary expressing "aspect", etc. This again is relative, varying from language to language, and it is extremely difficult in Pali to distinguish the uses of certain verbs as mere auxiliaries from parallel constructions where they retain their proper meanings.

ordinarily in nominal sentences. The 1st and 2nd persons also may be omitted when the corresponding pronoun is used. Examples :—

niggahīto 'si, " you are refuted "

(cf. also with p.p. in a *bahubbīhi* : *katapuñño 'si*, " you have done well ")

kilanto 'smi, " I am tired "

so 'mhi etarahi . . . mutto, " now I am freed "

micchā paṭipanno tvam asi, aham asmi sammā paṭipanno, " you have proceeded wrongly, I have proceeded rightly "

jit' amhā, " we are beaten "

vañcit' amhā, " we are tricked "

amhā āgatā, " we have come "

With pronoun (no auxiliary) :—

mayaṃ . . . upasaṃkantā, " we have come "

pasanno ahaṃ, " I have confidence " (*pasanna* is p.p. of (*p*)*pa-sīd*)

The present participle of *as* is used in the same way, but it is also used as present participle of *hū* as auxiliary in the second type of usage described below :—

satto . . . itthattaṃ āgato samāno, " a being . . . which has come to this world "

so . . . pabbajito samāno, " he . . . having gone forth "

eke samaṇabrāhmaṇā . . . pañhaṃ puṭṭhā samānā, " some priests and philosophers . . . having been asked a question "

The future (of *bhū* : *bhavissati*) is used in similar statements about future situations. For examples see the end of the first section on *hū* (*bhū*) below.

The optative of *as* is used when the statement is hypothetical, but it is more often used as optative of *hū* in the second type of usage discussed below. In this case the 3rd person also is used :—

puriso . . . nisinno assa, " a man might be seated "

n' āssa kiñ ci . . . apphuṭaṃ[1] *assa*, " no part of it . . . would be unpervaded "

[1] P.p. of (*p*)*phar* (I), " to pervade."

A similar construction is used with a future passive participle, the perfective aspect being modified into a continuous or durative ("imperfective") aspect :—

> *n' amhi kena ci upasaṃkamitabbo*, "I am not to be approached (visited) by anyone"—implying "not at any time."

It may be remarked that the main verb (participle) may be transitive or intransitive. In the former case the meaning is passive, in the latter active, just as in the case of the simple past participle (e.g. in the above examples : *mutto* is transitive and passive, *pabbajito* intransitive and active).

hū as auxiliary has two senses. Firstly the perfective aspect as in the case of *as*, but at any time, any point in time ("future-perfect", "past-perfect" = "pluperfect"). In this case the present tense of *hū* is usually a "historical" present expressing past time, hence whereas *as* as auxiliary expresses present time *hū* is used for past or future time. In dialogue and direct speech we find *as* as auxiliary, in narrative *hū* (and also as described below). The aorist tense of *hū* is less common in these constructions. The "historical present" is often a "continuous" tense expressing what was going on at the past time referred to (a common construction is : *tena kho pana samayena* . . . p.p. + *hoti* [1]). Otherwise it may express the "pluperfect" : what had happened at that time, what had been done. Examples :—

> *tena kho pana samayena Kūṭadanto . . . divāseyyaṃ upagato hoti*, "at that time (expressed previously by aorists : *ekaṃ samayaṃ . . . avasari*,[2] etc.) Kūṭadanta . . . was having his siesta" ("was in his day-bed")
>
> *tena kho pana samayena Jīvako . . . tuṇhībhūto nisinno hoti*, "at that time (just expressed by *ahosi*) Jīvaka . . . was sitting silently"
>
> *tena kho pana samayena . . . Upavāṇo bhagavato purato ṭhito hoti*, "at that time . . . Upavāṇa was standing in front of the fortunate one"

[1] The historical present *hoti* is often found in sentences beginning *tena . . . samayena*.

[2] Aorist of *ava-sar* (I), "approach," "go down to" (see Vocabulary 25).

tena kho pana samayena Pāyāsissa . . . diṭṭhigatam uppannaṃ hoti, " at that time Pāyāsi . . . had had/had been of the opinion (literally: of P . . . the opinion had arisen) "—" pluperfect "

tena kho pena samayena Nigaṇṭho Nāṭaputto adhunā kālakato hoti, " at that time the Nigaṇṭha (= Jaina) Nāṭaputta [1] had just died " (*adhunā* = " now ", " just now ").

Aorist of *hū* (in all these cases the expression *tena . . . samayena* is absent) :—

dvare . . . tālo ṭhito ahosi, " a . . . palm tree stood by the gate", " there was a . . . palm tree near the gate "

attamanā ahesuṃ, " they were assured "

anuyuttā ahesuṃ, " they submitted " (probably = they all went on submitting : continuous)

tā (lotus pools) . . . *citā ahesuṃ,* ". . . were built (of bricks) " (continuous condition, not the action of building, which is expressed by a different verb in the preceding sentence : *māpesi*)

Imperative of *hū* :—

upasamena . . . kumāro samannāgato hotu, " may the prince be endowed . . . with calm " (again the durative aspect seems implied)

Future of *hū* (*bhū*) with the future passive participle of the main verb :—

na dāni tena ciraṃ jīvitabbaṃ bhavissati, " he hasn't long to live now," " he won't live much longer " (perfective aspect)

maggo kho me gantabbo bhavissati, " the road will have to be travelled by me," " I shall have had to travel along the road " (the latter version is probably more correct : in the context the speaker envisages that he will have become tired by the journey)

kammaṃ kho me kātabbaṃ bhavissati, " I shall have had to do some work "

[1] Presumably Mahāvīra, the founder of Jainism.

Secondly *hū* as auxiliary is used in general statements or " eternal truths ", in passages of didactic or philosophical direct speech. Here the action referred to is such as would or may take place at any time given the conditions described, and we have one of the regular uses of the present tense. This construction alternates with the optative in hypothetical descriptions or analogies. Usually the passage where *hū* is used as auxiliary opens with the word *idha,* " in this connection," which sets the tone or aspect of the whole section of text—sometimes one of considerable length. Several such passages will be found in the reading passage in Exercise 22, with the present tense (except for the " perfect " *āha,* a form which in fact generally seems to stand for present or indefinite (general) time). It would be possible in such contexts to translate *idha* as " supposing " or " whenever " (introducing an example or hypothesis). Similar passages begin with *tatra,* " in this connection," with *hoti* itself (placed initially) or with the optative *siyā* :—

idha . . . tapassī . . . parisuddho hoti, " in this connection (supposing) . . . an ascetic (*tapassin*) . . . has become purified "

idha . . . bhikkhunā kammaṃ kataṃ hoti . . . maggo gato hoti, " supposing . . . a monk has done some work . . . (or) has journeyed along a road "

idha . . . satthā . . . pabbajito hoti . . . ananuppatto hoti . . . deseti, " in this connection . . . a teacher . . . has gone forth . . . (but) has not attained . . . (yet) teaches " (this passage is followed by a quotation in direct speech in which such a teacher is reproached, and in which the two past participles are not accompanied by auxiliaries, being constructed in the 3rd person : cf. under *as* above)

idha . . . seyyathā . . . evaṃ apphuṭaṃ hoti, " in this connection . . . just as . . . so . . . has not been pervaded " (the *seyyathā* clause contains the optative *apphuṭaṃ assa* quoted above under *as*)

hoti . . . samayo yaṃ . . . loko vivaṭṭati . . . ettāvatā kho . . . vivaṭṭo hoti, " there is/there has been . . . a time when . . . the world evolves (note present tense) . . . so far . . . is evolved " *siyā . . ., na kho pana . . . evaṃ . . . samugghāto hoti*, " it might be (that . . .), but . . . would not be suppressed . . . in this way " (followed by a counter statement concluding with a sentence beginning *api ca kho* . . . stating that it would be suppressed, however, by a different policy—the example is from the second reading passage in Exercise 19)

With the future passive participle of the main verb :—

idha . . . bhikkhunā kammaṃ kātabbaṃ hoti . . . maggo gantabbo hoti, " supposing . . . a monk has had to do some work . . . (or again) has had to travel along a road."

As present participle in this type of construction *samāna* is used :—

tatra . . . satto . . . āgato samāno, " in this connection . . . a being . . . (which) has come "

car is very rare as an auxiliary in the Pali Canon. In the *Dīgha Nikāya* there seems to be only one example :—

santi hi . . . samaṇabrāhmaṇā paṇḍitā . . . vobhindantā maññe caranti, " for no doubt there are . . . wise priests and philosophers . . . (who) go shooting (as it were) "

This need not be regarded as " periphrastic ", nor *car* as an auxiliary, since the full meaning of *car*, " carry on," " go on a mission " can be understood.

(*ṭ*)*ṭhā* also need not be regarded as an auxiliary in the *Dīgha*, though like *car* it has a meaning conducive to close combination with another verb :—

devī . . . dvārabāhaṃ ālambitvā aṭṭhāsi, " the queen . . . stayed/stopped/stood leaning/resting against the door-post (*dvārabāhā*) " (*ālambitvā*, gerund, " leaning against," " resting on ")

Ānando . . . rodamāno aṭṭhāsi, " Ānanda . . . stood weeping "

vatt may be very close to *car* in meaning :—

ko ime dhamme . . . samādāya vattati, " who conducts himself/goes on conforming . . . to these customs ? "

vi-har again has a durative meaning liable to combine with other actions. Its meaning, however, may fade into mere duration in certain combinations, making it then much more like a pure auxiliary than the above verbs. This use of *vi-har* is fairly frequent in all its tenses, usually with the gerund, but also with the present or past participle, of another verb :—

so . . . paṭhamajjhānaṃ upasampajja viharati, " he . . . dwells having entered into the first meditation," " he remains in the first meditation " (here we may on the other hand regard the gerund *upasampajja* as a mere postposition meaning " in ")

cetasā . . . pharitvā viharati, " he dwells pervading . . . with his mind "

anuyutto viharati, " he lives practising (fasting and other forms of asceticism) "

api pana tumhe . . . ekantasukhaṃ lokaṃ jānaṃ passaṃ viharatha, " but do you . . . live knowing, seeing the world as extremely happy ? "

bhikkhū Rājagahaṃ upanissāya viharanti, " monks live depending on Rājagaha (for support) " (here as in the first example the gerund of *upa-ni-(s)sī* resembles a postposition)

yathā ahaṃ subhaṃ vimokkhaṃ upasampajja vihareyyaṃ, " that I may live entered into/in glorious freedom "

upasampajja viharissati, " he will live in "

subhaṃ vimokkhaṃ upasampajja viharituṃ, " to live in glorious freedom "

ni-sīd, being durative, may enter into periphrastic constructions, as in the example given above :—

tuṇhībhūto nisinno hoti, " was sitting silently," — which, since *tuṇhībhūta* is p.p. of *tuṇhī-bhū,* " to be silent," may be regarded as a combination of three verb forms, a double periphrastic. Another example is :—

puriso . . . vatthena sasīsaṃ pārupitvā nisinno assa, " a man . . . might be seated covered with a garment right over his head " (*(p)pa-ā-rup* (I*) = " to cover ", " to wear ")

ni-pad likewise may enter into a periphrastic construction :—

so . . . sasīsaṃ pārupitvā nipajjeyya, " he . . . might lie down covering his head "

Vocabulary

Verbs :—

anu-mud (I)	*anumodati*	approve, express appreciation
abhi-nand (I)	*abhinandati*	be pleased with (acc.), appreciate
abhi-yā (I)	*abhiyāti*	attack, invade
ā-rabh (I)	*ārabhati*	begin, initiate
ā-han (I)	*āhanati*	strike
u(d)-chid (III)	*ucchijjati*	annihilate
kit (I)	*tikicchati* (reduplication, see also Lesson 30)	cure (Ipv. 2 sing. : *tikicchāhi*)
(p)pa-ā-vad (I)	*pāvadati*	tell
(p)paṭi-o-ruh (I)	*paccorohati*	get down, alight
pari-hā (I)	caus : *parihāpeti* =	bring to an end, rescind
pes (VII)	*peseti*	send, drive
vand (I)	*vandati*	salute, pay respect
vas (I)	caus. = make live with	
saṃ-vi-dhā (I)	*saṃvidahati*	arrange
saṃ-(d)dis	passive : *sandissati* = be seen, appear	
saṃ-u(d)-chid (II)	*samucchindati*	abrogate, abolish

Nouns :—

adhigamo	acquisition, getting
anukampā	compassion
avihiṃsā	harmlessness, non-injuring
ātaṅko	sickness, fever
ānisaṃso	benefit
ānubhāvo	power, magnificence, might
uṭṭhānaṃ	rising

upalāpanaṃ	propaganda
kiriyā	action
kulo	tribe
cariyā	conduct, way of life
cetiyaṃ	shrine, pagoda
thero	elder monk
dussaṃ	cloth
nivesanaṃ	house, building
patti (fem.)	attainment
pattiko	pedestrian, infantryman
parihāni (fem.)	decrease, decline, loss
passaddhi (fem.)	calmness, tranquillity
peto	one who has passed away, dead man
balaṃ	strength
mahallako	elder
milātaṃ	palanquin, litter
yuddhaṃ	battle, war
rattaññū (masc.)	one of long standing, senior
vasanaṃ	wearing
vaso	control
vicayo	discrimination
vitathaṃ	untruth
viriyaṃ	energy
vuddhi (fem.)	increase
sacchikiriyā	observation, experience
sannipāto	assembly
sikkhāpadaṃ	training, (moral) rule, precept
→ *hiraññaṃ*	gold (money)

Adjectives :—

akaraṇīya	impossible
aparihāniya	imperishable, leading to prosperity
appatta	unobtained
abbhantara	internal, home
āraññaka	forest
āroga	well
kīdisa	like what ?, of what sort ?
kusīta	indolent, lazy
paññatta	authorized, customary

pāṭikaṅkha	probable
pesala	congenial
ponobhavika	leading to rebirth
bahula	frequent, abundant (at end of compound = fond of, cultivating, devoted to)
bāhira	external, foreign
bhaṇḍu	shaven-headed
mithu	opposed
yāvataka (fem. -*ikā*)	as far as, as many as
ratta	coloured
samagga	united, unanimous
sāpekha	wishing for, desiring, preferring

Pronouns :—

ekameka	each one
pubba	former

Gerunds :—

upanissāya (*upa-ni-*(*s*)*sī*)	depending on
okkassa (*o-*(*k*)*kass* (VII))	having dragged down, having dragged away
nisajja (*ni-sīd*)	having sat down
pasayha ((*p*)*pa-sah* (I))	having forced

Infinitive :—

daṭṭhuṃ ((*d*)*dis*)	to see

Indeclinables :—

aññatra	except for (is also constructed with the dative)
abhiṇhaṃ	frequently
ko pana vādo	how much more (so), not to speak of
nānā	variously
pure	before, in advance, at first
yāvakīvaṃ	as long as

EXERCISE 24

Passages for reading :—

1. evam me sutaṃ. ekaṃ samayaṃ bhagavā Rājagahe viharati Gijjhakūṭe pabbate. tena kho pana samayena rājā Māgadho Ajātasattu Vedehiputto[1] Vajjī abhiyātukāmo hoti. so evam āha : āhañch' ime Vajjī evaṃmahiddhike evaṃmahānubhāve, ucchecchāmi Vajjī vināsessāmi Vajjī anayavyasanaṃ āpādessāmi Vajjī ti.

atha kho rājā Māgadho Ajātasattu Vedehiputto Vassakāraṃ brāhmaṇaṃ Magadhamahāmattaṃ āmantesi : ehi tvaṃ brāhmaṇa yena bhagavā ten' upasaṃkama, upasaṃkamitvā mama vacanena bhagavato pāde sirasā vandāhi, appābādham appātaṅkaṃ lahuṭṭhānaṃ balaṃ phāsuvihāraṃ puccha : rājā bhante Māgadho Ajātasattu Vedehiputto bhagavato pāde sirasā vandati, appābādhaṃ appātaṅkaṃ lahuṭṭhānaṃ balaṃ phāsuvihāraṃ pucchatī ti, evañ ca vadehi : rājā bhante Māgadho Ajātasattu Vedehiputto Vajjī abhiyātukāmo. so evam āha : āhañch' ime Vajjī evaṃmahiddhike evaṃmahānubhāve, ucchecchāmi Vajjī vināsessāmi Vajjī anayavyasanaṃ āpādessāmi Vajjī ti ; yathā ca te bhagavā vyākaroti taṃ sādhukaṃ uggahetvā mamaṃ āroceyyāsi, na hi tathāgatā vitathaṃ bhaṇantī ti.

evaṃ bho ti kho Vassakāro brāhmaṇo Magadhamahāmatto rañño Māgadhassa Ajātasattussa Vedehiputtassa paṭissutvā, bhaddāni bhaddāni yānāni yojāpetvā, bhaddaṃ yānaṃ abhirūhitvā, bhaddehi bhaddehi yānehi Rājagahamhā niyyāsi, yena Gijjhakūṭo pabbato tena pāyāsi, yāvatikā yānassa bhūmi yānena gantvā yānā paccorohitvā pattiko va yena bhagavā ten' upasaṃkami, upasaṃkamitvā bhagavatā saddhiṃ sammodi, sammodanīyaṃ kathaṃ sārāṇīyaṃ vītisāretvā ekamantaṃ nisīdi. ekamantaṃ nisinno kho Vassakāro brāhmaṇo Magadhamahāmatto bhagavantaṃ etad avoca : rājā bho Gotama Māgadho Ajātasattu Vedehiputto bhoto Gotamassa pāde sirasā vandati, appābādham appātaṅkaṃ lahuṭṭhānaṃ balaṃ phāsuvihāraṃ pucchati. rājā bho Gotama Māgadho

[1] Son of Bimbisāra, reigned — 494 to — 469. Started Magadha decisively on its imperial career by his conquest of the Vajjī republic in — 483, about three years after the events of the present narrative. The Vajjī republic lay to the north of the Ganges, which formed the frontier between it and Magadha.

Ajātasattu Vedehiputto Vajjī abhiyātukāmo. so evam āha: āhañch' ime Vajjī evaṃmahiddhike evaṃmahānubhāve, ucchecchāmi Vajjī vināsessāmi Vajjī anayavyasanaṃ āpādessāmi Vajjī ti.

tena kho pana samayena āyasmā Ānando bhagavato piṭṭhito ṭhito hoti bhagavantaṃ vījamāno. atha kho bhagavā āyasmantaṃ Ānandaṃ āmantesi: kin ti te Ānanda sutaṃ, Vajjī abhiṇhaṃ sannipātā sannipātabahulā ti. sutaṃ me taṃ bhante Vajjī abhiṇhaṃ sannipātā sannipātabahulā ti. yāvakīvañ ca Ānanda Vajjī abhiṇhaṃ sannipātā sannipātabahulā bhavissanti, vuddhi yeva Ānanda Vajjīnaṃ pāṭikaṅkhā no parihāni. kin ti te Ānanda sutaṃ, Vajjī samaggā sannipatanti samaggā vuṭṭhahanti samaggā Vajjikaraṇīyāni karontī ti. sutaṃ me taṃ bhante Vajjī samaggā sannipatanti samaggā vuṭṭhahanti samaggā Vajjikaraṇīyāni karontī ti. yāvakīvañ ca Ānanda Vajjī samaggā sannipatissanti samaggā vuṭṭhahissanti samaggā Vajjikaraṇīyāni karissanti, vuddhi yeva Ānanda Vajjīnaṃ pāṭikaṅkhā no parihāni. kin ti te Ānanda sutaṃ Vajjī appaññattaṃ na paññāpenti, paññattaṃ na samucchindanti, yathā paññatte porāṇe Vajjidhamme samādāya vattantī ti. sutaṃ me taṃ bhante Vajjī appaññattaṃ na paññāpenti, paññattaṃ na samucchindanti, yathā paññatte porāṇe Vajjidhamme samādāya vattantī ti. yāvakīvañ ca Ānanda Vajjī appaññattaṃ na paññāpessanti, paññattaṃ na samucchindissanti, yathā paññatte porāṇe Vajjidhamme samādāya vattissanti, vuddhi yeva Ānanda Vajjīnaṃ pāṭikaṅkhā no parihāni. kin ti te Ānanda sutaṃ Vajjī ye te Vajjīnaṃ Vajjimahallakā te sakkaronti garukaronti mānenti pūjenti tesañ ca sotabbaṃ maññantī ti. sutaṃ me taṃ bhante Vajjī ye te Vajjīnaṃ Vajjimahallakā te sakkaronti garukaronti mānenti pūjenti tesañ ca sotabbaṃ maññantī ti. yāvakīvañ ca Ānanda Vajjī ye te Vajjīnaṃ Vajjimahallakā te sakkarissanti garukarissanti mānessanti pūjessanti tesañ ca sotabbaṃ maññissanti, vuddhi yeva Ānanda Vajjīnaṃ pāṭikaṅkhā no parihāni. kin ti te Ānanda sutaṃ Vajjī yā tā kulitthiyo kulakumāriyo tā na okkassa pasayha vāsentī ti. sutaṃ me taṃ bhante Vajjī yā tā kulitthiyo kulakumāriyo tā na okkassa pasayha vāsentī ti. yāvakīvañ ca Ānanda Vajjī yā tā kulitthiyo kulakumāriyo tā na okkassa pasayha vāsessanti, vuddhi yeva Ānanda Vajjīnaṃ pāṭikaṅkhā no parihāni. kin ti te Ānanda sutaṃ Vajjī yāni tāni Vajjīnaṃ Vajjicetiyāni abbhantarāni c' eva bāhirāni ca tāni sakkaronti garukaronti mānenti pūjenti tesañ ca dinnapubbaṃ katapubbaṃ dhammikaṃ baliṃ no parihāpentī ti. sutaṃ me taṃ bhante Vajjī yāni tāni Vajjīnaṃ Vajjicetiyāni, abbhantarāni c'eva bāhirāni ca, tāni sakkaronti garukaronti mānenti pūjenti, tesañ ca dinnapubbaṃ katapubbaṃ dhammikaṃ baliṃ no parihāpentī ti. yāvakīvañ ca Ānanda Vajjī yāni tāni Vajjīnaṃ Vajjicetiyāni, abbhantarāni c' eva bāhirāni ca, tāni sakkarissanti garukarissanti mānessanti pūjessanti, tesañ ca dinnapubbaṃ katapubbaṃ dhammikaṃ baliṃ no parihāpessanti, vuddhi yeva Ānanda Vajjīnaṃ pāṭikaṅkhā no parihāni. kin ti te Ānanda sutaṃ Vajjīnaṃ arahantesu dhammikarakkhāvaraṇagutti susaṃvihitā, kin ti anāgatā ca arahanto vijitaṃ āgaccheyyuṃ āgatā ca arahanto vijite phāsuṃ vihareyyun ti. sutaṃ me taṃ bhante Vajjīnaṃ arahantesu dhammikarakkhāvaraṇagutti susaṃvihitā, kin ti anāgatā ca arahanto vijitaṃ āgaccheyyuṃ āgatā ca arahanto vijite phāsuṃ vihareyyun ti. yāvakīvañ ca Ānanda Vajjīnaṃ arahantesu dhammikarakkhāvaraṇagutti susaṃvihitā bhavissati, kin ti anāgatā ca arahanto vijitaṃ āgaccheyyuṃ āgatā ca arahanto vijite phāsuṃ vihareyyun ti, vuddhi yeva Ānanda Vajjīnaṃ pāṭikaṅkhā no parihānī ti.

atha kho bhagavā Vassakāraṃ brāhmaṇaṃ Magadhamahāmattaṃ āmantesi : ekam idāhaṃ brāhmaṇa samayaṃ Vesāliyaṃ [1] viharāmi Sārandade cetiye, tatrāhaṃ Vajjīnaṃ ime satta aparihāniye dhamme desesiṃ, yāvakīvañ ca brāhmaṇa ime satta aparihāniyā dhammā Vajjīsu ṭhassanti, imesu ca sattasu aparihāniyesu dhammesu Vajjī sandissanti, vuddhi yeva brāhmaṇa Vajjīnaṃ pāṭikaṅkhā no parihānī ti. evaṃ vutte Vassakāro brāhmaṇo Magadhamahāmatto bhagavantaṃ etad avoca : ekamekena pi bho Gotama aparihāniyena dhammena samannāgatānaṃ Vajjīnaṃ vuddhi yeva pāṭikaṅkhā no parihāni, ko pana vādo sattahi aparihāniyehi dhammehi. akaraṇīyā bho Gotama Vajjī raññā Māgadhena Ajātasattunā Vedehiputtena yadidaṃ yuddhassa aññatra upalāpanāya aññatra mithubhedāya. handa ca dāni mayaṃ bho Gotama gacchāma, bahukiccā mayaṃ bahukaraṇīyā ti. yassa dāni

[1] Vesālī : capital of the Vajjī republic.

tvaṃ brāhmaṇa kālaṃ maññasī ti. atha kho Vassakāro brāhmaṇo Magadhamahāmatto bhagavato bhāsitaṃ abhinanditvā anumoditvā uṭṭhāy' āsanā pakkāmi.

atha kho bhagavā acirapakkante Vassakāre brāhmaṇe Magadhamahāmatte āyasmantaṃ Ānandaṃ āmantesi : gaccha tvaṃ Ānanda yāvatakā bhikkhū Rājagahaṃ upanissāya viharanti, te sabbe upaṭṭhānasālāyaṃ sannipātehī ti. evaṃ bhante ti kho āyasmā Ānando bhagavato paṭissutvā yāvatakā bhikkhū Rājagahaṃ upanissāya viharanti te sabbe upaṭṭhānasālāyaṃ sannipātetvā yena bhagavā ten' upasaṃkami, upasaṃkamitvā bhagavantaṃ abhivādetvā ekamantaṃ aṭṭhāsi, ekamantaṃ ṭhito kho āyasmā Ānando bhagavantaṃ etad avoca : sannipatito bhante bhikkhusaṃgho, yassa dāni bhante bhagavā kālaṃ maññasī ti.

atha kho bhagavā uṭṭhāy' āsanā yena upaṭṭhānasālā ten' upasaṃkami, upasaṃkamitvā paññatte āsane nisīdi, nisajja kho bhagavā bhikkhū āmantesi : satta vo bhikkhave aparihāniye dhamme desessāmi, taṃ suṇātha sādhukaṃ manasikarotha bhāsissāmī ti. evaṃ bhante ti kho te bhikkhū bhagavato paccassosuṃ. bhagavā etad avoca : yāvakīvañ ca bhikkhave bhikkhū abhiṇhaṃ sannipātā sannipātabahulā bhavissanti, vuddhi yeva bhikkhūnaṃ pāṭikaṅkhā no parihāni. yāvakīvañ ca bhikkhave bhikkhū samaggā sannipatissanti samaggā vuṭṭhahissanti samaggā saṅghakaraṇīyāni karissanti, vuddhi yeva bhikkhave bhikkhūnaṃ pāṭikaṅkhā no parihāni. yāvakīvañ ca bhikkhave bhikkhū appaññattaṃ na paññāpessanti, paññattaṃ na samucchindissanti, yathāpaññattesu sikkhāpadesu samādāya vattissanti, vuddhi yeva bhikkhave bhikkhūnaṃ pāṭikaṅkhā no parihāni. yāvakīvañ ca bhikkhave bhikkhū ye te bhikkhū therā rattaññū cirapabbajitā saṅghapitaro saṅghapariṇāyakā te sakkarissanti garukarissanti mānessanti pūjessanti tesañ ca sotabbaṃ maññissanti, vuddhi yeva bhikkhave bhikkhūnaṃ pāṭikaṅkhā no parihāni. yāvakīvañ ca bhikkhave bhikkhū uppannāya taṇhāya ponobhavikāya na vasaṃ gacchanti, vuddhi yeva bhikkhave bhikkhūnaṃ pāṭikaṅkhā no parihāni. yāvakīvañ ca bhikkhave bhikkhū āraññakesu senāsanesu sāpekhā bhavissanti, vuddhi yeva bhikkhave bhikkhūnaṃ pāṭikaṅkhā no parihāni. yāvakīvañ ca bhikkhave bhikkhū paccattaṃ yeva satiṃ upaṭṭhāpessanti, kin ti anāgatā ca pesalā sabrahmacārī āgaccheyyuṃ āgatā ca pesalā sabrahmacārī phāsuṃ vihareyyun ti, vuddhi yeva bhikkhave bhikkhūnaṃ pāṭikaṅkhā no parihāni. yāvakīvañ ca bhikkhave ime satta aparihāniyā dhammā bhikkhūsu ṭhassanti imesu ca sattasu aparihāniyesu dhammesu bhikkhū sandissanti, vuddhi yeva bhikkhave bhikkhūnaṃ pāṭikaṅkhā no parihāni.

. . . apare pi kho bhikkhave satta aparihāniye dhamme desessāmi, taṃ suṇātha, sādhukam manasikarotha, bhāsissāmī ti. evaṃ bhante ti kho te bhikkhū bhagavato paccassosuṃ, bhagavā etad avoca: yāvakīvañ ca bhikkhave bhikkhū satisambojjhaṅgaṃ bhāvessanti, dhammavicayasambojjhaṅgaṃ bhāvessanti, viriyasambojjhaṅgaṃ bhāvessanti, pītisambojjhaṅgaṃ bhāvessanti, passaddhisambojjhaṅgaṃ bhāvessanti, samādhisambojjhaṅgaṃ bhāvessanti, upekhāsambojjhaṅgaṃ bhāvessanti, vuddhi yeva bhikkhave bhikkhūnaṃ pāṭikaṅkhā no parihāni. yāvakīvañ ca bhikkhave ime satta aparihāniyā dhammā bhikkhūsu ṭhassanti imesu ca sattasu aparihāniyesu dhammesu bhikkhū sandissanti, vuddhi yeva bhikkhave bhikkhūnaṃ pāṭikaṅkhā no parihāni . . .

tatra sudaṃ bhagavā Rājagahe viharanto Gijjhakūṭe pabbate etad eva bahulaṃ bhikkhūnaṃ dhammiṃ kathaṃ karoti: iti sīlaṃ iti samādhi iti paññā, sīlaparibhāvito samādhi mahapphalo hoti mahānisaṃso, samādhiparibhāvitā paññā mahapphalā hoti mahānisaṃsā, paññāparibhāvitaṃ cittaṃ sammad eva āsavehi vimuccati, seyyathīdaṃ kāmāsavā bhavāsavā diṭṭhāsavā avijjāsavā ti.

2. addasā kho bhikkhave Vipassī kumāro uyyānabhūmiṃ niyyanto mahājanakāyaṃ sannipatitaṃ; nānārattānañ ca dussānaṃ milātaṃ kayiramānaṃ. disvā sārathiṃ āmantesi: kin nu kho so samma sārathi mahājanakāyo sannipatito; nānārattānañ ca dussānaṃ milātaṃ kayiratī ti. eso kho deva kālakato nāmā ti. tena hi samma sārathi yena so kālakato tena rathaṃ pesehī ti. evaṃ devā ti kho bhikkhave sārathi Vipassissa kumārassa paṭissutvā yena so kālakato tena rathaṃ pesesi. addasā kho bhikkhave Vipassī kumāro petaṃ kālakataṃ. disvā sārathiṃ āmantesi: kim panāyaṃ samma sārathi kālakato nāmā ti. eso kho deva kālakato nāma: na dāni taṃ dakkhinti mātā vā pitā vā aññe vā ñātisālohitā, so pi na dakkhis-

sati mātaraṃ vā pitaraṃ vā aññe vā ñātisālohite ti. kim pana samma sārathi aham pi maraṇadhammo maraṇaṃ anatīto, mam pi na dakkhinti devo vā devī vā aññe vā ñātisālohitā, aham pi na dakkhissāmi devaṃ vā deviṃ vā aññe vā ñātisālohite ti. evañ ca deva mayañ c' amhā sabbe maraṇadhammā maraṇaṃ anatītā. tam pi na dakkhinti devo vā devī vā aññe vā ñātisālohitā. tvam pi na dakkhissasi devaṃ vā deviṃ vā aññe vā ñātisālohite ti. tena hi samma sārathi alan dān' ajja uyyānabhūmiyā, ito va antepuraṃ paccāniyyāhī ti. evaṃ devā ti kho bhikkhave sārathi Vipassissa kumārassa paṭissutvā tato va antepuraṃ paccāniyyāsi. tatra sudaṃ bhikkhave Vipassī kumāro antepuragato dukkhī dummano pajjhāyati: dhir atthu kira bho jāti nāma, yatra hi nāma jātassa jarā paññāyissati, vyādhi paññāyissati, maraṇaṃ paññāyissatī ti.

. . . addasā kho bhikkhave Vipassī kumāro uyyānabhūmiṃ niyyanto purisaṃ bhaṇḍuṃ pabbajitaṃ kāsāyavasanaṃ. disvā sārathiṃ āmantesi: ayam pana samma sārathi puriso kiṃ kato, sīsam pi 'ssa na yathā aññesaṃ, vatthāni pi 'ssa na yathā aññesan ti. eso kho deva pabbajito nāmā ti. kim pan' eso samma sārathi pabbajito nāmā ti. eso kho deva pabbajito nāma: sādhu dhammacariyā sādhu samacariyā sādhu kusalakiriyā sādhu puññakiriyā sādhu avihiṃsā sādhu bhūtānukampā ti. sādhu kho so samma sārathi pabbajito nāma sādhu hi samma sārathi dhammacariyā sādhu samacariyā sādhu kusalakiriyā sādhu puññakiriyā sādhu avihiṃsā sādhu bhūtānukampā. tena hi samma sārathi yena so pabbajito tena rathaṃ pesehī ti. evaṃ devā ti kho bhikkhave sārathi Vipassissa kumārassa paṭissutvā yena so pabbajito tena rathaṃ pesesi. atha kho bhikkhave Vipassī kumāro taṃ pabbajitaṃ etad avoca: tvaṃ pana samma kiṃ kato, sīsam pi te na yathā aññesaṃ, vatthāni pi te na yathā aññesan ti. ahaṃ kho deva pabbajito nāmā ti. kiṃ pana tvaṃ samma pabbajito nāmā ti. ahaṃ kho deva pabbajito nāma: sādhu dhammacariyā sādhu samacariyā sādhu kusalakiriyā sādhu puññakiriyā sādhu avihiṃsā sādhu bhūtānukampā ti. sādhu kho tvaṃ samma pabbajito nāma, sādhu hi samma dhammacariyā sādhu samacariyā sādhu kusalakiriyā sādhu puññakiriyā sādhu avihiṃsā sādhu bhūtānukampā ti. atha kho bhikkhave Vipassī kumāro sārathiṃ āmantesi: tena hi samma sārathi rathaṃ ādāya ito va antepuraṃ paccāniyyāhi. ahaṃ pana idh' eva kesamassuṃ ohāretvā kāsāyāni vatthāni acchādetvā agārasmā anagāriyaṃ pabbajissāmī ti. evaṃ devā ti kho sārathi Vipassissa kumārassa paṭissutvā, rathaṃ ādāya tato va antepuraṃ paccāniyyāsi. Vipassī pana kumāro tatth' eva kesamassuṃ ohāretvā kāsāyāni vatthāni acchādetvā agārasmā anagāriyaṃ pabbaji.

3. idh' avuso bhikkhunā kammaṃ kātabbaṃ hoti. tassa evaṃ hoti — kammaṃ kho me kātabbaṃ bhavissati, kammaṃ kho pana me karontassa kāyo kilamissati, handāhaṃ nipajjāmī ti. so nipajjati, na viriyaṃ ārabhati appattassa pattiyā anadhigatassa adhigamāya asacchikatassa sacchikiriyāya. idaṃ paṭhamaṃ kusītavatthuṃ. puna ca paraṃ āvuso bhikkhunā kammaṃ kataṃ hoti. tassa evaṃ hoti — ahaṃ kho kammaṃ akāsiṃ, kammaṃ kho pana me karontassa kāyo kilanto, handāhaṃ nipajjāmī ti. so nipajjati, na viriyaṃ ārabhati . . . pe . . . idaṃ dutiyaṃ kusītavatthuṃ. puna ca paraṃ āvuso bhikkhunā maggo gantabbo hoti. tassa evaṃ hoti — maggo kho me gantabbo bhavissati, maggaṃ kho pana me gacchantassa kāyo kilamissati, handāhaṃ nipajjāmī ti. so nipajjati, na viriyaṃ ārabhati . . . idaṃ tatiyaṃ kusītavatthuṃ. puna ca paraṃ āvuso bhikkhunā maggo gato hoti. tassa evaṃ hoti — ahaṃ kho maggaṃ agamāsiṃ, maggaṃ kho pana me gacchantassa kāyo kilanto, handāhaṃ nipajjāmī ti. so nipajjati, na viriyaṃ ārabhati . . . idaṃ catutthaṃ kusītavatthuṃ.

Translate into Pali :—

Now at that time in Sāketa [1] the wife of a moneylender had (present tense) an illness-of-the-head (which-had-lasted-for-) seven-years (use suffix *-ika*). Many great, foremost-of-(all-) regions, doctors had come (but) could not make (her) well. They went (off) taking much gold.

Then Jīvaka Komārabhacca entered Sāketa (and) asked people : " Who, I say, (is) ill ? Whom (shall) I cure ? " " This, O teacher, moneylender's wife has a seven-years-old head-illness. Go, teacher, cure the moneylender's wife." Then Jīvaka

[1] A city in the kingdom of Kosala, North-West of Magadha.

approached the house of the moneylender, who was a householder, (and) having approached ordered the porter: "Go, I say, O porter, tell the moneylender's wife: A doctor, lady, (has) come; he wishes to see you." (Saying:) "Yes, teacher," the porter, having assented to Jīvaka Komārabhacca, approached the moneylender's wife, (and) having approached said this to the moneylender's wife: "A doctor, lady, (has) come; he wishes to see you." "What sort, I say, porter, (of) doctor?" "Young, lady." "Enough! I say, porter; what use is a young doctor to me?[1] Many great, internationally-leading doctors have come (and) could not make (me) well. They went taking much gold."

Then the porter (returned to Jīvaka for further instructions) . . . said this to the moneylender's wife: "The doctor, lady, has spoken (*āha*) thus: Don't now (*kira*) lady give anything in advance. When you have become (aorist) well (fem.), then (you) may give me what you wish." "Now I say, porter, let the doctor come."

LESSON 25

Derivation

It was mentioned on p. 6 above that in theory all words are "derived" from roots, the roots being irreducible meaningful elements of the language. It may be noted here that the Buddhist theory of language (accepted by all Schools of Buddhism, though they differ on details) is that it is conventional (*vohāra*). Sounds in themselves are meaningless, but meanings are arbitrarily assigned to groups of sounds by social convention. Quite often these meanings change through usage (*rūḷhi*). The Brahmanical (Mīmāṃsā) tradition on the other hand holds that language (the Vedic language) is eternal and existed before men made use of it. It is clear that on the Buddhist view analysis and the setting up of roots, suffixes,

[1] *kiṃ . . . karissati*, "what will/can he/it do?" means much the same as "what's the use of?"

and inflections is pure abstraction: there are no roots in reality, but we find it convenient to group words around them for descriptive purposes. Some Brahmanical grammarians likewise held that analysis is pure abstraction and that in reality only sentences exist.

The suffixes by the addition of which "derivation" takes place are also meaningful elements, but of a different kind and with much more general meanings (or "grammatical meanings": thus *-ta* is such a suffix, meaning "past participle", "completed action"). A third and last group of meaningful elements, still more general in meaning, is the inflections of verbs and nouns. In the case of verbs it is essential to learn the roots (or prefix + roots, i.e. "verbs") to which the manifold tense stems and participle stems belong, carrying the same meaning with only distinctions of time and mode. In the case of nouns, however, it is usually more convenient to learn the separate words without much attention to derivation, especially as the meanings of nouns derived from a common root are often widely divergent and it is these distinctions of meaning, rather than any similarity, which it is essential to discover and remember.

Primary Derivation

The derivation of a stem directly from a root is called "primary" (*kita*) derivation, and nouns derived in this way are called primary nouns (*kitakanāma*). They include participles, gerunds, infinitives, the agent noun, action nouns, possessive nouns (the *kita* suffix *-in*) and a number of nouns having the suffix *-a* forming their stems. For theoretical purposes several distinct suffixes *-a* are assumed, since their "meanings" are distinct (thus one means "action noun"), or, in some cases, the process of derivation includes an alteration to the root. At least one of these must be noticed as yielding a group of words close to their roots in meaning and forming important nouns from them. To distinguish one suffix from another of the same form a fictitious addition, called an "exponent" (*anubandha*) is attached to it, being a letter not likely to cause confusion by any resemblance to another word or morpheme. A prefixed *ṇ* is a common exponent, since no words begin with *ṇ*. In the present group of words the suffix *-a* is labelled: *ṇa*.

The words thus formed cannot stand alone, but only as the second members of compounds. When *ṇa* is added a root must be strengthened (lengthened) as for the seventh conjugation (*vuddhi* : *a* > *ā*, *i* > *e*, *u* > *o*) ; if the root ends in *ā*, *y* is inserted between the root and the suffix. Thus from *kar* we have *-kāra*, " maker," " doer " (as in *kumbhakāro*, " potter ") ; from *dā* *-dāya*, " giver." (Compare the action noun suffix *a*—no exponent—yielding, e.g., *-kara*—no root strengthening.) The suffix called *ra* requires the elision of the final consonant and proceeding vowel of the root. It is used, e.g., with *gam* and *jan*, yielding the words *-ga* and *-ja*. (The zero suffix which is added for example to the root *bhū* in forming *abhibhū* is called *kvi* (all of which is thus exponent). When *kvi* is added to a root ending in a consonant (e.g. *gam*, *han*) the final consonant is dropped : *ura-ga* (*urago* = " snake "), *saṃ-gha* (*saṃgho*).)

Secondary Derivation

If a new word is derived not directly from a root but secondarily from another word-stem the derivation is called " secondary " (*taddhita*). Nouns thus derived are called secondary nouns (*taddhitanāma*). The suffixes used are distinguished from the primary suffixes, though sometimes they coincide in form with these. Among the secondary nouns (or adjectives) are some possessives (some of those in *in* and all of those in *mant* and *vant* [1]), various numeral forms (ordinals, etc.), comparatives in *tara*, abstract nouns and a miscellaneous group. (A number of suffixes forming indeclinables also belong to secondary derivation.) Abstract and other secondary nouns are formed freely in Pali, in principle from any noun or adjective, and their derivation is an important feature of the grammar of the language as well as a useful source of vocabulary.

Abstract Nouns

Abstract nouns are formed by the addition of the suffixes *-tā* (always feminine) or *-tta(ṃ)* (almost always neuter) to existing stems.

[1] These suffixes are known as *ī* (*taddhita*) or *ṇī* (*kita*), *mantu*, and *vantu*, where *n* and *u* are exponents (the feminine suffix *-ī* is also known as *ī* by some grammarians, but others label it *ṅī* ; the feminine possessive is given as *inī*).

devatā (" deity ", " any divine being "—whether " god " or " goddess ") < *devo*
vepullatā (" abundance ") < *vepullaṃ*
itthattaṃ (" this world ", lit. " thus-ness ") < *itthaṃ*
nānattaṃ (" variety ", " diversity ") < *nānā*
mandattaṃ (" ineptitude ") < *manda*
sattattaṃ (" existence ", " being-hood ") double abstract < *sant* + *-tta* + *-tta*

Various Secondary Nouns (including Adjectives)

Other secondary nouns are formed by the suffixes *ṇa* (i.e. *-a*, which if the stem already ends in *a* makes no change), *ṇeyya* (i.e. *-eyya*), *(ṇ)ika*,[1] *(ṇ)iya*, *(ṇ)aka*, *(ṇ)ya*, *ima*, *ssa*, and others, with strengthening (lengthening, *vuddhi*) of the first vowel of the word. They are extremely common and a good many have occurred already in the exercises, being listed in the vocabularies as independent words. They may be nouns or adjectives. In the latter case the feminine form usually has its stem in *ī*.

akālika (" timeless ") < *a* + *kālo* + *(ṇ)ika*
aṭṭhaṅgika (" having eight factors ") < *aṭṭha* + *aṅgaṃ* + *(ṇ)ika*
ākiñcaññaṃ (" nothingness ") < *a* + *kiṃ* + *cana* (= *ci*) + *(ṇ)ya*
ānañcaṃ (" infinity ") < *a* + *anto* + *(ṇ)ya*
ānupubba (feminine *ānupubbī*) (" systematic ") < *anupubba* + *(ṇ)a*
ābādhika (" ill ") < *ābādho* + *(ṇ)ika*
āraññaka (" living in the forest ") < *araññaṃ* + *(ṇ)aka*
ārogyaṃ (" health ") < *a* + *rogo* + *(ṇ)ya*
āsabha (feminine : *āsabhī*) (" bold ", lit. : " bull-like ") < *usabho* (" bull ") + *(ṇ)a* (irregular *vuddhi*)
ehipassika (" verifiable ") < *ehi* (" come ! ") + *passa* (" see ! ") + *(ṇ)ika*
opanayika (" fruitful ", lit. : " leading to ") < *upanayo* + *(ṇ)ika*
kāveyyaṃ (" poetry ") < *kavi* + *(ṇ)eyya*

[1] From here the exponents are enclosed in brackets.

Kosinārako (" inhabitant/citizen of *Kusinārā* ") : suffix (*ṇ*)*aka*
gamma (" vulgar ") < *gāmo* + (*ṇ*)*ya* (*ā* shortened before conjunct)
gāravo (" respect ") < *garu* + (*ṇ*)*a*
gelaññaṃ (" illness ") < *gilāna* + (*ṇ*)*ya* (with assimilation, *ny* > *ññ*)
cātummahābhūtika (" compounded of the four elements ") < *catu*(*r*) + *mahābhūtaṃ* + (*ṇ*)*ika*
jānapado (" countryman ", " country dweller ") < *janapado* + (*ṇ*)*a*
dāsavyaṃ (" slavery ") < *dāso* + *vya*
dhamma (feminine : *dhammī*) (" doctrinal ") < *dhammo* + (*ṇ*)*ya* (with assimilation of *y* to *m*)
negamo (" burgher ", " bourgeois ", " town dweller ") < *nigamo* (" town ") + (*ṇ*)*a*
Pāṭaligāmiyo (" inhabitant of *Pāṭaligāmo* ") : suffix (*ṇ*)*iya*
pāsādika (" lovely ") < *pasāda* + (*ṇ*)*ika*
ponobhavika (" leading to rebirth ") < *puna*(*r*) + *bhavo* + (*ṇ*)*ika*
majjhima (" middling ", " medium ") < *majjha* + *ima*
Māgadho (" of *Magadho* ", " Magadhan ") < *Magadho* + (*ṇ*)*a*
Vāseṭṭho (" descendant of *Vasiṭṭho* ", " member of the V. clan ") < *Vasiṭṭho* + (*ṇ*)*a* (irregular change of *i* > *e*)
vī̆riyaṃ [1] (" energy ") < *vīro* + (*ṇ*)*ya* (or (*ṇ*)*iya* according to some grammarians, but the best explanation appears to be by the junction *r* + *y* > *riy*, since the language tends to avoid such conjunct consonants)
sandiṭṭhika (" visible ") < *sandiṭṭha* + (*ṇ*)*ika*
sāpateyyaṃ (" property ") < *sa* (" own ") + *pati* (" lord ") + (*ṇ*)*eyya*
somanassaṃ (" joy ") < *su* + *manas* + *ssa*

Sometimes the distinction of these derived words can be inferred only from the context. E.g. *Gotamo* (clan) = *Gotamo* (the ancestor of the clan) + (*ṇ*)*a*.

[1] Usually written with the first *i* short, but it seems in fact to have been pronounced long. (In verse this word sometimes scans as only two syllables : *vir*[*i*]*yaṃ* ; here the first *i* might be written short because a conjunct follows it, cf. Lesson 23.

Junction Consonants

A junction consonant is a non-morphological consonant appearing between two vowels in junction. Certain finals given in brackets in this book might be classed as morphological or non-morphological, the exact dividing line being arbitrary. (This bracketing system could be extended.) All are regarded as non-morphological in the medieval grammars, whereas here we have preferred to show some of them as if belonging to certain words by adding them in brackets in cases where only those, and not other junction consonants, appear regularly with these words. Examples are *u(d)*, *du(r)*, *puna(d)*, and *saki(d)*.

Usually hiatus between two vowels is avoided in close junction, and if vowel junction (by elision, etc.) is not made a junction consonant is inserted. These consonants include *t, d, m, y, r*.

t may appear after *tasmā* : *tasmātiha*
d may appear after *sammā*, with shortening of *ā* : *bahudeva* (see Vocabulary), *sammadaññā* (cf. *puna, saki*, above) ; it may also appear between two words in a compound : *aññadatthu*
m may appear especially where a word is repeated, particularly in forming a compound : *ekameka*
y may appear after or before *i* (vowel > semi-vowel in junction with another vowel [1]) : *pariyā, nayidaṃ*
r may appear instead of *y* in similar positions : *yathariva*
v may appear before *u* : *jānapadovuṭṭhāsi*.
(Very rarely, *h* appears before *e* : *hevaṃ*—this should perhaps be taken as emphatic and as in fact the indeclinable *ha*, not a phonetic phenomenon).

Avyayībhāva *Compounds*

Compounds used as adverbs are fairly common, and we have noted that *bahubbīhis*, like other adjectives, may be so used. Another form of compound, which is always indeclinable, is the *avyayībhāva* (" indeclinable-nature "). In these the first member is an indeclinable or a prefix, the second usually a noun, and the

[1] Cf. in Lesson 23 *te* > *ty*, *su* > *sv*, *iti* > *ity* > *icc*, etc.

compound functions as an indeclinable (cf. in English " alongside "). Whereas in a *tappurisa* or *kammadhāraya* the second member may be said to predominate, and the first to be subordinated to it, in an *avyayībhāva* it is the first member which predominates. The second (final) member regularly has the inflexion of the neuter nominative/accusative singular as indeclinable form.

With a prefix as first member we have for example :—

ajjhattaṃ " internally " (*adhi* + *attan*, transferred to *-a* stem)
atibāḷhaṃ " too much "
anulomaṃ " in natural order ", " in normal order " (lit. : " along the hair "—*lomaṃ* = " hair (of the body) ")
paccattaṃ " individually ", " personally "
paṭipathaṃ " in the opposite direction ", " the other way "
paṭilomaṃ " in reverse order "

With an indeclinable as first member we have :—

tiropabbataṃ " through a mountain " (*tiro* = " through " : rarely used as a separate word)
pacchābhattaṃ " after the meal ", " after eating "
yathābalaṃ " according to one's ability "
yathābhūtaṃ " as it really is ", " according to nature "
yathāmittaṃ " with one's friends "
yāvajīvaṃ " as long as one lives ", " all one's life "
yāvadatthaṃ " as much as one wants " (*d* is junction consonant).

Vocabulary

Verbs :—

adhi-vas (I)	causative *adhivāseti* = agree to stay (i.e. reside, put up, in = acc.), accept an invitation	
anu-(k)kam (I)	*anukkamati*	walk along
anu-(s)su (V)	*anussuṇāti*	hear of
abhi-saṃ-budh (III)	*abhisambujjhati*	become enlightened, attain enlightenment

ava-sar (I) (*ava* is an alternative form of the prefix *o*)	*avasarati*	go down to, approach
ā-pucch (I)	*āpucchati*	ask leave (of absence)
u(d)-yuj (II)	causative *uyyojeti* = dismiss	
u(d)-har (I)	*uddharati*	dig up
jar (III)	*jīyati*	grow old
nam (I)	*namati*	bend, incline
ni-gam (I)	*nigacchati*	undergo, incur
ni(r)-pac (I)	*nippacati*	concoct
ni-vās (VII)	*nivāseti*	dress
(p)pa-(k)khal (VII)	*pakkhāleti*	wash
(p)paṭi-u(d)-ā-vatt (I)	*paccudāvattati*	turn back again
(p)paṭi-u(d)-(ṭ)ṭhā (I)	*paccuṭṭhāti*	rise
pari-(g)gah (V)	*parigganhāti*	occupy
(p)pa-hi (V)	*pahiṇāti*	send (aorist: *pāhesi*)
mar (III)	*mīyati*	die
māp (VII)	*māpeti*	build
saṃ-har (I)	*saṃharati*	gather
saṃ-thar (I)	*santharati*	strew, spread, carpet (the process is not clear, but appears to be a temporary but decorative floor covering)
saṃ-(d)dis	causative *sandasseti* = instruct	
saṃ-(p)pa-haṃs (VII)	*sampahaṃseti*	delight (transitive)
saṃ-ā-dā	causative *samādapeti* = exhort	
saṃ-u(d)-tij (VII)	*samuttejeti*	excite, fill with enthusiasm
saṃ-lakkh (VII)	*sallakkheti*	observe

Nouns :—

adhikaraṇaṃ	case, affair
adhivāsanaṃ	acceptance of an invitation
anvayo	inference
apāyo	misery
abhisamayo	insight
ambaṃ	mango fruit (usually neut.)

ambo	mango tree (usually masc.)
āvasathāgāraṃ	rest house, hostel (maintained by a local council as a public service)
udakamaṇi (masc.)	water-jar
uddāpo	foundations
uddeko	sickness, vomiting
upakkileso	corruption
kasāvaṃ	astringent
kitti (fem.)	fame
toraṇaṃ	gateway
thambho	column
duggati (fem.)	a bad fate, evil destiny
dussīlo	bad character
dūto	messenger
nādo	roar
nāmarūpaṃ	matter plus mind, sentient body (cf. Lesson 29)
nirayo	purgatory
nissakkanaṃ	escaping, leaving
nīvaraṇaṃ	obstacle (there are five obstacles to escaping from mental attachment to the world : desire, aversion, stupidity, pride—i.e. concern about the opinion of others—and uncertainty)
paṭibāho	repulse, repelling
paṭṭhānaṃ	basis
paṇḍurogo	jaundice
padakkhiṇā	reverence, veneration, circumambulation
padīpo	lamp
pākāro	city wall, ramparts
puṭo	bag, package (of merchandise)
phasso	touch, contact
biḷāro	cat
bodhi (fem.)	enlightenment
bodhisatto	being (destined) for enlightenment, future Buddha, Bodhisattva
bhitti (fem.)	wall
bhedanaṃ	opening

muhuttaṃ (or masc.)	moment
vaṇippatho	trade
vanaṃ	a wood
vāhanaṃ	mount (animal or vehicle)
vāhanāgāraṃ	stable, coach-house, mews
vikāro	disorder
vinipāto	ruin
vipatti (fem.)	failure
vivaraṃ	hole
saḷāyatanaṃ	the six spheres (of the senses: five senses + the mind)
sugati (fem.)	good destiny

Adjectives :—

atikkanta	surpassing
anāgata	(means also) future
anupariyāya	circling (*-patho* = the walk on top of a city wall)
abhikkanta	excellent
abhiñña	learned
abhimukha	facing
avisārada	diffident
uḷāra	mighty
ekaṃsa	definite, decided, confident
kevala	entire, whole
caṇḍa	fierce, irascible
jeguccha	disgusting
tādisa	this sort (of)
dubbalīkaraṇa	weakening
nīca	low, inferior
paccuppanna	present (time)
paṭikkūla	distasteful, disagreeable
pariya	encompassing
pāpaka	bad
bahu	much, many
majjhima	middle, intermediate
medhāvin	intelligent
visārada	confident
visuddha	pure, clear

vūpakaṭṭha	withdrawn, secluded
sabbasanthari	entirely strewn, having complete carpeting
sambahula	many
sīlavant	virtuous, well conducted

Past Participles :—

nadita (*nad*)	roared
pasanna ((*p*)*pa-sīd* I)	confident in, trusting
pīta (*pā*)	drunk
vipanna (*vi-pad*)	failed, lacking, without
sammūḷha (*saṃ-muh*)	bewildered

Present Participle :—

pariṇāment (causative of *pari-nam*)	digesting

Numeral :—

caturāsīti (fem.)	eighty (inflected like *jāti*)

Gerunds :—

paricca (*pari-i*)	going to, going round, encompassing
purakkhatvā (*pura*(*s*)-*kar*) (the prefix *pura*(*s*) means "before")	facing

Indeclinables :—

ajjatanāya	for to-day
antamaso	even
kudā	when ?
carahi	therefore, then
paṭigacc' eva	as a precaution
puratthā	east
yathābhirantaṃ	according to one's pleasure, (as long) as one likes
yāvatā	as far as
vinā	without (precedes ins.)
sādhu	(also means) please

EXERCISE 25

Passages for reading :—

1. atha kho bhagavā mahatā bhikkhusaṃghena saddhiṃ yena Nāḷandā [1] tad avasari. tatra sudaṃ bhagavā Nāḷandāyaṃ viharati Pāvārikambavane. atha kho āyasmā Sāriputto [2] yena bhagavā ten' upasaṃkami, upasaṃkamitvā bhagavantaṃ abhivādetvā ekamantaṃ nisīdi. ekamantaṃ nisinno kho āyasmā Sāriputto bhagavantaṃ etad avoca : evaṃpasanno ahaṃ bhante bhagavati na cāhu [3] na ca bhavissati na c' etarahi vijjati añño samaṇo vā brāhmaṇo vā bhagavatā bhiyyo 'bhiññataro yad idaṃ sambodhiyan ti.

uḷārā kho te ayaṃ Sāriputta āsabhī vācā bhāsitā, ekaṃso gahito sīhanādo nadito : evaṃpasanno ahaṃ bhante bhagavati na cāhu na ca bhavissati na c' etarahi vijjati añño samaṇo vā brāhmaṇo vā bhagavatā bhiyyo 'bhiññataro yad idaṃ sambodhiyan ti. kin nu Sāriputta ye te ahesuṃ atītam addhānaṃ arahanto sammāsambuddhā, sabbe te bhagavanto cetasā ceto paricca viditā evaṃsīlā te bhagavanto ahesuṃ iti pi, evaṃdhammā evaṃpaññā evaṃvihārī evaṃvimuttā te bhagavanto ahesuṃ iti pī ti. no h' etaṃ bhante. kiṃ pana Sāriputta ye te bhavissanti anāgatam addhānaṃ arahanto sammāsambuddhā, sabbe te bhagavanto cetasā ceto paricca viditā evaṃsīlā te bhagavanto bhavissanti iti pi, evaṃdhammā evaṃpaññā evaṃvihārī evaṃvimuttā te bhagavanto bhavissanti iti pī ti. no h' etaṃ bhante. kiṃ pana Sāriputta ahaṃ te etarahi arahaṃ sammāsambuddho cetasā ceto paricca vidito evaṃsīlo bhagavā iti pi, evaṃdhammo evaṃpañño evaṃvihārī evaṃvimutto bhagavā iti pī ti. no h' etaṃ bhante. etth' eva hi te Sāriputta atītānāgatapaccuppannesu arahantesu sammāsambuddhesu cetopariyañāṇaṃ n' atthi. atha kiñ carahi te ayaṃ Sāriputta uḷārā āsabhī vācā bhāsitā ekaṃso gahito sīhanādo nadito, evaṃpasanno ahaṃ bhante bhagavati na cāhu na ca bhavissati na c' etarahi vijjati añño samaṇo vā brāhmaṇo vā bhagavatā bhiyyo 'bhiññataro yad idaṃ sambodhiyan ti.

[1] A town about a league (*yojanaṃ*) north of Rājagaha, later the site of the most famous Buddhist university.

[2] The Buddha's leading disciple, who seems to have been largely responsible for the systematic study of his master's doctrines. He predeceased the Buddha, dying at Nāḷandā shortly after the present episode.

[3] *ahu*, 3rd singular " root " aorist of *hū* (see Lesson 30), " there was."

na kho me bhante atītānāgatapaccuppannesu arahantesu sammāsambuddhesu cetopariyañāṇaṃ atthi. api ca dhammanvayo vidito. seyyathā pi bhante rañño paccantimaṃ nagaraṃ daḷhuddāpaṃ daḷhapākāratoraṇaṃ ekadvāraṃ, tatr' assa dovāriko paṇḍito viyatto medhāvī aññātānaṃ nivāretā ñātānaṃ pavesetā. so tassa nagarassa samantā anupariyāyapathaṃ anukkamamāno na passeyya pākārasandhiṃ vā pākāravivaraṃ vā antamaso biḷāranissakkanamattam pi. tassa evam assa, ye kho keci oḷārikā pāṇā imaṃ nagaraṃ pavisanti vā nikkhamanti vā, sabbe te iminā va dvārena pavisanti vā nikkhamanti vā ti. evam eva kho me bhante dhammanvayo vidito. ye te bhante ahesuṃ atītam addhānaṃ arahanto sammāsambuddhā, sabbe te bhagavanto pañca nīvaraṇe pahāya cetaso upakkilese paññāya dubbalīkaraṇe, catusu satipaṭṭhānesu supatiṭṭhitacittā satta bojjhaṅge yathābhūtaṃ bhāvetvā anuttaraṃ sammāsambodhiṃ abhisambujjhiṃsu. ye pi te bhante bhavissanti anāgataṃ . . . abhisambujjhissanti. bhagavā pi bhante etarahi . . . abhisambuddho ti . . .

atha kho bhagavā Nāḷandāyaṃ yathābhirantaṃ viharitvā āyasmantaṃ Ānandaṃ āmantesi : āyām' Ānanda yena Pāṭaligāmo ten' upasaṃkamissāmā ti. evaṃ bhante ti kho āyasmā Ānando bhagavato paccassosi. atha kho bhagavā mahatā bhikkhusaṃghena saddhiṃ yena Pāṭaligāmo tad avasari. assosuṃ kho Pāṭaligāmiyā upāsakā bhagavā kira Pāṭaligāmaṃ anuppatto ti. atha kho Pāṭaligāmiyā upāsakā yena bhagavā ten' upasaṃkamiṃsu, upasaṃkamitvā bhagavantaṃ abhivādetvā ekamantaṃ nisīdiṃsu. ekamantaṃ nisinnā kho Pāṭaligāmiyā upāsakā bhagavantaṃ etad avocuṃ : adhivāsetu no bhante bhagavā āvasathāgāran ti. adhivāsesi bhagavā tuṇhībhāvena. atha kho Pāṭaligāmiyā upāsakā bhagavato adhivāsanaṃ viditvā uṭṭhāy' āsanā, bhagavantaṃ abhivādetvā, padakkhiṇaṃ katvā, yena āvasathāgāraṃ ten' upasaṃkamiṃsu, upasaṃkamitvā sabbasanthariṃ āvasathāgāraṃ santharitvā āsanāni paññāpetvā udakamaṇiṃ patiṭṭhāpetvā telappadīpaṃ āropetvā yena bhagavā ten' upasaṃkamiṃsu, upasaṃkamitvā bhagavantaṃ abhivādetvā ekamantam aṭṭhaṃsu. ekamantaṃ ṭhitā kho Pāṭaligāmiyā upāsakā bhagavantaṃ etad avocuṃ : sabbasanthariṃ santhataṃ bhante āvasathāgāraṃ, āsanāni paññattāni, udakamaṇiko patiṭṭhāpito, telappadīpo āropito, yassa dāni bhante bhagavā kālaṃ maññatī ti.

atha kho bhagavā nivāsetvā pattacīvaraṃ ādāya saddhiṃ bhikkhusaṃghena yena āvasathāgāraṃ ten' upasaṃkami, upasaṃkamitvā pāde pakkhāletvā āvasathāgāraṃ pavisitvā majjhimaṃ thambhaṃ nissāya puratthābhimukho nisīdi. bhikkhusaṃgho pi kho pāde pakkhāletvā āvasathāgāraṃ pavisitvā pacchimaṃ bhittiṃ nissāya puratthābhimukho nisīdi bhagavantaṃ yeva purakkhatvā. Pāṭaligāmiyā pi kho upāsakā pāde pakkhāletvā āvasathāgāraṃ pavisitvā puratthimaṃ bhittiṃ nissāya pacchābhimukhā nisīdiṃsu bhagavantaṃ yeva purakkhatvā. atha kho bhagavā Pāṭaligāmiye upāsake āmantesi : pañc' ime gahapatayo ādīnavā dussīlassa sīlavipattiyā. katame pañca. idha gahapatayo dussīlo sīlavipanno pamādādhikaraṇaṃ mahatiṃ bhogajāniṃ nigacchati. ayaṃ paṭhamo ādīnavo dussīlassa sīlavipattiyā. puna ca paraṃ gahapatayo dussīlassa sīlavipannassa pāpako kittisaddo abbhuggacchati. ayaṃ dutiyo ādīnavo dussīlassa sīlavipattiyā. puna ca paraṃ gahapatayo dussīlo sīlavipanno yaṃ yad eva parisaṃ upasaṃkamati, yadi khattiyaparisaṃ yadi brāhmaṇaparisaṃ yadi gahapatiparisaṃ yadi samaṇaparisaṃ, avisārado upasaṃkamati maṅkubhūto. ayaṃ tatiyo ādīnavo dussīlassa sīlavipattiyā. puna ca paraṃ gahapatayo dussīlo sīlavipanno sammūḷho kālaṃ karoti. ayaṃ catuttho ādīnavo dussīlassa sīlavipattiyā. puna ca paraṃ gahapatayo dussīlo sīlavipanno kāyassa bhedā param maraṇā apāyaṃ duggatiṃ vinipātaṃ nirayaṃ upapajjati. ayaṃ pañcamo ādīnavo dussīlassa sīlavipattiyā. ime kho gahapatayo pañca ādīnavā dussīlassa sīlavipattiyā.

pañc' ime gahapatayo ānisaṃsā sīlavato sīlasampadāya. katame pañca. idha gahapatayo sīlavā sīlasampanno appamādādhikaraṇaṃ mahantaṃ bhogakkhandhaṃ adhigacchati. ayaṃ paṭhamo ānisaṃso sīlavato sīlasampadāya. puna ca paraṃ gahapatayo sīlavato sīlasampannassa kalyāṇo kittisaddo abbhuggacchati. ayaṃ dutiyo ānisaṃso sīlavato sīlasampadāya. puna ca paraṃ gahapatayo sīlavā sīlasampanno yaṃ yad eva parisaṃ upasaṃkamati, yadi khattiyaparisaṃ yadi brāhmaṇaparisaṃ yadi gahapatiparisaṃ yadi samaṇaparisaṃ, visārado upasaṃkamati amaṅkubhūto. ayaṃ tatiyo ānisaṃso sīlavato sīlasampadāya. puna ca paraṃ gahapatayo sīlavā sīlasampanno asammūḷho kālaṃ karoti. ayaṃ catuttho ānisaṃso sīlavato sīlasampadāya. puna ca paraṃ gahapatayo sīlavā sīlasampanno kāyassa bhedā param maraṇā sugatiṃ saggaṃ lokaṃ upapajjati. ayaṃ pañcamo ānisaṃso sīlavato sīlasampadāya. ime kho gahapatayo pañca ānisaṃsā sīlavato sīlasampadāyā ti. atha kho bhagavā Pāṭaligāmiye upāsake bahud eva rattiṃ dhammiyā kathāya sandassetvā samādapetvā samuttejetvā sampahaṃsetvā uyyojesi, abhikkantā kho gahapatayo ratti, yassa dāni kālaṃ maññathā ti. evam bhante ti kho Pāṭaligāmiyā upāsakā bhagavato paṭissutvā uṭṭhāy' āsanā bhagavantaṃ abhivādetvā padakkhiṇaṃ katvā pakkamiṃsu. atha kho bhagavā acirapakkantesu Pāṭaligāmiyesu upāsakesu suññāgāraṃ pāvisi.

tena kho pana samayena Sunīdha-Vassakārā Magadhamahāmattā Pāṭaligāme nagaraṃ māpenti Vajjīnaṃ paṭibāhāya. tena kho pana samayena sambahulā devatāyo sahass' eva Pāṭaligāme vatthūni pariggaṇhanti. yasmiṃ padese mahesakkhā devatā vatthūni pariggaṇhanti, mahesakkhānaṃ tattha raññaṃ rājamahāmattānaṃ cittāni namanti nivesanāni māpetuṃ. yasmiṃ padese majjhimā devatā vatthūni pariggaṇhanti, majjhimānaṃ tattha raññaṃ rājamahāmattānaṃ cittāni namanti nivesanāni māpetuṃ. yasmiṃ padese nīcā devatā vatthūni pariggaṇhanti, nīcānaṃ tattha raññaṃ rājamahāmattānaṃ cittāni namanti nivesanāni māpetuṃ.

addasā kho bhagavā dibbena cakkhunā visuddhena atikkantamānusakena tā devatāyo sahass' eva Pāṭaligāme vatthūni pariggaṇhantiyo. atha kho bhagavā rattiyā paccūsasamayaṃ paccuṭṭhāya āyasmantaṃ Ānandaṃ āmantesi: ko nu kho Ānanda Pāṭaligāme nagaraṃ māpetī ti. Sunīdha-Vassakārā bhante Magadhamahāmattā Pāṭaligāme nagaraṃ māpenti Vajjīnaṃ paṭibāhāyā ti.

seyyathā pi Ānanda devehi Tāvatiṃsehi saddhiṃ mantetvā, evam eva kho Ānanda Sunīdha-Vassakārā Magadhamahāmattā Pāṭaligāme nagaraṃ māpenti Vajjīnaṃ paṭibāhāya. idhāhaṃ Ānanda addasaṃ dibbena cakkhunā visuddhena atikkantamānusakena sambahulā devatāyo sahass' eva Pāṭaligāme vatthūni pariggaṇhantiyo . . . nivesanāni māpetuṃ. yāvatā

Ānanda ariyaṃ āyatanaṃ yāvatā vaṇippatho idaṃ agganagaraṃ bhavissati Pāṭaliputtaṃ puṭabhedanaṃ. Pāṭaliputtassa kho Ānanda tayo [1] antarāyā bhavissanti, aggito vā udakato vā mithubhedā vā ti.

atha kho Sunīdha-Vassakārā Magadhamahāmattā yena bhagavā ten' upasaṃkamiṃsu, upasaṃkamitvā bhagavatā saddhiṃ sammodiṃsu sammodanīyaṃ kathaṃ sārāṇīyaṃ vītisāretvā ekamantaṃ aṭṭhaṃsu. ekamantaṃ ṭhitā kho Sunīdha-Vassakārā Magadhamahāmattā bhagavantaṃ etad avocuṃ : adhivāsetu no bhavaṃ Gotamo ajjatanāya bhattaṃ saddhiṃ bhikkhusaṃghenā ti. adhivāsesi bhagavā tuṇhībhāvena.

atha kho Sunīdha-Vassakārā Magadhamahāmattā bhagavato adhivāsanaṃ viditvā yena sako āvasatho ten' upasaṃkamiṃsu upasaṃkamitvā sake āvasathe paṇītaṃ khādaniyaṃ bhojaniyaṃ paṭiyādāpetvā bhagavato kālaṃ ārocāpesuṃ kālo bho Gotama niṭṭhitaṃ bhattan ti.

2. atha kho bhikkhave Vipassī bodhisatto aparena samayena eko gaṇasmā vūpakaṭṭho vihāsi. aññen' eva tāni caturāsītipabbajitasahassāni agamaṃsu, aññena Vipassī bodhisatto. atha kho bhikkhave Vipassissa bodhisattassa vāsupagatassa rahogatassa patisallīnassa evaṃ cetaso parivitakko udapādi : kicchaṃ vatāyaṃ loko āpanno, jāyati ca jīyati ca mīyati ca cavati ca upapajjati ca. atha ca pan' imassa dukkhassa nissaraṇaṃ na ppajānāti jarāmaraṇassa, kudā ssu nāma imassa dukkhassa nissaraṇaṃ paññāyissati jarāmaraṇassā ti.

atha kho bhikkhave Vipassissa bodhisattassa etad ahosi : kimhi nu kho sati jarāmaraṇaṃ hoti, kimpaccayā jarāmaraṇan ti. atha kho bhikkhave Vipassissa bodhisattassa yonisomanasikārā ahu [2] paññāya abhisamayo : jātiyā kho sati jarāmaraṇaṃ hoti, jātipaccayā jarāmaraṇan ti. atha kho bhikkhave Vipassissa bodhisattassa etad ahosi : kimhi nu kho sati jāti hoti, kimpaccayā jātī ti. atha kho bhikkhave Vipassissa bodhisattassa yonisomanasikārā ahu paññāya abhisamayo : bhave kho sati jāti hoti, bhavapaccayā jātī ti. atha kho bhikkhave Vipassissa bodhisattassa etad ahosi : kimhi nu kho

[1] " Three "—see next Lesson.
[2] " There was " : " root " aorist of *hū*, sec Lesson 30.

sati bhavo hoti, kimpaccayā bhavo ti. atha kho bhikkhave Vipassissa bodhisattassa yonisomanasikārā ahu paññāya abhisamayo : upādāne kho sati bhavo hoti, upādānapaccayā bhavo ti. atha kho bhikkhave Vipassissa bodhisattassa etad ahosi : kimhi nu kho sati upādānaṃ hoti, kimpaccayā upādānan ti. atha kho bhikkhave Vipassissa bodhisattassa yonisomanasikārā ahu paññāya abhisamayo : taṇhāya kho sati upādānaṃ hoti, taṇhāpaccayā upādānan ti. atha kho bhikkhave Vipassissa bodhisattassa etad ahosi : kimhi nu kho sati taṇhā hoti, kimpaccayā taṇhā ti. atha kho bhikkhave Vipassissa bodhisattassa yonisomanasikārā ahu paññāya abhisamayo : vedanāya kho sati taṇhā hoti, vedanāpaccayā taṇhā ti. atha kho bhikkhave Vipassissa bodhisattassa etad ahosi : kimhi nu kho sati vedanā hoti, kimpaccayā vedanā ti. atha kho bhikkhave Vipassissa bodhisattassa yonisomanasikārā ahu paññāya abhisamayo : phasse kho sati vedanā hoti, phassapaccayā vedanā ti. atha kho bhikkhave Vipassissa bodhisattassa etad ahosi : kimhi nu kho sati phasso hoti, kimpaccayā phasso ti. atha kho bhikkhave Vipassissa bodhisattassa yonisomanasikārā ahu paññāya abhisamayo : saḷāyatane kho sati phasso hoti, saḷāyatanapaccayā phasso ti. atha kho bhikkhave Vipassissa bodhisattassa etad ahosi : kimhi nu kho sati saḷāyatanaṃ hoti, kimpaccayā saḷāyatanan ti. atha kho bhikkhave Vipassissa bodhisattassa yonisomanasikārā ahu paññāya abhisamayo : nāmarūpe kho sati saḷāyatanaṃ hoti, nāmarūpapaccayā saḷāyatanan ti. atha kho bhikkhave Vipassissa bodhisattassa etad ahosi : kimhi nu kho sati nāmarūpaṃ hoti, kimpaccayā nāmarūpan ti. atha kho bhikkhave Vipassissa bodhisattassa yonisomanasikārā ahu paññāya abhisamayo : viññāṇe kho sati nāmarūpaṃ hoti, viññāṇapaccayā nāmarūpan ti. atha kho bhikkhave Vipassissa bodhisattassa etad ahosi : kimhi nu kho sati viññāṇaṃ hoti, kimpaccayā viññāṇan ti. atha kho bhikkhave Vipassissa bodhisattassa yonisomanasikārā ahu paññāya abhisamayo : nāmarūpe kho sati viññāṇaṃ hoti, nāmarūpapaccayā viññāṇan ti.

atha kho bhikkhave Vipassissa bodhisattassa etad ahosi : paccudāvattati kho idaṃ viññāṇaṃ nāmarūpamhā, nāparaṃ gacchati. ettāvatā jāyetha vā jīyetha vā mīyetha vā cavetha vā upapajjetha vā, yad idaṃ nāmarūpapaccayā viññāṇaṃ, viññāṇapaccayā nāmarūpaṃ, nāmarūpapaccayā saḷāyatanaṃ, saḷāyatanapaccayā phasso, phassapaccayā vedanā, vedanāpaccayā taṇhā, taṇhāpaccayā upādānaṃ, upādānapaccayā bhavo, bhavapaccayā jāti, jātipaccayā jarāmaraṇaṃ sokaparidevadukkhadomanassupāyāsā sambhavanti, evam etassa kevalassa dukkhakkhandhassa samudayo hoti. samudayo samudayo ti kho bhikkhave Vipassissa bodhisattassa pubbe ananussutesu dhammesu cakkhuṃ udapādi ñāṇaṃ udapādi paññā udapādi vijjā udapādi āloko udapādi.

atha kho bhikkhave Vipassissa bodhisattassa etad ahosi: kimhi nu kho asati jarāmaraṇaṃ na hoti, kissa nirodhā jarāmaraṇanirodho ti. atha kho bhikkhave Vipassissa bodhisattassa yonisomanasikārā ahu paññāya abhisamayo: jātiyā kho asati jarāmaraṇaṃ na hoti, jātinirodhā jarāmaraṇanirodho ti. atha kho bhikkhave Vipassissa bodhisattassa etad ahosi: kimhi nu kho asati jāti na hoti . . . nāmarūpanirodhā viññāṇanirodho, viññāṇanirodhā nāmarūpanirodho, nāmarūpanirodhā saḷāyatananirodho, saḷāyatananirodhā phassanirodho, phassanirodhā vedanānirodho, vedanānirodhā taṇhānirodho, taṇhānirodhā upādānanirodho, upādānanirodhā bhavanirodho, bhavanirodhā jātinirodho, jātinirodhā jarāmaraṇaṃ sokaparidevadukkhadomanassupāyāsā nirujjhanti, evam etassa kevalassa dukkhakkhandhassa nirodho hoti. nirodho nirodho ti kho bhikkhave Vipassissa bodhisattassa pubbe ananussutesu dhammesu cakkhuṃ udapādi ñāṇaṃ udapādi paññā udapādi vijjā udapādi āloko udapādi.

Translate into Pali :—

Now at that time king Pajjota [1] had jaundice. Many great, internationally-leading doctors came and could not make (him) well. They took much gold and went. Then king Pajjota sent a messenger into the presence of king Māgadha Seniya Bimbisāra : " I have this sort (of) illness, let the king (*devo*) please (put first) command Jīvaka the doctor, he will cure me." Then king Bimbisāra commanded Jīvaka : " Go, I say, Jīvaka, to Ujjenī [2] and cure king Pajjota." " Yes, O king," Jīvaka assented to king Bimbisāra, went to Ujjenī, approached king Pajjota,

[1] King of Avantī, western India.
[2] Capital of Avantī.

having approached and observed the disorder of king Pajjota said this to king Pajjota: "O king (place second), I will concoct ghee, the king (*devo*) will drink it." "(I) won't, I say, Jīvaka. If (*yaṃ*) it is possible for you to make (me) well without ghee, do it. Disgusting to me (is) ghee, distasteful."

Then Jīvaka thought: "This sort (of) illness of this king (it) is not possible to make well without ghee. Suppose I concoct ghee (so that it has) astringent-colour, astringent-odour, astringent-taste." Then Jīvaka concocted ghee with-various-drugs (so that it was) astringent-colour, astringent-odour, astringent-taste. Then Jīvaka thought: "To this king ghee, when drunk (and) digesting, will give vomiting. This king (is) irascible (put first), he may have me killed. Suppose I ask for leave as a precaution." Then Jīvaka approached king Pajjota and having approached said this to king Pajjota: "O king, we doctors, you know (*nāma*), at this sort (of) moment dig up roots, gather medicines. O king, please command at (loc.) the stables and gates: let Jīvaka go by any mount he likes, let him go by any gate he likes, let him go any time (acc.) he likes, let him enter any time he likes."

LESSON 26

Numerals [1]

The numeral stem *ti*, "three," is inflected in three genders as follows, and used like an adjective :—

	Masculine	Neuter	Feminine
Nom. / Acc.	*tayo*	*tīṇi*	*tisso*
Ins.	*tīhi*		*tīhi*
Dat.	*tiṇṇaṃ*		*tissannaṃ*
Abl.	*tīhi*		*tīhi*
Gen.	*tiṇṇaṃ*		*tissannaṃ*
Loc.	*tīsu*		*tīsu*

[1] See also Lessons 17, 18, and 20.

Of the remaining numerals, the following are inflected and used in the same way as *pañca*, "five" (see Lesson 17) :—

cha(ḷ)	six	(the final *ḷ* appears only in close junction as in compounds, e.g. *chaḷaṅga-*; it is assimilated to a following consonant; in certain compounds the form *sa(ḷ)* is current)
satta	seven	
aṭṭha	eight	
nava	nine	
dasa	ten	
ekādasa	eleven	
dvādasa	twelve	
teḷasa	thirteen	
cuddasa	fourteen	
paṇṇarasa	fifteen	
soḷasa	sixteen	
sattarasa	seventeen	
aṭṭhādasa	eighteen	

The following numerals are used as nouns, they are feminine singular and are inflected like *jāti* (Lesson 20) :—

vīsati	twenty
saṭṭhi	sixty
sattati	seventy
asīti	eighty
navuti	ninety

The following are neuter nouns, they are usually inflected (in the singular) like other neuters in *a*, but may also be used undeclined in the stem form :—

(t)tiṃsa	thirty	(usually *tt* in compounds)
cattārīsa	forty	(also found in a feminine form *cattārīsā* inflected like *kathā*: Lesson 17)
paññāsa	fifty	(also *-ā* feminine).

The remaining intermediate numbers are compounds having the usual inflections of the last member :—

ekūnavīsati	19	(*ekūna* = one less than-) (*ekūnapaññāsa* 49)
ekavīsati	21	(*ekanavuti* 91, and *ekatiṃsa* against the usual doubling)
dvāvīsati	22	(*dvāsaṭṭhi* 62, but *dvattiṃsa* 32 and *dvecattārīsaṃ* 42)
tevīsati	23	(*tettiṃsa* 33)
catuvīsati	24	(*caturāsīti* 84, *catucattārīsā* 44)
pañcavīsati	25	
chavīsati	26	(*chattiṃsa* 36 with doubling of the *t*)
sattavīsati	27	
aṭṭhavīsati	28	(*aṭṭhasaṭṭhi* 68)
ekūnatiṃsa	29	

Numerals which are nouns are generally used appositionally in the same case (but singular) as the noun they refer to (cf. *sata* and *sahassa*, Lesson 17). They may also form compounds with these nouns.

Fractions :—

aḍḍho (masc. or adjective, also spelt *addho*) " half " :—
aḍḍhayojanaṃ, " half a league "
upaḍḍha (adjective or neuter) " half " :—
upaḍḍhaṃ divasaṃ, " half a day "
upaḍḍhapathaṃ, " halfway " (adverb)

—" and a half " is expressed by prefixing *aḍḍha*- to the next higher numeral :—

(*diyaḍḍho*, " one and a half," not found in *Dīgha*)
aḍḍhateyya, " two and a half "
(*aḍḍhuḍḍha*, " three and a half," only in later texts) (the rest are regular)
aḍḍhateḷasa, " twelve and a half "

—for other fractions the ordinals are used, and they may be compounded with *bhāgo*, " part " :—

catuttha, " a quarter "
catutthabhāgo, " one fourth," " a quarter "

(On *sataṃ* and *sahassaṃ* see Lesson 17.)

The formation of numerals above 100 is somewhat fluid, and may be illustrated by the following examples.

101–199 may be formed by making compounds in which the odd amount is prefixed to the hundred, just as in 21, etc., the units are prefixed to the tens. Often, however, the word specifying what is enumerated is inserted between the odd amount and the hundred :—

saṭṭhivassasata 160 years
(*chasaṭṭhisata* 166—not in the *Dīgha*)

Alternatively the odd amount may follow the hundred as a separate word, followed by *ca*, " and," as connective (this method is rare in prose and may be characterized as poetic and elevated).

200, etc., are generally expressed by two words (note agreement : *tīṇi*, etc., neuter) :—

dve satāni 200
tīṇi satāni 300
cattāri satāni 400
pañca satāni 500

Here also compounds may be formed, though the simple compound seems rare and probably does not occur in the *Dīgha* (it would be liable to confusion if singular collective or part of a larger compound : *dvisata* = 102 or 200, though *dvisatāni* would be clear). Frequently a construction with *-matta* (" measure ") is used, including the objects enumerated (cf. the preceding paragraph) as follows :—

timattāni paribbājakasatāni " 300 wanderers "

201, etc., may be formed like 101, etc., as a compound including a compound for the hundreds or as separate groups of words joined by *ca*. In the former case the regular construction is of the type :—

vīsatitivassasata- [1] " 320 years "
cattārīsachabbassasata- [1] " 640 years "

[1] The examples quotable from the *Dīgha* are in larger compounds (*bahubbīhis*), e.g. : *vīsatitivassasatāyukā puttā*, " sons having a life of 320 years." In independent compounds in *-sata* we would expect the plural *-satāni*.

For 250, etc., there is a special construction using the fraction *aḍḍha* and the next higher hundred (cf. " two and a half " above) :—

aḍḍhateyyavassasatāni " 250 years "

1,001, etc., may be formed in the same ways as 101, etc. Note for example :—

aḍḍhateyyavassasahassāni " 2,500 years "

2,000, etc., are formed like 200, etc. :—

dve sahassāni 2,000

—or in compound form *dvevassasahassa-*

cattāri sahassāni 4,000

One also finds a continuing reckoning by hundreds above 1,000 :—

saddhiṃ tiṃsamattehi paribbājakasatehi " with 3,000 wanderers "

aḍḍhateḷasāni bhikkhusatāni " 1,250 monks "

Through the ten thousands we have :—

vīsati bhikkhusahassāni " 20,000 monks " (may also be written in compound with *vīsati*)
tiṃsa bhikkhusahassāni " 30,000 monks "
cattārīsa bhikkhusahassāni " 40,000 monks "
saṭṭhi bhikkhusahassāni " 60,000 monks "
sattati vassasahassāni " 70,000 years "
asīti vassasahassāni " 80,000 years "

(these may all be written as compounds, with plural inflection).
Likewise the intermediate numbers :—

dvecattārīsa nāgasahassāni " 42,000 elephants "
caturāsīti itthisahassāni " 84,000 women "
caturāsītināgasahassāni " 84,000 elephants "

100,000 is *satasahassaṃ*, which is used like *sataṃ* and *sahassaṃ* and like them is prominent in reckoning (1,000,000 is not prominent, being merely ten hundred thousands). Higher numbers are formed in the same way as between 1,000 and 100,000 :—

aṭṭhasaṭṭhibhikkhusatasahassaṃ (N.B. singular) " 168,000 monks "
cuddasa satasahassāni saṭṭhi ca sahassāni cha ca satāni 1,460,600
catuvīsati satasahassāni 2,400,000
asīti bhikkhusatasahassāni " 8,000,000 monks "

If such compounds are used as adjectives (*ṇ*)*ika* may be added.

The ordinals not yet given are usually formed by adding the suffix *ma* (fem. *mī*) to the cardinals. Sometimes the cardinals themselves are used with ordinal meaning.

Miscellaneous numeral expressions :—

" more than " : *paropaññāsa*(*ṃ*), " more than fifty "
" many " : *aneka* either compounded or *anekāni satāni*, etc.

The pronoun *katama*, " which ? ", " which one ? ", usually introduces an enumeration with explanations.

kati, " how many ? ", is inflected in the plural only like an adjective in *i*, but the nominative-accusative is *kati* for all genders.

" times " : *sakiṃ* or *sakid eva* " once " or " only once "
dvikkhattuṃ " twice "
tikkhattuṃ " three times "
chakkhattuṃ " six times "
katikkhattuṃ " how many times ? "
(these are all indeclinables)

" fold," etc. : *tividha* " triple ", " threefold "
dvidhā (ind.) " in two " (division)
sattadhā (ind.) " in seven "

multiples : *diguṇaṃ* (or *dvi-*) " double "
catugguṇa " fourfold ", " quadruple " (e.g. four thicknesses).

Distributive numbers (" x each ") are formed by simple repetition (*āmeṇḍita*).

The full declension of *ubho*, " both," is :—

Nominative and accusative	*ubho*
Instrumental	*ubhohi*
Dative	*ubhinnaṃ*
Ablative	*ubhohi*
Genitive	*ubhinnaṃ*
Locative	*ubhosu*

(Note also *ubhato*, " on both sides ")

Digu *Compounds*

The last of the six classes of compound (cf. Lesson 13) is the *digu*,[1] which may be regarded as a sub-variety of the *kammadhāraya*. Here the first member is a numeral, the second a noun, and the compound functions as a noun (cf. in English " twelvemonth "). The compound may be either a neuter singular (collective) noun or a plural (individual) of the gender of the second member (cf. the *dvanda*, Lesson 15). As collectives we have for example :—

catuddisaṃ, " the four directions " (*catu*(*r*) + *disā*)
saḷāyatanaṃ, " the six spheres," " the six senses " (*cha*(*ḷ*)/*sa*(*ḷ*) + *āyatanaṃ*)
sattāhaṃ, " seven days," " a week "

As plural with unchanged gender we have :—

catuddisā, " the four directions "

Past Participle Active

Past participles which are active (of either transitive or intransitive verbs) are formed by the addition of two suffixes, usually to the same form of the root as is used in the ordinarily passive past participle. Very few of them are used. Like other participles they may be used either as verbs or as adjectives. In the former construction they take an agent in the nominative and may take a patient in the accusative.

[1] *digu* = *dvi* + *go* (" cow " : cf. Lesson 29), an example of the class. It means " a two-cow ", " a pair of cows ", and may be explained as *dve gāvo* (*gāvo* is the plural of *go*).

The less infrequent suffix is *tāvin*, which is inflected like other stems in *in* :—

bhuj	*bhuttāvin*	having eaten, who has eaten
vi-ji	*vijitāvin*	who has conquered, who had conquered

The suffix *tavant*(*u*) may be considered as the possessive suffix *vant*(*u*) (whose declension it follows) added to the past participle in *ta* [1] :—

vas	*vusitavant*	who has lived (well)

(this appears to be the only example in regular use ; it has a special meaning, applying to the life of monks ; it is always an adjective).

Example of construction with patient :—

gahapatissa . . . bhojanam bhuttāvissa . . ., " of a householder . . . who has eaten a meal . . ."

Vocabulary

Verbs :—

anu-kamp (I)	*anukampati*	be compassionate, have compassion (acc.)
anu-bandh (I)	*anubandhati*	follow
anu-budh (III)	*anubujjhati*	understand
apa-lok (VII)	*apaloketi*	take leave, give notice
from the noun *udānaṃ*, cf. Lesson 28 on denominatives	*udāneti*	speak with exaltation, speak with joy
u(*d*)-*ā-har* (I)	*udāharati*	speak, say, promulgate
upa-nam (I)	causative *upanām̐eti* = offer, serve (dat. of person and acc. of thing)	
upa-saṃ-har (I)	*upasaṃharati*	visualize as, imagine as (2 acc's.)
o-lup (II)	causative *olumpeti* = scrape off	
o-lok (VII)	*oloketi*	look at
ni(*r*)-*pat* (I)	*nippatati*	flee
ni-vatt (I)	causative *nivatteti* = turn back (transitive)	

[1] The past participle suffix is sometimes labelled *kta*, or in our notation (*k*)*ta*.

(p)pa-kās (I)	(*pakāsati*, shine : poetic only, and not in the *Dīgha*) causative *pakāseti* = show	
(p)paṭi-ā-sis [1] (II)	*paccāsiṃsati*	hope for, expect
(p)paṭi-(g)gah (V)	causative *paṭiggaheti* = make receive, accept	
(p)paṭi-(p)pa-nam (I)	*paṭippaṇamati*	abate (causative = check)
(p)paṭi-(p)pa-(s)sambh (I)	*paṭippassambhati*	abate, be allayed
(p)paṭi-bhā (I)	*paṭibhāti*	be clear
(p)paṭi-vaṭṭ (I)	*paṭivaṭṭati*	turn back
(p)paṭi-vidh (III)	*paṭivijjhati*	penetrate, comprehend
(p)pa-bandh (I)	*pabandhati*	bind
pari-ni(r)-vā (I) (or III)	*parinibbāti*	attain extinction, attain liberation
pari-har (I)	*pariharati*	watch over, protect
poṭh (VII)	*poṭheti*	snap (fingers)
vi-ci (V)	*vicināti*	investigate, search out
saṃ-tapp (VII)	*santappeti*	(also) satisfy
saṃ-(p)pa-var (VII)	*sampavāreti*	feast (transitive)
saṃ-bhū (VII)	*sambhāveti*	catch up with (acc.)

Nouns :—

akkho	axle
abhijjhā	desire (with loc. of object)
ambakā	mango woman
ayyaputto	master, Mr., (plur :) gentlemen (especially when addressed by ladies, including their wives)
alaṅkāro	ornament, adornment
assāso	reassurance
āmalakaṃ	emblic myrobalan (a medicinal fruit)
ārāmo	park
āhāro	district

[1] Or *(p)paṭi-āsis* since *sis* never appears by itself and *ā* may not be a prefix here (but part of the root).

udānaṃ	exalted utterance, joyful utterance
upaṭṭhāko	attendant, follower
uḷumpo	boat, canoe
okāro	meanness, degradation, vanity
-jāto	become
tittham	landing place, jetty, crossing place, ferry, beach (for bathing and drinking)
dīpo	island
domanassaṃ	(may also mean) aversion
nekkhammaṃ	renunciation
netti (fem.)	leading, tendency
paṭipadā	way
paṭivedho	penetration, comprehension
pallalaṃ	pool
pānīyaṃ	water (drinking water)
punabbhavo	rebirth
pubbaṇho	morning
malaṃ	dirt
māyā	trick
yugaṃ	yoke
rajanaṃ	dye
velā	bank, time, occasion
saṃkileso	defilement
saṃkhāro	force, energy, activity, combination, process, instinct, habit (a very difficult word to find an exact equivalent for; "force", with a restricted technical sense attached to it, is probably the best. *saṃkhāro* means the force, or forces, manifested in the combination of atoms into all the things in the universe, in the duration of such combinations—as in the life-span of a living being—and in the instincts and habits of living beings, which are to be allayed by the practice of meditation (*jhāna*). It is one of the five basic groups (*khandha*) of kinds of things in the universe: matter, sensation, perception and consciousness being the others)

saraṃ	lake
sikkhā	training
hatthinikā	she-elephant

Adjectives :—

anupassin	observing
udagga	lofty, elated
uddesika	referring to
odāta	white
kalla	proper
gāmin	going
jara	old, aged
duṭṭha	evil, vile, corrupt
nīla	blue
pīta	yellow
madhuraka	drunk, intoxicated
mudu	supple
vuddha	old
saññata	restrained
sāmukkaṃsaka	exalted, sublime

Past Participles :—

adhivuttha (*adhi-vas*)	accepted
āṇatta (*āṇa* causative)	ordered
onīta (*o-nī*)	withdrawn, removed
suddha (*sudh* (III))	cleaned

Future Passive Participle :—

peyya (*pā*)	to be drunk, drinkable

Gerunds :—

adhiṭṭhāya (*adhi-*(*ṭ*)*ṭhā*)	having fixed one's attention on, having resolved on
paṭicca ((*p*)*paṭi-i*)	conditioned by, because of (usually with acc. ; sometimes spelt *paticca*)

bhojetvā (*bhuj* (II) causative)	having fed
vatvā (*vac*)	having said
vineyya (*vi-nī*)	having eliminated, having disciplined
visajja (*vi-sajj*)	getting over, leaving behind

Indeclinables :—

anantaraṃ	without omission
aparaṃ	further
aparāparaṃ	successively
abāhiraṃ	without exclusion, without excluding anyone
dūrato	in the distance
yathāsandiṭṭhaṃ	with one's acquaintances
yathāsambhattaṃ	with one's comrades
yāva (also means)	until, as long as
viya	like (enclitic : this is the usual prose form ; in verse we find also *va*)
sadā	always
svātanāya	for tomorrow

EXERCISE 26

Passages for reading :—

1. atha kho bhagavā pubbaṇhasamayaṃ nivāsetvā pattacīvaram ādāya saddhiṃ bhikkhusaṃghena yena Sunīdha-Vassakārānaṃ Magadhamahāmattānaṃ āvasatho ten' upasaṃkami, upasaṃkamitvā paññatte āsane nisīdi. atha kho Sunīdha-Vassakārā Magadhamahāmattā Buddhapamukhaṃ bhikkhusaṃghaṃ paṇītena khādaniyena bhojaniyena sahatthā santappesuṃ sampavāresuṃ. atha kho Sunīdha-Vassakārā Magadhamahāmattā bhagavantaṃ bhuttāviṃ onītapattapāṇiṃ aññataraṃ nīcaṃ āsanaṃ gahetvā ekamantaṃ nisīdiṃsu. ekamantaṃ nisinne kho Sunīdha-Vassakāre Magadhamahāmatte bhagavā imāhi gāthāhi anumodi :—

yasmiṃ padese kappeti vāsaṃ paṇḍitajātiko
sīlavant' ettha bhojetvā saññate brahmacārino,

yā tattha devatā assu tāsaṃ dakkhiṇam ādise,[1]
tā pūjitā pūjayanti [2] mānitā mānayanti [2] naṃ.

tato naṃ anukampanti mātā puttaṃ va orasaṃ
devānukampito poso [3] sadā bhadrāni [3] passatī ti.

atha kho bhagavā Sunīdha-Vassakāre Magadhamahāmatte imāhi gāthāhi anumoditvā uṭṭhāy' āsanā pakkāmi.

tena kho pana samayena Sunīdha-Vassakārā Magadhamahāmattā bhagavantaṃ piṭṭhito piṭṭhito anubaddhā honti, yen' ajja samaṇo Gotamo dvārena nikkhamissati taṃ Gotamadvāraṃ nāma bhavissati, yena titthena Gaṅgaṃ nadiṃ tarissati taṃ Gotamatitthaṃ bhavissatī ti. atha kho bhagavā yena dvārena nikkhami taṃ Gotamadvāraṃ nāma ahosi.

atha kho bhagavā yena Gaṅgā nadī ten' upasaṃkami. tena kho pana samayena Gaṅgā nadī pūrā hoti samatitthikā kākapeyyā. app ekacce manussā nāvaṃ pariyesanti app ekacce uḷumpaṃ pariyesanti app ekacce kullaṃ bandhanti aparāparaṃ gantukāmā. atha kho bhagavā seyyathā pi nāma balavā puriso sammiñjitaṃ vā bāhaṃ pasāreyya pasāritaṃ vā bāhaṃ sammiñjeyya, evam evaṃ Gaṅgāya nadiyā orimatīre antarahito pārimatīre paccuṭṭhāsi saddhiṃ bhikkhusaṃghena. addasā kho bhagavā te manusse app ekacce nāvaṃ pariyesante app ekacce uḷumpaṃ pariyesante app ekacce kullaṃ bandhante aparāparaṃ gantukāme. atha kho bhagavā etam atthaṃ viditvā, tāyaṃ velāyaṃ imaṃ udānaṃ udānesi :—

ye taranti aṇṇavaṃ saraṃ ; setuṃ katva [4] visajja pallalāni,
kullaṃ hi jano pabandhati, nittiṇṇā medhāvino janā ti.

atha kho bhagavā āyasmantaṃ Ānandaṃ āmantesi : āyām' Ānanda yena Koṭigāmo ten' upasaṃkamissāmā ti. evaṃ bhante ti kho āyasmā Ānando bhagavato paccassosi. atha kho bhagavā mahatā bhikkhusaṃghena saddhiṃ yena Koṭigāmo tad avasari. tatra sudaṃ bhagavā Koṭigāme viharati. tatra kho bhagavā bhikkhū āmantesi : catunnaṃ bhikkhave ariyasaccānaṃ ananubodhā appaṭivedhā evam idaṃ dīgham

[1] Poetic form of optative of *ā-dis* (I) " dedicate ", 3rd singular.
[2] In verse frequently *e* > *aya*.
[3] Poetic forms, *poso* = *puriso* and *bhadrāni* = *bhaddāni*.
[4] Poetic form of *katvā*.

addhānaṃ sandhāvitaṃ saṃsaritaṃ mamañ c' eva tumhākañ ca. katamesaṃ catunnaṃ. dukkhassa bhikkhave ariyasaccassa ananubodhā appaṭivedhā evam idaṃ dīgham addhānaṃ sandhāvitaṃ saṃsaritaṃ mamañ c' eva tumhākañ ca. dukkhasamudayassa bhikkhave ariyasaccassa ananubodhā appaṭivedhā evam idaṃ dīgham addhānaṃ sandhāvitaṃ saṃsaritaṃ mamañ c' eva tumhākañ ca. dukkhanirodhassa bhikkhave ariyasaccassa . . . pe . . . dukkhanirodhagāminiyā paṭipadāya bhikkhave ariyasaccassa ananubodhā appaṭivedhā evam idaṃ dīgham addhānaṃ sandhāvitaṃ saṃsaritaṃ mamañ c' eva tumhākañ ca. tayidaṃ bhikkhave dukkhaṃ ariyasaccaṃ anubuddhaṃ paṭividdhaṃ, dukkhasamudayaṃ ariyasaccaṃ anubuddhaṃ paṭividdhaṃ, dukkhanirodhaṃ ariyasaccaṃ anubuddhaṃ paṭividdhaṃ, dukkhanirodhagāminī paṭipadā ariyasaccaṃ anubuddhaṃ paṭividdhaṃ, ucchinnā bhavataṇhā, khīṇā bhavanetti, n' atthi dāni punabbhavo ti. idam avoca bhagavā, idaṃ vatvā sugato athāparaṃ etad avoca satthā :—

catunnaṃ ariyasaccānaṃ yathābhūtaṃ adassanā
saṃsitaṃ [1] dīgham addhānaṃ tāsu tās' eva jātisu.
tāni etāni diṭṭhāni bhavanetti samūhatā
ucchinnaṃ mūlaṃ dukkhassa n' atthi dāni punabbhavo ti.

* * *

assosi kho Ambapālī gaṇikā bhagavā kira Vesāliyaṃ anuppatto Vesāliyaṃ viharati mayhaṃ ambavane ti. atha kho Ambapālī gaṇikā bhaddāni bhaddāni yānāni yojāpetvā, bhaddaṃ yānaṃ abhirūhitvā bhaddehi bhaddehi yānehi Vesāliyā niyyāsi, yena sako ārāmo tena pāyāsi. yāvatikā yānassa bhūmi yānena gantvā yānā paccorohitvā pattikā va yena bhagavā ten' upasaṃkami, upasaṃkamitvā bhagavantaṃ abhivādetvā ekamantaṃ nisīdi. ekamantaṃ nisinnaṃ kho Ambapāliṃ gaṇikaṃ bhagavā dhammiyā kathāya sandassesi samādapesi samuttejesi sampahaṃsesi. atha kho Ambapāligaṇikā bhagavatā dhammiyā kathāya sandassitā samādapitā samuttejitā sampahaṃsitā bhagavantaṃ etad avoca :—

adhivāsetu me bhante bhagavā svātanāya bhattaṃ saddhiṃ

[1] Poetic form of the past participle of *saṃ-sar*.

bhikkhusaṃghenā ti. adhivāsesi bhagavā tuṇhībhāvena. atha kho Ambapāligaṇikā bhagavato adhivāsanaṃ viditvā uṭṭhāy' āsanā bhagavantaṃ abhivādetvā padakkhiṇaṃ katvā pakkāmi.

assosuṃ kho Vesālikā Licchavī bhagavā kira Vesāliṃ anuppatto Vesāliyaṃ viharati Ambapālivane ti. atha kho te Licchavī bhaddāni bhaddāni yānāni yojāpetvā bhaddaṃ yānaṃ abhirūhitvā bhaddehi bhaddehi yānehi Vesāliyā niyyiṃsu. tatr' ekacce Licchavī nīlā honti nīlavaṇṇā nīlavatthā nīlālaṅkārā, ekacce Licchavī pītā honti pītavaṇṇā pītavatthā pītālaṅkārā, ekacce Licchavī lohitakā honti lohitavaṇṇā lohitavatthā lohitālaṅkārā, ekacce Licchavī odātā honti odātavaṇṇā odātavatthā odātālaṅkārā.

atha kho Ambapāligaṇikā daharānaṃ daharānaṃ Licchavīnaṃ akkhena akkhaṃ cakkena cakkaṃ yugena yugaṃ paṭivaṭṭesi. atha kho Licchavī Ambapāliṃ gaṇikaṃ etad avocuṃ : kiñ je Ambapāli daharānaṃ daharānaṃ Licchavīnaṃ akkhena akkhaṃ cakkena cakkaṃ yugena yugaṃ paṭivaṭṭesī ti. tathā hi pana me ayyaputtā bhagavā nimantito svātanāya bhattaṃ saddhiṃ bhikkhusaṃghenā ti. dehi je Ambapāli etaṃ bhattaṃ satasahassenā ti. sace pi me ayyaputtā Vesāliṃ sāhāraṃ dassatha evaṃmahantaṃ bhattaṃ na dassāmī ti. atha kho te Licchavī aṅgulī poṭhesuṃ jit' amhā vata bho ambakāya, vañcit' amhā vata bho ambakāyā ti. atha kho te Licchavī yena Ambapālivanaṃ tena pāyiṃsu.[1]

addasā kho bhagavā te Licchavī dūrato va āgacchante, disvā bhikkhū āmantesi : yesaṃ bhikkhave bhikkhūnaṃ devā Tāvatiṃsā adiṭṭhā, oloketha bhikkhave Licchaviparisaṃ, avaloketha [2] bhikkhave Licchaviparisaṃ upasaṃharatha bhikkhave Licchaviparisaṃ Tāvatiṃsaparisan ti. atha kho te Licchavī yāvatikā yānassa bhūmi yānena gantvā yānā paccorohitvā, pattikā va yena bhagavā ten' upasaṃkamiṃsu, upasaṃkamitvā bhagavantaṃ abhivādetvā ekamantaṃ nisīdiṃsu. ekamantaṃ nisinne kho te Licchavī bhagavā dhammiyā kathāya sandassesi samādapesi samuttejesi sampahaṃsesi. atha kho te Licchavī bhagavatā dhammiyā kathāya sandassitā samādapitā samuttejitā sampahaṃsitā bhagavantaṃ etad avocuṃ : adhivāsetu no bhante bhagavā svātanāya bhattaṃ

[1] Irregular 3rd plural aorist of *yā*.
[2] *ava* is poetic form of *o*.

saddhiṃ bhikkhusaṃghenā ti. adhivutthaṃ kho me Licchavī svātanāya Ambapāligaṇikāya bhattan ti. atha kho te Licchavī aṅgulī poṭhesuṃ : jit' amhā vata bho ambakāya, vañcit' amhā vata bho ambakāyā ti. atha kho te Licchavī bhagavato bhāsitaṃ abhinanditvā anumoditvā uṭṭhāy' āsanā bhagavantaṃ abhivādetvā padakkhiṇaṃ katvā pakkamiṃsu.

atha kho Ambapāligaṇikā tassā rattiyā accayena sake ārāme paṇītaṃ khādaniyaṃ bhojaniyaṃ paṭiyādāpetvā bhagavato kālaṃ ārocāpesi : kālo bhante niṭṭhitaṃ bhattan ti. atha kho bhagavā pubbaṇhasamayaṃ nivāsetvā pattacīvaraṃ ādāya saddhiṃ bhikkhusaṃghena yena Ambapāligaṇikāya parivesanā ten' upasaṃkami, upasaṃkamitvā paññatte āsane nisīdi. atha kho Ambapāligaṇikā Buddhapamukhaṃ bhikkhusaṃghaṃ paṇītena khādaniyena bhojaniyena sahatthā santappesi sampavāresi. atha kho Ambapāligaṇikā bhagavantaṃ bhuttāviṃ onītapattapāṇiṃ aññataraṃ nīcaṃ āsanaṃ gahetvā ekamantaṃ nisīdi. ekamantaṃ nisinnā kho Ambapāligaṇikā bhagavantaṃ etad avoca : imāhaṃ bhante ārāmaṃ Buddhapamukhassa bhikkhusaṃghassa dammī [1] ti. paṭiggahesi bhagavā ārāmaṃ. atha kho bhagavā Ambapāligaṇikaṃ dhammiyā kathāya sandassetvā samādapetvā samuttejetvā sampahaṃsetvā uṭṭhāy' āsanā pakkāmi.

tatra pi sudaṃ bhagavā Vesāliyaṃ viharanto Ambapālivane etad eva bahulaṃ bhikkhūnaṃ dhammiṃ kathaṃ karoti : iti sīlaṃ iti samādhi iti paññā, sīlaparibhāvito samādhi mahapphalo hoti mahānisaṃso, samādhiparibhāvitā paññā mahapphalā hoti mahānisaṃsā, paññāparibhāvitaṃ cittaṃ sammad eva āsavehi vimuccati seyyathīdaṃ kāmāsavā bhavāsavā diṭṭhāsavā avijjāsavā ti.

atha kho bhagavā Ambapālivane yathābhirantaṃ viharitvā āyasmantaṃ Ānandaṃ āmantesi : āyām' Ānanda yena Beluvagāmako ten' upasaṃkamissāmā ti. evaṃ bhante ti kho āyasmā Ānando bhagavato paccassosi. atha kho bhagavā mahatā bhikkhusaṃghena saddhiṃ yena Beluvagāmako tad avasari. tatra sudaṃ bhagavā Beluvagāmake viharati.

tatra kho bhagavā bhikkhū āmantesi : etha tumhe bhikkhave, samantā Vesāliṃ yathāmittaṃ yathāsandiṭṭhaṃ yathā-

[1] " I give," elevated form of *demi*.

sambhattaṃ vassaṃ[1] upetha, ahaṃ pana idh' eva Beluvagāmake vassaṃ upagacchāmī ti. evaṃ bhante ti kho te bhikkhū bhagavato paṭissutvā samantā Vesāliṃ yathāmittaṃ yathāsandiṭṭhaṃ yathāsambhattaṃ vassaṃ upagañchuṃ, bhagavā pana tatth' eva Beluvagāmake vassaṃ upagañchi.

atha kho bhagavato vassūpagatassa kharo ābādho uppajji, bāḷhā vedanā vattanti māraṇantikā. tā sudaṃ bhagavā sato sampajāno adhivāseti avihaññamāno. atha kho bhagavato etad ahosi: na kho me taṃ patirūpaṃ[2] yo 'haṃ anāmantetvā upaṭṭhāke anapaloketvā bhikkhusaṃghaṃ parinibbāyeyyaṃ. yan nunāhaṃ imaṃ ābādhaṃ viriyena paṭippaṇāmetvā jīvitasaṃkhāraṃ adhiṭṭhāya vihareyyan ti. atha kho bhagavā taṃ ābādhaṃ viriyena paṭippaṇāmetvā jīvitasaṃkhāraṃ adhiṭṭhāya vihāsi. atha kho bhagavato so ābādho paṭippassambhi.

atha kho bhagavā gilānā vuṭṭhito aciravuṭṭhito gelaññā vihārā nikkhamma vihārapacchāyāyaṃ paññatte āsane nisīdi. atha kho āyasmā Ānando yena bhagavā ten' upasaṃkami, upasaṃkamitvā bhagavantaṃ abhivādetvā ekamantaṃ nisīdi. ekamantaṃ nisinno kho āyasmā Ānando bhagavantaṃ etad avoca: diṭṭhā me bhante bhagavato phāsu, diṭṭhaṃ me bhante bhagavato khamanīyaṃ. api hi me bhante madhurakajāto viya kāyo, disā pi me na pakkhāyanti, dhammā pi maṃ na paṭibhanti bhagavato gelaññena, api ca me bhante ahosi kā cid eva assāsamattā, na tāva bhagavā parinibbāyissati na yāva bhagavā bhikkhusaṃghaṃ ārabbha kiñ cid eva udāharatī ti.

kim pan' Ānanda bhikkhusaṃgho mayi paccāsiṃsati. desito Ānanda mayā dhammo anantaraṃ abāhiraṃ karitvā; na tatth' Ānanda tathāgatassa dhammesu ācariyamuṭṭhi. yassa nūna Ānanda evam assa ahaṃ bhikkhusaṃghaṃ pariharissāmī ti vā mamuddesiko bhikkhusaṃgho ti vā so nūna Ānanda bhikkhusaṃghaṃ ārabbha kiñ cid eva udāhareyya. tathāgatassa kho Ānanda na evaṃ hoti ahaṃ bhikkhusaṃghaṃ pariharissāmī ti vā mamuddesiko bhikkhusaṃgho ti vā. kiṃ Ānanda tathāgato bhikkhusaṃghaṃ ārabbha kiñ cid eva udāharissati. ahaṃ kho pan' Ānanda etarahi jiṇṇo vuddho mahallako addhagato vayo anuppatto, asītiko me vayo vattati. seyyathā pi Ānanda

[1] Wanderers put up for the rainy season when travel was impossible. The word *vassaṃ* came to be used for this putting up.

[2] In some words *pati-* is sometimes found instead of *paṭi-*.

jarasakaṭaṃ veghamissakena [1] yāpeti, evam eva kho Ānanda veghamissakena maññe tathāgatassa kāyo yāpeti. yasmiṃ Ānanda samaye tathāgato sabbanimittānaṃ amanasikārā ekaccānaṃ vedanānaṃ nirodhā animittaṃ cetosamādhiṃ upasampajja viharati, phāsukato Ānanda tasmiṃ samaye tathāgatassa kāyo hoti.

tasmāt ih' Ānanda attadīpā viharatha attasaraṇā anaññasaraṇā, dhammadīpā dhammasaraṇā anaññasaraṇā. kathañ c' Ānanda bhikkhu attadīpo viharati attasaraṇo anaññasaraṇo, dhammadīpo dhammasaraṇo anaññasaraṇo. idh' Ānanda bhikkhu kāye kāyānupassī viharati ātāpī sampajāno satimā, vineyya loke abhijjhādomanassaṃ, vedanāsu vedanānupassī viharati ātāpī sampajāno satimā, vineyya loke abhijjhādomanassaṃ, citte cittānupassī viharati ātāpī sampajāno satimā, vineyya loke abhijjhādomanassaṃ, dhammesu dhammānupassī viharati ātāpī sampajāno satimā, vineyya loke abhijjhādomanassaṃ, evaṃ kho Ānanda bhikkhu attadīpo viharati attasaraṇo anaññasaraṇo, dhammadīpo dhammasaraṇo anaññasaraṇo. ye hi keci Ānanda etarahi vā mamaṃ vā accayena attadīpā viharissanti attasaraṇā anaññasaraṇā, dhammadīpā dhammasaraṇā anaññasaraṇā, tamatagge [2] me te Ānanda bhikkhū bhavissanti ye keci sikkhākāmā ti.

2. tesaṃ Vipassī bhagavā arahaṃ sammāsambuddho ānupubbikathaṃ kathesi, seyyathīdaṃ dānakathaṃ sīlakathaṃ saggakathaṃ kāmānaṃ ādīnavaṃ okāraṃ saṃkilesaṃ nekkhamme ānisaṃsaṃ pakāsesi. yadā te bhagavā aññāsi kallacitte muducitte vinīvaraṇacitte udaggacitte pasannacitte, atha yā Buddhānaṃ sāmukkaṃsikā dhammadesanā tam pakāsesi, dukkhaṃ samudayaṃ nirodhaṃ maggaṃ. seyyathā pi nāma suddhaṃ vatthaṃ apagatakāḷakaṃ sammad eva rajanaṃ paṭigganheyya, evam eva Khaṇḍassa ca rājaputtassa Tissassa ca purohitaputtassa tasmiṃ yeva āsane virajaṃ vītamalaṃ dhammacakkhuṃ udapādi : yaṃ kiñci samudayadhammaṃ, sabban taṃ nirodhadhamman ti.

[1] " held together with straps," " bound up with bands " (?)—the precise meaning of *vegha*, which occurs only in this expression, seems to be unknown ; *missaka* = " mixed with," " combined with."

[2] " Highest of all " : according to the Commentary this is *tama* = " most " + *agge* joined by a junction consonant ; another explanation is that we have here *tamatā*, " mostness."

Translate into Pali :—

Now at that time king Pajjota had a she-elephant called Bhaddavatikā, a fifty-league-er (per day). Then Jīvaka offered ghee to king Pajjota (saying :) " Let the king (*devo*) drink astringent (put first)." Then Jīvaka having made king Pajjota drink ghee went to the elephant-hall and fled from the city on the she-elephant Bhaddavatikā. Then to king Pajjota that ghee (which was) drunk (and) digesting gave vomiting. Then king Pajjota said this to people : " I say, I have been made to drink ghee by the vile Jīvaka. Now ! I say, search out doctor Jīvaka ! " " O king, (he has) fled from the city on Bhaddavatikā the she-elephant."

At that time king Pajjota had a slave called Kāka, a sixty-league-er, born of [1] non-human beings. Then king Pajjota ordered Kāka the slave : " Go, I say, Kāka, turn back doctor Jīvaka (saying :) ' Teacher, the king has you turned back (double causative).' These doctors now (*nāma*) I say, Kāka, have-many-tricks, don't accept anything of him (gen.)." Then Kāka the slave caught up with Jīvaka whilst on the road, at Kosambī,[2] having (*kar*, present participle) breakfast. Then the slave Kāka said this to Jīvaka : " Teacher, the king has you turned back." " Wait, I say, Kāka, until I have eaten (present tense). Well ! I say, Kāka, have-something-to-eat-yourself ! [3] " " Enough, teacher ! I am ordered by (gen.) the king : ' These doctors now, Kāka, I say, have many tricks, don't accept anything from him.' " At that time Jīvaka Komārabhacca was eating (present tense) an emblic myrobalan (after) scraping off the medicine (medicinal part) with (his) nail, and was drinking water. Then Jīvaka said this to the slave Kāka : " Well ! I say, Kāka, eat (some) emblic myrobalan and drink (some) water yourself ! " [4]

[1] *paṭicca.*
[2] On the Yamunā near its confluence with the Ganges ; capital of Vatsa, a kingdom situated centrally between Avantī, Magadha, and Kosala.
[3] *bhuñjassu*, 2nd singular imperative " middle " or reflexive of *bhuj* (II) (cf. Lesson 28).
[4] *pivassu.*

LESSON 27

Text, Sentence, and Clause

The doctrine that what is given in language consists of sentences (*vākya* or *vyañjana*), and that smaller pieces such as words are grammatical abstractions, has been noted in earlier lessons. It will have been noticed in the earlier exercises that the sentence itself, though in a sense complete, is often obscure in the absence of any context : that is to say a genuine sentence, especially a short sentence, taken from the texts at our disposal has a strongly prehensive and dependent quality, the meaning being only vaguely given by the sentence alone. The precise meaning with which a sentence is charged in its context drains out of it when it is detached. The wholeness of a sentence is at best a grammatical independence (with certain reservations) and a more or less vague meaning cohering in this grammatical complex. We have to begin from a much larger piece of text in order to discover the precise meaning of a sentence. In our exercises the longer reading passages are fairly adequate for this, but some of the shorter ones are for example stories told in a wider context which is not given, in order to enforce some point, or parts of discourses in which the protagonist is unknown or the general trend of argument not given.

The actual textual units of the *Dīghanikāya* are its thirty-four *suttantas* or dialogues (or *pariyāyas*, discourses), which are independent in their contexts (though interlocking as regards the Buddhist doctrines enunciated, to the exposition of which all the arguments and narratives tend, and having many passages in common). These are of varying length, the longer ones being subdivided into chapters (*bhāṇavāra*) as convenient portions for reading at a stretch. A *bhāṇavāra* is said to contain 8,000 syllables. Each *suttanta* begins with the statement *evam me sutaṃ*, which is traditionally ascribed to Ānanda as the first reciter of the *Nikāyas* when they were compiled (orally at first) after the *Parinibbāna*. This is followed by an introductory narrative (*nidāna*) *ekaṃ samayaṃ* . . . giving the situation, and this by the dialogue (*sutta*). The main dialogue usually develops from a leading question (*pañha* or *pucchā*). The elaborate exposition (*niddesa*) of a question of doctrine is a unit of discourse intermediate between the *suttanta* and the sentence, which is prominent in the traditional exegesis of Pali texts. Sometimes we can distinguish sections of text intermediate in length between the *niddesa* and the sentence, marked by a uniformity of tenses (e.g. the " historical present ", etc.) and other elements. (Lesson 24 on the use of auxiliary verbs contains some indications of " aspect ", etc., running through sections of text.) These sections are usually much longer than the conventional modern paragraph, and may run to as much as ten pages.

Such larger units relate to broad trends in meaning and the wider contexts in which the texts have to be interpreted. Whatever concerns grammatical structure is dealt with in terms of the sentence. In Pali this may extend to a " period " of some complexity and of the length of a " paragraph ". No higher grammatical unit than the sentence being distinguished in our grammars, we may regard a series of " sentences " separated by the conventional punctuation, if linked by conjunctive indeclinables, anaphoric pronouns, etc., as a single " sentence " for our purposes, though a distinct term such as " period " may be useful to distinguish it from the minimal grammatically independent unit. The traditional punctuation is light, somewhat fluid, and not highly articulated : there is simply a half stop and a full stop. Modern editors have often disregarded it and introduced conventions of their own, the passages in this book being taken from such an edition, with some moderation in the direction of the tradition. The punctuation is thus not decisive in determining sentences, and grammatical considerations override it.

" A sentence (*vākya* or *vyañjana*) is a group of words (*padasamūha*) which is unified in meaning (*atthasambaddha*) and of limited extent (*padesapariyosāna*) "—Aggavaṃsa. The " meaning " intended here is primarily grammatical meaning : the words in the sentence prehend one another syntactically, the full grammatical explanation of one word relates it to other words and all those words which are thus interlocked constitute one sentence. The object of adding " of limited extent " is presumably to indicate that we should distinguish as sentences the smallest units which can be separated without breaking any syntactical connection, disregarding the looser connections with the wider context. The simple sentence is unified by grammatical relations and concord, e.g. between a verb and its agent and nouns in other cases relating to the action, between nouns by the genitive case relation or by compounding, between nouns and attributes by concord of case, sometimes gender, and number or by compounding, and so on. It may be affirmative or negative, interrogative, etc., as shown by indeclinables. A sentence may have a verb or be nominal, it may also have more than one verb (e.g. a string of verbs grammatically parallel to one another).

More complex sentences or " periods " may be organized in a number of ways. We can perhaps distinguish seven main elements of period construction as follows :—

(1) conjunction (connection by conjunctive indeclinables : Lesson 17),

(2) " paratax " (connection by the anaphoric pronoun : Lesson 5),

(3) subordination (" hypotax ", connection of a relative—" bound "—clause to a main—" free "—clause by a relative pronoun or indeclinable : Lesson 12),

(4) compounding (a compound, especially a *bahubbīhi*, equivalent to a subordinate clause : Lesson 19),

(5) the infinite verb (participles, including absolute constructions, the gerund and the infinitive may be used to connect a subordinate action to the main action : Lessons 8, 10, 16, and 19 ; it should be noted that the distinction between participles and adjectives is not absolute and that some words listed as adjectives may function as participle " predicates "),

(6) direct speech (concluded by the indeclinable marker *ti*, sometimes *iti* : Lesson 6),

(7) chaining (by a repeated word, see examples below ; other forms of parallelism also are used).

All these elements can be repeated and combined. With the exception of subordination and chaining they have been described above. Here we may note a few examples of them in the Passages for Reading :—

(1) conjunction : Exercise 19, first Passage, towards the end of the second paragraph—*pi* (repeated several times, but with

abbreviation) ;—Exercise 23, third Passage, sixth paragraph, towards the end—*ca* (repeated) ;—Exercise 25, first Passage, first paragraph—*na ca* repeated,

(2) paratax : Exercise 19, first Passage—opens with *te* referring to the characters already introduced (see Exercise 17),

(3) subordination : Exercise 19, first Passage, last sentence of second paragraph—*ye* (pronoun) ;—third paragraph—*yadā* (indeclinable),

(4) compounding : Exercise 19, first Passage, first paragraph—*dvīhatīhapāyāto* = " when . . .", series of *bahubbīhis* in the middle of the same sentence = " who . . .",

(5) infinite verbs : Exercise 19, first Passage, second paragraph—gerunds : *paṭissutvā, chaḍḍetvā* ;—second Passage, near beginning—present participle : *caramāno* ;—fourth paragraph, towards the end—past participle : *adhigato* ;—third Passage, near beginning—past participle : *jāto* ;—Exercise 24, first Passage, sixth paragraph—gerunds and past participles ; Exercise 19, third Passage—opens with locative absolute ; Exercise 18, second Passage, about two-thirds down—past participle *bhuttā* and infinitive *pariyesituṃ* ; Exercise 24, first Passage, fourth paragraph—adjective equivalent to a participle : *pāṭikaṅkha* (in this case in the main clause),

(6) direct speech : Exercise 19, first Passage—numerous *ti* clauses ;—also Exercise 23, third Passage, sixth and following paragraphs,

(7) chaining : Exercise 24, first Passage—*yāvakīvaṃ* repeated many times in parallel sentences ;—Exercise 26, first Passage, end of fourth paragraph after the break—*jit' amhā vata bho ambakāya, vañcit' amhā vata bho ambakāya* ;—Exercise 18, second Passage, in the sentence *bhuttā* . . . referred to just above, the words *kāmā* . . . *kāme* link the two clauses. A detailed investigation of chaining, including repeated (or contrasted) forms (e.g. Exercise 23, third Passage, end of sixth paragraph from the end, three " asyndetic " aorists : *nisedhesuṃ* . . . *akaṃsu* . . . *chindiṃsu*—of contrasting forms—the following paragraph closing with the three corresponding futures), would take us further into the field of stylistics and poetics than would be convenient here.

Relative Clauses

The subordinate or relative clause, or " bound clause " (terminology varies), is the most important and most frequent of all the elements in Pali period building. It is also the most complex and varied in structure and meaning and requires careful study. The formal indication of such clauses is that they open with a relative pronoun or indeclinable, that is the pronouns and indeclinables in *ya-* and certain other indeclinables which may be classed as relatives : *sace, ce* (enclitic), *hi* (enclitic), *seyyathā*. Similarly the relative adjective *yāvataka* (/*-ikā*) may open a relative clause. The usages governing the relative pronoun (concord) have been briefly stated in Lesson 12. The doubled relative expressing a generalization should be noted. The subordinate clauses with indeclinables, classified according to the indeclinables which introduce them, are as follows (the use of correlative demonstratives is fairly free, and quite frequently they are omitted altogether) :—

yaṃ is the most general or " empty " relative, and may serve simply as marker of a relative clause (in which case it may be translated " that ") much as *ti* marks direct speech. It may also introduce indirect speech (which, however, is extremely rare compared with direct), a supposition (*parikappa*), a concession (*anumati*), a cause, or merely a qualification (*araha, satti*)—cf. the relative pronoun. The optative tense appears as usual in hypothetical cases (cf. Lesson 14). Examples :—

anacchariyaṃ kho pan' etaṃ Ānanda, yaṃ manussabhūto kālaṃ kareyya = " but this is not surprising, Ānanda—that a human being should die "

yaṃ passanti . . . brāhmaṇā candimasuriye . . ., pahonti candimasuriyānaṃ sahavyatāya maggaṃ desetuṃ = " whereas priests . . . see the sun and moon . . ., can they teach the way to union with the sun and moon ? "

yaṃ taṃ jātaṃ . . . taṃ vata mā palujjī ti, n' etaṃ ṭhānaṃ vijjati = " that that (which is) born . . . it should not decay (lit. : ' indeed let it not decay ! '—direct speech) is impossible "

ṭhānaṃ kho pan' etaṃ Kassapa vijjati, yaṃ viññū . . . evaṃ vadeyyuṃ . . . = " but there exists the case, Kassapa, that discerning persons . . . may say thus . . . "

yaṃ pi bho samaṇo Gotamo Campaṃ anuppatto . . . atith' amhākaṃ samaṇo Gotamo = " and since, sir, the philosopher Gotama has arrived at Campā . . . the philosopher Gotama is our guest "

yaṃ sukho bhavaṃ taṃ sukhā mayaṃ = " if his honour is happy we are happy "

Some combinations of *yaṃ* (= *yad*) with other indeclinables may be exemplified briefly :—

yad agge (= " since ", " since the day that/when ") : *yad agge ahaṃ Mahāli bhagavantaṃ upanissāya viharāmi, na ciraṃ tīṇi vassāni, dibbāni hi kho rūpāni passāmi . . . no ca kho dibbāni saddāni suṇāmi* . . . = " Mahāli, since I have lived depending on (as pupil) the fortunate one, nearly three years, though I have seen divine forms (sights : *rūpaṃ* is applied to any object of vision) . . . I have not heard divine sounds . . . "

yad idaṃ (= " such as," " as," " to wit," " i.e.," " namely "—identification or specification) : *akaraṇīyā va . . . Vajjī raññā . . . yad idaṃ yuddhassa* = " the Vajjīs . . . are quite invincible (' impossible ') by the king . . . i.e. by war " ; *cirassaṃ* [1] *kho bhante bhagavā imaṃ pariyāyam akāsi yad idaṃ idh' āgamanāya* = " after a long time/at last, sir, the fortunate one has taken (' made ') this course, namely (for) coming here "

yathā is the next most general or empty relative after *yaṃ*, but with consecutive sense and that of manner, or sometimes of comparison, reason, or purpose :—

yathā te khameyya tathā naṃ vyākareyyāsi = " as it may please you (as you like) so you may explain it ", " you may explain it as you please "

yathā bhante devatānaṃ adhippāyo, tathā hotu = " let it be as the gods wish, sir ! "

yathā . . . vyākaroti taṃ . . . āroceyyāsi = " you must inform (me) . . . how he explains it "

[1] Indeclinable : " at last," " after a long time."

atthi paṭipadā yathā paṭipanno sāmaṃ yeva ñassati = " there is a way following which one will find out oneself "

yathā va pan' eke bhonto samaṇabrāhmaṇā . . . evarūpaṃ bījagāmabhūtagāmasamārambhaṃ anuyuttā viharati . . . iti evarūpā bījagāmabhūtagāmasamārambhā paṭivirato samaṇo Gotamo = " but (where)as, sirs, some priests and philosophers . . . live practising such destroying (*samārambho* = ' undertaking ', ' falling upon ') of living beings (*bhūtagāmo*) and plants (*bījagāmo*) . . . so the philosopher Gotama is abstaining from such destroying of living beings and plants " (*evarūpa* = *evaṃrūpa* = " of such a kind ", *bahubbīhi*—cf. Lesson 22)

yathā nu kho imāni bhante puthusippāyatanāni . . . sakkā nu kho bhante evam evaṃ diṭṭhe va dhamme sandiṭṭhikaṃ sāmaññaphalaṃ paññāpetuṃ = " sir, as/like these many (*puthu* = many, various) craft-circles (men of various trades) . . . is it possible, sir, in the same way to declare a visible fruit of the profession of philosophy in the visible world (*dhammo*) ? "

tena hi bho mama pi suṇātha, yathā mayam eva arahāma taṃ bhavantaṃ Gotamaṃ dassanāya upasaṃkamituṃ = " now listen to me, how/why we ought to (*eva* = it is we who ought to) go to see the honourable Gotama "

pahoti me samaṇo Gotamo tathā dhammaṃ desetuṃ yathā ahaṃ imaṃ kaṅkhādhammaṃ pajaheyyaṃ = " the philosopher Gotama can teach me the doctrine so that (or : ' in such a way that ') I may renounce this element/idea of doubt (*kaṅkhā*) "

The remaining relatives are more specialized in meaning :—

seyyathā introduces a simile :—

atha kho bhagavā seyyathā pi nāma balavā puriso . . . bāhaṃ pasāreyya . . . evaṃ evaṃ . . . pārimatīre paccuṭṭhāsi = " then the fortunate one, just as a strong man . . . might stretch out his arm, just so . . . he arose on the further shore " (for a more complex example see the first Passage of Exercise 25, third paragraph).

sace introduces a condition, concession, or hypothesis (observe use of tenses : cf. Lesson 14 and the notes below) :—

sace te agaru, bhāsassu = " if (it is) not troublesome (*garu*) to you, speak "

sace . . . yāceyyāsi . . . atha . . . adhivāseyya = " if you were to ask (request, *yāc* (I)) . . . then . . . he might accept "

sace kho ahaṃ yo yo . . . ādiyissati tassa tassa dhanam anuppadassāmi, evam idaṃ adinnādānaṃ pavaḍḍhissati = " if I grant money to whoever takes . . ., in that way this stealing will increase "

sace na vyākarissasi, aññena vā aññaṃ paṭicarissasi, tuṇhī vā bhavissasi, pakkamissasi vā ; etth' eva te sattadhā muddhā phalissati = " if you don't explain, or evade (*paṭi-car* (I)) irrelevantly, or are silent, or go away ;— your head will split in seven right here "

sace pana tumhākaṃ . . . evaṃ hoti . . . tiṭṭhatha tumhe = " if you . . . think thus . . . don't trouble "

sace agāraṃ ajjhāvasati, rājā hoti . . . sace kho pana . . . pabbajati, arahaṃ hoti . . . = " if he lives at home he will be a king . . . but if he goes forth he will be a perfected one . . . "

ce (enclitic) is similar :—

ito ce pi so . . . yojanasate viharati, alam eva . . . upasaṃkamituṃ = " even if he . . . lives a hundred leagues from here, it is proper . . . to approach "

te ce me evaṃ puṭṭhā āmo ti paṭijānanti = " if they are so questioned by me they admit ' yes ' "

taṃ ce te purisā evam āroceyyuṃ . . . api nu tvaṃ evaṃ vadeyyāsi . . . = " then if men were to inform you . . . would you perhaps say thus . . . ? "

ahañ ce va kho pana . . . abhivādeyyaṃ, tena maṃ sā parisā paribhaveyya = " but if I . . . were to salute, that assembly might despise me for it (therefore) "

yadi, " whether," is associated in meaning with *sace* :—

taṃ kim maññasi mahārāja, yadi evaṃ sante hoti vā sandiṭṭhikaṃ sāmaññaphalaṃ no vā = " then what do you think, great king—whether, that being so, it is a visible fruit of the profession of philosophy or not ? "

jānāhi yadi vā taṃ bhavantaṃ Gotamaṃ tathā santaṃ yeva saddo abbhuggato yadi vā no tathā, yadi vā so bhavaṃ Gotamo tādiso yadi vā na tādiso = " learn whether the report disseminated about that honourable Gotama is true, or whether not true, whether that honourable Gotama (is) this sort or not this sort "

yaṃ yad eva parisaṃ upasaṃkamati, yadi khattiyaparisaṃ, yadi brāhmaṇaparisaṃ, yadi gahapatiparisaṃ, yadi samaṇaparisaṃ ; visārado upasaṃkamati, amaṅkubhūto = " whatever assembly he may go to, whether of the nobility, of the priests, of householders, of philosophers, he approaches confidently, unashamed."

Notes on Tenses.—It appears from the above examples that if the condition, etc., and its result are purely hypothetical (in the view of the speaker or narrator) the verbs in both relative and main clauses will be in the optative. If the result is considered certain the (" indicative " tenses) present and future are used : the present for an " eternal truth " (result which is always true or certain) and the future for a particular case (which is certain, but might not be under different circumstances), the same tense being used in both clauses. Variations on the latter construction are the use of other tenses or infinite verbs in place of the present if the main clause is an injunction or command or wish (imperative), if there is a special infinite construction (such as *alaṃ* with the infinitive above, expressing an injunction), or if a past participle is used to express the condition, presumably recognizing or stressing that the antecedent action is completed (" present-perfect ") before the resulting action takes place. With *yadi* the present tense (or present or past participle or a nominal clause) is used, since the disjunction as a whole is certain (one alternative at least, even all the alternatives, being true).

yadā indicates time and/or a condition, in the latter case with the tense usage just noted :—

yadā aññāsi . . . satthaṃ pāyāpesi = " when he knew . . . he made the caravan set out "

yadā aññāsi . . . atha . . . pakāsesi = " when he knew . . . then he showed " *yadā bhagavā tamhā samādimhā vuṭṭhito hoti, atha mama vacanena bhagavantaṃ abhivādehi* = " when the fortunate one has come out from that concentration, then greet the fortunate one with my words (' speech ') "

yadā . . . nikkhamati . . . pātubhavanti = " when . . . he leaves . . . they appear "

yadā . . . nikkhamati, tadā . . . kampati = " when . . . he leaves, then . . . it quakes "

(the above are similar constructions with and without the correlative *tadā*, which evidently is optional)

yadā . . . passeyyāsi . . . atha me āroceyyāsi = " if/when . . . you should see . . . then you should inform me."

yato usually introduces a cause, sometimes the place of origin :—

yato kho Vāseṭṭhā sattā . . . upakkamiṃsu paribhuñjituṃ, atha tesaṃ sattānaṃ sayampabhā antaradhāyi = " because, Vāseṭṭhas, beings fell upon . . . to eat, then the self-luminosity of those beings disappeared "

yato kho bho ayaṃ attā . . . vinassati, na hoti param maraṇā, ettāvatā kho bho ayaṃ attā sammā samucchinno hoti = " since, sir, this soul . . . perishes utterly, is not after death, so far, sir, this soul has been completely annihilated "

yato . . . brāhmaṇo sīlavā ca hoti . . . sammā vadeyya = " because . . . a priest is well conducted . . . he may rightly say "

yato . . . bhikkhu averaṃ avyāpajjhaṃ mettacittaṃ bhāveti . . . ayaṃ vuccati Kassapa bhikkhu samaṇo iti . . . = " because . . . a monk develops a benevolent mind, without hatred, non-violent . . . this monk, Kassapa, is called a philosopher . . . "

yato kho bho ayaṃ attā . . . paricāreti, ettāvatā . . . patto hoti = " since, sir, this soul . . . enjoys itself, to that extent it has attained . . . "

yato ca candimasuriyā uggacchanti yattha ca ogacchanti . . . anuparivattanti = " whence the sun and moon rise and where they set . . . they (priests) turn towards " *yasmā*, " because," " since," is a rarely used synonym of *yato*. It is used with the correlative *tasmā* :—

yasmā ca kho Kassapa aññatr' eva imāya mattāya . . . sāmaññaṃ vā hoti brahmaññaṃ vā dukkaraṃ sudukkaraṃ, tasmā etaṃ kallaṃ vacanāya : dukkaraṃ sāmaññaṃ . . . ti = " and because, Kassapa, apart from this merely (' this measure ') . . . the profession of philosophy or the profession of priesthood (is) a hard task, a very hard task, therefore it is proper to say : ' The profession of philosophy is a hard task . . . ' "

hi also usually introduces a cause or reason (but is enclitic), though this sense is sometimes imprecise, extending to the adducing of a relevant factor ; *hi* clauses generally follow their main clauses, and a series of such *hi* clauses may be adduced :—

suppaṭipann' attha mārisā [1] *. . . mayam pi hi mārisā evam pi paṭipannā ekantasukhaṃ lokaṃ upapannā* = " be practising good, dear sirs, . . . for we, dear sirs, thus practising have been reborn in a world of extreme happiness "

āroceyyāsi, na hi tathāgatā vitathaṃ bhaṇanti = " you should inform (me—of what he says), for thus-gone ones do not speak untruth "

acchariyaṃ vata bho abbhutaṃ vata bho puññānaṃ gati puññānaṃ vipāko ; ayaṃ hi rājā . . . manusso, aham pi manusso ; ayaṃ hi rājā . . . paricāreti devo maññe, aham pan' amhi 'ssa dāso . . . = " surprising, methinks (this is a soliloquy), wonderful, methinks, is the destiny of merits, the result of merits ; for this king . . . is a man, I too am a man ;—for this king . . . enjoys himself as if a god, but I am his slave . . . "

. . . sabbapāṇabhūtahitānukampī viharatī ti ; iti vā hi . . . vaṇṇaṃ vadamāno vadeyya = " ' . . . he lives compassionate for the welfare of all living beings ' ; or thus, for example, . . . he may speak, speaking praise."

[1] *mārisa* (only vocative, singular and plural) polite and affectionate address customary among the gods, used also by gods addressing men (as here) : " sir," " dear sir," " my friend," " dear boy."

yāva (the *yāva* clause often follows its main clause) :—

yāv' assa kāyo ṭhassati tāva naṃ dakkhinti devamanussā = " as long as his body remains, so long gods and men will see him "

tasmāt iha Cunda yaṃ vo mayā cīvaraṃ anuññātaṃ, alaṃ vo taṃ yāvad eva sītassa paṭighātāya . . . = " therefore, in this case, Cunda, the robe which is allowed you by me is sufficient for you just as long as it keeps off the cold . . . " (lit. : for the keeping off, *paṭighāto*, of cold, *sītaṃ*)

na tāva bhagavā parinibbāyissati na yāva bhagavā bhikkhusaṃghaṃ ārabbha kiñ cid eva udāharati = " the fortunate one will not attain *nibbānaṃ* as long as the fortunate one has something to promulgate about the community of monks "

na tāva . . . pajjalissati yāva . . . na vandissati = " it will not light as long as . . . he has not paid respect . . ."

yāvakīvaṃ :—

yāvakīvaṃ . . . samaggā sannipatissanti . . . vuddhi yeva Ānanda Vajjīnaṃ pāṭikaṅkhā . . . = " as long as . . . they assemble united . . . only increase of the Vajjīs (is) probable, Ānanda, . . . "

yāvatā :—

yāvatā Ānanda ariyaṃ āyatanaṃ . . . idaṃ agganagaraṃ bhavissati = " Ānanda, as far as the Āryan sphere (extends) . . . this will be the supreme city."

yattha :—

yattha Himavantapasse . . . tattha vāsaṃ kappesuṃ = " where on the side of the Himālaya . . . there they arranged a dwelling place "

yattha sīlaṃ tattha paññā, yattha paññā tattha sīlaṃ = " where there is virtue there is wisdom, where wisdom, virtue "

te . . . jāneyyuṃ yatth' ime cattāro mahābhūtā aparisesā nirujjhanti = " they . . . may know where these four elements absolutely end "

yattha pan' āvuso sabbaso vedayitaṃ n' atthi, api nu kho

tattha asmī ti siyā = " but where, sir, experience is completely absent (" not "), would there be there the thought ' I am ' ? "

mayam . . . na jānāma yattha vā brahmā yena vā brahmā yahiṃ vā brahmā = " we . . . do not know where God is or which way God is or whereabouts God is "

yena (cf. last example) :—

yena Nāḷandā tad avasari = " he went down to(wards) Nāḷandā "

Relative adjective :—

yāvataka (feminine *-ikā*) :—

yāvatikā yānassa bhūmi yānena gantvā, yānā paccorohitvā, . . . upasaṃkami = " having gone by carriage as far as (there was) ground for a carriage, having alighted from the carriage, . . . approached "

Examples of Complex Sentences

Examples of the combination of various elements in a larger sentence or period :—

yathā kathaṃ pana te mahārāja vyākaṃsu, sace te agaru, bhāsassu (two subordinate clauses ; the whole connected to its wider, dialogue, context by *pana*)

kin nu Sāriputta ye te ahesuṃ atītam addhānaṃ arahanto sammāsambuddhā, sabbe te bhagavanto cetasā ceto paricca viditā, evaṃsīlā te bhagavanto ahesuṃ iti pi, evaṃdhammā evaṃpaññā evaṃvihārī evaṃvimuttā te bhagavanto ahesuṃ iti pī ti (subordinate clause and two direct speech clauses with *iti* ; the whole is interrogative direct speech)

yadā aññāsi dutiyo satthavāho bahunikkhanto kho dāni so sattho ti bahuṃ tiṇañ ca kaṭṭhañ ca udakañ ca āropetvā satthaṃ pāyāpesi (subordinate clause containing a direct speech clause, followed by infinite clause with gerund and main clause : the clauses here, as frequently in manuscripts and printed editions, are not separated by punctuation)

yadā bhagavā aññāsi Kūṭadantaṃ brāhmaṇaṃ kallacittaṃ muducittaṃ vinīvaraṇacittaṃ udaggacittaṃ pasannacittaṃ, atha yā Buddhānaṃ sāmukkaṃsikā dhammadesanā taṃ pakāsesi : dukkhaṃ, samudayaṃ, nirodhaṃ, maggaṃ (subordinate clause containing a series of *bahubbīhis*, with main clause containing another subordinate clause ; the last four words specify *taṃ*)

Channo Ānanda bhikkhu yaṃ iccheyya taṃ vadeyya, so bhikkhūhi n' eva vattabbo na ovaditabbo [1] *na anusāsitabbo* (two clauses joined by paratax, the first containing a subordinate clause, the second a " chain " of future passive participles equivalent to a string of " parallel " verbs)

cirapaṭikāhaṃ bhante bhagavantaṃ dassanāya upasaṃkamitukāmo, api ca devānaṃ Tāvatiṃsānaṃ kehi ci kehi ci kiccakaraṇīyehi vyāvaṭo evāhaṃ nāsakkhiṃ bhagavantaṃ dassanāya upasaṃkamituṃ (conjunction, and infinite constructions depending on a main verb).

Order

The normal order of clauses is that a subordinate clause precedes its main clause. Inversion of this order, like inversion of word order, may be used to emphasize the words thus placed first. For example :—

tassa te āvuso lābhā, tassa te suladdhaṃ, yassa te tathāgato pacchimaṃ piṇḍapātaṃ bhuñjitvā parinibbuto = " it is a gain for you, sir, it was well obtained for you, that the thus-gone attained liberation after eating your last offering of alms " (*lābhā* can be taken as an indeclinable form, or as plural)—here instead of a plain statement that this circumstance is a gain we have an emotive assertion (intended to reassure the person spoken to) stressing the words *lābhā* and *suladdhaṃ*.

The clause order is inverted when the whole sentence is interrogative :—

katame ca pana te bhikkhave dhammā gambhīrā . . . ye tathāgato . . . pavedeti = " now which, monks, are those profound doctrines . . . which the thus-gone . . . makes known ? "

[1] Future passive participle of *o-vad* I, " admonish."

In connection with word order [1] (*ṭhāna*, " position ") we may add here two rules.

Vocatives are usually placed second, like enclitics, except when following one or more enclitics (as in the two examples just quoted). They are never sentence or clause initials, but may be displaced to the end of a clause, as in the sentence quoted earlier in this lesson :—

anacchariyaṃ kho pan' etaṃ Ānanda, yaṃ manussabhūto kālaṃ kareyya

which is also an example of rhetorical inversion of both clause order and word order stressing the word *anacchariyaṃ*. Here perhaps the close link between *etaṃ* and *anacchariyaṃ* (= " this is not surprising "), or more probably the fact that *etaṃ* as correlative (with *yaṃ*) would normally be initial, displaces *Ānanda* to the end (the two enclitics occupy the second position in the inverted clause).

The length of words (number of syllables) may decide the order of words where this is not otherwise determined (as in a string of grammatically parallel words) :—

taṃ jātaṃ bhūtaṃ saṅkhataṃ palokadhammaṃ = " that which is born, become, synthesised, subject to the law of decay "

atītānāgatapaccuppanna = " past, future and present ".

Vocabulary

Verbs :—

añch (I)	*añchati*	turn (on a lathe)
anu-rakkh (I)	*anurakkhati*	look after, retain
ā-bhuj (I*)	*ābhujati*	fold the legs
ā-sev (I)	*āsevati*	practice
upa-ā-dā (III)	*upādiyati*	be attached
ni(r)-car (VII)	*nicchāreti*	bring up
ni(r)-yat (VII)	*niyyādeti*	hand over, give in charge of
ni-vatt (I)	*nivattati*	go back
(p)pa-(g)gah (V)	*paggaṇhāti*	apply
(p)paṭi-ā-vam (I)	*paccāvamati*	swallow back

[1] Cf. Lessons 1, 6, 10, 11, and 12 (interrogation).

(*p*)*pa-dhā* (I)	*padahati*	exert
(*p*)*pa-luj* (III)	*palujjati*	decay
(*p*)*pa-*(*s*)*sambh* (I)	*passambhati*	become calm (causative = make calm)
(*p*)*pa-*(*s*)*sas* (I)	*passasati*	breathe out
pā	(aorist *apāyi*)	
bahulī-kar (VI)	*bahulīkaroti*	cultivate
bhī (I)	(*bhāyati*, aorist *bhāyi* [1])	be afraid
yāc (I)	*yācati*	request, ask (for—not a question)
vi-ā-yam (I)	*vāyamati*	exercise, practice

Nouns :—

attho	(means also) matter, affair
anālayo	not clinging
antevāsin	apprentice
ayanaṃ	way, path
avyāpādo	non-violence
asammoso	not-forgetting
āgamanaṃ	coming
ājīvo	livelihood
uddhaccaṃ	pride, vanity
uddhaccakukkuccaṃ	pride, vanity, conceit
kukkuccaṃ	vanity, worry, anxiety
ghānaṃ (or *ghāṇaṃ*)	nose
cāgo	abandoning
jivhā	tongue
ñāyo	method
thīnaṃ	mental deficiency, stupidity, inertia
thīnamiddhaṃ	stupidity (and inertia)
nisīdanaṃ	seat (a cloth or groundsheet for sitting on on the ground)
paṭinissaggo	rejecting, renouncing
patissati (fem.) (or *paṭi-*)	recollectedness, mindfulness
paloko	decay
pallaṅko	sitting cross-legged

[1] In the *Dīgha* only the p.p. *bhīta* occurs.

passo	side
pādo	(also means) basis
pāripūri (fem.)	perfection
phoṭṭhabbaṃ	touchable (object), sensation (f.p.p. of (*p*)*phus*, but used only as noun)
bījagāmo	plants, the vegetable kingdom, the community of plants
bhamakāro	turner
bhāvanaṃ	development
bhūtagāmo	living beings, the community of living beings, the animal kingdom
middhaṃ	stupidity, mental derangement
mutti (fem.)	freeing
moho	delusion
vayo	loss
varaṃ	boon
vāyāmo	exercise
vicikicchā	uncertainty
visuddhi (fem.)	clarity, purification
veramaṇī	abstention
vyāpādo	violence, malevolence
saṃkappo	intention, object
saccaṃ	truth
samārambho	undertaking, falling upon, destroying
sāvako	pupil
sotaṃ	ear

Adjectives :—

addhaniya	roadworthy, enduring
anissita (neg. p.p. of *ni*-(*s*)*si*)	unattached
uttara	(also means) higher, further
garu	(also means) troublesome
dakkha	skilful
nirāmisa	non-sensual
paripakka	ripe
puthu	many, various
mahaggata	sublime, elevated

vikkhitta	diffuse, vain
vyāvaṭa	concerned, busy, worried
saṃkhitta	limited, narrow (instrumental = briefly, in short)
sāmisa	sensual

Past Participles :—

ossaṭṭha (*o*-(*s*)*saj*[1] (I, to pour out))	dispelled
catta (*caj*)	abandoned, thrown away
paccupaṭṭhita ((*p*)*paṭi-upa*-(*t*)*ṭhā*)	set up
paṭinissaṭṭha ((*p*)*paṭi-ni*(*r*)-(*s*)*saj*[1])	rejected, renounced
paṇihita ((*p*)*pa-ni-dhā*)	held
vanta (*vam*)	vomited
saṃkhata (*saṃ-kar*)	synthesized (cf. *saṃkhāro*)

Present Participle :—

sayāna (*si*)	lying down

Gerund :—

paṇidhāya ((*p*)*pa-ni-dhā*)	having held

Indeclinables :—

āyatiṃ	in future
cirassaṃ	at last, after a long time
parimukhaṃ	in front
bhadante	sir ! (polite address by Buddhist monks to the Buddha)
labbhā	possible, conceivable, is it conceivable ? (usually in the idiom *taṃ kut' ettha labbhā*, therefore how (whence) could this be possible ?, so how could one expect this ?, what is surprising in this ? : which may be used as affirmative or negative)
suṭṭhu	well (done)

EXERCISE 27

Passages for reading :—

1. atha kho bhagavā pubbaṇhasamayaṃ nivāsetvā pattacīvaram ādāya Vesāliṃ piṇḍāya pāvisi, Vesāliyaṃ piṇḍāya caritvā pacchābhattaṃ piṇḍapātapaṭikkanto āyasmantaṃ Ānandaṃ āmantesi : gaṇhāhi Ānanda nisīdanaṃ. yena Cāpālaṃ cetiyaṃ ten' upasaṃkamissāmi divāvihārāyā ti. evaṃ bhante ti kho āyasmā Ānando bhagavato paṭissutvā nisīdanaṃ ādāya bhagavantaṃ piṭṭhito piṭṭhito anubandhi.

atha kho bhagavā yena Cāpālaṃ cetiyaṃ ten' upasaṃkami, upasaṃkamitvā paññatte āsane nisīdi. āyasmā pi kho Ānando bhagavantaṃ abhivādetvā ekamantaṃ nisīdi. ekamantaṃ nisinnaṃ kho āyasmantaṃ Ānandaṃ bhagavā etad avoca : ramaṇīyā Ānanda Vesālī, . . . ramaṇīyaṃ Cāpālaṃ cetiyaṃ.

* * *

nanu evaṃ Ānanda mayā paṭigacc' eva akkhātaṃ, sabbeh' eva piyehi manāpehi nānābhāvo vinābhāvo aññathābhāvo. taṃ kut' ettha Ānanda labbhā. yaṃ taṃ jātaṃ bhūtaṃ saṅkhataṃ palokadhammaṃ taṃ vata mā palujjī ti n' etaṃ ṭhānaṃ vijjati. yaṃ kho pan' etaṃ Ānanda tathāgatena cattaṃ vantaṃ muttaṃ pahīnaṃ paṭinissaṭṭhaṃ, ossaṭṭho āyusaṅkhāro. ekaṃsena vācā tathāgatena bhāsitā : na ciraṃ tathāgatassa parinibbānaṃ bhavissati, ito tiṇṇaṃ māsānaṃ accayena tathāgato parinibbāyissatī ti. taṃ vacanaṃ tathāgato jīvitahetu puna paccāvamissatī ti, n' etaṃ ṭhānaṃ vijjati. āyām' Ānanda yena Mahāvanaṃ Kūṭāgārasālā ten' upasaṃkamissāmā ti. evaṃ bhante ti kho āyasmā Ānando bhagavato paccassosi.

atha kho bhagavā āyasmatā Ānandena saddhiṃ yena Mahāvanaṃ Kūṭāgārasālā ten' upasaṃkami. upasaṃkamitvā āyasmantaṃ Ānandaṃ āmantesi : gaccha tvaṃ Ānanda, yāvatakā bhikkhū Vesāliṃ upanissāya viharanti, te sabbe upaṭṭhānasālāyaṃ sannipātehī ti. evaṃ bhante ti kho āyasmā Ānando bhagavato paṭissutvā, yāvatakā bhikkhū Vesāliṃ upanissāya viharanti, te sabbe upaṭṭhānasālāyaṃ sannipātetvā, yena bhagavā ten' upasaṃkami, upasaṃkamitvā bhagavantaṃ abhivādetvā ekamantaṃ aṭṭhāsi. ekamantaṃ ṭhito kho āyasmā Ānando bhagavantaṃ etad avoca : sannipatito bhante bhikkhusaṃgho. yassa dāni bhante bhagavā kālaṃ maññatī ti.

atha kho bhagavā yena upaṭṭhānasālā ten' upasaṃkami, upasaṃkamitvā paññatte āsane nisīdi. nisajja kho bhagavā bhikkhū āmantesi : tasmāt iha bhikkhave ye vo mayā dhammā abhiññāya desitā, te vo sādhukaṃ uggahetvā āsevitabbā bhāvetabbā bahulīkātabbā, yathayidaṃ brahmacariyaṃ addhaniyaṃ assa ciraṭṭhitikaṃ, tad assa bahujanahitāya bahujanasukhāya lokānukampāya atthāya hitāya sukhāya devamanussānaṃ. katame ca te bhikkhave dhammā mayā abhiññāya desitā, ye vo sādhukaṃ uggahetvā āsevitabbā bhāvetabbā bahulīkātabbā yathayidaṃ brahmacariyaṃ addhaniyaṃ assa ciraṭṭhitikaṃ, tad assa bahujanahitāya bahujanasukhāya lokānukampāya atthāya hitāya sukhāya devamanussānaṃ. seyyathīdaṃ cattāro satipaṭṭhānā, cattāro sammappadhānā, cattāro iddhipādā, pañc' indriyāni, pañca balāni, satta bojjhaṅgā, ariyo aṭṭhaṅgiko maggo, ime kho bhikkhave dhammā mayā abhiññāya desitā, te vo sādhukaṃ uggahetvā āsevitabbā bhāvetabbā bahulīkātabbā yathayidaṃ brahmacariyaṃ addhaniyaṃ assa ciraṭṭhitikaṃ tad assa bahujanahitāya bahujanasukhāya lokānukampāya atthāya hitāya sukhāya devamanussānan ti.

atha kho bhagavā bhikkhū āmantesi : handa dāni bhikkhave āmantayāmi vo, vayadhammā saṅkhārā, appamādena sampādetha, na ciraṃ tathāgatassa parinibbānaṃ bhavissati, ito tiṇṇaṃ māsānaṃ accayena tathāgato parinibbāyissatī ti. idam avoca bhagavā, idaṃ vatvā sugato athāparaṃ etad avoca satthā :—

paripakko vayo mayhaṃ, parittaṃ mama jīvitaṃ,
pahāya vo gamissāmi, katam me saraṇam attano,
appamattā satīmanto [1] susīlā hotha bhikkhavo
susamāhitasaṃkappā sacittam anurakkhatha.
yo imasmiṃ dhammavinaye appamatto vihessati [2]
pahāya jātisaṃsāraṃ dukkhass' antaṃ karissatī ti.

[1] *satimant-* with the vowel *i* preceding the suffix *-mant* lengthened by poetic licence, see Lesson 30.
[2] Contracted poetic form of *viharissati*.

2. evam me sutaṃ. ekaṃ samayaṃ bhagavā Kurūsu[1] viharati. Kammāssadhammaṃ nāma Kurūnaṃ nigamo. tatra kho bhagavā bhikkhū āmantesi bhikkhavo ti. bhadante ti te bhikkhū bhagavato paccassosuṃ. bhagavā etad avoca: ekāyano ayaṃ bhikkhave maggo sattānaṃ visuddhiyā sokaparidevānaṃ samatikkamāya dukkhadomanassānaṃ atthagamāya ñāyassa adhigamāya nibbānassa sacchikiriyāya, yadidaṃ cattāro satipaṭṭhānā. katame cattāro. idha bhikkhave bhikkhu kāye kāyānupassī viharati ātāpī sampajāno satimā, vineyya loke abhijjhādomanassaṃ — vedanāsu vedanānupassī viharati ātāpī sampajāno satimā, vineyya loke abhijjhādomanassaṃ — citte cittānupassī viharati ātāpī sampajāno satimā, vineyya loke abhijjhādomanassaṃ — dhammesu dhammānupassī viharati ātāpī sampajāno satimā, vineyya loke abhijjhādomanassaṃ.

kathañ ca bhikkhave bhikkhu kāye kāyānupassī viharati. idha bhikkhave bhikkhu araññagato vā rukkhamūlagato vā suññāgāragato vā nisīdati pallaṅkaṃ ābhujitvā ujuṃ kāyaṃ paṇidhāya parimukhaṃ satiṃ upaṭṭhapetvā. so sato va assasati, sato passasati. dīghaṃ vā assasanto dīghaṃ assasāmī ti pajānāti, dīghaṃ vā passasanto dīghaṃ passasāmī ti pajānāti. rassaṃ vā assasanto rassaṃ assasāmī ti pajānāti, rassaṃ vā passasanto rassaṃ passasāmī ti pajānāti. sabbakāyapaṭisaṃvedī assasissāmī ti sikkhati sabbakāyapaṭisaṃvedī passasissāmī ti sikkhati. passambhayaṃ kāyasaṃkhāraṃ assasissāmī ti sikkhati, passambhayaṃ kāyasaṃkhāraṃ passasissāmī ti sikkhati.

seyyathā pi bhikkhave dakkho bhamakāro vā bhamakārantevāsī vā dīghaṃ vā añchanto dīghaṃ añchāmī ti pajānāti, rassaṃ vā añchanto rassaṃ añchāmī ti pajānāti, evam eva kho bhikkhave bhikkhu dīghaṃ vā assasanto . . . sikkhati. iti ajjhattaṃ vā kāye kāyānupassī viharati, bahiddhā vā kāye kāyānupassī viharati, ajjhattabahiddhā vā kāye kāyānupassī viharati. samudayadhammānupassī vā kāyasmiṃ viharati, vayadhammānupassī vā kāyasmiṃ viharati, samudayavayadhammānupassī vā kāyasmiṃ viharati. atthi kāyo ti vā pan' assa sati paccupaṭṭhitā hoti yāvad eva ñāṇamattāya patis-

[1] Kuru, a small kingdom to the west of the upper Yamunā, about half way between Vatsa and Gandhāra.

satimattāya. anissito ca viharati na ca kiñ ci loke upādiyati. evam pi bhikkhave bhikkhu kāye kāyānupassī viharati.

puna ca paraṃ bhikkhave bhikkhu gacchanto vā gacchāmī ti pajānāti, ṭhito vā ṭhito 'mhī ti pajānāti, nisinno vā nisinno 'mhī ti pajānāti, sayāno vā sayāno 'mhī ti pajānāti. yathā yathā vā pan' assa kāyo paṇihito hoti, tathā tathā naṃ pajānāti. iti ajjhattaṃ vā kāye kāyānupassī viharati . . . na ca kiñ ci loke upādiyati. evam pi bhikkhave bhikkhu kāye kāyānupassī viharati. . . .

kathañ ca bhikkhave bhikkhu vedanāsu vedanānupassī viharati. idha bhikkhave bhikkhu sukhaṃ vedanaṃ vedayamāno sukhaṃ vedanaṃ vedayāmī ti pajānāti, dukkhaṃ vedanaṃ vedayamāno dukkhaṃ vedanaṃ vedayāmī ti pajānāti. adukkhamasukhaṃ vedanaṃ vedayamāno adukkhamasukhaṃ vedanaṃ vedayāmī ti pajānāti. sāmisaṃ vā sukhaṃ vedanaṃ vedayamāno sāmisaṃ sukhaṃ vedanaṃ vedayāmī ti pajānāti. nirāmisaṃ vā sukhaṃ vedanaṃ vedayamāno nirāmisaṃ sukhaṃ vedanaṃ vedayāmī ti pajānāti. sāmisaṃ vā dukkhaṃ vedanaṃ vedayamāno sāmisaṃ dukkhaṃ vedanaṃ vedayāmī ti pajānāti. nirāmisaṃ vā dukkhaṃ vedanaṃ vedayamāno nirāmisaṃ dukkhaṃ vedanaṃ vedayāmī ti pajānāti. sāmisaṃ vā adukkhamasukhaṃ vedanaṃ vedayamāno sāmisaṃ adukkhamasukhaṃ vedanaṃ vedayāmī ti pajānāti. nirāmisaṃ vā adukkhamasukhaṃ vedanaṃ vedayamāno nirāmisaṃ adukkhamasukhaṃ vedanaṃ vedayāmī ti pajānāti.

iti ajjhattaṃ vā vedanāsu vedanānupassī viharati, bahiddhā vā vedanāsu vedanānupassī viharati, ajjhattabahiddhā vā vedanāsu vedanānupassī viharati. samudayadhammānupassī vā vedanāsu viharati, vayadhammānupassī vā vedanāsu viharati, samudayavayadhammānupassī vā vedanāsu viharati. atthi vedanā ti vā pan' assa sati paccupaṭṭhitā hoti yāvad eva ñāṇamattāya patissatimattāya. anissito ca viharati na ca kiñ ci loke upādiyati. evaṃ kho bhikkhave bhikkhu vedanāsu vedanānupassī viharati.

kathañ ca bhikkhave bhikkhu citte cittānupassī viharati. idha bhikkhave bhikkhu sarāgaṃ vā cittaṃ sarāgaṃ cittan ti pajānāti, vītarāgaṃ vā cittaṃ vītarāgaṃ cittan ti pajānāti, sadosaṃ vā cittaṃ sadosaṃ cittan ti pajānāti, vītadosaṃ vā cittaṃ vītadosaṃ cittan ti pajānāti, samohaṃ vā cittaṃ samohaṃ cittan ti pajānāti, vītamohaṃ vā cittaṃ vītamohaṃ cittan ti pajānāti, saṃkhittaṃ vā cittaṃ saṃkhittaṃ cittan ti pajānāti, vikkhittaṃ vā cittaṃ vikkhittaṃ cittan ti pajānāti, mahaggataṃ vā cittaṃ mahaggataṃ cittan ti pajānāti, amahaggataṃ vā cittaṃ amahaggataṃ cittan ti pajānāti, sauttaraṃ vā cittaṃ sauttaraṃ cittan ti pajānāti, anuttaraṃ vā cittaṃ anuttaraṃ cittan ti pajānāti, samāhitaṃ vā cittaṃ samāhitaṃ cittan ti pajānāti, asamāhitaṃ vā cittaṃ asamāhitaṃ cittan ti pajānāti, vimuttaṃ vā cittaṃ vimuttaṃ cittan ti pajānāti, avimuttaṃ vā cittaṃ avimuttaṃ cittan ti pajānāti.

iti ajjhattaṃ vā citte cittānupassī viharati, bahiddhā vā citte cittānupassī viharati, ajjhattabahiddhā vā citte cittānupassī viharati. samudayadhammānupassī vā cittasmiṃ viharati, vayadhammānupassī vā cittasmiṃ viharati, samudayavayadhammānupassī vā cittasmiṃ viharati. atthi cittan ti vā pan' assa sati paccupaṭṭhitā hoti yāvad eva ñāṇamattāya patissatimattāya. anissito ca viharati na ca kiñ ci loke upādiyati. evaṃ kho bhikkhave bhikkhu citte cittānupassī viharati.

kathañ ca bhikkhave bhikkhu dhammesu dhammānupassī viharati. idha bhikkhave bhikkhu dhammesu dhammānupassī viharati pañcasu nīvaraṇesu. kathañ ca bhikkhave bhikkhu dhammesu dhammānupassī viharati pañcasu nīvaraṇesu.

idha bhikkhave bhikkhu santaṃ vā ajjhattaṃ kāmacchandaṃ atthi me ajjhattaṃ kāmacchando ti pajānāti, asantaṃ vā ajjhattaṃ kāmacchandaṃ n' atthi me ajjhattaṃ kāmacchando ti pajānāti. yathā ca anuppannassa kāmacchandassa uppādo hoti tañ ca pajānāti, yathā ca uppannassa kāmacchandassa pahānaṃ hoti tañ ca pajānāti, yathā ca pahīnassa kāmacchandassa āyatiṃ anuppādo hoti tañ ca pajānāti.

santaṃ vā ajjhattaṃ vyāpādaṃ atthi me ajjhattaṃ vyāpādo ti pajānāti, asantaṃ vā ajjhattaṃ vyāpādaṃ n' atthi me ajjhattaṃ vyāpādo ti pajānāti. yathā ca anuppannassa vyāpādassa uppādo hoti tañ ca pajānāti, yathā ca uppannassa vyāpādassa pahānaṃ hoti tañ ca pajānāti, yathā ca pahīnassa vyāpādassa āyatiṃ anuppādo hoti tañ ca pajānāti.

santaṃ vā ajjhattaṃ thīnamiddhaṃ atthi me ajjhattaṃ thīnamiddhan ti pajānāti, . . . thīnamiddhassa āyatiṃ anuppādo hoti tañ ca pajānāti.

santaṃ vā ajjhattaṃ uddhaccakukkuccaṃ atthi me ajjhattaṃ

uddhaccakukkuccan ti pajānāti, . . . uddhaccakukkuccassa āyatiṃ anuppādo hoti tañ ca pajānāti.

santaṃ vā ajjhattaṃ vicikicchaṃ atthi me ajjhattaṃ vicikicchā ti pajānāti, . . . yathā ca pahīnāya vicikicchāya āyatiṃ anuppādo hoti tañ ca pajānāti.

iti ajjhattaṃ vā dhammesu dhammānupassī viharati, bahiddhā vā dhammesu dhammānupassī viharati, ajjhatta-bahiddhā vā dhammesu dhammānupassī viharati. samudaya-dhammānupassī vā dhammesu viharati, vayadhammānupassī vā dhammesu viharati, samudayavayadhammānupassī vā dhammesu viharati. atthi dhammā ti vā pan' assa sati paccupaṭṭhitā hoti yāvad eva ñāṇamattāya patissatimattāya. anissito ca viharati na ca kiñ ci loke upādiyati. evaṃ kho bhikkhave bhikkhu dhammesu dhammānupassī viharati pañcasu nīvaraṇesu.

puna ca paraṃ bhikkhave bhikkhu dhammesu dhammānupassī viharati pañcas' upādānakkhandhesu. kathañ ca bhikkhave bhikkhu dhammesu dhammānupassī viharati pañcas' upādānakkhandhesu. idha bhikkhave bhikkhu iti rūpaṃ, iti rūpassa samudayo, iti rūpassa atthagamo — iti vedanā, iti vedanāya samudayo, iti vedanāya atthagamo — iti saññā, iti saññāya samudayo, iti saññāya atthagamo — iti saṃkhārā, iti saṃkhārāṇaṃ [1] samudayo, iti saṃkhārāṇaṃ atthagamo — iti viññāṇaṃ, iti viññāṇassa samudayo, iti viññāṇassa atthagamo ti, iti ajjhattaṃ vā dhammesu dhammānupassī viharati, . . . evaṃ kho bhikkhave bhikkhu dhammesu dhammānupassī viharati pañcas' upādānakkhandhesu.

puna ca paraṃ bhikkhave bhikkhu dhammesu dhammānupassī viharati chasu ajjhattikabāhiresu āyatanesu. kathañ ca bhikkhave bhikkhu dhammesu dhammānupassī viharati chasu ajjhattikabāhiresu āyatanesu. idha bhikkhave bhikkhu cakkhuñ ca pajānāti, rūpe ca pajānāti, yañ ca tadubhayaṃ paṭicca uppajjati saṃyojanaṃ tañ ca pajānāti, yathā ca anuppannassa saṃyojanassa uppādo hoti tañ ca pajānāti, yathā ca uppannassa saṃyojanassa pahānaṃ hoti tañ ca pajānāti, yathā ca pahīnassa saṃyojanassa āyatiṃ anuppādo hoti tañ ca pajānāti . . . sotañ ca pajānāti, sadde ca pajānāti . . . pe . . . ghānañ ca pajānāti, gandhe ca pajānāti . . . pe . . . jivhañ

[1] Cerebralization of *n* after a *r* in the same word.

ca pajānāti, rase ca pajānāti . . . pe . . . kāyañ ca pajānāti, phoṭṭhabbe ca pajānāti . . . pe . . . manañ ca pajānāti, dhamme ca pajānāti, yañ ca tad ubhayaṃ paṭicca uppajjati saṃyojanaṃ tañ ca pajānāti, yathā ca anuppannassa saṃyojanassa uppādo hoti tañ ca pajānāti, yathā ca uppannassa saṃyojanassa pahānaṃ hoti tañ ca pajānāti, yathā ca pahīnassa saṃyojanassa āyatiṃ anuppādo hoti tañ ca pajānāti. iti ajjhattaṃ vā dhammesu dhammānupassī viharati, bahiddhā vā dhammesu dhammānupassī viharati, ajjhattabahiddhā vā dhammesu dhammānupassī viharati. samudayadhammānupassī vā dhammesu viharati, vayadhammānupassī vā dhammesu viharati, samudayavayadhammānupassī vā dhammesu viharati. atthi dhammā ti vā pan' assa sati paccupaṭṭhitā hoti yāvad eva ñāṇamattāya patissatimattāya. anissito ca viharati na ca kiñ ci loke upādiyati. evaṃ kho bhikkhave bhikkhu dhammesu dhammānupassī viharati ajjhattikabāhiresu āyatanesu.

puna ca paraṃ bhikkhave bhikkhu dhammesu dhammānupassī viharati sattasu bojjhaṅgesu. kathañ ca bhikkhave bhikkhu dhammesu dhammānupassī viharati sattasu bojjhaṅgesu. idha bhikkhave bhikkhu santaṃ vā ajjhattaṃ satisambojjhaṅgaṃ atthi me ajjhattaṃ satisambojjhaṅgo ti pajānāti. asantaṃ vā ajjhattaṃ satisambojjhaṅgaṃ n' atthi me ajjhattaṃ satisambojjhaṅgo ti pajānāti. yathā ca anuppannassa satisambojjhaṅgassa uppādo hoti tañ ca pajānāti, yathā ca uppannassa satisambojjhaṅgassa bhāvanāya pāripūrī hoti tañ ca pajānāti. . . . santaṃ vā ajjhattaṃ dhammavicayasambojjhaṅgaṃ . . . pe . . . santaṃ vā ajjhattaṃ viriyasambojjhaṅgaṃ . . . pe . . . santaṃ vā ajjhattaṃ pītisambojjhaṅgaṃ . . . pe . . . santaṃ vā ajjhattaṃ passaddhisambojjhaṅgaṃ . . . pe . . . santaṃ vā ajjhattaṃ samādhisambojjhaṅgaṃ . . . pe . . . santaṃ vā ajjhattaṃ upekhāsambojjhaṅgaṃ atthi me ajjhattaṃ upekhāsambojjhaṅgo ti pajānāti. asantaṃ vā ajjhattaṃ upekhāsambojjhaṅgaṃ n' atthi me ajjhattaṃ upekhāsambojjhaṅgo ti pajānāti. yathā ca anuppannassa upekhāsambojjhaṅgassa uppādo hoti tañ ca pajānāti, yathā ca uppannassa upekhāsambojjhaṅgassa bhāvanāya pāripūrī hoti tañ ca pajānāti. iti ajjhattaṃ vā dhammesu dhammānupassī viharati, bahiddhā vā dhammesu dhammānupassī viharati, ajjhattabahiddhā vā dhammesu dhammānupassī viharati.

samudayadhammānupassī vā dhammesu viharati, vayadhammānupassī vā dhammesu viharati, samudayavayadhammānupassī vā dhammesu viharati. atthi dhammā ti vā pan' assa sati paccupaṭṭhitā hoti yāvad eva ñāṇamattāya patissatimattāya. anissito ca viharati na ca kiñ ci loke upādiyati. evaṃ kho bhikkhave bhikkhu dhammesu dhammānupassī viharati sattasu sambojjhaṅgesu.

puna ca paraṃ bhikkhave bhikkhu dhammesu dhammānupassī viharati catusu ariyasaccesu. kathañ ca bhikkhave bhikkhu dhammesu dhammānupassī viharati catusu ariyasaccesu. idha bhikkhave bhikkhu idaṃ dukkhan ti yathābhūtaṃ pajānāti, ayaṃ dukkhasamudayo ti yathābhūtaṃ pajānāti, ayaṃ dukkhanirodho ti yathābhūtaṃ pajānāti, ayaṃ dukkhanirodhagāminī paṭipadā ti yathābhūtaṃ pajānāti.

katamañ ca bhikkhave dukkhaṃ ariyasaccaṃ. jāti pi dukkhā, jarā pi dukkhā, vyādhi pi dukkhā, maraṇam pi dukkhaṃ. sokaparidevadukkhadomanassupāyāsā pi dukkhā, yam p' icchaṃ na labhati tam pi dukkhaṃ, saṃkhittena pañcupādānakkhandhā dukkhā. . . .

katamañ ca bhikkhave dukkhasamudayaṃ ariyasaccaṃ. yā 'yaṃ taṇhā ponobhavikā. . . . seyyathīdaṃ kāmataṇhā bhavataṇhā vibhavataṇhā . . .

katamañ ca bhikkhave dukkhanirodhaṃ ariyasaccaṃ. yo tassā yeva taṇhāya asesavirāganirodho cāgo paṭinissaggo mutti anālayo . . .

katamañ ca bhikkhave dukkhanirodhagāminīpaṭipadā ariyasaccaṃ. ayam eva ariyo aṭṭhaṅgiko maggo, seyyathīdaṃ sammādiṭṭhi sammāsaṃkappo sammāvācā sammākammanto sammāājīvo sammāvāyāmo sammāsati sammāsamādhi.

katamā ca bhikkhave sammādiṭṭhi. yaṃ kho bhikkhave dukkhe ñāṇaṃ dukkhasamudaye ñāṇaṃ dukkhanirodhe ñāṇaṃ dukkhanirodhagāminiyā paṭipadāya ñāṇaṃ, ayaṃ vuccati bhikkhave sammādiṭṭhi.

katamo ca bhikkhave sammāsaṃkappo. nekkhammasaṃkappo avyāpādasaṃkappo avihiṃsāsaṃkappo, ayaṃ vuccati bhikkhave sammāsaṃkappo.

katamā ca bhikkhave sammāvācā. musāvādā veramaṇī, pisuṇāya vācāya veramaṇī, pharusāya vācāya veramaṇī, samphappalāpā veramaṇī, ayaṃ vuccati bhikkhave sammāvācā.

katamo ca bhikkhave sammākammanto. pāṇātipātā veramaṇī, adinnādānā veramaṇī, kāmesu micchācārā veramaṇī, ayaṃ vuccati bhikkhave sammākammanto.

katamo ca bhikkhave sammāājīvo. idha bhikkhave ariyasāvako micchāājīvaṃ pahāya sammāājīvena jīvikaṃ kappeti, ayaṃ vuccati bhikkhave sammāājīvo.

katamo ca bhikkhave sammāvāyāmo. idha bhikkhave bhikkhu anuppannānaṃ pāpakānaṃ akusalānaṃ dhammānaṃ anuppādāya chandaṃ janeti vāyamati, viriyaṃ ārabhati, cittaṃ paggaṇhāti padahati. uppannānaṃ pāpakānaṃ akusalānaṃ dhammānaṃ pahānāya chandaṃ janeti vāyamati, viriyaṃ ārabhati, cittaṃ paggaṇhāti padahati. anuppannānaṃ kusalānaṃ dhammānaṃ uppādāya chandaṃ janeti vāyamati, viriyaṃ ārabhati, cittaṃ paggaṇhāti padahati. uppannānaṃ kusalānaṃ dhammānaṃ ṭhitiyā asammosāya bhiyyobhāvāya vepullāya bhāvanāya pāripūriyā chandaṃ janeti vāyamati, viriyaṃ ārabhati, cittaṃ paggaṇhāti padahati. ayaṃ vuccati bhikkhave sammāvāyāmo.

katamā ca bhikkhave sammāsati. idha bhikkhave bhikkhu kāye kāyānupassī viharati ātāpī sampajāno satimā vineyya loke abhijjhādomanassaṃ, vedanāsu . . . pe . . . citte . . . pe . . . dhammesu dhammānupassī viharati ātāpī sampajāno satimā vineyya loke abhijjhādomanassaṃ. ayaṃ vuccati bhikkhave sammāsati.

katamo ca bhikkhave sammāsamādhi. idha bhikkhave bhikkhu vivicc' eva kāmehi vivicca akusalehi dhammehi savitakkaṃ savicāraṃ vivekajaṃ pītisukhaṃ paṭhamajjhānaṃ upasampajja viharati. vitakkavicārānaṃ vūpasamā ajjhattaṃ sampasādanaṃ cetaso ekodibhāvaṃ avitakkaṃ avicāraṃ samādhijaṃ pītisukhaṃ dutiyajjhānaṃ upasampajja viharati. pītiyā ca virāgā upekhako viharati sato ca sampajāno, sukhañ ca kāyena patisaṃvedeti yan taṃ ariyā ācikkhanti : upekhako satimā sukhavihārī ti tatiyajjhānaṃ upasampajja viharati. sukhassa ca pahānā dukkhassa ca pahānā pubb' eva somanassadomanassānaṃ atthagamā adukkhaṃ asukhaṃ upekhāsatipārisuddhiṃ catutthajjhānaṃ upasampajja viharati. ayaṃ vuccati bhikkhave sammāsamādhi.

idaṃ vuccati bhikkhave dukkhanirodhagāminīpaṭipadā ariyasaccaṃ.

Translate into Pali :—

1. Then the slave Kāka (thinking) : " this doctor is eating (present tense) emblic myrobalan and drinking water, there shouldn't be (*arah* with infinitive) anything bad (in it)," ate half an emblic myrobalan and drank water. (When he) had eaten (*khāyita*, the form is irregular) the half emblic myrobalan he brought (it) up right there. Then the slave Kāka said this to Jīvaka Komārabhacca : " Shall I (*atthi me*) live (noun), teacher ? " " Don't be afraid, I say, Kāka, and you will be well. The king is irascible, that king might have me killed, therefore I don't go back." Having handed over Bhaddavatikā the she-elephant to Kāka he went to Rājagaha. In due course he approached Rājagaha (and) king Māgadha Seniya Bimbisāra. Having approached he informed this matter (acc.) to the king (dat.). " You did well, I say, Jīvaka, that (you have) not gone back. Irascible (is) that king (and he) might have you killed."

Then king Pajjota, being well, sent a messenger into the presence of Jīvaka : " Let Jīvaka come, I shall give a boon."

2. Whom, however (*kho pana*), this assembly should despise, his reputation also would be diminished ; whose, however, reputation were diminished, his properties also would be diminished. (In the Pali of this " his " follows " also ", " reputation " and " properties " being placed first for emphasis.)

LESSON 28

" *Middle* " *Conjugation*

Special inflections of verbs, called " middle " or " reflexive " (*attanopada*), are occasionally used in place of the ordinary inflections (which are called " active " or " transitive "[1] : *parassapada*). They may be regarded as poetic forms rather than as a regular reflexive, the name applying literally only to the usage of cognate forms in other languages. They are very

[1] This translation does not distinguish the term from " transitive " in the narrower sense of " taking a patient " (*sakammaka*).

rare in prose, a little less rare in verse. The following reflexive forms are idiomatic in prose. Some forms found in verse are added in brackets.

Present tense (in place of the transitive terminations *ti* . . . *āma* the following reflexive terminations are reckoned : *te, ante ; se, vhe ; e, mhe* or *mhase*) :—

(*labhate,* " he obtains "—verse)
maññe, " I think," " I suppose," " no doubt," " as if "
ex. *devo maññe,* " I suppose (he is) a god," " just like a god " (note that *ti* is not used here)
bhaṇe " I say ! " (cf. Exercise 16)
(In the verse collections in the Canon, especially the *Jātaka,* a variety of " middle " forms will be found, e.g. 2nd singular *labhase*).

Imperative tense (*taṃ, antaṃ ; ssu, vho ; e,* (*ā*)*mase*) :—

labhataṃ, " let him obtain ! "
bhāsassu, " speak ! " (this word is fairly common)
saṃvidahassu (*dhā*), " organize ! "
mantavho, " take counsel ! "

Optative tense (*etha, eraṃ ; etho, eyyavho ; eyyaṃ,*[1] *eyyāmase* or (*ā*)*mase*) :—

jāyetha, " he would be born," " it would arise "
āgametha, " he might come "
labhetha, " he should obtain "
chijjeraṃ, " they would be cut " (by themselves), " they would break " (e.g. straps)
(*vademase* (in verse), " we would speak ").

Aorist tense (*ttha* or *tha, re ; ttho, vhaṃ ; a, mhase* or *mase*) :—

sandittha, " it flowed " (*sand*)
abhāsittha, " he spoke " (with augment)
akampittha, " it trembled," " it quaked " (*kamp*)
abhiramittha, " he enjoyed," " he took pleasure in " (*ram*)
pucchittho, " you asked "
(*karomase* (in verse), " we did ").

[1] It is alleged that only *eyyāmi* is the 1st singular *parassapada* termination—doubtful.

[The present participle in *māna* is sometimes called reflexive. Its use, however, is hardly to be distinguished [1] from that of the form in *ant*, and it is fairly frequent (far more so than the above reflexive inflections).]

All the above are active. The passive reflexive is extremely rare. Examples :—

abhihariyittha,[2] " it was brought," " it was presented "
paññāyittha, " it was discerned "
(the 3rd plural used in exactly parallel sentences, however, is *paññāyiṃsu*).

A survey of the usage of " reflexive " forms in Pali, and particularly in the *Dīgha*, leads to the conclusion that the shade of meaning they carry is simply a poetic, dramatic or elevated one, adding emphasis or dignity : note especially *bhāsassu* and the slightly pompous *bhaṇe*.

Denominative Conjugation

In principle any root can be used as a verb by adding conjugational suffixes. Other stems, such as noun stems, and even onomatopoeic elements, can also be used as verbs if required. The verbs thus derived are called denominative, or more exactly " word used as a root " (*dhāturūpakasadda*). They are usually conjugated according to the seventh conjugation (substituting the suffix *e/aya*, or adding *ya* to the stem), sometimes according to the first conjugation. They are rare except in poetry or exaggerated speech.

Examples :—

Noun stem, etc.	Denominative verb, 3rd singular present
sukha	*sukheti*, " he is happy "
tīra	*tīreti*, " he accomplishes," " he finishes " (e.g. business), lit. " (reaches) the shore (of) "

[1] It is favoured by certain verbs, some of which (*labh*, *sand*, *bhās*) are used with reflexive inflections, and it is specially associated with the passive.
[2] Variant readings :—*harīyittha, harayittha, and -hār-* (latter causative).

udāna	*udāneti*, " he speaks with exaltation," " he speaks joyfully "
ussukka (neuter : " eagerness," " impatience ")	*ussukkati*, " he is eager," " he is impatient "
gaḷa-gaḷa	*gaḷagaḷāyati*, " it pours down " (rain) (onomatopoeic : *ga-ḷa-ga-ḷa* imitating large drops of water beating down on the earth, repetition suggesting quantity)
	Aorist of denominative
udāna	*udānesi*
	Causative of denominative
dukkha	*dukkhāpeti*, " he makes unhappy "

Fourth Conjugation

The fourth or (*s*)*su* conjugation (*svādi gaṇa*) includes only one root at all frequently used. Moreover that root, (*s*)*su*, itself usually follows the fifth conjugation (> *suṇāti*, cf. Lesson 15). The fourth conjugation has a present stem formed with the suffix *ṇo*. From the root (*s*)*su*, " to hear," we may have :—

	Singular	Plural
3rd person	(*suṇoti*)	(*suṇonti* ? ?—hypothetical)
2nd person	(*suṇosi*)	(*suṇotha*)
1st person	(*suṇomi*)	(*suṇoma*)

The root *sak* may be classed here (*sak* + *ṇo* > *sakko* by assimilation), though it is equally convenient to regard it as sixth conjugation : *sak*(*k*) + *o* > *sakko* (cf. Lesson 6). Likewise the root *ap* or *ap*(*p*) may be classed here (*ap* + *ṇo* > *appo*).

Of (*s*)*su* only the imperative 2nd singular *suṇohi* according to the fourth conjugation is found in the *Dīgha Nikāya*, some forms of the present tense being found only (and very rarely) in other Canonical books.

Vocabulary

Verbs :—

ati-(k)kam (I)	*atikkamati*	pass over
anu-pa-gam (I)	*anupagacchati* (sic [1])	amalgamate with (accusative)
anu-pa-i (I)	*anupeti* (sic [1])	coalesce with (accusative)
adhi-o-gāh (I)	*ajjhogāhati* (also means)	plunge into (Gerund: *-etvā*)
ava-(ṭ)ṭhā (I)	*avatiṭṭhati*	remain
ava-sis (III)	*avasissati*	remain, be left over
upa-dah (I)	*upadahati*	torment, worry
o-tar (I)	*otarati*	pass down, collate (causative = check)
ci (V)	(passive *cīyati* = be piled up, be built up)	
ni-khaṇ (I)	*nikhaṇati*	bury
(p)paṭi-(k)kus (I)	*paṭikkosati*	decry, criticize (in bad sense)
(p)paṭi-u(d)-tar (I)	*paccuttarati*	come (back) out (after bathing)
(p)paṭi-labh (I)	*paṭilabhati*	obtain, acquire
(p)paṭi-vi-nī (I)	*paṭivineti*	dispel
(p)paṭi-saṃ-cikkh (I)	*paṭisaṃcikkhati*	reflect, consider
pari-vis (I*)	*parivisati*	serve (with food)
vi-sudh (III)	*visujjhati*	become purified
saṃ-yam (I)	*saṃyamati*	control oneself
saṃ-vatt (I)	*saṃvattati*	lead to (dative)
saṃ-(k)kam (I)	*saṃkamati*	pass into
saṃ-kilis (III)	*saṃkilissati*	become defiled
sand (I)	*sandati*	flow
saṃ-(d)dis	causative (also means)	review
sev (I)	*sevati*	indulge in, pursue

[1] A variant reading *anupigacchati* suggests *anu-(a)pi-gam*, also *anu-(a)pi-i* (there is a prefix *api* or *pi* meaning " over ", " covered ").

Nouns :—

abhijāti (fem.)	class of birth
abhiññā	insight
āgamo	(also means) body of doctrine, tradition (and the p.p. *āgata* likewise may refer to the handing down, receiving, of such a tradition)
ādi (masc.)	beginning, opening
ādhipateyyaṃ	lordship, supremacy
āvāso	living in, dwelling
ottappaṃ	shame, fear of blame
karuṇā	compassion
kasiraṃ	difficulty
kilamatho	tiring, wearying, weariness
gattaṃ	limb
gocaro	pasture, territory, proper place, range
caraṇaṃ	conduct, good conduct
thāmo	vigour
nadikā	stream
nāgo	elephant
niṭṭhā	conclusion
niyati (fem.)	Fate, Destiny
pakkhandikā	dysentery
pajā	the creation, the created universe ("created" according to the Brahmanical tradition)
paṭilābho	acquisition
pabbajito	one who has gone forth (left the world)
pabbajjā	going forth
pamāṇaṃ	measure, size
parakkamo	courage, valour
pariṇāmo	digestion
pariyosānaṃ	ending, conclusion
parivaṭṭaṃ	circle
pātimokkho	liberation
mātikā	matrix, notes (for remembering doctrine)
Māro	the god of death and passion (leading to rebirth)

muditā	sympathetic joy (joy at the well-being of others), sympathy, gladness
mettā	love (only in the spiritual and non-sexual sense), kindness, loving-kindness, benevolence, goodwill, friendliness
yiṭṭhaṃ (p.p. *yaj* (I))	sacrifice, offering
lohitaṃ	blood
vajjaṃ	fault
vidū (masc.)	knower
vyañjanaṃ	expression (speech: contrasted with meaning: *attho*), sentence
saṃghāṭi (fem.)	cloak
sabbattatā	non-discrimination ("all = self-ness"), unselfishness
sampajaññaṃ	consciousness
sambodho	enlightenment
sukhallikā	pleasure, enjoyment
suttaṃ	(also means) (a record of a) dialogue, (eventually the entire) collection of dialogues (of the Buddha made by his followers)
sobbhaṃ	pit
hiri (fem.)	modesty, self-respect, conscience
hutaṃ	oblation

Adjectives :—

accha	clear, bright, sparkling
acchariya	surprising
anariya	barbarian
anupādisesa	with no attachment remaining
anuyoga	practising
abbhuta	wonderful, marvellous
avasa	powerless
āvila	turbid, muddy
odaka (fem. *-ikā*)	having water
-karaṇa (fem. *-ī*)	making
damma	trainable, educable

dassāvin	seeing, who would see
pabāḷha	violent
pamāṇakata	measurable, finite
pipāsita	thirsty
pothujjanika	common (*puthu* + *jano* + (*ṇ*)*ika*)
maddava	tender
yasassin	reputable, respected
likhita	polished
luḷita	stirred up
vippasanna	very clear
vyāpajjha	violent, malevolent
sabbāvant	all-inclusive, whole
sambādha	confined
sahagata	charged with, suffused with
sāta	sweet
sīta	cool
supatittha	having good beaches (stream : for getting water to drink)
setaka	clear, clean

Past Participles :—

abhisambuddha (*abhi-saṃ-budh*)	illuminated (fig.)
avasiṭṭha (*ava-sis*)	left over, remaining
upacita (*upa-ci* (V))	accumulated
gutta (*gup*)	protected, guarded
paccājāta ((*p*)*paṭi-ā-jan* (III))	reborn
parinibbuta (*pari-ni*(*r*)-*vā*)	attained extinction, attained liberation
laddha (*labh*)	got, obtained
saṃvuta (*saṃ-var* (I))	controlled
saṃhita (*saṃ-dhā*)	joined, connected

Gerunds :—

accādhāya (*ati-ā-dhā*)	putting on top of
nahatvā (*nhā* (III))	having bathed (also written *nhātvā*)

Indeclinables :—

ativiya	very much
avidūre	not far, near
majjhe	in the middle
sabbadhi	everywhere

EXERCISE 28

Passages for reading :—

1. atha kho bhagavā pubbaṇhasamayaṃ nivāsetvā patta-cīvaram ādāya Vesāliṃ piṇḍāya pāvisi, Vesāliyaṃ piṇḍāya caritvā pacchābhattaṃ piṇḍapātapaṭikkanto nāgāpalokitaṃ Vesālim apaloketvā āyasmantaṃ Ānandaṃ āmantesi : idaṃ pacchimakaṃ Ānanda tathāgatassa Vesālidassanaṃ bhavissati, āyām' Ānanda yena Bhaṇḍagāmo ten' upasaṃkamissāmā ti. evaṃ bhante ti kho āyasmā Ānando bhagavato paccassosi. atha kho bhagavā mahatā bhikkhusaṃghena saddhiṃ yena Bhaṇḍagāmo tad avasari. tatra sudaṃ bhagavā Bhaṇḍagāme viharati.

tatra kho bhagavā bhikkhū āmantesi : catunnaṃ bhikkhave dhammānaṃ ananubodhā appaṭivedhā evam idaṃ dīgham addhānaṃ sandhāvitaṃ saṃsaritaṃ mamañ c' eva tumhākañ ca : katamesaṃ catunnaṃ. ariyassa bhikkhave sīlassa ananubodhā appaṭivedhā evam idaṃ dīgham addhānaṃ sandhāvitaṃ saṃsaritaṃ mamañ c' eva tumhākañ ca. ariyassa bhikkhave samādhissa ananubodhā appaṭivedhā evam idaṃ dīgham addhānaṃ sandhāvitaṃ saṃsaritaṃ mamañ c' eva tumhākañ ca. ariyāya bhikkhave paññāya ananubodhā appaṭivedhā evam idaṃ dīgham addhānaṃ sandhāvitaṃ saṃsaritaṃ mamañ c' eva tumhākañ ca. ariyāya bhikkhave vimuttiyā ananubodhā appaṭivedhā evam idaṃ dīgham addhānaṃ sandhāvitaṃ saṃsaritaṃ mamañ c' eva tumhākañ ca. tayidaṃ bhikkhave ariyaṃ sīlam anubuddhaṃ paṭividdhaṃ, ariyo samādhi anubuddho paṭividdho, ariyā paññā anubuddhā paṭividdhā, ariyā vimutti anubuddhā paṭividdhā, ucchinnā bhavataṇhā khīṇā bhavanetti, n' atthi dāni punabbhavo ti. idam avoca bhagavā, idaṃ vatvā sugato athāparaṃ etad avoca satthā :—

sīlaṃ samādhi paññā ca vimutti ca anuttarā,
anubuddhā ime dhammā Gotamena yasassinā.
iti Buddho abhiññāya dhammam akkhāsi bhikkhŭnaṃ,[1]
dukkhass' antakaro satthā cakkhumā parinibbuto ti.

tatrā pi sudaṃ bhagavā Bhaṇḍagāme viharanto etad eva bahulaṃ bhikkhūnaṃ dhammiṃ kathaṃ karoti : iti sīlaṃ iti samādhi iti paññā, sīlaparibhāvito samādhi mahapphalo hoti mahānisaṃso, samādhiparibhāvitā paññā mahapphalā hoti mahānisaṃsā, paññāparibhāvitaṃ cittaṃ sammad eva āsavehi vimuccati, seyyathīdaṃ kāmāsavā bhavāsavā diṭṭhāsavā avijjāsavā ti.

atha kho bhagavā Bhaṇḍagāme yathābhirantaṃ viharitvā āyasmantaṃ Ānandaṃ āmantesi : āyām' Ānanda yena Hatthigāmo . . . pe . . . Ambagāmo . . . Jambugāmo . . . yena Bhoganagaraṃ ten' upasaṃkamissāmā ti. evaṃ bhante ti kho āyasmā Ānando bhagavato paccassosi. atha kho bhagavā mahatā bhikkhusaṃghena saddhiṃ yena Bhoganagaraṃ tad avasari.

tatra sudaṃ bhagavā Bhoganagare viharati Ānande cetiye. tatra kho bhagavā bhikkhū āmantesi : cattāro me bhikkhave mahāpadese desessāmi, taṃ suṇātha sādhukaṃ manasikarotha bhāsissāmī ti. evaṃ bhante ti kho te bhikkhū bhagavato paccassosuṃ. bhagavā etad avoca : idha bhikkhave bhikkhu evaṃ vadeyya : sammukhā me taṃ āvuso bhagavato sutaṃ sammukhā paṭiggahītaṃ ayaṃ dhammo ayaṃ vinayo idaṃ satthu sāsanan ti, tassa bhikkhave bhikkhuno bhāsitaṃ n' eva abhinanditabbaṃ na paṭikkositabbaṃ. anabhinanditvā appaṭikkositvā tāni padavyañjanāni sādhukaṃ uggahetvā sutte otāretabbāni vinaye sandassetabbāni. tāni ce sutte otāriyamānāni vinaye sandassiyamānāni na c' eva sutte otaranti na vinaye sandissanti, niṭṭham ettha gantabbaṃ : addhā idaṃ na c' eva tassa bhagavato vacanaṃ, imassa ca bhikkhuno duggahītan ti, iti h' etaṃ bhikkhave chaḍḍeyyātha. tāni ce sutte otāriyamānāni vinaye sandassiyamānāni sutte c' eva otaranti vinaye ca sandissanti, niṭṭham ettha gantabbaṃ :

[1] Metrical shortening.

addhā idaṃ tassa bhagavato vacanaṃ imassa ca bhikkhuno suggahītan ti. idaṃ bhikkhave paṭhamaṃ mahāpadesaṃ dhāreyyātha. idha pana bhikkhave bhikkhu evaṃ vadeyya: amukasmiṃ nāma āvāse saṃgho viharati satthero sapāmokkho. tassa me saṃghassa sammukhā sutaṃ sammukhā paṭiggahītaṃ, ayaṃ dhammo ayaṃ vinayo ... addhā idaṃ tassa bhagavato vacanaṃ, tassa ca saṃghassa suggahītan ti. idaṃ bhikkhave dutiyaṃ mahāpadesaṃ dhāreyyātha. idha pana bhikkhave bhikkhu evaṃ vadeyya: amukasmiṃ nāma āvāse sambahulā therā bhikkhū viharanti bahussutā āgatāgamā dhammadharā vinayadharā mātikādharā. tesaṃ me therānaṃ sammukhā sutaṃ sammukhā paṭiggahītaṃ, ayaṃ dhammo ayaṃ vinayo ... idaṃ bhikkhave tatiyaṃ mahāpadesaṃ dhāreyyātha. idha pana bhikkhave bhikkhu evaṃ vadeyya: amukasmiṃ nāma āvāse eko thero bhikkhu viharati bahussuto āgatāgamo dhammadharo vinayadharo mātikādharo. tassa me therassa sammukhā sutaṃ sammukhā paṭiggahītaṃ ayaṃ dhammo ayaṃ vinayo ... idaṃ bhikkhave catutthaṃ mahāpadesaṃ dhāreyyāthā ti. ime kho bhikkhave cattāro mahāpadese dhāreyyāthā ti ...

atha kho bhagavā Bhoganagare yathābhirantaṃ viharitvā āyasmantaṃ Ānandaṃ āmantesi: āyām' Ānanda yena Pāvā [1] ten' upasaṃkamissāmā ti. evaṃ bhante ti kho āyasmā Ānando bhagavato paccassosi. atha kho bhagavā mahatā bhikkhusaṃghena saddhiṃ yena Pāvā tad avasari. tatra sudaṃ bhagavā Pāvāyaṃ viharati Cundassa kammāraputtassa ambavane. assosi kho Cundo kammāraputto: bhagavā kira Pāvaṃ anuppatto Pāvāyaṃ viharati mayhaṃ ambavane ti. atha kho Cundo kammāraputto yena bhagavā ten' upasaṃkami, upasaṃkamitvā bhagavantaṃ abhivādetvā ekamantaṃ nisīdi, ekamantaṃ nisinnaṃ kho Cundaṃ kammāraputtaṃ bhagavā dhammiyā kathāya sandassesi samādapesi samuttejesi sampahaṃsesi. atha kho Cundo kammāraputto bhagavatā dhammiyā kathāya sandassito samādapito samuttejito sampahaṃsito bhagavantaṃ etad avoca: adhivāsetu me bhante bhagavā svātanāya bhattaṃ saddhiṃ bhikkhusaṃghenā ti. adhivāsesi bhagavā tuṇhībhāvena. atha kho Cundo kammāraputto bhagavato adhi-

[1] Capital of the southern Malla republic, about 30 leagues north-west of Vesālī in the foothills of the Himālaya.

vāsanaṃ viditvā, uṭṭhāy' āsanā bhagavantaṃ abhivādetvā padakkhiṇaṃ katvā pakkāmi. atha kho Cundo kammāraputto tassā rattiyā accayena sake nivesane paṇītaṃ khādaniyaṃ bhojaniyaṃ paṭiyādāpetvā pahūtañ ca sūkaramaddavaṃ bhagavato kālaṃ ārocāpesi : kālo bhante niṭṭhitaṃ bhattan ti. atha kho bhagavā pubbaṇhasamayaṃ nivāsetvā pattacīvaram ādāya saddhiṃ bhikkhusaṃghena yena Cundassa kammāraputtassa nivesanaṃ ten' upasaṃkami, upasaṃkamitvā paññatte āsane nisīdi, nisajja kho bhagavā Cundaṃ kammāraputtaṃ āmantesi : yan te Cunda sūkaramaddavaṃ paṭiyattaṃ, tena maṃ parivisa, yaṃ pan' aññaṃ khādaniyaṃ bhojaniyaṃ paṭiyattaṃ, tena bhikkhusaṃghaṃ parivisā ti. evaṃ bhante ti kho Cundo kammāraputto bhagavato paṭissutvā, yaṃ ahosi sūkaramaddavaṃ paṭiyattaṃ, tena bhagavantaṃ parivisi, yaṃ pan' aññaṃ khādaniyaṃ bhojaniyaṃ paṭiyattaṃ tena bhikkhusaṃghaṃ parivisi. atha kho bhagavā Cundaṃ kammāraputtaṃ āmantesi : yan te Cunda sūkaramaddavaṃ avasiṭṭhaṃ, taṃ sobbhe nikhaṇāhi nāhan taṃ Cunda passāmi sadevake loke samārake sabrahmake sassamaṇabrāhmaṇiyā pajāya sadevamanussāya yassa taṃ paribhuttaṃ sammāpariṇāmaṃ gaccheyya aññatra tathāgatassā ti. evaṃ bhante ti kho Cundo kammāraputto bhagavato paṭissutvā, yaṃ ahosi sūkaramaddavaṃ avasiṭṭhaṃ taṃ sobbhe nikhaṇitvā, yena bhagavā ten' upasaṃkami, upasaṃkamitvā bhagavantaṃ abhivādetvā ekamantaṃ nisīdi, ekamantaṃ nisinnaṃ kho Cundaṃ kammāraputtaṃ bhagavā dhammiyā kathāya sandassetvā samādapetvā samuttejetvā sampahaṃsetvā uṭṭhāy' āsanā pakkāmi.

atha kho bhagavato Cundassa kammāraputtassa bhattaṃ bhuttāvissa kharo ābādho uppajji lohitapakkhandikā pabāḷhā vedanā vattanti māraṇantikā. tā sudaṃ bhagavā sato sampajāno adhivāsesi avihaññamāno. atha kho bhagavā āyasmantaṃ Ānandaṃ āmantesi : āyām' Ānanda yena Kusinārā ten' upasaṃkamissāmā ti. evam bhante ti kho āyasmā Ānando bhagavato paccassosi.

atha kho bhagavā maggā okkamma yen' aññataraṃ rukkhamūlaṃ ten' upasaṃkami, upasaṃkamitvā āyasmantaṃ Ānandaṃ āmantesi : iṅgha me tvaṃ Ānanda catugguṇaṃ saṃghāṭiṃ paññāpehi, kilanto 'smi Ānanda, nisīdissāmī ti.

evaṃ bhante ti kho āyasmā Ānando bhagavato paṭissutvā catugguṇaṃ saṃghāṭiṃ paññāpesi. nisīdi bhagavā paññatte āsane, nisajja kho bhagavā āyasmantaṃ Ānandaṃ āmantesi, iṅgha me tvaṃ Ānanda pānīyaṃ āhara, pipāsito 'smi, Ānanda, pivissāmī ti. evaṃ vutte āyasmā Ānando bhagavantaṃ etad avoca : idāni bhante pañcamattāni sakaṭasatāni atikkantāni, taṃ cakkacchinnaṃ udakaṃ parittaṃ luḷitaṃ āvilaṃ sandati. ayaṃ bhante Kakutthā nadī avidūre acchodikā sātodikā sītodikā setakā supatitthā ramaṇīyā. ettha bhagavā pānīyañ ca pivissati, gattāni ca sītaṃ karissatī ti. dutiyam pi kho bhagavā āyasmantaṃ Ānandaṃ āmantesi : iṅgha me tvaṃ Ānanda pānīyaṃ āhara, . . . gattāni ca sītaṃ karissatī ti. tatiyam pi kho bhagavā āyasmantaṃ Ānandaṃ āmantesi : iṅgha me tvaṃ Ānanda pānīyaṃ āhara, pipāsito 'smi Ānanda, pivissāmī ti. evaṃ bhante ti kho āyasmā Ānando bhagavato paṭissutvā pattaṃ gahetvā yena sā nadikā ten' upasaṃkami. atha kho sā nadikā cakkacchinnā parittā luḷitā āvilā sandamānā āyasmante Ānande upasaṃkamante acchā vippasannā anāvilā sandittha. atho kho āyasmato Ānandassa etad ahosi : acchariyaṃ vata bho, abbhutaṃ vata bho, tathāgatassa mahiddhikatā mahānubhāvatā. ayaṃ hi sā nadikā cakkacchinnā parittā luḷitā āvilā sandamānā, mayi upasaṃkamante acchā vippasannā anāvilā sandatī ti. pattena pānīyaṃ ādāya yena bhagavā ten' upasaṃkami, upasaṃkamitvā bhagavantaṃ etad avoca : acchariyaṃ bhante abbhutaṃ bhante tathāgatassa mahiddhikatā mahānubhāvatā. idāni sā bhante nadikā cakkacchinnā parittā luḷitā āvilā sandamānā, mayi upasaṃkamante acchā vippasannā anāvilā sandittha. pivatu bhagavā pānīyaṃ, pivatu sugato pānīyan ti. atha kho bhagavā pānīyaṃ apāyi.

* * *

atha kho bhagavā mahatā bhikkhusaṃghena saddhiṃ yena Kakutthā nadī ten' upasaṃkami, upasaṃkamitvā Kakutthaṃ nadiṃ ajjhogāhetvā nahātvā ca pivitvā ca paccuttaritvā yena Ambavanaṃ ten' upasaṃkami, upasaṃkamitvā āyasmantaṃ Cundakaṃ āmantesi : iṅgha me tvaṃ Cundaka catugguṇaṃ saṃghāṭiṃ paññāpehi, kilanto 'smi Cundaka, nipajjissāmī ti. evaṃ bhante ti kho āyasmā Cundaka bhagavato paṭissutvā catuggunaṃ saṃghāṭiṃ paññāpesi. atha kho bhagavā dakkhiṇena passena sīhaseyyaṃ kappesi, pāde pādaṃ accādhāya, sato sampajāno uṭṭhānasaññaṃ manasikaritvā. āyasmā pana Cundako tatth' eva bhagavato purato nisīdi.

atha kho bhagavā āyasmantaṃ Ānandaṃ āmantesi : siyā kho pan' Ānanda Cundassa kammāraputtassa ko ci vippaṭisāraṃ upadaheyya : tassa te āvuso Cunda alābhā, tassa te dulladdhaṃ, yassa te tathāgato pacchimaṃ piṇḍapātaṃ bhuñjitvā parinibbuto ti. Cundassa Ānanda kammāraputtassa evaṃ vippaṭisāro paṭivinetabbo : tassa te āvuso lābhā, tassa te suladdhaṃ, yassa te tathāgato pacchimaṃ piṇḍapātaṃ bhuñjitvā parinibbuto. sammukhā me taṃ āvuso Cunda bhagavato sutaṃ sammukhā paṭiggahītaṃ, dve 'me piṇḍapātā samasamaphalā samasamavipākā ativiya aññehi piṇḍapātehi mahapphalatarā ca mahānisaṃsatarā ca. katame dve. yañ ca piṇḍapātaṃ bhuñjitvā tathāgato anuttaraṃ sammāsambodhiṃ abhisambujjhati, yañ ca piṇḍapātaṃ bhuñjitvā tathāgato anupādisesāya nibbānadhātuyā parinibbāyati. ime dve piṇḍapātā samasamaphalā samasamavipākā ativiya aññehi piṇḍapātehi mahapphalatarā ca mahānisaṃsatarā ca. āyusaṃvattanikaṃ āyasmatā Cundena kammāraputtena kammaṃ upacitaṃ, vaṇṇasaṃvattanikaṃ āyasmatā Cundena kammāraputtena kammaṃ upacitaṃ, sukhasaṃvattanikaṃ āyasmatā Cundena kammāraputtena kammaṃ upacitaṃ, yasasaṃvattanikaṃ āyasmatā Cundena kammāraputtena kammaṃ upacitaṃ, saggasaṃvattanikaṃ āyasmatā Cundena kammāraputtena kammaṃ upacitaṃ, ādhipateyyasaṃvattanikaṃ āyasmatā Cundena kammāraputtena kammaṃ upacitan ti. Cundassa Ānanda kammāraputtassa evaṃ vippaṭisāro paṭivinetabbo ti. atha kho bhagavā etam atthaṃ viditvā tāyaṃ velāyaṃ imam udānaṃ udānesi :—

> dadato puññaṃ pavaḍḍhati, saṃyamato veraṃ na cīyati,
> kusalo ca jahāti pāpakaṃ, rāga<d>dosakhayā [1] sa nibbuto ti.

2. cattāro iddhipādā. idh' āvuso bhikkhu chandasamādhipadhānasaṃkhārasamannāgataṃ iddhipādaṃ bhāveti. citta-

[1] The metre requires that we give this word the rhythm – – – ⏑ ⏑ –, hence we may read *(d)dosa-* and *khayā*.

samādhipadhānasaṃkhārasamannāgataṃ iddhipādaṃ bhāveti. viriyasamādhipadhānasaṃkhārasamannāgataṃ iddhipādaṃ bhāveti. vīmaṃsāsamādhipadhānasaṃkhārasamannāgataṃ iddhipādaṃ bhāveti.

3. pañc' indriyāni. saddhindriyaṃ, viriyindriyaṃ, satindriyaṃ, samādhindriyaṃ, paññindriyaṃ.

4. cattāri balāni. viriyabalaṃ, satibalaṃ, samādhibalaṃ, paññābalaṃ.

5. satta balāni. saddhābalaṃ, viriyabalaṃ, hiribalaṃ, ottappabalaṃ, satibalaṃ, samādhibalaṃ, paññābalaṃ.

6. idha mahārāja tathāgato loke uppajjati, arahaṃ sammāsambuddho vijjācaraṇasampanno sugato lokavidū anuttaro purisadammasārathi satthā devamanussānaṃ buddho bhagavā. so imaṃ lokaṃ sadevakaṃ samārakaṃ sabrahmakaṃ sassamaṇabrāhmaṇiṃ pajaṃ sadevamanussaṃ sayaṃ abhiññā [1] sacchikatvā pavedeti. so dhammaṃ deseti ādikalyāṇaṃ majjhekalyāṇaṃ pariyosānakalyāṇaṃ sātthaṃ savyañjanaṃ, kevalaparipuṇṇaṃ parisuddhaṃ brahmacariyaṃ pakāseti.

taṃ dhammaṃ suṇāti gahapati vā gahapatiputto vā aññatarasmiṃ vā kule paccājāto. so taṃ dhammaṃ sutvā tathāgate saddhaṃ paṭilabhati. so tena saddhāpaṭilābhena samannāgato iti paṭisaṃcikkhati : sambādho gharāvāso rajopatho, abbhokāso pabbajjā. na idaṃ sukaraṃ agāraṃ ajjhāvasatā ekantaparipuṇṇaṃ ekantaparisuddhaṃ saṃkhalikhitaṃ brahmacariyaṃ carituṃ. yan nūnāhaṃ kesamassuṃ ohāretvā kāsāyāni vatthāni acchādetvā agārasmā anagāriyaṃ pabbajeyyan ti. so aparena samayena appaṃ vā bhogakkhandhaṃ pahāya mahantaṃ vā bhogakkhandhaṃ pahāya, appaṃ va ñātiparivaṭṭaṃ pahāya mahantaṃ vā ñātiparivaṭṭaṃ pahāya, kesamassuṃ ohāretvā kāsāyāni vatthāni acchādetvā agārasmā anagāriyaṃ pabbajati.

evaṃ pabbajito samāno pātimokkhasaṃvarasaṃvuto viharati ācāragocarasampanno aṇumattesu vajjesu bhayadassāvī samādāya sikkhati sikkhāpadesu kāyakammavacīkammena samannāgato kusalena parisuddhājīvo sīlasampanno indriyesu guttadvāro satisampajaññena samannāgato santuṭṭho.

[1] Gerund, cf. footnote at beginning of Exercise 22.

7. so mettāsahagatena cetasā ekaṃ disaṃ pharitvā viharati, tathā dutiyaṃ, tathā tatiyaṃ, tathā catutthaṃ. iti uddham adho tiriyaṃ sabbadhi sabbattatāya sabbāvantaṃ lokaṃ mettāsahagatena cetasā vipulena mahaggatena appamāṇena avereṇa [1] avyāpajjhena pharitvā viharati. seyyathā pi Vāseṭṭha balavā saṅkhadhamo appakasiren' eva catuddisā viññāpeyya, evaṃ bhāvitāya kho Vāseṭṭha mettāya cetovimuttiyā yaṃ pamāṇakataṃ kammaṃ na taṃ tatrāvasissati na taṃ tatrāvatiṭṭhati. ayam pi kho Vāseṭṭha brahmāṇaṃ [1] sahavyatāya maggo. puna ca paraṃ Vāseṭṭha bhikkhu karuṇāsahagatena cetasā . . . pe . . . muditāsahagatena cetasā . . . pe . . . upekhāsahagatena cetasā ekaṃ disaṃ pharitvā viharati, . . . evaṃ bhāvitāya kho Vāseṭṭha upekhāya cetovimuttiyā yaṃ pamāṇakataṃ kammaṃ na taṃ tatrāvasissati na taṃ tatrāvatiṭṭhati. ayam pi kho Vāseṭṭha brahmāṇaṃ sahavyatāya maggo.

Translate into Pali :—

(Three Doctrines)

These two (put first, for emphasis) extremes, monks, should not be pursued by one who has gone forth. Which two ? This (*ayaṃ*), which (put relative first) (is) among passions practising the-enjoyment-of-passions, inferior, vulgar, common, barbarian, not-connected-with-welfare, and this, which (is) devoted-to-weariness-of-oneself (*attan*), unhappy, barbarian, not-connected-with-welfare. Monks, not having gone to (*-gamma*) both these (put first) extremes, the intermediate way, illuminated by the thus-gone, making-an-eye (*-karaṇa*), making-knowledge, leads to calm, to insight, to enlightenment, to liberation. And which, monks, (is) that intermediate way illuminated by the thus-gone . . . to liberation ? It (*ayaṃ*) (is) just the excellent way having eight factors, as follows : right-theory,[2] right-intention, right-speech, right-work, right-livelihood, right-exercise, right-self-possession, right-concentration.

Makkhali Gosāla [3] said this to me : " O great king, there is no cause, there is no condition, for the defilement of beings.

[1] Sometimes when the stem of a word contains the letter *r* a following *n* in a suffix or inflection is " cerebralised " to *ṇ*.
[2] *sammā* = right(ly) is used as a prefix to nouns as well as to verbs.
[3] The Ājīvaka leader : see first footnote in Exercise 21.

From-no-cause-(and)-no-condition beings are defiled. There is no cause, there is no condition, for the purification of beings. From-no-cause-(and)-no-condition beings are purified. There is no self-making (*-kāro*), there is no other-making, there is no making-by-man. There is no strength, there is no energy, there is no vigour-of-man, there is no courage-of-man. All beings, all life (plural), all living beings, all souls, powerless, without-strength, without-energy, changed-in-nature-by-the-combinations-of-Fate, experience happiness-and-unhappiness in the six classes of birth."

Ajita Kesakambalin [1] said this to me : " O great king, there is no (merit in) giving (*dinnaṃ*),[2] there is no sacrifice, there is no oblation. There is no fruit, result, of actions (which are) well-done-(or)-ill-done. There is no other world. There is no mother, there is no father, there are (use singular) no beings transmigrating. There are (singular) no priests and philosophers in the world (who have) rightly-gone, (who are) rightly-practising, who, having themselves known, observed this world and the other world make (it) known. This man is-compounded-of-the-four-elements. When he dies, the earth coalesces with, amalgamates with, the earth-substance, the water coalesces with, amalgamates with, the water-substance, the heat coalesces with, amalgamates with, the heat-substance, the air coalesces with, amalgamates with, the air-substance, the faculties pass into space . . . Fools and wise men (after = ablative) the splitting up of the body are annihilated, perish utterly, are not after death."

[1] A Lokāyata (" naturalism " : materialism) philosopher contemporary with the Buddha. His doctrine as given here agrees as far as it goes with that of the classical *Lokāyata Sūtra* of " Bṛhaspati ", but does not state the aim of the school, which is " happiness " (*sukhaṃ*), of course in this life. On this and other philosophical schools of the time of the origin of Buddhism see the essay : " On the relationships between early Buddhism and other contemporary systems," *Bulletin of the School of Oriental and African Studies*, London, 1956, where an attempt is made to define the original doctrines of Buddhism in the light of these relationships.

[2] *dinnaṃ*, given (thing), giving, almsgiving, is here used " pregnantly " (a kind of metonymy not uncommon in Pali) to refer to the giving which is understood, by the Brahmanical priests and the Buddhists, as a meritorious action leading to well-being of the giver, not to the mere everyday action,

LESSON 29

Intensive Conjugation

A special conjugation (cf. the causative as another special or " secondary " conjugation) is very occasionally used to mean that the action of the verb is done very strongly or frequently, or that the state signified is severe. It is called the " intensive " conjugation.[1] Few intensives are idiomatic in prose, except for an unusual emphasis (as to say : " he is exceedingly stupid "). In the intensive the inflections are those of the first conjugation, but the root is reduplicated : a sometimes stronger form (always a long syllable) of the root being prefixed. Gutturals reduplicate as palatals :—

(*k*)*kam* *caṅkamati* he walks up and down, he walks about (this is commonly used of taking exercise)

—present participle *caṅkamant*.

A complete conjugation is possible. E.g. aorist intensive 3rd plural from *anu*-(*k*)*kam* *anucaṅkamiṃsu*, " they followed up and down."

Conditional Tense

The conditional[2] (*kālātipatti*) tense is rarely used, though it appears regularly when a false or impossible hypothesis (in the view of the speaker, and usually of the hearer also) is stated. It is formed from the future stem with inflections of the aorist type (cf. the aorist of (*d*)*dis*, Lesson 11), and the augment is used. Unlike the aorist, the conditional has the augment regularly except when there is a prefix :—

	Singular	Plural
3rd person	*abhavissa* (or -*ssā*) " if it were "	*abhavissaṃsu*
2nd person	*abhavissa*	*abhavissatha*
1st person	*abhavissaṃ*	*abhavissāma*

[1] The medieval Pali grammars do not recognize this as a separate conjugation, classing the forms simply as irregular verbs of the ordinary conjugation. As the formation is a distinct strong reduplication with special meaning, and derivatives (including adjectives) from it are used with this meaning distinctly felt, it is worth noticing separately.

[2] The term " conditional " is much too wide for this tense, and was adopted

The 3rd singular conditional reflexive, or " middle ", is also occasionally used, and is identical in form with the 2nd plural " active " or " transitive " :—

	Singular
3rd person	*abhavissatha*

The conditional " active " of verbs other than *bhū* is extremely rare, but the conditional " middle " (3rd singular) may be exemplified as follows :—

abhi-ni(r)-vatt (I)	*abhinibbattissatha*	if it were produced (no augment) (in interrogative sentence : would it be produced ?)
u(d)-pad (III)	*uppajjissatha*	if it had arisen (no augment)
labh (I)	*alabhissatha*	if it were obtained
vi-o-chid (III)	*vocchijjissatha* [1]	if it were cut off (no augment) (passive)

With the conditional tense it is not usual to introduce the subordinate (conditional) clause with a relative indeclinable. The conditional tense often appears in the main clause as well, otherwise the optative. The subordination of the conditional clause is marked simply by the use of the conditional tense in one or both clauses, the subordinate coming first. Sometimes the main clause is interrogative (rhetorical, there being no doubt as to the answer expected).

Examples of the use of the conditional :—

viññāṇaṃ va hi . . . vocchijjissatha . . . api nu kho nāmarūpaṃ . . . āpajjissatha = " for if consciousness . . . were cut off . . . would a sentient body (' matter plus mind ') . . . be produced ? "

by philologists on the grounds of comparative morphology. On the expression of conditions in Pali cf. the " Notes on Tenses " in Lesson 27.

[1] *ch* is regularly doubled to *cch* after a vowel in close junction.

(*nāmarūpaṃ* is a technical term meaning the combination of material and mental elements in a sentient body, *nāmaṃ* here means not " name " but all aspects of mental activity : sensation, perception, volition, contact, attention. The context here is the general one that the existence of sentient bodies depends on the presence of " consciousness " and that in fact " consciousness " continues after birth, hence the sentient body continues. The supposition of the cutting off of " consciousness " whilst the sentient body continues is hence regarded as impossible.)

oḷāriko ca hi Poṭṭhapāda attā abhavissa rūpī . . ., = " for if your soul were gross, material . . ., Poṭṭhapāda . . ." (here Poṭṭhapāda had suggested that it was, but the Buddha speaks of this as false and convinces him that it is impossible by adducing a consequence).

A more complex case with two conjoined main clauses :—

imāya ca Kassapa mattāya . . . sāmaññaṃ . . . abhavissa . . . dukkaraṃ . . . n' etam abhavissa kallaṃ vacanāya : dukkaraṃ sāmaññaṃ . . . ti. sakkā ca pan' etaṃ abhavissa kātuṃ gahapatinā . . . antamaso kumbhadāsiyā pi . . . ti, = " if, Kassapa, (only) to this degree . . . asceticism were a hard task . . . it would not be proper to say this : 'Asceticism is a hard task . . .'. Moreover it would be possible for a householder . . . even a pot-(carrying)-slave-girl to do this . . ."

The conditional is also used in speaking of a hypothetical event which did not in fact take place.

The system of using the tenses is thus : if the condition and its result are purely hypothetical the optative is used ; if true, the indicative (present or future) ; if false, the conditional. In simply denying the possibility of something, however, without positing it as condition with a result, a speaker may use *n' etaṃ ṭhānaṃ vijjati yaṃ* with the optative, or *sak(k)* negated, or an infinite form such as *akaraṇīya* or *abhabba*, or *na sakkā*.

Aorist of labh

The root *labh,* " to obtain," has besides a regular aorist of the " first " form (Lesson 4), *labhi*, etc., an irregular and perhaps " elevated " aorist as follows :—

	Singular	Plural
3rd person	*alattha*	*alatthuṃ*
2nd person	(*alattha*)	—
1st person	*alatthaṃ*	(*alatthamhă*)

The bracketed forms are not found in the *Dīgha*, but the others are used quite regularly in prose, e.g. for obtaining an interview with the Buddha or entrance to the Community—*saṃgho*—of monks.

Declension of go *and* sakhā

The stem *go-*, " cow," " bull," " cattle," which is masculine and feminine (cf. *Sd.* 207 ff. for a discussion on this controversial point), has a somewhat irregular declension only sporadically used (more specific words for " bull ", " cow ", and " ox " are commonly used). Before vowel inflections *-o* becomes *-av* :—

Stem *go-* (used in compounds)

	Singular	Plural
Nom. Voc.	(*go*)	*gāvo* (Nom., Voc., Acc.)
Acc.	(*gavaṃ*)	
Ins.	(*gavena*)	(*gohi*)
Dat.	(*gavassa*)	(*gunnaṃ*)
Abl.	*gavā*	(*gohi*)
Gen.	(*gavassa*)	(*gunnaṃ* or, in verse, *gavaṃ*)
Loc.	(*gave*)	(*gosu*)

(Bracketed forms not found in the *Dīgha*.)

The stem *gava-* as well as *go-* is occasionally used in compounds.

A specifically feminine form *gāvī*, " cow," is inflected like *devī*.

An irregular (" poetic ") noun *sakhā* (masc.), " friend," is rarely used instead of the ordinary word *sahāyo* (the forms show a mixture of the *-i* and *-ar* declensions) :—

	Singular	Plural
Nom. / Voc.	*sakhā*	(*sakhāro*)
Acc.	(*sakhāraṃ*)	(*sakhāro*)
Ins.	(*sakhinā*)	(*sakhārehi*—Grammarians)
Dat.	(*sakhino*)	(*sakhīnaṃ*)
Abl.	(*sakhinā* or *sakhārasmā*)	(*sakhārehi*—Grammarians)
Gen.	*sakhino*	(*sakhīnaṃ*)
Loc.	(*sakhe*—Grammarians)	(*sakhāresu*—Grammarians)

(At the end of compounds we have the usual transfer to the *-a* declension : *-sakho*.)

(Bracketed forms not in *Dīgha*.)

Vocabulary

Verbs :—

ati-vatt (I)	*ativattati*	escape
u(d)-kujj (I)	*ukkujjati*	set upright
upa-labh (I)	(passive *upalabbhati* = exist)	
o-vad (I)	*ovadati*	admonish
(k)khā (III)	*khāyati*	seem
(p)paṭi-i (I)	*pacceti*	assume

→

pari-tas (III)	*paritassati*	long (for), desire
vaṭṭ (I)	*vaṭṭati*	turn, roll, circle
var (VII)	*vāreti*	prevent, hinder, obstruct, stop
vi-var (I)	*vivarati*	open
vi-o-(k)kam (I)	*vokkamati*	pass away, break away
vi-o-chid (III)	*vocchijjati*	cut off, separate from
saṃ-anu-pass (I)	*samanupassati*	envisage
saṃ-u(d)-ā-car (I)	*samudācarati*	speak to, converse with
saṃ-mucch (I)	*sammucchati*	coagulate, form (intransitive)

Nouns :—

adhivacanaṃ	designation, name
ape(k)khā	intention, expectation
abhiseko	consecration
avabhāso	splendour, illumination
upasampadā	entrance
kucchi (masc.)	womb
kumārikā	girl
kumbho	pot
catuppado	quadruped
(ṭ)ṭhiti (fem.)	(also means) station
tantaṃ	loom
nāmaṃ	(also means) mind, mental being (in the most general sense, as contrasted with *rūpaṃ*, matter, physical being)
pajjoto	lamp
paññāpanaṃ	preparation
paṭigho	(also means) reaction, resistance (as property of matter)
paṭiññā	admission, assertion
patiṭṭhā	resting place, perch
patho	road, way
payirupāsanaṃ	attending on (action noun from *pari-upa-ās* (I), where *payir* is a junction form of *pari(y)*)
pācariyo	teacher's teacher
puggalo	person

babbajaṃ	a coarse grass (used in making ropes and slippers)
brahmacariyaṃ	God-like life, best life, celibate life
mañcako	bed
muñjaṃ	a kind of rush (used for making ropes, girdles, and slippers)
yamakaṃ	pair
yāmo	watch (of the night)
vaṭṭaṃ	rolling, circulation, cycle, cycling (of the universe)
(*v*)*vataṃ*	vow (in compound > *-bbataṃ*)
vinipātiko	unhappy spirit (reborn in purgatory, or as an animal, ghost, or demon)
vimati (fem.)	perplexity
→ *virūḷhi* (fem.)	growth
vihesā	trouble, harassing
vemattatā	difference, distinction
saṃsāro	transmigration
samuppādo	origination
samphasso	contact, union
sallāpo	talk
sālo	(a kind of tree : *Shorea robusta*)
siriṃsapo	snake

Adjectives :—

akalla	unsound
adhimutta	intent on
anuesin	seeking (from *is*(*a*) (I))
anukhuddaka	very minor
appaṭisaṃvedana	not feeling, not experiencing
appamatta	not-negligent
ākula	confused, tangled
uttānaka	shallow (and figuratively "easily understood", "simple")
kalla	sound, proper
niyata	constant, certain
paṭicchanna	covered, concealed
-vattin	setting going, deploying, operating, conducting, governing, developing

saṃvejanīya	emotional, inspiring, stirring (future passive participle of *saṃ-vij*)
saddha	trusting, believing
sotāpanna	in the stream, on the Way (from *sotas*, "stream")

Pronoun :—

añña . . . añña	one . . . another, the . . . is a different thing from the . . .

Past Participles :—

abhisitta (*abhi-sic* (II))	consecrated
āraddha (*ā-rādh* (VII))	pleased, satisfied
nikkujjita (*ni*(*r*)-*kujj*)	overturned
pahita ((*p*)*pa-dhā* (I))	exerted
mūḷha (*muh*)	lost
vuttha (*vas* (I))	spent (time) (cf. *vusita* from the same root but with a different meaning, "lived well")

Indeclinables :—

atha	(is also used in introducing a deduction) : thence, (if) so
ubhato	in both ways, on both sides, both
evaṃ santaṃ	in that case, in such case
kira (enclitic)	(may be used to introduce, as enclitic, a report or rumour, and might then be translated) it is said that, they say (and also a discovery, meaning then) in fact, actually
ca pana (enclitic)	moreover
yatthicchakaṃ	wherever one wishes
yadicchakaṃ	whatever one wishes
yāvaticchakaṃ	as far as one wishes
sakkhī	in person, personally
sabbathā	in all ways

EXERCISE 29

Passages for reading :—

1. atha kho bhagavā āyasmantaṃ Ānandaṃ āmantesi: āyām' Ānanda yena Hiraññavatiyā nadiyā pārimatīraṃ yena Kusinārā-Upavattanaṃ [1] Mallānaṃ sālavanaṃ ten' upasaṃkamissāmā ti. evaṃ bhante ti kho āyasmā Ānando bhagavato paccassosi.

atha kho bhagavā mahatā bhikkhusaṃghena saddhiṃ yena Hiraññavatiyā nadiyā pārimatīraṃ yena Kusinārā-Upavattanaṃ Mallānaṃ sālavanaṃ ten' upasaṃkami, upasaṃkamitvā āyasmantaṃ Ānandaṃ āmantesi: iṅgha me tvaṃ Ānanda antarena yamakasālānam uttarasīsakaṃ mañcakaṃ paññāpehi, kilanto 'smi Ānanda, nipajjissāmī ti. evaṃ bhante ti kho āyasmā Ānando bhagavato paṭissutvā antarena yamakasālānaṃ uttarasīsakaṃ mañcakaṃ paññāpesi. atha kho bhagavā dakkhiṇena passena sīhaseyyaṃ kappesi pāde pādaṃ accādhāya sato sampajāno.

* * *

pubbe bhante disāsu vassaṃ vutthā bhikkhū āgacchanti tathāgataṃ dassanāya, te mayaṃ labhāma manobhāvanīye bhikkhū dassanāya labhāma payirupāsanāya. bhagavato pana mayaṃ bhante accayena na labhissāma manobhāvanīye bhikkhū dassanāya na labhissāma payirupāsanāyā ti. cattār' imāni Ānanda saddhassa kulaputtassa dassanīyāni saṃvejanīyāni ṭhānāni. katamāni cattāri. idha tathāgato jāto ti Ānanda saddhassa kulaputtassa dassanīyaṃ saṃvejanīyaṃ ṭhānaṃ. idha tathāgato anuttaraṃ sammāsambodhiṃ abhisambuddho ti Ānanda saddhassa kulaputtassa dassanīyaṃ saṃvejanīyaṃ ṭhānaṃ. idha tathāgatena anuttaraṃ dhammacakkaṃ pavattitan ti Ānanda saddhassa kulaputtassa dassanīyaṃ saṃvejanīyaṃ ṭhānaṃ. idha tathāgato anupādisesāya nibbānadhātuyā parinibbuto ti Ānanda saddhassa kulaputtassa dassanīyaṃ saṃvejanīyaṃ ṭhānaṃ. imāni kho Ānanda cattāri saddhassa kulaputtassa dassanīyāni saṃvejanīyāni ṭhānāni.

[1] Kusinārā : capital of the northern Malla republic, three quarters of a league north-west of Pāvā ; Upavattanaṃ : a wood near the city.

āgamissanti kho Ānanda saddhā bhikkhubhikkhuniyo upāsakaupāsikāyo idha tathāgato jāto ti pi, idha tathāgato anuttaraṃ sammāsambodhiṃ abhisambuddho ti pi, idha tathāgatena anuttaraṃ dhammacakkaṃ pavattitan ti pi, idha tathāgato anupādisesāya nibbānadhātuyā parinibbuto ti pi. ye hi ke ci Ānanda cetiyacārikaṃ āhiṇḍantā pasannacittā kālaṃ karissanti, sabbe te kāyassa bhedā param maraṇā sugatiṃ saggaṃ lokaṃ upapajjissantī ti.

* * *

tena kho pana samayena Subhaddo nāma paribbājako Kusinārāyaṃ paṭivasati. assosi kho Subhaddo paribbājako: ajj' eva kira rattiyā pacchime yāme samaṇassa Gotamassa parinibbānaṃ bhavissatī ti. atha kho Subhaddassa paribbājakassa etad ahosi. sutaṃ kho pana m' etaṃ paribbājakānaṃ vuddhānaṃ mahallakānaṃ ācariyapācariyānaṃ bhāsamānānaṃ: kadā ci karaha ci tathāgatā loke uppajjanti arahanto sammāsambuddhā ti. ajja ca rattiyā pacchime yāme samaṇassa Gotamassa parinibbānaṃ bhavissati. atthi ca me ayaṃ kaṅkhādhammo uppanno, evaṃ pasanno ahaṃ samaṇe Gotame, pahoti me samaṇo Gotamo tathā dhammaṃ desetuṃ yathā ahaṃ imaṃ kaṅkhādhammaṃ pajaheyyan ti.

atha kho Subhaddo paribbājako yena Upavattanaṃ Mallānaṃ sālavanaṃ yen' āyasmā Ānando ten' upasaṃkami, upasaṃkamitvā āyasmantaṃ Ānandaṃ etad avoca: sutaṃ m' etaṃ bho Ānanda paribbājakānaṃ . . . yathā ahaṃ imaṃ kaṅkhādhammaṃ pajaheyyaṃ. svāhaṃ bho Ānanda labheyyaṃ samaṇaṃ Gotamaṃ dassanāyā ti. evaṃ vutte āyasmā Ānando Subhaddaṃ paribbājakaṃ etad avoca: alaṃ āvuso Subhadda, mā tathāgataṃ viheṭhesi. kilanto bhagavā ti. dutiyam pi kho Subhaddo paribbājako . . . pe . . . tatiyam pi kho Subhaddo paribbājako . . . tatiyam pi kho āyasmā Ānando Subhaddaṃ paribbājakaṃ etad avoca: alaṃ āvuso Subhadda, mā tathāgataṃ viheṭhesi. kilanto bhagavā ti. assosi kho bhagavā āyasmato Ānandassa Subhaddena paribbājakena saddhiṃ imaṃ kathāsallāpaṃ. atha kho bhagavā āyasmantaṃ Ānandaṃ āmantesi: alaṃ Ānanda, mā Subhaddaṃ vāresi, labhataṃ Ānanda Subhaddo tathāgataṃ dassanāya. yaṃ kiñci maṃ Subhaddo pucchissati, sabban taṃ aññāpekho va pucchissati no vihesāpekho, yañ c' assāhaṃ puṭṭho vyākarissāmi taṃ khippam eva ājānissatī ti. atha kho āyasmā Ānando Subhaddaṃ paribbājakaṃ etad avoca : gacch' āvuso Subhadda, karoti te bhagavā okāsan ti.

atha kho Subhaddo paribbājako yena bhagavā ten' upasaṃkami, upasaṃkamitvā bhagavatā saddhiṃ sammodi, sammodanīyaṃ kathaṃ sārāṇīyaṃ vītisāretvā ekamantaṃ nisīdi. ekamantaṃ nisinno kho Subhaddo paribbājako bhagavantaṃ etad avoca : ye me bho Gotama samaṇabrāhmaṇā saṃghino gaṇino gaṇācariyā ñātā yasassino titthakarā sādhusammatā ca bahujanassa, seyyathīdaṃ Pūraṇo Kassapo,[1] Makkhali Gosālo,[2] Ajitakesakambalī,[3] Pakudho Kaccāyano,[4] Sañjayo Belaṭṭhiputto,[5] Nigaṇṭho Nāthaputto,[6] sabbe te sakāya paṭiññāya abbhaññaṃsu, sabbe va na abbhaññaṃsu, ekacce abbhaññaṃsu ekacce na abbhaññaṃsū ti. alaṃ Subhadda. tiṭṭhat' etaṃ sabbe te sakāya paṭiññāya abbhaññaṃsu, sabbe va na abbhaññaṃsu, udāhu ekacce abbhaññaṃsu ekacce na abbhaññaṃsū ti. dhammaṃ te Subhadda desessāmi, taṃ suṇāhi, sādhukaṃ manasikarohi, bhāsissāmī ti. evaṃ bhante ti kho Subhaddo paribbājako bhagavato paccassosi. bhagavā etad avoca : yasmiṃ kho Subhadda dhammavinaye ariyo aṭṭhaṅgiko maggo na upalabbhati, samaṇo [7] pi tattha na upalabbhati, dutiyo pi tattha samaṇo na upalabbhati, tatiyo pi tattha samaṇo na upalabbhati, catuttho pi tattha samaṇo na upalabbhati. yasmiñ ca kho Subhadda dhammavinaye ariyo aṭṭhaṅgiko maggo upalabbhati, samaṇo pi tattha upalabbhati, dutiyo pi tattha samaṇo upalabbhati, tatiyo pi tattha samaṇo upalabbhati, catuttho pi tattha samaṇo upalabbhati. imasmiṃ kho Subhadda dhammavinaye ariyo aṭṭhaṅgiko maggo upalabbhati,

[1] The Ājīvaka leader, see footnote in Exercise 21.
[2] See footnotes in Exercises 21 and 28.
[3] The materialist, see Exercise 28 (English into Pali).
[4] An Ājīvaka leader.
[5] A philosopher who followed the method of perpetual equivocation in debate, which is exemplified in Exercise 22.
[6] The founder of the Jaina sect, which seceded from the Ājīvakas.
[7] According to the Commentary, the *samaṇo* here is one who is *sotāpanna*, "on the Way," which is the first stage of the Buddhist Way ; the second, third and fourth *samaṇos* are those in the remaining three stages, which are : *sakadāgāmin*, "once-returning" (to the world) ; *anāgāmin*, "non-returning" ; and *arahant*.

idh' eva Subhadda samaṇo, idha dutiyo samaṇo, idha tatiyo samaṇo, idha catuttho samaṇo. suññā parappavādā samaṇehi aññe, ime ca Subhadda bhikkhū sammā vihareyyuṃ, asuñño loko arahantehi assa.

ekūnatiṃso vayasā Subhadda
yaṃ pabbajiṃ kiṃkusalānuesī.
vassāni paññāsasamādhikāni [1]
yato ahaṃ pabbajito Subhadda
ñāyassa dhammassa padesavattī.
ito bahiddhā samaṇo pi n' atthi.

dutiyo pi samaṇo n' atthi, tatiyo pi samaṇo n' atthi, catuttho pi samaṇo n' atthi. suññā parappavādā samaṇehi aññe, ime ca Subhadda bhikkhū sammā vihareyyuṃ, asuñño loko arahantehi assā ti.

evaṃ vutte Subhaddo paribbājako bhagavantaṃ etad avoca : abhikkantaṃ bhante, abhikkantaṃ bhante. seyyathā pi bhante nikkujjitaṃ vā ukkujjeyya, paṭicchannaṃ vā vivareyya, mūḷhassa vā maggaṃ ācikkheyya, andhakāre vā telappajjotaṃ dhāreyya cakkhumanto rūpāni dakkhintī ti, evam eva bhagavatā anekapariyāyena dhammo pakāsito. esāhaṃ bhante bhagavantaṃ saraṇaṃ gacchāmi dhammañ ca bhikkhusaṃghañ ca. labheyyāhaṃ bhagavato santike pabbajjaṃ, labheyyaṃ upasampadan ti. yo kho Subhadda aññatitthiyapubbo imasmiṃ dhammavinaye ākaṅkhati pabbajjaṃ, ākaṅkhati upasampadaṃ, so cattāro māse parivasati. catunnaṃ māsānaṃ accayena āraddhacittā bhikkhū pabbājenti upasampādenti bhikkhubhāvāya. api ca m' ettha puggalavemattatā viditā ti.

sace bhante aññatitthiyapubbā imasmiṃ dhammavinaye ākaṅkhantā pabbajjaṃ, ākaṅkhantā upasampadaṃ, cattāro māse parivasanti, catunnaṃ māsānaṃ accayena āraddhacittā bhikkhū pabbājenti upasampādenti bhikkhubhāvāya, ahaṃ cattāri vassāni parivasissāmi, catunnaṃ vassānaṃ accayena āraddhacittā bhikkhū pabbājentu upasampādentu bhikkhubhāvāyā ti. atha kho bhagavā āyasmantaṃ Ānandaṃ āmantesi : tena h' Ānanda Subhaddaṃ pabbājethā ti. evaṃ bhante ti kho āyasmā Ānando bhagavato paccassosi.

[1] *samādhika*, " more than," is *sam-adhika* with metrical lengthening in the junction.

atha kho Subhaddo paribbājako āyasmantaṃ Ānandaṃ etad avoca : lābhā vo āvuso Ānanda, suladdhaṃ vo āvuso Ānanda, ye ettha satthārā sammukhā antevāsābhisekena abhisittā ti. alattha kho Subhaddo paribbājako bhagavato santike pabbajjaṃ, alattha upasampadaṃ. acirūpasampanno kho pan' āyasmā Subhaddo eko vūpakaṭṭho appamatto ātāpī pahitatto viharanto. na cirass' eva yass' atthāya kulaputtā sammad eva agārasmā anagāriyaṃ pabbajanti, tad anuttaraṃ brahmacariyapariyosānaṃ diṭṭhe va dhamme sayaṃ abhiññā [1] sacchikatvā upasampajja vihāsi : khīṇā jāti, vusitaṃ brahmacariyaṃ, kataṃ karaṇīyaṃ, nāparaṃ itthattāyā ti abbhaññāsi. aññataro kho pan' āyasmā Subhaddo arahataṃ ahosi. so bhagavato pacchimo sakkhisāvako ahosī ti.

atha kho bhagavā āyasmantaṃ Ānandaṃ āmantesi : siyā kho pan' Ānanda tumhākam evam assa : atītasatthukaṃ pāvacanaṃ, n' atthi no satthā ti. na kho pan' etaṃ Ānanda evaṃ daṭṭhabbaṃ. yo vo Ānanda mayā dhammo ca vinayo ca desito paññatto, so vo mam' accayena satthā. yathā kho pan' Ānanda etarahi bhikkhū aññamaññaṃ āvusovādena samudācaranti, na vo mam' accayena evaṃ samudācaritabbaṃ. theratarena Ānanda bhikkhunā navakataro bhikkhu nāmena vā gottena vā āvusovādena vā samudācaritabbo, navakatarena bhikkhunā therataro bhikkhu bhante ti vā āyasmā ti vā samudācaritabbo. ākaṅkhamāno Ānanda saṃgho mam' accayena khuddānukhuddakāni sikkhāpadāni samūhanatu. Channassa Ānanda bhikkhuno mam' accayena brahmadaṇḍo kātabbo ti. katamo pana bhante brahmadaṇḍo ti. Channo Ānanda bhikkhu yaṃ iccheyya taṃ vadeyya, so bhikkhūhi n' eva vattabbo na ovaditabbo na anusāsitabbo ti.

atha bhagavā bhikkhū āmantesi : siyā kho pana bhikkhave ekabhikkhussa [2] pi kaṅkhā vā vimati vā Buddhe vā dhamme vā saṃghe vā magge vā paṭipadāya vā. pucchatha bhikkhave. mā pacchā vippaṭisārino ahuvattha : sammukhībhūto no satthā ahosi, na mayaṃ sakkhimha bhagavantaṃ sammukhā paṭipucchitun ti. evaṃ vutte te bhikkhū tuṇhī ahesuṃ. dutiyam pi kho bhagavā . . . tatiyam pi kho bhagavā bhikkhū āmantesi : siyā kho pana bhikkhave ekabhikkhussa pi kaṅkhā vā vimati

[1] Gerund of *abhi-(ñ)ñā*, cf. footnote at beginning of Exercise 22.
[2] Inflection of *a* declension.

vā Buddhe vā dhamme vā saṃghe vā magge vā paṭipadāya vā. pucchatha bhikkhave. mā pacchā vippaṭisārino ahuvattha : sammukhībhūto no satthā ahosi, na mayaṃ sakkhimha bhagavantaṃ sammukhā paṭipucchitun ti. tatiyam pi kho te bhikkhū tuṇhī ahesuṃ. atha kho bhagavā bhikkhū āmantesi : siyā kho pana bhikkhave satthugāravena pi na puccheyyātha. sahāyako pi bhikkhave sahāyakassa ārocetū ti. evaṃ vutte te bhikkhū tuṇhī ahesuṃ.

atha kho āyasmā Ānando bhagavantaṃ etad avoca : acchariyaṃ bhante abbhutaṃ bhante. evaṃ pasanno ahaṃ bhante imasmiṃ bhikkhusaṃghe, n' atthi ekabhikkhussa pi kaṅkhā vā vimati vā Buddhe vā dhamme vā saṃghe vā magge vā paṭipadāya vā ti. pasādā kho tvaṃ Ānanda vadesi. ñāṇam eva h' ettha Ānanda tathāgatassa : n' atthi imasmiṃ bhikkhusaṃghe, n' atthi ekabhikkhussa pi kaṅkhā vā vimati vā Buddhe vā dhamme vā saṃghe vā magge vā paṭipadāya vā. imesaṃ hi Ānanda pañcannaṃ bhikkhusatānaṃ yo pacchimako bhikkhu so sotāpanno avinipātadhammo niyato sambodhiparāyano ti. atha kho bhagavā bhikkhū āmantesi : handa dāni bhikkhave āmantayāmi vo : vayadhammā saṃkhārā, appamādena sampādethā ti. ayaṃ tathāgatassa pacchimā vācā.

atha kho bhagavā paṭhamajjhānaṃ samāpajji. paṭhamajjhānā vuṭṭhahitvā dutiyajjhānaṃ samāpajji. dutiyajjhānā vuṭṭhahitvā tatiyajjhānaṃ samāpajji. tatiyajjhānā vuṭṭhahitvā catutthajjhānaṃ samāpajji. catutthajjhānā vuṭṭhahitvā ākāsānañcāyatanaṃ samāpajji. ākāsānañcāyatanasamāpattiyā vuṭṭhahitvā viññāṇañcāyatanaṃ samāpajji. viññāṇañcāyatanasamāpattiyā vuṭṭhahitvā ākiñcaññāyatanaṃ samāpajji. ākiñcaññāyatanasamāpattiyā vuṭṭhahitvā nevasaññānāsaññāyatanaṃ samāpajji. nevasaññānāsaññāyatanasamāpattiyā vuṭṭhahitvā saññāvedayitanirodhaṃ samāpajji.

atha kho āyasmā Ānando āyasmantaṃ Anuruddhaṃ etad avoca : parinibbuto bhante Anuruddha bhagavā ti. na āvuso Ānanda bhagavā parinibbuto, saññāvedayitanirodhaṃ samāpanno ti. atha kho bhagavā saññāvedayitanirodhasamāpattiyā vuṭṭhahitvā nevasaññānāsaññāyatanaṃ samāpajji. nevasaññānāsaññāyatanasamāpattiyā vuṭṭhahitvā ākiñcaññāyatanaṃ samāpajji. ākiñcaññāyatanasamāpattiyā vuṭṭhahitvā viññāṇañcāyatanaṃ samāpajji. viññāṇañcāyatanasamāpattiyā vuṭṭhahitvā ākāsānañcāyatanaṃ samāpajji. ākāsānañcāyatanasamāpattiyā vuṭṭhahitvā catutthajjhānaṃ samāpajji. catutthajjhānā vuṭṭhahitvā tatiyajjhānaṃ samāpajji. tatiyajjhānā vuṭṭhahitvā dutiyajjhānaṃ samāpajji. dutiyajjhānā vuṭṭhahitvā paṭhamajjhānaṃ samāpajji. paṭhamajjhānā vuṭṭhahitvā dutiyajjhānaṃ samāpajji. dutiyajjhānā vuṭṭhahitvā tatiyajjhānaṃ samāpajji. tatiyajjhānā vuṭṭhahitvā catutthajjhānaṃ samāpajji. catutthajjhānā vuṭṭhahitvā samanantarā bhagavā parinibbāyi.

2. evam me sutaṃ. ekaṃ samayaṃ bhagavā Kurūsu viharati, Kammāssadhammaṃ nāma Kurūnaṃ nigamo. atha kho āyasmā Ānando yena bhagavā ten' upasaṃkami, upasaṃkamitvā bhagavantaṃ abhivādetvā ekamantaṃ nisīdi. ekamantaṃ nisinno kho āyasmā Ānando bhagavantaṃ etad avoca: acchariyaṃ bhante abbhutaṃ bhante yāva gambhīro cāyaṃ bhante paṭiccasamuppādo gambhīrāvabhāso ca. atha ca pana me uttānakuttānako viya khāyatī ti. mā h' evaṃ Ānanda avaca, mā h' evaṃ Ānanda avaca. gambhīro cāyaṃ Ānanda paṭiccasamuppādo gambhīrāvabhāso ca. etassa Ānanda dhammassa ananubodhā appaṭivedhā evam ayaṃ pajā tantākulakajātā guḷāguṇṭhikajātā [1] muñjababbajabhūtā apāyaṃ duggatiṃ vinipātaṃ saṃsāraṃ nātivattati.

atthi idappaccayā jarāmaraṇan ti. iti puṭṭhena satā Ānanda, atthī ti 'ssa vacanīyaṃ. kim paccayā jarāmaraṇan ti. iti ce vadeyya, jātipaccayā jarāmaraṇan ti icc assa vacanīyaṃ. atthi idappaccayā jātī ti. iti puṭṭhena satā Ānanda, atthī ti 'ssa vacanīyaṃ. kim paccayā jātī ti. iti ce vadeyya, bhavappaccayā jātī ti icc assa vacanīyaṃ. atthi idappaccayā bhavo ti. iti puṭṭhena satā . . . upādānapaccayā bhavo ti icc assa vacanīyaṃ. atthi idappaccayā upādānan ti. iti puṭṭhena satā . . . taṇhāpaccayā upādānan ti icc assa vacanīyaṃ. atthi idappaccayā taṇhā ti. iti puṭṭhena satā . . . vedanāpaccayā taṇhā ti icc assa vacanīyaṃ. atthi idappaccayā vedanā ti. iti puṭṭhena satā . . . phassapaccayā vedanā ti icc assa vacanīyaṃ. atthi idappaccayā phasso ti. iti puṭṭhena satā . . . nāmarūpapaccayā phasso ti icc assa vacanīyaṃ. atthi idappaccayā nāmarūpan

[1] The meaning of *guḷāguṇṭhika* is uncertain. It refers probably to knotted or twisted threads in weaving, or perhaps to a bird's nest of tangled construction.

ti. iti puṭṭhena satā Ānanda atthī ti 'ssa vacanīyaṃ. kim paccayā nāmarūpan ti. iti ce vadeyya, viññāṇapaccayā nāmarūpan ti icc assa vacanīyaṃ. atthi idappaccayā viññāṇan ti. iti puṭṭhena satā Ānanda atthī ti 'ssa vacanīyaṃ. kim paccayā viññāṇan ti. iti ce vadeyya, nāmarūpapaccayā viññāṇan ti icc assa vacanīyaṃ.

iti kho Ānanda nāmarūpapaccayā viññāṇaṃ, viññāṇapaccayā nāmarūpaṃ, nāmarūpapaccayā phasso, phassapaccayā vedanā, vedanāpaccayā taṇhā, taṇhāpaccayā upādānaṃ, upādānapaccayā bhavo, bhavapaccayā jāti, jātipaccayā jarāmaraṇaṃ, jarāmaraṇapaccayā sokaparidevadukkhadomanassupāyāsā sambhavanti. evam etassa kevalassa dukkhakkhandhassa samudayo hoti.

jātipaccayā jarāmaraṇan ti iti kho pan' etaṃ vuttaṃ, tad Ānanda iminā p' etaṃ pariyāyena veditabbaṃ yathā jātipaccayā jarāmaraṇaṃ. jāti va hi Ānanda nābhavissa sabbena sabbaṃ sabbathā sabbaṃ kassa ci kimhi ci, seyyathīdaṃ devānaṃ vā devattāya, gandhabbānaṃ [1] vā gandhabbattāya, yakkhānaṃ [2] vā yakkhattāya, bhūtānaṃ vā bhūtattāya, manussānaṃ vā manussattāya, catuppadānaṃ vā catuppadattāya, pakkhīnaṃ vā pakkhattāya, siriṃsapānaṃ vā siriṃsapattāya, tesaṃ tesaṃ va hi Ānanda sattānaṃ tathattāya jāti nābhavissa, sabbaso jātiyā asati jātinirodhā api nu kho jarāmaraṇaṃ paññāyethā ti. no h' etaṃ bhante. tasmāt ih' Ānanda es' eva hetu etaṃ nidānaṃ esa samudayo esa paccayo jarāmaraṇassa, yadidaṃ jāti. . . . bhavo va hi Ānanda nābhavissa sabbena sabbaṃ sabbathā sabbaṃ kassa ci kimhi ci, seyyathīdaṃ kāmabhavo [3] rūpabhavo arūpabhavo vā, sabbaso bhave asati bhavanirodhā api nu kho jāti paññāyethā ti. no h' etaṃ bhante. tasmāt ih' Ānanda es' eva hetu etaṃ nidānaṃ esa samudayo esa paccayo jātiyā, yadidaṃ bhavo . . . upādānaṃ va hi Ānanda nābhavissa sabbena sabbaṃ sabbathā sabbaṃ kassa ci kimhi ci, seyyathīdaṃ kāmūpādānaṃ vā

[1] *gandhabbo*, "heavenly musician" (a class of minor gods).

[2] *yakkho*, "spirit," "god," "fairy," "genie" (usually applied to minor deities such as tree spirits, or to servants of greater gods).

[3] Three forms or levels of existence are recognised, the *arūpa*, "immaterial," *rūpa*, "material," and *kāma*, "sensual." The *kāma* is really the lower part of the *rūpa*, but they are usually separated and the *rūpa* restricted to the fine or imponderable matter of the worlds of the gods.

diṭṭhūpādānaṃ vā sīlabbatūpādānaṃ vā attavādūpādānaṃ vā, sabbaso upādāne asati upādānanirodhā api nu kho bhavo paññāyethā ti. no . . . taṇhā va hi Ānanda nābhavissa sabbena sabbaṃ sabbathā sabbaṃ kassa ci kimhi ci, seyyathīdaṃ rūpataṇhā saddataṇhā gandhataṇhā rasataṇhā phoṭṭhabbataṇhā dhammataṇhā, sabbaso taṇhāya asati taṇhānirodhā api nu kho upādānaṃ paññāyethā ti. no . . . vedanā va hi Ānanda nābhavissa sabbena sabbaṃ sabbathā sabbaṃ kassa ci kimhi ci, seyyathīdaṃ cakkhusamphassajā vedanā sotasamphassajā vedanā ghānasamphassajā vedanā jivhāsamphassajā vedanā kāyasamphassajā vedanā manosamphassajā vedanā, sabbaso vedanāya asati vedanānirodhā api nu kho taṇhā paññāyethā ti. no . . .

* * *

. . . phasso va hi Ānanda nābhavissa sabbena sabbaṃ sabbathā sabbaṃ kassa ci kimhi ci, seyyathīdaṃ cakkhusamphasso sotasamphasso ghānasamphasso jivhāsamphasso kāyasamphasso manosamphasso, sabbaso phasse asati phassanirodhā api nu kho vedanā paññāyethā ti. no . . .

nāmarūpapaccayā phasso ti iti kho pan' etam vuttaṃ, tad Ānanda iminā p'etaṃ pariyāyena veditabbaṃ, yathā nāmarūpapaccayā phasso. yehi Ānanda ākārehi yehi liṅgehi yehi nimittehi yehi uddesehi nāmakāyassa paññatti hoti, tesu ākāresu tesu liṅgesu tesu nimittesu tesu uddesesu asati, api nu kho rūpakāye adhivacanasamphasso paññāyethā ti. no h' etaṃ bhante. yehi Ānanda ākārehi yehi liṅgehi yehi nimittehi yehi uddesehi rūpakāyassa paññatti hoti, tesu ākāresu tesu liṅgesu tesu nimittesu tesu uddesesu asati, api nu kho nāmakāye paṭighasamphasso paññāyethā ti. no h' etaṃ bhante. yehi Ānanda ākārehi yehi liṅgehi yehi nimittehi yehi uddesehi nāmakāyassa ca rūpakāyassa ca paññatti hoti, tesu ākāresu tesu liṅgesu tesu nimittesu tesu uddesesu asati, api nu kho adhivacanasamphasso vā paṭighasamphasso vā paññāyethā ti. no h' etaṃ bhante. yehi Ānanda ākārehi yehi liṅgehi yehi nimittehi yehi uddesehi nāmarūpassa paññatti hoti, tesu ākāresu tesu liṅgesu tesu nimittesu tesu uddesesu asati, api nu kho phasso paññāyethā ti. no h' etaṃ bhante. tasmāt ih'

Ānanda es' eva hetu etaṃ nidānaṃ esa samudayo esa paccayo phassassa, yadidaṃ nāmarūpaṃ.

viññāṇapaccayā nāmarūpan ti iti kho pan' etaṃ vuttaṃ, tad Ānanda iminā p' etaṃ pariyāyena veditabbaṃ yathā viññāṇapaccayā nāmarūpaṃ. viññāṇaṃ va hi Ānanda mātu kucchiṃ na okkamissatha, api nu kho nāmarūpaṃ mātu kucchismiṃ sammucchissathā ti. no h' etaṃ bhante. viññāṇaṃ va hi Ānanda mātu kucchiṃ okkamitvā vokkamissatha, api nu kho nāmarūpaṃ itthattāya abhinibbattissathā ti. no h' etaṃ bhante. viññāṇaṃ va hi Ānanda daharass' eva sato vocchijjissatha kumārassa vā kumārikāya vā, api nu kho nāmarūpaṃ vuddhiṃ virūḷhiṃ vepullaṃ āpajjissathā ti. no h' etaṃ bhante. tasmāt ih' Ānanda es' eva hetu etaṃ nidānaṃ esa samudayo esa paccayo nāmarūpassa, yadidaṃ viññāṇaṃ.

nāmarūpapaccayā viññāṇan ti iti kho pan' etaṃ vuttaṃ, tad Ānanda iminā p' etaṃ pariyāyena veditabbaṃ, yathā nāmarūpapaccayā viññāṇaṃ. viññāṇaṃ va hi Ānanda nāmarūpe patiṭṭhaṃ nālabhissatha, api nu kho āyatiṃ jātijarāmaraṇadukkhasamudayasambhavo paññāyethā ti. no h' etaṃ bhante. tasmāt ih' Ānanda es' eva hetu etaṃ nidānaṃ esa samudayo esa paccayo viññāṇassa, yadidaṃ nāmarūpaṃ. ettāvatā kho Ānanda jāyetha vā jīyetha vā mīyetha vā cavetha vā upapajjetha vā, ettāvatā adhivacanapatho, ettāvatā niruttipatho, ettāvatā paññattipatho, ettāvatā paññāvacaraṃ, ettāvatā vaṭṭaṃ vaṭṭati itthattaṃ paññāpanāya, yadidaṃ nāmarūpaṃ saha viññāṇena.

* * *

yato kho Ānanda bhikkhu n' eva vedanaṃ attānaṃ samanupassati, no pi appaṭisaṃvedanaṃ attānaṃ samanupassati, no pi attā me vedayati, vedanādhammo hi me attā ti samanupassati, so evaṃ asamanupassanto na kiñ ci loke upādiyati, anupādiyaṃ na paritassati, aparitassaṃ paccattaṃ yeva parinibbāyati, khīṇā jāti, vusitaṃ brahmacariyaṃ, kataṃ karaṇīyaṃ, nāparaṃ itthattāyā ti pajānāti. evaṃvimuttacittaṃ kho Ānanda bhikkhuṃ yo evaṃ vadeyya hoti tathāgato param maraṇā ti, iti 'ssa diṭṭhī ti tad akallaṃ. na hoti tathāgato . . . tad akallaṃ. taṃ kissa hetu. yāvat' Ānanda adhivacanaṃ yāvatā adhivacanapatho, yāvatā nirutti yāvatā niruttipatho, yāvatā paññatti yāvatā paññattipatho, yāvatā paññā yāvatā paññāvacaraṃ, yāvatā vaṭṭaṃ yāvatā vaṭṭaṃ vaṭṭati, tad abhiññā [1] vimutto bhikkhu, tad abhiññā vimutto bhikkhu na jānāti na passati iti 'ssa diṭṭhī ti tad akallaṃ.

satta kho imā Ānanda viññāṇaṭṭhitiyo, dve ca āyatanāni. katamā satta. sant' Ānanda sattā nānattakāyā nānattasaññino, seyyathā pi manussā ekacce ca devā ekacce ca vinipātikā. ayaṃ paṭhamā viññāṇaṭṭhiti. sant' Ānanda sattā nānattakāyā ekattasaññino, seyyathā pi devā brahmakāyikā paṭhamābhinibbattā. ayaṃ dutiyā viññāṇaṭṭhiti. sant' Ānanda sattā ekattakāyā nānattasaññino, seyyathā pi devā ābhassarā.[2] ayaṃ tatiyā viññāṇaṭṭhiti. sant' Ānanda sattā ekattakāyā ekattasaññino, seyyathā pi devā subhakiṇṇā.[3] ayaṃ catutthā viññāṇaṭṭhiti. sant' Ānanda sattā sabbaso rūpasaññānaṃ samatikkamā paṭighasaññānaṃ atthagamā nānattasaññānaṃ amanasikārā ananto ākāso ti ākāsānañcāyatanūpagā. ayaṃ pañcamī viññāṇaṭṭhiti. sant' Ānanda sattā sabbaso ākāsānañcāyatanaṃ samatikkamma anantaṃ viññāṇan ti viññāṇañcāyatanūpagā. ayaṃ chaṭṭhā viññāṇaṭṭhiti. sant' Ānanda sattā sabbaso viññāṇañcāyatanaṃ samatikkamma n' atthi kiñ cī ti ākiñcaññāyatanūpagā. ayaṃ sattamī viññāṇaṭṭhiti.

asaññasattāyatanaṃ nevasaññānāsaññāyatanam eva dutiyaṃ.

tatr' Ānanda y' āyaṃ paṭhamā viññāṇaṭṭhiti nānattakāyā nānattasaññino, seyyathā pi manussā ekacce ca devā ekacce ca vinipātikā, yo nu kho Ānanda tañ ca pajānāti, tassā ca samudayaṃ pajānāti, tassā ca atthagamaṃ pajānāti, tassā ca assādaṃ pajānāti, tassā ca ādīnavaṃ pajānāti, tassā ca nissaraṇaṃ pajānāti, kallaṃ nu kho tena tad abhinanditun ti. no h' etaṃ bhante. . . . pe . . . tatr' Ānanda y' āyaṃ sattamī viññāṇaṭṭhiti sabbaso viññāṇañcāyatanaṃ samatikkamma n' atthi kiñ cī ti ākiñcaññāyatanūpagā, yo nu kho Ānanda tañ ca pajānāti, . . . tassā ca nissaraṇaṃ pajānāti, kallaṃ nu kho tena

[1] Gerund, cf. footnote at beginning of Exercise 22.
[2] *ābhassara*, "the world of radiance," cf. second passage in Exercise 20.
[3] *subhakiṇṇa*, "the lustrous world," the inhabitants of which enjoy the highest, unalloyed happiness (the sole defect of which is that it is temporary, not eternal).

tad abhinanditun ti. no h' etaṃ bhante. tatr' Ānanda yam idaṃ asaññasattāyatanaṃ, yo nu kho Ānanda tañ ca pajānāti, . . . tassa ca nissaraṇaṃ pajānāti, kallaṃ nu kho tena tad abhinanditun ti. no h' etaṃ bhante. tatr' Ānanda yam idaṃ nevasaññānāsaññāyatanaṃ, yo nu kho Ānanda tañ ca pajānāti, . . . tassa ca nissaraṇaṃ pajānāti, kallaṃ nu kho tena tad abhinanditun ti. no h' etaṃ bhante. yato kho Ānanda bhikkhu imāsañ ca sattannaṃ viññāṇaṭṭhitīnaṃ imesañ ca dvinnaṃ āyatanānaṃ samudayañ ca atthagamañ ca assādañ ca ādīnavañ ca nissaraṇañ ca yathābhūtaṃ viditvā anupādā vimutto hoti, ayaṃ vuccati Ānanda bhikkhu paññāvimutto.

aṭṭha kho ime Ānanda vimokhā. katame aṭṭha. rūpī rūpāni passati.[1] ayaṃ paṭhamo vimokho. ajjhattaṃ arūpasaññī bahiddhā rūpāni passati. ayaṃ dutiyo vimokho. subhan t' eva adhimutto hoti. ayaṃ tatiyo vimokho. sabbaso rūpasaññānaṃ samatikkamā paṭighasaññānaṃ atthagamā nānattasaññānaṃ amanasikārā ananto ākāso ti ākāsānañcāyatanaṃ upasampajja viharati. ayaṃ catuttho vimokho. sabbaso ākāsānañcāyatanaṃ samatikkamma anantaṃ viññāṇan ti viññāṇañcāyatanaṃ upasampajja viharati. ayaṃ pañcamo vimokho. sabbaso viññāṇañcāyatanaṃ samatikkamma n' atthi kiñ cī ti ākiñcaññāyatanaṃ upasampajja viharati. ayaṃ chaṭṭho vimokho. sabbaso ākiñcaññāyatanaṃ samatikkamma nevasaññānāsaññāyatanaṃ upasampajja viharati. ayaṃ sattamo vimokho. sabbaso nevasaññānāsaññāyatanaṃ samatikkamma saññāvedayitanirodhaṃ upasampajja viharati. ayaṃ aṭṭhamo vimokho. ime kho Ānanda aṭṭha vimokhā.

yato kho Ānanda bhikkhu ime aṭṭha vimokhe anulomam pi samāpajjati, paṭilomam pi samāpajjati, anulomapaṭilomam pi samāpajjati, yatthicchakaṃ yadicchakaṃ yāvaticchakaṃ samāpajjati pi vuṭṭhāti pi, āsavānañ ca khayā anāsavaṃ cetovimuttiṃ paññāvimuttiṃ diṭṭhe va dhamme sayaṃ abhiññā sacchikatvā upasampajja viharati, ayaṃ vuccati Ānanda bhikkhu ubhatobhāgavimutto, imāya ca Ānanda ubhatobhāgavimuttiyā aññā ubhatobhāgavimutti uttaritarā vā paṇītatarā vā n' atthī ti. idam avoca bhagavā. attamano āyasmā Ānando bhagavato bhāsitaṃ abhinandī ti.

[1] These eight are stages in meditation. The first one is the simple contemplation of some material object in order to compose the mind.

Translate into Pali :—

(From the dialogue between the Buddha and the wanderer Poṭṭhapāda.)

" Sir, does (*nu*) the fortunate one declare just one summit (*aggo*)-of-perception, or (*udāhu*) (does he) declare many (*puthu*) summits-of-perception ? "

" I declare one summit-of-perception, Poṭṭhapāda, and I also declare many summits-of-perception."

" But in what way, sir, (does) the fortunate one declare one summit-of-perception and also declare many summits-of-perception ? "

" In whatever way, Poṭṭhapāda, (one) reaches (*phus*) peace of mind, just so I declare a summit-of-perception, thus, Poṭṭhapāda, I declare one summit-of-perception and also I declare many summits-of-perception."

" Sir, does (*nu*) perception occur first, afterwards knowledge, or (does) knowledge occur first, afterwards perception, or (do) perception and knowledge occur simultaneously ? "

" Perception, Poṭṭhapāda, occurs first, afterwards knowledge, moreover from-the-occurrence-of-perception is the-occurrence-of-knowledge (i.e. results from, expressed simply by the ablative and *hoti*). He (i.e. the person engaged in meditation, who was being discussed) understands thus : " In fact, from-this-condition (stem of pronoun assimilated to following *p* > *pp*) my knowledge occurred." Even (*api*) through this course, Poṭṭhapāda, it (*etaṃ*) (is) to be ascertained (*vid*) how perception occurs first, afterwards knowledge, from-the-occurrence-of-perception, moreover, is the-occurrence-of-knowledge."

" Is (*nu*) perception the soul of a man, sir, or (is) one (thing) perception, another the soul ? "

" What now (*kim pana*) (do) you, Poṭṭhapāda, assume a soul ? "

" I assume a gross soul, sir, material, which-is-(made)-of-the-four-elements, which-is-feeding-on-solid-food."

" Yet (*hi*) if your soul were (conditional tense) gross, Poṭṭhapāda, material, of-the-four-elements, feeding-on-solid-food, in that case, Poṭṭhapāda, for you (*te*) perception would be one thing, soul another. Then (*tad*) through this course.

Poṭṭhapāda, it (is) to be ascertained how perception will be one (thing), soul another. Just let this gross, material, four-element, solid-food-feeding soul be (*tiṭṭhatu*), Poṭṭhapāda : so (*atha*) this man's perceptions occur (as) one (thing), (his) perceptions cease (as) another. Through this course, Poṭṭhapāda, it (is) to be ascertained how perception will be one (thing), soul another."

LESSON 30

Desiderative Conjugation

A special conjugation and certain derivatives from it are sometimes used to express the desire to do an action. This conjugation is called the " desiderative " (*tumicchattha*). The root is reduplicated, the reduplicating syllable being in a weak form, and the suffix *sa* is added to form a stem which is inflected according to the first conjugation. An adjective (stem *sa*) and a feminine abstract noun (stem *sā*) are also formed. Apart from a few forms in ordinary use the desiderative may be regarded as a " poetic " conjugation, being largely restricted to verse. Examples :—

vi-kit (I) (" to cure ")	*vicikicchati*, *vicikicchā* (in common use), " be uncertain "
gup	*jigucchati*, *jegucha* (adj.) (in common use), " be disgusted with "
ghas	*jighacchati* (verse), " desire to eat," " be hungry "
vi-ji	*vijigīsati* (not in *Dīgha*), " desire to conquer "
tij (I) (" to sharpen ", " to bear ")	*titikkhā*, " forbearance "
pā	*pipāsita* (pp. in common use), *pipāsin* (adj.), " desire to drink," " be thirsty "
	pipāsa (adj., also common, has pejorative meaning) " drunken ", " drunkard "

man — *vīmaṃsati, vīmaṃsā, vīmaṃsin* (in common use), ("desire to think") "investigate"

vac — *vavakkhati* (verse), "desire to speak"

(s)su — *sussūsati, sussūsā* (in common use), "desire to hear"

har — *jigiṃsamāno* (irregular formation) (present participle, verse), "desire to take," "wish for"

ni-har — *nijigiṃsitar* (agent noun, in common use), "coveter," "acquisitor"

(*kit*, "cure" > *tikicchati* may also be classed here; it is not found in the *Dīgha*. The root has two alternative reduplications, with *ci-* or *ti-*, with different meanings.)

"Root" Aorist

The "root" aorist, which is rarely found except in verse, is so called by historical philologists because the inflections are added directly to the root, not to a stem (historically in the ordinary *-i* aorist the *-i* is a stem suffix, not an inflection, likewise in *addasā*, etc., we have an *-a* stem).

Examples :—

hū

	Singular	Plural
3rd person	*ahū̆, ahud* (junction form) "it was", "there was"	*ahuṃ* or *ahū* (both verse)
2nd person	(*ahū̆*)	—
1st person	(*ahuṃ*)	(*ahuṃ*) (*ahumhā̆* belongs to the ordinary aorist system : Lesson 4)

(In *Dīgha* prose the final *-u* is short in the 3rd singular.)

gam

	Singular	Plural
3rd person	*agā̆*	*agū̆* (verse)
2nd person	(*agā̆*)	(*aguttha*—Grammarians)
1st person	(*agaṃ*)	(*agamhā*)

(In *Dīgha* prose only from *adhi-gam* > *ajjhagā*.)

ahu(*d*) is generally used impersonally: " there was " (e.g. with possessive genitive).

Verse

So far we have restricted ourselves (except for a few incidental verses in the reading passages) to the ordinary prose language of the *Dīgha Nikāya*, which is sufficiently typical of the Pali prose in which most of the Canon is written. We must, however, to complete this introductory survey of Pali, consider the main features of Pali verse, which likewise are well exemplified in the *Dīgha*. The Canon contains probably 15,000–20,000 verses. These are mostly collected in books consisting entirely, or almost entirely, of verse, but some are scattered about in the prose texts as in the *Dīgha Nikāya* itself. The verses of the *Dīgha Nikāya* illustrate their most important linguistic and metrical characteristics. The linguistic features to remark are twofold: poetic licence and the use of archaic forms obsolete in everyday speech. The main characteristic of the metres is that they are quantitative, that is that the rhythm is determined purely by the lengths of the syllables, the effect of any stress (" accent ") being negligible.

Poetic licence is most noticeable in the freedom of word order in verse. Since the inflections generally show the relations between the words in a sentence almost any deviation from the prose order is possible without serious change of meaning (the emphasis will be different, and indeed the metrical form provides special possibilities for emphasis by placing words in rhythmically prominent positions), though for beginners it adds greatly to the difficulty of disentangling the meaning. Secondly, the need to fit the sentence to the metre influences the choice of vocabulary, so that unusual synonyms and rare words may be used. Thirdly, superfluous or redundant words may be inserted to fill up lines of verse, especially indeclinables (*nipāta*) of merely emphatic or otherwise vague meaning. A prefix may be dropped or added where the meaning of the sentence will tolerate a slight change of nuance. Fourthly, the making of junction (*sandhi*) is more variable than in prose, and may be decided by metrical requirements rather than grammatical usage. Fifthly, certain syllables may be lengthened or shortened to suit the rhythm of the metre. Vowels linking suffixes to roots (less often prefixes) as well as final vowels are especially susceptible to this treatment, though this form of licence is not of very frequent occurrence.

Examples of poetic licence :—

Lengthened final :

ramatī (3rd singular present of *ram* (I), " delight ")
heṭhayī (aorist of *heṭh* (VII), " harass ")

Shortened final :

gihi (for *gihī* : *gihin* = " house-dwelling ")
santŏ (perhaps we should write *santa*)
Buddhāna (genitive plural, for *-ānaṃ*)
kammăṃ (perhaps we should write *kamma*)
chetva (for *-tvā*, gerund of *chid*).

Junction between root and suffix lengthened :

satīmanto

—shortened :

jānahi

Junction between prefix and root lengthened :

sūgatiṃ.

Archaic forms are kept alive to a limited extent by being preserved in poems and songs handed down from past centuries. Though not acceptable in ordinary speech, they may be felt appropriate for poetic expression just because of their purely poetic associations. They may also be felt to have greater dignity and power than everyday forms. The obscurity which may result is not always avoided by poets, on the contrary a certain mystification and portentousness may be deliberately sought. We thus meet in Pali verse with a residue of ancient grammatical forms, among which we may note here some characteristic or frequent ones :—

Nominative plural in *āse* : *sāvakāse* (= *sāvakā*)
gatāse (= *gatā*)
Imperative 1st plural in *mu* instead of *ma* : *jānemu*
Optative 3rd singular in *e* instead of *eyya* : *ādise* (= *ādiseyya;* from *ā-dis* (I), "dedicate")
Optative 1st plural in *mu* instead of *yyāma* : *pucchemu*
Use of root aorist, e.g. 3rd plural in *uṃ* : *akaruṃ* (for *akaṃsu*), *āpāduṃ* (for *āpādiṃsu*)
Another unusual aorist : *abhida* (for *abhindi*)
Future of *hū* : *hessati* (= *bhavissati*)
Infinitive in *tāye* : *dakkhitāye* (= *daṭṭhuṃ*)
Gerund in (*t*)*vāna* rare in prose : *caritvāna*, *disvāna*, *katvāna*, *sutvāna*

Middle (*attanopada*) forms not current in prose :—

vande (= *vandāmi*)
amhāse (= *amhā*)
karomase (= *karoma*)
ārabhavho (= *ārabhatha*, imperative)
vademase (= *vadeyyāma*)
āsīne (locative singular of the present participle middle of the verb *ās*, "to sit," itself almost extinct—replaced by *ni-sīd*).

We have noted in Lessons 28 and 29 and earlier in this lesson that the denominative, intensive, desiderative, and "root" aorist are more frequent in verse.

Where two parallel forms exist, one with assimilation and consequent obscurity and one with a clear articulation through a linking vowel between stem and suffix, the form with assimilation will usually be more frequent in verse and sometimes extinct in prose :—

dajjā (optative of *dā*, from the reduplicated stem *dad* + the ancient optative inflection *yā*(*t*), 3rd singular)
jaññā (= *jāneyya*)
kassāma (= *karissāma*).

Other archaic forms :—

diviyā (= *dibbā*, ablative)
poso (= *puriso*)
tuvaṃ (= *tvaṃ*)
duve (= *dve*)
addakkhiṃ (= *addasaṃ*)
-bhi (= *-hi*, instrumental plural).

Other poetic forms :—

caviya (= *cavitvā*)
ramma (= *ramaṇīya*).

As examples of vocabulary not used in prose we may list a few words here.

brū (I)	*brūhi* (imperative 2nd singular) " say ", " call "
ram (I)	*ramati* (also present middle 1st singular *rame*) " delight ", " enjoy "
vid (II)	*vindati* " find " (for *labh*)
ambujo	fish (" water-born ")
mahī	the earth
suro	god
have (ind.)	truly, surely
ve (ind.)	surely.

In scanning Pali verse the following two rules apply :—

(1) A syllable having its vowel short and followed by not more than one consonant is short (*lahu*).
(2) A syllable having its vowel long, or followed by *ṃ* or by more than one consonant, is long (*garu*).

There are also certain complications arising from minor discrepancies between the standard orthography and the original pronunciation. These arose over variant pronunciations of the semi-vowels *y*, *r*, and *v* in some combinations (more rarely over the nasals). Some examples are :—

-cariya = —⏑ (**-carya*)
iriyati = —⏑⏑ (**iryati*)
sirīmant (" beautiful ", " fortunate ") = —— (**srīmant*)
(but *sirī̆*, " beauty, " fortune " = ⏑⏓)
vya- = ⏑⏑ (*viya-*, as sometimes written)
veḷuriyo (" lapis lazuli ") = —⏑⏑—
ariya = usually —⏑ (**arya*), sometimes = —⏑⏑ (**āriya*)
viriya = sometimes —⏑ (**virya*) but sometimes —⏑⏑ (*vīriya*, which is sometimes so written)
suriyo = sometimes —— (**suryo*) but sometimes —⏑— (*sūriyo*, which is sometimes so written).

In the word *brāhmaṇo*, *br-* does not function as two consonants, hence a preceding syllable will be short if its vowel is short (**bamhaṇo* ?). Occasionally other conjuncts also fail to " make position " (make a preceding syllable long).

Though all Pali metres are quantitative, a new style of poetry had come into fashion in the 5th or 4th century B.C. which may be called the " musical " style. In the metres of this style the opposition of long and short syllables, that one long equals two shorts, is exact and inflexible in the same way as a note and two notes of half its value in music. The new metres had in fact taken their rhythms from music. In the older metres, which remained in use, though not uninfluenced by the new, the opposition of quantities is approximate only, so that the number of syllables in a line is still felt to be of decisive importance.

A " verse " usually contains four lines (*pādas*), being a quatrain, much more rarely six lines. Rhyme is not used.

Most important metres :—

" Old " metres (number of syllables per line constant, with only rare " resolution " of a long into two shorts, giving an extra syllable, under the influence of the " new " metres) :—

vatta (epic narrative metre : only approximately quantitative) eight syllables per line, the contrasting cadences of alternate lines giving a verse of two dissimilar lines repeated ; in the epic style there is a tendency to use this as a line of sixteen syllables not organized in verses, which is very appropriate and flexible for continuous narrative

⏓ (or ⏑⏑) ⏓ ⏓ ⏓ ⏑ ⏑⏑/– – ⏓ | ⏓ ⏓ ⏓ ⏓ ⏑ – ⏑ ⏓ × 2

(with these usually) ⏓ – ⏑ – { ⏑ ⏑ ⏑ / – ⏑ ⏑ / – ⏑⏑/– – / – ⏑ – / ⏑ ⏑ – / – – ⏑ }

anuṭṭhubha (the archaic form of *vatta*, in which the alternate lines are not contrasted)

⏓ ⏓ ⏓ ⏓ ⏑ – ⏑ ⏓ × 4 (the cadences of the prior *vatta* line are also admitted)

tuṭṭhubha-jagatī, normally eleven (*tuṭṭhubha*) or twelve (*jagatī*) syllables per line ; these two metres, which have different cadences, are freely mixed, though they may also be used separately ; there is a caesura (slight pause) after either the fourth or the fifth syllable

⏓ (or ⏑⏑) – ⏑ –, ⏓, ⏑ ⏓ – ⏑ – ⏓ × 4 (*tuṭṭhubha*) (caes. in one of the marked positions)

⏓ (or ⏑⏑) – ⏑ –, ⏓, ⏑ ⏓ – ⏑ – ⏑ ⏓ × 4 (*jagatī*) (caes. in one of the marked positions)

by mixture of an opening with caesura at the fifth with a continuation as per caesura at the fourth we occasionally find a *tuṭṭhubha* of twelve syllables or a *jagatī* of thirteen :

⏓ – ⏑ – –, ⏓ ⏑ ⏓ – ⏑ – ⏓ (*tu.*)

⏓ – ⏑ – –, ⏓ ⏑ ⏓ – ⏑ – ⏑ ⏓ (*ja.*).

" New " metres (total quantity of each line constant, the unit in counting being the *mattā* = quantity of one short syllable ; number of syllables variable) :—

mattāchandas (" measure-metre "), (cadence fixed, being the last five or six syllables, rest widely variable provided the total quantity is constant ; there are always two dissimilar lines repeated) :

vetālīya (lines one and three contain fourteen *mattās*, two and four contain sixteen ; cadence — ⏑ — ⏑ ⏓)

opacchandasaka (as *vetālīya*, but with two extra *mattās* in each line resulting from the longer cadence — ⏑ — ⏑ — ⏓)

(very rarely, *vetālīya* and *opacchandasaka* are mixed) (another metre originally of this class is the *svāgatā*, which being less flexible is usually classified under *akkharacchandas*, see below)

gaṇacchandas (" bar-metre ") (not found in the *Dīgha Nikāya* : strictly musical and exactly quantitative like musical rhythms) :

gīti (two or three lines of thirty *mattās* each, each only theoretically divisible into two quarter verses ; each of the two lines is organized in eight bars, called *gaṇa*, of four *mattās* each, there being a " rest " of two *mattās* at the end ; the characteristic rhythm is | ⏑⏑ — | ⏑ — ⏑ | = 2 bars, though this is simply a base on which variation is very freely made)

ariyā (a line of thirty *mattās*, as in *gīti*, followed by a line of twenty-seven *mattās*, the cadence being syncopated).

Derived metres (these represent a third phase, which subsequently became the dominant style in the literature, along with a somewhat restricted form of the *vatta* for continuous narrative ; the tendency is for both the quantity and the number of syllables to be fixed. In the Pali Canon these metres still retain a good deal of flexibility, whilst in later Indian literature they are given forms absolutely fixed except for the last syllable of each line) :—

akkharacchandas ("syllable-metre")

samavutta (four similar lines) :—

upajāti (a form of *tuṭṭhubha*, fixed)

⏓–⏑––⏑⏑–⏑–⏓ × 4

rathoddhatā (a form of *vetālīya* line, fixed)

–⏑–⏑⏑⏑–⏑–⏑⏓ × 4

vaṃsaṭṭhā (a form of *jagatī*, fixed)

⏓–⏑––⏑⏑–⏑–⏑⏓ × 4

pamitakkharā (derived from *gaṇacchandas*)

⏕–⏑–⏑ ⏑⏑–⏑⏑⏓ × 4

rucirā (derived from *jagatī* by resolution of fifth syllable)

⏓–⏑–⏑⏑⏑⏑–⏑–⏑⏓ × 4

aḍḍhasamavutta (two dissimilar lines, repeated) :—

pupphitaggā (a particular form of *opacchandasaka*, fixed)

⏑⏑ ⏑⏑ ⏑⏑–⏑–⏑–⏓ | ⏑⏑ ⏑⏑ – ⏑⏑ – ⏑–⏑–⏓ × 2

svāgatā

– ⏑–⏑ / ⏑⏑– – – ⏕ ⏓ | – ⏑–⏑ / ⏑⏑– – – ⏑⏑–⏓ × 2

visamavutta (four dissimilar lines) :—

upaṭṭhitappacupita (probably derived from *mattāchandas*)

– – – ⏑⏑–⏑–⏑–⏑⏑– – | ⏕– ⏑⏑ ⏑⏑–⏑–⏑–... |
⏑⏑ ⏑⏑ ⏑⏑ ⏑⏑– | ⏑⏑ ⏑⏑ ⏑⏑ ⏑⏑ ⏑⏑–⏑⏑–⏓ × 1

uggatā (derived from *gaṇacchandas*)

⏑⏑–⏑–⏑ ⏑⏑–⏑ | ⏑ ⏑⏑ ⏑⏑ –⏑–⏑– |
⏕ ⏑ ⏕ ⏑ ⏑⏑–⏑⏑– | ⏑⏑–⏑–⏑ ⏑⏑–⏑–⏑⏓ × 1

Vocabulary (N.B.—Some of these words and forms are found only in poetry)

Verbs :—

adhi-(ṭ)ṭhā (I)	*adhiṭṭhāti*	fix one's attention on, resolve on
abhi-ni(r)-dis (I*)	*abhiniddisati*	declare
abhi-pāl (VII)	*abhipāleti*	protect
abhi-bhū (I)	*abhibhavati*	conquer, rule over
abhi-vass (I)	*abhivassati*	rain on
abhi-vi-(s)saj[1] (I)	*abhivi(s)sajati*	dispense
ā-car (I)	*ācarati*	conduct oneself
ā-vas (I)	*āvasati*	dwell in, live in
iriy (I*)	*iriyati*	move, move about, go on (lit. and fig.)
o-gāh (I)	*ogāhati*	plunge into
ghas (I)	*ghasati*	devour
(j)jal (I)	*jalati*	blaze
nand (I)	*nandati*	rejoice, be pleased
nī (I)	*neti*	lead, draw (passive: *nīyati*)
(p)paṭi-gam (I)	*paṭigacchati*	go back
pari-(s)saj[2] (I)	*palissajati*	embrace
(p)pa-vap (I)	*pavapati*	sow
(v)vaj (I)	*vajati*	go
var (I)	*varati*	choose
(or (VII) *vā̆reti*—preferred by Aggavaṃsa, *Sd.* 559)		
vi-pac (III)	*vipaccati*	ripen, have a result, bear fruit
(s)saj [2] (I)	*sajati*	embrace
subh (I)	*sobhati*	shine, be glorious
heṭh (VII)	*heṭheti/heṭhayati*	harass

Nouns :—

aggatā	pre-eminence, supremacy
anvāyiko	follower
apanū̆danaṃ	driving away, removing (this word occurs only in a few verses where the metre requires *ū*, which may be licence—though this is unusual in a root vowel: root *nud*, "drive")

asāhasaṃ	non-violence
ahiṃsā	harmlessness
aheṭhako	non-harasser
ādhipati (masc.)	lord
ānando	joy
ālayo	home
-āvaho	bringing
indakhīlo	royal stake (marking the royal threshold, also as a symbol of firmness : Inda is the old name of Sakka, king of the gods, hence a title for any king)
uttāso	terror
udaraṃ	belly, lap, bosom
udikkhitar (masc.)	looker at
uposatho	observance day, sabbath
ubbādhanā	imprisonment
ubbego	apprehension, anxiety
ūru (fem.)	thigh
oṭṭhavacittaka	a kind of bird
kanakaṃ	gold
karo	hand
kiñjakkhaṃ	stamen, filament
kukkuṭako	cock (wild cock)
kulīrako	a kind of bird
kokilo	cuckoo (Indian cuckoo)
koñco	heron
(*k*)*kodho*	anger
khantī	forgivingness, toleration
khīlo	stake (for marking boundaries : ~ *chid* = to cut down a stake, to obliterate a boundary, figuratively break out of confinement)
-gamo	going
ghammo	summer
caraṇaṃ	foot
janatā	the people
jananī	bearer (birth), producer
jīvaṃjīvako	a kind of partridge (said to cry *jīva* = " live ! ")

taco	skin
tanu (neut.)	body
tapas	asceticism
tuṇḍikīro	gourd (used as a pot—i.e. a natural pot, not man-made)
tuttaṃ	goad (for driving elephants or cattle)
tomaraṃ	lance
thanaṃ	breast
daṇḍamānavakaṃ	a kind of bird
dijo	bird (" twice-born ")
divo	sky, heaven
naṅgalo	plough
nayanaṃ	eye
nalinī	lotus pool
nāsanaṃ	destroying
nibhā	lustre, brilliance
paritajjanā	threatening, intimidation
paligho	bar (holding a door)
pekkhitar (masc.)	looker on, watcher, observer
pokkharaṇī	lotus pool
pokkharasātako	a kind of bird
macco	mortal
manujo	human being
mamattaṃ	(" mine-ness "), possessiveness, selfishness
mayūro	peacock
mahī	the earth
mānuso	man, human being
mudutā	suppleness
muni (masc.)	recluse
reṇu (masc.)	pollen
lakkhaṇaṃ	mark, special quality, excellence, shapeliness, definition
locanaṃ	eye
vaṅkaṃ	hook
vāto	wind
vāri (neut.)	water
sālikā	myna
suko	parrot
suro	god

susu (masc.)	boy, young (of animals)
soceyyaṃ	purity

Adjectives :

aṅgīrasa (fem. -*ī*)	radiant
accaṃkusa	beyond the hook (*aṃkuso*, elephant hook), defying the hook (an elephant in " rut ")
aneja	imperturbable
appaka	little
abhitatta (from *tap*, p.p.)	overheated, exhausted by heat
abhiyogin	expert, proficient
abhiruda	resounding with
amata	deathless (neut. = immortality ; ambrosia, the drink of the immortals according to the Brahmanical myths—in this latter sense, with metonymy, the word is used by Buddhists as a poetic synonym for *nibbāna*) [1]
amama (= *a-mama*, " not-mine ")	not possessive, unselfish
āyuta	full of (p.p. *ā-yu* (I), " mix ")
uttama	highest
upaghātin	harming
ussuka	eager
ekodi	concentrated
etādisa	this sort (of)
kaṅkhin	doubting, in doubt
kovida	learned, knowing thoroughly
gihin	house-dwelling, one living " in the world "
jālin	net-like (Buddhas and other " great men ", i.e. emperors, are said to have net-like hands and feet, amongst other extraordinary bodily marks : their four fingers are straight and of equal length, giving the impression of network)

[1] According to the Buddhists the gods are not immortal. Liberation from existence, from transmigration, however understood, means no more dying.

dassaneyya	beautiful
nipaka	wise
pariggaha	possessing
pākima	fruitful, ripening
piyadassana	lovable sight, whose appearance inspires affection
pubba	before, former
purima	former, earlier
phulla	blossoming, blossomed
bhogin	possessing, enjoying
-maya	consisting of, made of
missa	mixed
mogha	false, erroneous, excluded
rucira	splendid
vaggu	soft (especially of sounds)
vara	excellent, good
vāma	lovely
viceyya	inscrutable (this meaning is probably correct, but the form is uncertain)
-vidha	kind (of, manner), -fold
vimala	free from dirt
visāci	sidelong, furtive
vediya	known (as noun "thing known", "information")
vellita	wavy
sacca	true
sammatta	intoxicated, maddened
sukumāra	delicate
sukhuma	fine, subtle
succhavi	pleasant to the skin (*chavi* fem.)
sudassana	beautiful
sumedhasa	very intelligent
sedaka	sweating

Past Participles:

abhipatthita (*abhi-patth* (VII))	yearned for
abhirata (*abhi-ram*)	enjoying, taking pleasure in

avyākata (*vi-ā-kar*, negative)	unexplained, undetermined, indeterminate
gathita (*gath* (II))	tied
ghasta (*ghas* (I))	devoured
danta (*dam*)	tamed, restrained
pasaṭa ((*p*)*pa-sar*)	stretched out, frank, open
piyāyita (denom. from *piya*)	held dear, beloved
purakkhata (*pura*(*s*)-*kar*)	facing, in front
visaṭa (*vi-sar*)	spread, staring

Gerunds:

ūhacca (*u*(*d*)-*han* or *o-han*)	having knocked out
caviya (*cu*)	having passed away
patvā ((*p*)*pa-ap*(*p*) or (*p*)*pa-āp*)	having attained

Future Passive Participle:

ramma (*ram*)	delightful

Pronoun:

ta(*d*) . . . *ta*(*d*) . . .	that/the . . . (is) the same thing as that/the . . .

Indeclinables:

ahe	ah !
iva (enclitic)	like
u	emphatic enclitic particle added to other indeclinables, thus *atha* + *u* > *atho*
kasmā	why ?, wherefore ?
puratthā	(also means) formerly
samattaṃ	completely, perfectly

Prefixes:

ati-	very, exceedingly (prefixed to adjectives in poetry)
du(*r*)-	(also means) hard, difficult
su-	(also means) very (prefixed to adjectives in poetry)

EXERCISE 30

Passages for reading :—

(*vatta*, or *anuṭṭhubha* in transition to *vatta*)

yena Uttarakurū [1] rammā, Mahā-Neru [1] sudassano,
manussā tattha jāyanti amamā apariggahā.

na te bījaṃ pavapanti, na pi nīyanti naṅgalā,
akaṭṭhapākimaṃ sāliṃ paribhuñjanti mānusā.

akaṇaṃ athusaṃ suddhaṃ sugandhaṃ taṇḍulapphalaṃ
tuṇḍikīre pacitvāna, tato bhuñjanti bhojanaṃ.

* * * * *

tattha niccaphalā rukkhā nānādijagaṇāyutā
mayūrakoñcābhirudā kokilābhi hi [2] vaggubhi.

jīvaṃjīvakasadd' ettha atho oṭṭhavacittakā
kukkuṭakā kuḷīrakā vane pokkharasātakā. (*anuṭṭhubha*)

sukasālikasadd' ettha daṇḍamānavakāni ca,
sobhati sabbakālaṃ sā Kuveranalinī sadā.

ito sā uttarā disā iti naṃ ācikkhatī jano. (*anuṭṭhubha*)
yaṃ disaṃ abhipāleti, mahārājā yasassi so —

yakkhānaṃ ādhipati Kuvero iti nāma so
ramati naccagītehi yakkhehi purakkhato.[3]

[1] In ancient times it was believed that there were four continents, India, called in Pali Jambudīpo, being the southern continent bordered on the north by the Himālaya. Beyond the impenetrable mountains lay the semi-mythical northern continent, called Uttarakuru—normally inflected in the plural as the name of the people living there. In Uttarakuru, or perhaps on its border, was Mount Neru, standing at the centre of the land mass of the earth. This was a mythical or cosmological conception, and the mountain was supposed to be inhabited by gods. Later, as geographical knowledge extended, the Utopian Uttarakuru receded to the antipodes and Neru was assimilated to the concept of the North Pole as the Earth's axis. Thus the Commentary (*Sumaṅgala Vilāsinī*) tells us that when it is midnight in Jambudīpo it is midday in Uttarakuru, sunrise in the eastern continent and sunset in the western continent. In the first line there is resolution of fourth syllable, or read *yen'*.

[2] An easier variant is *-ādīhi*, " etc." There is a rare use of *abhi* as indeclinable with accusative, meaning " on ", " among " (the trees), but no accusative here.

[3] Two lines of this verse are a syllable short, add emphatic particles? There are parallel verses with different gods, for the four directions, some of which fit the metre, so this may be a clumsy substitution of names.

(*vatta*)

vande te pitaraṃ, bhadde, Timbaruṃ, Suriyavaccase,
yena jātā 'si kalyāṇi, ānandajananī mama.

vāto va sedakaṃ [1] kanto pānīyaṃ va pipāsino
aṅgīrasī piyā me 'si dhammo arahatām [2] iva,

āturass' eva bhesajjaṃ, bhojanaṃ va jighacchato,
parinibbāpaya bhadde jalantam iva vārinā.

sītodakiṃ pokkharaṇiṃ yuttaṃ kiñjakkhareṇunā
nāgo ghammābhitatto va ogāhe te thanūdaraṃ.

accaṃkuso va nāgo ca jitaṃ me tuttatomaraṃ,
kāraṇaṃ na ppajānāmi sammatto lakkhaṇūruyā.

tayi gathitacitto 'smi cittaṃ vipariṇāmitaṃ,
paṭigantuṃ na sakkomi vaṅkaghasto va ambujo.

vāmūru saja maṃ bhadde saja maṃ mandalocane,
palissaja maṃ kalyāṇi etam me abhipatthitaṃ.

appako vata me santo kāmo vellitakesiyā
anekabhāgo sampādi arahante va dakkhiṇā.

yam me atthi kataṃ puññaṃ arahantesu tādisu,
tam me sabbaṅgakalyāṇi tayā saddhiṃ vipaccataṃ.

yam me atthi kataṃ puññaṃ asmiṃ paṭhavimaṇḍale,
tam me sabbaṅgakalyāṇi tayā saddhiṃ vipaccataṃ.

Sakyaputto [3] va jhānena ekodi nipako sato
amataṃ muni jigiṃsāno tam ahaṃ Suriyavaccase.

[1] There is a variant reading *sedataṃ* here which is perhaps preferable. It would be the present participle of a verb *sid* (I) *sedati*, "sweat."

[2] This is a rare case of the lengthening of the vowel of a final *aṃ* under stress of metre, a phenomenon of historical interest. Metrically *aṃ* would be equally satisfactory, and is found in some manuscripts.

[3] The Sakyas were the tribe (living in an independent city state) among whom the Buddha was born, hence he is called *Sakyaputto*.

yathā pi muni nandeyya patvā sambodhim uttamaṃ,
evaṃ nandeyyaṃ kalyāṇi missībhāvaṃ gato tayā.

Sakko [1] ca me varaṃ dajjā Tāvatiṃsānam [2] issaro,
tāhaṃ [3] bhadde vareyyāhe [3] evaṃ kāmo daḷho mama.

sālaṃ va na ciraṃ phullaṃ pitaraṃ te sumedhase
vandamāno namassāmi [4] yassa s' etādisī pajā.

(*tuṭṭhubha*)

pucchāmi brahmānaṃ Sanaṃkumāraṃ [5]
kaṅkhī akaṅkhiṃ paravediyesu
kattha ṭṭhito kimhi ca sikkhamāno
pappoti macco amataṃ brahmalokan ti.[6]

hitvā mamattaṃ manujesu brahme [7]
ekodibhūto karuṇādhimutto
ettha ṭṭhito ettha ca sikkhamāno
pappoti macco amataṃ brahmalokan ti.

(*opacchandasaka* [8])

khantī paramaṃ tapo titikkhā, nibbānaṃ paramaṃ vadanti
Buddhā ;
na hi pabbajito parūpaghātī samaṇo hoti paraṃ viheṭhayanto.

(*rathoddhatā* [9])

geham āvasati ce tathāvidho
aggataṃ vajati kāmabhogīnaṃ,
tena uttaritaro na vijjati,
Jambudīpam abhibhuyya iriyati.

[1] The king of the gods.
[2] *Tāvatiṃsā*, the collective name (plural) of the traditional gods.
[3] Unusual junction of *taṃ* + *ahaṃ*, likewise of *vareyyaṃ* + *ahe*.
[4] Denominative from *namas*, the stem of the indeclinable *namo*.
[5] A name of *brahman*.
[6] This *ti* does not form part of the verse.
[7] *brahme* here means *brāhmaṇa* (a priest is here questioning *brahman*, who replies in this verse), perhaps as polite substitute.
[8] For examples of *vetālīya* see Exercises 18 and 28, ends of first Passages. For an example of mixed *vetālīya-opacchandasaka* see Exercise 26, fourth verse.
[9] For example of *upajāti* see the first verse in Exercise 29.

(*vaṃsaṭṭhā*)

sacce ca dhamme ca dame ca saṃyame
soceyyasīlālayuposathesu ca,
dāne ahiṃsāya asāhase rato
daḷhaṃ samādāya samattam ācari.

pure puratthā purimāsu jātisu,
manussabhūto bahūnaṃ sukhāvaho,
ubbegauttāsabhayāpanūdano
guttīsu rakkhāvaraṇesu ussuko.[1]

(*pamitakkharā*)

pubbaṅgamo [2] sucaritesu ahu
dhammesu dhammacariyābhirato,
anvāyiko bahujan' assa ahu,
saggesu vedayitha puññaphalaṃ.

(*rucirā*)

na pāṇinā na ca pana daṇḍaleḍḍunā
satthena vā maraṇavadhena vā puna,
ubbādhanāya ca paritajjanāya vā
na heṭhayī janatam aheṭhako ahu.

(*pupphitaggā*)

caviya punar idhāgato samāno
karacaraṇāmudutañ ca jālino ca,
atirucirasuvaggudassaneyyaṃ
paṭilabhatī daharo susūkumāro.

(*svāgatā*)

chetvā khīlāṃ chetvā palighaṃ | indakhīlam ūhaccamanejā [3] |
te caranti suddhā vimalā | cakkhumatā [4] dantā susunāgā ||

[1] Note the alliteration in this verse—an ornament prominent in early Indian poetic theory.

[2] In this word the accusative inflection is retained irregularly in the first member of the compound (and *ṃ* is assimilated to *g*, becoming *ṅ*) ; the meaning is " going before ", " leading ".

[3] *m* here is junction consonant.

[4] i.e. by the Buddha, and in the metaphor by the driver.

(*upaṭṭhitappacupita*)

akkodhañ ca adhiṭṭhahī adāsi ca dānaṃ |
vatthāni ca sukhumāni succhavīnī |
purimatarabhavaṭhito |
abhivisaji mahim iva suro abhivassaṃ ||

taṃ katvāna ito cuto divaṃ upapajja |
sukataṃ ca phalavipākam ānubhotvā |
kanakatanunibhataco |
idha bhavati suravarataroriva [1] Indo ||

(*uggatā*)

na ca vīsaṭaṃ na ca visāci |
na ca pana viceyyapekkhitā |
ujju [2] tatha pasaṭam ujjumano |
piyacakkhunā bahujanaṃ udikkhitā ||

abhiyogino ca nipuṇā ca |
bahu pana nimittakovidā |
sukhumanayanakusalā manujā |
piyadassano ti abhiniddisanti naṃ ||

piyadassano gihi pi santŏ |
bhavati bahŭnaṃ piyāyito |
yadi ca na bhavati gihī, samaṇo |
bhavatī piyo bahŭnăṃ sokanāsano ||

Translate into Pali :—

" I assume a mental soul, sir, having-all-limbs-and-parts (use suffix *-in*), (having-)not-inferior-faculties (i.e. its faculties are perfect)."

" Yet if your soul were mental, Poṭṭhapāda, having-all-limbs-and-parts, having-not-inferior-faculties, in that case also, Poṭṭhapāda, for you perception would be one thing, soul another. Then through this course, Poṭṭhapāda, it is to be ascertained how perception will be one thing, soul another.

[1] The last *r* here is a junction consonant.
[2] In *u(j)ju* the quantity of the first syllable is variable.

Just let this mental soul be, having-all-limbs-and-parts, having-not-inferior-faculties, Poṭṭhapāda: so this man's perceptions occur as one thing, his perceptions cease as another. Through this course, Poṭṭhapāda, it is to be ascertained how perception will be one thing, soul another."

" I assume an immaterial soul, sir, consisting-of-perception."

" Yet if your soul were consisting-of-perception . . . perception would be one thing, soul another . . ."

" But is it possible, sir, for me (ins.) to know this: ' Perception (is) a man's soul,' or ' Perception (is) one (thing), soul another ' ? "

" This (is) hard-knowing (present participle, and sentence initial for emphasis), Poṭṭhapāda, by you (who-)have-other-opinions . . ."

" If, sir, this is by me hard-knowing (not initial), (who-)have-other-opinions . . . however, sir, is (*kiṃ*) the universe eternal ? Only this (is) true, the other false (?) "

" (It is) undetermined, Poṭṭhapāda, by me: the universe (is) eternal, only this (is) true, the other false."

" But, sir, is (*kiṃ*) the universe non-eternal . . ."

" Undetermined . . ."

. . . finite . . . Undetermined . . . non-finite . . . Undetermined . . .

" But, sir, is the life-principle (*jīvaṃ* here is neuter) (the same thing as: use *ta*(*d*) repeated) the body ? Only this (is) true, the other false (?) "

" Undetermined . . ."

" But, sir, is the life-principle one (thing), the body another ? . . ."

" This also, Poṭṭhapāda, (is) undetermined by me . . ."

. . . is the thus-gone after death ? . . . Undetermined . . . is not the thus-gone after death ? . . . Undetermined . . . is and is not the thus-gone after death ? . . . Undetermined . . . neither is nor is not the thus-gone after death ? . . .

" This also, Poṭṭhapāda, (is) undetermined by me . . ."

" Why, sir, (is it) undetermined by the fortunate one ? "

" Poṭṭhapāda, this (is) not (*na h' etaṃ*) connected-with-welfare, not connected-with-the-doctrine . . . does not lead to liberation."

" But what, sir, is determined (explained) by the fortunate one ? "

" ' This (is) unhappiness,' Poṭṭhapāda, (is) determined by me, ' This (is) the-origin-of-unhappiness,' . . . ' This (is) the-cessation-of-unhappiness,' . . . ' This (is) the unhappiness-cessation-going way,' Poṭṭhapāda, (is) determined by me."

PRINCIPAL PARTS OF VERBS

Root	*Con.*	*Pres. 3rd sing.*	*P.p.*	*Aor. 3rd sing.*	*Fut. 3rd sing.*	*Causative*	*Infinitive*	*Gerund*	*F.p.p.*	*Passive*	*Miscellaneous*
añch	(I)	añchati									
atth	(VII)	attheti	atthita								
ap	(IV)	appoti	atta								
ap(p)	(VI)	appoti	atta					-atvā			
app	(VII)		appita								
arah	(I)	arahati									
as	(I)	atthi	bhūta	āsi	bhavissati	(rest from bhū or hū)					pres. part. : samāna, sant opt. : assa, siyā
ah	(substitute for brū)										perfect : āha 3rd sing.
āṇa	(only causative)					āṇāpeti					p.p. of caus. : āṇatta
āp	(V)	āpuṇāti	atta	āpuṇi		āpeti		-atvā			
ās	(I)	āsati	(āsita)	(āsi)			(āsituṃ)				
āsis	(II)	āsiṃsati				āsiṃsāpeti					
i	(I)	eti	ita					-āya -icca			ipv. 2nd sing. : ehi
ikkh	(I)	ikkhati	ikkhita								
iñj	(I)	iñjati	iñjita								
idh	(III)	ijjhati	iddha	ijjhi							
iriy	(I*)	iriyati									
is(a)	(I)	esati	iṭṭha esita				esituṃ				
is(u)	(I)	icchati	icchita		icchissati				(icchitabba)		
kaṅkh	(I)	kaṅkhati	kaṅkhita								
kaḍḍh	(I)	kaḍḍhati						kaḍḍhitvā			
kath	(VII)	katheti	(kathita)	kathesi	(kathessati)		(kathetuṃ)				
kapp	(VII)	kappeti	kappita	kappesi		kappāpeti		kappetvā			
(k)kam	(I)	kamati	kanta	-kami	kamissati		kamituṃ	kamitvā -kamma	kamitabba		intensive : caṅkamati
kam	(VII)	kāmeti	kanta						kamanīya		
kamp	(I)	kampati	kampita			kampeti					
kar	(VI)	karoti	kata	akāsı	karissati	kāreti kārāpeti	kātuṃ	katvā karitvā	kātabba karaṇīya kicca	karīyati kayirati	ipv. 2nd sing. : karohi
(k)kass	(VII)							kassa			
kās	(I)	(kāsati)				kāseti					
ki	(V)	kiṇāti						(kiṇitvā)			
kit	(I)										desid. : vi-cikicchā (tikicchhti)
kir	(I*)	kirati	kiṇṇa	-kiri				-kiriya			
kilam	(I)	kilamati	kilanta		kilamissati	kilameti					
kilis	(III)	kilissati	kiliṭṭha								
kujj	(I)	kujjati	kujjita					kujjitvā			
kuṭ	(VII)	koṭeti		koṭesi							
kup	(III)	kuppati	kupita	kuppi	(kuppissati)						
(k)kus	(I)	kosati		-kosi				kositvā	kositabba		
khaṇ	(I)	khaṇati						khaṇitvā			ipv. 2nd sing. : khaṇāhi
(k)kham	(I)	khamati							khamanīya		
(k)khal	(VII)	khāleti						khāletvā			

Root	Con.	Pres. 3rd sing.	P.p.	Aor. 3rd sing.	Fut. 3rd sing.	Causative	Infinitive	Gerund	F.p.p.	Passive	Miscellaneous
(k)khā	(I)	khāti	khāta	-khāsi			khātuṃ	-khāya		khāyati	
(k)khā	(III)	khāyati									
khād	(I)	khādati	khāyita	khādi					khādanīya		
(k)khip	(I*)	khipati	khitta		khipissati			khipitvā			
(k)khī	(III)	khīyati	khīṇa	khīyi					khīyitabba		
gath	(II)	ganthati	gathita								
gam	(I)	gacchati	gata	agamāsi -gacchi -gañchi	gamissati	gameti	gantuṃ	gantvā -gamma	gantabba gamanīya		root aor. : agā, ipv. of caus. 2nd sing. : gamehi
garah	(I)	garahati	garahita	garahi					garahitabba		
gaves	(I)	gavesati			gavesissati						
(g)gah	(V)	gaṇhāti	gahīta	gahesi		gāheti		gahetvā -gayha			ipv. 2nd sing. : gaṇhāhi
gādh	(I)	gādhati	gāḷha								
gāh	(I)	gāhati	gāḷha	(gāhi)				gāhetvā			
gil	(I*)	gilati									
gup			gutta								desid. : jigucchati
ge	(I)	gāyati	gīta						gāyitabba		
(g)ghar	(I)	gharati									
ghas	(I)	ghasati	ghasta								desid. : jighacchati
ghā	(III)	ghāyati						ghāyitvā			
caj			catta								
car	(I)	carati	carita	acari	carissati	cāreti	carituṃ	caritvā	caritabba		
ci	(V)	cināti	cita						(-ceyya)	cīyati	
cikkh	(I)	cikkhati		-cikkhi	cikkhissati		(cikkhituṃ)				
cu	(I)	cavati	cuta			cāveti		cavitvā			
chaḍḍ	(VII)	chaḍḍeti	chaḍḍita		chaḍḍessati			chaḍḍetvā	chaḍḍetabba		
chad	(VII)	chādeti	(chādita)	chādesi				chādetvā			
chid	(II)	chindati }	chinna	chindi	chindissati checchati }	chedāpeti		chinditvā		chijjati	
chid	(III)	chijjati }									
jan	(III)	jāyati	jāta	-jāyi		janeti					
jar	(III)	jīyati									
(j)jal	(I)	jalati	jalita	-jali	jalissati	jāleti		jalitvā			
ji	(I)	jayati									
ji	(V)	jināti	jita	-jini				-jiya -jinitvā			p.p. active : jitāvin (desid. : jigīsati)
jīr	(I)	jīrati	jiṇṇa								
jīv	(I)	jīvati	jīvita				jīvituṃ		jīvitabba		ipv. 2nd sing. : jīvāhi
(j)jhe	(I)	jhāyati	jhāyita	jhāyi		jhāpeti	jhāyituṃ				
(ñ)ñap	(VII)	ñāpeti	ñatta	ñāpesi	ñāpessati		ñāpetuṃ				
(ñ)ñā	(V)	jānāti	ñāta	jāni aññāsi	jānissati ñassati	ñāpeti	ñātuṃ	ñatvā -ñāya	jānitabba -ñeyya	ñāyati	ipv. 2nd sing. : jānāhi
(ṭ)ṭhā	(I)	tiṭṭhati -ṭhāti -ṭhahati	ṭhita	aṭṭhāsi	ṭhassati -ṭhahissati	ṭhāpeti ṭhapayati	ṭhātuṃ	-ṭhāya -ṭhahitvā			p.p. of caus. : ṭhāpita
takk	(VII)	takketi	takkita								
tacch	(I)	tacchati		tacchi							
tan	(VI)	tanoti									aor. pass. 3rd sing. : atāni
tap	(I)	tapati	tatta								
tapp	(VII)	tappeti		tappesi							
tar	(I)	tarati	tiṇṇa	-tari	tarissati	tāreti	tarituṃ	taritvā			
tas	(III)	tassati	tasita								

tij	(I)										desid. : titikkhā
tij	(VII)	tejeti	tejita	tejesi				tejetvā			
tus	(III)	tussati	tuṭṭha								
(t)thar	(I)	tharati	thata			tharāpeti		tharitvā			
(t)thu	(V)	thunāti		-thuni							
dam			danta								
dah	(I)	dahati	daḍḍha				dahituṃ				
dā	(I)	deti dadāti	dinna (-diṇṇa)	adāsi	dassati	dāpeti	dātuṃ	datvā -dāya	dātabba deyya	dīyati	p.p. of caus. : dapita ipv. 2nd sing. : dehi
dā	(III)	diyati	dinna	-diyi	diyissati	diyāpeti		diyitvā -dāya			
div	(III)	dibbati		dibbi	dibbissati						
dis	(I*)	disati					(disituṃ)	-dissa			
dis	(III)	dissati									
(d)dis	—	passati	diṭṭha	addasā	dakkhiti dakkhissati	dasseti	daṭṭhuṃ	disvā	daṭṭhabba dassanīya	dissati	aor. of caus. : dassesi p.p. of caus. : dassita
dis	(VII)	deseti	desita	desesi	desessati		desetuṃ				
dev	(VII)			devesi							
dhar	(VII)	dhāreti			dhāressati						
dhā	(I)	dahati	hita	-dahi			-dahituṃ	-dahitvā			
dhā	(III)	dhāyati		-dhāyi			dhātuṃ	-dhāya			
dhāv	(I)	dhāvati	dhāvita					dhāvitvā			
dhū	(V)	dhunāti		-dhuni							
nat	(III)	naccati				nacceti					
nand	(I)	nandati		-nandi			nandituṃ	nanditvā	nanditabba		
nam	(I)	namati	nata			nāmeti					
nas	(III)	nassati	naṭṭha			nāseti					
nah	(II)	nandhati	naddha	-nandhi				-nandhitvā			
nī	(I)	neti	nīta	-nayi	(nessati)	nāyeti	netuṃ	netvā -neyya	netabba	nīyati	
nhā	(III)	n(a)hāyati				nahāpeti		n(a)hatvā			
pac	(I)	pacati	pakka	-paci	pacissati	pāceti		pacitvā			
pac	(III)	paccati									
pat	(I)	patati	patita	-pati	patissati	pāteti		patitvā			ipv. of caus. 2nd sing. : pātehi
pad	(III)	pajjati	panna	pajji apādi	pajjissati	pādeti	pajjituṃ	-pajja	pajjitabba		
pabb	(I)	pabbati									
pass	(I)	passati	(rest from (d)dis)								
pā	(I)	pivati	pīta	apāyi	pivissati	pāyeti	pātuṃ	pivitvā	pātabba peyya		desid. : pipāsati, ger. of caus. : pāyetvā, p.p. of caus. : pāyita
pāy	(I)	pāyati									
pāl	(VII)	pāleti									
pucch	(I)	pucchati	puṭṭha	pucchi	pucchissati		pucchituṃ		pucchitabba		
poth	(VII)	potheti		pothesi							
pus	(VII)	poseti		posesi		posāpeti	posetuṃ				p.p. of caus. : posāpita
pūj	(VII)	pūjeti	pūjita		pūjessati				pūjetabba		
pūr	(I)	(pūrati)	puṇṇa	(pūri)		pūreti					
pes	(VII)	peseti		pesesi							

Root	Con.	Pres. 3rd sing.	P.p.	Aor. 3rd sing.	Fut. 3rd sing.	Causative	Infinitive	Gerund	F.p.p.	Passive	Miscellaneous
phand	(I)	phandati	phandita			phandāpeti					
(p)phar	(I)	pharati	phuṭa					pharitvā			
(p)phal	(I)	phalati		phali	phalissati	phāleti					
(p)phus	(I*)	phusati	phuṭṭha	(-phusi)			phusituṃ	phusitvā phussa	phoṭṭhabba		
bandh	(I)	bandhati	baddha	bandhi	bandhissati			bandhitvā			
budh	(III)	bujjhati	buddha	-bujjhi	bujjhissati				bodhabba		
brū	(I*)	(brūti)									ipv. 2nd sing. : brūhi (cf. ah)
bhakkh	(VII)	bhakkheti	bhakkhita	bhakkhesi				bhakkhayitvā			
bhaj	(I)	bhajati		bhaji	bhajissati			bhajitvā			
bhaṇ	(I)	bhaṇati	(bhaṇita)	(abhaṇi)		bhaṇāpeti		bhaṇitvā		bhaññati	pres. middle 1st sing. : bhaṇe
bhar	(I)		bhata		bharissati						
bhā	(I)	bhāti						-bhāya			
bhās	(I)	bhāsati	bhāsita	abhāsi	bhāsissati		bhāsituṃ		bhāsitabba		ipv. 2nd sing. middle : bhāsassu
bhid	(II)	bhindati	bhinna	(abhida)				bhinditvā (bhetvā)			
bhī	(I)	(bhāyati)	bhīta	(bhāyi)							
bhuj	(I*)	bhujati						bhujitvā			
bhuj	(II)	bhuñjati	bhutta	-bhuñji	bhuñjissati	bhojeti	bhuñjituṃ	bhuñjitvā	bhojanīya		p.p. active : bhuttāvin
bhū	(I)	bhavati -bhoti after paccanu-	bhūta	-bhosi	bhavissati	bhāveti	bhavituṃ	-bhavitvā -bhotvā -bhutvā (-bhuyya)	bhabba		p.p. of caus. : bhāvita
bhū	(VII)	bhāveti		bhāvesi							
makkh	(VII)	makkheti	makkhita								
mad	(III)	majjati	matta						madanīya		
man	(III)	maññati	-mata muta	amaññi	maññissati						desid. : vīmaṃsati pres. middle 1st sing. : maññe
man	(VI)	mannati	mata								
mant	(VII)	manteti	mantita	mantesi		mantāpeti	mantetuṃ	mantetvā			
mar	(III)	mīyati	mata				marituṃ				
mas	(I)	masati	maṭṭha	-masi				masitvā -massa			
mā	(V)	miṇāti	mita								
mān	(VII)	māneti	mānita		mānessati				mānetabba		
māp	(VII)	māpeti	māpita	māpesi	māpessati		māpetuṃ				
muc	(II)	muñcati		(muñci)	muñcissati	muñcāpeti	muñcituṃ				
muc	(III)	muccati	mutta			moceti					
mucch	(I)	mucchati	mucchita		mucchissati				mucchanīya		
mud	(I)	modati	(modita)	modi				moditvā	modanīya		
muh			mūḷha								
yaj	(I)	yajati	yiṭṭha			yajāpeti yājeti	yajituṃ	yajitvā			
yat[1]	(VII)	yādeti	yatta			yādāpeti		yādetvā			ger. of caus. : yādāpetvā
yam	(I)	yamati	yata		yamissati						

[1] *yat* > *yad* is regarded as a sporadic substitution of *d* for *t*, though *d* is generally written.

yā	(I)	yāti	yāta	-yāsi		yāpeti	yātuṃ				ipv. 2nd sing. : yāhi aor. 3rd plur. : ayiṃsu
yāc	(I)	yācati		yāci							
yuj	(II)	yuñjati	yutta			yojeti					
yuj	(VII)	yojeti	yutta	yojesi		yojāpeti					
rakkh	(I)	rakkhati	rakkhita		rakkhissati						
rañj	(I)	rañjati				rañjeti			rajanīya		
rabh	(I)	rabhati	raddha	-rabhi				-rabbha			
ram	(I)	ramati	rata						ramaṇīya		
rādh	(VII)	rādheti	raddha		rādhessati		rādhetuṃ				
ruc	(VII)	roceti		rocesi	rocessati	rocāpeti					
rud	(I*)	rudati									
rudh	(III)	rujjhati	ruddha								
rup	(I*)	rupati						rupitvā			
ruh	(I*)	rūhati ā-ruhati abhi/vi- rŭhati	rūḷha			ropeti ropāpeti		ā-ruyha abhi-rŭhitvā			p.p. of caus. : ropita
ruh	(I)	o-rohati						o-rohitvā			
lakkh	(VII)	lakkheti						lakkhetvā			
labh	(I)	labhati	laddha	labhi alattha	labhissati lacchati			labhitvā	labbha	labbhati	
lip	(II)	limpati	litta								
luj	(III)	lujjati		-lujji							
lup	(II)	lumpati				lumpeti					ger. of caus. : lumpetvā
lū	(V)		lūna								
lok	(VII)	loketi	lokita	lokesi				loketvā			
ḷas	(VII)	ḷāseti						ḷāsitvā			
vac	(I)	vacati	vutta	avoca		vāceti		vatvā	vattabba vacanīya	vuccati	desid. : vavakkhati
(v)vaj	(I)	vajati	vajita	-vaji	vajissati	vājeti	vajituṃ				
vajj	(VII)	vajjeti							vajja		
vañc	(VII)	vañceti	vañcita								
vaṭṭ	(I)	vaṭṭati	vaṭṭa			vaṭṭeti					
vaḍḍh	(I)	vaḍḍhati			vaḍḍhissati	vaḍḍheti					
vatt	(I)	vattati	vatta	vatti	vattissati	vatteti vattāpeti					ipv. 2nd sing. : vattāhi ipv. of caus. 2nd sing. : vattehi p.p. of caus. : vattita
vatt	(VII)	vatteti						vattetvā			
vad	(I)	vadati				vādeti			vaditabba		ipv. 2nd sing. : vadehi pass. of caus. : vajjeti pres. act. 2nd. sing. often vadesi
vad	(VII)	vādeti						vādetvā			
vand	(I)	vandati		vandi	vandissati	vandāpeti					ipv. 2nd sing. : vandāhi
vap	(I)	vapati									
vam	(I)	vamati	vanta		vamissati						
var (choose)	(I ?) or (VII)	varati vareti									

Root	Con.	Pres. 3rd sing.	P.p	Aor. 3rd sing.	Fut. 3rd sing.	Causative	Infinitive	Gerund	F.p.p.	Passive	Miscellaneous
var	(I)	varati	vuta	-vari	varissati			varitvā			
var	(VII)	vāreti		vāresi	vāressati						
vas	(I)	vasati	vuttha vusita	-vasi	vasissati	vāseti	(vasituṃ)	-vasitvā			p.p. active : vusitavant
vass	(I)	vassati	vaṭṭa	avassi	vassissati						
vah	(I)	vahati				vāheti				vuyhati	
vā	(I)	vāti									
vā	(III)	vāyati	vuta	-vāyi	vāyissati	vāpeti					
vās	(VII)	vāseti	vuttha					vāsetvā			
vic	(VII)		vitta					vicca			
vid	(I*)	(not used)				vedeti					
vid	(II)	(vindati)	vidita		vedissati		vindituṃ	viditvā	veditabba vedanīya		
vid	(III)	vijjati									
vid	(VII)	vedeti		vedesi	vedissati						
vidh	(III)	vijjhati	viddha				vijjhituṃ				
vis	(I*)	visati		avisi		veseti	visituṃ	-visitvā -vissa			
vīj	(I)	vījati									
veṭh	(VII)	veṭheti						veṭhetvā			
vedh	(I)	vedhati									
saṃs	(I)	saṃsati	sattha								
sak	(IV)	sakkoti		asakkhi							
sak(k)	(VI)	sakkoti									
sakk	(I)	sakkati	sakkita								
(s)saj [1]	(I)	sajati	saṭṭha	-saji							
(s)saj [2]	(I)	sajati									
sajj								sajja			
sand	(I)	sandati									
sam	(III)		santa								
sambh	(I)	sambhati		-sambhi		sambheti					
sar	(I)	sarati	saṭa saṃ- sarita	-sari		sāreti		sitvā			
(s)sar	(I)	sarati	sarita								
(s)sas	(I)	sasati			sasissati						
sah	(I)	sahati		-sahi				-sayha			
sā	(III)	sāyati	sāyita	sāyi				sāyitvā	sāyanīya		
sār	(VII)	sāreti						sāretvā			
sās	(I)	sāsati	siṭṭha	-sāsi	sāsissati			sāsitvā	sāsitabba		
si	(I)	seti	sayita								pres. part.: sayāna
(s)si			sita								
sikkh	(I)	sikkhati	sikkhita			sikkhāpeti	sikkhituṃ		sikkhitabba		
sic	(II)	siñcati	sitta	-siñci	siñcissati						
sidh	(I)					sedheti					
sis	(II)	siṃsati				siṃsāpeti					
sis	(III)	sissati	siṭṭha								
sis	(VII)	seseti	siṭṭha	sesesi							
(s)sī								-sāya			
sīd	(I)	sīdati	ni-sinna pa-sanna	-sīdi	sīdissati	sīdāpeti sādeti		-sajja			
su	(I)	savati									

(s)su	(IV)	(suṇoti)									ipv. 2nd sing. : suṇohi
(s)su	(V)	suṇāti	suta	assosi	sossati	sāveti	sotuṃ	sutvā	sotabba	sūyati	desid. : sussūsati ipv. 2nd sing. : suṇāhi
suc	(I)	socati		soci		soceti					
sudh	(III)	sujjhati	suddha			sodheti					
subh	(I)	sobhati			sobhissati						
sev	(I)	sevati	sevita	-sevi			sevituṃ		sevitabba		
haṃs	(VII)	haṃseti	haṃsita	haṃsesi				haṃsetvā			
han	(I)	hanati	hata		hanissati hañchati	ghāteti ghātāpeti		(-hacca)	hantabba	haññati	p.p. of caus. : ghāta
har	(I)	harati	hata	ahāsi -hari	harissati	hāreti	harituṃ	haritvā		harīyati	aor. 3rd. sing. : ā/vi-hāsi aor. 1st plur. : ā-harāma desid. : jigiṃsati
hā	(I)	jahati	hīna	-hāsi	(jahissati)	hāpeti		hitvā -hāya	hātabba	hāyati hīyati	
hi	(V)	hiṇāti		ahesi							
hiṇḍ	(I)	hiṇḍati									
his	(II)	hiṃsati	(hiṃsita)								
hū	(I)	hoti	bhūta	ahosi ahu(d)	(hessati) bhavissati		hotuṃ	hutvā			ipv. 2nd sing. : hohi root aor. : ahŭ(d)
heṭh	(VII)	heṭheti		heṭhesi	heṭhessati						

BIBLIOGRAPHY

A choice of authorities on the language, texts, and reference books for further study.

LANGUAGE

Saddanīti (*Sd.*, by Aggavaṃsa, + twelfth century, in Pali. Beautifully and exactly edited by H. Smith, Lund, Gleerup, 1928 . . . the last part of the indices being in preparation by N. Simonsson, with exhaustive indices including a concise dictionary not confined to *Sd.* itself and a synopsis of the grammatical system) : The finest and most comprehensive grammar, and standard authority on all questions of grammatical analysis (usually followed in this book).

Pali Literature and Language (by W. Geiger, originally in German. English translation by Ghosh, perfectly correct except when too literal, University of Calcutta, 1943, and since reprinted) : A historical phonology and morphology with a brief survey of the literature.

A Critical Pali Dictionary (*CPD*, by Trenckner, Andersen, Smith, and others. Vol. I = words beginning with *a*-, Copenhagen, 1924–48, in twelve parts ; Vol. II, Copenhagen, 1960, in progress) : The only comprehensive dictionary, but its scale and careful method have resulted in slow progress.

Pali Tipiṭakaṃ Concordance (F. L. Woodward and others, PTS 1952, in progress) : A basic tool for the study of the grammar and lexis of the Canon.

Abhidhānappadīpikā (by Moggallāna, + twelfth century, in Pali. Edited by the Thera Subhūti with English equivalents, an index, and notes, Colombo, fifth edition, 1938) : A dictionary of the medieval rather than of the Canonical language.

Pali–English Dictionary (*PED*, by T. W. Rhys Davids and W. Stede, PTS, 1921–25, since reprinted) : The fullest dictionary yet completed, but concentrates on etymology rather than on actual usage.

A Dictionary of the Pali Language (by Childers, London, Kegan Paul, Trench, Trübner, 1875) : A dictionary which is old but still important as it gives some words and meanings (Canonical as well as medieval) missed by *PED* ; largely dependent on the *Abhidhānappadīpikā*.

English–Pali Dictionary (by A. P. Buddhadatta, PTS, 1955) : Modern Pali.

A Pali Reader (by Andersen, Copenhagen, 1901) : An introduction to the medieval language of the commentaries, about 1,000 years posterior to the *Dīgha*, consisting mainly of narratives from the Commentary on the *Jātaka* (see below under *Khuddaka Nikāya*).

TEXTS

Tipiṭaka = the Canon of the Theravāda School of Buddhism in Pali (complete editions : in romanized script mostly published by the PTS, in Siamese script, Bangkok, which is more accurate but gives few variant readings, in Sinhalese script, Colombo, in Burmese script, Rangoon ; new ones in Cambodian script, Pnompenh, and in the *devanāgarī* script, Nāḷandā, now in progress) : Consists of the *Vinaya*, *Suttanta*, and *Abhidhamma Piṭakas*.

Vinaya Piṭaka (ed. Oldenberg, London, 1879–83 ; translated by I. B. Horner as the *Book of the Discipline*, five volumes, PTS, 1938–52) : After being originally subordinate to the *dhamma* (*Suttanta*) the book of monastic discipline was promoted to first place by the Theravāda monks. Consequently its commentary and sub-commentaries are of primary importance in exegesis.

Samanta Pāsādikā (by Buddhaghosa, + fifth century, ed. Takakusu, Nagai and Mizuno, PTS, 1924–47) : Commentary (*aṭṭhakathā*) on the *Vinaya Piṭaka*.

Sāratthа Dīpanī (by Sāriputta, + twelfth century, complete edition in 4 vols., Rangoon, 1902–24, unfinished edition in Sinhalese script, ed. Devarakkhita and Medhaṅkara, Colombo, 1914, 1933) : A sub-commentary (*ṭīkā*) on the *Vinaya*, i.e. a commentary on the *Samanta Pāsādikā*, which became the most authoritative exegetical work.

Suttanta Piṭaka (PTS : mostly reprinted 1947–61) : The collection of *dhamma* made after the Parinibbāna of the Buddha. Divided into five *nikāyas* : *Dīgha*, *Majjhima*, *Saṃyutta*, *Aṅguttara*, and *Khuddaka*.

Dīgha Nikāya (three vols. ed. T. W. Rhys Davids and J. E. Carpenter, PTS, reprinted 1947–60) : Translated by T. W. and C. A. F. Rhys Davids as *Dialogues of the Buddha*, PTS, reprinted several times : a very interesting and stimulating translation and notes, though rather free.

" Commentary " = *Sumaṅgala Vilāsinī* (by Buddhaghosa, + fifth century, ed. Rhys Davids, Carpenter and Stede, PTS, 1886–1932).

Līnattha Pakāsinī, Book I, ed. Lily de Silva, 3 vols., PTS, 1970 (by Dhammapāla, + ninth century (?), published in three vols., Rangoon, 1924): The "old" *ṭīkā* (sub-commentary) on the *Dīgha* (i.e. a commentary on the *Sumaṅgala Vilāsinī*).

Sādhu[jana] Vilāsinī (by Ñāṇābhivaṃsa, + eighteenth to nineteenth century, two vols. of this have been published in Rangoon, 1913–23) : The " new " *ṭīkā* on the *Dīgha*.

Majjhima Nikāya (three vols. ed. Trenckner and Chalmers, PTS, reprint 1948–51): Nearest text to *Dīgha* in language and style. Translated by I. B. Horner as *Middle Length Sayings*, PTS, 1954–59.

Saṃyutta Nikāya (five vols. ed. Feer, PTS, reprinted 1960).

Khuddaka Nikāya (twenty-three vols., including) : *Jātaka* (ed. with its commentary in six vols. by Fausbøll, London, Trübner, 1877–96) : The most popular book of the Canon, consisting of about 550 stories or reminders of stories in verse (partly epic in style), which the commentary completes in medieval prose where necessary. Translation, very free, by various scholars, reprinted PTS (three vols.) as *Jātaka Stories*, 1956, including both text and commentary except for the introductory narrative of the commentary, which was translated separately by Rhys Davids as *Buddhist Birth Stories*, Routledge (second-hand copies of this are fairly common). *Ten Jātaka Stories* (I. B. Horner, London, 1957), texts with literal translations printed opposite.

: *Dhammapada* (ed. Fausbøll, 2nd ed., London, 1900) : Lyric verses on *dhamma*. The Glossary to Andersen's *Pali Reader* (see above) includes the vocabulary of this text.

: *Sutta Nipāta* (ed. Andersen and Smith, PTS, reprinted 1948) : longer lyric poems.

Abhidhamma Piṭaka (ed., PTS, 1883–1923, also more correct and complete editions from Bangkok) : Seven systematic works on philosophy elaborated from the ancient lists of topics of the *dhamma* called *Mātikā* (which were in their original form common to all schools of Buddhism, whereas the *Abhidhamma* was elaborated during the period of the great schisms of the — 4th to — 2nd century and maintains the strictly Theravāda doctrine) : *Dhammasaṅgaṇi, Vibhaṅga, Dhātukathā, Puggalapaññatti, Kathāvatthu, Yamaka* and *Paṭṭhāna.*

Dhammasaṅgaṇi (PTS, 1885) : Translated by C. A. F. Rhys Davids as *A Buddhist Manual of Psychological Ethics* (London, Royal Asiatic Society, second ed. 1923).

Vibhaṅga (PTS, 1904) : The most ancient *Abhidhamma* text and closest in content to the *Suttanta.* Translated by U Thittila, PTS, 1969.

Kathāvatthu (ascribed to Moggaliputta Tissa, fl. — 250, ed. Taylor, PTS, 1894–97, two vols., best PTS edition of an *Abhidhamma* text) : Translated by S. Z. Aung and C. A. F. Rhys Davids as *Points of Controversy* (PTS, reprinted 1960), contains Theravāda refutations of the special doctrines of other schools of Buddhism.

Mohavicchedanī (by Kassapa, + twelfth century, ed. A. P. Buddhadatta and A. K. Warder, PTS, 1961) : A detailed synopsis of the entire *Abhidhamma Piṭaka*, together with Buddhaghosa's commentaries on it, in the guise of a commentary on the *Mātikā.*

Abhidhammatthasaṅgaha (by Anuruddha, + twelfth century, published *Journal PTS,* 1884) : A very concise compendium of the *Abhidhamma.* Translated rather freely as *Compendium of Philosophy* by S. Z. Aung and C. A. F. Rhys Davids (PTS, reprint 1956).

Guide through the Abhidhamma Piṭaka (by Nyanatiloka, in English, Colombo, 1938) : A very useful survey.

Netti (PTS, 1902, ed. Hardy) : An early post-canonical systematic work on exegesis and methodology which also surveys the Canon. Translated by Ñāṇamoli as *The Guide* (PTS in the press).

Visuddhimagga (by Buddhaghosa, + fifth century, ed. Warren and D. Kosambi, Harvard Oriental Series, 1950). A systematic and comprehensive exposition of the Theravāda Buddhist doctrine as understood in Ceylon in Buddhaghosa's time, based on old commentaries and the traditions of the monks. It was Buddhaghosa who prepared, in fact translated and edited in Pali from the older Sinhalese materials, the standard commentaries on the Canon which are now in use. These often refer to the *Visuddhimagga* for detailed explanations of doctrine, hence it is a necessary complement to them, being originally part of the same ancient body of commentarial texts. It is, however, complete in itself and may be read first as an introduction to the study of the medieval phase of Theravāda. There is an excellent and exact translation by Ñāṇamoli under the title *The Path of Purification* (Colombo, Semage, 1956).

LITERATURE AND REFERENCE

(Cf. *Pali Literature and Language*, above, and also the Epilegomena to *CPD* Vol. I, pp. 37* ff., which gives a full bibliography of the literature in Pali.)

History of Indian Literature (by Winternitz, English edition published by the University of Calcutta) : Vol. II includes Pali literature. This is the best modern work on Indian literature.

Early History of Buddhism in Ceylon (by Adikāram, Migoda, Ceylon, 1946) : A basic work for the history and chronology of the Theravāda School in Ceylon, as well as a detailed piece of research on the nature and origins of the old (pre-Buddhaghosa and no longer extant in its original form) commentarial literature.

Pali Literature of Ceylon (G. P. Malalasekera, London, Royal Asiatic Society, 1928).

Dictionary of Pali Proper Names (by G. P. Malalasekera, PTS reprint 1960) : Detailed information and references for the names in the whole field of Pali literature.

University of Ceylon Review (1943 . . . a journal which frequently carries articles on Pali literature and the history of Buddhism).

Hinduism and Buddhism (by C. Eliot, London, 1921, reprinted 1954) : Includes in its first volume an interesting commentary on the doctrines of the Pali Canon in their historical setting.

The Central Conception of Buddhism and the Meaning of the Word " Dharma " (by Stcherbatsky, London, Royal Asiatic Society, 1923 : the Calcutta reprint is seriously defective as the diacritical marks are omitted) : Although based on the Sanskrit texts of the Sarvāstivāda (Sabbatthivāda) School this book contains the soundest introduction to the study of the philosophies of all schools of Buddhism.

The Wonder that was India (by A. L. Basham, London, Sidgwick and Jackson, 1954, since reprinted) : General background to Indian studies.

Pali Metre (by A. K. Warder, PTS, 1967). A historical study of the development of Pali metres in the context of Indian metrics generally, leading to conclusions about the history of literature.

Indian Buddhism (by A. K. Warder, Delhi, Motilal Banarsidass, 1970). A general introduction to Buddhism, its original doctrine, the 'eighteen' early schools, including Theravāda or Sthaviravāda, and Mahāyāna and Mantrayāna. Buddhist philosophy is systematically presented from the original texts, along with its ethics or social teaching.

Indian Kāvya Literature (by A. K. Warder, Delhi, Motilal Banarsidass, 1972 in progress). Volume II (1974) includes two chapters on the Pali Canon from the literary point of view.

Encyclopaedia of Buddhism (edd. G. P. Malalasekera, O. H. de A. Wijesekera, Government of Ceylon, 1961, in progress). Articles by numerous contributors on Buddhist names and terms.

PALI–ENGLISH VOCABULARY

Verbs are given as prefix + root. The prefixes are shown unmodified by junction, but the verbs are placed as they would be after the junction of prefix and root.

Nouns in *-a/ā* are given in the form of the nominative singular to show the gender, whereas the adjectives in *-a* are given in the stem form. Other nouns are usually given in the stem form with the gender indicated, except those in *-ī* and *-ū*, which are feminine unless otherwise marked. All stems in *-as* are nouns, masculine or neuter.

For the order, initial bracketed letters indicating the possibility of doubling are not counted.

a

a- not, non, un-
akaṭṭha uncultivated, unploughed
akaṇa without the red coating which lies underneath the husk (of rice)
akaraṇīya impossible, invincible
akalla unsound
akālika timeless
akiccaṃ what should not be done
akiriyaṃ inaction
akusala bad
ā-(k)kus (I) abuse, scold
akkhadhutto gambler
akkharaṃ expression (word, locution)
ā-(k)khā (I) tell, report (esp. tradition)
akkhātar (masc.) reporter
akkhi (neut.) eye
akkho die (dice)
akkho axle
agāraṃ house, home
aggañña knowing the beginning, primeval, original
aggatā pre-eminence, supremacy
ā-(g)gah (V) seize
aggi (masc.) fire
agge (ind.) since
aggo top, tip, the supreme
aṅgaṃ limb, characteristic, factor
aṅgīrasa (fem. *-ī*) radiant (poetic)
aṅguli (fem.) finger, toe
acelo naked ascetic
accaṃkusa beyond the hook, defying the hook (elephant)
accayena (ind.) after, through (time gen.)
accādhāya (gerund *ati-ā-dhā*) putting on top of
accha clear, bright, sparkling
acchariya surprising
ā-(c)chād (VII) dress
ajo goat
ajja (ind.) today
ajjatanāya (ind.) for today
ajjhatta inner
ajjhattaṃ (ind.) internally
adhi-ā-vas (I) live on, exploit, subsist by
adhi-upa-gam (I) join, adhere to
adhi-o-gāh (I) put out to (sea), cross over (ocean), plunge into
añch (I) turn (on a lathe)
añña (pronoun) other (repeated =) one . . . another, the . . . is a different thing from the . . .
aññatara (pronoun) a certain, a
aññatra (ind.) except for, apart from (ins., dat., abl.)
aññathā (ind.) otherwise
aññadatthu (ind.) absolutely, universally
aññā knowledge, insight
aññātar (masc.) learner, grasper
aññāto stranger
aññena aññaṃ (ind.) irrelevantly
aṭṭha eight
aṭṭhaṅgika having eight factors
aṭṭhādasa eighteen
aṭṭhāhaṃ eight days
aṭṭhikaṃ bone
aḍḍha rich
aḍḍhamāso fortnight
aḍḍho (or adj.) half,
aṇu minute, atomic
aṇu (masc.) atom
aṇṇavo flood
ati (prefix) over, very, exceedingly, (may be prefixed to adjectives in poetry)
ati-(k)kam (I) pass over
atikkanta surpassing

atithi (masc.) guest
ati-pat (caus. = slay, kill)
atipātin slaying, killing
atipāto slaying, killing
atibāḷhaṃ (ind.) too much
ati-man (III) despise
atimāno arrogance, contempt
ati-vatt (I) escape
ativiya (ind.) very much
ativela excessive
ativelaṃ (ind.) too long, excessively
ati-sar (I) pass over, ignore
atīta past
attan (masc. and pronoun, see Lesson 22) self, soul
attamana assured
attarūpa personal (see Vocab. 20)
atthagamo setting, extinction
atthika aspiring, wishful, desirous
attho prosperity, wealth, welfare, purpose, meaning, matter, affair; *atthāya* = for the sake of
atha (ind.) then; thence, (if) so
atha kho (ind.) then, moreover, rather
athusa without husk
aduṃ (pronoun) it, that, yon
addhan road, time
addhaniya roadworthy, enduring
addhā (ind.) certainly
addho (variant for *aḍḍho*)
adhana poor
adhammo false doctrine; bad nature; bad custom, injustice; bad mental object, bad idea
adhi (prefix) over
adhikaraṇaṃ case, affair
adhi-gam (I) understand, acquire, get
adhigamo acquisition, getting
adhicca spontaneous, causeless
adhi-(ṭ)ṭhā (I) fix one's attention on, resolve on
adhiṭṭhāya (ger.) having fixed one's attention on, having resolved on
adhimutta intent on
adhivacanaṃ designation, name
adhi-vas (I) (caus. = agree to stay/reside/put up, in = acc., accept)
adhivāsanaṃ acceptance of an invitation
adhivutti (fem.) expression, description
adhivuttha (p.p. *adhi-vas*) accepted
adhunā (ind.) now, just now
adho (ind.) below (abl.)
anagāriyaṃ homelessness
anatīta not-passing, not escaping
anattamana disturbed, worried
anattamanatā worry, disquiet, anxiety
ananta infinite
anantaraṃ (ind.) without omission
anabhibhūta (p.p. *abhi-bhū* (I)) unconquered
anabhirati (fem.) discontent, loneliness
anayo misfortune, misery
anariya barbarian
anāgata future (also neg. p.p. of *ā-gam*)
anālayo not clinging
anidassana indefinable, invisible
anissita unattached
anīkaṭṭho soldier
anu (prefix) after, following
anuesin seeking
anu-kamp (I) be compassionate, have compassion (acc.)
anukampā compassion
anu-(k)kam (I) walk along
anukhuddaka very minor
anugati (fem.) following, imitation
anu-ge (I) sing after
anu-car (I) follow, practice
anu-(ñ)ñā (V) allow
anuttara unsurpassed, supreme
anu-(t)thu (V) lament, complain
anudiṭṭhin contemplating, theorizing
anudisaṃ (ind.) in all directions
anudisā intermediate direction
anu-pa-i (I) (*anupeti*, cf. Vocab. 28) coalesce with (acc.)
anu-pa-(k)khand (I) (*anupa-*) go over to, be converted to, join
anu-pa-gam (I) (*anupaggachati*, cf. Vocab. 28) amalgamate with (acc.)
anu-pat (I) follow, chase after
anupariyāya circling
anupassin observing
anupādā (ind.) without attachment, through non-attachment
anupādisesa with no attachment remaining
anupubbena (ind.) in due course, in succession
anu-(p)pa-dā (I) grant
anu-(p)pa-āp (V) arrive at

anu-bandh (I) follow
anu-budh (III) understand
anubodho understanding
anu-bhās (I) say after
anu-bhū (I) experience, enjoy, observe
anu-mud (I) approve, express appreciation
anu-yuj (II) submit
anuyoga practising
anuyogo practice, examination
anu-rakkh (I) look after, retain
anulomaṃ (ind.) in natural order, in normal order
anu-vac (I) (caus. = recite after)
anu-(s)sar (I) recollect
anu-sās (I) advise, instruct
anu-(s)su (V) hear of
aneka many
aneja imperturbable
aneḷaka pure
anta finite
antamaso (ind.) even
antara (prefix) within
antara-dhā (III) disappear
antarā (ind.) within, between (acc.), meanwhile, whilst (loc.)
antarāyo obstacle, danger, plague
antarena (ind.) between (gen.)
antalikkhaṃ sky
antavant- finite
antepuraṃ citadel, palace
antevāsin apprentice
anto side, end, extreme
andhakāro darkness, obscurity
annaṃ food
anvad (*eva*) (ind.) behind, after
anvayo inference
anvāya (ger. *anu-i*) following, in consequence of (acc.)
anvāyiko follower
apa (prefix) off, away
apa-(k)kam (I) go off, withdraw
apagata- without, free from
apacco offspring
apadānaṃ reaping, harvest
apa-nah (II) tie back, untie
apa-nī (I) lead away
apanūdanaṃ driving away, removing (poetic)
apara (pronoun) another
aparaṃ (ind.) further, afterwards
aparaddha failed, offended
aparanto the future, the end, a future or final state
aparāparaṃ (ind.) successively
apạriyanta unlimited
aparisesa without remainder, complete, absolute
aparihāniya imperishable, leading to prosperity
apa-lok (VII) take leave, give notice
apa-vad (I) disparage
apāyo misery
apāraṃ hither, this world
apāruta open
api (ind.) (sentence/clause initial) with opt. = perhaps, with ind. is polite interrog. = does ?, do ?, did ? (in junction also *app* and *ap'*)
api ca (ind.) nevertheless
apuññaṃ demerit, evil
apubbaṃ acarimaṃ (ind.) simultaneously
apa-i (I) go from, go away (poetic)
ape(k)khā intention, expectation
app (= *api*)
ap(p) (VI) reach (= *ap* (IV))
appa little
appaka little (poetic)
appaṭisaṃvedana not feeling, not experiencing
appatta unobtained
appamatta not-negligent
appamāṇa immeasurable
appamādo diligence, care
appesakkha inferior
abāhiraṃ (ind.) without exclusion, without excluding anyone
abbhantara internal, home
abhi-ā-cikkh (I) slander, calumniate
abhi-u(d)-kir (I*) sprinkle
abhi-u(d)-gam (I) be disseminated
abbhuta wonderful, marvellous
abbhokāsa open, free, out of doors, open air
abhabba unable, incapable (with dat. of the action)
abhi (prefix) towards, about
abhi-(k)kam (I) go forward, advance
abhikkanta excellent
abhijāti (fem.) class of birth
abhijjhā desire (with loc. of object)
abhijjhālu (sometimes *-ū* masc. ; fem. : *-unī*) covetous

abhiñña learned
abhiññā insight
abhi-(ñ)ñā (V) know, be aware of, ascertain, discover
abhiṇhaṃ frequently
abhitatta overheated, exhausted by heat
abhi-nand (I) be pleased with (acc.), appreciate
abhi-ni(r)-dis (I*) declare
abhi-ni(r)-vatt (I) be produced
abhinibbatti (fem.) production, origin
abhi-ni-vajj (VII) avoid
abhipatthita (p.p. abhi-patth (VII)) yearned for
abhi-pāl (VII) protect
abhi-(p)pa-vass (I) rain down on, pour down (heavy rain, cloudburst)
abhi-bhū (I) conquer, rule over
abhibhū (masc.) overlord, conqueror
abhimukha facing
abhi-yā (I) attack, invade
abhiyogin expert, proficient
abhi-ram (I) enjoy, take pleasure in (loc.) (elevated)
abhiruda resounding with
abhi-ruh (I*) mount, get into, board
abhirūpa handsome
abhi-vaḍḍh (I) increase
abhi-vad (I) proclaim
abhi-vad (VII) salute, greet, take leave
abhi-vass rain on
abhi-vi-ji (V) conquer
abhi-vi-(s)saj[1] (I) dispense
abhisaṭa (p.p. *abhi-sar*) visited, met
abhisamayo insight
abhisamparāyo future state
abhi-saṃ-budh (III) become enlightened, attain enlightenment
abhisambuddha illuminated (fig.)
abhisitta (p.p. *abhi-sic* (II)) consecrated
abhiseko consecration
amacco minister (privy councillor)
amata deathless
amataṃ immortality, ambrosia (see Vocab. 30)
amanāpa displeasing
amanusso non-human being
amama not possessive, unselfish
amarā perpetuity
amu- (pronoun) he, she, it, that, yon
amuka (adj.) such and such
amutra (ind.) there, yonder
ambaṃ mango (fruit, usually neut.)
ambakā mango woman
ambo mango tree (usually masc.)
ambujo fish (poetic)
ambho (ind.) sir ! (not very respectful, may express surprise)
ayaṃ (pronoun) he, she, this
ayanaṃ way, path
ayoniso (ind.) haphazardly, erratically, unmethodically, inconsequentially, unscientifically
ayyaputto master, Mr. (pl. :) gentlemen (esp. when addressed by ladies, including their wives)
ayye (voc.) lady ! (polite or respectful address, used also to nuns)
araññaṃ forest
araṇi (fem.) kindling stick
arah (I) deserve, must, ought
arahant- (masc.) worthy one, perfected one
ariya excellent, exalted, noble, Āryan
arūpin- formless, immaterial
alaṃ (ind.) sufficient, enough, adequate, proper, perfected, enough !, stop !, I won't (dat.)
alaṅkāro ornament, adornment
alasa lazy
alla wet
ava (prefix : alternative, more poetic form of *o*)
avacaro scope
ava-(ṭ)ṭhā (I) remain
avabhāso splendour, illumination
avasa powerless
ava-sar (I) go down to, approach
ava-sis (III) remain, be left over
avasesako one who remains, survivor
avijjā ignorance
avidūre (ind.) not far, near
avisārada diffident
avihiṃsā harmlessness, non-injuring
avyākata (p.p. *vi-ā-kar*, neg.) unexplained, undetermined, indeterminate
avyāpādo non-violence
as (I) be
asañña insentient

asammoso not-forgetting
asāhasaṃ non-violence
asīti (fem.) eighty
asu (pronoun) he, she, that, yon
asuci impure, dirty, vile
asubha foul
asesa without remainder, complete, absolute
assamo hermitage
ā-(s)sas (I) breathe in
assādo tasting, enjoyment
assāso reassurance
ah (only perfect) say
ahaṃ (pronoun) I
ahata new
ahi (masc.) snake
ahiṃsā harmlessness
ahicchattako mushroom, toadstool
ahitaṃ disadvantage, hardship
ahe (ind.) ah ! (poetic)
aheṭhako non-harasser
aho (ind.) ah ! (expresses surprise—approving—and delight)

ā

ā (prefix) to
ā-kaṅkh (I) wish
ākappo deportment, style
ākāro feature, peculiarity
ākāso sky, space
ākiñcaññaṃ nothingness
ā-kuṭ (VII) strike
ākula confused, tangled
āgatāgataṃ (ind.) each time (it) came
ā-gam (I) come (caus.—or (VII)—= wait)
āgamanaṃ coming
āgamo coming, body of doctrine, tradition
āgamma (ger. *ā-gam*) depending on, as a result of (acc.) [*āgantvā* = having come, having returned]
āghatanaṃ death
ā-car (I) conduct oneself
ācariyo teacher
ācāro conduct
ā-cikkh (I) call, describe
ājīvin living by
ājīvo livelihood
ā-(ñ)ñā (V) learn, grasp (fig.)
āṇa (caus.) order, command
āṇatta (p.p. *āṇa* caus.) ordered
ātaṅko sickness, fever
ātappo energy (purifying ascetic energy)
ātāpin energetic
ātura afflicted
ā-dā (I) or (III) take
ādānaṃ taking
ādi (masc.) beginning, opening
ādīnavo disadvantage
ādhipati (masc.) lord
ādhipateyyaṃ lordship, supremacy
ānañcaṃ infinity
ānando joy
ānisaṃso benefit
ānupubba (fem. *-ī*) systematic
ānubhāvo power, magnificence, might
ā-pad (III) acquire, produce, get, have (intransitive)
āpas- water
ā-pucch (I) ask leave (of absence)
ābādhika ill
ābādho illness
ā-bhar (only p.p.) bring, carry
ā-bhuj (I*) fold the legs
ābhogo enjoyment
āma (ind.) yes
ā-mant (VII) address
āmalakaṃ emblic myrobalan (medicinal fruit)
āyatanaṃ sphere
āyatiṃ (ind.) in future
āyasmant venerable
ā-yā (I) come, approach
āyāmo length
āyu (neut.) life, age
āyuta full of (poetic)
ārakā (ind.) far from (abl.)
āraññaka forest, living in the forest
āraddha (p.p. *ā-rabh* (I) and *ā-rādh* (VII))
ārabbha (ger. *ā-rabh* (I)) with reference to, about (acc.)
ā-rabh (I) begin, initiate
ā-rādh (VII) please, satisfy (acc.)
ārāmo park
ā-ruc (VII) inform (dat.)
ā-ruh (I*) climb, mount (caus. : put on top of, load, show, show up, disprove)
āroga well (healthy)
ārogyaṃ health
āropita disproved

ālayo home
ālumpaṃ bit, piece
āloko light (illumination)
āvaraṇaṃ shelter
ā-vas (I) dwell in, live in
āvasathāgāraṃ rest house, hostel (maintained by a local council)
āvasatho room, cell, dwelling, residence
-āvaho bringing
āvāso living in, dwelling
āvila turbid, muddy
āvuso (ind.) sir ! (polite address between equals)
āsaṅkā apprehension, doubt, fear
āsanaṃ seat
āsabha (fem. *-ī*) bold
āsavo influx, influence
ā-sic (II) shower over, pour over
ā-sev (I) practice
ā-han (I) strike
ā-har (I) bring, fetch
āhāro food (incl. figurative), gathering ; district
ā-hiṇḍ (I) wander

i

i (I) go (poetic)
iṅgha (ind.) here !
iti (ind.) this, that, thus
ito (ind.) from this, than this
itthaṃ (ind.) thus, in this way
itthattaṃ this world
itthī (fem.) woman
idaṃ (pronoun) it, this (ind. = here)
iddha powerful
iddhi (fem.) power (marvellous)
idha (ind.) here, in this connection
indakhīlo royal stake (see Vocab. 30)
indriyaṃ faculty
ibbha domestic
iriy (I*) move, move about, go on (lit. and fig.) (poetic)
iva (ind., enclitic) like
is (I) wish, desire ("*isu*")
isi (masc.) *sage, seer*
issaro lord, god
iha (ind.) here, in this case

u

u (ind. : emphatic enclitic particle added to other indeclinables, poetic)
u (prefix) (= *u*(*d*)) up
uju straight, erect
utu (neut.) (the gender fluctuates) season
uttama highest
uttara northern, higher, further
uttarāsaṅgo cloak
uttari (ind.) beyond, further, more
uttāna stretched out, lying down
uttānaka shallow (and fig. : "easily understood," "simple")
uttāso terror
u(*d*) (prefix) up
udaraṃ belly, lap, bosom
u(*d*)*-ā-har* (I) speak, say, promulgate
u(*d*)*-kujj* (I) set upright
u(*d*)*-*(*g*)*gah* (V) learn, memorize
u(*d*)*-*(*g*)*ghar* (I) ooze
u(*d*)*-chid* (III) annihilate (passive = be annihilated)
ucchedo annihilation
u(*d*)*-*(*ṭ*)*ṭhā* (I) stand up, get up, rise up, arise, come out from, emigrate
uṭṭhānaṃ rising
u(*d*)*-tar* (I) cross
udakaṃ water
udakamaṇi (masc.) water-jar
udagga lofty, elated
udānaṃ exalted utterance, joyful utterance (denom. *udāneti* speak with exaltation, speak with joy)
udāhu (ind.) or
udikkhitar (masc.) looker at
uddāpo foundations
uddeko sickness, vomiting
uddesika referring to
uddeso synopsis, summary, summarized description
uddhaṃ (ind.) above, up, after, beyond (abl.)
uddhaggika uplifting
uddhaccaṃ pride, vanity
uddhaccakukkuccaṃ pride, vanity, conceit
u(*d*)*-har* (I) dig up, collect, raise
upa (prefix) up to, towards
upa-i (I) go to (poetic)
upa-(*k*)*kam* (I) attack, fall upon, go into
upakaraṇaṃ resources
upakkileso corruption
-upaga going to

upa-gam (I) go to
upaghātin harming
upacita (p.p. *upa-ci* (V)) accumulated
upa-jīv (I) live by, live upon
upa-(ṭ)ṭhā (I) serve, attend on/to (usually caus.; dat.)
upaṭṭhāko attendant, follower
upaṭṭhānaṃ serving, attending on, audience
upaḍḍha (or neut.) half
upaḍḍhapathaṃ (ind.) halfway
upa-dah (I) torment, worry
upa-nam (I) (caus. = offer, serve—dat. of person and acc. of thing)
upa-ni-(j)jhe (I) observe, think about
upa-ni(r)-vatt (I) derive
upanissāya (gerund of *upa-ni-(s)sī*) depending on
upa-pad (III) transmigrate, be reborn
upapīḷā oppression, trouble
upamā simile
upari (ind.) on top (of) (precedes the word it relates to, which is usually in the loc.)
upa-rudh (III) stop, cease, end
upa-labh (I) (pass. = exist)
upalāpanaṃ propaganda
upa-ḷas (VII) play (instrument, etc.), sound
upa-saṃ-har (I) visualize as, imagine as (two accs.)
upa-saṃ-(k)kam (I) go to, approach
upasamo calm
upa-saṃ-pad (III) enter into
upasampadā entrance
upa-subh (I) appear beautiful, shine
upa-ā-dā (III) be attached
upādānaṃ attachment
upāyāso misery, despair
upāsako lay disciple
upāsikā female lay disciple
upe(k)khaka detached
upe(k)khā equanimity, detachment
uposatho observance day, sabbath
u(d)-pad (III) happen, occur, arise, become
uppādo occurrence, arising, production
u(d)-vah (I) (*ubbahati*) carry off
ubbādhanā imprisonment
ubbilāvitattaṃ elation, exultation
ubbego apprehension, anxiety
ubhato (ind.) in both ways, on both sides, both
ubhaya (pronoun) both
ubho (numeral) both
ummatta mad
uyyānaṃ park
u(d)-yuj (II) (caus. = dismiss)
ura bosom, own (e.g. child)
uḷāra mighty
uḷumpo boat, canoe
usabho bull
ussado abundance
u(d)-sah (I) try, undertake, take up
u(d)-sīd (caus. *ussādeti* = lift onto)
ussuka eager
ussukkaṃ eagerness, impatience (denom. *ussukkati* be eager, be impatient)

ū

ūru (fem.) thigh
ūhacca (ger. *u(d)-han* or *o-han*) having knocked out

e

ā-i (I) come (poetic)
eka (pronoun, numeral) one, a, pl. some
ekaṃsa definite, decided, confident
ekaṃsena (ind.) for certain; certainly, definitely
ekaka (adj.) alone, single
ekacca (pronoun) someone, something(s)
ekato (ind.) on one side, together, on either side
ekattaṃ unity
ekanta extreme
ekantikena (ind.) finally, conclusively
ekameka (pronoun) each one
ekāgāriko burglar, burglary
ekādasa eleven
ekūnavīsati nineteen (*ekūna* = "one less than")
ekodakī-bhū (I) consist entirely of water
ekodi concentrated
ekodibhāvo singleness, concentration
eta(d) (pronoun) he, she, it, this
etarahi (ind.) now, at present
etādisa (adj.) this sort (of)

ettāvatā (ind.) so far, to that extent, to this extent
ettha (ind.) here, in this case
enaṃ (pronoun) him (acc. sg. masc. only, enclitic)
eva (ind. : enclitic ; in close junction sometimes ***va*** or ***yeva***) only, alone, just, surely
evaṃ (ind.) thus, so, yes
evam eva (ind.) just so, likewise
evaṃ santaṃ (ind.) in that case, in such case
esikaṃ pillar
esikaṭṭhāyin- firm as a pillar
eso this
ehipassika verifiable

o

o (prefix) down, off
o-(k)kam (I) descend into, arise within
okkassa (ger. of ***o-(k)kass*** (VII)) having dragged down, having dragged away
okāro meanness, degradation, vanity
okāso opportunity
o-gāh (I) plunge into
oṭṭhavacittako a kind of bird
o-tar (I) pass down, collate (caus. = check)
ottappaṃ shame, fear of blame
odaka (fem. ***-ikā***) having water
odano boiled rice
odāta white
o-dhā (I) put down
onīta (p.p. ***o-nī***) withdrawn, removed
opanayika fruitful
opapātika transmigrating
obhāso radiance
orasa own (cf. ***ura***)
orima nearer, this side
o-ruh (I) descend
o-lup (II) (caus. = scrape off)
o-lok (VII) look at
oḷārika coarse, gross, material
o-vad (I) admonish
o-sakk (I) draw back, retire
ossaṭṭha (p.p. ***o-(s)saj*** [1] (I)) dispelled
o-har (I) (caus. = shave off)

k

ka- (***kiṃ***) (pronoun) who ?, which ?, what ?
kaṅkhā doubt
kaṅkhin doubting, in doubt
kacci (ind.) perhaps ?, did ?, I doubt whether ?, I hope ?, aren't you ?
kaṭukaṃ bitterness
kaṭṭhaṃ firewood
kaṇiṭṭha (or ***kan-***) younger, youngest
kaṇo the fine red powder between the grain and husk of rice
kaṇṭakaṃ ("thorn") subversive element, rebel, bandit
kaṇha black, dark
katama (pronoun) which ?, which one ?
kati how many ? (Lesson 26)
kattar (masc.) maker
kattarasuppo old winnowing-basket
kattha (ind.) where ?
kath (VII) relate, tell
kathaṃ (ind.) how ?, why ?
kathā talk, story
kadā (ind.) when ?
kadā ci (ind.) at any time, at some time, ever
kaddamo mud
kanakaṃ gold
kanta agreeable, lovely
kantāro wilderness, semi-desert
kapp (VII) arrange, put in order, organize
kappo arrangement, order, rule, aeon
kabaḷiṅkāro solid matter, solid (food)
kam (VII) love
(k)kam (I) walk ; intensive = walk up and down, walk about, take exercise
kamanīya lovely
kammaṃ work, action
kamman (neut.) action
kammanto work, undertaking, business
kammāro smith
kar (VI) make, do, work
-karaṇa (fem. ***-ī***) making
karaṇīyaṃ duty, business
karaha ci (ind.) at some time
karīsaṃ excrement
karuṇā compassion
-karo doing, working
karo hand (poetic)
kalambukā a creeper : *Convolvulus repens* ?

kalāpo bundle, quiver
kali (masc.) unlucky die, bad luck, the "iron age"
kalyāṇa beautiful, good
kalyāṇī a beautiful girl
kalla proper, sound
kavi poet
kasāvaṃ astringent
kasi (fem.) cultivation, agriculture
kasiraṃ difficulty
kasmā (ind.) why ?, wherefore ?
kahaṃ (ind.) whereabouts ?
kāko crow
kāmo love, passion, liking, pleasure
kāyo body, substance
kārako doer
kāraṇaṃ cause
-kārin doing
-kāro making
kālo time, opportunity, proper time
kāḷa black
kāveyyaṃ poetry
kāsāya brown, orange, saffron
(k)ki (V) buy
kiṃ (ind.) why ?, ? (i.e. marks interrogative sentence)
kiṃ (pronoun) who ?, which ?, what ?
kiccaṃ business, what should be done
kicchaṃ difficulty
kiñjakkhaṃ stamen, filament
kit (I) (*tikicchati* : desid.) cure
kitti (fem.) fame
kir (I*) scatter
kira (ind. ; enclitic) really, now ; it is said that, they say ; in fact, actually
kiriyā action
kilam (I) tire
kilamatho tiring, wearying, weariness
kīdisa (adj.) like what ?, of what sort ?
kukkuccaṃ vanity, worry, anxiety
kukkuṭako cock (wild cock)
kukkuravatiko canine (ascetic), dog-vower
kukkuro dog
kucchi (masc.) womb
kujj (I) bend, fold
kuto (ind.) whence ?
kuto pana (ind.) much less, let alone
kudā (ind.) when ?
kup (III) be angry (dat.)
kumārikā girl
kumārī girl, princess (girl of the military-aristocratic class)
kumāro boy, prince
kumudaṃ white water-lily
kumbho pot
kummāso barley bread
-kulīna (adj.) by tribe
kulo tribe
kullo raft
kuḷīrako a kind of bird
kusala good, good at
kusalaṃ good
kusīta indolent, lazy
kuhiṃ (ind.) where to ?
kūṭaṭṭha (or *kūt-*) immovable as a peak
kūṭo point, peak, ridge, gable
kevala entire, whole
keso hair (of the head)
ko pana vādo (ind.) how much more (so), not to speak of
kokilo cuckoo (Indian cuckoo)
koñco heron
koṭṭhāgāraṃ granary, storehouse
(k)kodho anger
kovida learned, knowing thoroughly (poetic)
koso treasury

kh

khattar- (masc.) steward (nom. sing. *khattā*, acc. *khattaṃ*, voc. *khatte*)
khattiyo warrior, noble (member of the military-aristocratic class)
khantī forgivingness, toleration
(k)khandho group, collection, mass
(k)kham (I) please, suit, approve, like
khamanīyaṃ pleasure, contentment
(k)khayo exhaustion
khara rough, harsh
kharattaṃ roughness
khalaṃ threshing (floor)
khalu (ind., enclitic) indeed
khā (III) seem
khād (I) eat, bite, chew
khādanīyaṃ foods, dishes
khiḍḍā play
(k)khip (I*) throw
khippaṃ (ind.) quickly
(k)khī (III) exhaust, waste, perish, become indignant
khīlo stake (boundary)
khudda minor, small

khuddaṃ honey (of wild bees)
khuraṃ razor
khettaṃ field, territory, land
khema secure, safe
kho (ind., enclitic) indeed
khomaṃ flax

g

gaṇako mathematician, treasurer
gaṇikā courtesan, geisha
gaṇībhūta crowded together
gaṇo group, aggregate
gatako goer
gati (fem.) future career, destiny, future course
gattaṃ limb
gathita (p.p. ***gath*** (II)) tied
gadrabho donkey
gandho scent, perfume, odour
gabbhin- pregnant
gabbho embryo
gam (I) go
gamanaṃ going
-gamo going
gambhīra profound
gamma vulgar
garah (I) blame
garahā blame, reproof, threat
garu heavy, troublesome
garu-kar (VI) give respect to
gaḷagaḷāyati (onomatopoeic verb) pour down (rain)
gaves (I) look for, search for
(g)gah (V) seize, grasp, take
gahaṇaṃ seizing, keeping
gahapati (masc.) householder
gahapatiko householder
gādh (I) be firm, stand fast, hold tight
gāmapadaṃ site of a village
gāmin going
gāmo village
gāravo respect
gāvī cow
-(g)gāho seizing, eclipse
gimhika summer
gil (I*) swallow
gilāna ill
gihin house-dwelling, one living "in the world"
gītaṃ singing
guṇaṃ (sometimes masc.) string, strand, quality
gutta (pp. ***gup***) protected, guarded
gutti (fem.) protection
gup (desid.: be disgusted with)
gūtho dung
gelaññaṃ illness
gehaṃ house, building
go (masc. and fem.) cow, bull, cattle
gocaro pasture, territory, proper place, range
gottaṃ clan
gopānasī (roof) bracket
gomayaṃ cow dung
gorakkhā cattle breeding
govatiko bovine (ascetic), cow-vower

gh

ghaccā destruction
ghammo summer
gharaṃ house
ghas (I) devour (desid. desire to eat, be hungry)
ghā (III) smell (trans.)
ghāṇaṃ = ***ghānaṃ***
ghātetar (masc.) instigator to kill
ghāto attacking, destruction
ghānaṃ nose

c

ca (ind., enclitic) and
ca pana (ind., enclitic) moreover
cakkavatti (masc.) emperor
cakkaṃ wheel
cakkhu (neut.) eye, sense of sight
cakkhumant- having eyes, having insight, intelligent
caṇḍa fierce, irascible
catasso see ***catu(r)***
catu(r) four
catugguṇa fourfold, quadruple
catuttha fourth, a quarter
catuppado quadruped
caturāsīti (fem.) eighty-four
catuhaṃ four days
catta (p.p. ***caj***) abandoned, thrown away
cattārīsā (fem.) or ***-a*** (neut.) forty
cattāro, cattāri see ***catu(r)***
candimā (masc.) moon
cando moon
car (I) proceed, live, conduct oneself, carry on, go on a mission
-cara living

caraṇaṃ conduct, good conduct
caraṇaṃ foot (poetic)
carahi (ind.) therefore, then
cariyā conduct, way of life
cavanaṃ passing away
cāgo abandoning
cārikā travel, journey, mission
-cārin living, behaving, carrying on, going on
ci (V) (passive *cīyati* = be piled up, be built up)
cittaṃ thought, mind, "heart"
cira long (time)
ciraṃ (ind.) for a long time, after a long time
cirapaṭika (as *bahubbīhi*, or *-kā* (fem.)) since long, a long time back, long
cirassaṃ (ind.) at last, after a long time
cīvaraṃ robe
cu (I) fall from, pass away (from a form of existence)
cuddasa fourteen
ce (ind., enclitic) if
cetas- mind
cetiyaṃ shrine, pagoda

ch

cha(ḷ) six
chaṭṭha sixth
chaḍḍ (VII) throw away, abandon
chatta(ka)ṃ sunshade
chad (VII) be pleased
chandas- will
chamā earth, ground
chid (II), (III) cut, cut down, cut off

j

-ja born (of)
-jacca (adj.) by birth
jan (III) be born (caus. : produce)
janatā the people
jananī bearer (birth), producer
janapado country
jano person, people (collective singular)
jayo victory
jar (III) grow old
jara old
jarā old age
(j)jal (I) blaze
jātarūpaṃ gold
jāti (fem.) birth
-jātika of the genus/kind/class/nature
-jāto become
jānapado country dweller
jāni (fem.) confiscation
jālin net-like
ji (I) conquer, win, defeat
ji (V) win
jivhā tongue
jīr (I) become old, age
jīv (I) live, be alive, make a living
jīvaṃjīvako a kind of partridge
jīvikā livelihood
jīvitaṃ life
jīvo life-principle, soul
je (ind., enclitic) you! (form of address by a master/mistress to a slave woman ; preceded by ***handa***, ***kiñ***, etc., or by ***gaccha***)
jeguccha disgusting
jeṭṭha elder, eldest, (most) senior

jh

(j)jhānaṃ meditation
(j)jhe (I) meditate
(j)jhe (I) burn (caus. : set fire to)

ñ

(ñ)ñap (VII) (see *pa-(ñ)ñap*)
(ñ)ñā (V) know, learn, find out
ñāṇaṃ knowledge
ñāti (masc.) relative, kinsman
ñāto friend
ñāyo method
ñeva = *eva* (junction form sometimes used after *ṃ*)

ṭh

(ṭ)ṭhā (I) stand, remain, stay (caus. : erect, establish ; except)
(ṭ)ṭhānaṃ place, case
-(ṭ)ṭhāyin staying, remaining
(ṭ)ṭhiti (fem.) duration, persistence, station

t

ta(d) (pronoun) he, it, that
ta(d) . . . ***ta(d)*** . . . that/the . . . (is) the same thing as that/the . . .
tad agge (ind.) since then
ta(d) (pronoun) you (thou)

taṃ (pronoun) it, that (also as ind.: then, so, now)
takkin- deducing (as masc. noun = deducer, logician)
takko deduction
taggha (ind.) certainly, assuredly
taco skin
tacch (I) chop, carve
taṇḍulaṃ rice grain, husked rice
taṇhā desire, "thirst," "drive"
tatiya (numeral) third
tato (ind.) thence, then, from there, from that
tatta (p.p. *tap*) hot
tattha (ind.) there, in that/this connection
tatra (ind.) there, in this connection
tathā (ind.) thus, true
tathāgato thus-gone (title of the Buddha)
ta(d) (ind.) then, so (as pronoun see above at beginning of *t*)
tadā (ind.) then
tan (VI) expand, stretch
tanu (neut.) body
tantaṃ loom
tap (I) heat
tapas asceticism
tayidaṃ (ind.) with reference to this
tayo see *ti-*
tar (I) cross
tasmā (ind.) therefore
tāta (ind.) my son! (affectionate address)
tādisa (adj.) this sort (of)
tārakā star
tāva (ind.) so much, so long, first, now
ti (ind.) end quote
ti- three (Lesson 26)
(t)tiṃsa (neut.) thirty
tikicchati (see *kit* (I))
tikkhattuṃ (ind.) thrice
tiṇaṃ grass
tiṇha sharp
titikkhā forbearance (desid. *tij* (I))
titthaṃ landing place, jetty, crossing place, ferry, beach (for bathing and drinking)
timisā darkness
tiracchāno animal
tiriyaṃ (ind.) horizontally
tiro- (prefix) through
tividha threefold, triple
tisso see *ti-*
tīṇi see *ti-*
tīraṃ shore, bank (denom. *tīreti* accomplish, finish)
tīradassi shore-sighting, land-sighting
tīhaṃ three days
tuṇḍikīro gourd (used as a pot)
tuṇhī (ind.) silent, silently
tuttaṃ goad (for driving elephants or cattle)
tumhe (pronoun) you (pl.)
tus (III) be pleased
tejas- heat, energy, potency
tena (ind.) therefore, this way (with *yena*)
tena hi (ind.) now! (admonitory)
telaṃ oil (sesame oil)
teḷasa thirteen
t' eva (ind.) = *ti* + *eva* (cf. *tv eva*)
tevijja having the triple knowledge (= the verses, music and prayers of the Three Vedas)
tomaraṃ lance
toraṇaṃ gateway (arched)
tvaṃ (pronoun) thou, you (sing.)
tv eva [1] (ind.) = *ti* + *eva* "end quote" + emphasis, "definitely" (cf. italics, and see Vocab. 20)
tv eva [2] (ind., enclitic) but (emphatic)

th

thanaṃ breast
thambho column
thalaṃ land, dry land
thāmo vigour
thīnaṃ mental deficiency, stupidity, inertia
thīnamiddhaṃ stupidity (and inertia)
thuso husk, chaff
thūpo monument, pagoda
thūla gross, large
theyyaṃ theft
thero elder monk

d

dakkha skilful
dakkhiṇa right (hand), southern
dakkhiṇā gift, donation
dakkhin seeing (fem. *dakkhiṇī*)
daṇḍamānavakaṃ a kind of bird
daṇḍo stick, force, punishment

danta (p.p. *dam*) tamed, restrained
damo taming, restraint
damma trainable, educable
daliddiyaṃ poverty
daḷha strong, firm
dasa ten
-dasa seeing
dassanaṃ seeing
dassanīya beautiful
dassaneyya beautiful (poetic)
dassāvin seeing, who would see
dassu (masc.) brigand, thief
dahara young, baby
dā (I) give
dātar (masc.) giver
dānaṃ gift, donation, alms
dāni (ind.) now (enclitic)
dāyajjaṃ inheritance
dāyādo inheritor, heir
dāyo gift
dārako boy
dāro (sometimes *-ā*) wife
dāsavyaṃ slavery
dāsī slave-woman, slave girl
dāso slave
diguṇaṃ double
dijo bird (poetic = "twice-born")
dittha visible
diṭṭhā (ind.) excellent !, splendid !, it's lucky, it's wonderful
diṭṭhi (fem.) opinion, theory
diṭṭhin- seeing
dibba divine, heavenly
div (III) play, gamble
divas- day
divā (ind.) by day
divāseyyā day-bed, siesta bed
divo sky, heaven
dis (VII) teach
(d)dis (I > *pass*) see (caus. = show)
disā direction, region
dīgha long
dīghaṃ (ind.) long
dīgharattaṃ (ind.) long (time)
dīpo island
du(r)- (prefix) ill, bad, hard, difficult
dukkaraṃ hard task
dukkhaṃ unhappiness, misery, suffering (denom. *dukkheti* be unhappy)
dukkhita afflicted
dukkhin- unhappy
duggati (fem.) a bad fate, evil destiny
duccaritaṃ bad conduct
duṭṭha evil, vile, corrupt
dutiya (numeral) second
dubbaṇṇa discoloured, ugly
dubbalīkaraṇa weakening (making weak)
dummana depressed
dullabha rare
dussaṃ cloth
dussīlo bad character
duhano robbery
dūto messenger
dūrato (ind.) in the distance
dūrā (ind.) from far
deyyaṃ gift
devatā deity, divine being, spirit (male as well as female)
devī queen
devo god, king
deso point (topic)
domanassaṃ depression, melancholy ; aversion
dovāriko porter, doorkeeper
doso aversion, anger
dvādasa twelve
dvāraṃ doorway, gateway (the opening, not the obstruction)
dvi (num.) two (nom. *dve*)
dvikkhattuṃ (ind.) twice
dviguṇaṃ double
dvidhā (ind.) twofold, twice, in two
dvīhaṃ two days

dh

dhaññaṃ grain
dhanaṃ money, wealth
dhammika just
dhamma (fem. *-ī*) doctrinal
dhammo (basic meaning approx. "nature", hence the following usages :) (true, natural) doctrine ; natural phenomenon, natural element, natural substance, natural principle, phenomenon, element ; custom, way, law of nature, quality, justice ; world, nature ; mental object, mental phenomenon, idea; virtue; good mental object, good mental phenomenon, good idea (when opposed to bad :

adhammo ; as "natural phenomenon" it includes bad as well as good)
dhar (VII) hold, wear, have, accept (2 accs. : x as y), remember
-dharo holding, remembering, memorizer
dhāti nurse
dhātu (fem.) element
dhi(r) (ind.) fie !, confound ! (acc. or → nom.)
dhuva fixed

n

na (ind.) not
na kiñ ci (pronoun) nothing, none at all
na cirass' eva (ind.) soon
na- (pronoun) he, that
nakkhattaṃ constellation, lunar mansion
nakho fingernail, toenail
nagaraṃ city
naṅgalo plough
naccaṃ dancing
nat (III) dance
natthu (fem.) nose
nadikā stream
nadī river
nanu (ind.) isn't ?, isn't it ?
nand (I) rejoice, be pleased
nam (I) bend, incline
namo (ind.) hail ! (dat.)
nayanaṃ eye (poetic)
nalinī lotus pool
nava nine
nava new
navanītaṃ butter
navuti (fem.) ninety
nas (III) perish
nahatvā (ger. *nhā* (III)) having bathed
nāgo elephant
nādo roar
nānattaṃ diversity
nānā (ind.) variously
nāma (ind.) by name, indeed
nāmaṃ name ; mind, mental being
nāmarūpaṃ matter plus mind, sentient body (see Lesson 29)
nāvā boat, ship
nāsanaṃ destroying
ni (prefix) down (cf. *ni(r)*)
nikkujjita (p.p. *ni(r)-kujj*) overturned
ni(r)-kam (*r* + *k* > *kkh*) (I) go out, leave
ni-khaṇ (I) bury
ni-(k)khip (I*) discard, put down, throw down
ni-gam (I) undergo, incur
ni-(g)gah (V) refute
nigamo town
nicca permanent
ni(r)-car (VII) (*nicchāreti*) bring up
nijigiṃsitar (desid. *ni-har*) coveter, acquisitor
niṭṭhā conclusion
niṭṭhita completed, ready
ni(r)-tar (I) cross over
nittharaṇaṃ crossing over
nidānaṃ cause, source, origin
nipaka wise
ni-pat (I) fall down (caus. : drop, put down)
ni-pad (III) lie down
nipuṇa subtle
ni(r)-pac (I) concoct
ni(r)-pat (I) flee
ni(r)-vatt (VII) produce
ni(r)-vah (I) lead out
ni(r)-vā (III) become cool, go out, become extinguished
nibbānaṃ extinction (of existence), liberation (from existence), "Nirvāṇa" (from *ni(r)-vā*)
nibbuti (fem.) extinguishing, calming, liberating (from *ni(r)-vā*)
nibbusitattā unsettlement, uneasiness
ni(r)-veṭh (VII) unravel, explain, rebut
nibhā lustre, brilliance
ni-mant (VII) invite, ask (*āsanena* ~ to sit down, offer a seat)
nimitto sign, omen, portent
nimmātar (masc.) creator
niyata constant, certain
niyati (fem.) Fate, Destiny
ni(r)-yat (VII) (*niyyādeti*) hand over, give in charge of
ni(r)-yā (I) go out (to)
ni(r) (prefix) out, without
nirayo purgatory
nirāmisa non-sensual
nirutti (fem.) language
ni-rudh (III) stop, cease, end
nirodho cessation, peace of mind, calm
ni(r)-mā create

nillopo plunder
ni-vatt (I) go back (caus. = turn back, transitive)
nivāretar (masc.) keeper away
ni-vās (VII) dress
nivāso life, existence
nivesanaṃ house, building
ni-sidh (I) caus. = prevent, prohibit
ni-sīd (I) sit down
nisīdanaṃ seat (on the ground)
nisedho prevention, prohibition
nissakkanaṃ escaping, leaving
nissaraṇaṃ liberation
nissāya (ger. of *ni-(s)sī* (I)) depending on, leaning on
nī (I) lead, draw
nīca inferior, low
nīla blue
nīvaraṇaṃ obstacle
ni(r)-har (I) (*nīharati*) take out, take away
→ *nu* (ind., enclitic) ?, does ? (see Vocab. 12)
nekkhammaṃ renunciation
negamo town dweller, bourgeois
netti (fem.) leading, tendency
netvā (ger. *nī*) having led
nemitto diviner, prognosticator, astrologer, soothsayer
no (ind.) not (emphatic)
nhā (III) bathe

p

(p)pa (prefix) out, away
paṃsu (masc.) dust, mud
(p)pa-kapp (VII) dispense
(p)pa-kās (I) (shine : poetic) caus. = show
pakka ripe
(p)pa-(k)kam (I) go away
pakkhandikā dysentery
(p)pa-(k)khal (VII) wash
(p)pa-(k)khā (III) be clear to, be visible to, be apparent to (dat.)
(p)pa-(k)khip (I*) put into
pakkhin (masc.) bird
pag eva (ind.) how much more so, let alone, still more, still less
(p)pa-(g)gah (V) apply
(p)pa-(g)ghar (I) trickle, drip
pac (I) cook, torture, torment
paccaṅgaṃ part
paccatta individual, personal, independent
paccattaṃ individually, personally
paccatthiko enemy
paccantajo borderer, foreigner
paccantima bordering, foreign
(p)paccayo condition, cause
(p)paṭi-ā-gam (I) return
paccājāta (p.p. *(p)paṭi-ā-jan* (III)) reborn
(p)paṭi-ā-ni(r)-yā (I) go back, return
(p)paṭi-ā-vam (I) swallow back
(p)paṭi-ā-sis (or *-āsis*) (II) hope for, expect
(p)paṭi-u(d)-(ṭ)ṭhā (I) (*-ṭṭheti*) rise
(p)paṭi-u(d)-tar (I) come (back) out (after bathing)
(p)paṭi-u(d)-ā-vatt (I) turn back again
paccupaṭṭhita (p.p. *(p)paṭi-upa-(ṭ)ṭhā*) set up
(p)paccuppanna present (time)
(p)paṭi-i (I) (*pacceti*) assume
(p)paṭi-o-ruh (I) get down, alight
pacchima last, western
pacchā (ind.) afterwards, back, behind, west
pacchāyā shade
pajā the creation, the created universe (Brahmanical theory)
pajānanā understanding
pajjoto lamp
(p)pa-(j)jhe (I) be consumed with regret
pañca five
pañcama fifth
paññatta authorized, customary
paññatti (fem.) concept
(p)pa-(ñ)ñap (VII) prepare, declare
(p)pa-(ñ)ñā (V) understand, have insight ; passive = be discerned
paññā understanding, wisdom
paññāpanaṃ preparation
paññāsā (fem.) (or *-a* neut.) fifty
pañho question
(p)paṭi (prefix) towards, back
(p)paṭi-(k)kus (I) decry, criticize (in " bad " sense)
(p)paṭikkūla distasteful, disagreeable
paṭigacc' eva (ind.) as a precaution
(p)paṭi-gam (I) go back
(p)paṭi-(g)gah (V) accept (caus. = make receive, accept)

paṭiggahetar (masc.) receiver, recipient
(*p*)*paṭigho* repulsion, reacting, reaction, resistance
paṭicca (ger. (*p*)*paṭi-i*) conditioned by, because of (usually with acc.)
paṭicchanna covered, concealed
→ *paṭi-*(*ñ*)*ñā* (V) admit
paṭiññā admission, assertion
paṭinissaggo rejecting, renouncing
(*p*)*paṭinissaṭṭha* (p.p. *paṭi-ni*(*r*)-(*s*)*saj*[1]) rejected, renounced
paṭipathaṃ (ind.) the opposite way, in the opposite direction, the other way
(*p*)*paṭi-*(*p*)*pa-nam* (I) abate (caus. = check)
(*p*)*paṭi-pad* (III) engage in, follow, practise, behave (habitually)
paṭipadā way
(*p*)*paṭi-*(*p*)*pa-*(*s*)*sambh* (I) abate, be allayed
→ *paṭibāho* repulse, repelling
(*p*)*paṭibhayaṃ* danger, terror
(*p*)*paṭi-bhā* (I) be clear
(*p*)*paṭibhānaṃ* intuition, inspiration
(*p*)*paṭi-yat* prepare (only caus. form: *paṭiyādāpeti*, except for p.p. *paṭiyatta*)
(*p*)*paṭi-rājan* (masc.) hostile king
(*p*)*paṭirūpa* proper
(*p*)*paṭi-labh* (I) obtain, acquire
paṭilābho acquisition
(*p*)*paṭilomaṃ* (ind.) in reverse order
(*p*)*paṭi-vaṭṭ* (I) turn back
(*p*)*paṭi-vas* (I) dwell
(*p*)*paṭi-vid* (I) only caus.: inform, announce
(*p*)*paṭi-vidh* (III) penetrate, comprehend
(*p*)*paṭi-vi-nī* (I) dispel
(*p*)*paṭi-vi-ram* (I) abstain
(*p*)*paṭi-vi-ruh* (I*) grow again
(*p*)*paṭivedho* penetration, comprehension
(*p*)*paṭi-saṃ-vid* (VII) feel, experience
paṭisaṃvedana feeling, experiencing
(*p*)*paṭisaṃvedin-* feeling, experiencing
(*p*)*paṭi-saṃ-cikkh* (I) reflect, consider
paṭissati = *pati-*
(*p*)*paṭi-*(*s*)*su* (V) agree, assent to (dat.)
(*p*)*paṭi-sev* (I) indulge in
paṭṭhānaṃ basis

N

paṭhama (numeral) first
paṭhamaṃ (ind.) first, firstly
paṭhavī earth
paṇavo drum
paṇidhi (masc.) aspiration, determination
paṇiyaṃ commodity
paṇihita (p.p. (*p*)*pa-ni-dhā*) held
paṇīta excellent, delightful, delicious
paṇḍita wise, astute
paṇḍito wise man
paṇḍurogo jaundice
paṇṇarasa fifteen
pati (masc.) lord
paticca (= *paṭicca*)
(*p*)*paṭi*(> *pati*)-(*ṭ*)*ṭhā* (I) set up, station oneself
patiṭṭhā resting place, perch
patisallānaṃ retirement, seclusion (sometimes spelt *paṭi-*)
patisallīna retired, secluded (sometimes spelt *paṭi-*)
patissati (fem.) recollectedness, mindfulness
(*p*)*patta* (p.p. (*p*)*pa-āp* and *-ap*(*p*)) attained
patti (fem.) attainment
pattiko pedestrian, infantryman
patto bowl
(*p*)*pa-*(*t*)*thar* (I) spread out
patho road, way
padaṃ word
padakkhiṇa dextrous, skilful in, good at (loc.)
padakkhiṇā reverence, veneration, circumambulation
(*p*)*pa-dā* (I) give to, hand over
padīpeyyaṃ lamp
padīpo lamp
padeso place, locality, region
padoso anger
(*p*)*pa-dhā* (I) exert
padhānaṃ exertion
pana (ind., enclitic) but, however, now
pantho road
pappaṭako fungus
(*p*)*pa-ap*(*p*) (VI) attain, arrive (poetic)
(*p*)*pa-bandh* (I) bind
pabāḷha violent
pabb (I) thrive, flourish

(*p*)*pa-*(*v*)*vaj* (I) go forth (from ordinary life to wandering) (caus. : banish)
pabbajito one who has gone forth
pabbajjā going forth
pabbato mountain
pabbājanā banishment
pabhā radiance, luminosity
pamāṇaṃ measure, size
pamāṇakata measurable, finite
(*p*)*pamādo* negligence, pastime
payas- milk
(*p*)*pa-yā* (I) set out
payirupāsanaṃ attending on
(*p*)*pa-yuj* (VII) undertake
para (pronoun) other, another
parakkamo courage, valour
parama most, highest
paraṃ (ind.) after (abl.)
parā (prefix) on, on to
parā-mas (I) hold on to, be attached to
parāyana depending on
pari (prefix) round, around
pari-(*k*)*khī* (III) exhaust, eliminate
pari-(*g*)*gah* (V) occupy, possess
pariggaha possessing
pari-car (I) tend (caus. = enjoy oneself)
paricca (gerund) going to, going round, encompassing
parijeguccho disgust
pari-nam (I) (*pariṇam-*) change, develop (caus. = digest)
pariṇata (p.p. *pari-nam* (I)) changed, developed
pariṇāmo digestion
pariṇāyako leader
paritajjanā threatening, intimidation
pari-tas (III) long (for), desire
paritassanā longing
paritta small, restricted
pari-dev (VII) lament, grieve
paridevo lamentation, grief
pari-ni(*r*)*-vā* (I) (or (III)) attain extinction, attain liberation
parinibbānaṃ attainment of *nibbānaṃ*, especially the Parinibbānaṃ of the Buddha in 486 B.C.
parinibbuta (p.p. *pari-ni*(*r*)*-vā*)
pari-nī (I) lead round
paripakka ripe
paripantho ambush
paripāko ripening
pari-pucch (I) ask about, ask advice
paripuṇṇa full, perfect
paribbājako wanderer
pari-bhās (I) defame, slander
paribhāsā slander
pari-bhuj (II) eat, enjoy
pari-bhū (I) despise (caus. : treat with, penetrate with, fill with)
parimukhaṃ (ind.) in front
pariya (adj.) encompassing
pariyanta bordered, encircled
pari-ā-dā (III) (*pariyā-*) use up, exhaust
pariyāyo course
pariyāhata deduced
pari-is(*a*) (I) (*pariyes-*) seek, look for, search
pariyeṭṭhi (fem.) seeking, looking for, search
pari-o-nah (II) (*pariyonandhati*) cover up, envelop
pariyosānaṃ ending, conclusion
pari-rakkh (I) guard
pariḷāho burning, lust
parivaṭuma limited, circumscribed
parivaṭṭaṃ circle
pari-vas (I) live among
parivitakko reflection, idea
pari-vis (I*) serve (with food)
→ *parisā* assembly
pari-sudh (III) become pure
pari-har (I) watch over, protect
pari-hā (I) passive = be eliminated, come to an end ; caus. = bring to an end, rescind
parihāni (fem.) decrease, decline, loss
paro- more than
palāpo nonsense
palālaṃ straw
palāso foliage
pari (> *pali*)*-kujj* (I) squat down
paligho bar (holding a door)
palipanna (p.p. *pari-pad* (III)) fallen into
pari(> *pali*)*-*(*s*)*saj* [2] (I) embrace
(*p*)*pa-luj* (III) decay
paloko decay
pallaṅko sitting cross-legged
pallalaṃ pool
(*p*)*pa-vaḍḍh* (I) increase
(*p*)*pa-vatt* (I) set going, start, get

going, revolve, go on, continue, proceed
pavattar (masc.) proclaimer
(*p*)*pa-vap* (I) sow
(*p*)*pa-vass* (I) rain heavily
(*p*)*pavādo* debate
(*p*)*pa-vid* (I) (only caus.: make known)
(*p*)*pa-vis* (I*) enter
pavuttaṃ recitation
(*p*)*pa-vedh* (I) tremble
pavesetar (masc.) shower in, usher
pasanna confident in, trusting
(*p*)*pa-*(*s*)*sambh* I become calm (caus. = make calm)
pasayha (gerund of (*p*)*pa-sah* (I)) having forced
(*p*)*pa-saṃs* (I) praise
pasaṭa (pp. (*p*)*pa-sar*) stretched out, frank, open
(*p*)*pa-sar* (I) stretch out, intrans. (caus. = stretch out, trans.)
(*p*)*pa-*(*s*)*sas* (I) breathe out
→ (*p*)*pa-sās* (I) govern
(*p*)*pa-su* (I) generate
pasu (masc.) animal (esp. domestic)
pasuta intent on
pass (I) (and (*d*)*dis*) see
passaddhi (fem.) calmness, tranquillity
passena (ind.) on its side
passo side
(*p*)*pa-har* (I) hit, beat
(*p*)*pa-hā* (I) give up, renounce
pahānaṃ abandoning
(*p*)*pa-hi* (V) send
pahita (p.p. (*p*)*pa-dhā* (I)) exerted
(*p*)*pa-hū* (I) can
pahūta much, many
pā (I) (*pivati*) drink, desid. = be thirsty
pāka ripe, ripened
pākāro city wall, ramparts
pākima fruitful, ripening
pācariyo teacher's teacher
pāṭikaṅkha probable
pāṇi (masc.) hand
pāṇo breath, life, living (breathing) being
pātarāso breakfast, morning meal
pātavyatā indulgence
pātimokkho liberation
pātu(*r*) (prefix) manifest
pātubhāvo appearance, manifestation
pātu(*r*)*-bhū* (I) appear (to: dat.), be(come) manifest
pāto (ind.) in the morning (in compound before a vowel *pātar*)
-pāto dropping, offering, collecting
pādo foot, basis
pānaṃ drink
pānīyaṃ (drinking) water
pāpa bad, evil
pāpaka bad
pāpīya worse
(*p*)*pa-āp* (may also be considered as *-ap*) (V) attain (in figurative sense)
pābhataṃ present, gratuity, capital, grant →
pāmokkha foremost
pāraṃ (ind.) thither, across, beyond
pāripūri (fem.) perfection
pārima further, other side
pārisajjo councillor, member of an assembly
pārisuddhi (fem.) purity
pa-ā-vad (I) tell →
pāsādika lovely
pāsādo palace
pi (ind. enclitic) also, too, even
piṭṭhito (ind.) behind (gen.)
piṇḍo alms
pitar (masc.) father
pipāsu thirsty, drunken, drunkard
pipāsita thirsty
pipāsin thirsty
piya dear (to: dat.)
piyadassana lovable sight, whose appearance inspires affection
piyāyita (p.p. of denom.) held dear, beloved
pisuṇa malicious
pih (VII) long for (dat.)
pīṇ (I) please (only caus.)
pīta yellow
pīti (fem.) joy
puggalo person
pucch (I) ask
pucchitar (masc.) asker
puñjo heap
puññaṃ merit, good, goodness, meritorious action
puṭo bag, package (of merchandise)
putto son
puthu many, various

puna(d) (ind.) again
punabbhavo rebirth
pubba before, former
pubbaka former, old
pubbaṇho morning
pubbanto origin
pubbe (ind.) before, (as) formerly
puman- man
purakkhata (p.p. *pura(s)-kar*) facing, in front
purakkhatvā (gerund) facing
purato (ind.) before, in front of (gen.)
puratthā (ind.) east, formerly
puratthima east
purāṇa old
purima former, earlier
puriso man, person
pure (ind.) before, in advance, at first
purohito high priest, prime minister
pus (VII) rear, look after
pūj (VII) honour
pūra full
pe (ind.) and so on, etc.
(p)pa-ikkh (I) look on, watch
pekkhitar (masc.) looker on, watcher, observer
peto one who has passed away, dead man
pettika paternal
peyya (f.p.p. *pā*) to be drunk, drinkable
pes (VII) send, drive
pesala congenial
pokkharaṇī lotus pool
pokkharatā complexion
pokkharasātako a kind of bird
poṭh (VII) snap (fingers)
pothujjanika common
ponobhavika leading to rebirth
porāṇaṃ antiquity, ancient tradition
porisaṃ service
posako rearer, breeder
poso (poetic form of *puriso*)

ph

phand (I) throb, quiver
phar (I) pervade
pharusa harsh, rough
(p)phal (I) split (intrans.)
phalaṃ fruit
phasso touch, contact
phāsu comfortable
phīta prosperous
phulla blossoming, blossomed
phus (I*) touch, reach, attain
phoṭṭhabbaṃ touchable (object), sensation, tangible object

b

badālatā creeper
bandh (I) bind
bandhanaṃ bond, fetter
bandhu (masc.) Kinsman, a name of God (*brahmā* as father or grandfather of all creatures)
→ *babbajaṃ* a coarse grass (used in making ropes and slippers)
balaṃ strength
balavant strong
bali (masc.) tithe, religious tax or contribution
bahiddhā (ind.) outside, apart
bahu much, many
bahuka much, plenty
bahukāra very useful
bahula frequent, abundant (at end of compound = fond of, devoted to, cultivating)
bahulī-kar (VI) cultivate
bāla foolish
bālo fool
bāḷha strong, excessive, violent
bāhā arm
bāhira external, foreign
biḷāro cat
bījaṃ seed
bījagāmo plants, the vegetable kingdom, the community of plants
budh (III) know, be aware of, be enlightened
bodhi (fem.) enlightenment
brahmakāyika having a God-like body, of the substance of God (the gods who are the companions, retinue or courtiers of God)
brahmacariyaṃ God-like life, best life, celibate life
brahmacārin celibate, having the best way of life
brahmadeyyaṃ ("gift to God": i.e. grant of land/villages to a priest of the Brahmanical religion) grant, fief, benefice

brahmā (masc.) (*brahman-*) the best, supreme, God
brāhmaṇī (priestess) woman of the hereditary priest-class
brāhmaṇo priest, brahman (member of the hereditary priesthood)
brū (I) say, call (poetic)

bh

bhakkh (VII) eat, devour
-bhakkha eating, feeding on
bhagavā (*bhagavant-*) (masc.) the fortunate (title of the Buddha), the Master, the bountiful
bhaj (I) resort to
bhaṇ (I) say
bhaṇe (ind.) I say !
bhaṇḍaṃ goods, stores, supplies
bhaṇḍikā parcel, bundle
bhaṇḍu shaven-headed
bhattaṃ meal
bhadante (ind.) sir ! (polite address by Buddhist monks to the Buddha)
bhadda good (repeated = very good)
bhaddaṃ (ind.) good luck ! (dat.)
bhante (ind.) sir ! (polite address to a monk)
bhabba capable (with dat.)
bhamakāro turner
bhayaṃ danger, fear
bhavant (pronoun) you, sir, your honour, his honour
bhavaṃ (ind.) good fortune ! best wishes ! (greeting, with acc. of person and ipv. of *as*)
bhavo existence, good fortune
bhavyo being, future being
bhāgineyyo nephew (sister's son)
bhāgo share, part
bhātar (masc.) brother
bhāro burden, load
bhāvanaṃ development
bhāvo nature, state, status
bhās (I) say, speak
bhāsitaṃ speech, saying
bhāsitar (masc.) speaker
bhikkhu (masc.) monk
bhikkhunī nun
bhiṅkāro vase, ceremonial water vessel
bhitti (fem.) wall
bhid (II) split (trans.)
bhiyya more
bhiyyo (ind.) more
bhiyyoso (ind.) still more (so), still greater
bhiyyoso mattāya (= abl.) to a still greater extent/degree
bhī (I) be afraid
bhuj (II) eat
bhū (I) be, exist (caus. : develop)
bhūto living being
bhūtagāmo living beings, the community of living beings, the animal kingdom
bhūtapubbaṃ (ind.) formerly, once upon a time
bhūmi (fem.) earth, ground, place
bhedanaṃ opening
bhedo division, splitting up
bhesajjaṃ medicine, drug
bhogin possessing, enjoying
bhogo property
bhogga bent
bhoggaṃ property, proprietary rights
bhojanaṃ meal, food
bhojanīyaṃ (soft) foods

m

ma(d) (pronoun) I
maṃsaṃ flesh, meat
makkh (VII) smear
maggo road, way
maṅku shamefaced
macco mortal
majjaṃ intoxicant, liquor, drink
majjhima middle, intermediate, medium
majjhe (ind.) in the middle
mañcako bed
maññe (ind.) I think, no doubt, I suppose, as if
maṇḍalaṃ circle, disc
mataṃ opinion
mattā measure
madanīya intoxicating
mado drink (intoxicating), excess
maddava tender
madhu (adj.) sweet, (neut. = honey)
madhuraka drunk, intoxicated
man (III) think, desid. = investigate
man (VI) consider
manas- mind
manasikāro attention

manāpa pleasing
manujo human being (poetic)
manusso human being, person
mant (VII) take counsel, discuss (confidentially)
manda slow, dull, inept
mandattaṃ dullness, ineptitude
manomaya mental, spiritual ("consisting of mind")
manto prayer, hymn
mamattaṃ possessiveness, selfishness
-maya consisting of, made of
mayaṃ (pronoun) we
mayūro peacock
mar (III) die
maraṇaṃ death
mariyādā boundary
malaṃ dirt
massu (neut.) beard
mahaggata sublime, elevated
mahant- great
mahallako elder
mahājano the people
mahābhūto element
mahāmatto minister
mahārājo great king, king
mahī the earth (poetic)
mahesakkha superior
mā (ind.) don't
mā (V) measure
māṇavo boy, young priest
mātar (fem.) mother
mātikā matrix, notes
mān (VII) honour, respect, revere
mānusaka human
mānuso man, human being (poetic)
māno pride, conceit
māp (VII) build
māyā trick
mārisa (voc.) sir !, dear sir !, my friend !, dear boy ! (polite and affectionate address customary among the gods, used also by gods addressing men)
Māro the god of death and passion (leading to rebirth), the Devil
mālā garland
māso month
migo beast, deer
micchā (ind. or fem.) badly, wrongly ; wrong, misconduct
mitto friend
mithu opposed
middhaṃ stupidity, mental derangement
milātaṃ palanquin, litter
missa mixed
mukhaṃ mouth
muc (II) become free
muñjaṃ a kind of rush (used for making ropes, girdles, and slippers)
muṭṭhi (masc.) fist
muṇḍa shaven
muṇḍaka shaven-headed
muttaṃ urine
mutti (fem.) freeing
mud (I) rejoice
muda glad, joyful
muditā sympathetic joy, sympathy, gladness (joy at the well-being of others)
mudu supple
mudutā suppleness
muddhan- (masc.) head
muni (masc.) recluse (poetic)
musā falsehood
muhuttaṃ (or masc.) moment
mūlaṃ root, base, capital (money)
mūḷha (p.p. *muh*) lost
megho cloud
mettā love (non-sexual, spiritual), kindness, loving kindness, benevolence, goodwill, friendliness
methuna sexual
medhāvin intelligent, wise
mogha false, erroneous, excluded
momūha extremely stupid
momūhattaṃ extreme stupidity
moho delusion

y

ya(d) (pronoun) who, which (as ind. : *yaṃ* that, what, since, if, whereas ; *yena* which may, towards)
yad agge (ind.) since, since the day that/when
yaṃ kiñ ci (pronoun) whatever
yad idaṃ (ind.) such as, as, to wit, i.e., namely
yan nūna (ind.) what now if ?, what if ?, now if, supposing ?
yakkho god, demon
yagghe (ind.) hear !

yaj (I) sacrifice
yañño sacrifice (ritual)
yato (ind.) because, since, whence
yattha (ind.) where
yatthicchakaṃ (ind.) wherever one wishes
yatra (ind.) where
yatra hi nāma (ind.) in as much as (may express wonder, etc.)
yathā (ind.) as, how
yathā kathaṃ (ind.) in what way ?
yathā yathā (ind.) in whatever way, however
yathākata usual, customary
yathābalaṃ (ind.) according to one's ability
yathābhirantaṃ (ind.) according to one's pleasure, (as long) as one likes
yathābhucca real, proper
yathābhūtaṃ (ind.) as it really is, in its true nature, according to nature
yathāsandiṭṭhaṃ (ind.) with one's acquaintances
yathāsambhattaṃ (ind.) with one's comrades
yadā (ind.) when
yadi (ind.) whether
yadicchakaṃ (ind.) whatever one wishes
yamakaṃ pair
yasas- reputation
yasassin reputable, respected
yasmā (ind.) because, since
yahiṃ (ind.) whereabouts
yā (I) go
yāc (I) request, ask (for—not a question)
yājetar (masc.) sacrificer
yānaṃ carriage
-yāniya leading to
yāmo watch (of the night)
yāva (ind.) as far as, up to (abl.), as much, to what extent, until, as long as
yāvakīvaṃ (ind.) as long as
yāvajīvaṃ (ind.) as long as one lives, all one's life
yāvataka (fem. *-ikā*) as far as, as many as
yāvatā (ind.) as far as
yāvaticchakaṃ (ind.) as far as one wishes
yāvadatthaṃ (ind.) as much as one wants
yiṭṭhaṃ (p.p. *yaj* (I)) sacrifice, offering
yugaṃ yoke
yuj (VII) yoke
yuddhaṃ battle, war
yuvan (masc.) youth
yena (ind.) which way, towards
yebhuyyena (ind.) mostly, the majority of
yeva (= *eva*)
yoggaṃ draught animal, ox
yojanaṃ league (about 4·5 miles)
yoni (fem.) womb, origin, source
yoniso (ind.) methodically, consequently
yobbanaṃ youth (state of)

r

rakkhā safety
rajataṃ silver
rajanaṃ dye
rajanīya exciting
rajas- dust
rajjaṃ kingdom
rajju (fem.) rope
rañj (I) be excited, be glad, be delighted
ratanaṃ gem, precious thing
ratta coloured
rattaññū (masc.) one of long standing, senior
ratti (fem.) night
rathiyā street
ratho chariot, cart
ram (I) delight, enjoy (poetic)
ramaṇīya delightful
ramma delightful (poetic)
raso taste, piquancy, enjoyment (aesthetic experience, source of aesthetic experience)
rassa short
rassaṃ (ind.) shortly
rahogata alone, in privacy
rāgo passion, desire
rājakulaṃ royal court
rājadāyo gift by the king, royal endowment
rājaputto prince
rājabhoggaṃ crown property
rājā (masc.) (*rājan-*) king
rāsiko accumulation

rukkho tree
rucira splendid
rud (I*) weep
ruh (I*) grow (caus. : plant)
rūpaṃ form (usually as property of matter), matter, sight (object)
-rūpa kind, sort
rūpabhavo existence in the imponderable world (of the gods)
rūpin- formed, material
re (ind.) hey !, damn you ! (contemptuous address)
reṇu (masc.) pollen
rogo illness

l

lakkhaṇaṃ mark, special quality, excellence, shapeliness, definition
laddha (p.p. *labh* (I))
labbhā (ind.) possible, conceivable, is it conceivable ? (see Vocab. 27)
labh (I) get, obtain, find
lahu light (weight)
lābho gain
(*lābhā* in the idiom *tassa te* . . . ~ . . . *suladdhaṃ* is taken by the Commentary as plural : " gains for you . . ." ; some philologists maintain that it is an indeclinable ; it is in any case elevated or emotive)
likhita polished
liṅgaṃ characteristic
lip (II) smear
luḷita stirred up
lūna (p.p. *lū* (V)) reaped, mown
leḍḍu (masc.) clod
loko world, people, universe
locanaṃ eye (poetic)
lomaṃ hair (of the body)
lola restless, fickle, wanton
lohita red
lohitaṃ blood

v

va (= *eva*) (ind., enclitic) only, just, surely
va (ind., enclitic) like (poetic : a variant for *viya* and *iva* occasionally used in verse)
vaggu soft (especially of sounds)
vaṅka crooked
vaṅkaṃ hook
vac (I) say
vacanaṃ saying, speech, words (sing. collective)
vacī speech
(*v*)*vaj* (I) go (poetic)
vañc (VII) deceive
vañjha barren, sterile
vaṭumaṃ road
vaṭṭ (I) turn, roll, circle
vaṭṭaṃ rolling, circulation, cycle, cycling (of the universe)
vaṇijjā commerce
vaṇippatho trade
vaṇṇavant- beautiful, handsome
vaṇṇo colour, beauty, praise, class
vata (ind., enclitic) surely, indeed ! (emphatic and emotive : mild expletive expressing a wish, regret, reproach or surprise : cf. " alas ! ", " my word ! ", " I say ! ", " good heavens ! ", and the like)
(*v*)*vataṃ* vow
vatt (I) proceed, conduct oneself, go on (doing)
vattaṃ conduct, duty, government
vattar (masc.) speaker
-vattin setting going, deploying, operating, conducting, governing, developing
vatthaṃ garment (pl. clothes, dress)
vatthu (neut.) thing, (building) site, position, mode (of argument)
vad (I) say, speak
vadhū (fem.) bride
vadho execution
vanaṃ a wood
vanta (p.p. *vam*) vomited
vand (I) salute, pay respect
vayas- age, period of life
vayo loss
var (I) (or (VII) irreg.) choose
var (VII) prevent, hinder, obstruct, stop
vara excellent, good (poetic)
varaṃ boon
vas (I) live (caus. = make live with)
vasanaṃ wearing
vasavattin- wielding power
vasin- master, authority
vaso control
vassaṃ rain, rainy season (plur.), year
vassika rainy (for the rainy season)

-vassuddesika about the age of (numeral-)
vā (ind., enclitic) or, either
vācā speech
vācetar (masc.) causer to speak
vāṇijo merchant
vāto wind
vāditaṃ instrumental music
vādin- speaking
vādo debate, argument, statement
vāma lovely (poetic)
vāma left
vi-ā-yam (I) (*vāyamati*) exercise, practice
vāyas- air
vāyāmo exercise
vāri (neut.) water
vālo wild animal
vās (VII) dress
vāsī hatchet
vāso dwelling place, camp
vāhanaṃ mount (animal or vehicle)
vāhanāgāraṃ stable, coach-house, mews
vi (prefix) apart, asunder, strongly, without
vikāro disorder
vi-kit desid. = be uncertain
vikkhitta diffuse, vain
vikkhepo confusion, equivocation
vigata- without, free from
viggaho quarrel, strife
vighāto remorse
vicayo discrimination
vicārita (p.p. caus. *vi-car* (I)) excogitated, pondered
vicāro cogitation, pondering
vi-ci (V) investigate, search out
vicikicchā uncertainty
viceyya inscrutable
vi-jan (III) give birth
vijitaṃ realm, kingdom
vijjā science, knowledge
vi-(ñ)ñā (V) be conscious of, discern
viññāṇaṃ consciousness
viññāpetar causer of discernment
viññutā discernment, discretion
viññū (masc.) discerning person
vitakkita (pp. *vi-takk*) reasoned
vitakko reasoning
vitathaṃ untruth
vitti (fem.) pleasure
vitthāro breadth
vid (II) find (poetic)
vid (III) be, occur, be found
vid (VII) feel
vid (I) know (present not used; caus. = inform)
vidita (p.p. *vid* (II)) found, known, discovered, ascertained
vidū (masc.) knower
-vidha kind (manner), -fold
vinayo discipline
vi-nas (III) perish utterly
vinā (ind.) without (precedes ins.)
vināso destruction
vinipātiko unhappy spirit (reborn in purgatory or as an animal, ghost or demon)
vinipāto ruin
vineyya (ger. *vi-nī*) having eliminated, having disciplined
vi-pac (III) ripen, have a result, bear fruit
vipatti (fem.) failure
vipanna failed, lacking, without
vi-pari-nam (I) (*vipariṇamati*) change
vipāko result
vipula large, abundant
vippaṭisāro regret
vippasanna very clear
vi-bhaj (I) divide
vibhavo non-existence
vimati (fem.) perplexity
vimala free from dirt
vimāno palace, mansion (only of divine beings, in the sky)
vi-muc (III) become free (caus. = set free)
vimutti (fem.) release, liberation
viya (ind., enclitic) like
viyatta (alternative spelling of *vyatta*)
virāgo dispassion
viriyaṃ energy
virūḷhi (fem.) growth
vilepanaṃ ointment, cosmetic
vi-vaṭṭ (I) evolve
vivaṭṭaṃ evolution
vivaraṃ hole
vi-var (I) open
vivādo dispute
vivicca (ger. *vi-vic* (VII)) having become separated from, having become isolated

→

vivitta (p.p. *vi-vic* (VII)) separated, isolated
viveko separation, seclusion, discrimination
visaṃ poison
visajja (ger. *vi-sajj*) getting over, leaving behind
visaṭa (p.p. *vi-sar*) spread, staring
visāci (adj.) sidelong, furtive
visārada confident
visuddha pure, clear
visuddhi (fem.) clarity, purification
vi-sudh (III) become purified
vi-han (I) distress, trouble
vi-har (I) dwell, live
-vihārin living, dwelling, being
vihāro life, way of life, dwelling
vihita (p.p. *vi-dhā*) arranged
vi-heṭh (VII) harass
vihesā trouble, harassing
vīj (I) fan
vīta- without, removed
vi-ati-sār (VII) converse, make (conversation)
vīmaṃsā investigation
vīmaṃsin- (as masc. noun = investigator, exegete, metaphysician)
vīsati (fem.) twenty
vuṭṭh- (see note on *u-/vu-* Vocab. 14)
vuttha (p.p. *vas* (I)) spent (time)
vuddha (sometimes written *vuḍḍha* or *buḍḍha*) old
vuddhi (fem.) increase
vusitavant- having lived (properly), having (truly) lived (as a monk)
vūpakaṭṭha withdrawn, secluded
vūpasamo calming
ve (ind., enclitic) surely (poetic)
veceta daft
vejjo doctor, physician
veṭh (VII) twist, wrap
vetanaṃ wages, pay
vedanā sensation
vedayitaṃ sensation, experience
vediya known (~*aṃ* as noun : thing known, information)
vedhin- shooter, archer
vepullaṃ prevalence
vepullatā abundance
vemattatā difference, distinction
veyyākaraṇaṃ explanation, analysis
veraṃ hatred
veramaṇī abstention
velā bank, time, occasion
vellita wavy
veḷuriyo lapis lazuli
vevaṇṇatā discolouration
vesso husbandman, farmer, merchant, bourgeois (member of the hereditary agricultural-mercantile class : see footnote to Vocab. 20)
(*vo-* : cf. *vi-o*)
vokiṇṇa (p.p. *vi-o-kir*) mixed (with)
vi-o-(k)kam (I) pass away, break away
vi-o-chid (III) cut off, separate from
vi-o-bhid (II) shoot
vyañjanaṃ expression, sentence
vyatta intelligent
vyasanaṃ disaster
vi-ā-kar (VI) explain
vyādhi (masc.) disease
vyādhita diseased, ill
vyāpajjha violent, malevolent
vyāpanna malevolent, violent
vyāpādo violence, malevolence
vyāvaṭa concerned, busy, worried

s

sa- with, possessing
sa- own
saṃ (prefix) together
saṃ-yam (I) control oneself
saṃyamo self-control, abstinence
saṃyojanaṃ connection, union
saṃvaccharaṃ year
saṃ-vaṭṭ (I) involve, dissolve
saṃvaṭṭaṃ dissolution, involution
saṃvaṭṭanika involved in, dissolved in
saṃ-vatt (I) lead to (dat.)
saṃvattanika leading to
saṃvaro restraint
saṃ-vid (III) be, occur, be found
saṃ-vi-dhā (I) arrange, organize
saṃvidhānaṃ arrangement, policy
saṃ-vi-bhaj (I) share
saṃ-vis (I*) go home (caus. = take home)
saṃvuta (p.p. *saṃ-var* (I)) controlled
saṃvejanīya (f.p.p. *saṃ-vij*) emotional, inspiring, stirring
saṃ-sar (I) transmigrate (circulate indefinitely)
saṃsāro transmigration
saṃ-har (I) gather

saṃhita (p.p. *saṃ-dhā*) joined, connected
saka (adj.) own
sak(k) (VI) can, be able (= *sak* (IV))
sakaṭo (also *-ṭaṃ*) cart
saki(d) (*eva*) (ind.) once
sakiṃ (ind.) once
sakuṇo bird
sat-kar (VI) entertain
sakkā (ind.) it is possible, is it possible ?
sakkāro entertainment
sakkhī (ind.) in person, personally
sakhā (masc.) friend
saggo heaven
saṃ-kaḍḍh (I) collect
saṃkappo intention, object
saṃ-(k)kam (I) pass into
saṃkārakūṭo rubbish heap
saṃ-kilis (III) become defiled
saṃkileso defilement
saṃkhata (p.p. *saṃ-kar*) synthesized, activated
saṅkhadhamo conch blower
saṃkhā (= *saṃkhyā*)
-saṃkhāta known as, called (p.p. of *saṃ-(k)khā* (I))
saṃkhāro force, energy, activity, combination, process, instinct, habit (see Vocab. 26)
saṃkhitta limited, narrow (instrumental = briefly, in short)
saṅkho conch
saṃkhyā enumeration, calculation, denomination, classification
saṃghāṭi (fem.) cloak
saṃghāsaṃghin in groups
saṃghāsaṃghīgaṇībhūta clustered in groups
saṃgho community
sace (ind.) if
sacca true
saccaṃ truth
saccaṃ (ind.) it is true that ; is it true that ?
saccavajjaṃ speaking the truth, truthfulness
sacchi-kar (VI) perceive, observe, experience, examine
sacchikiriyā observation, experience
(s)saj [1] (I) pour out
(s)saj [2] (I) embrace
sajjhāyo learning, studying, study
sajjhu (neut.) silver
saṃ-jan (III) be produced
sañjitar (masc.) ordainer
saññata restrained
saṃ-(ñ)ñā (V) experience, perceive
saññā perception
saññin- having perception, sentient
saṭṭhi (fem.) sixty
saṇḍo cluster
sata self-possessed, mindful
sataṃ hundred
(s)sati (fem.) self-possession, mindfulness
satimant- self-possessed, mindful
satta seven
sattati (fem.) seventy
sattattaṃ existence
sattama seventh
sattarasa seventeen
sattāhaṃ week
satto being, creature
satthaṃ sword
satthar (masc.) teacher
satthavāho caravan-merchant
satthiko caravan-merchant
sattho caravan
sadattho the true (good) purpose, the true (good) objective
sadā (ind.) always
sadisa (adj.) like, of such sort
saddo noise, sound, report (rumour)
saddha trusting, believing
saddhā confidence, trust, conviction
saddhiṃ (ind.) with (ins.)
san- (masc.) dog
sant- existing, true (more rarely " good ", particularly in compounds)
santa (p.p. *sam*) calmed
saṃ-tan (VI) stretch out, spread out
saṃ-tapp (VII) gratify, please, satisfy
santānakaṃ film, skin
santikā (ind.) (directly) from (gen.) (at first hand)
santike (ind.) into the presence of (gen. or acc.)
saṃ-tus be contented, be satisfied (only p.p.)
saṃ-(t)thar (I) strew, spread, carpet (with temporary decorative floor covering)

sand (I) flow
sandiṭṭhika visible
saṃ-(d)dis (passive = be seen, appear ; caus. = instruct, review)
sandhātar (masc.) peacemaker
saṃ-dhāv (I) transmigrate (pass on)
sandhi (masc.) junction, joint, breach
saṃ-dhu (V) shake
saṃ-nah (II) tie up
sannidhi (masc.) store
saṃ-ni-pat (I) assemble
sannipāto assembly
sap (I) (not used in the *Dīgha*) curse
sappi (neut.) ghee
sabba (pronoun) all, entire
sabbato (ind.) all round
sabbattatā non-discrimination (" all-self-ness "), considering all beings as like oneself, putting oneself in the place of others
sabbathā (ind.) in all ways
sabbadhi (ind.) everywhere
sabbasanthari (adj.) entirely strewn, completely carpeted
sabbaso (ind.) completely
sabbāvant all-inclusive, whole
sabbena sabbaṃ (ind.) completely, thoroughly
sabhā assembly hall
sama even, equal to, up to, like, impartial
samaṃ (ind.) equally, like
saṃagga united, unanimous
samaṅgī-bhū (I) supply with, provide with
samaññā designation, agreed usage
samaṇo ascetic, wanderer, philosopher (other than a brahman)
saṃ-ati-(k)kam (I) pass beyond, transcend
samatikkamo passing beyond, transcending
samattaṃ (ind.) completely, perfectly
saṃ-anu-ā-gam (I) be endowed with, acquire
saṃ-anu-(g)gah (V) (caus. = ask for reasons, cross-examine)
saṃ-anu-pass (I) envisage
saṃ-anu-bhās (I) criticize, refute
saṃ-anu-yuj (II) take up, cross-question
saṃ-anu-sās (I) install, appoint (as ruler)
samantā (ind.) on all sides, all round, anywhere, in any direction
samappita (p.p. *saṃ-app* (VII) " to fix in ", " to apply to ") presented with
samayo time, occasion (any time, time of an event)
saṃ-ā-dā (III) conform (to a rule or way of life) (caus. = exhort)
samādhi (masc.) concentration
samāpatti (fem.) attainment
saṃ-ā-pad (III) attain
samārambho undertaking, falling upon, destroying
samāhita (p.p. *saṃ-ā-dhā*) concentrated
samihitaṃ collection
samugghāta (p.p. of caus. of *saṃ-u(d)-han*)
saṃ-u(d)-chid (II) abrogate, abolish
samucchinna (p.p. *saṃ-u(d)-chid* (III)) utterly annihilated
saṃ-u(d)-tij (VII) excite, fill with enthusiasm
samudayo origin, origination
saṃ-u(d)-ā-car (I) speak to, converse with
samuddo ocean
samuppanna (p.p. *saṃ-u(d)-pad* (III)) originated
samuppādo origination
saṃ-u(d)-han (I) (*samūhanati*) suppress, abolish
sampajaññaṃ consciousness: deliberation
sampajāna conscious :deliberate
saṃ-pad (III) be endowed with, have
sampadā success
samparikiṇṇa (p.p. *saṃ-pari-kir*) surrounded by, covered with
saṃ-(p)pa-var (VII) feast
sampasādanaṃ serenity
saṃ-(p)pa-haṃs (VII) delight (transitive)
saṃ-pāy (I) maintain one's position, defend one's thesis
samphaṃ frivolity, chatter
samphasso contact, union
sambahula many

sambādha confined
sambuddha enlightened
sambodhi (fem.) enlightenment, complete enlightenment
sambodho enlightenment
sambhavo origin, production
saṃ-bhū (VII) catch up with (acc.)
samma (ind.) my dear ! (fam.)
sammatta intoxicated, maddened
saṃ-man (VI) agree on, elect
sammā (ind.) rightly, perfectly
saṃ-iñj (I) (usually *sammiñj-*) draw in, bend
sammukhā (ind.) in the presence of (gen.)
saṃ-mucch (I) coagulate, form (intrans.)
saṃ-mud (I) greet, exchange greetings with (*saddhiṃ* and instrumental)
sammūḷha bewildered
sammodanīya agreeable, pleasant
sayaṃ (ind.) oneself, self
sayāna (pres. p. *si*) lying down
sar (I) move
(*s*)*sar* (I) remember
saraṃ lake
saraṇaṃ protection, refuge
sarīraṃ body (pl. also " relics ")
(*s*)*saro* sound, voice
saṃ-lakkh (VII) observe
sallāpo talk
saḷāyatanaṃ the six spheres (of the senses : five senses + the mind)
savanaṃ hearing
sassata eternal
sassati (fem.) eternal thing, eternity
sassatisamaṃ (ind.) eternally
saha (ind.) along with, according to (ins.)
sahagata charged with, suffused with
sahavyatā association, condition, union (with gen.)
sahassaṃ thousand
sahāyako friend
sahāyo friend
sahitaṃ kindling block
sā (III) taste
sā (pronoun) she
sākhā branch
sāṇaṃ hemp
sāta sweet
sādhu good
sādhu (ind.) well, please
sādhuka good
sādhukaṃ (ind.) well
sāpateyyaṃ property
sāpekha wishing for, desiring, preferring
sāmaṃ (ind.) oneself, self
sāmaññaṃ state of being a wanderer/ascetic/philosopher, profession of asceticism, etc.
sāmisa sensual
sāmukkaṃsaka exalted, sublime
sāmuddika oceanic, ocean going
sāyaṃ (ind.) in the evening
sāyaṇho evening
sāyamāso evening meal
sārathi (masc.) charioteer
sārāgo passion
sārāṇīya polite
sāro value (also the valuable/best part of anything)
sālā hall
sāli (fem.) rice
sālikā myna
sālo a kind of tree : *Shorea robusta*
sālohito blood relation
sāvako pupil
sāvetar (masc.) reciter
sās (I) rule
sāsanaṃ instruction, doctrine
si (I) lie down
sikkh (I) train, study, learn
sikkhā training
sikkhāpadaṃ training, (moral) rule, precept
siṅghāṭako crossroads, square
sic (II) sprinkle
sippaṃ craft, trade, profession
siras- head
siriṃsapo snake
sirīmant beautiful, fortunate (poetic)
sis (VII) leave
sīghaṃ (ind.) fast (repeated = very fast)
sīta cool
sīlaṃ virtue, good conduct
sīlavant virtuous, well conducted
sīsaṃ lead
sīsaṃ head
sīho lion
su (I) crush, extract (liquids), produce

su- (prefix) well, good (meaning " very ", may be prefixed to adjectives in poetry)
(*s*)*su* (V) (rarely (IV)) hear, desid. = desire to hear
(*s*)*su* (ind.) even, isn't it ? (or merely emphatic)
sukara easy
sukumāra delicate
suko parrot
sukka white, light coloured
sukkha dry
sukha happy (denom. *sukheti*, be happy)
sukhaṃ happiness
sukhallikā pleasure, enjoyment
sukhin- happy
sukhuma fine, subtle
sugati (fem.) good destiny
sugato well-gone (title of the Buddha)
suc (I) grieve, sorrow
sucaritaṃ good conduct
succhavi pleasant to the skin (*chavi* fem.)
suñña empty
suṭṭhu (ind.) well (done)
suṇo dog
suttaṃ thread, (record of a) dialogue, collection of dialogues
(*s*)*sudaṃ* (ind.) even
sudassana beautiful (poetic)
suddo helot (member of the servile or working class : see footnote to Vocab. 20)
sudh (III) become pure, become clean
supatittha having good beaches (for getting water to drink, etc.)
subh (I) make clear, shine, be glorious
subha lustrous, fair
subhaṃ lustre, glory
subhāsita well-spoken
sumedhasa very intelligent (poetic)
suriyo sun
suro god (poetic)
suvaṇṇaṃ gold
susu (masc.) boy, young (of animals)
sussūsā desire to hear
sūkaro pig
seṭṭha best
seṭṭhi (fem. ?) ash
setaka clear, clean
setu (masc.) causeway, dam, bridge
sedaka sweating →
senāsanaṃ abode, resting place
seyya better
seyyathā (ind.) as, just like (introducing a simile)
seyyathīdaṃ (ind.) as, to wit, as follows
seyyā bed
seyyo (ind.) better
sev (I) indulge in, pursue
so (pronoun) he
soko grief, sorrow
soceyyaṃ purity
sotaṃ ear
sotar (masc.) hearer
sotāpanna (*sotas-* " stream ") in the stream, on the Way
sotthi (ind.) safety, safely (dat.)
sotthinā (ind.) safely
sobbhaṃ pit
somanassaṃ joy, elation
soḷasa sixteen
sovaggika heavenly, leading to heaven
svāgataṃ (ind.) welcome ! (dat.)
svātanāya (ind.) for tomorrow

h

ha (ind.) indeed, truly
hatthinikā she-elephant
hattho hand
han (I) kill
hanu (fem.) jaw(s)
hantar (masc.) killer
handa (ind.) well !
handa je (ind.) you there ! (cf. *je*)
har (I) take, desid. (irreg.) = desire to take, wish for
haritaka green, fresh
have (ind.) truly, surely (poetic)
hā (I) abandon, diminish, be eliminated
hi (ind., enclitic) for, because, though
hitaṃ benefit, welfare
hiraññaṃ gold (money)
hiri (fem.) modesty, self-respect, conscience
his (II) injure
hīna inferior
hutaṃ oblation
hū (I) be
heṭh (VII) harass
hetu (masc.) cause
hemantika winter

ENGLISH–PALI VOCABULARY

The first apparent synonym given is generally the nearest to the English, the most usual and the least " elevated ", though the others may have special shades of meaning appropriate for certain contexts. The Pali–English Vocabulary will in many cases give a clearer idea of the meanings of the various Pali words, but the precise meanings can be gleaned only from their use in the texts.

The Pali parts of speech and genders are indicated as in the Pali–English Vocabulary. Verbs are given first. The English parts of speech have not been noticed.

a

a (usually no equivalent) ***aññatara*** (pronoun), ***eka*** (pronoun, numeral : see Lesson 17)
abandon ***hā*** (I), ***chaḍḍ*** (VII)
abandoned ***catta*** (p.p. ***caj***)
abandoning ***pahānaṃ***, ***cāgo***
abate ***(p)paṭi-(p)pa-(s)sambh*** (I)
according to one's ability ***yathābalaṃ*** (ind.)
abode ***senāsanaṃ***
abolish ***saṃ-u(d)-han*** (I), ***saṃ-u(d)-chid*** (II)
about ***ārabbha*** (acc., ger. ***ā-rabbh*** (I)), ***abhi*** (prefix)
above ***uddhaṃ*** (ind.)
abrogate ***saṃ-u(d)-chid*** (II)
absolute ***aparisesa***, ***asesa***
absolutely ***aññadatthu*** (ind.)
abstain ***(p)paṭi-vi-ram*** (I)
abstention ***veramaṇī***
abstinence ***saṃyamo***
abundant ***vipula***, ***bahula***
abundance ***ussado***, ***vepullatā***
abuse ***ā-(k)kus*** (I)
accept ***dhar*** (VII) (2 accs. : x as y), ***(p)paṭi-(g)gah*** (V) or caus., ***adhi-vas*** caus. (invitation to stay at = acc.)
accepted ***adhivuttha*** (p.p. ***adhi-vas***)
accomplish ***tīreti*** (denom.)
according to ***saha*** (ind., ins.)
accumulated ***upacita*** (p.p. ***upa-ci*** (V))
accumulation ***rāsiko***
acknowledge ***(p)paṭi-(ñ)ñā*** (V)
with one's acquaintances ***yathāsandiṭṭhaṃ*** (ind.)
acquire ***adhi-gam*** (I), ***ā-pad*** (III), ***(p)paṭi-labh*** (I), ***saṃ-anu-ā-gam*** (I)
acquisition ***adhigamo***, ***paṭilābho***
acquisitor ***nijigiṃsitar*** (masc.)
across ***pāraṃ*** (ind.)
action ***kamman*** (neut.), ***kiriyā***
activated ***saṃkhata*** (pp. ***saṃ-kar***)
activity ***saṃkhāro*** (see Vocab. 26)
actually ***kira*** (ind., enclitic)
address ***ā-mant*** (VII)
adequate ***alaṃ*** (ind.)
adhere to ***adhi-upa-gam*** (I)
admit ***(p)paṭi-(ñ)ñā*** (V)
admission ***paṭiññā***
admonish ***o-vad*** (I)
adornment ***alaṅkāro***
advance ***abhi-(k)kam*** (I)
in advance ***pure*** (ind.)
advise ***anu-sās*** (I)
aeon ***kappo***
aesthetic experience (or source of aesthetic experience) ***raso***
affair ***adhikaraṇaṃ***, ***attho***
whose appearance inspires affection ***piyadassana***
afflicted ***ātura***, ***dukkhita***
afraid ***bhīta*** (p.p. ***bhī*** (I))
be afraid ***bhī*** (I)
after (as time relation often expressed merely by the use of a gerund) ***accayena*** (ind. : time = gen.), ***paraṃ*** (ind., abl.) ; (space :) ***anvad eva*** (ind.), ***anu*** (prefix), ***uddhaṃ*** (ind.)
afterwards ***pacchā*** (ind.)
again ***puna(d)*** (ind.)
age ***jīr*** (I), ***vayas-***, ***āyu*** (neut.)
aged ***jara***
about the age of ***-vassudesika*** (num.-)
aggregate ***gaṇo***
agree on ***saṃ-man*** (VI)
agree ***(p)paṭi-(s)su*** (V)
agreed usage ***samaññā***
agreeable ***kanta***, ***sammodanīya*** (speech)

agriculture *kasi* (fem.)
ah ! *aho* (ind.) (expresses surprise—approving—and delight), *ahe* (poetic)
air *vāyas-*
alas ! *vata* (ind., enclitic)
alight *(p)paṭi-o-ruh* (I)
be alive *jīv* (I)
be allayed *(p)paṭi-(p)pa-(s)sambh* (I)
allow *anu-(ñ)ñā* (V)
all *sabba* (pronoun)
all except *yebhuyyena ṭhapetvā*
all-inclusive *sabbāvant*
all round *sabbato* (ind.)
alms *piṇḍo, dānaṃ*
alone *ekaka* (adj.), *eva* (ind., enclitic), *rahogata*
also *pi* (ind., enclitic)
always *sadā* (ind.)
amalgamate with *anu-pa-gam* (I) (*anupagacchati*—see Vocab. 28) (acc.)
ambrosia *amataṃ*
ambush *paripantho*
analysis *veyyākaraṇaṃ*
ancient tradition *porāṇaṃ*
and *ca* (ind., enclitic)
and so on *pe* (ind.)
anger *(k)kodho, doso, padoso*
be angry *kup* (III) (dat.)
animal *tiracchāno* ; *pasu* (masc.) (esp. domestic)
the animal kingdom *bhūtagāmo*
annihilate *u(d)-chid* (III) (passive = be annihilated)
utterly annihilated *samucchinna* (p.p. *saṃ-u(d)-chid*)
annihilation *ucchedo*
announce *(p)paṭi-vid* (I) caus.
another *apara* (pronoun), *para* (pronoun)
antiquity *porāṇaṃ*
anywhere *samantā* (ind.)
anxiety *anattamanatā, ubbego, kukkuccaṃ*
apart *bahiddhā* (ind.), *vi* (prefix)
apart from *aññatra* (ind., ins., dat., abl.)
be apparent to *(p)pa-(k)khā* (III) (dat.)
appear *pātu(r)-bhū* (I) (to : dat.), *saṃ-(d)dis* passive
appear beautiful *upa-subh* (I)
appearance *pātubhāvo*
apply *(p)pa-(g)gah* (V)
apply to *saṃ-app* (VII)
appoint (as ruler) *saṃ-anu-sās* (I)
appreciate *abhi-nand* (I)
express appreciation *anu-mud* (I)
apprehension *āsaṅkā, ubbego*
apprentice *antevāsin*
approach *upa-saṃ-(k)kam* (I), *ava-sar* (I), *ā-yā* (I)
approve *anu-mud* (I), *(k)kham* (I)
archer *vedhin-* (masc.)
aren't you ? *kacci* (ind.)
argument *vādo*
arise *u(d)-(ṭ)ṭhā* (I), *u(d)-pad* (III) (fig.)
arise within *o-(k)kam* (I)
arising *uppādo*
arm *bāhā*
around *pari* (prefix)
arrange *kapp* (VII), *saṃ-vi-dhā* (I)
arranged *vihita* (p.p. *vi-dhā*)
arrangement *kappo, saṃvidhānaṃ*
arrive *(p)pa-ap(p)* (VI) (poetic)
arrive at *anu-(p)pa-āp* (V)
arrogance *atimāno*
aryan *ariya*
as *yathā* (ind.), *yad idaṃ* (ind.), *seyyathā* (ind.), *seyyathīdaṃ* (ind.)
as if *maññe* (ind.)
as much *yāva* (ind.)
ascertain *abhi-(ñ)ñā* (V)
ascertained *vidita* (p.p. *vid* (II)), f.p.p. *veditabba* also current = to be ascertained
ascetic *samaṇo*
ascetic (bovine) *govatiko*
ascetic (naked) *acelo*
asceticism *tapas*
profession of asceticism *sāmaññaṃ*
ash *seṭṭhi* (fem. ?)
ask *pucch* (I) (question), *yāc* (I) (for something), *ni-mant* (VII) (to sit down, etc.)
ask about, ask advice *pari-pucch* (I)
asker *pucchitar* (masc.)
aspiring *atthika*
aspiration *paṇidhi* (masc.)
assemble *saṃ-ni-pat* (I)
assembly *parisā, sannipāto*
assembly hall *sabhā*

assent to *(p)paṭi-(s)su* (V) (dat.)
assertion *paṭiññā*
association *sahavyatā*
assume *(p)paṭi-i* (I) (*pacceti*)
assured *attamana*
assuredly *taggha* (ind.)
astringent *kasāvaṃ*
astrologer *nemitto*
astute *paṇḍita*
asunder *vi* (prefix)
atom *aṇu* (masc.)
atomic *aṇu*
attachment *upādānaṃ*
without attachment (through non-attachment) *anupādā* (ind.)
with no attachment remaining *anupādisesa*
be attached *upa-ā-dā* (III)
be attached to *parā-mas* (I)
attack *abhi-yā* (I), *upa-(k)kam* (I)
attacking *ghāto*
attain *phus* (I*), *saṃ-ā-pad* (III), *(p)pa-ap(p)* (VI) (poetic), *(p)pa-āp* (V) (fig.)
attained *(p)patta* (p.p. *(p)pa-ap(p)* (VI) or *(p)pa-āp* (V))
attainment *samāpatti* (fem.), patti (fem.)
attainment of *nibbānaṃ*, esp. the Parinibbānaṃ of the Buddha in 486 B.C. *parinibbānaṃ*
attendant *upaṭṭhāko*
attending on *upaṭṭhānaṃ*, *payirupāsanaṃ*
attention *manasikāro*
fix one's attention on *adhi-(ṭ)ṭhā* (I)
audience *upaṭṭhānaṃ*
authorized *paññatta*
authority *vasin-*
aversion *doso*, *domanassaṃ*
avoid *abhi-ni-vajj* (VII)
be aware of *budh* (III), *abhi-(ñ)ñā* (V)
away *apa* (prefix), *(p)pa* (prefix)
axle *akkho*

b

baby *dahara* (adj.)
back *pacchā* (ind.), *(p)paṭi* (prefix)
go back *ni-vatt* (I), *(p)paṭi-ā-ni(r)-yā* (I), *(p)paṭi-gam* (I)
bad *pāpa*, *pāpaka*, *akusala*, *du(r)-* (prefix)
badly *micchā* (ind.)
bad character *dussīlo*
bad conduct *duccaritaṃ*
bad luck *kali* (masc.)
bad thing *adhammo*
bag *puṭo*
bandit *kaṇṭakaṃ*
banish *(p)pa-(v)vaj* (I) caus.
banishment *pabbājanā*
bank *tīraṃ*, *velā*
bar *paligho* (holding a door)
barbarian *anariya*
barley bread *kummāso*
barren *vañjha*
base *mūlaṃ*
basis *paṭṭhānaṃ*, *pādo*
having bathed *nahatvā* (ger. *nhā* (III), also written *nhatvā*)
battle *yuddhaṃ*
be *as* (I) (exist), *hū* (I) (happen, have, become, cf. *u(d)-pad* and Lessons 5 and 24), *bhū* (I), *vid* (III) (occur), *saṃ-vid* (III)
beach *titthaṃ*
having good beaches *supatittha*
bear fruit *vi-pac* (III)
beard *massu* (neut.)
bearer (giving birth) *jananī*
beat *(p)pa-har* (I)
beast *migo*
beauty *vaṇṇo*
appear beautiful *upa-subh* (I)
beautiful *kalyāṇa*, *vaṇṇavant-*, *dassanīya*, *sirīmant* (poetic), *dassaneyya* (poetic), *sudassana* (poetic)
a beautiful girl *kalyāṇī*
because *yato* (ind.), *hi* (ind., enclitic), *yasmā* (ind.)
because of *paṭicca* (gerund : acc.)
become *u(d)-pad* (III), *-jāto*
bed *seyyā*, *mañcako*
before *purato* (ind. : space), *pure* (ind. : time), *pubba* (adj.)
begin *ā-rabh* (I)
beginning *ādi* (masc.)
knowing the beginning *aggañña*
behave (habitually) *(p)paṭi-pad* (III)
behaving *-cārin*
behind *piṭṭhito* (ind. : space, gen.), *anvad eva* (ind. : space, "following"), *pacchā* (ind. : time)

being *satto* (creature) (cf. " existence ", " state," " nature," " be ")
future being *bhavyo*
living being *bhūto*
believing *saddha*
beloved *piyāyita* (p.p. of denom.)
below *adho* (ind., abl.)
belly *udaraṃ*
bend *saṃ-iñj* (I) (usually *sammiñj-*), *kujj* (I), *nam* (I)
benefice *brahmadeyyaṃ*
benefit *ānisaṃso*
benevolence *mettā*
bent *bhogga*
best *seṭṭha*
the best *brahman-*
better *seyya, seyyo* (ind.)
between *antarena* (ind., gen.), *antarā* (ind.)
bewildered *sammūḷha*
beyond *uttari* (ind.), *pāraṃ* (ind.), *uddhaṃ* (ind., abl.)
bind *bandh* (I), (*p*)*pa-bandh* (I)
bird *pakkhin* (masc.), *sakuṇo, dijo* (poetic)
birth *jāti* (fem.)
by birth *-jacca* (adj.)
class of birth *abhijāti* (fem.)
give birth *vi-jan* (III)
bit (piece) *ālumpaṃ*
bite *khād* (I)
bitterness *kaṭukaṃ*
black *kaṇha, kāḷa*
blame *garah* (I), *garahā*
blaze (*j*)*jal* (I)
blood *lohitaṃ*
blossomed *phulla*
blossoming *phulla*
blue *nīla*
board *abhi-ruh* (I*)
boat *nāvā* (large, or ship), *uḷumpo* (small)
body *sarīraṃ, kāyo* (general and theoretical, " substance "), *tanu* (neut.)
sentient body *nāmarūpaṃ*
bold *āsabha* (fem. *-ī*)
bond *bandhanaṃ*
bone *aṭṭhikaṃ*
boon *varaṃ*
bordered *pariyanta*
borderer *paccantajo*
bordering *paccantima*
born (of) *-ja, jātika*
be born *jan* (III) (caus. = produce)
bosom *udaraṃ*
bosom (e.g. own child) *ura*
both *ubhaya* (pronoun), *ubho* (numeral), *ubhato* (ind.)
in both ways *ubhato* (ind.)
on both sides *ubhato* (ind.)
boundary *mariyādā*
boundary stake *khīlo*
bourgeois *negamo* (town dweller), *vesso* (member of the hereditary agricultural-mercantile class: see footnote to Vocab. 20)
bovine (ascetic) *govatiko*
bowl *patto*
boy *dārako, kumāro* (aristocratic), *māṇavo* (priestly), *susu* (masc.)
bracket (roof) *gopānasī*
brahman (member of the hereditary priesthood) *brāhmaṇo*
branch *sākhā*
breach *sandhi* (masc.)
bread (barley) *kummāso*
break away *vi-o-*(*k*)*kam* (I)
breakfast *pātarāso*
breast *thanaṃ*
breath *pāṇo*
breathe in *ā-*(*s*)*sas* (I)
breathe out (*p*)*pa-*(*s*)*sas* (I)
breeder *posako*
bride *vadhū* (fem.)
bridge *setu* (masc.)
briefly *saṃkhittena* (ind.)
brigand *dassu* (masc.)
bright *accha*
brilliance *nibhā*
bring *ā-har* (I), *ā-bhar* (only p.p.)
bring up *ni*(*r*)*-car* (VII) (*nicchāreti*) (vomit)
bringing *-āvaho*
brother *bhātar* (masc.)
brown *kāsāya*
build *māp* (VII)
building *gehaṃ, nivesanaṃ*
be built up *ci* (V) passive (*cīyati*)
bull *usabho, go* (masc. and fem.)
bundle *kalāpo* (bunch, quiver), *bhaṇḍikā* (parcel)
burden *bhāro*
burgher (cf. bourgeois) *negamo*

burglar, burglary *ekāgāriko*
burn *(j)jhe* (I) (caus. : set fire to)
burning *pariḷāho* (lust)
bury *ni-khaṇ* (I)
business *kammanto* (work), *karaṇīyaṃ* (duty), *kiccaṃ* (what should be done)
busy *vyāvaṭa*
but *pana* (ind., enclitic), (emphatic :) *tv eva* (ind., enclitic)
butter *navanītaṃ*
buy *ki* (V)

C

calculation *saṃkhyā*
call *ā-cikkh* (I)
called *-saṃkhāta* (p.p. of *saṃ-(k)khā* (I))
calm *nirodho, upasamo*
become calm *(p)pa-(s)sambh* (I)
calmed *santa* (p.p. *sam*)
calming *nibbuti* (fem.), *vūpasamo*
calmness *passaddhi* (fem.)
make calm *(p)pa-(s)sambh* (I) caus.
calumniate *abhi-ā-cikkh* (I)
camp *vāso*
can *(p)pa-hū* (I), *sak(k)* (VI)
canine (ascetic) *kukkuravatiko*
canoe *uḷumpo*
capable *bhabba* (with dat.)
capital (money) *mūlaṃ, pābhataṃ*
caravan *sattho*
caravan merchant *satthiko*
care *appamādo*
future career *gati* (fem.)
carpet (with temporary decorative floor-covering) *saṃ-(t)thar* (I)
completely carpeted *sabbasanthari* (adj.)
carriage *yānaṃ*
carry *ā-bhar* (only p.p.)
carry off *u(d)-vah* (I)
carry on *car* (I)
carrying on *-cārin*
cart *sakaṭo* (also *-taṃ*), *ratho*
carve *tacch* (I)
case *adhikaraṇaṃ, (ṭ)ṭhānaṃ*
in this case *iha* (ind.), *ettha* (ind.)
in that case *evaṃ santaṃ* (ind.)
in such case *evaṃ santaṃ* (ind.)
cat *biḷāro*
catch up with (acc.) *saṃ-bhū* (VII)
cattle *go* (masc., and fem.)
cattle breeding *gorakkhā*
cause *hetu* (masc.), *kāraṇaṃ, nidānaṃ, (p)paccayo*
causeless *adhicca*
causeway *setu* (masc.)
cease *ni-rudh* (III), *upa-rudh* (III)
celibate *brahmacārin*
celibate life *brahmacariyaṃ*
cell *āvasatho*
certain (constant) *niyata*
a certain *aññatara* (pronoun)
for certain *ekaṃsena* (ind.)
certainly *ekaṃsena* (ind.), *taggha* (ind.), *addhā* (ind.)
cessation *nirodho*
chaff *thuso*
give in charge of *ni(r)-yat* (VII) (*niyyādeti*)
charged with *sahagata*
chase after *anu-pat* (I)
change *vi-pari-nam* (I) (*vipariṇam-*)
changed *pariṇata* (p.p. *pari-nam* (I))
having a good character *sīlavant*
bad character (person) *dussīlo*
characteristic *liṅgaṃ, aṅgaṃ*
chariot *ratho*
charioteer *sārathi* (masc.)
chatter *samphaṃ*
check *o-tar* (I) caus.
chew *khād* (I)
choose *var* (I) or (VII) (*vāreti*—grammarians) (poetic)
chop *tacch* (I)
circle *vaṭṭ* (I), *parivaṭṭaṃ, maṇḍalaṃ*
circling *anupariyāya*
circulation *vaṭṭaṃ*
circumambulation *padakkhiṇā*
circumscribed *parivaṭuma*
citadel *antepuraṃ*
city *nagaraṃ*
city wall *pākāro*
clan *gottaṃ*
clarity *visuddhi* (fem.)
class *vaṇṇo*
class of birth *abhijāti*
classification *saṃkhyā*
clean *setaka*
become clean *sudh* (III)
cleaned *suddha*
clear *accha, visuddha, setaka*
be clear *(p)paṭi-bhā* (I)

be clear to (*p*)*pa-*(*k*)*khā* (III) (dat.)
make things clear *subh* (I) (intrans.)
very clear *vippasanna*
climb *ā-ruh* (I*)
not clinging *anālayo*
cloak *uttarāsaṅgo, saṃghāṭi* (fem.)
clod *leḍḍu* (masc.)
cloth *dussaṃ*
cloud *megho*
cluster *saṇḍo*
clustered in groups *saṃghāsaṃghī-gaṇībhūta*
coach-house *vāhanāgāraṃ*
coagulate *saṃ-mucch* (I)
coalesce with *anu-pa-i* (I) (*anupeti*—see Vocab. 28) (acc.)
coarse *oḷārika*
cock (wild) *kukkuṭako*
coercion *daṇḍo*
collate *o-tar* (I)
collect *saṃ-kaḍḍh* (I), *u*(*d*)*-har* (I)
collecting *-pāto*
collection *samihitaṃ*, (*k*)*khandho*
colour *vaṇṇo*
coloured *ratta*
column *thambho*
combination *saṃkhāro* (see Vocab. 26)
→ come *ā-gam* (I), *ā-yā* (I), *ā-i* (I) (poetic)
having come *āgantvā* (ger.)
each time it came *āgatāgataṃ* (ind.)
coming *āgamanaṃ, āgamo*
come back out (*p*)*paṭi-u*(*d*)*-tar* (I)
come out from *u*(*d*)-(*t*)*ṭhā* (I)
comfortable *phāsu*
command *āṇa* (caus.)
commerce *vaṇijjā*
commodity *paṇiyaṃ*
common *pothujjanika*
community *saṃgho*
compassion *anukampā, karuṇā*
be compassionate, have compassion (on = acc.) *anu-kamp* (I)
complain *anu-*(*t*)*thu* (V)
complete *aparisesa, asesa*
completed *niṭṭhita*
completely *sabbaso* (ind.), *samattaṃ* (ind.), *sabbena sabbaṃ* (ind.)
complexion *pokkharatā*
comprehend (*p*)*paṭi-vidh* (III)
comprehension *paṭivedho*
with one's comrades *yathāsambhattaṃ*

concealed *paṭicchanna*
conceit *māno, uddhaccakukkuccaṃ*
conceivable, is it conceivable ? *labbhā* (ind.) (see Vocab. 27)
concentrated *samāhita* (p.p. *saṃ-ā-dhā*), *ekodi*
concentration *samādhi* (masc.), *ekodi-bhāvo*
concept *paññatti* (fem.)
concerned *vyāvaṭa*
conch *saṅkho*
conch blower *saṅkhadhamo*
conclusion *niṭṭhā* (deduced), *pari-yosānaṃ* (ending)
conclusively *ekantikena* (ind.)
concoct *ni*(*r*)*-pac* (I)
condition (*p*)*paccayo* (basis), *sahav-yatā* (state)
conditioned by *paṭicca* (ger. : acc.)
conduct *ācāro, cariyā, vattaṃ, caraṇaṃ* (good)
(good) conduct *caraṇaṃ*
conduct oneself *ā-car* (I), *car* (I), *vatt* (I)
well conducted *sīlavant*
conducting *-vattin*
confidence *saddhā, pasādo*
confident *visārada, ekaṃsa*
confident in *pasanna*
confined *sambādha*
confiscation *jāni* (fem.)
conform (to a rule or way of life) *saṃ-ā-dā* (III)
confound (it) ! *dhi*(*r*) (ind., acc., or nom.)
confused *ākula*
confusion *vikkhepo*
congenial *pesala*
connected *saṃhita* (p.p. *saṃ-dhā*)
connection *saṃyojanaṃ*
in this/that connection *idha* (ind.), *tattha* (ind.), *tatra* (ind.)
conquer *abhi-vi-ji* (V), *ji* (I), *abhi-bhū* (I)
conqueror *abhibhū* (masc.)
conscience *hiri* (fem.)
conscious *sampajāna*
be conscious of *vi-*(*ñ*)*ñā* (V)
consciousness *viññāṇaṃ, sampajañ-ñaṃ*
consecrated *abhisitta* (p.p. *abhi-sic* (II))
consecration *abhiseko*

in consequence of (acc.) *anvāya* (ger. *anu-i*)
consequently (methodically) *yoniso* (ind.)
consider *man* (VI), (*p*)*paṭi-saṃ-cikkh* (I)
consisting of *-maya*
constant *niyata*
constellation *nakkhattaṃ*
contact *samphasso, phasso*
contempt *atimāno*
contemplating *anudiṭṭhin-*
be contented *saṃ-tus* (only p.p.)
contentment *khamanīyaṃ*
continue (*p*)*pa-vatt* (I)
control *vaso*
control oneself *saṃ-yam* (I)
controlled *saṃvuta* (p.p. *saṃ-var* (I))
contribution *bali* (masc.)
converse *vi-ati-sār* (VII)
converse with *saṃ-u*(*d*)*-ā-car* (I)
make conversation *vi-ati-sār* (VII)
be converted to *anu-pa-*(*k*)*khand* (I)
conviction *saddhā*
Convolvulus repens *kalambukā* (?)
cook *pac* (I)
cool *sīta*
become cool *ni*(*r*)*-vā* (III)
corrupt *duṭṭha*
corruption *upakkileso*
cosmetic *vilepanaṃ*
councillor *pārisajjo*
(take) counsel *mant* (VII)
country *janapado*
country dweller *jānapado*
courage *parakkamo*
course *pariyāyo*
in due course *anupubbena* (ind.)
future course *gati* (fem.)
courtesan *gaṇikā*
covered *paṭicchanna*
covered with *samparikiṇṇa* (p.p. *saṃ-pari-kir*)
cover up *pari-o-nah* (II) (*pariyonandhati*)
coveter *nijigiṃsitar*
covetous *abhijjhālu* (sometimes *-ū* masc.; fem. *-unī*)
cow *gāvī, go* (masc. and fem.)
cow dung *gomayaṃ*
cow vower *govatiko*
craft *sippaṃ*
create *ni*(*r*)*-mā* (V)
creation *pajā* (the created universe, in sense of theists)
creator *nimmātar* (masc.)
creature *satto*
creeper *badālatā*
criticize *saṃ-anu-bhās* (I), (*p*)*paṭi-*(*k*)*kus* (I) (decry)
crooked *vaṅka*
cross-examine *saṃ-anu-*(*g*)*gah* (V) caus.
cross *u*(*d*)*-tar* (I), *tar* (I)
cross over *ni*(*r*)*-tar* (I), (ocean:) *adhi-o-gāh* (I)
crossing over *nittharaṇaṃ*
crossing place *titthaṃ*
cross-question *saṃ-anu-yuj* (II)
crossroads *siṅghāṭako*
crow *kāko*
crowded together *gaṇībhūta*
crown property *rājabhoggaṃ*
crush *su* (I)
cuckoo (Indian) *kokilo*
cultivate *bahulī-kar* (VI)
cultivating *-bahula* (at end of compound)
cultivation *kasi* (fem.)
cure *kit* (I) desid. (*tikicchati*)
curse *sap* (I)
custom *dhammo*
customary *yathākata* (usual), *paññatta* (authorized)
cut, cut down, cut off *chid* (II), (III)
cut off *vi-o-chid* (III)
cycle *vaṭṭaṃ* (of the universe)
cycling *vaṭṭaṃ* (of the universe)

d

dance *nat* (III)
dancing *naccaṃ*
daft *veceta*
dam *setu* (masc.)
damn you! (contemptuous address) *re* (ind.)
danger *bhayaṃ,* (*p*)*paṭibhayaṃ, antarāyo*
dark *kaṇha*
darkness *andhakāro, timisā*
day *divas-*
by day *divā* (ind.)
day-bed *divāseyyā*
dear *piya* (to: dat.)

held dear *piyāyita* (p.p. of denom.)
my dear ! (familiar) *samma* (ind.)
dead man *peto*
death *āghatanaṃ*
deathless *amata*
debate *vādo*, *(p)pavādo*
decay *(p)pa-luj* (III), *paloko*
deceive *vañc* (VII)
decided *ekaṃsa*
declare *(p)pa-(ñ)ñap* (VII), *abhi-ni(r)-dis* (I*)
decline *parihāni* (fem.)
decrease *parihāni* (fem.)
decry *(p)paṭi-(k)kus* (I)
deduced *pariyāhata*
deducing *takkin-*
deducer *takkin-* (as masc. noun)
deduction *takko*
deer *migo*
defame *pari-bhās* (I)
defeat *ji* (I)
defend one's thesis *saṃ-pāy* (I)
become defiled *saṃ-kilis* (III)
defilement *saṃkileso*
definite *ekaṃsa*
definitely *ekaṃsena* (ind.), *tu eva* (ind.: follows a word to be strongly emphasized)
definition *lakkhaṇaṃ*
degradation *okāro*
deity *devatā*
delicate *sukumāra*
delicious *paṇīta*
delight *saṃ-(p)pa-haṃs* (VII) (transitive)
delight in *ram* (I) (poetic)
be delighted *rañj* (I)
delightful *ramaṇīya*, *paṇīta*, *ramma* (poetic)
delusion *moho*
demerit *apuññaṃ*
demon *yakkho*
denomination *saṃkhyā*
depending on *parāyana*, *upanissāya* (ger. of *upa-ni-(s)sī*), *nissāya* (ger. of *ni-(s)sī* (I)), *āgamma* (ger. *ā-gam*)
deploying *-vattin*
deportment *ākappo*
depressed *dummana*
depression *domanassaṃ*
derive *upa-ni(r)-vatt* (I)
descend *o-ruh* (I)
descend into *o-(k)kam* (I)
describe *ā-cikkh* (I)
description *adhivutti* (fem.)
deserve *arah* (I)
designation *adhivacanaṃ*, *samaññā*
desire *pari-tas* (III), *is(u)* (I), *abhijjhā*, *taṇhā*, *rāgo*
desiring *sāpekha*
desirous *atthika*
despair *upāyāso*
despise *ati-man* (III), *pari-bhū* (I)
destiny *gati* (fem.) (in general, any future existence)
Destiny *niyati* (fem.) (inevitable, in sense of determinists)
evil destiny *duggati* (fem.)
good destiny *sugati* (fem.)
destroying *nāsanaṃ*, *samārambho*
destruction *vināso*, *ghaccā*, *ghāto*
detached *upe(k)khaka*
detachment *upe(k)khā*
determination *paṇidhi* (masc.)
develop *bhū* (I) caus.
developed *pariṇata* (p.p. *pari-nam* (I))
developing *-vattin*
development *bhāvanaṃ*
devoted to *-bahula* (at end of compound)
devour *bhakkh* (VII), *ghas* (I)
devoured *ghasta* (p.p. *ghas*)
dexterous *padakkhiṇa*
dialogue *suttaṃ*
did ? *api* (ind.), *kacci* (ind.)
die (dice) *akkho*
die *mar* (III)
difference *vemattatā*
different : the . . . is a different thing from the . . . *añña* . . . *añña* . . . (pronouns)
difficult *du(r)-* (prefix)
difficulty *kicchaṃ*, *kasiraṃ*
diffident *avisārada*
diffuse *vikkhitta*
dig up *u(d)-har* (I)
digest *pari-nam* caus. (*pariṇām-*)
digestion *pariṇāmo*
diligence *appamādo*
diminish *hā* (I)
direction *disā*, in any direction : *samantā* (ind.), intermediate : *anudisā*, in all directions : *anudisaṃ* (ind.)

dirt *malaṃ*
free from dirt *vimala*
dirty *asuci*
disadvantage *ahitaṃ*, *ādīnavo*
disagreeable *(p)paṭikkūla*
disappear *antara-dhā* (III)
disaster *vyasanaṃ*
disc *maṇḍalaṃ*
discard *ni-(k)khip* (I*)
discern *vi-(ñ)ñā* (V)
be discerned *(p)pa-(ñ)ñā* (V) passive
discerning person *viññū* (masc.)
discernment *viññutā*
causer of discernment *viññāpetar*
discipline *vinayo*
having disciplined *vineyya* (gerund)
discoloured *dubbaṇṇa*
discolouration *vevaṇṇatā*
discontent *anabhirati* (fem.)
discover *abhi-(ñ)ñā* (V)
discovered *vidita* (p.p. *vid* (II)) (f.p.p. *veditabba* also current)
discretion *viññutā*
discrimination (philosophical, logical) *vicayo*, *viveko*
non-discrimination (ethical : between self and others) *sabbattatā*
discuss confidentially *mant* (VII)
disease *vyādhi* (masc.)
diseased *vyādhita*
disgust *parijegucchо*
be disgusted with *gup* desid.
disgusting *jeguccha*
dishes *khādaniyaṃ*
dismiss *u(d)-yuj* (II) caus.
disorder *vikāro*
disparage *apa-vad* (I)
dispassion *virāgo*
dispel *(p)paṭi-vi-nī* (I)
dispelled *ossaṭṭha* (p.p. *o-(s)saj* [1] (I))
dispense *(p)pa-kapp* (VII) (pay out), *abhi-vi-(s)saj* [1] (I) (gifts)
displeasing *amanāpa*
disprove *ā-ruh* (I) caus.
disproved *āropita*
dispute *vivādo*
disquiet *anattamanatā*
dissolve *saṃ-vaṭṭ* (I)
dissolved in *saṃvaṭṭanika*
dissolution *saṃvaṭṭaṃ*
disseminate : be disseminated *abhi-u(d)-gam* (I)
in the distance *dūrato* (ind.)
distasteful *(p)paṭikkūla*
distinction *vemattatā* (difference)
distress *vi-han* (I)
district *āhāro*
disturbed *anattamana*
diversity *nānattaṃ*
divide *vi-bhaj* (I) (share), *bhid* (II) (split)
divine *dibba*
divine being *devatā*
diviner *nemitto*
division *bhedo*
do *kar* (VI)
do ? *api* (ind.)
what should be done *kiccaṃ*
what should not be done *akiccaṃ*
doctor *vejjo*
doctrine *dhammo*, *sāsanaṃ*
received doctrine (tradition) *āgamo*
doctrinal *dhamma* (fem. *-ī*)
doer *kārako*
does ? *nu* (ind., enclitic), *kiṃ* (ind.), *api* (ind.)
doing *-karo*, *-kārin*
dog *kukkuro*, *suṇo*, *san-* (masc.)
dog-vower *kukkuravatiko*
domestic *ibbha*
donation *dānaṃ*, *dakkhiṇā*
donkey *gadrabho*
don't *mā* (ind.)
doorkeeper *dovāriko*
doorway (i.e. the opening) *dvāraṃ*
double *diguṇaṃ* (or *dvi-*)
doubt *kaṅkhā*, *āsaṅkā* (apprehension)
in doubt *kaṅkhin*
I doubt whether ? *kacci* (ind.)
no doubt *maññe* (ind.)
doubting *kaṅkhin*
down *ni* (cf. *ni(r)*) (prefix), *o* (prefix)
having dragged down, having dragged away *okkassa* (ger. of *o-(k)kass* (VII))
draught animal *yoggaṃ*
draw *nī* (I) (ploughs, etc.)
draw in *saṃ-iñj* (I) (usually *sam-miñj-*)
draw back *o-sakk* (I)
dress *ā-(c)chād* (VII), *ni-vās* (VII), *vās* (III)
drink *pā* (I) (*pivati*), *pānaṃ* (general), *majjaṃ* (alcoholic)

drinking water *pānīyaṃ*
drip *(p)pa-(g)ghar* (I)
drive *pes* (VII)
" drive " (= desire) *taṇhā*
driving away *apanūdanaṃ* (poetic)
drop *ni-pat* caus.
dropping *-pāto*
drug *bhesajjaṃ*
drum *paṇavo*
drunk *madhuraka, pipāsa*
drunkard *pipāsa*
dry *sukkha*
dry land *thalaṃ*
in due course *anupubbena* (ind.)
dull *manda*
dullness *mandattaṃ*
dung *gūtho*
duration *(t)ṭhiti* (fem.)
dust *paṃsu* (masc.), *rajas-*
duty *karaṇīyaṃ, vattaṃ*
dwell *vi-har* (I), *(p)paṭi-vas* (I)
dwell in *ā-vas* (I)
dwelling *āvasatho* (place, building), *āvāso* (~ in), *vihāro* (mode of life)
dwelling place *āvasatho* (building), *vāso* (temporary camp, etc.)
dye *rajanaṃ*
dysentery *pakkhandikā*

e

each one *ekameka* (pronoun)
eager *ussuka*
be eager *ussukkati* (denom.)
eagerness *ussukkaṃ*
ear *sotaṃ* (esp. as sense of hearing)
earlier *purima*
earth *paṭhavī* (the ~, the element ~), *bhūmi* (fem.) (ground), *chamā*, *mahī* (poetic)
east *puratthā* (ind.)
easy *sukara*
eat *khād* (I), *pari-bhuj* (II), *bhakkh* (VII)
eating *-bhakkha*
eclipse *-(g)gāho*
educable *damma*
eight *aṭṭha* (num.)
eighteen *aṭṭhādasa* (num.)
eight days *aṭṭhāhaṃ*
having eight factors *aṭṭhaṅgika*
eighty *asīti* (fem.)
eighty-four *caturāsīti* (fem.)
either *vā* (ind., enclitic)
elated *udagga*
elation *ubbilāvitattaṃ, somanassaṃ*
elder (monk) *thero*
elder *jeṭṭha, mahallako*
eldest *jeṭṭha*
elect *saṃ-man* (VI)
element *dhātu* (fem.), *mahābhūto*, *dhammo*
elephant *nāgo*
she-elephant *hatthinikā*
elevated *mahaggata*
eleven *ekādasa* (num.)
eliminate *pari-(k)khī* (III)
having eliminated *vineyya* (ger.)
be eliminated *pari-hā* (I) passive, *hā* (I)
embrace *pari(> pali)-(s)saj* [2] (I), *(s)saj* [2] (I)
emigrate *u(d)-(ṭ)ṭhā* (I)
emotional *saṃvejanīya*
emperor *cakkavatti* (masc.)
empty *suñña*
encircled *pariyanta*
encompassing *pariya* (adj.), *paricca* (gerund)
end *ni-rudh* (III), *upa-rudh* (III), *anto*
the end (future) *aparanto*
come to an end *pari-hā* (I) pass.
bring to an end *pari-hā* (I) caus.
ending *pariyosānaṃ* (conclusion)
be endowed with *saṃ-anu-ā-gam* (I), *saṃ-pad* (III)
end quote *ti* (ind.), (emphasizing one word or expression :) *tv eva* (ind.)
enduring *addhaniya*
enemy *paccatthiko*
energy *viriyaṃ, saṃkhāro* (see Vocab. 26), *ātappo* (ascetic energy which burns up defilements and purifies the faculties), *tejas-*
energetic *ātāpin* (ascetic)
engage in *(p)paṭi-pad* (III)
enjoy *anu-bhū* (I), *pari-bhuj* (II), *abhi-ram* (I) (elevated, with loc.)
enjoying *bhogin, abhirata* (p.p. *abhi-ram*)
enjoyment *ābhogo, sukhallikā, assādo, raso*
enjoy oneself *pari-car* (I) caus.
enlightened *sambuddha, buddha*

become enlightened *abhi-saṃ-budh* (III)
attain enlightenment *abhi-saṃ-budh* (III)
enlightenment *bodhi* (fem.), *sambodhi* (fem.), *sambodho*
complete enlightenment *sambodhi* (fem.)
enough (!) *alaṃ* (ind.)
enter *(p)pa-vis* (I*), *vis* (I*)
enter into *upa-saṃ-pad* (III)
entertain *sat-kar* (VI)
entertainment *sakkāro*
entire *kevala*, *sabba* (pronoun)
entrance *upasampadā*
enumeration *saṃkhyā*
envelop *pari-o-nah* (II) (*pariyonandhati*)
envisage *saṃ-anu-pass* (I)
equal to *sama*
equally *samaṃ* (ind.)
equanimity *upe(k)khā*
equivocation *vikkhepo*
erect *(ṭ)ṭhā* (I) caus., *uju*
erratically *ayoniso* (ind.)
erroneous *mogha*
escape *ati-vatt* (I)
escaping *nissakkanaṃ* (not escaping: *anatīta*)
establish *(ṭ)ṭhā* (I) caus.
etc. *pe*
eternal *sassata*
eternal thing *sassati* (fem.)
eternity *sassati* (fem.)
eternally *sassatisamaṃ* (ind.)
even *antamaso* (ind.: merely, mere), *sama* (adj.: not uneven, equal), *pi* (ind.: too), *(s)su* (ind.), *(s)sudaṃ* (ind.)
evening *sāyaṇho*
in the evening *sāyaṃ* (ind.)
evening meal *sāyamāso*
ever *kadā ci* (ind.)
everywhere *sabbadhi* (ind.)
evil *pāpa*, *duṭṭha*, *apuññaṃ*
evil destiny *duggati* (fem.)
evolve *vi-vaṭṭ* (I)
evolution *vivaṭṭaṃ*
speak with exaltation *udāneti* (denom.)
exalted *sāmukkaṃsaka*, *ariya*
exalted utterance *udānaṃ*
examine *sacchi-kar* (VI)
examination *anuyogo*
exceedingly *ati-* (prefix to adjectives, poetic)
excellence *lakkhaṇaṃ*
excellent *abhikkanta*, *paṇīta*, *ariya*, *vara* (poetic)
excellent ! *diṭṭhā* (ind.)
except *(ṭ)ṭhā* (I) caus.
except for *aññatra* (ind., ins., dat., or abl.)
excess *mado*
excessive *ativela*, *bāḷha*
excessively *ativelaṃ* (ind.)
exchange greetings with *saṃ-mud* (I) (preceded by ins. and *saddhiṃ*)
excite *saṃ-u(d)-tij* (VII)
be excited *rañj* (I)
exciting *rajanīya*
excluded (false) *mogha*
without excluding anyone *abāhiraṃ* (ind.)
excogitated *vicārita* (p.p. of caus. *vi-car* (I))
excrement *karīsaṃ*
execution *vadho*
exegete *vīmaṃsin-* (as masc. noun)
exercise *vi-ā-yam* (I) (*vāyamati*), *vāyāmo*
take exercise (walking) *(k)kam* (I) intensive
exert *(p)pa-dhā* (I)
exertion *padhānaṃ*
exhaust *(k)khī* (III), *pari-(k)khī* (III), *pari-ā-dā* (III)
exhaustion *(k)khayo*
exhausted by heat *abhitatta*
exhort *saṃ-ā-dā* (I) caus.
exist *upa-labh* (I) pass., *as* (I), *bhū* (I)
existing *sant-*
existence *sattattaṃ*, *bhavo*, *nivāso*
expand *tan* (VI)
expect *(p)paṭi-ā-sis* (II), cf. also *labbhā* (ind.) (Vocab. 27)
expectation *ape(k)khā*
experience *(p)paṭi-saṃ-vid* (VII), *anubhū* (I), *sacchi-kar* (VI), *saṃ-(ñ)ñā* (V), *vedayitaṃ*, *sacchikiriyā*
experiencing *paṭisaṃvedin-*, *paṭisaṃvedana*
expert *abhiyogin*
explain *vi-ā-kar* (VI), *ni(r)-veṭh* (VII)

explanation *veyyākaraṇaṃ*
exploit *adhi-ā-vas* (I)
expression (verbal) *akkharaṃ, vyañjanaṃ, adhivutti* (fem.)
external *bāhira*
extinction *atthagamo, nibbānaṃ*
attain extinction *pari-ni(r)-vā* (I) or (III)
become extinguished *ni(r)-vā* (III)
extinguishing *nibbuti* (fem.)
extract (liquids) *su* (I)
extreme *anto, ekanta*
exultation *ubbilāvitattaṃ*
eye *akkhi* (neut.), *cakkhu* (neut.) (esp. as sense of sight), *nayanaṃ* (poetic), *locanaṃ* (poetic)
having eyes *cakkhumant-*

f

facing *abhimukha, purakkhatvā* (ger.), *purakkhata* (p.p. *pura(s)-kar*)
in fact *kira* (ind., enclitic)
factor *aṅgaṃ*
faculty *indriyaṃ*
failed *vipanna, aparaddha*
failure *vipatti* (fem.)
fair *subha*
fall down *ni-pat* (I)
fall from *cu* (I)
fall upon *upa-(k)kam* (I)
falling upon *samārambho*
fallen into *palipanna* (p.p. *pari-pad* (III))
false *mogha*
falsehood *musā*
fame *kitti* (fem.)
fan *vīj* (I)
as far as *yāva* (ind.), *yāvatā* (ind.), *yāvataka* (fem. *-ikā*)
as far as one wishes *yāvaticchakaṃ* (ind.)
from far *dūrā* (ind.)
far from *ārakā* (ind., abl.)
not far *avidūre* (ind.)
farmer *vesso*
fast *sīghaṃ* (ind., repeated = very fast)
fate *gati* (fem.) (in general, any future existence, result of actions)
a bad fate *duggati* (fem.)
Fate *niyati* (fem.) (inevitable, in sense of determinists)
father *pitar* (masc.)
fear *bhayaṃ, āsaṅkā, ottappaṃ* (of blame)
feast *saṃ-(p)pa-var* (VII) (transitive)
feature *ākāro*
feeding on *-bhakkha*
having fed *bhojetvā* (ger., transitive)
feel *(p)paṭi-saṃ-vid* (VII), *vid* (VII)
feeling *paṭisaṃvedin-, paṭisaṃvedana*
fellow-feeling *muditā* (joyful)
ferry *titthaṃ*
fetch *ā-har* (I)
fetter *bandhanaṃ*
fever *ātaṅko*
fickle *lola*
fie ! *dhi(r)* (ind., acc., or nom)
fief *brahmadeyyaṃ*
field *khettaṃ*
fierce *caṇḍa*
fifteen *paṇṇarasa* (num.)
fifth *pañcama*
fifty *paññāsā* (fem. or *-a* neut.)
filament *kiñjakkhaṃ*
fill with *pari-bhū* (I) caus.
film *santānakaṃ*
finally *ekantikena* (ind.)
find *labh* (I), *vid* (II) (poetic)
find out *(ñ)ñā* (V)
fine *sukhuma* (subtle)
finger *aṅguli* (fem.)
fingernail *nakho*
finish *tīreti* (denom.)
finite *anta, antavant-, pamāṇakata*
fire *aggi* (masc.)
firewood *kaṭṭhaṃ*
firm *daḷha*
be firm *gādh* (I)
firm as a pillar *esikaṭṭhāyin-*
first *tāva* (ind.)
first (numeral) *paṭhama*
firstly *paṭhamaṃ* (ind.)
at first *pure* (ind.)
fist *muṭṭhi* (masc.)
five *pañca* (num.)
fixed *dhuva*
fix in *sam-app* (VII)
flax *khomaṃ*
flee *ni(r)-pat* (I)
flesh *maṃsaṃ*
flood *aṇṇavo*
flourish *pabb* (I)
flow *sand* (I)

fold *kujj* (I)
fold the legs *ā-bhuj* (I*)
-fold *-guṇa(ṃ)*, *-vidha*
foliage *palāso*
follow *anu-bandh* (I), *anu-pat* (I), *(p)paṭi-pad* (III) (fig.), *anu-car* (I) (fig.)
follow about *anu-(k)kam* (I) intensive
follower *upaṭṭhāko* (attendant), *anvāyiko*
following *anugati* (fem.), *anvāya* (ger. *anu-i*), *anu* (prefix)
as follows *seyyathīdaṃ* (ind.)
fond of *-bahula* (at end of compound)
food *annaṃ*, *bhojanaṃ*, *āhāro* (incl. general and fig.), *bhojanīyaṃ* (soft foods
foods (dishes) *khādanīyaṃ*
solid food *kabaḷiṅkāro*
fool *bālo*
foolish *bāla*
foot *pādo*, *caraṇaṃ* (poetic)
forbearance *titikkhā*
force *daṇḍo* (coercion), *saṃkhāro* (natural—see Vocab. 26)
having forced *pasayha* (gerund of *(p)pa-sah* (I))
foreign *paccantima*, *bāhira*
foreigner *paccantajo*
foremost *pāmokkha*
forest *araññaṃ*, *āraññaka*
living in the forest *āraññaka*
not-forgetting *asammoso*
forgivingness *khantī*
form *saṃ-mucch* (I) (intrans.), *rūpaṃ*
formed, having form *rūpin-*
former *pubba* (adj.), *pubbaka*, *purima*
formerly *pubbe* (ind.), *bhūtapubbaṃ* (ind.), *puratthā* (ind., poetic)
formless *arūpin*
(good) fortune *bhavo*
(good) fortune (to you!) *bhavaṃ* (ind. with *atthu* and acc. of person)
fortnight *aḍḍhamāso*
fortunate *sirīmant* (poetic)
the fortunate *bhagavant* (masc.) (title of the Buddha)
forty *cattārīsā* (fem. or *-a* neut.)
foul *asubha*
found *vidita* (p.p. *vid* (II), f.p.p. *veditabba* also current);
be found *vid* (III), *saṃ-vid* (III)
foundations *uddāpo*
four *catu(r)*
fourteen *cuddasa* (num.)
fourth *catuttha*
four days *catuhaṃ*
frank *pasaṭa* (p.p. *(p)pa-sar*)
free *muc* (II), *abbhokāsa*
become free *vi-muc* (III)
free from *vigata-*, *apagata-*
set free *vi-muc* (III) caus.
freeing *mutti* (fem.)
frequent *bahula*
frequently *abhiṇhaṃ* (ind.)
fresh *haritaka*
friend *sahāyo*, *mitto*, *ñāto*, *sakhā* (masc.)
friendliness *mettā*
frivolity *samphaṃ*
from that, from these *tato* (ind.)
from this *ito* (ind.)
(directly) from *santikā* (ind.)
in front *purakkhata* (p.p. *pura(s)-kar*), *parimukhaṃ* (ind.)
in front of *purato* (ind., gen.)
fruit *phalaṃ*
bear fruit *vi-pac* (III)
fruitful *pākima*, *opanayika*
full *pūra*, *paripuṇṇa* (also fig.)
full of *āyuta* (poetic)
fungus *pappaṭako*
further *pārima*, *uttara*, *uttari* (ind.), *aparaṃ* (ind.)
furtive *visāci*
future *anāgata* (also neg. p.p. of *ā-gam*)
(the) future *aparanto*
in future *āyatiṃ* (ind.)
future career or course *gati* (fem.) (in present or subsequent lives)
(a) future or final state *aparanto*
future state *abhisamparāyo*

g

gable *kūṭo*
gain *lābho*
gamble *div* (III)
gambler *akkhadhutto*
garland *mālā*
garment *vatthaṃ*
gateway *dvāraṃ*
gateway (arched) *toraṇaṃ*
gather *saṃ-har* (I)
gathering *āhāro*

geisha *gaṇikā*
gem *ratanaṃ*
generate *(p)pa-su* (I)
get *adhi-gam* (I), *ā-pad* (III), *labh* (I)
getting *adhigamo*
get down *(p)paṭi-o-ruh* (I)
get into *abhi-ruh* (I*)
get going *(p)pa-vatt* (I)
get up *u(d)-(ṭ)ṭhā* (I)
getting over *visajja* (ger.)
ghee *sappi* (neut.)
gift *dānaṃ, deyyaṃ, dakkhiṇā, dāyo*
" gift to God " : i.e. grant of land/villages to a priest of the Brahmanical religion *brahmadeyyaṃ*
gift by the king *rājadāyo*
girl *kumārikā, kumārī* (of the military-aristocratic class) ; a beautiful girl : *kalyāṇī*
give *dā* (I)
giver *dātar* (masc.)
give up *(p)pa-hā* (I)
give in charge of *ni(r)-yat* (VII) (*niyyādeti*)
glad *muda*
be glad *rañj* (I)
gladness *muditā* (fellow-feeling)
be glorious *subh* (I)
glory *subhaṃ*
go *gam* (I), *yā* (I), *i* (I) (*poetic*), *(v)vaj* (I) (poetic)
going *gamanaṃ, -gamo, gāmin*
go away *(p)pa-(k)kam* (I)
go back *ni-vatt* (I), *(p)paṭi-ā-ni(r)-yā* (I), *(p)paṭi-gam* (I)
go down to *ava-sar* (I)
go forward *abhi-(k)kam* (I)
go on *(p)pa-vatt* (I), *iriy* (I*) (lit., and fig., poetic)
go off *apa-(k)kam* (I)
go out *ni(r)-(k)kam* (I) ($r + k > kkh$), *ni(r)-vā* (III)
go out to *ni(r)-yā* (I)
go on (doing) *vatt* (I)
go home *saṃ-vis* (I*)
going to *-upaga, paricca* (ger.)
going on *-cārin*
go forth (from ordinary life to wandering) *(p)pa-(v)vaj* (I)
going forth *pabbajjā*
one who has gone forth *pabbajito*
go on a mission *car* (I)
go over to *anu-pa-(k)khand* (I)
go to *upa-saṃ-(k)kam* (I), *upa-gam* (I), *upa-i* (I)
go into *upa-(k)kam* (I)
going round *paricca* (ger.)
goad *tuttaṃ*
goat *ajo*
god *devo, yakkho, issaro, suro* (poetic)
God *brahman* (masc.)
goer *gatako*
gold *suvaṇṇaṃ, jātarūpaṃ, hiraññaṃ* (money), *kanakaṃ*
good *bhadda* (= good of its kind, repeated = very good), *kusala* (morally), *sādhuka* (proper, doing a thing well : more often used as ind. : ~ *aṃ*), *kalyāṇa* (aesthetically or morally or both), *vara* (poetic), *sant-* (usually " true ", sometimes = " good " in compounds), *su-* (prefix)
goodness, good (noun) *puññaṃ, kusalaṃ*
good at *kusala, padakkhiṇa* (loc.)
goodbye (host speaking) *yassa dāni kālaṃ maññasi* (approximate equivalent in certain circumstances, see Lesson 12)
good conduct *sucaritaṃ, sīlaṃ*
good fortune (see " fortune ")
good heavens ! *vata* (ind., enclitic)
good luck *bhaddaṃ* (dat.)
goods *bhaṇḍaṃ*
goodwill *mettā*
gourd *tuṇḍikīro* (pot)
govern *(p)pa-sās* (I)
governing *-vattin*
government *vattaṃ*
grain *dhaññaṃ*
granary *koṭṭhāgāraṃ*
grant *anu-(p)pa-dā* (I), *pābhataṃ, brahmadeyyaṃ*
grasp *(g)gah* (V), *ā-(ñ)ñā* (V) (fig.)
grasper (fig.) *aññātar* (masc.)
grass *tiṇaṃ, babbajaṃ* (a coarse variety for rope and slipper making)
gratify *saṃ-tapp* (VII)
gratuity *pābhataṃ*
great *mahant-*
green *haritaka*
greet *abhi-vad* (VII), *saṃ-mud* (I) (preceded by ins. and *saddhiṃ*)

greetings ! (see " (best) wishes ! ")
grief *soko* (sorrow), *paridevo* (lamentation)
grieve *suc* (I), *pari-dev* (VII)
gross *oḷārika*
ground *chamā*, *bhūmi* (fem.)
groundsheet *nisīdanaṃ*
group *gaṇo*, *(k)khandho*
in groups *saṃghāsaṃghin*
grow *ruh* (I*)
grow again *(p)paṭi-vi-ruh* (I*)
grow old *jar* (III)
growth *virūḷhi* (fem.)
guard *pari-rakkh* (I)
guarded *gutta* (p.p. *gup*)
guest *atithi* (masc.)

h

habit *saṃkhāro* (see Vocab. 26)
hail ! *namo* (ind., dat.)
hair (of the head) *keso*
hair (of the body) *lomaṃ*
half *aḍḍho* (or adj., also spelt *addho*), *upaḍḍha* (or neut.)
halfway *upaḍḍhapathaṃ* (ind.)
hall *sālā*
hand *hattho*, *pāṇi* (masc.), *karo* (poetic)
hand over *(p)pa-dā* (I), *ni(r)-yat* (VII) (*niyyādeti*)
handsome *abhirūpa*, *vaṇṇavant-*
haphazardly *ayoniso* (ind.)
happen *u(d)-pad* (III)
happy *sukha*, *sukhin-*
be happy *sukheti* (denom.)
happiness *sukhaṃ*
harass *heṭh* (VII)
be harassed *vi-heṭh* (VII)
harasser *heṭhako*
harassing *vihesā*
hard *du(r)-* (prefix) (difficult)
hardship *ahitaṃ*
hard task *dukkaraṃ*
harming *upaghātin*
harmlessness *avihiṃsā*, *ahiṃsā*
harsh *pharusa*, *khara*
harvest *apadānaṃ*
hatchet *vāsī*
hatred *veraṃ*
have (often expressed by the gen. case + *hū* (I)) *ā-pad* (III) (intrans.), *dhar* (VII)

he *ta(d)* (*so*), *eta(d)*, *idam-*(*ayaṃ*), *amu-* (*asu*), *na-*, *bhavant* (his honour)
head *sīsaṃ*, *siras-*, *muddhan-* (poetic)
health *ārogyaṃ*
heap *puñjo*
hear *(s)su* (V)
desire to hear *(s)su* (desid.), *sussūsā*
hear of *anu-(s)su* (V)
hearer *sotar* (masc.)
hearing *savanaṃ* (action), *sotaṃ* (sense)
hear ! *yagghe*
" heart " *cittaṃ* (fig.)
heat *tap* (I), *tejas-*
exhausted by heat *abhitatta*
heaven *saggo*, *divo* (poetic)
heavenly *sovaggika*, *dibba*
leading to heaven *sovaggika*
heavy *garu*
heir *dāyādo*
helot (member of the servile or working class: see footnote to Vocab. 20) *suddo*
hemp *sāṇaṃ*
here *ettha* (ind.), *idha* (ind.), *iha* (ind.)
here ! *iṅgha* (ind.)
hermitage *assamo*
heron *koñco*
hey ! *re* (ind.)
high priest *purohito*
higher *uttara*
highest *uttama*, *parama*
him (see " he ") *enaṃ* (pronoun, acc., sg. masc. only, enclitic)
hinder *var* (VII)
hit *(p)pa-har* (I)
hither *apāraṃ* (ind.)
hold *dhar* (VII)
held *paṇihita* (p.p. *(p)pa-ni-dhā*)
holding *-dharo*
hold on to *parā-mas* (I)
hold tight *gādh* (I)
hole *vivaraṃ*
home *ālayo*, *agāraṃ*, *abbhantara*
go home *saṃ-vis* (I*)
take home *saṃ-vis* (I*) caus.
homelessness *anagāriyaṃ*
your honour, his honour *bhavant*
honour *pūj* (VII), *mān* (VII)
honey *madhu* (neut.), *khuddaṃ* (wild)
hook *vaṅkaṃ*
elephant hook *aṃkuso*

beyond/defying the hook *accaṃkusa*
hope for *(p)paṭi-ā-sis* (II)
I hope ? *kacci* (ind.)
horizontally *tiriyaṃ* (ind.)
hostel (maintained by a local council) *āvasathāgāraṃ*
hostile king *paṭirājan* (masc.)
hot *tatta* (p.p. *tap*)
house *gharaṃ, gehaṃ, agāraṃ, nivesanaṃ*
house-dwelling *gihin*
householder *gahapati* (masc.), *gahapatiko*
how *yathā* (ind.)
how ? *kathaṃ* (ind.)
however *pana* (= but : ind., enclitic), *yathā yathā* (=whatever way : ind.)
how much ! (to what an extent) *yāva* (ind.)
how much more (so) *pag eva* (ind.), *ko pana vādo* (ind.)
human *mānusaka*
human being *manusso, manujo* (poetic), *mānuso* (poetic)
non-human being *amanusso*
hundred *sataṃ*
hundred thousand *satasahassaṃ*
be hungry *ghas* desid.
husbandman *vesso*
husk *thuso*
without husk *athusa*
husked rice *taṇḍulaṃ*
hymn *manto*

i

I *ma(d)*- (*ahaṃ*)
idea *parivitakko, dhammo*
i.e. *yad idaṃ* (ind.)
if *sace* (ind.), *ce* (ind., enclitic), *yaṃ* (ind.)
what (now) if ? *yan nūna* (ind.)
if so *atha* (ind.)
ignorance *avijjā*
ignore *ati-sar* (I)
ill *ābādhika, gilāna, vyādhita, du(r)*- (prefix)
illness *ābādho, gelaññaṃ, rogo*
illuminated *abhisambuddha* (fig.)
illumination *avabhāso*
imagine as *upa-saṃ-har* (I) (2 accs.)
imitation *anugati* (fem.)
immaterial *arūpin*
immeasurable *appamāṇa*
immortality *amataṃ*
immovable as a peak *kūṭaṭṭha*
impatience *ussukkaṃ*
be impatient *ussukkati* (denom.)
imperishable *aparihāniya*
imperturbable *aneja*
impossible *akaraṇīya*
imprisonment *ubbādhanā*
impure *asuci*
inaction *akiriyaṃ*
incapable *abhabba* (with dat. of the action)
incline *nam* (I)
inconsequentially *ayoniso* (ind.)
increase *(p)pa-vaḍḍh* (I), *abhi-vaḍḍh* (I)
incur *ni-gam* (I)
indeed *kho* (ind., enclitic), *khalu* (ind., enclitic), *u* (ind., enclitic to other indeclinables, poetic)
indefinable *anidassana*
independent *paccatta*
indeterminate *avyākata* (neg. p.p. *vi-ā-kar*)
become indignant *(k)khī* (III)
individual *paccatta*
individually *paccattaṃ*
indolent *kusīta*
indulge in *(p)paṭi-sev* (I), *sev* (I)
indulgence *pātavyatā*
inept *manda*
ineptitude *mandattaṃ*
inertia *thīnaṃ* (mental), *thīnamiddhaṃ* (mental)
infantryman *pattiko*
inference *anvayo*
inferior *appesakkha, hīna, nīca*
infinite *ananta*
infinity *ānañcaṃ*
influence *āsavo*
influx *āsavo*
inform *ā-ruc* (VII) (dat.), *vid* (I) caus., *(p)paṭi-vid* (I) caus.
information *vediyaṃ*
inheritance *dāyajjaṃ*
inheritor *dāyādo*
initiate *ā-rabh* (I)
injure *his* (II)
inner *ajjhatta*
inscrutable *viceyya*
insentient *asañña*
insight *abhisamayo, abhiññā, aññā*

have insight *(p)pa-(ñ)ñā* (V)
having insight *cakkhumant-*
inspiration *paṭibhānaṃ*
inspiring *saṃvejanīya*
instigate (use caus. or agent noun of caus., e.g. : instigator to kill *ghātetar* (masc.))
instinct *saṃkhāro* (see Vocab. 26)
instruct *saṃ-(d)dis* caus., *anu-sās* (I)
instruction *sāsanaṃ*
intelligent *vyatta, viyatta* (alternative spelling of *vyatta*), *medhāvin, cakkhumant-*
very intelligent *sumedhasa* (poetic)
intent on *pasuta, adhimutta*
intention *saṃkappo, ape(k)khā*
intermediate *majjhima*
intermediate direction *anudisā*
internal *abbhantara*
internally *ajjhattaṃ*
intimidation *paritajjanā*
intoxicant *majjaṃ*
intoxicated *madhuraka, sammatta*
intoxicating *madanīya*
intoxicating drink *mado*
intuition *paṭibhānaṃ*
invade *abhi-yā* (I)
investigate *vi-ci* (V), *man* desid.
investigating *vīmaṃsin-*
investigation *vīmaṃsā*
investigator *vīmaṃsin-* (as masc. noun)
invisible *anidassana*
invite *ni-mant* (VII)
involve *saṃ-vaṭṭ* (I)
involved in *saṃvaṭṭanika*
involution *saṃvaṭṭaṃ*
irascible *caṇḍa*
the " iron age " (that of misfortune) *kali* (masc.)
irrelevantly *aññena aññaṃ* (ind.)
island *dīpo*
isn't, isn't it ? *nanu* (ind.), *(s)su* (ind.)
isolated *vivitta* (p.p. *vi-vic* (VII))
having become isolated *vivicca* (ger. *vi-vic* (VII))
it *ta(d)* (*taṃ/tad*), *eta(d)*, *idaṃ*, *amu-* (*aduṃ*)

j

jaundice *paṇḍurogo*
jaw(s) *hanu* (fem.)
jetty *titthaṃ*
join *adhi-upa-gam* (I) (adhere to person/party), *anu-pa-(k)khand* (I) (*anupa-*) (go over to, be converted to)
joined *saṃhita* (p.p. *saṃ-dhā*)
joint *sandhi* (masc.)
journey *cārikā*
joy *pīti* (fem.), *ānando, somanassaṃ, muditā* (sympathetic—at well-being of others)
speak with joy *udāneti* (denom.)
joyful *muda*
joyful utterance *udānaṃ*
junction *sandhi* (masc.)
just *dhammika* (practising justice), *eva* (ind., enclitic : " only "), *va* (junction form of *eva*)
just now *adhunā* (ind.)
just so *evam eva* (ind.)
justice *dhammo*
just like *seyyathā* (ind., introducing a simile)

k

keeping *gahaṇaṃ*
keeper away *nivāretar* (masc.)
kill *han* (I), *ati-pat* caus.
killing *atipāto*
killer *hantar* (masc.)
kind (of) *-rūpa, -vidha*
kindling block *sahitaṃ*
kindling stick *araṇi* (fem.)
kindness *mettā*
king *rājā* (masc.) (*rājan-*), *mahārājo* (" great king "), *devo* (used for polite address)
kingdom *rajjaṃ, vijitaṃ*
kinsman *ñāti* (masc.), *bandhu* (masc.) (as name of God, poetic)
having knocked out *ūhacca* (ger. *u(d)-han* or *o-han*)
know *(ñ)ñā* (V), *abhi-(ñ)ñā* (V), *budh* (III), (*vid* (I), present not used, is used in caus. = " inform ")
knower *vidū* (masc.)
knowing thoroughly *kovida* (poetic)
known *vidita* (p.p. *vid* (II) : (f.p.p. *veditabba* also current), *vediya* (esp. that which is known : ~ *aṃ*)
make known *(p)pa-vid* (I) (only caus.)

known as *-saṃkhāta* (p.p. of *saṃ-(k)khā* (I))
knowledge *ñāṇaṃ*, *aññā* (the quality of, insight), *vijjā* (body of, science)
having the triple knowledge *tevijja* (= the verses, music and prayers of the Three Vedas)

l

lacking *vipanna*
lady ! *ayye* (voc.) (polite or respectful address, used also to nuns)
lake *saraṃ*
lament *pari-dev* (VII), *anu-(t)thu* (V)
lamentation *paridevo*
lamp *padīpeyyaṃ*, *padīpo*, *pajjoto*
lance *tomaraṃ*
land *khettaṃ* (field, territory, etc.), *thalaṃ* (dry land)
landing place *titthaṃ*
land-sighting *tīradassi*
language *nirutti* (fem.)
lap *udaraṃ*
lapis lazuli *veḷuriyo*
large (cf. " great ") *thūla*, *vipula*
last *pacchima*
at last *cirassaṃ* (ind.)
law of nature *dhammo*
lay disciple *upāsako* (masc.), *upāsikā* (fem.)
lazy *alasa*, *kusīta*
lead *sīsaṃ*
lead *nī* (I)
lead away *apa-nī* (I)
lead out *ni(r)-vah* (I)
lead to *saṃ-vatt* (I) (dat.)
leader *pariṇāyako*
leading *netti* (fem.)
leading to *-yāniya*, *saṃvattanika*
league *yojanaṃ* (about 4·5 miles)
leaning on *nissāya* (ger. of *ni-(s)sī* (I))
learn *ā-(ñ)ñā* (V) (grasp), *u(d)-(g)gah* (V) (memorize), *(ñ)ñā* (V) (find out), *sikkh* (I) (train)
learned *abhiññā*, *kovida* (poetic)
learning *sajjhāyo* (studying)
learner *aññātar* (masc.)
leave *ni(r)-kam* (I) (*r* + *k* > *kkh*)
take leave *abhi-vad* (VII), *apa-lok* (VII) (give notice)
ask leave (of absence) *ā-pucch* (I)
leaving *nissakkanaṃ*
leaving behind *visajja* (ger.)
having led *netvā* (ger. *nī*)
left (hand, etc.) *vāma*
be left over *sis* (VII), *ava-sis* (III)
left over *avasiṭṭha*
length *āyāmo*
let alone (much less) *kuto pana* (ind.), *pag eva* (ind.)
liberating *nibbuti* (fem.) (*from ni(r)-vā* (I))
liberation *pātimokkho*
liberation (from existence) *nibbānaṃ*, *nissaraṇaṃ*, *vimutti* (fem.)
attain liberation *pari-ni(r)-vā* (I) (or III)
lie down *ni-pad* (III), *si* (I)
life *jīvitaṃ*, *pāṇo* (breath), *āyu* (neut.) (length of, age), *nivāso* (kind of, sphere of, particular existence), *vihāro* (way of)
all one's life *yāvajīvaṃ* (ind.)
life principle *jīvo*
way of life *vihāro*
" best " (celibate) life *brahmacariyaṃ*
lift onto *u(d)-sīd* caus. (*ussādeti*)
light (illumination) *āloko*
light (weight) *lahu*
light coloured *sukka*
like *(k)kham* (I), *sadisa* (adj.), *sama* (adj.), *samaṃ* (ind.), *viya* (ind., enclitic), *iva* (ind., enclitic), *va* (ind., enclitic, poetic)
liking *kāmo*
likewise *evam eva* (ind.)
like what ? *kīdisa* (adj.)
as long as one likes *yathābhirantaṃ* (ind.)
limb *gattaṃ*, *aṅgaṃ*
limited *parivaṭuma*, *saṃkhitta*
lion *sīho*
liquor *majjaṃ*
litter (palanquin) *milātaṃ*
little *appa*, *appaka* (poetic)
live *jīv* (I) (be alive), *vi-har* (I) (dwell), *vas* (I) (dwell), *car* (I) (conduct oneself, carry on)
live among *pari-vas* (I)
live in *ā-vas* (I)
live on *adhi-ā-vas* (I)
live upon, live by *upa-jīv* (I)
make live with *vas* (I) caus.

as long as one lives *yāvajīvaṃ* (ind.)
having lived properly *vusitavant-*
having truly lived (as a monk) *vusitavant-*
lived well *vusita* (p.p. *vas* (I))
livelihood *ājīvo, jīvikā*
living *-vihārin* (dwelling, being), *-cārin* (going on), *-cara*
living by *ājīvin*
living in *āvāso*
make a living *jīv* (I)
living being *bhūto, pāṇo*
living beings *bhūtagāmo*
load *ā-ruh* (I) caus., *bhāro*
locality *padeso*
lofty *udagga*
logician *takkin-*
loneliness *anabhirati* (fem.)
long *dīgha*
long (adv.) *dīghaṃ* (ind.)
so long *tāva* (ind.)
long (for) *pari-tas* (III), *pih* (VII) (dat.)
too long *ativelaṃ* (ind.)
long time *cira, dīgharattaṃ* (ind.)
for a long time *ciraṃ* (ind.) (*cira-paṭikāhaṃ* = " I have long ")
after a long time *ciraṃ* (ind.), *cirassaṃ* (ind.)
as long as *yāva* (ind.), *yāvakīvaṃ* (ind.)
longing *paritassanā*
as long as one lives *yāvajīvaṃ* (ind.)
look at *o-lok* (VII)
looker at *udikkhitar* (masc.)
looker on *pekkhitar* (masc.)
look for *pari-is(a)* (I) (*pariyes-*)
looking for *pariyeṭṭhi* (fem.)
look after *pus* (VII), *anu-rakkh* (I)
look on *(p)pa-ikkh* (I)
loom *tantaṃ*
lord *ādhipati* (masc.), *pati* (masc.), *issaro*
lordship *ādhipateyyaṃ*
loss *vayo, parihāni* (fem.)
lost (strayed) *mūḷha* (p.p. *muh*)
lotus pool *pokkharaṇī, nalinī*
(of) lovable sight/appearance *piya-dassana*
love *kam* (VII), *kāmo* (sexual or otherwise possessive), *mettā* (spiritual and non-sexual)
lovely *kanta, kamanīya, pāsādika, vāma* (poetic)
lovingkindness *mettā*
low *nīca*
it's lucky *diṭṭhā* (ind.)
luminosity *pabhā*
lunar mansion *nakkhattaṃ*
lust *pariḷāho*
lustre *subhaṃ, nibhā*
lustrous *subha*
lying down *uttāna, sayāna* (pres. p. *si*)

m

mad *ummatta*
maddened *sammatta*
magnificence *ānubhāvo*
the majority of *yebhuyyena* (ind.)
malicious *pisuṇa*
make *kar* (VI)
made of *-maya*
maker *kattar* (masc.)
making *-kāro, -karaṇa* (fem. *-ī*)
malevolence *vyāpādo*
malevolent *vyāpanna, vyāpajjha*
man *puriso, puman-, mānuso* (poetic)
mango (fruit) *ambaṃ* (usually neut.)
mango (tree) *ambo* (usually masc.)
mango woman *ambakā*
manifest *pātu(r)* (prefix)
become manifest *pātu(r)-bhū* (I)
manifestation *pātubhāvo*
manner (of) *-vidha*
mansion *vimāno* (only of divine beings, in the sky; cf. lunar ~, palace)
many *aneka, sambahula, pahūta, bahu, puthu*
how many? *kati* (adj., but see Lesson 26)
as many as *yāvataka* (fem. *-ikā*)
mark *lakkhaṇaṃ*
marvellous *abbhuta*
mass *(k)khandho*
master *vasin-, ayyaputto* (= " Mr. ": polite address, esp. by ladies, including wives)
the Master *bhagavant* (title of the Buddha)
material *oḷārika, rūpin-*
mathematician *gaṇako*
matrix *mātikā* (for remembering doctrine)

matter *rūpaṃ, attho* (affair)
meal *bhattaṃ, bhojanaṃ*
meaning *attho*
meanness *okāro*
meanwhile *antarā* (ind.)
measurable *pamāṇakata*
measure *mā* (V), *mattā, pamāṇaṃ* (size)
meat *maṃsaṃ*
medicine *bhesajjaṃ*
meditation *(j)jhānaṃ*
meditate *(j)jhe* (I)
medium *majjhima*
melancholy *domanassaṃ*
member of an assembly *pārisajjo*
memorize *u(d)-(g)gah* (V)
memorizer *-dharo*
mental *manomaya*
mental being *nāmaṃ*
mental deficiency *thīnaṃ*
mental derangement *middhaṃ*
mental object *dhammo*
mental phenomenon *dhammo*
mental state *dhammo*
merchant *vāṇijo, vesso*
merit *puññaṃ*
meritorious action *puññaṃ*
messenger *dūto*
met *abhisaṭa* (p.p. *abhi-sar*)
metaphysician *vīmaṃsin*
method *ñāyo*
methodically *yoniso* (ind.)
mews *vāhanāgāraṃ*
middle *majjhima*
in the middle *majjhe* (ind.)
might *ānubhāvo*
mighty *uḷāra*
milk *payas-*
mind *manas-, cetas-, cittaṃ, nāmaṃ*
mindful *sata, satimant-*
mindfulness *(s)sati* (fem.), *patissati* (fem.)
minister *mahāmatto*
minister (privy councillor) *amacco*
minor *khudda*
very minor *anukhuddaka*
minute (infinitesimal) *aṇu*
misconduct *micchā*
misery *apāyo, upāyāso, dukkhaṃ, anayo*
misfortune *anayo*
mission *cārikā*
go on a mission *car* (I)
mixed *missa*
mixed (with) *vokiṇṇa* (p.p. *vi-o-kir*)
mode (of argument) *vatthu* (neut.)
modesty *hiri* (fem.)
moment *muhuttaṃ* (or masc.)
money *dhanaṃ*
monk *bhikkhu* (masc.) (elder : *thero*)
month *māso* →
monument *thūpo*
moon *candimā* (masc.), *cando*
more *bhiyya, bhiyyo* (ind.), *uttari* (ind.)
more than (-numeral) *paro-*
moreover *ca pana* (ind., enclitic), *atha kho* (ind.)
morning *pubbaṇho*
morning meal *pātarāso*
in the morning *pāto* (ind., in compound before a vowel *pātar*)
mortal *macco*
most *parama*
mostly *yebhuyyena* (ind.)
mother *mātar* (fem.)
mount *abhi-ruh* (I*), *ā-ruh* (I*), *vāhanaṃ* (animal or vehicle)
mouth *mukhaṃ*
mountain *pabbato*
move *sar* (I), *iriy* (I*) (poetic)
move about *iriy* (I*) (poetic)
mown *lūna* (p.p. *lū* (V))
much *pahūta, bahu, bahuka*
very much *ativiya* (ind.)
as much *yāva* (ind.)
so much *tāva* (ind.)
in as much as *yatra hi nāma* (ind.) (may express wonder, etc.)
much less (= " let alone ") *kuto pana* (ind.)
mud *kaddamo, paṃsu* (masc.)
muddy *āvila* (turbid)
mushroom *ahicchatako*
(instrumental) music *vāditaṃ*
must *arah* (I) (or ipv.)
myna *sālikā*

n

nail *nakho* (finger-)
name *nāmaṃ, adhivacanaṃ*
narrow *saṃkhitta*
natural element *dhammo*
natural phenomenon *dhammo*
natural principle *dhammo*

in natural order *anulomaṃ* (ind.)
nature *bhāvo, dhammo*
in its true nature, according to nature *yathābhūtaṃ* (ind.)
near *avidūre* (ind.)
nearer *orima*
negligence *(p)pamādo*
negligent *(p)pamatta*
neither *n' eva*
nephew (sister's son) *bhāgineyyo*
net-like *jālin*
nevertheless *api ca* (ind.)
new *ahata, nava*
night *ratti* (fem.)
nine *nava* (num.)
nineteen *ekūnavīsati* (fem.)
ninety *navuti* (fem.)
" Nirvana " *nibbānaṃ* (from *ni(r)-vā* (I))
noble *ariya*
noise *saddo*
non *a-*
through non-attachment *anupādā* (ind.)
non-existence *vibhavo*
non-harasser *aheṭhako*
non-injuring *avihiṃsā*
non-sensual *nirāmisa*
non-violence *avyāpādo, asāhasaṃ*
none at all *na kiñ ci* (pronoun)
nonsense *palāpo*
nor *na, na pana, no ca kho*
in normal order *anulomaṃ* (ind.)
northern *uttara*
nose *natthu* (fem.), *ghānaṃ* (esp. as sense of smell)
not *a-, na* (ind.)
not (emphatic) *no* (ind.)
don't *mā* (ind.)
not to speak of *ko pana vādo* (ind.)
notes *mātikā* (sing.)
nothing *na kiñ ci* (pronoun)
nothingness *ākiñcaññaṃ*
give notice *apa-lok* (VII)
now *etarahi* (ind. = at present), *dāni* (ind., enclitic), *adhunā* (ind. = " just now "), *kira* (ind.), *taṃ* (ind.), *tāva* (ind.)
now ! *tena hi* (ind., admonitory)
nun *bhikkhunī*
nurse *dhātī*

O

object (cf. " sight ", etc., " purpose ") *saṃkappo* (intention)
the true/good objective *sadattho*
oblation *hutaṃ*
obscurity *andhakāro*
observance day *uposatho*
observe *saṃ-lakkh* (VII), *sacchi-kar* (VI), *upa-ni-(j)jhe* (I), *anu-bhū* (I)
observation *sacchikiriyā*
observer *pekkhitar* (masc.)
observing *anupassin*
obstacle *nīvaraṇaṃ, antarāyo*
obstruct *var* (VII)
obtain *labh* (I), *(p)paṭi-labh* (I)
occasion *samayo, velā*
occupy *pari-(g)gah* (V)
occur *u(d)-pad* (III), *vid* (III), *saṃ-vid* (III)
occurrence *uppādo*
ocean *samuddo*
oceanic, ocean going *sāmuddika*
odour *gandho*
of what sort ? *kīdisa* (adj.)
off *apa* (prefix), *o* (prefix)
offended *aparaddha*
offer *upa-nam* (I) caus. (dat. of person and acc. of thing)
offer a seat *āsanena ni-mant* (VII)
offering *-pāto* (alms), *yiṭṭhaṃ* (sacrificial, ritual)
offspring *apacco*
oil *telaṃ* (sesame)
ointment *vilepanaṃ*
old *purāṇa, pubbaka, jara* (aged), *vuddha* (aged, senior)
grow old *jar* (III)
old age *jarā*
omen *nimitto*
without omission *anantaraṃ* (ind.)
on *parā* (prefix)
oneself *sayaṃ* (ind.), *sāmaṃ* (ind.), *attan* (pronoun)
one *eka* (prn. num.)
one . . . another *añña . . . añña* (prn.)
once *saki(d)* *(eva)* (ind.), *sakiṃ* (ind.)
once upon a time *bhūtapubbaṃ* (ind.)
only *eva* (ind., enclitic), *va* (ind., enclitic)
on to *parā* (prefix)
ooze *u(d)-(g)ghar* (I)

open *vi-var* (I)
open *apāruta* (door, etc.), *abbhokāsa* (air), *pasaṭa* (frank gaze)
opening *bhedanaṃ* (unpacking), *ādi* (masc.) (beginning)
open air *abbhokāsa*
operating (something) *-vattin*
opinion *mataṃ, diṭṭhi* (fem.)
opportunity *okāso, kālo*
opposed *mithu*
in the opposite direction, the opposite way *paṭipathaṃ* (ind.)
oppression *upapīḷā*
or *vā* (ind., enclitic), *udāhu* (ind.)
orange *kāsāya*
order *āṇa* caus. (" command "), *kappo* (arrangement)
in normal or natural order *anulomaṃ* (ind.)
in reverse order *paṭilomaṃ* (ind.)
ordered *āṇatta* (p.p. *āṇa* caus.)
ordainer *sañjitar* (masc.)
organize *kapp* (VII), *saṃ-vi-dhā* (I)
origin *samudayo, sambhavo, pubbanto, abhinibbatti* (fem.), *nidānaṃ, yoni* (fem.)
originated *samuppanna* (p.p. *saṃ-u(d)-pad* (III))
origination *samuppādo, samudayo*
original *aggañña*
ornament *alaṅkāro*
other side *pārima*
other *añña* (pronoun), *para* (pronoun)
the other way *paṭipathaṃ* (ind.)
otherwise *aññathā* (ind.)
ought *arah* (I)
out *ni(r)* (prefix), *(p)pa* (prefix)
out of doors *abbhokāsa*
outside *bahiddhā* (ind.)
over *adhi* (prefix), *ati* (prefix)
overheated *abhitatta*
overlord *abhibhū* (masc.)
overturned *nikkujjita* (p.p. *ni(r)-kujj* (I))
own *sa-, saka,* (~ child, etc. :) *ura, orasa, attan* (pronoun)
ox *yoggaṃ*

P

package *puṭo* (of merchandise)
pagoda *thūpo, cetiyaṃ*
pair *yamakaṃ*
palace *pāsādo, antepuraṃ, vimāno* (of divine beings)
palanquin *milātaṃ*
parcel *bhaṇḍikā*
park *uyyānaṃ, ārāmo*
parrot *suko*
part *paccaṅgaṃ* (of body), *bhāgo* (share)
partridge *jīvaṃjīvako*
pass into *saṃ-(k)kam* (I)
pass over *ati-(k)kam* (I), *ati-sar* (I) (ignore)
pass away *vi-o-(k)kam* (I)
pass away (from a form of existence) *cu* (I)
one who has passed away *peto*
passing away *cavanaṃ*
pass beyond *saṃ-ati-(k)kam* (I)
pass down *o-tar* (I)
not passing *anatīta*
passing beyond *samatikkamo*
passion *rāgo, kāmo, sārāgo*
past *atīta*
pastime *(p)pamādo*
pasture *gocaro*
paternal *pettika*
path *ayanaṃ*
pay *(p)pa-kapp* (VII) (wages), *vetanaṃ*
peace of mind *nirodho*
peacemaker *sandhātar* (masc.)
peacock *mayūro*
peak *kūṭo*
peculiarity *ākāro*
pedestrian *pattiko*
penetrate *(p)paṭi-vidh* (III) (comprehend)
penetrate with *pari-bhū* (I) caus.
penetration *(p)paṭivedho* (comprehension)
people *loko*
the people *mahājano, janatā*
perceive *sacchi-kar* (VI), *saṃ-(ñ)ñā* (V)
perception *saññā*
having perception *saññin-*
perch *patiṭṭhā*
perfect *paripuṇṇa*
perfectly *sammā* (ind. : " rightly "), *samattaṃ* (ind. : " completely ")
perfected *alaṃ* (ind.)
perfected one *arahant-* (masc.)
perfection *pāripūri* (fem.)

perfume *gandho*
perhaps *api* (ind., with opt.)
perhaps ? *kacci* (ind.)
perish *(k)khī* (III), *nas* (III)
perish utterly *vi-nas* (III)
permanent *nicca*
perpetuity *amarā*
perplexity *vimati* (fem.)
persistence *(ṭ)ṭhiti* (fem.)
person *puriso, manusso, puggalo, jano*
people *jano* (collective singular)
personal *attarūpa, paccatta*
pervade *phar* (I)
phenomenon *dhammo* (physical or mental, but natural)
philosopher (other than a brahman) *samaṇo*
physician *vejjo*
piece *ālumpaṃ*
pig *sūkaro*
be piled up *ci* (V) passive (*cīyati*)
pillar *esikaṃ*
firm as a pillar *esikaṭṭhāyin-*
piquancy *raso*
pit *sobbhaṃ*
place *(ṭ)ṭhānaṃ, padeso, bhūmi* (fem.)
proper place *gocaro*
plague *antarāyo*
plant *ruh* (I) caus.
plants *bījagāmo*
play *div* (III) (gamble), *upa-ḷas* (VII) (instrument, etc.), *khiḍḍā*
pleasant to the skin *succhavi*
please *ā-rādh* (VII) (acc.), *(k)kham* (I) (dat.), *saṃ-tapp* (VII) (acc.), *pīṇ* (I) (only caus.)
as you please *yathā te khameyya*
pleased *āraddha* (p.p. *ā-rādh* (VII))
be pleased *chad* (VII), *tus* (III), *nand* (I)
be pleased with (acc.) *abhi-nand* (I)
pleasing *manāpa*
pleasure *kāmo, khamanīyaṃ, vitti* (fem.), *sukhallikā*
according to one's pleasure *yathābhirantaṃ* (ind.)
take pleasure in *abhi-ram* (I) (elevated) (loc.)
taking pleasure in *abhirata* (p.p. *abhiram*)
pleasant *sammodanīya*
plenty *bahuka*
plough *naṅgalo*
plunder *nillopo*
plunge into *o-gāh* (I), *adhi-o-gāh* (I)
poet *kavi* (masc.)
poetry *kāveyyaṃ*
point *kūṭo, deso* (topic)
poison *visaṃ*
policy *saṃvidhānaṃ*
polished *likhita*
polite *sārāṇīya*
pollen *reṇu* (masc.)
pondered *vicārita* (p.p. of caus. *vi-car* (I))
pool *pallalaṃ*
lotus pool *pokkharaṇī, nalinī*
poor *adhana*
portent *nimitto*
porter *dovāriko*
position *vatthu* (neut.)
maintain one's position (thesis) *sampāy* (I)
possess *pari-(g)gah* (V)
possessing *pariggaha, bhogin, sa-*
not possessive *amama*
possessiveness *mamattaṃ*
possible *labbhā* (ind.) (see Vocab. 27)
it is possible, is it possible ? *sakkā* (ind.)
pot *kumbho* (clay), *tuṇḍikīro* (gourd)
potency *tejas-*
pour over *ā-sic* (II)
pour down (heavy rain, cloudburst) *abhi-(p)pa-vass* (I), *gaḷagaḷāyati* (denom.-onomat.)
poverty *daliddiyaṃ*
power *ānubhāvo, iddhi* (fem.) (marvellous)
powerful *iddha*
powerless *avasa*
practice *anuyogo*
practise *(p)paṭi-pad* (III), *anu-car* (I), *ā-sev* (I), *vi-ā-yam* (I) (*vāyamati*)
practising *anuyoga*
praise *(p)pa-saṃs* (I), *vaṇṇo*
prayer *manto*
as a precaution *paṭigacc' eva* (ind.)
precept *sikkhāpadaṃ*
precious thing *ratanaṃ*
pre-eminence *aggatā*
preferring *sāpekha*
pregnant *gabbhin-*
preparation *paññāpanaṃ*

prepare (*p*)*pa*-(*ñ*)*ñap* (VII), (*p*)*paṭi-yat* (only caus. : *paṭiyādāpeti*)
in the presence of *sammukhā* (ind., gen.)
at present *etarahi* (ind.)
present *pābhataṃ* (gratuity), *paccup-panna* (time)
presented with *samappita*, (p.p. *saṃ-app* (VII))
prevalence *vepullaṃ*
prevent *var* (VII), *ni-sidh* (I) caus.
prevention *nisedho*
pride *māno*, *uddhaccaṃ*, *uddhaccakuk-kuccaṃ*
priest *brāhmaṇo*
young priest *māṇavo*
high priest *purohito*
priestess *brāhmaṇī* (woman of the hereditary priest class)
prime minister *purohito*
primeval *aggañña*
prince *kumāro*, *rājaputto*
princess *kumārī* (girl of the military-aristocratic class)
principle (natural) *dhammo*
in privacy *rahogata*
probable *pāṭikaṅkha*
proceed *car* (I), *vatt* (I), (*p*)*pa-vatt* (I)
process *saṃkhāro* (see Vocab. 26)
proclaim *abhi-vad* (I)
proclaimer *pavattar* (masc.)
produce *ni*(*r*)-*vatt* (VII), *su* (I), *ā-pad* (III)
be produced *abhi-ni*(*r*)-*vatt* (I), *saṃ-jan* (III)
produced from *jātika*
producer *janani* (poetic)
production *abhinibbatti* (fem.), *uppādo*, *sambhavo*
profession *sippaṃ*
proficient *abhiyogin*
profound *gambhīra*
prognosticator *nemitto*
prohibit *ni-sidh* (I) caus.
prohibition *nisedho*
promulgate *u*(*d*)-*ā-har* (I)
propaganda *upalāpanaṃ*
proper *paṭirūpa*, *kalla* (sound), *yathā-bhucca* (real)
proper time *kālo*
property *bhogo*, *sāpateyyaṃ*, *bhoggaṃ*
proprietary rights *bhoggaṃ*
prosperity *attho*
leading to prosperity *aparihāniya*
prosperous *phīta*
protect *abhi-pāl* (VII), *pari-har* (I) (watch over)
protected *gutta* (p.p. *gup*)
protection *gutti* (fem.), *saraṇaṃ*
provide with *samaṅgī-bhū* (I)
punishment *daṇḍo*
pupil *sāvako*
pure *visuddha*, *aneḷaka*
become pure *pari-sudh* (III), *sudh* (III)
purgatory *nirayo*
purification *visuddhi* (fem.)
become purified *vi-sudh* (III)
purity *pārisuddhi* (fem.), *soceyyaṃ*
purpose *attho*
the true/good purpose *sadattho*
pursue *sev* (I) (indulge in)
put on top of *ā-ruh* (I) caus.
put down *o-dhā* (I), *ni*-(*k*)*khip* (I*), *ni-pat* (I) caus.
put in order *kapp* (VII)
put out (to sea) *adhi-o-gāh* (I)
put into (*p*)*pa*-(*k*)*khip* (I*)
putting on top of *accādhāya* (ger. *ati-ā-dhā*)

q

quadruped *catuppado*
quadruple *catugguṇa*
quake *kamp* (I)
quality *guṇaṃ* (sometimes masc.), *dhammo*
special (peculiar) quality *lakkhaṇaṃ*
quarrel *viggaho*
quarter *catutthabhāgo*, *catuttha*
queen *devī*
question *pañho*
quickly *khippaṃ*
quiver *phand* (I), *kalāpo*
end quote *ti* (ind.), (emphasizing one word or expression :) *tv eva* (ind.)

r

radiance *obhāso*, *pabhā*
radiant *aṅgīrasa* (fem. -*ī*)
raft *kullo*
rain *vassaṃ*
rain down on *abhi*-(*p*)*pa-vass* (I)
rain heavily (*p*)*pa-vass* (I)
rain on *abhi-vass* (I)

rainy season *vassaṃ* (plur.)
rainy (for the rainy season) *vassika* (adj.)
raise *u(d)-har* (I)
ramparts *pākāro*
range *gocaro*
rare *dullabha*
rather *atha kho* (ind.)
razor *khuraṃ*
reach *phus* (I*), *ap(p)* (VI)
reacting *(p)paṭigho*
reaction *(p)paṭigho*
ready *niṭṭhita*
real *yathābhucca*
really *kira* (ind.)
as it really is *yathābhūtaṃ* (ind.)
realm *vijitaṃ*
reaped *lūna* (p.p. *lū* (V))
reaping *apadānaṃ*
rear *pus* (VII)
rearer *posako*
ask for reasons *saṃ-anu-(g)gah* (V) caus.
reasoned *vitakkita* (p.p. *vi-takk*)
reasoning *vitakko*
reassurance *assāso*
rebel *kaṇṭakaṃ*
rebirth *punabbhavo*
leading to rebirth *ponobhavika*
reborn *paccājāta* (p.p. *(p)paṭi-ā-jan* (III))
be reborn *upa-pad* (III)
rebut *ni(r)-veṭh* (VII)
make receive *(p)paṭi-(g)gah* (V) caus.
received (doctrine) *āgata*
receiver *paṭiggahetar* (masc.)
recipient *paṭiggahetar* (masc.)
recite after *anu-vac* (I) caus.
recitation *pavuttaṃ*
reciter *sāvetar* (masc.)
recluse *muni* (masc.) (poetic)
recollect *anu-(s)sar* (I)
recollectedness *patissati* (fem.)
red *lohita*
reference *padeso*
with reference to *ārabbha* (ger. *ā-rabh* (I))
with reference to this *tayidaṃ* (ind.)
referring to *uddesika*
reflect *(p)paṭi-saṃ-cikkh* (I)
reflection *parivitakko*
refuge *saraṇaṃ*
refute *ni-(g)gah* (V), *saṃ-anu-bhās* (I)
region *padeso, disā*
regret *vippaṭisāro*
be consumed with regret *pa-(j)jhe* (I)
rejected *paṭinissaṭṭha* (p.p. *(p)paṭi-ni(r)-(s)saj* [1])
rejecting *paṭinissaggo*
rejoice *mud* (I), *nand* (I)
relate *kath* (VII)
relative *ñāti* (masc.)
blood relation *salohito*
release *vimutti* (fem.)
relics *sarīraṃ* (plur.)
religious tax *bali* (masc.)
remain *(ṭ)ṭhā* (I) (stay), *sis* (VII) (be left over), *ava-sis* (III) (be left over), *ava-(ṭ)ṭhā* (I)
remaining *(ṭ)ṭhāyin-*, *avasiṭṭha*
without remainder *aparisesa, asesa*
one who remains *avasesako*
remember *dhar* (VII), *(s)sar* (I)
remembering *-dharo*
remorse *vighāto*
removed *onīta, vīta-*
removing *apanūdanaṃ* (poetic)
renounce *(p)pa-hā* (I)
renounced *paṭinissaṭṭha* (p.p. *(p)paṭi-ni(r)-(s)saj* [1])
renouncing *paṭinissaggo*
renunciation *nekkhammaṃ*
repelling *paṭibāho*
report *ā-(k)khā* (I) (esp. tradition) *saddo* (rumour)
reporter *akkhātar* (masc.)
reproof *garahā*
repulse *paṭibāho*
repulsion *(p)paṭigho*
reputable *yasassin*
reputation *yasas-*
request *yāc* (I)
rescind *pari-hā* (I) caus.
residence *āvasatho*
resistance *(p)paṭigho*
resolve on *adhi-(ṭ)ṭhā* (I)
resort to *bhaj* (I)
resounding with *abhiruda*
resources *upakaraṇaṃ*
respect *mān* (VII), *gāravo*
give respect to *garu-kar* (VI)
pay respect *vand* (I)
respected *yasassin*
resting place *senāsanaṃ, patiṭṭhā*

rest house *āvasathāgāraṃ*
restless *lola*
restrained *saññata, danta* (p.p. *dam*)
restraint *saṃvaro, damo*
restricted *paritta*
result *vipāko*
have a result *vi-pac* (III)
as a result of *āgamma* (acc., ger. *ā-gam*)
retain *anu-rakkh* (I)
retire *o-sakk* (I)
retired *patisallīna* (sometimes spelt *paṭi-*)
retirement *patisallānaṃ* (sometimes spelt *paṭi-*)
return *(p)paṭi-ā-gam* (I), *(p)paṭi-ā-ni(r)-yā* (I)
having returned *āgantvā* (ger.)
revere *mān* (VII)
reverence *padakkhiṇā*
in reverse order *paṭilomaṃ* (ind.)
review *saṃ-(d)dis* caus.
revolve *(p)pa-vatt* (I)
rice *sāli* (fem.), *odano* (boiled) (the fine red powder between the grain and husk of rice : *kaṇo*)
rice grain *taṇḍulaṃ*
rich *aḍḍha*
ridge *kūṭo*
right (hand) *dakkhiṇa*
right (cf. just, true)
rightly *sammā* (ind.)
ripe, ripened *pakka, pāka, paripakka*
ripen *vi-pac* (III)
ripening *paripāko, pākima*
rise *(p)paṭi-(u)d-(ṭ)ṭhā* (I) (*paccuṭṭheti*)
rise up *u(d)-(ṭ)ṭhā* (I)
rising *uṭṭhānaṃ*
rite *yañño* (sacrifice)
river *nadī*
road *addhan-, patho, pantho, maggo, vaṭumaṃ*
roadworthy *addhaniya*
roar *nādo*
robbery *duhano*
robe *cīvaraṃ*
roll *vaṭṭ* (I) (intrans.)
rolling *vaṭṭaṃ*
roof bracket *gopānasī*
room *āvasatho*
root *mūlaṃ*
rope *rajju* (fem.)
rough *khara, pharusa*
roughness *kharattaṃ*
round *pari* (prefix)
all round *samantā* (ind.)
royal court *rājakulaṃ*
royal endowment *rājadāyo*
royal stake (marking the royal threshold) *indakhilo*
rubbish heap *saṃkārakūṭo*
ruin *vinipāto*
rule *sās* (I), *kappo*
moral rule *sikkhāpadaṃ*
rule over *abhi-bhū* (I)
rumour *saddo*
rush (plant) *muñjaṃ*

S

sabbath *uposatho*
sacrifice (ritual) *yaj* (I), *yañño* (rite), *yiṭṭhaṃ* (offering)
sacrificer *yājetar* (masc.)
safe *khema*
safely *sotthi* (ind., dat.), *sotthinā* (ind.)
safety *rakkhā, sotthi* (ind., dat.)
sage *isi* (masc.)
for the sake of *atthāya* (ind.)
salute *vand* (I)
same : that/the . . . (is) the same thing as that/the . . . *ta(d)* . . . *ta(d)* . . .
satisfy *ā-rādh* (VII) (acc.), *saṃ-tapp* (VII) (acc.)
be satisfied *saṃ-tus* (only p.p.)
say *vad* (I), *bhās* (I), *vac* (I) (aorist), *bhaṇ* (I), *ah* (only perfect), *u(d)-ā-har* (I)
saying *vacanaṃ, bhāsitaṃ*
say after *anu-bhās* (I)
I say ! *bhaṇe* (ind., enclitic : arrogant or lordly), *vata* (ind., enclitic : polite, mild expletive)
they say (it is said that) *kira* (ind., enclitic)
scatter *kir* (I*)
scent *gandho*
science *vijjā*
scold *ā-(k)kus* (I)
scope *avacaro*
scrape off *o-lup* (II) caus.
sea *samuddo*
put out to sea *adhi-o-gāh* (I)
search *pariyeṭṭhi* (fem.)

search for *gaves* (I), *pari-is(a)* (I) (*pariyes-*)
search out *vi-ci* (V)
season *utu* (neut.) (the gender fluctuates)
seat *āsanaṃ* (raised), *nisīdanaṃ* (groundsheet, etc.)
offer a seat *āsanena ni-mant* (VII)
secluded *patisallīna* (sometimes spelt *paṭi-*), *vūpakaṭṭha*
seclusion *patisallāṇaṃ* (sometimes spelt *paṭi-*), *viveko*
second *dutiya*
secure *khema*
see *pass* (I), *(d)dis* (I) (present system from *pass*, rest from *(d)dis*)
seed *bījaṃ*
seeing *dassanaṃ*, *dakkhin* (fem. *-iṇī*), *diṭṭhin*, *-dasa*, *dassāvin* (who would see)
be seen *saṃ-(d)dis* passive
seek *pari-is(a)* (I) (*pariyes-*)
seeking *pariyeṭṭhi* (fem.), *anuesin* (adj.)
seem *(k)khā* (III)
seer *isi* (masc.)
seize *(g)gah* (V), *ā-(g)gah* (V)
seizing *-(g)gāho*
self *attan* (masc. and pronoun: Lesson 22), *sayaṃ* (ind.), *sāmaṃ* (ind.)
self-control *saṃyamo*
selfishness *mamattaṃ*
self possessed *sata*, *satimant-*
self possession *(s)sati* (fem.)
self-respect *hiri* (fem.)
semi-desert *kantāro*
send *(p)pa-hi* (V), *pes* (VII)
(most) senior *jeṭṭha*
sensation *vedanā*, *vedayitaṃ*, *phoṭṭhabbaṃ*
sensual *sāmisa*
sentence *vyañjanaṃ*
sentient *saññin-*
sentient body *nāmarūpaṃ*
separated *vivitta* (p.p. *vi-vic* (VII))
separate from *vi-o-chid* (III)
having become separated from *vivicca* (ger. *vi-vic* (VII))
separation *viveko*
serenity *sampasādanaṃ*
serve *upa-(ṭ)ṭhā* (I), *upa-nam* (I) caus. (dat. of person and acc. of thing), *pari-vis* (I*) (with food)
service *porisaṃ*
serving *upaṭṭhānaṃ*
set going *(p)pa-vatt* (I)
setting going *-vattin*
set out *(p)pa-yā* (I)
set up *(p)paṭi(> pati)-(ṭ)ṭhā* (I), *(p)paccupaṭṭhita* (p.p. *(p)paṭi-upa-(ṭ)ṭhā*)
set upright *u(d)-kujj* (I)
setting *atthagamo*
seven *satta* (num.)
seventeen *sattarasa* (num.)
seventh *sattama*
seventy *sattati* (fem.)
sexual *methuna*
shade *pacchāyā*
shake *saṃ-dhu* (V)
shallow *uttānaka*
shame *ottappaṃ*
shamefaced *maṅku*
shapeliness *lakkhaṇaṃ*
sharp *tiṇha*
share *saṃ-vi-bhaj* (I), *bhāgo*
shave off *o-har* (I) caus.
shaven *muṇḍa*
shaven-headed *muṇḍaka*, *bhaṇḍu*
she *ta(d)* (*sā*), *eta(d)*, *idaṃ-* (*ayaṃ*), *amu-* (*asu*), *bhotī* (honorific)
shelter *āvaraṇaṃ*
shine *subh* (I), *upa-subh* (I)
ship *nāvā*
shoot *vi-o-bhid* (II)
shooter *vedhin-*
shore *tīraṃ*
shore sighting *tīradassi*
short *rassa*
in short *saṃkhittena* (ind.)
shortly *rassaṃ*
show *(d)dis* (I) caus., *(p)pa-kās* (I) caus., *ā-ruh* (I) caus.
show up *ā-ruh* (I) caus.
shower in (usher) *pavesetar* (masc.)
shower over (sprinkle) *ā-sic* (II)
shrine *cetiyaṃ*
sickness *ātaṅko*, *uddeko* (vomiting)
side *passo*, *anto* (extreme)
on one side *ekato* (ind.)
on either side *ekato* (ind.)
on its side *passena* (ind.)
on all sides *samantā* (ind.)

sidelong *visāci*
siesta bed *divāseyyā*
sight *rūpaṃ* (object), *cakkhu* (neut.) (sense)
sign *nimitto*
silent, silently *tuṇhī* (ind.)
silver *sajjhu* (neut.), *rajataṃ*
simile *upamā*
simple *uttānaka*
simultaneously *apubbaṃ acarimaṃ* (ind.)
since *agge* (ind. : time), *yato* (ind. : cause), *yaṃ* (ind.), *yasmā* (ind. : cause)
since then *tad agge* (ind.)
sing after *anu-ge* (I)
singing *gītaṃ*
single *ekaka* (adj.)
singleness *ekodibhāvo*
sir ! (polite address to a monk) *bhante* (ind.)
sir ! (polite address by Buddhist monks to the Buddha) *bhadante* (ind.)
sir ! (not very respectful, may express surprise) *ambho* (ind.)
(dear) sir ! (polite and affectionate address between gods, or by gods to men) *mārisa* (pl. *mārisā*) (voc.)
sir ! (polite address between equals), *bho* (voc. of *bhavant*—used also to a senior person), *āvuso* (ind.) (used also to a junior person)
sir (honorific pronoun) *bhavant*
sit down *ni-sīd* (I)
sitting cross-legged *pallaṅko*
site of a village *gāmapadaṃ*
building site *vatthu* (neut.)
six *cha(ḷ)* (num.)
the six spheres *saḷāyatanaṃ* (of the senses : 5 senses + the mind)
sixth *chaṭṭha*
sixteen *soḷasa* (num.)
sixty *saṭṭhi* (fem.)
size *pamāṇaṃ*
skilful *dakkha*
skilful in *padakkhiṇa* (loc.)
skin *taco, chavi* (fem.)
skin (film) *santānakaṃ*
sky *antalikkhaṃ, ākāso* (space), *divo* (poetic)
slander *abhi-ā-cikkh* (I), *pari-bhās* (I), *paribhāsā*
slave *dāso*
slavery *dāsavyaṃ*
slave girl *dāsī*
slave woman *dāsī*
slay *ati-pat* caus.
slaying *atipāto*
slow *manda*
small *paritta, khudda*
smear *makkh* (VII), *lip* (II)
smell *ghānaṃ* (sense of)
smith *kammāro*
snake *ahi* (masc.), *siriṃsapo*
snap *poṭh* (VII) (fingers)
so *evaṃ* (ind.), *taṃ* (ind.), *tad* (ind.)
if so *atha* (ind.)
so far *ettāvatā* (ind.)
soft *vaggu* (usually of beautiful sounds)
soldier *anīkaṭṭho*
solid matter *kabaḷiṅkāro*
some *eka* (pl. pronoun)
someone *ekacca* (pronoun)
some thing(s) *ekacca* (pronoun)
son *putto*
my son ! *tāta* (ind., affectionate address)
soon *na cirass' eva* (ind.)
soothsayer *nemitto*
sorrow *suc* (I), *soko*
sort *-rūpa*
this sort of *tādisa* (adj.), *etādisa* (adj.)
of such sort *sadisa* (adj.)
of what sort ? *kīdisa* (adj.)
soul *attan* (masc.), *jīvo*
sound (audible) *upa-ḷas* (VII), *saddo, (s)saro*
sound (proper) *kalla*
source *nidānaṃ, yoni* (fem.)
southern *dakkhiṇa*
sow *(p)pa-vap* (I)
space *ākāso*
sparkling *accha*
speak *bhās* (I), *vad* (I), *u(d)-ā-har* (I)
not to speak of *ko pana vādo* (ind.)
speak with exaltation, with joy *udāneti* (denom. of *udānaṃ*)
speaker *bhāsitar* (masc.), *vattar* (masc.)
causer to speak *vācetar* (masc.)
speak to *saṃ-u(d)-ā-car* (I)
speaking *vādin-*

speech *bhāsitaṃ* (saying), *vacanaṃ* (saying, words), *vācā* (language, action), *vacī* (language, action: used in compounds)
spent (time) *vuttha* (p.p. *vas* (I))
sphere *āyatanaṃ*
spirit *devatā* (male as well as female)
unhappy spirit *vinipātiko* (reborn in purgatory, or as an animal, ghost or demon)
spiritual *manomaya* ("consisting of mind")
splendid *rucira*
splendid! *diṭṭhā* (ind.)
splendour *avabhāso*
split *bhid* (II) (trans.), *(p)phal* (I) (intrans.)
splitting up *bhedo*
spontaneous *adhicca*
spread *saṃ-(t)thar* (I)
spread out *(p)pa-(t)thar* (I), *saṃ-tan* (VI)
sprinkle *abhi-u(d)-kir* (I*), *sic* (II)
square *siṅghāṭako*
squat down *pari* (> *pali*)-*kujj* (I)
stable *vāhanāgāraṃ*
stake *khīlo* (boundary)
stamen *kiñjakkhaṃ*
stand *(ṭ)ṭhā* (I)
stand up *u(d)-(ṭ)ṭhā* (I)
stand fast *gādh* (I)
one of long standing *rattaññū* (masc.)
star *tārakā*
staring *visaṭa* (adj., from p.p. *vi-sar*)
start *(p)pa-vatt* (I)
state *bhāvo* (nature)
mental state *dhammo*
statement *vādo*
state of being a wanderer/ascetic/philosopher *sāmaññaṃ*
station *(ṭ)ṭhiti* (fem.)
station oneself *(p)paṭi*(> *pati*)-*(ṭ)ṭhā* (I)
status *bhāvo*
stay *(ṭ)ṭhā* (I)
staying *(ṭ)ṭhāyin-*
sterile *vañjha*
steward *khattar-* (nom. sing. *khattā*, acc. *khattaṃ*, voc. *khatte*)
stick *daṇḍo*
to a still greater extent/degree *bhiyyoso mattāya* (= abl., ind.)
still greater *bhiyyoso* (ind.)
still less *pag eva* (ind.)
still more *pag eva* (ind.)
still more so *bhiyyoso* (ind.)
stirred up *luḷita*
stirring *saṃvejanīya* (inspiring)
stop! *alaṃ* (ind.)
stop *ni-rudh* (III), *upa-rudh* (III), *var* (III) (trans.)
store *sannidhi* (masc.)
stores *bhaṇḍaṃ*
storehouse *koṭṭhāgāraṃ*
story *kathā*
straight *uju*
strand *guṇaṃ* (sometimes masc.)
stranger *aññāto*
straw *palālaṃ*
stream *nadikā*
street *rathiyā*
stretch *tan* (VI)
stretch out *(p)pa-sar* (I) (intrans.), *saṃ-tan* (VI) (intrans.), *(p)pa-sar* (I) caus. (trans.)
strength *balaṃ*
strew *saṃ-(t)thar* (I)
entirely strewn *sabbasanthari*
strike *ā-kuṭ* (VII), *ā-han* (I)
string *guṇaṃ* (sometimes masc.)
strong *balavant*, *daḷha*
strongly *vi* (prefix)
study *sikkh* (I), *sajjhāyo*
studying *sajjhāyo*
extremely stupid *momūha*
stupidity *thīnamiddhaṃ*, *middhaṃ* (mental derangement), *thīnaṃ* (mental deficiency)
extreme stupidity *momūhattaṃ*
style *ākappo*
sublime *sāmukkaṃsaka*, *mahaggata*
submit *anu-yuj* (II)
subsist by *adhi-ā-vas* (I)
substance *kāyo*
subtle *nipuṇa* (reasoning), *sukhuma* (matter)
subversive element *kaṇṭakaṃ*
success *sampadā*
in succession *anupubbena* (ind.)
successively *aparāparaṃ* (ind.)
such as *yad idaṃ* (ind.)
such and such *amuka* (adj.)
suffering *dukkhaṃ*
sufficient *alaṃ* (ind.)

suffused with *sahagata*
suit (*k*)*kham* (I)
summary *uddeso*
summarized description *uddeso*
summer *ghammo* (noun), *gimhika* (adj.)
sun *suriyo*
sunshade *chatta*(*ka*)*ṃ*
superior *mahesakkha*
supple *mudu*
suppleness *mudutā*
supply with *samaṅgī-bhū* (I)
supplies *bhaṇḍaṃ*
suppose (usual equivalent is simply use of the optative tense; for " suppose I were to . . ." there is *yan nūna* + opt.) I suppose: *maññe* (ind.)
supposing ? *yan nūna* (ind.)
suppress *saṃ-u*(*d*)*-han* (I)
supremacy *ādhipateyyaṃ*, *aggatā*
supreme *anuttara*
the supreme *aggo*
surely *eva* (ind., enclitic), *va* (ind., enclitic), *vata* (ind.), *ve* (ind., poetic), *have* (ind., poetic)
surpassing *atikkanta*
surprising *acchariya* (cf. also *labbhā* (ind.), Vocab. 27)
surrounded by *samparikiṇṇa* (p.p. *saṃ-pari-kir*)
survivor *avasesako*
swallow *gil* (I*)
swallow back (*p*)*paṭi-ā-vam* (I)
sweating *sedaka*
sweet *madhu* (adj.), *sāta*
sword *satthaṃ*
sympathy *muditā* (with happiness; otherwise see " compassion ")
synopsis *uddeso*
synthesized *saṃkhata* (p.p. *saṃ-kar*)
systematic *ānupubba* (fem. *-ī*)

t

take *ā-dā* (I) or (III), *har* (I), (*g*)*gah* (V)
taking *ādānaṃ*
take away *ni*(*r*)*-har* (I) (*nīharati*)
take out *ni*(*r*)*-har* (I) (*nīharati*)
take up *u*(*d*)*-sah* (I) (undertake), *saṃ-anu-yuj* (II) (cross-question)
talk *kathā*, *sallāpo*
tamed *danta* (p.p. *dam*)
taming *damo*
tangled *ākula*
taste *sā* (III), *raso* (object), *jivhā* (sense)
tasting *assādo*
tax (religious) *bali* (masc.)
teach *dis* (VII)
teacher *ācariyo*, *satthar* (masc.)
teacher's teacher *pācariyo*
tell *kath* (VII), *ā-*(*k*)*khā* (I), (*p*)*pa-ā-vad* (I)
ten *dasa* (num.)
tend *pari-car* (I)
tendency *netti* (fem.)
tender *maddava*
territory *khettaṃ*, *gocaro*
terror (*p*)*paṭibhayaṃ*, *uttāso*
than (expressed by the abl.)
than this *ito* (ind.)
that *ta*(*d*) (anaphoric), *eta*(*d*) (deictic), *idaṃ* (deictic), *amu-* (deictic and more remote), *na-*, *iti* (ind.), *yaṃ* (ind.)
that is (i.e.) *yad idaṃ* (ind.)
the (usually no equivalent: see Lesson 5) *ta*(*d*)
theft *theyyaṃ*
then *tadā* (ind.), *atha* (ind.), *atha kho* (ind.), *tato* (ind.), *carahi* (ind.), *taṃ* (ind.), *tad* (ind.)
thence *tato* (ind.), *atha* (ind.)
theory *diṭṭhi* (fem.)
theorizing *anudiṭṭhin-*
there *tattha* (ind.), *tatra* (ind.), *amutra* (ind., more remote)
therefore *tena* (ind.), *tasmā* (ind.), *carahi* (ind.)
thief *dassu* (masc.)
thigh *ūru* (fem.)
thing *vatthu* (neut.)
good thing *dhammo*
think gen. + *evaṃ hū* (I) followed by direct speech, *man* (III)
I think *maññe* (ind.)
think about *upa-ni*(*-j*)*jhe* (I)
third *tatiya*
" thirst " (fig.) *taṇhā*
be thirsty *pā* desid.
thirsty *pipāsita*, *pipāsin*
thirteen *teḷasa* (num.)
thirty (*t*)*tiṃsa* (neut.)

this *idaṃ*, *eta(d)*, *iti* (ind.)
this side *orima*
thither *pāraṃ* (ind.)
" thorn " (i.e., subversive element) *kaṇṭakaṃ*
thoroughly *sabbena sabbaṃ* (ind.)
thou *tvaṃ* (*ta(d)*-)
thought *cittaṃ*
thousand *sahassaṃ*
thread *suttaṃ*
threat *garahā*
threatening *paritajjanā*
three *ti*- (nom. masc. *tayo*, neut. *tīṇi*, fem. *tisso*)
threefold *tividha*
three days *tīhaṃ*
thrice *tikkhattuṃ* (ind.)
thrive *pabb* (I)
throb *phand* (I)
through (may be expressed by the ins.) *tiro*- (prefix), *accayena* (ind., time passed = gen.)
throw *(k)khip* (I*)
throw away *chaḍḍ* (VII)
thrown away *catta* (p.p. *caj*)
throw down *ni-(k)khip* (I*)
thus *evaṃ* (ind.), *tathā* (ind.), *itthaṃ* (ind.), *iti* (ind.)
thus-gone *tathāgato* (title of the Buddha)
tie *gath* (II)
tie back *apa-nah* (II)
tie up *saṃ-nah* (II)
tied *gathita* (p.p. *gath* (II))
time *kālo* (opportunity, proper time), *samayo* (any time, occasion, time of an event, accidental time), *addhan*- (extent of time, period), *velā* (occasion)
timeless *akālika*
at any time *kadā ci* (ind.)
at some time *kadā ci* (ind.), *karaha ci* (ind.)
each time it came *āgatāgataṃ* (ind.)
tip *aggo*
tire *kilam* (I)
tiring *kilamatho*
tithe *bali* (masc.)
to *ā* (prefix)
toadstool *ahicchattako*
today *ajja* (ind.)
for today *ajjatanāya* (ind.)
toe *aṅguli* (fem.)
toenail *nakho*
together *ekato* (ind.), *saṃ* (prefix)
toleration *khanti*
for tomorrow *svātanāya* (ind.)
tongue *jivhā* (incl. as sense of taste)
too (" also ") *pi* (ind., enclitic)
too much *atibāḷhaṃ* (ind.)
top *aggo*
on top of *upari* (ind., precedes the word it relates to, which is usually in the loc.)
torment *pac* (I), *upa-dah* (I)
torture *pac* (I)
touch *phus* (I*), *phasso* (for sense of touch, *kāyo* is used)
touchable *phoṭṭhabbaṃ* (object)
towards *yena* (ind. with nom. and *tena*), *abhi* (prefix), *upa* (prefix), *(p)paṭi* (prefix)
town *nigamo*
town dweller *negamo*
trade *vaṇippatho* (commerce), *sippaṃ* (craft)
tradition *āgamo*
train *sikkh* (I)
trainable *damma*
training *sikkhā*, *sikkhāpadaṃ*
transcend *saṃ-ati-(k)kam* (I)
transcending *samatikkamo*
transmigrate *upa-pad* (III), *saṃ-sar* (I) (circulate indefinitely), *saṃ-dhāv* (I) (pass on)
transmigrating *opapātika*
transmigration *saṃsāro*
travel *cārikā*
treasurer *gaṇako*
treasury *koso*
treat with *pari-bhū* caus.
tree *rukkho*
tremble *(p)pa-vedh* (I), *kamp* (I)
tribe *kulo*
by tribe *-kulīna* (adj.)
trick *māyā*
trickle *(p)pa-(g)ghar* (I)
triple *tividha*
trouble *vi-han* (I), *upapīḷā*, *vihesā*
troublesome *garu*
true *sacca*, *sant*-, *tathā* (ind.)
it is true that, is it true that? *saccaṃ* (ind.)
truly *ha* (ind.), *have* (ind.), (poetic)

trust *saddhā*
trusting *saddha, pasanna*
truth *saccaṃ*
speaking the truth, truthfulness *saccavajjaṃ*
try *u(d)-sah* (I)
turbid *āvila*
turn *vaṭṭ* (I), *añch* (I) (on a lathe)
turn back *(p)paṭi-vaṭṭ* (I) (intransitive, transitive = caus.), caus. of *ni-vatt* (I) (transitive)
turn back again *paṭi-u(d)-ā-vatt* (I)
turner *bhamakāro*
twelve *dvādasa* (num.)
twenty *vīsati* (fem.)
twice *dvikkhattuṃ* (ind.), *dvidhā* (in two) (ind.)
twist *veṭh* (VII)
two *dvi* (num. : nom. *dve*)
in two *dvidhā* (ind.)
two days *dvihaṃ*
twofold *dvidhā* (ind.)

u

ugly *dubbaṇṇa*
un- *a-*
unable *abhabba*
unanimous *samagga*
unattached *anissita*
be uncertain *vi-kit* desid.
uncertainty *vicikicchā*
unconquered *anabhibhūta* (p.p. *abhi-bhū* (I))
uncultivated *akaṭṭha*
undergo *ni-gam* (I)
understand *adhi-gam* (I), *(p)pa-(ñ)ñā* (V), *anu-budh* (III)
understanding *paññā, pajānanā, anubodho*
undertake *(p)pa-yuj* (VII), *u(d)-sah* (I)
undertaking *kammanto, samārambho*
undetermined *avyākata* (neg. p.p. *vi-ā-kar*)
uneasiness *nibbusitattā*
unexplained *avyākata* (neg. p.p. *vi-ā-kar*)
unhappy *dukkhin-*
be unhappy *dukkheti* (denom.)
unhappiness *dukkhaṃ*
union *saṃyojanaṃ, samphasso, sahavyatā* (with gen.)
united *samagga*

unity *ekattaṃ*
universe *loko*
universally *aññadatthu* (ind.)
unlimited *apariyanta*
unlucky die *kali* (masc.)
unmethodically *ayoniso* (ind.)
unobtained *appatta*
unploughed *akaṭṭha*
unravel *ni(r)-veṭh* (VII)
unscientifically *ayoniso* (ind.)
unselfish *amama*
unselfishness *sabbattatā*
unsettlement *nibbusitattā*
unsound *akalla*
unsurpassed *anuttara*
untie *apa-nah* (II)
until *yāva* (ind.)
untruth *vitathaṃ*
up *uddhaṃ* (ind.), *u(d)* (prefix)
uplifting *uddhaggika*
set upright *u(d)-kujj* (I)
up to *sama* (adj.), *yāva* (ind., abl.), *upa* (prefix)
urine *muttaṃ*
what's the use of ? *kiṃ . . . karissati* (of = nom.)
use up *pari-ā-dā* (III)
very useful *bahukāra*
usher *pavesetar* (masc.)
usual *yathākata*
exalted or joyful utterance *udānaṃ*

v

vain *vikkhitta*
valour *parakkamo*
value *sāro*
vanity *uddhaccaṃ, kukkuccaṃ, uddhaccakukkuccaṃ, okāro*
various *puthu*
variously *nānā* (ind.)
vase *bhiṅkāro*
the vegetable kingdom *bījagāmo*
veneration *padakkhiṇā*
verifiable *ehipassika*
very (cf. " excessive ") (an adjective may be repeated, so may an " adverbial accusative " ; see Lesson 21) *ativiya* (ind.), *su-* (prefix to adjectives, poetic), *ati-* (prefix to adjectives, poetic), (*vi-* and *(p)pa-* occasionally may be translated " very ")

very much *ativiya* (ind.)
victory *jayo*
vigour *thāmo*
vile *duṭṭha, asuci*
village *gāmo*
violence *vyāpādo* [non ~ see s.v.]
violent *vyāpajjha, vyāpanna, pabāḷha, bāḷha*
virtue *sīlaṃ*
virtuous *sīlavant*
visible *sandiṭṭhika, diṭṭha*
be visible to *(p)pa-(k)khā* (III) (dat.)
visited *abhisaṭa* (p.p. *abhi-sar*)
visualize as *upa-saṃ-har* (I) (2 accs.)
voice *(s)saro*
vomited *vanta* (p.p. *vam*)
vomiting *uddeko*
vow *(v)vataṃ*
vulgar *gamma*

W

wages *vetanaṃ*
wait *ā-gam* (I) caus.
walk *(k)kam* (I)
walk about *(k)kam* (I) intensive
walk along *anu-(k)kam* (I)
walk up and down *(k)kam* (I) intensive
wall *bhitti* (fem.)
wander *ā-hiṇḍ* (I)
wanderer *paribbājako, samaṇo*
as much as one wants *yāvadatthaṃ* (ind.)
wanton *lola*
war *yuddhaṃ*
warrior (member of the military-aristocratic class) *khattiyo*
wash *(p)pa-(k)khal* (VII)
waste *(k)khī* (III)
watch *(p)pa-ikkh* (I), *yāmo* (of the night)
watch over *pari-har* (I)
watcher *pekkhitar* (masc.)
water *udakaṃ, pānīyaṃ* (drinking water), *āpas-* (as "element"), *vāri* (neut.)
having water *odaka* (fem. *-ikā*)
water-jar *udakamaṇi* (masc.)
ceremonial water vessel *bhiṅkāro*
consist entirely of water *ekodakī-bhū* (I)
wavy *vellita*
way *paṭipadā, maggo, patho, ayanaṃ, dhammo*
way of life *cariyā*
having the best way of life *brahmacārin*
on the Way *sotāpanna*
in this way *itthaṃ* (ind.)
this way *tena* (only with *yena* and nom.)
in what way ? *yathā kathaṃ* (ind.)
in whatever way *yathā yathā* (ind.)
in all ways *sabbathā* (ind.)
we *ma(d)-* (*mayaṃ*)
weakening (making weak) *dubbalīkaraṇa*
wealth *dhanaṃ, attho*
wear *dhar* (VII)
weariness *kilamatho*
wearing *vasanaṃ*
wearying *kilamatho*
week *sattāhaṃ*
weep *rud* (I*)
welcome ! *svāgataṃ* (ind., dat.)
well (done) *suṭṭhu* (ind.)
well *sādhukaṃ* (ind.), *su-* (prefix)
well ! *handa* (ind.)
well (healthy) *āroga*
well-gone *sugato* (title of the Buddha)
well-spoken *subhāsita*
welfare *hitaṃ, attho*
wet *alla*
west *pacchā* (ind.)
western *pacchima*
what *ya(d)* (pronoun), *yaṃ* (ind.)
what ? *kiṃ* (pronoun)
what if ? *yan nūna* (ind.)
like what ? *kīdisa* (adj.)
whatever *yaṃ kiñ ci* (pronoun)
what should be done *kiccaṃ*
wheel *cakkaṃ*
when *yadā* (ind.)
when ? *kadā* (ind.), *kudā* (ind.)
whence *yato* (ind.)
whence ? *kuto* (ind.)
where *yattha* (ind.), *yatra* (ind.), *yena* (ind.)
where ? *kattha* (ind.)
whereabouts *yahiṃ* (ind.)
whereabouts ? *kahaṃ* (ind.)
whereas *yaṃ* (ind.)
wherefore ? *kasmā* (ind.)
where to ? *kuhiṃ* (ind.)

whether *yadi* (ind.)
whilst *antarā* (ind.)
who *ya(d)* (pronoun)
who ? *kiṃ* (pronoun)
which *ya(d)* (pronoun)
which ? *kiṃ* (pronoun), *katama* (pronoun)
which one ? *katama* (pronoun)
which way *yena* (ind., nom.)
white *sukka, odāta*
white water-lily *kumudaṃ*
whole *kevala, sabbāvant*
why ? *kasmā* (ind.), *kiṃ* (ind.), *kathaṃ* (ind.)
wielding power *vasavattin-*
wife *dāro* (sometimes *-ā*)
wild animal *vālo*
wilderness *kantāro*
will *chandas-*
I won't *alaṃ* (ind., dat.)
win *ji* (V), *ji* (I)
wind *vāto*
old winnowing basket *kattarasuppo*
winter *hemantika* (adj.)
wisdom *paññā*
wise *paṇḍita, nipaka, medhāvin*
wise man *paṇḍito*
wish *ā-kaṅkh* (I), *is(u)* (I)
as far as one wishes *yāvaticchakaṃ* (ind.)
best wishes ! *bhavaṃ* (ind. with *atthu* and acc. of person)
wherever one wishes *yatthicchakaṃ* (ind.)
whatever one wishes *yadicchakaṃ* (ind.)
wishful *aṭṭhika*
wishing for *sāpekha, jigiṃsamāna* (poetic)
to wit *yad idaṃ* (ind.), *seyyathīdaṃ* (ind.)
with *saddhiṃ* (ind., ins.), *sa-*
withdraw *apa-(k)kam* (I)
withdrawn *vūpakaṭṭha* (secluded), *onīta* (removed)
within *antarā* (ind.), *antara* (prefix)
without *vinā* (ind., precedes ins.), *a-* (prefix), *ni(r)-* (prefix), *vi-* (prefix), *apagata-* (prefix), *vigata-* (prefix), *vīta-* (prefix), *vipanna* (adj.)
woman *itthī*
womb *yoni* (fem.), *kucchi* (masc.)
wonderful *abbhuta*
it's wonderful *diṭṭhā* (ind.)
a wood *vanaṃ* (" wood " = *kaṭṭhaṃ*, esp. firewood)
word *padaṃ*
words (speech) *vacanaṃ* (sing. collective)
work *kar* (VI), *kammanto, kammaṃ*
working *-karo*
world *loko*
this world *ayaṃ loko, itthattaṃ, apāraṃ* (ind.)
living " in the world " *gihin*
worthy one *arahant-* (masc.)
worry *upa-dah* (I), *anattamanatā, kukkuccaṃ*
worried *anattamana, vyāvaṭa*
worse *pāpīya*
wrap *veṭh* (VII)
wrong *micchā*
wrongly *micchā* (ind.)

y

year *vassaṃ, saṃvaccharaṃ*
yearned for *abhipatthita* (p.p. *abhipatth* (VII))
yellow *pīta*
yes *āma* (ind.), *evaṃ* (ind.)
yoke *yuj* (III), *yugaṃ*
yon *amu-*
yonder *amutra* (ind.)
you (sing. thou) *ta(d)-* (*tvam*), *bhavant* (honorific)
you there ! *handa je* (ind., cf. *je*)
you (plur. :) *ta(d)-* (*tumhe*), *bhavant* (honorific)
you ! *je* (enclitic) (form of address by a master/mistress to a slave woman ; preceded by *handa, kiñ,* etc., or by *gaccha*)
young *dahara*
young (of animals) *susu* (masc.)
younger, youngest *kaniṭṭha*
youth *yuvan* (masc.)
state of youth *yobbanaṃ*

ABBREVIATIONS

acc.	accusative
abl.	ablative
adj.	adjective
aor.	aorist
caus.	causative
con.	conjugation
CPD	*Critical Pali Dictionary*
dat.	dative
denom.	denominative
desid.	desiderative
fem.	feminine
fig.	figurative
f.p.p.	future passive participle
fut.	future
gen.	genitive
ger.	gerund
ind.	indeclinable
ins.	instrumental
intrans.	intransitive
ipv.	imperative
lit.	literal(ly)
loc.	locative
masc.	masculine
neut.	neuter
neg.	negative
nom.	nominative
num.	numeral
pass.	passive
PED	*Pali–English Dictionary*
plur.	plural
p.p.	past participle
pres.	present tense
pres. p.	present participle
PTS	Pali Text Society
Sd.	*Saddanīti*
sing.	singular
trans.	transitive
voc.	vocative

GRAMMATICAL INDEX

Additions to the Lessons

Page	
319	*apadeso* reference
127	*dhuttako* gambler, rascal
279	*nūna* if (enclitic)
335	*(p) paṭi-pucch* (I) *paṭipucchati* ask in return
336	*pasādo* confidence
65	*pāmujjaṃ* joy
336	*pāvacanaṃ* teaching
141	*bandho* imprisonment
337	*vimokho* freedom
119	*saṃ-ni-sīd* (I) *sannisīdanti* they sit down together
338	*samanantarā* (ind.) immediately
241	*seṭṭhi* (masc.) moneylender
128	*senā* army

Additions to Pali-English Vocabulary

388	*apadeso* reference
399	*dhuttako* gambler, rascal
400	*nūna* (ind., enclitic) if
401	*paṭicchādanā* concealment
401	*(p) paṭi-pucch* (I) ask in return
402	*parivesanā* food distribution
403	*pasādo* confidence
403	*pāmujjaṃ* joy
403	*pāvacanaṃ* teaching
404	*bandho* imprisonment
409	*vimokho* freedom
411	*saṅgati* (fem.) combination
412	*saṃ-ni-sīd* (I) sit down together
412	*samanantarā* (ind.) immediately
414	*senā* army

Additions to English-Pali Vocabulary

420	*read:* combination *saṅgati* (fem.), *saṃkhāro* (see Vocab. 26)
434	moneylender *seṭṭhi*
444	summit *aggo*

KEY TO PASSAGES FOR READING AND PALI SENTENCES

(All references are to *Dīgha Nikāya*)

EXERCISE 4

II 85
II 230–1
I 143

EXERCISE 5

II 231	II 252	I 50
II 75	II 233	I 50 [*sic*]
III 65	I 179	II 288
I 129	I 185	II 292
I 143	III 84	I 180
I 18		I 124

EXERCISE 6

I 231–2	I 179 [*sic*]	II 147, 170
II 104	III 117	I 50
I 67	II 38	II 142
I 179		I 211

EXERCISE 7

I 18	I 29	I 83
I 18 [*sic*]	cf. III 28 and I 194	III 117
II 100	III 39	II 128
III 66		II 357

EXERCISE 8

II 196	III 73	III 181
I 53	III 183	III 146
III 28	II 237	II 238
cf. I 222 and 85	I 236	II 43
III 39–40	III 16	I 148

EXERCISE 9

II 221	III 53	III 266
I 124	III 54	II 93
II 310	I 21	III 6
II 354	II 51	cf. I 179 and III 38
	I 214	

EXERCISE 10

II 114	I 8	I 105
I 10	I 137	II 73
III 81	II 139	III 255
I 54		II 16

EXERCISE 11

II 130	III 71	I 81
II 156	III 255	I 179
I 196	I 110	I 180
II 87	II 172	II 127
II 232	II 222	I 85
I 187	III 75	III 255
I 222	III 117	I 18

EXERCISE 12

II 337	II 185	III 146
II 89	II 216	I 50
II 28	I 55	I 51
III 285	II 356	II 150
II 162	III 61	III 43
	III 84	

EXERCISE 13

II 357–8	I 84	II 223
II 236	II 21	II 161
III 259	I 71	I 49
I 50	II 140	I 50

EXERCISE 14

II 349–50	III 249	II 67
I 51	II 320	III 283
I 20	III 61	I 91
II 56	I 72	II 233
III 73		I 224

EXERCISE 15

II 350	II 40	I 88
I 124	III 259	I 84
III 117	II 234	II 41
II 140		II 246

EXERCISE 16

1. II 350–1	I 237	I 138
2. II 347–8	I 47	I 196
I 47	II 22	II 340
II 319		II 223

EXERCISE 17

II 342–3	I 151	III 64
I 124	II 225	II 85
II 291	I 152	III 62
II 45		II 233

EXERCISE 18

1. II 348–9	III 99	II 15
2. III 59–62	I 56	III 52
III 81	III 9	II 223
I 98		I 185

EXERCISE 19

1. II 343–6	2. I 127–35	3. II 16, 19, 21

EXERCISE 20

1. II 21–2 2. III 80–6

EXERCISE 21

1. I 52–3 2. III 86–93 3. I 215–6

EXERCISE 22

I 12–38

EXERCISE 23

1. I 220–3	I 238	II 124
2. II 22–4	II 37	II 162
3. III 64–8	II 248	II 178

EXERCISE 24

1. II 72–81 2. II 25–9 3. III 255

EXERCISE 25

1. II 81–8 2. II 30–5

EXERCISE 26

1. II 88–101 2. II 41

EXERCISE 27

1. II 102, 118–21 2. II 290–313

EXERCISE 28

1. II 122–36
2. III 221–2
3. III 278
4. III 229
5. III 253
6. I 62–3
7. I 250–1

EXERCISE 29

1. II 137, 140–1, 148–56
2. II 55–71

EXERCISE 30

vatta III 199–200, 201 -2 and II 265–7
tuṭṭhubha II 241
opacchandasaka II 49
rathoddhatā III 155
vaṃsaṭṭhā III 147 and 148
pamitakkharā III 169
rucirā III 166
pupphitaggā III 153
svāgatā II 254
upaṭṭhitappacupita III 159–60
uggatā III 168–9

KEY TO PASSAGES FOR RETRANSLATION INTO PALI

EXERCISE 16
D I 118

EXERCISE 17
D I 120–4

EXERCISE 18
M I 387–8

EXERCISE 19
M I 134–5

EXERCISE 20
Vin I 268–9

EXERCISE 21
Vin I 269–70

EXERCISE 22
(Free essay)

EXERCISE 23
D II 340–1

EXERCISE 24
Vin I 270–1

EXERCISE 25
Vin I 276–7

EXERCISE 26
Vin I 277–8

EXERCISE 27
Vin I 278

EXERCISE 28
Vin I 10 = S V 421
D I 53
D I 55

EXERCISE 29
D I 185–6

EXERCISE 30
D I 186–9